AN

AMERICAN

IMPERATIVE

W9-CHI-486

AN

AMERICAN

IMPERATIVE

Accelerating

Minority Educational

Advancement

L. Scott Miller

Yale University Press

New Haven and London

Designed by Christopher Harris / Summer Hill Books

Set in Caledonia and Helvetica types by The Marathon Group, Inc.,
Durham, North Carolina.

Printed in the United States of America by Vail-Ballou Press, Binghamton, New York.

Library of Congress Cataloging-in-Publication-Data
Miller, L. Scott.
 An American imperative : accelerating minority educational advancement / L. Scott Miller..
    p.   cm.
 Includes bibliographical references and index.
 ISBN 0-300-05793-8 (cloth: alk. paper)
 0-300-07279-1 (pbk.: alk. paper)
  1. Minorities — Education — Social aspects — United States.   2. Academic achievement —
Social aspects — United States.   3. Pluralism (Social sciences) — United States.   4. Right to
education — United States.   I. Title.
LC3731.M54   1995
371.97'00973 — dc20   94-31669
                                                                                        CIP

A catalogue record for this book is available from the British Library.

The paper in this book meets the guidelines for permanence and durability
of the Committee on Production Guidelines for Book Longevity of the
Council on Library Resources.

10 9 8 7 6 5 4 3 2

To my mother, Betty Lou Laird Miller, and my father, Thomas Oskar Miller; to my sons, Cary Randolph Miller and Dana Laird Miller; and to the potential for one generation to improve the life chances of the next

Contents

List of Tables   ix

Preface   xiii

Acknowledgments   xix

1   Society's Interest in the Educational Advancement of Minorities   1

2   Trends in Majority and Minority Educational Attainment   26

3   Majority and Minority Educational Achievement Trends   45

4   Opportunity, Resources, and Intergenerational Advancement   84

5   Educational Achievement and Socioeconomic Status   121

6   An Analysis of Academic Achievement Patterns: Race/Ethnicity and Social Class   143

7   Standard Social Class Categories and the Mismeasurement of Education-Relevant Resources   160

8   The Origins, Evolution, and Contemporary Dimensions of Racial/Ethnic Prejudice   172

9   The Educational Impact of Racial/Ethnic Prejudice and Discrimination   202

10   Education-Relevant Cultural Differences Associated with Race/Ethnicity and Social Class   244

11   Estimating Current School and Family Resource Variations   287

12   Principles and Recommendations for Action   337

13   A Nation-Building, Region-Building Rationale for Accelerating the Educational Advancement of Minorities   377

Index   383

Tables

1.1 Estimated Racial/Ethnic Composition of the Under-18 Population   22

2.1 Years of School Completed by Individuals Aged 25 to 29, by Race: Selected Years 1920–88   27

2.2 Percent of Population Aged 25 to 29 That Has Completed Twelve or More Years of School, by Race/Ethnicity: Selected Years 1964–89   29

2.3 Percent of Population Aged 25 to 29 That Has Completed Two or More Years of College, by Race/Ethnicity: Selected Years 1968–89   31

2.4 Percent of Population Aged 25 to 29 That Has Completed Four or More Years of College, by Race/Ethnicity: Selected Years 1964–89   32

2.5 Percent of Population Aged 25 to 29 That Has Completed Five or More Years of College, by Race/Ethnicity: Selected Years 1964–89   32

2.6 Highest Level of Postsecondary Attainment of 1980 High School Seniors, by Race/Ethnicity, in the Spring of 1986   34

2.7 Bachelor's and Doctoral Degrees Awarded in 1979 and 1989, by Race/Ethnicity and Nonresident Alien Status   36

2.8 Bachelor's and Doctoral Degrees Awarded in the Natural Sciences, the Computer/Information Sciences, and Engineering in 1979 and 1989, by Race/Ethnicity and Nonresident Alien Status   39

2.9 Bachelor's Degrees Awarded in Education in 1979 and 1989, by Race/Ethnicity and Nonresident Alien Status   43

3.1 Anchor Points for NAEP Reading and Mathematics Tests   48

3.2 Average NAEP Reading Scores, by Race/Ethnicity: 1971–90   49

3.3 Percentages of Students Performing at Selected NAEP Reading Anchor Points at Age 9, by Race/Ethnicity: 1971–90   50

3.4 Percentages of Students Performing at Selected NAEP Reading Anchor Points at Age 17, by Race/Ethnicity: 1971–90   52

3.5 Average NAEP Mathematics Scores, by Race/Ethnicity: 1973–90   53

3.6 Percentages of Students Performing at Selected NAEP Mathematics Anchor Points at Age 9, by Race/Ethnicity: 1978–90   54

3.7 Percentages of Students Performing at Selected NAEP Mathematics Anchor Points at Age 17, by Race/Ethnicity: 1978–90   56

3.8 Selected Data from the 1990 NAEP Mathematics Assessment of Students in Grades 4 and 12   58

3.9 Selected SAT Math Section Data for 1981 and 1990, by Race/Ethnicity   61

3.10 Selected SAT Verbal Section Data for 1981 and 1990, by Race/Ethnicity   64

3.11 Selected 1990 SAT Information for Planned Education and Engineering Majors, by Race/Ethnicity   67

3.12 Selected GRE Verbal Section and Quantitative Section Data for U.S. Citizens (Only) in 1987, by Race/Ethnicity 69

3.13 Selected Data from the National Education Longitudinal Study of 1988, by Race/Ethnicity 71

3.14 Cumulative High School Grade Point Averages of 1990 SAT Test Takers, by Race/Ethnicity 73

3.15 SAT and High School Grade Data for Students in the ABET Engineering Study Who Were College Freshmen in the Fall of 1985, by Race/Ethnicity 75

3.16 Grade Point Averages for Students in the ABET Engineering Study Who Were College Freshmen in the Fall of 1985, by Race/Ethnicity 76

3.17 Academic Performance of Engineering Students in the ABET Study with a Combined SAT Score of 1100 or More and Those with a Combined Score of Less than 1100, by Race/Ethnicity 77

4.1 Percentages of Children under Age 18 Living in Various Family Circumstances, by Race/Ethnicity: 1970, 1980, 1989 107

5.1 Parent Education and Eighth-Grade Student Achievement Patterns in the National Education Longitudinal Study of 1988 123

5.2 Family Income and Eighth-Grade Student Achievement Patterns in the National Education Longitudinal Study of 1988 124

5.3 Average NAEP Reading Scores for 9- and 17-Year-Olds, by Parent Education Level: 1971–90 127

5.4 Average NAEP Mathematics Scores for 9- and 17-Year-Olds, by Parent Education Level: 1978–90 128

5.5 Average Verbal, Mathematics, and Combined SAT Scores for 1990, by Parent Education and Parent Income Levels 130

5.6 Selected Characteristics of Low, Medium, and High Poverty Concentration Elementary Schools 133

5.7 Selected Student Achievement Data for Low, Medium, and High Poverty Concentration Elementary Schools 134

6.1 Selected Reading and Mathematics Proficiency Data for High and Low Socioeconomic Status Eighth Graders from Each Racial/Ethnic Group in the National Education Longitudinal Study of 1988 145

6.2 Average NAEP Reading Scores for 9-Year-Olds, by Race/Ethnicity and Parent Education Level: 1971–88 147

6.3 Average NAEP Reading Scores for 13-Year-Olds, by Race/Ethnicity and Parent Education Level: 1971–88 148

6.4 Average NAEP Mathematics Scores for 9-Year-Olds, by Race/Ethnicity and Parent Education Level: 1978–90 150

6.5 Average NAEP Mathematics Scores for 13-Year-Olds, by Race/Ethnicity and Parent Education Level: 1978–90 151

6.6 NAEP Reading and Mathematics Test Sample Sizes for 9- and 13-Year-Olds, by Race/Ethnicity 152

6.7 Absolute Changes in Average NAEP Reading Scores, 1971–88, and in Average NAEP Mathematics Scores, 1978–90, for 9- and 13-Year-Olds, by Race/Ethnicity and Parent Income Level, 154

6.8 Average 1990 Verbal, Math, and Combined SAT Scores, by Race/Ethnicity and Selected Parent Education Levels 156

6.9 Average 1990 Verbal, Math, and Combined SAT Scores, by Race/Ethnicity and Selected Parent Income Levels 157

7.1 Average NAEP Reading Scores and Reading Anchor Point Percentages for Young Adults in 1985 and In-School 17-Year-Olds in 1980 163

9.1 Agreement of NELS:88 Eighth Graders with Various Statements about Their Relationships with Their Teachers and Schools, by Race/Ethnicity, Social Class, Gender, and Grades 229

9.2 Percentages of 1982 and 1987 High School Graduates Who Took Selected Math and Science Courses 235

9.3 Selected SAT Data for 1987 and 1992, by Race/Ethnicity 236

11.1 Current Expenditure per Pupil Averages in 1988–89 and the Racial/Ethnic Composition of the Public School Population in the Fall of 1989, by State 289

11.2 Selected Student Demographic, School Expenditure, High School Completion, and High School Dropout Data for Fourteen States 294

11.3 Average Math Scores of Eighth Graders in the NAEP 1990 Trial State Assessment 296

11.4 The Composition of the National, District of Columbia, North Dakota, and West Virginia Student Samples for the NAEP Trial State Assessment, by Race Ethnicity and Parent Education Level 300

11.5 Selected Math Performance Data for the Nation, the District of Columbia, North Dakota, and West Virginia for the NAEP Trial State Assessment, by Parent Education Level 301

11.6 Selected School Resource Data for the District of Columbia, North Dakota, West Virginia, and the Nation 304

11.7 Selected Family-Resource-Related Data for the District of Columbia, North Dakota, West Virginia, and the Nation 306

11.8 Hypothetical After-Tax Family Income Examples 311

11.9 Education Levels of Parents in Hypothetical Families 315

11.10 Estimates of the Time Parents Spend Making Educational Investments in Their Children 323

11.11 Monetary Value of the Educational Resource Investments that Parents in the Hypothetical Families Make in Their Children 324

11.12 Comparisons of School Resources with Family Resources 326

11.13 Combined School and Education-Relevant Family Resource Investments in the Children in Hypothetical Family A and Family E, from Birth to Age 18 335

Preface

This book is the product of a decade of work on the educational challenges posed by the rapidly changing racial and ethnic demographics of the United States. Its core assumption is that maintaining a humane, harmonious pluralistic society, while never easy, is especially problematic in periods when the composition of the population is changing rapidly.

Education is the primary prism through which the challenges of the changing demographics are viewed in this book, first because high levels of formal education are essential for the effective functioning of a democratic, technological, diverse society such as the American one and, second, because the constituent groups need high levels of education in order to reap the full benefits of membership in the nation. A third reason for my focus on education is that several of the country's racial and ethnic minority groups, including some of the largest and fastest growing, continue to be much less well educated, on average, than the majority population.

The central purpose of the book, very broadly, is to help leaders and professionals in government, education, business, foundations, and the media think clearly about what needs to be done to ensure that minorities reach educational parity with the majority population as soon as possible. However, the policy orientation of the book necessarily reaches beyond education to several other topics, for example, health care and child care.

The analysis presented here is strategic in the sense that it is concerned with developing a set of recommendations that, if acted on in combination, could reasonably be expected to lead to a much more rapid rate of educational advancement among minorities than is now the case; it focuses on changes in societal institutions that are fundamental to supporting the robust educational advancement of individuals and groups; it takes a long-term perspective, recognizing that even a very rapid rate of advancement is unlikely to produce full minority-majority educational parity within a few years or even a few decades; and, finally it attempts to make clear how large the national effort must be if the nation is to respond effectively to the challenges posed by the changing demographics.

The analysis is also integrative in that it links a discussion of the size of the educational gaps between the majority population and racial/ethnic minorities with an examination of underlying causes, described from economic, sociological, and cross-cultural perspectives and from both historical and contemporary vantage points. And it emphasizes the similarities and interconnections among the findings of research from different fields.

The emphasis on a strategic, integrative approach reflects the view that the more comprehensive the analysis can be, the more probable it is that an effective combination of policies can be identified and that a strong consensus can be built in support of this policy mix. It also reflects a belief that too few policy-oriented, cross-disciplinary analyses of research findings have been mounted in this area in recent years. For this reason, my book is concerned not only with informing the policy process but also with encouraging those with different perspectives and resources to undertake similar analyses.

I believe that American society will find it necessary to work energetically to bring about a convergence of minority-majority educational performance for several generations to come. Consequently, the nation will need a steady stream of thoughtful, strategic, integrative analyses to chart and rechart the most effective course to its destination and to muster and to maintain the resolve to stay that course.

Necessarily, there are some significant omissions in this book. One of the most important is that no data and research are presented on gender variations in educational attainment within racial/ethnic groups, owing to the paucity of available test score data broken down simultaneously by race/ethnicity, gender, and social class and to the limited time available for preparing the book. I believe, however, that the addition of gender to the line of inquiry presented here should receive the earliest possible attention. There is considerable research suggesting that the education-relevant school and nonschool experiences of male and female youngsters not only differ in general but also vary substantially by race/ethnicity and social class.

TERMINOLOGY

The term *race* is used here in the common but imprecise sense of describing groups of people who tend to share certain physical appearance characteristics: skin color, hair texture, facial features. *Ethnicity* is used to refer to groups of people who tend to share distinctive cultural attributes (language, religion, family customs, food preferences, and so on) a common national identity, and common historical origins.

The primary terms used to categorize the American population by race are white, black, Asian, and Native American. The descriptive value of these terms, of course, is inherently limited, owing to the diversity of individuals (and groups) to whom they are applied. One of the most problematic terms is *Asian* because it includes people who are as different in physical appearance and culture as are the typical residents of such countries as Pakistan, Cambodia, and Korea.

In some statistical reports, Asians are grouped with Pacific Islanders (for example, Tahitians) under the category Asians/Pacific Islanders. For reasons of brevity, however, I shall use the term *Asian* on some occasions even though the discussion concerns Pacific Islanders as well.

Blacks are sometimes referred to as African American, whites as European American or Anglo. For Native Americans, I sometimes use the term American Indian even though technically it does not include Eskimos and Aleuts.

Many of the terms used to identify ethnic categories are the same as those used to categorize people by race. For example, such terms as African American, Asian, European American, and American Indian tend to have both racial and ethnic/cultural usages.

One of the most important and complex ethnicity-related terms is Hispanic, which is used in the text to refer to people who self-identify or share cultural attributes with one or more Latin American societies. A synonym used frequently is Latino. For groups associated with specific Hispanic cultures, countries of origin, or regions, I sometimes use such terms as *Mexican American, Puerto Rican,* and *Central American.*

Hispanics fall into several racial categories. Many think of themselves as racially white; some think of themselves as black; a few think of themselves as Asian. A large percentage of Latinos in the United States think of themselves in racial terms as *other,* in part reflecting their descent from some combination of people of white, black, Native American, or Asian origins. The racial/ethnic complexity of Latinos in the United States leads to such phrases as non-Hispanic whites and non-Hispanic blacks in some statistical data sources and research documents. These phrases are used in the text on occasion. For convenience, however, I often use simply *white* or *black.*

Because Asians come from so many nations and cultural groups, there are a number of references to specific Asian subpopulations, for example, Chinese Americans, Japanese Americans, and Korean Americans.

Because African Americans and Native Americans are also quite pluralistic, there are occasional references to particular segments of these groups, for example, specific American Indian nations/tribes and specific black subpopulations, for example, recent immigrants from an African country.

Finally, I frequently use the terms *minority* and *majority. Majority* always refers to the non-Hispanic white population. In most contexts, *minority* refers collectively to African Americans, Latinos, and Native Americans, the racial/ethnic groups that are doing the least well educationally under existing societal arrangements. In some cases, *minority* also includes Asian/Pacific Islanders as well, even though educationally Asians—but not Pacific Islanders—are doing about as well as, if not better than, non-Hispanic whites.

VIEWPOINT

As I have mentioned, the maintaining of a healthy, humane society characterized by substantial racial/ethnic pluralism is almost always difficult. Certainly the history of the United States bears this out. The movement of millions of white immigrants from many European national and cultural groups into the mainstream of American life ranks as one of the greatest successes of American society. The exclusionary or harshly discriminatory treatment of nonwhites over most of the nation's history is one of its most tragic failures.

The progress minorities have made in recent decades toward securing full membership in American society gives one reason to feel optimistic about the nation's capacity to build a more humane society in the context of an increasingly heterogeneous population. Nevertheless, neither success nor failure in this undertaking is a foregone conclusion. The country has many options in attempting to meet the educational, economic, social, and political needs of individuals and groups. Some of the choices seem likely to lead toward a more rewarding environment for all; others seem likely to lead in the opposite direction. I hope this book will help point the way to wise and compassionate decisions.

PLAN OF THE BOOK

Chapter 1 discusses several reasons why it is in the interest of American society to make a much greater effort than ever before to improve the educational fortunes of racial/ethnic minorities. It also examines the changing demographics in some detail. In chapter 2 I turn to an examination of educational attainment trends for the minority and majority populations, as measured by years of schooling completed and degrees earned. Trends are examined for the twentieth century as a whole as well as for the past two or three decades—the period in which the demographic shift has been especially rapid.

In chapter 3, my focus shifts to educational achievement as measured by standardized test scores and school grades. Differences among racial/ethnic groups in both average scores and the distribution of scores are examined.

Chapter 4 lays the groundwork for a multichapter exploration of why large academic attainment and achievement gaps originally developed between whites and (non-Asian) minorities and why they persist. The chapter first reviews influential research showing that differences among racial/ethnic groups in standardized test score and grade patterns are correlated more highly with measures of socioeconomic status than with measures of school resources. I then present a conceptual explanation for the association between academic performance and social class and a definition of equal educational opportunity that emphasizes the production of similar distributions of academic achievement among racial/ethnic groups. I close the chapter with a discussion of the economic dimensions of the opportunity structure.

The relationship between socioeconomic status and student achievement is examined in much greater detail in chapter 5, which gives special attention to the connection between poverty and academic performance.

Chapter 6 focuses on whether standard measures of socioeconomic status (family income and parent education) account for most of the differences in academic achievement among racial/ethnic groups. I look at standardized achievement test score data broken down simultaneously by measures of socioeconomic status and race/ethnicity.

Chapter 7 begins an exploration of the large differences in standardized test score patterns between whites and some minority groups. The differences in the education-relevant resources available to majority and minority students and their families at most socioeconomic levels are emphasized.

Chapter 8 is the first part of a two-chapter analysis of the role racial/ethnic prejudice and discrimination continue to play in generating differences in academic achievement patterns. This chapter reviews the history of prejudice and discrimination in the United States as well as some of the reasons they persist. Chapter 9 reviews evidence regarding some specific ways in which prejudice and discrimination may undermine the academic achievement of minority students, regardless of social class.

In chapter 10, I explore the growing body of research on the relationship of cultural differences between groups of students and the school to academic achievement patterns. The focus is on cultural attributes that tend to be specific to racial/ethnic groups and social classes.

In chapter 11, I provide "order-of-magnitude" estimates of the variation in education-relevant family and school resources available to different groups of children.

Chapter 12 summarizes the central findings of the book in a way that can contribute to the development of more effective strategies for accelerating the educational advancement of minorities. It also offers a set of criteria that can be used to set priorities for efforts in this area. Further, it presents recommendations for action, based on the conviction that America has a compelling interest in substantially changing not just its educational system but several other institutional systems relevant to the educational performance of minority (and majority) students.

Chapter 13 offers some thoughts on the larger meaning of the changing demographics of the United States.

Acknowledgments

Most books have one or more godparents. One of the most prominent godparents of my book is Arnold Shore, who during his tenure as president of the Council for Aid to Education made it possible for me to undertake the several years of research and writing that this project entailed. For more than a decade Arnie has been an adviser and sounding board as I have examined alternative ways of thinking about the improvement of educational opportunities for disadvantaged and low-status populations.

Several other people generously offered an enormous amount of support and encouragement during the writing of this book—Edmund Gordon, John Goodlad, Carole Morning, Robert Egbert, and Edward Goldberg. These individuals not only have given me advice and counsel on minority education and related school reform issues for many years, but also have read and commented extensively on the manuscript as it evolved. No matter what the issue or problem, each was always ready to help. That several difficult, sensitive minority education issues are addressed in this book from several vantage points is owing in no small measure to the guidance and leadership provided by Ed Gordon over many years. The broad, synthetic approach taken in the book was strongly supported by John Goodlad.

I also would like to express my appreciation to William Baumol, Leonard Beckum, Raymond Castro, Judith Eaton, Jeanne Frankl, Michael MacDowell, Blandina Ramirez, Philip Uri Treisman, and Michael Usdan, each of whom read parts of the manuscript during its development and offered thoughtful reactions, suggestions, and encouragement.

Of enormous help in the preparation of this book was Daniel Humphrey, my research assistant for much of the project. Dan has an uncommonly firm grasp of a wide range of educational research and a remarkable willingness to delve into new topics. Even more important was the good judgment he offered, whether helping to sift through a seemingly endless number of books and articles or critiquing drafts of the manuscript.

Special thanks are extended to my friend and former colleague at the Council for Aid to Education, Priscilla Lewis, who read and commented on each draft of the manuscript and offered crucial editorial advice as the book took shape.

Catherine Cullar's logistical support for (and good humor about) the preparation of the manuscript proved invaluable. Others at the council, including James Butler, David Gile, Robert Jordan, Ellen Kramer, Carla Mikell, David Morgan, and Diana Rigden, also were very helpful in numerous ways.

I also would like to thank a number of people with whom I have worked in a variety of educational contexts over the years. Bernice Anderson, David Bergholz, Russell Edgerton, Gary Fenstermacher, Mark Fredisdorf, Paul Hechman, Norbert Hill, Harold Hodgkinson, Sol Hurwitz, David Imig, Marsha Levine, Gil Lopez, Arturo Madrid, the late Edward Meade, Deborah Meier, Frank Newman, Robert Payton, Thomas Phillips, Ann Marie Senior, Barbara Shade, Theodore Sizer, and Michael Timpane have each significantly influenced my thinking on school reform and minority education issues.

I am unusually indebted to my editor at Yale University Press, Gladys Topkis, her assistant, Janyce Beck, and my manuscript editor, Lawrence Kenney. Owing to their efforts, the book is much more readable—and shorter. They brought a firm but thoughtfully sympathetic approach to a very challenging editorial task.

Family members are among an author's most important sources of support, and my case is no exception. My wife, Sandy, frequently compensated at home for the extensive (excessive) amount of time her husband committed to this project. Our sons, Cary and Dana, did the same, even as they wondered when it would be done.

Some final comments about the godparents of this book. Although I grew up in a part of the country (southern Indiana) in which there were few members of racial/ethnic minorities, I was aware from a relatively early age that some groups did not have full membership in our society. My late mother, Betty Lou Laird Miller, and two close family friends, the late George and Dorothy Johnson, were responsible for much of this awareness. The Johnsons' participation in the March on Washington in 1963 made a powerful impression on me during my teens. (Widowed and in her midseventies, Dorothy participated in the twentieth-anniversary march in 1983.)

Later, as a young adult in places as diverse as Vietnam, urban America (New York City), and Kenya, I was able to observe all too similar patterns of racial/ ethnic prejudice, discrimination, and conflict as well as their interaction with such diverse factors as educational differences, cultural differences, war, intense poverty, and rapid population growth and migration. In each place, courageous, empathetic people were struggling with these problems.

Alfred Oxenfeldt, my mentor when I was a graduate student at Columbia University, demonstrated to me again and again the value of unromantic, rigorous, interdisciplinary analysis, whether one is attempting to solve the problems of individuals or those of groups, institutions, or society as a whole.

My hope is that the voices of people like Mom, George, Dorothy, and Al— wherever they may reside—can be heard in the pages of this book, along with those of the many extraordinary educators and researchers whose work I draw upon in addressing education-related aspects of the nation's pursuit of more humane conditions for all members of its increasingly pluralistic society.

AN

AMERICAN

IMPERATIVE

CHAPTER ONE

Society's Interest

in the

Educational Advancement

of Minorities

In April 1983, the National Commission on Excellence in Education submitted its report, *A Nation at Risk: The Imperative for Educational Reform,* to Secretary of Education Terrel H. Bell and in the process helped usher in a vigorous period of educational reform that has extended into the 1990s.[1] A major focus of *A Nation at Risk* was the perceived inadequate academic performance of American students in general; the specific educational problems facing many minority children were not discussed.

Other reports soon followed, however, that did raise minority issues directly. As early as June 1983, the Task Force on Education for Economic Growth released *Action for Excellence,* which, in addition to stressing the importance of improving education for all students, called attention to the need to improve urban schools because of their high concentration of minority students.[2] By the mid-1980s, a number of reform reports had begun to address the persistent gaps in academic achievement between majority students and those from several minority groups—especially African Americans, Latinos, and Native Americans.[3] Eventually, several major reports focused exclusively on issues related to

1. National Commission on Excellence in Education, *A Nation at Risk: The Imperative for Educational Reform* (Washington, D.C.: Department of Education, U.S. Government Printing Office, 1983).

2. Task Force on Education for Economic Growth, *Action for Excellence: A Comprehensive Plan to Improve Our Nation's Schools* (Denver: Education Commission of the States, 1983), pp. 22, 40. In September 1983, the National Science Board's Commission on Precollege Education in Mathematics, Science and Technology produced *Educating Americans for the 21st Century: A plan of action for improving mathematics, science and technology education for all American elementary and secondary students so that their achievement is the best in the world by 1995* (Washington, D.C.: National Science Board/National Science Foundation, 1983). This report also was concerned mainly with the need to improve education for all students, but—possibly reflecting the fact that several commission members, including the cochair were minority—its comments on minority students' educational needs were somewhat more extensive than those in *A Nation at Risk* and *Action for Excellence*. See pp. vi-vii and 12–14.

3. In the 1980s many educators, government leaders, business leaders, and others became aware of the demographic shift, thanks in part to a report on its educational implications by Harold L. Hodgkinson. See *All One System: Demographics of Education, Kindergarten through Graduate School* (Washington, D.C.: Institute for Educational Leadership, 1985).

One of the first commission reports to link school reform to minority education issues extensively

minority education. For example, in May 1988, the Commission on Minority Participation in Education and American Life released *One-Third of a Nation,* which opened with this provocative statement:

> America is moving backward—not forward—in its efforts to achieve the full participation of minority citizens in the life and prosperity of the nation.
>
> In education, employment, income, health, longevity, and other basic measures of individual and social well-being, gaps persist—and in some cases are widening—between members of minority groups and the majority population.
>
> If these disparities are allowed to continue, the United States inevitably will suffer a compromised quality of life and a lower standard of living. Social conflict will intensify. Our ability to compete in world markets will decline, our domestic economy will falter, our national security will be endangered. In brief, we will find ourselves unable to fulfill the promise of the American dream.[4]

Admittedly, it is common for commission reports on important issues of the day to forecast negative consequences should aggressive remedial action not be taken quickly. (A central purpose of such commissions is to sound the alarm regarding the issues they were convened to address.) Yet even by these standards *A Nation at Risk* and *One-Third of a Nation* are strongly worded documents. Their credibility has been enhanced by the similar assessments published subsequently by many other respected groups and organizations[5] and their persuasiveness reinforced by deteriorating social and economic conditions, particularly in the country's largest cities. In spite of the long period of economic growth in the mid- to late 1980s, many American families, especially those headed by individuals who are less than thirty years old and those with little formal education, currently have significantly lower real incomes than their counterparts of a generation ago.[6] Poverty-related problems confronting

---

was *A Nation Prepared: Teachers for the 21st Century* (1986), produced by the Carnegie Forum on Education and the Economy. The Forum's Task Force on Teaching as a Profession included a mix of government, business, and educational leaders, some of whom had been members of commissions that had produced earlier reports on school reform, such as *Action for Excellence.* The report gave a great deal of attention to the question of how to expand the number of minority teachers (pp. 79–86).

4. Commission on Minority Participation in Education and American Life, *One-Third of a Nation* (Washington, D.C.: American Council on Education/Education Commission of the States, 1988), p. 1.

5. See, for example, Carnegie Foundation for the Advancement of Teaching, *An Imperiled Generation: Saving Urban Schools* (Princeton, N.J.: Princeton University Press, 1988); *The Forgotten Half: Pathways to Success for America's Youth and Young Families, Final Report* (Washington, D.C.: William T. Grant Foundation Commission on Work, Family and Citizenship, 1988); Carnegie Council on Adolescent Development, *Turning Points: Preparing American Youth for the 21st Century* (New York: Carnegie Corporation of New York, 1989).

6. Real average weekly earnings in the private, nonagricultural work force dropped (in 1989 dollars) from $387.24 in 1969 to $335.20 in 1989, or over 13 percent. But families headed by well-educated individuals were generally earning more in the late 1980s than in the late 1960s, while families headed by poorly educated individuals were earning much less than they had. The decline in

minorities in central cities have worsened in several respects, and racial/ethnic conflict has intensified.

But there is a more positive side to the minority advancement story. Although educational gaps between the white majority and several minority groups were still large as we entered the 1990s, many of these gaps are currently much smaller than they were as recently as the mid-1970s. The gap in mean Scholastic Aptitude Test (SAT) scores between blacks and whites fell from 258 points in 1976 to 196 points in 1992, a 24 percent reduction.[7]

Minority advances in education have been paralleled by economic and social advances. In spite of high minority poverty rates, the number of black and Hispanic middle-class families is considerably larger now than it was only two or three decades ago.[8] Many more minorities are in positions of institutional leadership. For example, since the Voting Rights Act of 1965, significant changes have taken place in the racial/ethnic composition of the nation's elected officials at all levels of government.[9] Although they are still extremely underrepresented in leadership positions throughout society, minorities are long past the so-called token representation point in many sectors.[10] Consequently, the debate regarding minority advancement into leadership positions has been gradually shifting toward the question of how to attain proportional representation as quickly as possible.

---

earnings was especially acute among families headed by an individual under age thirty; their median income fell 13 percent between 1973 and 1989. See Commission on the Skills of the American Workforce, *America's Choice: High Skills or Low Wages* (Rochester, N.Y.: National Center on Education and the Economy, 1990), pp. 19–22; Aaron Bernstein et al., "What Happened to the American Dream?" *Business Week*, 19 August 1991, pp. 80–85.

7. *College Bound Seniors: 1992 Profile of SAT and Achievement Test Takers* (New York: College Entrance Examination Board, 1992), p. iv.

8. In 1989, 68 percent of white families, 42 percent of African American familes, and 47 percent of Latino families had annual incomes of $25,000 or more. As recently as 1967 only 32 percent of black families had an annual income of $25,000 or more (in 1989 dollars) compared to 63 percent of white families. (Income data for Hispanics were not available for 1967.) Edward J. Welniak, Jr., and Mark S. Littman, "Money Income and Poverty Status in the U.S. 1989," *Current Population Reports Series P-60, No. 168* (Washington, D.C.: Bureau of the Census, U.S. Government Printing Office, 1990), pp. 23–24. For an analysis of changes in the proportion and composition of the African American middle class, see Bart Landry, *The New Black Middle Class* (Berkeley: University of California Press, 1987).

9. For example, in the national elections of November 1992, an African American woman and an American Indian man were elected to the Senate. At the same time, thirty-eight blacks and seventeen Latinos were elected to the House of Representatives (up from twenty-five and ten, respectively, in the previous congressional election). The first Korean American was elected to the House—from a district with a small Asian population. See Gloria Borger, "The Storming of Capital Hill," *U.S. News & World Report*, 16 November 1992, p. 65; Clifford Krauss, "The Old Order Changes in Congress—A Little," *New York Times*, 8 November 1992, Section 4, p. 3. A few years earlier, an African American was elected governor of a southern state, and members of minority groups are currently mayors of several of the nation's largest cities. See Gerald D. Jaynes and Robin M. Williams, Jr., eds., *A Common Destiny: Blacks and American Society* (Washington, D.C.: National Academy Press, 1989), pp. 230–58.

10. The advancement of blacks into leadership positions may have been greatest in the U.S. Army. An African American army officer, Colin Powell, attained the most senior position within the U.S. military (head of the Joint Chiefs), and a significant number of blacks are generals. See Charles Moskos, "How Do They Do It?: The Army's Racial Success Story," *New Republic*, 5 August 1991, pp. 16–20.

Clear gains notwithstanding, however, minorities are not making enough progress, especially in education. Thus, the objectives of this book are to provide educators, government policymakers, corporate leaders, foundation professionals, journalists, and other interested parties with a clear understanding of the differences in educational performance patterns that continue to exist between major racial/ethnic groups in American society, an explanation for the persistence of these differences, and a set of recommendations for action to eliminate them as quickly as possible.

WHY CLOSING MINORITY-MAJORITY EDUCATIONAL GAPS IS IMPERATIVE

The continued existence of substantial minority-majority educational gaps is prohibitively costly, not only for minorities, but for the nation as a whole. Among the most compelling reasons for seeking to eliminate these gaps as soon as possible are the following: (1) the achievement of significantly higher minority education levels is essential to the long-term productivity and competitiveness of the U.S. economy; (2) if minorities are to enjoy the full benefits of their recently won civil rights, they need formal-education-dependent knowledge and skills much closer in quantity and quality to those held by whites; and (3) the maintenance of a humane and harmonious society depends to a considerable degree on minorities' reaching educational parity with whites.

The Nation's Long-Term Economic Productivity and Competitiveness   During the 1970s, the rate of productivity growth in the United States, as measured by gross domestic product (GDP) per work-hour, was somewhat lower than it had been in the 1950s and 1960s.[11] This decrease occurred at a time when Japan and several other countries were increasingly penetrating U.S. domestic markets for technology related goods at the expense of American manufacturers.[12] The nation's economy was also buffeted by the twin oil price shocks of the 1970s, stagflation (the simultaneous occurrence of low economic growth and high inflation) for much of that decade, and a severe recession in the early 1980s. Collectively, these events served to remind Americans that economic prosperity is not a natural right but something that must be earned daily, year in and year out, in a marketplace that is increasingly international.

With the publication of *A Nation at Risk* in 1983, Americans were also reminded that a principal determinant of a country's long-term economic pro-

11. Angus Maddison, *Phases of Capitalist Development* (New York: Oxford University Press, 1982), p. 212.

12. Between 1965 and 1985, Japan's trade surplus with the United States in technology-intensive products grew from $143 million to $13 billion. In 1985 surpluses were particularly large in radio/television-receiving equipment, communications equipment, office/computing machines, and professional/scientific instruments. In the broader category of high-technology products, the Japanese trade surplus with the United States was about $22 billion in 1986. About 75 percent of the Japanese surplus in high-technology products was in telecommunications equipment and electronic components. Maria Papadakis, *The Science and Technology Resources of Japan: A Comparison with the United States* (Washington, D.C.: National Science Foundation, 1988), pp. xii-xiii.

ductivity and competitiveness is the educational level of its population. The report strongly suggested that American students were generally not performing as well in school as students in a number of other industrialized countries.[13] It was already well known that students from several minority groups were, on average, much less successful in school than white students. By the mid-1980s there also was increasing awareness of the rapid growth in the minority proportion of the student-age population. Given these circumstances, it is not surprising that the authors of *One-Third of a Nation* saw connections among the changing demographics, the continuing educational problems of minorities, and the apparently declining economic health of the United States.

It is possible, of course, to overestimate the importance of the educational level of a population in determining the health of an economy and the role of school reform in correcting the economy's perceived deficiencies.[14] Clearly, factors other than education influence the overall health of an economy, including the society's savings and investment rate and the government's monetary and fiscal policies. Nevertheless, research on the sources of long-term productivity growth (and, therefore, economic competitiveness) in industrial societies has consistently found that the knowledge and skills of the population are very important.

In *Productivity and American Leadership: The Long View,* William Baumol, Sue Anne Blackman, and Edward Wolff noted that there was a convergence in productivity growth rates among sixteen industrialized nations, including the United States, between 1870 and 1979. However, during this same period the economic productivity gaps between industrialized nations and many less developed countries (LDCs) actually grew. In the view of Baumol and his associates, differences in the educational levels of nations' populations over time have played an important role in producing these results. According to these writers, in the contemporary world, a nation needs both an educated elite and a well-educated general population to maintain membership in the industrialized nations club. Educated elites can produce advances in science, technology, and other areas of the kinds that generate sources of new economic growth in the society as a whole, and they can quickly access and adapt new knowledge generated elsewhere. A well-educated general population is important because the overall level of knowledge and skill increasingly determines a society's ability to use new knowledge effectively throughout the economy.[15]

13. National Commission on Excellence in Education, *A Nation at Risk,* pp. 1–11.

14. Lawrence A. Cremin, *Popular Education and Its Discontents* (New York: Harper and Row, 1989), pp. 102–03.

15. William J. Baumol, Sue Anne Batey Blackman, and Edward N. Wolff, *Productivity and American Leadership: The Long View* (Cambridge: MIT Press, 1989), pp. 195–210. Many corporations have found that the knowledge and skill requirements their manufacturing employees must meet have been increasing rapidly owing to technological change and competitive pressures to turn out higher-quality products. For example, according to Motorola's vice president for training and education, the company's manufacturing employees "must have communication and computation skills at the seventh grade level, soon going up to eighth and ninth. They must be able to do basic problem solving—not only as individuals but also as members of a team." This means that Motorola's manufacturing employees must soon know basic algebra as well as have a grasp of some basic statistical

In the future, a country that is able to draw upon all three ways in which education can contribute to productivity growth will probably have a good chance to become a leading member in the club of industrialized nations. Interestingly, the generation of large amounts of new knowledge seems to be less essential for gaining or maintaining membership (as opposed to assuming a leadership position) in the club than the ability to access new knowledge generated elsewhere and to use it widely. A nation with a modest-size educated elite and a well-educated general population should be able to be a member of the club, all other things being equal. In contrast, a nation with a large educated elite and a relatively undereducated general population may find it increasingly difficult in the future to gain or maintain a leadership position among industrialized nations.

In the period immediately following World War II, Japan was among the most successful practitioners of an economic growth strategy that combined an educated elite that concentrated on accessing and using new knowledge developed elsewhere with a relatively well-educated general population that could make use of this knowledge to produce high-quality products. More recently the capacity of Japan's educated elite to develop new knowledge also has become very substantial. Thus, Japan has emerged as one of the leading members of the industrialized nations club. For the future, the Japanese appear to be very well positioned to use all three educational methods for ensuring robust productivity growth and a high level of economic competitiveness.[16]

In the past century the United States has been able to rely on all three educational strategies to a significant degree. The nation has been a leader in developing a large educated elite, able to generate new knowledge as well as to adapt advances made elsewhere. The United States has also benefited from a substantial number of well-educated immigrants, first from Europe and, more recently, from Asia. And its early provision of broad access to elementary and (subsequently) secondary education gave the United States a better educated general population than those of a number of other industrial societies.[17] Con-

---

concepts in order to perform their work. See William Wiggenhorn, "Motorola U: When Training Becomes an Education," *Harvard Business Review* 90 (July-August 1990): 71, 74.

16. "The first phase of Japan's S/T [science and technology] efforts, which occurred from the immediate postwar period through the early sixties, did not involve indigenous R&D investment so much as a reorientation of Japanese industry. Throughout the period, there was large-scale financial investment aimed at transforming Japan's economy from light manufactures to heavy industry. The acquisition of foreign technology was an integral part of this strategy, and technology was purchased which would allow Japan both to manufacture new products and to introduce new techniques for the production of existing goods. Once the new industrial base was established, Japan embarked on its own research and technology development" (Papadakis, *The Science and Technology Resources of Japan*, p. viii).

17. In 1910, less than 3 percent of the 25-and-over population had completed at least four years of college. This percentage had grown to over 6 percent in 1950, to 17 percent in 1980, and to more than 21 percent in 1988. See National Center for Education Statistics, U.S. Department of Education, *Digest of Education Statistics 1990* (Washington, D.C.: U.S. Government Printing Office, 1991), p. 17. As recently as 1950, only 5–10 percent of the students in most European nations, compared with over half of those in the United States, completed high school. See Torsten Husen, "Are Standards in U.S. Schools Really Lagging Behind Those in Other Countries?" *Phi Delta Kappan* 64 (March 1983): 457; National Center for Education Statistics, *Digest of Education Statistics 1990*, p. 17.

sequently, for most of the period America has enjoyed a competitive advantage in situations in which a significant number of people needed a relatively good education to make productive use of knowledge in the workplace.

In recent decades, however, America has evidently lost a good deal of its competitive edge. In the post–World War II period, several nations offered elementary and secondary education to all or most of their populations, and some surpassed the quality of schooling in America.[18] Further, rapidly changing demographics have increased the proportion of the U.S. student population that is educationally disadvantaged. The relative educational weakness of the general U.S. population has been demonstrated on a number of international tests of academic achievement in the past decade. The average test scores of U.S. students have typically placed them in the bottom half of the group of participating industrialized/industrializing nations. On many subject-area tests—especially in math and science—U.S. students often have finished in the bottom quarter of participating nations. In more than one instance, they have been among the lowest-scoring national groups of students.[19]

These test results demonstrate the need to raise the math and science performance of the U.S. student population as a whole and, even more urgently, of minority students, both because they do much less well academically than whites and because they represent a growing proportion of the student-age population. As we shall see in chapter 11, many African American and Latino students perform at levels similar to those usually attained by students in LDCs. Given that minority students currently make up about three in ten of the elementary- and secondary-school-age population in the United States and that at least two in ten of all American children have been living in poverty at any given time in recent years, it is understandable that the demographer Harold Hodgkinson has observed that the lowest performing third of America's students are "undoubtedly the worst 'bottom third' of any of the industrialized democracies."[20] This

18. The 1985 secondary school enrollment rate was 99 percent in the United States, 97 percent in Australia, 96 percent in France, 75 percent in Italy, 96 percent in Japan, 83 percent in Sweden, 85 percent in the United Kingdom, and 74 percent in West Germany. Kenneth Redd and Wayne Riddle, *Comparative Education: Statistics on Education in the United States and Selected Foreign Nations* (Washington, D.C.: Congressional Research Service of the Library of Congress, U.S. Government Printing Office, 1988), p. 17.

19. Curtis C. McKnight et al., *The Underachieving Curriculum: Assessing U.S. School Mathematics from an International Perspective* (Champaign, Ill.: Stipes, 1987), pp. vi-vii, 15–19; Archie E. Lapointe, Nancy A. Mead, and Gary W. Phillips, *A World of Differences: An International Assessment of Mathematics and Science* (Princeton, N.J.: Educational Testing Service, 1988), pp. 8, 13–14, 35–36; and International Association for the Evaluation of Educational Achievement, *Science Achievement in Seventeen Countries: A Preliminary Report* (Oxford: Pergamon Press, 1988), pp. 2–4. The actual experience of American companies with many of their employees provides additional support for the conclusion that U.S. students, in general, have not been doing as well academically as their counterparts in other countries. For example, in the early 1980s Motorola found that many of its employees, including recent high school and junior college graduates, lacked basic literacy and numeracy skills. Thus, Motorola has found it necessary to arrange for many employees to take remedial math and English courses. See Wiggenhorn, "Motorola U.: When Training Becomes an Education," pp. 71–72, 77–79.

20. Harold Hodgkinson, "Reform Versus Reality," *Phi Delta Kappan* 73 (September 1991): 10. Many are concerned about America's top students as well. See Daniel J. Singal, "The Other Crisis in

observation is made more powerful by the relative homogeneity of the academic achievement pattern of Japanese students: Japan simply does not have a sizable proportion of students doing very poorly. Relative to the United States, the academic middle of Japan's student population is both high performing and very large.[21]

The evidence regarding the importance of education to a nation's economic well-being coupled with the existence of large numbers of minority youngsters who are not doing well academically suggests that the United States has a compelling economic interest in accelerating the educational advancement of minorities. In the words of Baumol, Blackman, and Wolff,

> The likelihood that a markedly expanding proportion of the U.S. working population will be made up of persons drawn from groups whose amount of education and educational performance is significantly below that of the remainder of the nation presages a growing impediment to U.S. productivity performance. Thus, it may be that those of us who are affected only indirectly by the educational handicaps of underprivileged groups will nevertheless end up paying dearly if we do not provide the thought, the planning, the effort, and the resources needed to deal effectively with those educational problems.[22]

MINORITY EDUCATIONAL LEVELS AND THE OBJECTIVES OF THE CIVIL RIGHTS MOVEMENT

At the end of World War II the United States still had an elaborate race/ethnic-based caste system. Although circumstances varied by region, minorities—especially blacks—as a result of both law and custom and of the preferences (prejudices) of whites, were mostly relegated to subordinate positions. But over the next twenty years, the civil rights movement would succeed in dismantling the legal foundations of "separate but equal" institutional arrangements.

An early victory in this extraordinary period of reform came in 1948, when President Harry S. Truman issued *Executive Order 9981,* which provided the basis for integrating the U.S. armed forces and for ensuring equal treatment of minorities in the military.[23] The civil rights movement gathered momentum in

---

American Education," *Atlantic Monthly* (November 1991): 59–62, 65–67, 70, 73–74. However, others counter that, by the end of college or graduate school, the top American students are clearly among the best in the world. See, for example, Michael W. Kirst, "The Need to Broaden Our Perspective Concerning America's Educational Attainment," *Phi Delta Kappan* 73 (October 1991): 118–20.

21. Harold W. Stevenson, James W. Stigler, Shin-ying Lee et al., "Cognitive Performance and Academic Achievement of Japanese, Chinese and American Children," *Child Development* 56 (June 1985): 718–34.

22. *Productivity and American Leadership,* p. 209.

23. Historically, white political leaders have taken steps to increase the rights of African Americans "only in national emergencies or under extreme political pressure." In this case, President Truman acted after A. Philip Randolph had "called for black and white youths to boycott the draft in

1954, when the U.S. Supreme Court ruled unanimously in the *Brown* case that racially segregated public schools were "inherently unequal" and therefore unconstitutional.[24] The Civil Rights Act of 1964 barred discrimination in employment and public accommodations, and the Voting Rights Act of 1965 effectively ended the use of literacy tests to prevent African Americans from voting. Although many important changes in the legal and regulatory environment continued to be made in the 1970s, 1980s, and early 1990s, the period of legal change produced by the civil rights movement essentially ended in 1968 with the passage of federal legislation making discrimination in housing sales and rentals illegal.

A little more than a century after Lincoln issued the Emancipation Proclamation, the modern civil rights movement had finally been able to secure the legal rights necessary for blacks and other minorities to seek full participation in American life. And it had done so through the use of a mainstream-values and participation-oriented strategy that combined litigation, moral suasion, nonviolent civil disobedience, and interest-group lobbying.[25] Yet, ironically, 1968 was also the year in which President Lyndon B. Johnson established the National Advisory Commission on Civil Disorders (called the Kerner Commission after its chair, Gov. Otto Kerner of Illinois) to determine the causes of the race riots that had erupted in cities all over the country in the mid- to late 1960s—*after* most of the key victories in the civil rights movement. In its now-famous report, the Kerner Commission blamed the riots on the nation's long history of racism and the segregated society it had produced. The commission contended that the riots were grounded in large measure in rigid housing segregation in urban areas and a shortage of economic opportunities for undereducated African Americans.[26]

Beginning in 1965 with the uprising in Watts, a section of Los Angeles, there were more than fifty race riots in urban America in the latter half of the 1960s.[27] Apart from the human tragedies they represented, the riots are a clear reminder

---

1947." Earlier (1941), by threatening a march on Washington by blacks, Randolph had persuaded President Franklin Roosevelt to issue an executive order ending racial discrimination among defense contractors. Twenty-two years later (1963), it was Randolph who conceived the historic March on Washington to pressure the federal government into passing civil rights legislation. Lawrence H. Fuchs, *The American Kaleidoscope: Race, Ethnicity, and the Civic Culture* (Hanover, N.H.: Wesleyan University Press/University Press of New England, 1990), pp. 157–58, 165–66.

24. *Brown v. the Board of Education of Topeka, Kansas,* 347 U.S. 483 (1954).

25. Dr. Martin Luther King, Jr.'s "I Have a Dream" speech—an example of the highly effective use of moral suasion by a civil rights leader—drew heavily on the nation's most cherished political and economic values. For example, it emphasized the need to "let freedom ring" for blacks and other minorities in the form of a market economics metaphor—a promissary note that had come due. King, "I Have a Dream," speech delivered in Washington D.C., 28 August 1963, at the March on Washington for Civil Rights, reprinted in *Rhetoric of Racial Revolt,* ed. Roy L. Hill (Denver: Golden Bell Press, 1964), pp. 371–75.

26. National Advisory Commission on Civil Disorders, *Report of the National Advisory Commission on Civil Disorders* (New York: Bantam, 1968), pp. 236–50, 253.

27. Reynolds Farley and Walter R. Allen, *The Color Line and the Quality of Life in America* (New York: Russell Sage Foundation, 1987), p. 1.

that technical equality under the law is a necessary but insufficient condition for full participation in society. Individuals and groups must also possess the knowledge and skills necessary to exercise their legal rights effectively. The nature and mix of things people need to know, of course, varies from country to country. In a large, democratic, technology-based, organizationally complex nation, more and more people must possess verbal, quantitative, and scientific knowledge and skills of the kinds that are taught formally in the schools.

Historically it has been difficult for groups with little formal education to acquire substantial amounts of such knowledge and skills quickly. Even under favorable circumstances, most groups that have succeeded in America needed several generations to improve their educational fortunes sufficiently to become largely middle class.[28] Not only did the children in each generation need opportunities to attend school, but the adults had to have jobs that paid enough to support their families. Unfortunately, in spite of the expansion of their legal rights following World War II, by the 1960s the economic opportunity structure available to urban minorities with limited education was increasingly unfavorable. Adequately paying jobs for the low-skilled were harder to come by despite the general prosperity of the nation during those years.[29] This meant that the children born to the least well-educated adults, both minority and majority, in that period had to do better in school than their parents simply to hold even at their parents' modest income levels.[30] Indeed, available evidence suggests that the economic opportunity structure for inner city minorities with limited education has worsened in the quarter century since the Kerner Commission report, with devastating consequences for their ability to realize the promises of the victories of the civil rights movement.[31]

The obstacles that inadequate education and limited job opportunities have posed for the most disadvantaged members of minority groups are relatively easy to recognize. It is much harder to see that many middle-class minority group members face similar problems, albeit at a different stage in the intergenerational advancement process. In the past few decades, many minorities have moved into the lower and middle ranks of the middle class as defined by their educational attainment and occupational and income levels. Nevertheless, an examination of the standardized test scores and grades of their children shows that collectively these youngsters are performing much less well in

28. For an overview of the experiences of several racial and ethnic groups over time in the United States, see Thomas Sowell, *Ethnic America: A History* (New York: Basic Books, 1981).

29. This shortage of adequately paying jobs for minorities in the postwar period contrasts sharply with the opportunities many European immigrant groups found in the late nineteenth and early twentieth centuries. John Kasarda, "Caught in the Web of Change," *Society* 21 (November/December, 1983): 41–47.

30. A recent study of job seekers found that up to half had extremely low levels of literacy, which seriously limited their access to the labor market. These problems were most acute for blacks and Hispanics with a high school education or less. Irwin S. Kirsch, Ann Jungeblut, and Anne Campbell, *Beyond the School Doors: The Literacy Needs of Job Seekers Served by the U.S. Department of Labor* (Princeton, N.J.: Educational Testing Service/U.S. Department of Labor, 1992), pp. 9, 71.

31. Richard Bernstein, "20 Years after the Kerner Report: Three Societies, All Separate," *New York Times*, 29 February 1988, p. B8.

school than are middle-class white (and Asian) children. Moreover, relatively few middle-class minority students are performing at the highest academic levels in verbal or quantitative areas. Among minority groups this problem seems to be most acute for African American children. Among the diverse Latino communities, it may be most acute among Puerto Rican children.

Given these achievement patterns, one can anticipate that the current generation of middle-class minority students will find it difficult to expand their representation in many professional fields, especially those that are math- and science-based, and even more difficult to become well represented among those who demonstrate the highest levels of technical competence in these fields and who therefore reach the highest levels of authority in them. For example, until the nation achieves something much closer to minority/majority educational (achievement) parity, it seems certain that there will continue to be few African American physicists and a conspicuous absence of black theoretical physicists doing leading-edge work at internationally prominent research universities, government laboratories, and corporate research facilities. It also seems very likely that there will be few Mexican Americans pursuing careers in oceanography, much less holding senior research positions in this field. And it seems probable that there will be significant underrepresentation of Puerto Ricans in biochemistry. Similar statements could be made regarding these groups' prospects for progress in market research, medicine, computer software engineering, and numerous other professions.

Until there is minority middle-class convergence on white middle-class educational performance levels in these and other professions, significant minority underrepresentation in senior management positions is also likely to continue. High achievement in college or graduate/professional school is often a prerequisite for entry level positions that prepare people for careers in management.[32] As long as blacks, Hispanics, and American Indians remain underrepresented among high academic achievers, their access to positions at the beginning of the "fast track" for senior professionals, as well as their general ability to compete successfully on that track over the years, will remain truncated.

In summary, there appears to be a strong link between educational performance and the capacity of minority groups to climb all rungs of the intergenerational advancement ladder. Currently, many disadvantaged minorities are having difficulty climbing onto the first few rungs of this ladder, while many middle-class minorities are having difficulty moving up to the highest rungs. As long as this is the case, the dream of civil rights leaders for an America in which minorities can participate on an equal basis with the white majority in all realms of society will be difficult to realize fully.

---

32. On the admissions processes and academic performance experience of selective colleges and universities as well as a summary of the literature on the relationship between academic performance and work performance, see Robert Klitgaard, *Choosing Elites* (New York: Basic Books, 1985).

As noted earlier, the authors of *One-Third of a Nation* were very much concerned about the persistence and even the growth of "social well-being" gaps between the white majority and racial/ethnic minorities. They were fearful that, should current trends continue, the United States would find it progressively more difficult to be a society in which fairness, civility, and decency prevail for most, if not all. Clearly, both the economic competitiveness and civil rights rationales for accelerating minority educational advancement are closely related to the issue of societal humaneness and harmony. If the U.S. economy proves to be markedly less competitive in the years ahead, it is less likely that Americans will have sufficient material resources to meet the needs of the population. In such circumstances, poverty could be a worsening problem, especially among minority group members with little education. Similarly, should minority groups continue to be seriously limited in their capacity to compete successfully for good jobs and leadership positions, they are likely to become more alienated from the white majority, each other, and society as a whole.

But neither the economic competitiveness rationale nor the civil rights rationale is an adequate basis for acquiring a full understanding of the importance of minority educational advancement to the development and maintenance of a just, socially stable America. We must look simultaneously at social class and racial/ethnic differences in America at a time of rapid growth in knowledge (especially in science and technology), rapid transformation of the structure of the economy, and rapid change in the composition of the population.

In most contemporary technological societies, access to desirable positions has been allocated on the basis of merit—how well individuals can perform the tasks required by that position. Using the market mechanism, the scarcer a given set of skills is (and, therefore, the more valuable to society), the greater the economic, social status, or institutional power rewards usually provided to those who possess it. This means that some individuals receive significantly more (or fewer) benefits than others. A group of individuals who receive somewhat similar amounts of benefits in a society is referred to as a social class.[33] The differences in benefits between social classes have been among the most enduring and difficult sources of conflict in technological societies since the beginning of the industrial revolution. Governments—especially democratically elected ones—have tended to spend a great deal of time on the twin questions of how to expand the size of the benefits pie and ensure that these benefits are allocated among different strata of the population (classes) in a fair and conflict-minimizing fashion without undermining the system's capacity to generate benefits.[34]

Two economic trends suggest that social class differences will continue to be

33. On class, see *Encyclopedia of Sociology* (Guilford, Conn.: Dushkin, 1974), pp. 44–46. On the relationship between social class and educational achievement, see chapters 4, 5, 6, 7, 10, 11 below.

34. See Ralf Dahrendorf, *The Modern Social Conflict: An Essay on the Politics of Liberty* (Berkeley: University of California Press, 1990).

very salient in the United States: the growing divergence in income between those with few skills and little formal education and those with many skills and much formal education[35] and the slowdown in economic growth in the 1970s and 1980s.[36] These trends suggest that there may be increased pressure on government to direct resources to the less advantaged social classes as well as to redouble efforts to increase the economy's growth rate.

Racial/ethnic differences have been among the most enduring sources of human conflict historically and remain so today. Nevertheless, in the early 1980s the social scientist Richard D. Lambert observed, "Americans tend to downplay ethnic/racial conflict as a major world problem. In a recent survey, a national sample of American college and university seniors listed it as tenth out of 10 in a list of world problems. And yet it—not territory, forms of government, economic systems, or ideology—is the most common source of conflict involving nation-states."[37]

Similarly, Abdul A. Said and Luis R. Simmons commented in the middle 1970s that a "revived sense of ethnic identity has grown in the last few decades, and ethnic politics has emerged as a significant factor in the international polit-

35. Gary Burtless, "Introduction and Summary," in Burtless, ed., *A Future of Lousy Jobs? The Changing Structure of U.S. Wages* (Washington, D.C.: Brookings Institution, 1990), pp. 1–30. Although college graduates faired better in the labor market in the 1980s than people with relatively little formal education, this does not mean that the economy was able to provide good jobs for all college graduates. Moreover, should the economy grow more slowly over the next ten to fifteen years than it did in the 1980s, competition among college graduates for good jobs is expected to become more intense. See Daniel E. Hecker, "Reconciling Conflicting Data on Jobs for College Graduates," and Kristina J. Shelley, "The Future of Jobs for College Graduates," *Monthly Labor Review* 115 (July 1992): 3–12, 13–21.

36. From 1948 to 1973, economic growth averaged about 3.5 percent per year; from 1973 to 1990, about 2.5 percent per year. For the 1948–53 period, the rate was 3.9 percent per year; for 1953–57, it was 3.1 percent per year; for 1957–60, it was 2.7 percent per year; for 1960–66, it was 4.5 percent per year; for 1966–73, it was 3.2 percent per year; for 1973–79, it was 2.9 percent per year; and for 1979–90, it was 2.4 percent per year. Analysis of the annual growth trend in the 1980s is complicated by the fact that there were two years of negative growth, 1980 and 1982. If we look only at the 1983–90 period, we get a 3.1 percent growth average. Nonetheless, despite relatively robust economic growth in the mid- to late 1980s (which included a high for the decade in 1984 of 6.8 percent), the trend does seem to be down. In 1990, the annual growth fell to 1.0 percent as the economy entered a recession. Although positive growth had resumed by mid-1991, by late 1992 the strong upsurge in growth typical of most economic recoveries had not yet occurred. The Bureau of Labor Statistics (BLS) has developed three economic growth projections for the 1990–2005 period. The "low growth scenario" projects a 1.5 percent annual growth rate for the 15-year period, the "moderate growth scenario" 2.3 percent, and the "high growth scenario" 2.9 percent. If the rate of growth continues to slow, a lower rate of growth in per capita income is expected as well. In 1973–90, for example, income per capita grew at 1.7 percent per year. Under the three BLS projections, annual per capita growth would increase at 1.1 percent, 1.5 percent, and 2.3 percent in the low-growth, moderate-growth, and high-growth scenarios, respectively. See Dale W. Jorgenson, "Microeconomics and Productivity," in Ralph Landau and Nathan Rosenberg, eds., *The Positive Sum Strategy: Harnessing Technology for Economic Growth* (Washington, D.C.: National Academy Press, 1986), p. 61; Council of Economic Advisers, *Economic Indicators November 1991* (Washington, D.C.: U.S. Government Printing Office, 1991), p. 3; Norman C. Saunders, "The U.S. Economy into the 21st Century," *Monthly Labor Review* 114 (November 1991): 13, 25; and Robert D. Hershey, Jr., "The Economy's Final Report Card before Election," *New York Times,* 26 October 1992, pp. D1-D2.

37. "Ethnic/Racial Relations in the United States in Comparative Perspective," *Annals of the American Academy of Political and Social Science* 454 (March 1981): 190–91.

ical system. . . . Out of an estimated 164 disturbances of significant violence involving states between 1958 and May 1966, a mere 15 were military conflicts involving two or more states. The most significant violence after 1945 has found its *causus belli* in ethnic, tribal, and racial disputes that have often exerted a spillover effect in international politics."[38]

Although ten or fifteen years ago the pervasiveness and importance of racial/ethnic differences may not have been acknowledged by many Americans, these days we are all too aware of their central role in human affairs. Regular readers of a major newspaper or viewers of a nightly national news program are likely to be exposed frequently to this topic. One of the major stories of recent years has been the end of the former Soviet Union's hegemony in Eastern Europe and the surge in ethnic nationalism in that region and within the former Soviet Union itself.[39] The most visible source to date of ethnic-related blood-shed has been the tragic war in the former Yugoslavia—a war that has introduced the chilling term *ethnic cleansing*. Ethnic differences have also played a substantial role in the catastrophic civil war in Somalia, where very large numbers of people have died not only as a direct result of the fighting, but also indirectly through starvation.[40] And we can easily find ethnic tension and conflict in many other nations and regions of the world. Iraq, Kenya, South Africa, and India represent but a handful of the countries that continue to experience ethnic-related difficulties.

Racial/ethnic differences and the violent conflicts they produce frequently spill over into other nations and regions, partly because the hostilities often lead many people to leave their embattled countries, to seek what they hope will be temporary sanctuary.[41] Some have been forceably expelled from their country of origin with little prospect of ever returning, regardless of their preferences.[42] Still others are immigrants hoping to build a new life in a new country. If the influx of refugees or immigrants to a particular host country

38. "The Ethnic Factor in World Politics," in Said and Simmons, eds., *Ethnicity in an International Context* (New Brunswick, N.J.: Transaction Books, 1976), pp. 15–16.

39. See, for example, Serge Schmemann, "Declaring Death of Soviet Union, Russia and 2 Republics Form New Commonwealth," *New York Times*, 9 December 1991, pp. A1, A8. It is estimated that from the beginning of 1991 through late summer of 1992 more than three thousand people were killed in the former Soviet Union in ethnic or political violence. Only about one hundred were killed while fighting Soviet troops. Most of the deaths were the result of ethnic conflict in Georgia, in Tajikistan, and between Armenia and Azerbaijan. See "Better than Bosnia," *The Economist*, 5 September 1992, p. 54.

40. See Rakiya Omaar, "Somalia: At War with Itself," *Current History* 91 (May 1992): 230–34; Leslie H. Gelb, "Shoot to Feed Somalia," *New York Times*, 19 November 1992, p. A27.

41. By the summer of 1992, Germany had taken in two hundred thousand refugees from the Balkan war, Austria and Hungary fifty thousand each, Sweden forty thousand, Switzerland thirteen thousand, Italy seven thousand, and the Netherlands four thousand. Tens of thousands of others had gone to several other countries. See Sabrina Petra Ramet, "War in the Balkans," *Foreign Affairs* 71 (Fall 1992): 79.

42. Three countries that have expelled significant numbers of people in the past two decades are Vietnam, Cuba, and Uganda. Although not all were expelled for reasons that qualify as racial/ethnic conflict, many were. See Michael S. Teitelbaum, "Forced Migration: The Tragedy of Mass Expulsions," in Nathan Glazer, ed., *Clamor at the Gates: The New American Immigration* (San Francisco: ICS Press, 1985), pp. 261–83.

becomes large, the possibility of triggering resentment from the indigenous population is substantial.[43]

Beginning with the early encounters between Europeans and Native Americans, American history (as well as the history of most other nations and regions) can be viewed as a long, complex series of racial/ethnic collisions, at times with extremely high levels of intergroup violence. In some cases, the threat or use of physical force has had devastating consequences, as the experiences of blacks and American Indians with whites over the past several centuries attest. In most cases, acts of violence have been initiated by the majority population against a minority group. However, minorities have sometimes responded with violence against the majority and against each other.[44]

Since the 1960s, America has received an extraordinarily large and diverse group of immigrants. With so many newcomers, the potential for racial/ethnic conflict has increased dramatically. Depending on the region, these new conflicts may primarily involve a new minority group and the white majority or a new group and an older minority group. Whites and Vietnamese in Texas, (white) Cubans and blacks in Miami, and Koreans and African Americans in New York City are examples of new categories of group conflict. Fortunately, the level of physical conflict has been modest relative to the size and diversity of the pool of newcomers as well as to the violence produced by large-scale immigration in nineteenth-century America. Nevertheless, the potential remains.

Racial/ethnic conflict is often intertwined with social class conflict.[45] In conflicts between old groups, social class is most salient when the combatants are the white majority versus blacks, Mexican Americans, Puerto Ricans, or Native Americans because these minority groups tend to have the largest proportions and numbers of economically and educationally disadvantaged individuals. In conflicts involving new groups, the linkages with social class may be more complex. For example, some recent groups of Asian immigrants—Koreans and Asian Indians, among others—include a large proportion of well-educated individuals. Other new groups, including many recent immigrants from Latin America, are disproportionately made up of individuals with little formal edu-

43. About 500,000 individuals applied for political asylum in Western Europe in 1990, up from 250,000 as recently as 1985. Moreover, about 12 million political refugees and immigrants were living in West European countries in the early 1990s. These are large numbers for nations that, unlike the United States, have not typically received a large volume of refugees and immigrants over many decades. Given this history as well as the difficult economic environment of recent years several European countries have experienced a rise in antiforeigner sentiment and action. See Craig R. Whitney, "Europeans Look for Ways to Bar Door to Immigrants," *New York Times*, 29 December 1991, pp. A1, A8; Gregory F. Treverton, "The Year of European (Dis)Unification," *Current History* 91 (November 1992): 353–58; Judith Miller, "Strangers at the Gate," *New York Times Magazine*, 15 September 1991, pp. 32–37, 49–50, 86.

44. See Michael Newton and Judy Ann Newton, *Racial and Religious Violence in America: A Chronology* (New York: Garland, 1991). For a discussion of how whites in one state threatened and used violence against blacks in the Jim Crow years, see George C. Wright, *Racial Violence in Kentucky 1865–1940: Lynchings, Mob Rule, and "Legal Lynchings"* (Baton Rouge: Louisiana State University Press, 1990).

45. See John Stone, *Racial Conflict in Contemporary Society* (Cambridge: Harvard University Press, 1985).

cation.[46] Thus, some new groups are positioned for relatively rapid advancement into the mainstream, at least from an occupational and income perspective, while others are not. This means that new minority groups have emerging social class patterns that can bring them into conflict with the majority population in some cases and with older minority populations in others. The Los Angeles riot of 1992 included a mixture of racial/ethnic and social class conflict, as did the riots in urban America in the 1960s.

THE CHANGING RACIAL/ETHNIC DEMOGRAPHICS OF THE UNITED STATES

The History of Change   Changes in the racial/ethnic composition of the population have been an ongoing feature of American life since the first European settlements. But only in recent decades has the population become less rather than more white. The racial/ethnic diversity of Americans is not only much greater now than at any previous period in American history but seems destined to become progressively more diverse for some time to come.

At the time of the first census, in 1790, the total population of the country was a little less than 4 million, about 81 percent white and 19 percent black. (In 1790, Native Americans were not counted in the census, immigration from Asia had not yet begun, and few people in the United States were from parts of the Americas that were then controlled by Spain.) [47] From 1790 until about 1920, the white proportion of the population gradually grew to about 89 percent (about 94 million of a total population of 106 million).[48]

This gradual increase in the white share of the population was primarily the result of massive immigration from Europe from 1840 to 1930 as well as substantial immigration from Canada. (Of the 37 million immigrants to the United States in this period, 85 percent came from Europe and nearly 8 percent—3 million—from Canada.)[49] Early in the nineteenth century the legal slave trade

46. In the mid-1980s, the proportion of immigrants aged twenty-five to fifty-four with a high school diploma was 81 percent for Filipinos, 64 percent for Haitians, 61 percent for Vietnamese, 58 percent for Jamaicans, 24 percent for Central Americans, 24 percent for Dominicans, and 13 percent for Mexicans. In 1980, fewer than 3 percent of the Mexican immigrants but about one-third of the Filipinos had a college degree. See National Coalition of Advocates for Students, *New Voices: Immigrant Students in U.S. Public Schools* (Boston: National Coalition of Advocates for Students, 1988), p. 7; Carolyn Lochhead, "Give Me Your Skilled, Your Erudite," *Insight,* 28 May 1990, p. 22.

47. Bryant Robey, "Two Hundred Years and Counting: The 1990 Census," *Population Bulletin* 44 (April 1989): 6–9. In the census of 1790, only those American Indians who were paying taxes were included in the count. By 1860, those who were living off reservations were included in the census. The first universal counting of Native Americans in the United States was undertaken in the 1890 census. See ibid., p. 6; Dwight L. Johnson, Edna L. Paisano, and Michael J. Levin, *The First Americans* (Washington, D.C.: Bureau of the Census, U.S. Government Printing Office, 1988), p. 3.

48. Robert W. Gardner, Bryant Robey, and Peter C. Smith, "Asian Americans: Growth, Change, and Diversity," *Population Bulletin* 40 (October 1985): 8. The 89 percent figure for the white population excludes those thought to be of Mexican origin but "not definitely white" (about 0.7 percent of the total). Since all those of Mexican origin were categorized as white in the 1920 census, it was difficult to determine later how many were descended primarily from Spaniards (whites) versus Indian peoples. See Joseph A. Hill, "Composition of the American Population by Race and Country of Origin," *Annals of the American Academy of Political and Social Science* (November 1936): 177.

49. Data are derived from Leon F. Bouvier and Robert W. Gardner, "Immigration to the U.S.: The Unfinished Story," *Population Bulletin* 41 (November 1986): 11–12.

from Africa came to an end; thereafter, the growth of the black population in the United States was primarily a product of natural increase.[50] Immigration from Asia (which did not really begin until the mid–nineteenth century) was small throughout the period.[51] And, as a result of disease and conflict with whites, the American Indian population dropped throughout the nineteenth century and did not begin to grow again on a sustained basis until the 1920s.[52]

There was little change in the racial composition of the population in the 1920s and 1930s, primarily because immigration fell to low levels in the late 1920s and stayed at these levels throughout the 1930s. The initial cause of this drop was the passage of restrictive legislation in 1924 that not only continued to limit immigration from Asia but also began to limit immigration from Europe — especially eastern and southern Europe, which had been the greatest source of immigrants since the beginning of the twentieth century.[53] An added factor was the Great Depression, which discouraged immigration to the United States during the 1930s.

By the 1940s, the white proportion of the population had begun to fall. At first the decline was relatively slow, but it became rapid by the mid- to late 1960s. The initial downturn was due to a combination of continued low immigration and a growing divergence between whites and racial minorities (excluding Asians) in the rates of natural increase. A major factor in the downturn of the mid-1960s was the end of the baby boom (and the beginning of a baby bust), which pushed the rate of natural increase in the white population to much lower levels than before, not only in absolute terms but relative to minorities.[54]

50. See Farley and Allen, *The Color Line and the Quality of Life in America*, pp. 11–16; John Reid, "Black America in the 1980s," *Population Bulletin* 37 (December 1982): 4.

51. Beginning with the Chinese Exclusion Act of 1882, Asian immigration was heavily restricted. These restrictions began to ease during World War II, but not until the Immigration Act of 1965 was it possible for Asian immigration to build to high levels. For a brief summary of the history of U.S. immigration law from 1789 through 1965, see Bouvier and Gardner, "Immigration to the U.S.: The Unfinished Story," pp. 9–18; Glazer, *Clamor at the Gates: The New American Immigration*, pp. 3–13.

52. Estimates of the number of Native Americans at the time of the arrival of the Europeans about five hundred years ago range from a few million to several million people. Over the next several centuries, diseases common in Europe, Asia, and Africa at that time (including smallpox, cholera, and measles) but unknown in the so-called New World brought death to untold numbers of American Indians. The cumulative impact of disease and conflict with whites can be seen in the census of 1890, which counted only 248,000 American Indians. Their numbers fell to 237,000 in the census of 1900. Although the census of 1910 counted 277,000 Native Americans, the census of 1920 counted only 244,000. The first census in which more than 300,000 Native Americans were counted was 1930, when the total was 343,000. Harold L. Hodgkinson, with Janice Hamilton Outtz and Anita M. Obarakpor, *The Demographics of American Indians: One Percent of the People; Fifty Percent of the Diversity* (Washington, D.C.: Institute for Educational Leadership, 1990), p. 3; Johnson, Paisano, and Levin, "We, the First Americans," p. 3; Fuchs, *The American Kaleidoscope*, p. 84; William H. McNeill, *Plagues and Peoples* (New York: Doubleday Anchor, 1977): pp. 176–207.

53. Bouvier and Gardner, "Immigration to the U.S.: The Unfinished Story," p. 11.

54. During the 1920–40 period, whites and the nation's largest minority group, blacks, had a similar number of children under age five per one thousand women; in the 1940s a gap began to open up, in favor of the blacks. The African American baby boom between the mid-1940s and the mid-1960s was actually larger than the white. Both blacks and whites experienced a baby bust in the 1960s. However, the gap between the population growth rates of whites and African Americans

Another major factor was the immigration reform legislation of 1965, which made it possible for immigration from non-European nations to increase substantially. Legal immigration from Asia and Latin America grew rapidly after 1965.[55]

The impact of the increased rate of change in the racial composition of the United States was clearly in evidence by 1980, when the census showed that the white proportion of the population had fallen to about 83 percent. Racial minorities not only had grown in numbers and percentages but were much different in composition. In 1980, the African American proportion of the population had reached nearly 12 percent, up from less than 10 percent as recently as 1950. The Asian percentage had grown to 1.5 percent, up from less than 0.4 percent in the 1920–40 period. The American Indian proportion of the population had grown to 0.6 percent, up from a little more than 0.2 percent in 1920. In addition, about 3 percent of the population in 1980 was included in the "other" racial category. Most of these individuals were members of one of the Hispanic ethnic groups. In 1920, the equivalent "other" race Hispanic population had represented less than 1 percent of the population.[56]

The racial minority component of the population continued to grow rapidly throughout the 1980s. By 1990 the white population had fallen to 80 percent—almost the same level as in 1790. The racial minorities component comprised 12 percent of the population who were black, about 3 percent Asian, almost 1 percent Native American, and nearly 4 percent in the "other" race category (primarily reflecting the continued growth of the Latino population).[57]

At the time of the first census, individuals of English descent made up about three-fifths of the white population; the remaining two-fifths were mainly of German, Irish, French, Dutch, and Scottish descent.[58] The cultural pluralism among whites was tempered by the considerable degree of commonality in the important area of religion: in 1790, about 99 percent of the whites were Protestant, while only 1 percent (about 35,000 people) were Catholic. Over the next century, the white population continued to be primarily of northern European origins, but it became much more pluralistic, especially in religious terms,

---

widened during the 1960s and 1970s (Farley and Allen, *The Color Line and the Quality of Life in America*, p. 17).

55. The total number of immigrants to the United States recovered somewhat in the 1940s from the low level of the depression-dominated 1930s. Nonetheless, the flow of immigrants in the 1940s was still low by the standards of the previous hundred years. See Bouvier and Gardner, "Immigration to the U.S.: The Unfinished Story," p. 8–9.

56. Bureau of the Census, *1980 Census of Population Supplementary Report—Age, Sex, Race, and Spanish Origin of the Population by Regions, Divisions, and States: 1980* (Washington, D.C.: U.S. Government Printing Office, 1981), pp. 2–3; Reid, "Black America in the 1980s," p. 2; Gardner, Robey, and Smith, "Asian Americans: Growth, Change, and Diversity," p. 8; Johnson, Paisano, and Levin, "We, the First Americans," p. 3; Hill, "Composition of the American Population by Race and Country of Origin," p. 177.

57. Bureau of the Census, "Race and Hispanic Origin," *1990 Census Profile* 2 (Washington, D.C.: U.S. Department of Commerce, Economics and Statistics Administration, June 1991): 5.

58. Lawrence H. Fuchs, "Immigration, Pluralism, and Public Policy: The Challenge of the *Pluribus* to the *Unum*," in Mary M. Korty, ed., *U.S. Immigration and Refugee Policy* (Lexington, Mass.: D. C. Heath, 1983), p. 294.

owing to the fact that the largest immigrant groups during most of this period were the Irish and the Germans. (Most Irish immigrants and a large percentage of German immigrants were Catholic.) By 1860, the number of Catholics in the United States had grown to 3.1 million, or 10 percent of the total population. Unsurprisingly, religious diversity had become a considerable source of cultural tension by that time.[59]

Beginning in the late nineteenth century, European immigration shifted heavily toward people from the eastern and southern parts of the continent. This meant that several national groups (and cultures)—Italians, Hungarians, Poles, Russians, Greeks, and so forth—became well represented in America for the first time. The proportion of Catholic Americans also continued to grow, and for the first time a significant number of residents were Jewish—2 million Jewish immigrants had arrived in the United States between 1870 and 1914.[60]

Beginning in the mid–nineteenth century, Chinese immigrants and sojourners began to arrive on the West Coast in response to the demand for laborers in railroad construction and mining. Their numbers never became large, owing to anti-Chinese sentiments that resulted in the passage of the Chinese Exclusion Act in 1882. At the end of the nineteenth century, Japanese immigrants began to arrive, but this flow too was curbed by white prejudice that resulted in immigration restrictions. As a result of the Spanish-American War, the United States began to receive a small number of Filipino immigrants early in the twentieth century. However, the Chinese and Japanese were the only Asian groups represented in significant numbers in the United States in 1920.[61]

In the mid–nineteenth century, following the end of the Mexican-American War, substantial numbers of Hispanic people first became part of the United States. (At the signing of the Treaty of Guadalupe Hidalgo in 1848, America gained territory that today makes up all or part of the states of Arizona, California, Colorado, Nevada, New Mexico, Texas, and Utah.) The size of the Mexican population in the Southwest at the time of the signing of the treaty has been estimated at 80,000–100,000, or less than 0.5 percent of the U.S. population.[62]

The Latino proportion of the American population changed little until well into the twentieth century, primarily because there was little movement into the United States from Mexico and other Latin American societies until after 1900. The census of 1920 found only a little more than 700,000 people of Mexican origin, representing less than 1 percent of the total U.S. population. In 1920, there was no other large Latino group in the United States. Although America

59. Philip Gleason, "American Identity and Americanization," in Stephan Thernstrom, ed., *Concepts of Ethnicity* (Cambridge: Belknap Press of Harvard University Press, 1982), p. 68–79.

60. Ibid., p. 108; Fuchs, "Immigration, Pluralism, and Public Policy: The Challenge of the *Pluribus* to the *Unum*," pp. 300–01; Bouvier and Gardner, "Immigration to the U.S.: The Unfinished Story," pp. 8, 11.

61. Hill, "Composition of the American Population by Race and Country of Origin," p. 177; Gardner, Robey, and Smith, "Asian Americans: Growth, Change, and Diversity," pp. 7–9; Bouvier and Gardner, "Immigration to the U.S.: The Unfinished Story," pp. 8–12.

62. Frank D. Bean and Marta Tienda, *The Hispanic Population of the United States* (New York: Russell Sage Foundation, 1987), pp. 106–07. Also see Julian Samoro, "Introduction," in Samoro, ed., *La Raza: Forgotten Americans* (South Bend, Ind.: University of Notre Dame Press, 1969), p. xii.

had acquired Puerto Rico after the Spanish American War in 1898, large-scale migration from Puerto Rico did not begin until after World War II.[63]

As this brief review demonstrates, between the time of the first census in 1790 and the 1920–40 period, when the white share of the population reached its peak, America accommodated a relatively large number of ethnically and culturally different groups. However, most of the groups who came between 1790 and 1920 were from Europe. Very few were from Asian or Latin American cultures. Moreover, although blacks were one-tenth of the population in 1920, the group had become only slightly more diverse ethnically/culturally, owing to the virtual stoppage of African immigration in the nineteenth and early twentieth centuries.[64]

In recent decades, however, this state of affairs has changed dramatically. The census of 1980 identified people from more than twenty Asian and Pacific Island national and cultural groups. The census of 1990 counted nearly 7.3 million people of Asian background, almost 3 percent of the U.S. population.[65] Large numbers of Asian Americans identified themselves as being of Chinese, Filipino, Japanese, Asian Indian, Korean, or Vietnamese origin.

The Latino population had also become diverse by 1980, when Hispanics represented about twenty ethnic/national groups. The census of 1990 counted more than 22 million Hispanics, who collectively made up about 9 percent of the U.S. population. Mexican Americans made up about 58 percent of all Latinos in 1990, Puerto Ricans about 13 percent, Cubans about 7 percent, Central and South Americans about 14 percent, and other Hispanics about 9 percent.[66]

63. Legal immigration from Latin America ranged from 0.5 percent to 2.1 percent of the total number of legal immigrants to the United States in each of the five decades between 1850 and 1900. The percentages from Mexico in these decades ranged from 0.1 percent to 0.6 percent. By the 1920s, however, the percentage of all legal immigrants who were from Latin America had grown to 14.4 percent, while the percentage from Mexico alone had grown to 11.2 percent. To put this in perspective, in the 1871–80 decade, there were 5,192 legal immigrants to America from Mexico, while in the 1921–30 decade, the total was 459,287. Owing to the Great Depression, immigration from Latin America and Mexico fell dramatically; in the 1930s only 22,319 Mexicans came. However, by the 1950s Mexican immigration had recovered to 299,811. Bouvier and Gardner, "Immigration to the U.S.: The Unfinished Story," pp. 8–9; Bean and Tienda, *The Hispanic Population of the United States*, p. 106; Hill, "Composition of the American Population by Race and Country of Origin," p. 177; John H. Burma, *Spanish-Speaking Groups in the U.S.* (Durham: Duke University Press, 1954), pp. 157–59.

64. The percentage of African immigrants to the United States did not reach 0.1 percent until the decade of 1901–10. As recently as the decade of 1971–80, it had reached only 1.8 percent of all legal immigrants. Of course, significant populations of a number of Latin American nations are primarily of African origin. Therefore, blacks in America have become somewhat more culturally diverse as the result of the arrival of Latin American blacks—especially those from the Caribbean—over the course of the twentieth century. See Bouvier and Gardner, "Immigration to the U.S.: The Unfinished Story," pp. 8–9.

65. Dwight L. Johnson, Michael J. Levin, and Edna L. Paisano, *We, the Asian and Pacific Islander Americans* (Washington, D.C.: Bureau of the Census, U.S. Government Printing Office, 1988), p. 1; Bureau of the Census, "Race and Hispanic Origin," p. 4.

66. See Bean and Tienda, *The Hispanic Population of the United States*, pp. 109–15; Bureau of the Census, "Race and Hispanic Origin," p. 5. These percentages are derived not from 1990 census data but from March 1990 *Current Population Survey* data. Jesus M. Garcia and Patricia A. Montgomery, "The Hispanic Population in the United States: March 1990," *Current Population Reports, Population Characteristics*, Series P-20 No. 449 (Washington, D.C.: Bureau of the Census, U.S. Government Printing Office, 1991): 2.

So far I have been discussing the racial and ethnic minority components of the American population as though they were distinct. However, when one combines ethnicity with race, the majority proportion is significantly smaller and the minority population significantly larger than when these components are calculated on the basis of race alone, primarily because only about half of all Latinos consider themselves to be white in racial terms. More specifically, 56 percent of the Latinos categorized themselves as white in the 1980 census, and about 52 percent did so in the 1990 census. By contrast, about two-fifths of the Hispanics in both the 1980 and 1990 censuses placed themselves in the "other" race category.[67] The frequent use of this category undoubtedly reflects, in part, the fact that many Latinos are descended from a combination of people who, in current racial terminology, would be regarded as white, black, or Native American.

As previously mentioned, about 80 percent of the people counted in the 1990 census indicated that they were white. However, only about 76 percent indicated that they were *non-Hispanic* whites. (By comparison, about 83 percent of those counted in the 1980 census categorized themselves as white, while about 80 percent counted themselves as non-Hispanic whites.) If we define *majority* as non-Hispanic white rather than simply white, then the demographic shift from majority to minorities in the 1980s was 4 percent for the entire U.S. population (80 percent - 76 percent = 4 percent), or an average of 0.4 percent per year over the ten years. This would be a rapid rate of change in the racial/ethnic composition of any nation, but is especially so in one as populous as the United States.

The Changing Composition of the Student-Age Population   The changes in the racial/ethnic composition of the U.S. population are currently largest among its younger segments. First, as has been the case historically, a large proportion of the recent wave of newcomers are young adults, and many are children.[68] Because the large majority of these new arrivals are from Asia and Latin America, their collective impact has been to increase the minority component of the country's population as a whole and of the young in particular.

Second, many of the immigrant groups have higher fertility rates than native whites and native-born members of minority groups. This is in part a function of the fact that the immigrants are, on average, younger than the native-born population. Further, many immigrant groups have relatively low average levels of formal education and low incomes, factors that tend to be associated with above-average fertility rates.[69]

67. For 1980 percentages see Bureau of the Census, "Age, Sex, Race, and Spanish Origin of the Population by Regions, Divisions, and States: 1980," *1980 Census of Population Supplementary Reports* (Washington, D.C.: U.S. Government Printing Office, 1981): p. 2. Percentages for 1990 are derived from Bureau of the Census, "Race and Hispanic Origin," pp. 4–5.

68. For example, in 1988 a total of 640,000 legal immigrants arrived in the United States, of which more than 140,000 were of school age. See Lochhead, "Give Me Your Skilled, Your Erudite," p. 22; and *Diversity within American Schools: The Changing Student Population, 1968–2010* (Washington, D.C.: Joint Center for Political and Economic Studies, 1990), p. 25.

69. The fertility rates of immigrants from Latin America tend to be significantly higher than those of Asian immigrants, primarily because the Latin American immigrants have much less formal edu-

And third, native-born members of many minority groups still have higher fertility rates than whites, owing to many of the same factors that apply to recent immigrants: blacks and native-born Mexican Americans and Puerto Ricans have a lower average age than whites and tend to have less formal education and lower average incomes. Native-born Asians, on the other hand, tend to have fertility rates similar to those of whites, reflecting in part the similarity of their educational and economic levels.[70]

Table 1.1 summarizes changes in the racial/ethnic composition of the under-18 population between 1920 and 1990 and the probable changes between 1990 and 2020. Owing to limitations in the available data these figures should be regarded as order-of-magnitude estimates rather than as statistically precise information.[71] The objective is to provide a general sense of the trend line that has emerged since the white proportion of the U.S. population peaked around 1920.

Table 1.1
Estimated Racial/Ethnic Composition of the Under-18 Population

1: Majority/Minority Percentages, Selected Years, 1920–2020

Group	1920	1950	1980	1990	2020
Non-Hispanic whites	88	85	74	69	54?
All Minorities	12	15	26	31	46?

2: Breakdown of Minority/Majority Percentages, 1980 and 1990

Group	1980	1990
Non-Hispanic Whites	74	69
Non-Hispanic Blacks	14	15
Hispanics	9	12
Asians/Pacific Islanders	2	3
Native Americans	1	1

Source: See Note 71 of this chapter.

cation, on average. For a comparison of the fertility of native and foreign-born groups in America, see Amara Bachu, "Profile of the Foreign-Born Population in the United States," in *Studies in American Fertility*, Current Population Reports Special Studies Series P-23, No. 176 (Washington, D.C.: Bureau of the Census, U.S. Government Printing Office, 1991), pp. 19–67. For a more general discussion of the relationship between income, education, and other factors related to differences in fertility, see Reid, "Black America in the 1980s," pp. 8–14; Farley and Allen, *The Color Line and the Quality of Life in America*, pp. 59–102; Bean and Tienda, *The Hispanic Population of the United States*, pp. 205–32.

70. Frederick W. Hollman, "U.S. Population Estimates, by Race, and Hispanic Origin: 1989," *Current Population Reports Population Estimates and Projections Series P-25, No. 1057* (Washington, D.C.: Bureau of the Census, U.S. Government Printing Office, 1990), pp. 3–5, 26.

71. These estimates have been derived from a number of sources, most of which have already been cited in the text. Among the most important are (1) Bureau of the Census, "Age, Sex, Race, and

As the table shows, non-Hispanic whites are estimated to have made up about 88 percent of the under-18 population in 1920 and racial/ethnic minorities about 12 percent. This was slightly different from the 89 percent-11 percent majority-minority split for the population as a whole, primarily reflecting the somewhat higher fertility rates in the black community at that time. (Native Americans, Hispanics, and Asians had little impact on the overall minority fertility rate because collectively they made up only a little more than 1 percent of the U.S. population in 1920, while blacks represented almost 10 percent.)[72]

It is estimated that the share of the under-18 population made up of non-Hispanic whites had fallen to about 74 percent in 1980 and to about 69 percent by 1990—again, reflecting both higher fertility rates among (non-Asian) minorities than whites and high levels of immigration from Latin America and Asia.

The demographic shift from the majority to minorities in the under-18 population was about 5 percent during the 1980s. What will the future hold? As table 1.1 shows, if the average annual change in the majority/minority composition of the under-18 population of the 1980s were to continue at about 0.5 percent per year for another three decades, the majority component would be only 54 percent in 2020. The actual rate of the demographic shift, of course, will be influenced by several factors, some of which could change substantially in a relatively short time—for example, a large increase in the fertility rates of non-Hispanic whites or a significant drop in the fertility rates of blacks and Latinos could slow the shift. Alternatively, an increase in the number and percentage of immigrants from Latin America and Asia (or Africa) would make the rate of the demographic shift even higher in the future.[73]

One should be wary of giving great credence to any single long-term demographic forecast. Nevertheless, there are currently good reasons to believe that the majority-to-minority demographic shift in the U.S. population will continue. African Americans and Hispanics are much younger populations than whites, and they have substantially lower average incomes and education levels. Consequently, it seems likely that it will take much more than three decades for the natural population-growth rates of these groups to converge with that of whites. Even if large-scale immigration from Latin America ended, this would still be the case.[74] The demographic shift is almost certain to continue to be a powerful

Spanish Origin of the Population By Regions, Divisions, and States: 1980;" (2) Bureau of the Census, "Race and Hispanic Origin;" (3) unpublished 1990 census data on the under- and over-eighteen populations, provided by Patricia Montgomery of the Bureau of the Census; (4) Hollmann, "U.S. Population Estimates, by Age, Sex, Race, and Hispanic Origin, 1989;" and (5) Gregory Spencer, "Projections of the Hispanic Population: 1983 to 2080," *Current Population Reports, Series P-25, No. 995* (Washington, D.C.: Bureau of the Census, U.S. Government Printing Office, 1986).

72. Hill, "Composition of the American Population by Race and Country of Origin," p. 177.

73. A provision of the new immigration laws of 1990 calls for the admission of forty thousand immigrants from thirty-four specific nations, on the basis of a lottery. In late 1991, the U.S. government received nineteen million applications. Seth Mydans, "Foreign Millionaires in No Rush to Apply for Visas, U.S. Finds," *New York Times,* 22 December 1991, p. A18.

74. For an analysis of how the Latino population of the United States might vary over the next hundred years under different fertility and immigration assumptions, see Spencer, "Projections of the Hispanic Population: 1983–2080."

underlying rationale for accelerating the educational advancement of minorities for years to come.

POTENTIAL CHANGES IN THE MEANING OF *MAJORITY* AND *MINORITY*

In my discussion of recent changes in the composition of the U.S. population I have necessarily emphasized the fact that there are significant racial (physical appearance) and ethnic (cultural/group identity) differences between members of the majority in contemporary America and members of minority groups. Nevertheless, the nature and extent of these differences have changed over the nation's history and are likely to continue to do so. One might argue that the more we can accelerate the educational advancement of today's disadvantaged minority groups, the more likely we are to experience blurring of boundaries between these groups and the majority population, and the greater the changes are likely to be over time in the defining characteristics of *majority* and *minority*.

The potential for such change has been demonstrated most obviously by the experiences of the many white immigrant groups from Europe who were ethnic minorities when they arrived in the nineteenth and early twentieth centuries. The cultural differences among these groups as well as between them and the native white population were numerous and substantive. Differences in language and religion were two of the most obvious.

Successive generations of these originally diverse groups have had increasingly similar (but still far from identical) experiences with education, work, political participation, religion, leisure time, technology, and popular culture. Many have become friends, neighbors, and spouses of members of other groups. Yet we still routinely refer to a number of hyphenated white ethnics as, for example, Italian-Americans, Irish-Americans, and Polish-Americans. The national origin designation attests to the persistence of cultural diversity among whites in the United States, while the word *American* attests to the cultural similarity among them.[75]

The point is not to suggest that the growing racial/ethnic pluralism of the U.S. population can or should quickly reverse direction. Rather, it is to note that common experiences often produce widely shared attitudes, beliefs, and behaviors over a period of time, even as some cultural differences remain. Thus, if during the next several decades Americans of all varieties share similar educa-

---

75. See Fuchs, *The American Kaleidoscope*, pp. 1–75. Interestingly, many contemporary Jewish Americans are concerned about preserving their ethnic and religious identity in the face of what is perceived to be a continuing rapid melding with the majority culture, especially through intermarriage. This is a result of acceptance rather than rejection by the majority—no small irony for a group that was subjected to severe prejudice and discrimination by the non-Jewish white majority in the United States until recent decades. See Scott Heller, "5-Volume History Portrays Jewish Life in America: Books Explore Immigration, Economic Success, Culture, and Persisting Anxieties over Assimilation," *Chronicle of Higher Education*, 18 November 1992, pp. A8-A10; Paul R. Spickard, *Mixed Blood: Intermarriage and Ethnic Identity in Twentieth-Century America* (Madison: University of Wisconsin Press, 1989), pp. 161–228.

tional, occupational, political, and social experiences on increasingly equal terms, they are likely to reflect these experiences through an emergent new American majority culture. Many of these Americans of the future will be of some hyphenated variety. To the degree that individuals with widely different racial/cultural heritages have had a preponderance of positive common experiences, the existence of these hyphens will evidence their ongoing efforts to mediate and to gain strength from their commonalities as well as their differences. It is this possibility that gives us reason to believe that we can construct a more just, inclusive society.

CHAPTER TWO

Trends in

Majority and Minority

Educational Attainment

The twentieth century has been a period of enormous educational advancement for Americans. In 1900, only a small fraction of the student population completed high school, and even fewer graduated from college. Today the vast majority of young people earn a high school diploma or its equivalent, and 20–25 percent earn a bachelor's degree. At the beginning of the century, whites held huge educational attainment advantages over most minority groups, whether measured by years of formal education completed or degrees earned. Since that time, there has been a significant reduction in minority-majority educational attainment gaps, especially at the elementary and secondary school levels. However, sizable differences continue to exist—for example, in the percentages of whites and Hispanics who graduate from high school and in the percentages of whites, blacks, and Latinos who receive college degrees. Moreover, recent progress in closing the remaining gaps has been slow.

In this chapter, I explore minority-majority educational attainment patterns for the twentieth century as a whole and for the past twenty to thirty years—the period in which the demographic shift has become pronounced. I then look at the number and percentages of college degrees earned by the various racial/ethnic groups. I shall be particularly concerned with whether the recent rate of increase in minority educational attainment levels has been rapid enough to keep pace with the demographic shift.

TWENTIETH-CENTURY TRENDS

Until recent decades, few data were collected that allowed detailed tracking of national educational attainment trends on the basis of race or ethnicity. Some data, however, from the Bureau of the Census from as far back as 1920 make it possible to examine changes in years of school completed for both the white and nonwhite populations. Table 2.1 presents these data for the nation's 25–29-year-olds for selected years between 1920 and 1988. This age group has been chosen because most people have completed their formal schooling by their late twenties and because these are among the prime child-rearing years. Thus, by examining these rates at twenty-year intervals for most of this century, one is able to

Table 2.1
Years of School Completed by Individuals Aged 25 to 29, by Race:
Selected Years 1920–1988
(Percentages)

Year	Race	<5 Years Elementary School	≥ 4 Years High School	≥ 4 Years College	Median School Years Completed
1920	All Races	NA	NA	NA	NA
	White	12.9	22.0	4.5	8.5
	Black/other	44.6	6.3	1.2	5.4
1940	All Races	5.9	38.1	5.9	10.3
	White	3.4	41.2	6.4	10.7
	Black/other	27.0	12.3	1.6	7.1
1960	All Races	2.8	60.7	11.0	12.3
	White	2.2	63.7	11.8	12.3
	Black/other	7.2	38.6	5.4	10.8
1980	All Races	0.8	85.4	22.5	12.9
	White	0.8	86.9	23.7	12.9
	Black/other	1.0	77.0	15.2	12.7
1988	All Races	1.0	85.9	22.7	12.8
	White	1.0	86.6	23.5	12.9
	Black/other	1.2	82.0	18.1	12.6

Source: National Center for Education Statistics (NCES), U.S. Department of Education, *Digest of Education Statistics 1990* (Washington, D.C.: U.S. Government Printing Office, 1991), p. 17. The NCES assembled the data from various U.S. Bureau of Census reports and documents. The "black/other" group includes blacks, Native Americans, and Asians. Hispanics are included in either the white or the black/other category as appropriate.

assess the amount of advancement these populations have made over several successive generations.

As table 2.1 shows, in 1920 about 87 percent of whites had completed elementary school, but only about 22 percent had completed high school, and fewer than 5 percent had earned a four-year college degree. For blacks and other racial minorities collectively, only about half had completed elementary school, while only 6 percent and 1 percent had completed high school and college, respectively. However, as noted in chapter 1, African Americans made up the overwhelming majority of the nonwhite population in 1920, so the attainment rates for the "black/other" category in that year are essentially surrogates for the African American attainment rates; they tell us little about the educational levels of American Indians and Asians. Moreover, neither the white nor the black/other category in 1920 tells us anything directly about the attainment rates of Hispanics.

Over the ensuing years, the educational attainment pattern of white 25–29-year-olds improved dramatically. In 1988, six out of seven had completed high school, and almost 24 percent had completed at least four years of college.

Blacks and other racial minorities made even more dramatic progress. By 1988, they had collectively achieved close to the same high school graduation rate as whites, and about 18 percent had completed four or more years of college. In 1988 nonblack racial minorities made up a significant proportion of the black/other category. Therefore, the data for this category are not a clear surrogate for blacks or any other racial minority in that year. To understand the variations in educational attainment patterns among minority groups in the late 1980s, we need to examine different data sets.

Table 2.1 shows, first, that considerable progress was made by racial minorities prior to the culmination of the civil rights movement in the 1960s. Therefore, much of the minority educational advancement since the mid-1960s was platformed on advancement made earlier. For instance, by 1960 almost all of the 25–29-year-olds in the black/other category had completed elementary school, and nearly two in five had completed high school. Thus, the civil rights legislation of the 1960s was passed in a context in which racial minorities had reached much higher educational levels than they had one or two generations earlier.

Second, because racial minorities collectively started this century at a much lower average educational attainment level than whites, it is only within the past ten years that the high school graduation rates of the white and nonwhite populations have come close to converging—and the college graduation rates of the two groups continue to be quite far apart. This means that recent minority high school and college graduates are much less likely than whites to have parents who are also high school or college graduates. As we shall see, this helps to explain why many of the current generation of minority students have lower grades or standardized test scores than whites at each level of the educational system.

RECENT TRENDS

In the 1960s and 1970s, the Census Bureau began to collect data on a regular basis that allows tracking and analysis of the educational attainment patterns of the white majority and the nation's two largest racial/ethnic minorities, blacks and Latinos. There are still no comparable data for Native Americans and Asians, although some important snapshots have been taken of these groups via decennial censuses and individual education-related studies.

High School Completion Rates   Table 2.2 presents data on recent changes in the percentages of 25–29-year-old whites, blacks, and Hispanics who have completed at least twelve years of schooling for selected years, starting in 1964.[1] As the table shows, there were still extremely large differences in the

1. The Bureau of the Census collects data on educational attainment annually via its March Current Population Survey (CPS), which gathers economic and social information monthly from about sixty thousand American households. The education sections ask respondents about years of school completed rather than degrees earned. However, analyses of the CPS data commonly equate twelve years of school completed with a high school diploma, four years of college completed with a bach-

high school graduation rates of blacks and whites in 1964—the year in which the federal government enacted pivotal civil rights legislation. Over seven in ten whites in this age group had completed at least twelve years of school compared to less than half of the blacks. By 1989, this gap had largely been erased: over 82 percent of blacks compared to 86 percent of whites had completed high school.

Table 2.2
Percent of Population Aged 25 to 29 That Has Completed Twelve or More Years of School, by Race/Ethnicity: Selected Years 1964–89

Race/ Ethnicity	1964	1968	1971	1974	1977	1980	1983	1986	1989
White	72.1	75.3	79.5	83.4	86.8	86.9	86.9	86.4	86.0
Black	45.0	55.8	57.5	68.2	74.5	76.6	79.4	83.4	82.2
Hispanic	NA	NA	NA	52.4	58.1	57.8	58.3	59.0	61.1

Sources: Bureau of the Census, U.S. Department of Commerce, *Current Population Reports, Series P-20*, various years. Hispanics may be of any race. In this data set, both the white and black categories include Hispanics, but they represent a small fraction of each group.

The recent trend for Hispanics has been much less favorable than for blacks. In 1974 little more than half of the Hispanic 25–29-year-olds had completed at least twelve years of schooling, and the percentage had grown to only 61 percent in 1989. Apart from the large size of the current gap between Latinos, on the one hand, and Anglos and African Americans, on the other, this situation is troubling because the rate for Latinos in 1989 was far below the rate required for robust participation in the American work force that year—and even farther below the rate likely to be needed early in the next century (see chapter 4). Further, if the Hispanic high school completion percentage continues to increase at the relatively modest rate that characterized the 1980s, it will take seventy or eighty years for Latinos to reach the 86 percent level whites enjoyed in 1989.

There is an important caveat to this generally negative interpretation of the Hispanic data. Owing to the large number of immigrants from Mexico and other Latin American countries over the past quarter century, the aggregate Latino high school completion rate may underestimate the progress being made by second- and third-generation Hispanic Americans. For example, a Rand Corporation study in the mid-1980s found that there had been a great deal of intergenerational educational advancement among Mexican Americans in California since the 1950s, measured by comparing immigrants born in Mexico with the

---

elor's degree, and five or more years with at least some graduate or professional school experience. The analysis in this chapter follows this approach. It must be noted, however, that there may have been some modest erosion of the close relationship in CPS data between years of school completed and degrees earned as more individuals obtain a high school diploma via a GED or attend college full-time for more than four years to earn a bachelor's degree. See Nabeel Alsalam and Gayle Thompson Rogers, *The Condition of Education 1991, Vol. 2: Postsecondary Education* (Washington, D.C.: National Center for Education Statistics, Department of Education, U.S. Government Printing Office, 1991), pp. 259–61.

second and third generations on years of school completed. About four-fifths of the second- and third-generation Mexican Americans had completed high school, and many had at least attended college; the first-generation Mexican Americans typically had an eighth-grade education or less.[2]

Data from the student questionnaire of the Scholastic Aptitude Test confirm the intergenerational educational progress of many Mexican American children. As recently as 1985, almost 23 percent of those who took the SAT reported having a mother who had not completed elementary school; the comparable percentages for whites and blacks were 3 percent and 1 percent, respectively.[3] Yet the Rand study noted that this progress appeared to have been heavily dependent on the favorable job market for individuals with modest levels of formal education that prevailed in that period.[4] Frank Bean and his associates found that more recent groups of second- and third-generation Mexican Americans have had significantly less favorable intergenerational educational experiences. The third generation even appears to have somewhat lower levels of educational attainment than their parents.[5] Although these researchers were not able to offer a definitive explanation for this outcome, a major contributing factor may be that the labor market in much of the Southwest has become much less favorable for low-skilled workers over the past ten to twenty years.[6]

Completion Rates for Two or More Years of College   Completion of a significant amount of postsecondary education, even if it does not culminate in a bachelor's degree, is increasingly important for successful participation in the labor market. For example, nearly 22 percent of all employed persons in the United States in 1990 had completed between one and three years of college; another 24 percent had completed four or more years. Moreover, it has been estimated that 22 percent of all new jobs in the year 2000 will require one to three years of college, and another 30 percent will require a bachelor's degree or more.[7] Thus, more than half of the new jobs at the turn of the century are expected to require at least some postsecondary education.[8]

2. Kevin F. McCarthy and R. Burciaga Valdez, *Current and Future Effects of Mexican Immigration in California: Executive Summary* (Santa Monica, Cal.: Rand Corporation, 1985), pp. 28–31.

3. Leonard Ramist and Solomon Arbeiter, *Profiles, College-Bound Seniors, 1985* (New York: College Entrance Examination Board, 1986), pp. 46, 56, 76.

4. McCarthy and Valdez, *Current and Future Effects*, pp. 17–21.

5. Frank D. Bean, Jorge Chapa, Ruth Berg, and Kathryn Sowards, "Educational and Sociodemographic Incorporation among Hispanic Immigrants to the United States," in Barry Edmonston and Jeffrey S. Passel, eds., *Immigration and Ethnicity: The Integration of America's Newest Immigrants* (Forthcoming).

6. Roberto Suro, "Generational Chasm Leads to Cultural Turmoil for Young Mexicans in U.S.," *New York Times*, 20 January 1992, p. A16.

7. George Silvestri and John Lukasiewicz, "Occupational Employment Projections," *Monthly Labor Review* 114 (November 1991): 91; Bernard L. Madison and Therese A. Hart (for the Committee on the Mathematical Sciences in the Year 2000), *A Challenge of Numbers: People in the Mathematical Sciences* (Washington, D.C.: National Research Council, National Academy Press, 1990), p. 91.

8. Virtually all forecasts indicate that a large percentage of new jobs in the future will require postsecondary education. For example, the Bureau of Labor's most recent long-term employment growth forecast for the American economy indicates that for the 1990–2005 period, "more than 2 out of 3 of the 30 fastest growing occupations and nearly half of the 30 with the largest number of jobs

Table 2.3 presents trends in the percentages of 25–29-year-old whites, blacks, and Hispanics who have completed at least two years of college. I have chosen to present data for two or more years of college rather than one because so many college freshmen must take remedial/developmental course work.[9] By looking at those who have completed two or more years of college, I am more likely to exclude those who never get much beyond remedial courses.

Table 2.3
Percent of Population Aged 25 to 29 That Has Completed Two or More Years of
College, by Race/Ethnicity: Selected Years 1968–89

Race/Ethnicity	1968	1971	1974	1977	1980	1983	1986	1989
White	24.2	24.1	34.1	38.6	37.7	36.8	37.1	38.1
Black	10.4	2.6	17.0	22.9	24.0	25.6	28.0	27.3
Hispanic	NA	NA	14.9	16.4	17.0	19.8	19.4	21.4

Sources: Bureau of the Census, U.S. Department of Commerce, *Current Population Reports, Series P-20*, various years. Hispanics may be of any race. In this data set, both the white and black categories include Hispanics, but they represent a small fraction of each group.

Almost 25 percent of the whites, but only about 10 percent of the blacks, had completed two years of college in 1968. By 1974, 34 percent of whites, 17 percent of blacks, and 15 percent of Hispanics in the 25–29-year age group had reached this level. After 1974, whites continued to make rapid progress for another two or three years but plateaued thereafter. Consequently, the proportion of white 25–29-year-olds who had completed two or more years of college was essentially the same in 1989 as in 1977. But the comparable percentage of African Americans continued to grow, reaching about 27 percent in 1989. Hispanic 25–29-year-olds also continued to register gains throughout the period, but at a somewhat lower rate than African Americans.

Completion Rates for Four or More Years of College   Table 2.4 summarizes recent trends in the percentages of white, black, and Hispanic 25–29-year-olds who have completed four or more years of college.

About 14 percent of whites and 6 percent of blacks had completed four or more years of college in 1964. Over the next decade the gap actually grew in absolute terms, from 8 percent to 14 percent: by 1974, 22 percent of whites and 8 percent of blacks in the 25–29 age group had completed four or more years of college. That same year, less than 6 percent of Hispanics had completed four or more years of college, which translated into a 16 percent Latino-white gap.

---

added had a majority of workers with education or training beyond high school in 1990" (Silvestri and Lukasiewicz, "Occupational Employment Projections," p. 82).

9. Of all college freshmen in the fall of 1989, 30 percent took at least one remedial course. Moreover, 55 percent of the freshmen at predominantly minority institutions required remediation compared to only 27 percent at predominantly majority institutions. Wendy Mansfield and Elizabeth Farris, *College-Level Remedial Education in the Fall of 1989* (Washington, D.C.: Department of Education, U.S. Government Printing Office, 1991), pp. 4–5.

Table 2.4
Percent of Population Aged 25 to 29 That Has Completed Four or More Years of
College, by Race/Ethnicity: Selected Years, 1964–89

Race/ Ethnicity	1964	1968	1971	1974	1977	1980	1983	1986	1989
White	13.6	15.6	17.9	22.0	25.3	23.7	23.4	23.5	24.4
Black	5.5	5.4	6.4	7.9	12.6	11.5	12.9	11.8	12.7
Hispanic	NA	NA	NA	5.7	6.7	7.6	10.4	9.0	10.1

Sources: Bureau of the Census, U.S. Department of Commerce, *Current Population Reports, Series P-20,* various years. Hispanics may be of any race. In this data set, both the white and black categories include Hispanics, but they represent a small fraction of each group.

Between 1974 and 1989, the percentage of whites who had completed four or more years of college grew only 2 percent, to about 24 percent. In contrast, the rates for both African Americans and Latinos were significantly higher than they had been in 1974—13 percent and 10 percent, respectively. But the black-white and Latino-white gaps in 1989 were still very large (12 percent and 14 percent, respectively). This reflected the fact that the percentages of each group had barely changed since the late 1970s or early 1980s.

Completion Rates for Five or More Years of Higher Education　　Because many occupations require education beyond the bachelor's degree, it is appropriate to examine recent trends in the percentages of whites, blacks, and Hispanics completing five or more years of higher education.

Table 2.5
Percent of Population Aged 25 to 29 That Has Completed Five or More Years of
College, by Race/Ethnicity: Selected Years, 1964–89

Race/ Ethnicity	1964	1968	1971	1974	1977	1980	1983	1986	1989
White	4.7	5.2	6.4	7.4	8.6	8.1	7.9	6.9	6.9
Black	1.1	0.7	1.2	2.4	3.9	2.9	3.3	2.2	2.7
Hispanic	NA	NA	NA	1.6	2.8	3.1	2.7	3.2	3.0

Sources: Bureau of the Census, U.S. Department of Commerce, *Current Population Reports, Series P-20,* various years. Hispanics may be of any race. In this data set, both the white and black categories include Hispanics, but they represent a small fraction of each group.

As table 2.5 indicates, at the time of the civil rights legislation of 1964, 4.7 percent of white and 1.1 percent of black 25–29-year-olds had completed five or more years of college, a gap of 3.6 percent. By 1974 the white and African American percentages were 7.4 percent and 2.4 percent, respectively, and the black-white gap was a full 5 percent. In that year, 1.6 percent of the Hispanic 25–29-year-olds had completed five or more years of college, and the Latino-white completion gap was 5.8 percent.

In the years immediately following 1974, all three groups continued to have increases. However, none made further progress in the 1980s. In fact, the five-year completion rates of whites and African Americans in 1989 were lower than in the mid- to late 1970s.

As the 1990s began, the black-white and Latino-white five-year-or-more college completion gaps were 4.2 percent and 3.9 percent, respectively. These gaps represent formidable obstacles to expanded representation of African Americans and Hispanics in occupations that routinely require education beyond a bachelor's degree.

RECENT DATA FOR NATIVE AMERICANS AND ASIAN/PACIFIC ISLANDERS

Recent decennial census data indicate that Native Americans have attainment patterns much closer to those of Hispanics and blacks than to those of whites. Asian attainment patterns, however, tend to be much closer to those of whites and in some respects significantly stronger.

For example, in 1980 only 56 percent of Native Americans aged 25 and over had completed four years of high school, and only 8 percent had completed four or more years of college. Of those who were living on the twenty-five most populous reservations, only 43 percent had completed high school. However, there was considerable variation among reservations. For instance, 66 percent of the 25-and-over population at the Osage Reservation in Oklahoma had graduated from high school as compared to 34 percent at the Navajo Reservation in Arizona/New Mexico, 52 percent at the Crow Reservation in Montana, and 43 percent at the Eastern Cherokee Reservation in North Carolina. For the entire U.S. population aged 25 and over in 1980, high school and college completion percentages were 67 percent and 16 percent, respectively.[10]

The decennial census of 1980 found that 75 percent of the Asians/Pacific Islanders aged 25 and over had completed at least four years of high school, while 33 percent had completed four or more years of college.[11] The comparable white attainment rates were 71 percent and 18 percent, respectively.[12] Thus, from the standpoint of postsecondary educational attainment, Asians/Pacific Islanders were collectively the best-educated Americans in 1980. However, attainment patterns varied dramatically within this highly diverse group. For example, Japanese Americans had high school and college completion rates of 82 percent and 26 percent, respectively, while the comparable rates were 31 percent and 6 percent for Laotians, 71 percent and 37 percent for Chinese, 22 percent and 3 percent for Hmong, 80 percent and 52 percent for Asian Indians, and 62 percent and 13 percent for Vietnamese. Among the Pacific Islanders,

10. Dwight L. Johnson, Edna L. Paisano, and Michael J. Levin, *We, the First Americans* (Washington, D.C.: Bureau of the Census, U.S. Government Printing Office, 1988), pp. 5, 23.

11. Dwight L. Johnson, Michael J. Levin, and Edna L. Paisano, *We, the Asian and Pacific Islander Americans* (Washington, D.C.: Bureau of the Census, U.S. Government Printing Office, 1988), p. 12.

12. National Center for Educational Statistics, U.S. Department of Education, *Digest of Educational Statistics 1990* (Washington, D.C.: U.S. Government Printing Office, 1991), p. 17.

Native Hawaiians had high school and college completion rates of 69 percent and 10 percent, while the comparable rates were 47 percent and 11 percent for Melanesians and 61 percent and 7 percent for Samoans. In general, Asians had much higher levels of educational attainment than Pacific Islanders. For instance, the Asian-only high school and college completion percentages in 1980 were 75 percent and 34 percent, respectively, but the rates for Pacific Islanders were 67 percent and 9 percent.[13]

Other minority groups, especially Hispanics, also have considerable diversity in educational attainment among their subpopulations. For example, in 1990, among Mexican Americans aged 25 and older, 44 percent had completed at least twelve years of school and 5 percent had completed four or more years of college; the comparable rates were 56 percent and 10 percent for Puerto Ricans, 64 percent and 20 percent for Cuban Americans, and 59 percent and 16 percent for Central/South Americans.[14]

POSTSECONDARY EDUCATION

I have noted that minority-majority attainment gaps continue to be especially large at the higher education level. In this section, I want to look at data from the federal government's High School and Beyond (HS&B) survey (1986), which tracked the educational progress of a national representative sample of individuals who were high school seniors and sophomores in the spring of 1980. This data set allows us to examine in detail the differences in the educational trajectories of racial/ethnic groups in the years just after high school.

Table 2.6
Highest Level of Postsecondary Attainment of 1980 High School Seniors, by
Race/Ethnicity, in the Spring of 1986
(Percentages)

Degree	White	Black	Hispanic	Asian	Native American
Associate	6.6	5.3	7.3	8.7	9.3
Bachelor's	20.2	9.9	6.8	27.3	10.8
Graduate/Professional	0.9	0.2	0.1	1.7	0.0

Source: National Center for Education Statistics (NCES), U.S. Department of Education, *Digest of Education Statistics 1989* (Washington, D.C.: U.S. Government Printing Office, 1989), p. 277. Data are from the High School and Beyond Survey of NCES.

Table 2.6 presents data on postsecondary attainment patterns in the spring of 1986, by which time most of those who were high school seniors in the spring of 1980 would have been twenty-four or twenty-five.

13. Johnson, Levin, and Paisano, *We, the Asian and Pacific Islander Americans,* pp. 12, 15.
14. Jesus M. Garcia and Patricia A. Montgomery, "The Hispanic Population in the United States: March 1990," *Current Population Reports, Population Characteristics,* Series P-20 No.449 (March 1991): 6–7.

The data indicate that there were only small differences among racial/ethnic groups in the percentages for whom an associate degree was the highest attainment level. There is only a 4 percent spread between the group with the highest percentage (Native Americans) and the group with the lowest (blacks). Significantly, two of the three educationally disadvantaged groups, Hispanics and Native Americans, had higher percentages with an associate degree than whites did.

The situation is dramatically different at the bachelor's degree level. The spread between the group with the highest percentage of degree recipients (Asians) and the group with the lowest percentage (Hispanics) was almost 21 percent. The Asian percentage was much higher than that of any other group. Probably even more significant, blacks, Hispanics, and Native Americans in the sample were only one-third to one-half as likely as whites to have earned a bachelor's degree as their highest attainment level by their mid-twenties. These three minority groups collectively accounted for 75–80 percent of the demographic shift in the under-18 population in the 1980s. Moreover, Hispanics—the group that accounted for over half of the demographic shift in the 1980s—had the lowest percentage of bachelor's degree recipients in the sample.

Relatively few of the 1980 high school seniors, regardless of race/ethnicity, had completed a graduate or professional degree by the spring of 1986. Nevertheless, the significantly different bachelor's degree attainment patterns among the racial/ethnic groups were already having a demonstrable impact: almost no African Americans, Latinos, or Native Americans had earned a graduate or professional degree at that point, while nearly 2 percent of the Asians and almost 1 percent of the whites had done so.

The HS&B-derived data presented here are based on a sample of students who were high school seniors when the study began; they do not include those who dropped out of school prior to their senior year. This is especially important to understand when interpreting the data for such groups as Latinos, who have high dropout rates. We can reasonably infer that the HS&B data underestimate the postsecondary attainment gaps between Hispanics and Asians and between Hispanics and whites who were twenty-four or twenty-five years old in 1986.

BACHELOR'S AND DOCTORAL DEGREES

Up to this point, the analysis has focused on the percentages of racial/ethnic groups that reach specific educational levels as measured by years of formal schooling or degree level achieved. Two other ways of analyzing attainment are to examine trends in the absolute number of degrees earned and in the percentages of degrees earned by each group.

Recent Trends by Race/Ethnicity and Nonresident Alien Status   Table 2.7 presents information on the total number of bachelor's and doctoral degrees awarded in the academic years ending in 1979 and 1989 for the major racial/ethnic groups as well as for nonresident aliens. Since this period largely overlaps the decade of the 1980s, the data allow us to look at the relationship between changes in the number of degrees awarded to the various groups and the rapid demographic shift in the student-age population between 1980 and 1990.

Table 2.7
Bachelor's and Doctoral Degrees Awarded in 1979 and 1989,
by Race/Ethnicity and Nonresident Alien Status

Group	1979 Number	1979 % U.S Only	1979 % All	1989 Number	1989 % U.S Only	1989 % All
Bachelor's Degrees						
White	799,617	89.0	87.3	858,186	86.8	84.5
Black	60,125	6.7	6.6	58,016	5.9	5.7
Hispanic	20,029	2.2	2.2	29,800	3.0	2.9
Asian/Pacific Islander	15,336	1.7	1.7	38,219	3.9	3.8
Native American	3,404	0.4	0.4	4,046	0.4	0.4
Total U.S. Citizen/ Perm. Res.	898,511	100.0	98.2	988,267	100.0	97.3
Nonresident Alien	17,715		1.9	26,972		2.7
Total All	916,226		100.0	1,015,239		100.0
Doctoral Degrees						
White	26,128	90.9	80.0	24,895	88.9	69.7
Black	1,267	4.4	3.9	1,071	3.8	3.0
Hispanic	439	1.5	1.3	625	2.2	1.8
Asian/Pacific Islander	811	2.8	2.5	1,337	4.8	3.7
Native American	104	0.4	0.3	84	0.3	0.2
Total U.S. Citizen/ Perm. Res	28,749	100.0	88.0	28,012	100.0	78.4
Nonresident Alien	3,915		12.0	7,680		21.5
Total All	32,664		100.0	35,692		100.0

Source: William H. Freund, *Race/Ethnicity Trends in Degrees Conferred by Institutions of Higher Education: 1978-79 through 1988-89* (Washington, D.C.: National Center for Education Statistics, Department of Education, U.S. Government Printing Office, 1991), p. 4. Percentages may not add to 100.0% because of rounding.

The table shows that the total number of bachelor's degrees awarded by American colleges and universities grew nearly 11 percent between 1979 and 1989 (from 916,226 to 1,015,239) and that all groups but blacks shared in this increase to some degree. Excluding nonresident aliens, the number of bachelor's degrees increased 10 percent. The increase was over 7 percent for whites,

49 percent for Hispanics, an extraordinary 149 percent for Asians/Pacific Islanders, 19 percent for Native Americans, and 52 percent for nonresident aliens. In contrast, the number of degrees awarded to blacks fell almost 4 percent.

The absolute growth in the total number of bachelor's degrees awarded to minorities also represented absolute growth in the minority share of all such degrees awarded during the period. In 1979, African Americans, Latinos, Asians, and Native Americans received 10.9 percent of the bachelor's degrees, including those awarded to nonresident aliens; in 1989 they earned 12.8 percent. Unfortunately, this increase (about 2 percent) was equal to only two-fifths of the 5 percent increase in the minority component of the under-18 population and about half of the 4 percent increase in the minority share of the total population in the decade of the 1980s. (When nonresident aliens are excluded from the analysis, the increase in the minority component of bachelor's degree recipients between 1979 and 1989 was only slightly larger: 11.0 percent to 13.2 percent of the total.)

The largest single component of the increase in the minority share of all bachelor's degree recipients was Asian/Pacific Islanders, the one minority segment that was not underrepresented among bachelor's degree recipients at the start of the period. This group more than doubled its share in the 1979–89 interval, from 1.7 percent to 3.8 percent. As a result, it actually became overrepresented among all bachelor's degree recipients. (Asians/Pacific Islanders made up about 3 percent of the under-18 population in 1990.) However, if we were able to differentiate segments of this highly diverse category, we would find that it is the Asians who are overrepresented among bachelor's degree recipients, not the Pacific Islanders. And within the Asian population, we would find that some groups are doing extremely well while others are not.

When Asians/Pacific Islanders are excluded from the calculations, the educationally disadvantaged minorities (blacks, Hispanics, and Native Americans) saw their share of all bachelor's degree recipients fall from 9.2 percent to 9.0 percent of the total between 1979 and 1989. This, of course, was a direct function of the 0.9 percent drop in the African American share. However, even the 0.7 percent increase experienced by Latinos was far less than the estimated increase in the Hispanic component of the under-18 population between 1980 and 1990 from 9 percent to 12 percent.

Table 2.7 also shows a very mixed picture as regards doctoral degrees. Between 1979 and 1989, the total number of recipients increased over 9 percent (from 32,664 to 35,692). However, this increase was due essentially to the growth in the number of nonresident aliens who earned such degrees. Indeed, the absolute increase in nonresident alien doctoral degree recipients was larger than the total growth in doctoral degree recipients in the period (3,765 versus 3,028). That is to say, excluding nonresident aliens, the total number of doctoral degrees awarded to American citizens and permanent residents actually fell nearly 3 percent, from 28,749 in 1979 to 28,012 in 1989.

The trends in the 1979–89 period varied a great deal among the major racial/ethnic categories. For example, the total number of doctoral degrees awarded to whites, blacks, and Native Americans fell during the period, but the number awarded to Asians/Pacific Islanders and Hispanics increased. For minorities as a whole, the total number of doctoral degrees grew about 19 percent.

The net result of these changes was to increase the minority share of all doctoral degree recipients, from 8.0 percent to 8.7 percent. Moreover, if we exclude degrees awarded to nonresident aliens, the minority share of doctoral degrees earned by U.S. citizens and permanent residents grew even more—from 9.1 percent to 11.1 percent. But regardless of which calculation is emphasized, the increase in the minority share of doctoral recipients lagged far behind the majority-to-minority demographic shift in the 1980s.

As in the case of bachelor's degrees, the increases in the minority shares of all doctoral degrees and of those awarded to U.S. citizens and permanent residents were heavily dependent on the growth in the number of Asian/Pacific Islander degree recipients. Excluding this group from the calculations, the minority (African American, Latino, and Native American) share of all doctoral degree recipients actually fell, from 5.5 percent to 5.0 percent; their share of degrees awarded to U.S. citizens and permanent residents, however, remained unchanged at 6.3 percent. The drop in the minority share was due for the most part to a drop in the black share, from 3.9 percent to 3.0 percent, although a small drop in the Native American share also occurred. Hispanics were able to muster a modest gain during the period—from 1.3 percent to 1.8 percent. However, this increase was a small fraction of the growth in the share of the overall Hispanic population in the 1980s.

Interestingly, the largest absolute drop in the share of doctoral degrees awarded in the period was experienced by whites: from 80 percent of all doctoral degree recipients in 1979 to a little less than 70 percent in 1989. (This large drop in the white pool of doctoral recipients accounts for the fact that the black/Hispanic/Native American percentage of doctoral degrees earned by American citizens and permanent residents did not change in the period.) Nevertheless, the share of doctoral degree recipients accounted for by whites in 1989 was still about the same as their estimated 69 percent share of the total under-18 population in 1990. Moreover, their 88.9 percent share of the doctoral degrees awarded to U.S. citizens and permanent residents was far in excess of the white component of the student-age population as the 1990s began.

Recent Trends in Key Fields   The underrepresentation of non-Asian minorities among bachelor's and doctoral degree recipients in such fields as engineering, computer/information sciences, and natural sciences (physical sciences, life sciences, and mathematical sciences) is significant for several reasons. These fields are crucial to the long-term economic competitiveness of the American economy, and they are fields in which the rate of job growth is expected to be markedly above average over the next ten to fifteen years.[15] The likelihood that job demand will be generally strong in these fields over the long term gives us good reason to believe that the nation will need to turn increasingly to the growing minority population to meet this demand. And, as noted in chapter 1, they are fields that provide important avenues to leadership positions in many sectors of society—leadership positions in which minorities remain greatly underrepresented.

Table 2.8 presents data on degrees in these areas awarded in 1979 and 1989, broken down by race/ethnicity and nonresident alien status. As to bachelor's

Table 2.8
Bachelor's and Doctoral Degrees Awarded in the Natural Sciences,
the Computer/Information Sciences, and Engineering in 1979 and 1989,
by Race/Ethnicity and Nonresident Alien Status

Group	1979 Number	1979 % U.S Only	1979 % All	1989 Number	1989 % U.S. Only	1989 % All
Bachelor's Degrees						
White	132,701	90.6	86.5	144,909	83.1	78.6
Black	6,091	4.2	4.0	9,247	5.3	5.0
Hispanic	2,914	2.0	1.9	5,308	3.0	2.9
Asian/Pacific Islander	4,303	2.9	2.8	14,288	8.2	7.7
Native American	425	0.3	0.3	643	0.4	0.3
Total U.S. Citizen/ Perm. Res.	146,434	100.0	95.5	174,395	100.0	94.5
Nonresident Alien	6,964		4.5	10,035		5.4
Total All	153,398		100.0	184,430		100.0
Doctoral Degrees						
White	7,494	91.5	74.2	7,758	87.9	58.2
Black	136	1.7	1.3	130	1.5	1.0
Hispanic	80	1.0	0.8	155	1.8	1.2
Asian/Pacific Islander	468	5.7	4.6	760	8.6	5.7
Native American	16	0.2	0.2	27	0.3	0.2
Total U.S. Citizen/ Perm. Res.	8,194	100.0	81.1	8,830	100.0	66.3
Nonresident Alien	1,907		18.9	4,508		33.8
Total All	10,101		100.0	13,338		100.0

Source: William H. Freund, *Race/Ethnicity Trends in Degrees Conferred by Institutions of Higher Education: 1978-79 through 1988-89* (Washington, D.C.: National Center for Education Statistics, Department of Education, U.S. Government Printing Office, 1991), pp. 5–8, 13–16. Percentages may not add to 100.0% because of rounding.

15. For estimates of job growth in these areas for 1990–2005, see Silvestri and Lukasiewicz,

degrees, the table shows that the number awarded in these fields grew about 20 percent from 1979 to 1989. The number awarded to U.S. citizens/permanent residents increased about 19 percent. All groups shared in this growth, but not uniformly. The total number of bachelor's degrees earned in these fields by whites grew 9 percent; comparable rates of increase were 52 percent for blacks, 82 percent for Hispanics, a phenomenal 232 percent for Asian/Pacific Islanders, 51 percent for Native Americans, and 44 percent for nonresident aliens.

Yet all minorities except Asians continued to be significantly underrepresented in these areas in 1989. Blacks, Hispanics, and Native Americans collectively accounted for 8.2 percent of the bachelor's degree recipients in these fields in 1989, up from 6.2 percent in 1979. These percentages look modestly more favorable when nonresident aliens are excluded from the analysis: African Americans, Latinos, and Native Americans received 8.7 percent of the degrees awarded in these areas to U.S. citizens and permanent residents in 1989, up from 6.5 percent in 1979. Regardless of which approach one uses, the resulting 2 percent or so increase in the black, Hispanic, and Native American share of degree recipients in these fields lagged the demographic shift in the student-age population for these groups in the 1980s by a large amount.

The Asian/Pacific Islander experience was much different. This population segment began the period modestly overrepresented among degree recipients in these fields: in 1980, Asians accounted for about 2 percent of the under-18 population and for 2.8 percent of all degrees awarded in the natural sciences, computer/information sciences, and engineering in 1979 and 2.9 percent of those awarded to U.S. citizens and permanent residents. By 1990, Asians/Pacific Islanders represented about 3 percent of the under-18 population; by 1989, they accounted for 7.7 percent of all degree recipients in these fields and 8.2 percent of the degrees awarded to American citizens and permanent residents. Thus, as the 1990s began, Asians were overrepresented in these key fields by a factor of two to three.

The increase in the absolute number of Asian degree recipients in these fields was also impressive, from 4,303 to 14,288. By comparison, in 1989 blacks, Hispanics, and Native Americans collectively received 15,198 degrees in the natural sciences, the computer/information sciences, and engineering. These data show that as of the beginning of the 1990s Asians, who constitute one-tenth of the nation's minority population, were earning almost as many degrees in these fields as the other 90 percent.

The total number of doctoral degrees awarded in the natural sciences, the computer/information sciences, and engineering increased 32 percent over the decade. Again, most groups shared in this increase. However, the doctoral

---

"Occupational Employment Projections," p. 92. These fields, of course, have tended to have above-average growth rates for many years. The number of employed engineers and scientists of all kinds doubled in 1976–86, going from 2,331,200 to 4,626,500. See National Science Foundation, *Women and Minorities in Science and Engineering* (Washington, D.C.: National Science Foundation, 1988), pp. 79–80.

growth pattern diverged in important respects from the bachelor's degree pattern. First, the nonresident alien share of degrees in these areas grew much more rapidly than any other group—136 percent. Second, the number of degrees awarded to African Americans actually declined 4 percent. Third, the increase among whites at the doctoral degree level was much smaller than it was at the bachelor's degree level; the number of doctoral degrees awarded to whites grew less than 4 percent. And fourth, although the number of doctoral degrees awarded to Asians grew from 468 to 760, the 62 percent increase this represented was only about one-quarter of the 232 percent increase Asians achieved at the bachelor's level.

An important result of these factors is that the percentage of doctoral degrees in these key fields awarded to nonresident aliens mushroomed, from 19 percent to 34 percent of the total. Another is that the underrepresentation of blacks, Hispanics, and Native Americans among degree recipients in these fields was only slightly less extreme in 1989 than in 1979. These three minority groups accounted for 2.4 percent of all the doctoral degrees in these fields awarded in 1989, up from 2.3 percent in 1979. Excluding nonresident aliens, these groups accounted for 3.6 percent of the doctoral degrees in these fields awarded to American citizens and permanent residents in 1989, up from 2.9 percent in 1979. Again, regardless of which method of measuring change is used, the demographic shift in the 1980s was far in excess of the increase in representation these groups achieved at the doctoral level in these fields. Only Asian/Pacific Islanders improved their relative position significantly, from 4.6 percent to 5.7 of all doctoral degrees awarded. Among American citizens/permanent residents, the Asian share was 8.6 in 1989, up from 5.7 percent. Moreover, given their large increase in bachelor's degrees in these fields in the 1979–89 period, one can reasonably expect their share of the doctoral degrees to continue to grow.

Ironically, because so many nonresident alien doctoral degree recipients are from Asian nations, the actual Asian American share of these degrees seems much larger than it really is. For example, out of 1,723 individuals on temporary visas in 1988 who earned a doctoral degree in engineering, 1,125—or about 65 percent—were from an Asian country.[16]

Depending on how one looks at the data, the overall position of whites at the doctoral level in these fields either continues to be reasonably strong or is weakening rapidly. The white share of doctoral degrees awarded to U.S. citizens/permanent residents in 1989 was nearly 88 percent, down modestly from a little less than 92 percent in 1979. However, the white share of all doctoral degrees earned in these fields fell from 74 percent to 58 percent in the period. The modest rise in the number of whites who earned doctoral degrees in these fields in 1989 would seem to support the view that whites are holding their own at the doctoral level. The growth in the number of whites who earned bachelor's degrees in these fields—9 percent between 1979 and 1989—also supports this

16. Deborah J. Carter and Reginald Wilson, *Eighth Status Report on Minorities in Higher Education* (Washington, D.C.: American Council on Education, 1989), p. 32.

view. However, if we look at the number of bachelor's degrees in the natural sciences, the computer/information sciences, and engineering awarded to whites since the mid-1980s, we have good reason to believe that the situation could weaken noticeably over the next decade. (The data for the mid-1980s are not shown in table 2.8.) Between 1985 and 1989, the number of bachelor's degrees whites earned in these areas fell almost 16 percent—after increasing about 30 percent between 1979 and 1985.[17] On the basis of the drop after 1985 alone, we can expect some pullback in the number of doctoral degrees awarded to whites in these fields in the 1990s. In addition, the recent drop at the bachelor's level does not appear to be a fluke: The baby-bust generation had begun to reach traditional college age by the mid-1980s.[18] Unless higher proportions of future white cohorts choose to pursue degrees in these fields, it will be difficult to avoid further declines in the white share of degrees as the demographic shift continues. Unless racial/ethnic minorities can pick up the slack, the United States is likely to find it increasingly difficult to meet the growing demand for professionals in technical fields with American citizens and permanent residents.[19]

I want to shift attention now to recent trends in bachelor's degrees in education. Teaching (from preschool through high school) is expected to experience substantial job growth over the next decade. Minorities are currently significantly underrepresented in the teaching profession. Thus, many minority students (and most majority students) have too few minority teachers in their school careers.[20] Table 2.9 presents data on bachelor's degrees awarded in teacher education in 1979 and 1989, by race/ethnicity and nonresident alien status.

The total number of bachelor's degrees awarded in education fell 23 percent over this period. All groups but Asians, who experienced a 44 percent increase, shared in this drop. The decline was especially sharp for African Americans (over 63 percent). As a result, the overall minority share fell from 12.6 percent to 8.6 percent, with the black share alone falling from 9.1 percent to 4.4 percent. As these data show in startling fashion, the demographic shift in bachelor's degrees in the 1979–89 period was roughly equal in size to the demographic

17. For data on the academic year ending in 1985, see William H. Freund, *Race/Ethnicity Trends in Degrees Conferred by Institutions of Higher Education: 1978–79 thorough 1988–89* (Washington, D.C.: National Center for Education Statistics, Department of Education, U.S. Government Printing Office, 1991), pp. 5–8.

18. In the first half of the 1990s, white high school graduates are expected to be fewer in number than they were in the mid-1980s. An increase in the number of white graduates is expected in the mid-1990s, due to the "echo" of the baby boom. This increase, however, is not expected to change the overall trend of the demographic shift from the majority toward minorities. See Western Interstate Commission for Higher Education and the College Board, *The Road to College: Educational Progress by Race and Ethnicity* (Boulder, Col.: Western Interstate Commission for Higher Education and the College Board, 1991), pp. 39–41.

19. Our society could choose to meet growing demand primarily via an immigration strategy focused on admitting immigrants who already hold degrees in technical fields or who are academically very well prepared to pursue these. However, as long as several American minority groups—and women—remain significantly underrepresented in these fields, such a policy would probably be politically difficult to pursue. For a discussion of this issue from the perspective of minorities and women, see National Science Foundation, *Women and Minorities in Science and Engineering*.

20. Silvestri and Lukasiewicz, "Occupational Employment Projections," pp. 82, 92.

Table 2.9
Bachelor's Degrees Awarded in Education in 1979 and 1989,
by Race/Ethnicity and Nonresident Alien Status

| | | 1979 | | | 1989 | |
Group	Number	% U.S Only	% All	Number	% U.S. Only	% All
White	108,949	87.2	86.6	88,152	91.5	90.9
Black	11,509	9.2	9.1	4,233	4.4	4.4
Hispanic	3,029	2.4	2.4	2,293	2.4	2.4
Asian/Pacific Islander	785	0.6	0.6	1,127	1.2	1.2
Native American	645	0.5	0.5	537	0.6	0.6
Total U.S. Citizen/ Perm. Res	124,917	100.0	99.2	96,342	100.0	99.5
Nonresident Alien	869		0.7	646		0.7
Total All	125,786		100.0	96,988		100.0

Source: William H. Freund, *Race/Ethnicity Trends in Degrees Conferred by Institutions of Higher Education: 1978–79 through 1988–89* (Washington, D.C.: National Center for Education Statistics, Department of Education, U.S. Government Printing Office, 1991), pp. 5–8. Percentages may not add to 100.0% because of rounding.

shift in the student-age population between 1980 and 1990—but in the opposite (wrong) direction.

These data need to be interpreted with caution because significant numbers of new teachers enter the profession each year without a bachelor's degree in education. (Many have a combination of a master's degree in education and a bachelor's degree in a particular subject; others have a bachelor's degree in a subject area and a minor in education; and some enter via an "alternative certification" process that requires a college degree in some field but relatively little formal coursework in education.) However, there is no reason to believe that there has been a large increase in the proportion of minorities relative to whites who enter teaching without a bachelor's degree in education. Available evidence suggests the opposite. For example, the drop in the total number of master's degrees in education awarded between 1979 and 1989 was disproportionately large among African Americans.[21]

SUMMARY AND CONCLUSIONS

Over the course of the twentieth century, essentially all racial/ethnic groups in the United States have experienced substantial educational advancement, as measured by increases in attainment levels. Yet some extremely large minority-majority gaps remain, and relatively little progress has been made in closing

21. Freund, *Race/Ethnicity Trends in Degrees Conferred*, pp. 9–12.

them. For blacks, Hispanics, and Native Americans, recent progress (if any) does not seem to have been as rapid as the demographic shift. In some respects, the most severe attainment-gap problem is being experienced by Latinos. Both the high school and the college graduation rates for young Hispanic adults are far below those of whites, while for blacks most of the attainment gap is now centered in higher education. Native Americans also are experiencing serious gaps at both levels.

The severity of the attainment-gap problem in higher education is evident in the general underrepresentation of African Americans, Latinos, and American Indians not only among degree recipients in general but also among those in such key areas as the natural sciences, the computer/information sciences, engineering, and teacher education. In spite of substantial increases in minority enrollment, there is little reason to believe that the attainment gaps in these areas or in higher education as a whole will be reduced significantly in the next several years.[22]

Charting attainment trends is an important way to gauge minority educational advancement, both in absolute terms and relative to the white majority. However, attainment data are not designed to provide direct information about variations among individuals and groups in the mastery of specific knowledge, skills, and ways of thinking that are at the heart of the formal schooling process. In the next chapter, I examine two of the most common sources of information concerned with assessing specific skills and capacities that schools are charged with developing—standardized test scores and grades.

22. Black, Hispanic, and Native American enrollment in schools of engineering grew 49 percent between the 1986–87 and the 1990–91 academic years. However, since only about one-third of the engineering students from these groups have typically been able to earn a bachelor's degree, the increase in enrollment may produce a relatively modest increase in the minority proportion of engineering degree recipients. George Campbell, Jr., Ronni Denes, Douglas L. Friedman, and Lynn Miyazaki, "Minority Graduation Rates: Comparative Performance of American Engineering Schools," *NACME Research Letter* 2 (December 1991). For a discussion of minority college enrollment trends in general, see Deborah J. Carter and Reginald Wilson, *Tenth Annual Status Report on Minorities in Higher Education* (Washington, D.C.: American Council on Education, 1992).

CHAPTER THREE

Majority and Minority

Educational Achievement

Trends

In the previous chapter, I looked at the outcomes of formal schooling for various racial/ethnic groups by examining educational attainment trend data. In this chapter, I examine the degree to which individuals and groups have acquired specific knowledge and skills that are taught in the schools, as measured by standardized achievement test scores for the elementary and secondary school population as a whole, for college-bound high school students, and for those planning to pursue education beyond the bachelor's degree. I then shift the focus to data on school grades for elementary and secondary students, for the college-bound population, for college students, and finally for graduate students.

INTERPRETING STANDARDIZED TEST SCORES AND SCHOOL GRADES

Standardized test and school grade data can make valuable contributions to our understanding of differences among racial/ethnic groups in their mastery of knowledge and skills that the schools are expected to teach. Some standardized tests are especially valuable because they have been designed to be administered to representative samples of students over a period of many years. These tests therefore provide a means of monitoring changes in student performance over time in a number of academic areas. School-grade data are most useful as single-point assessments of academic competencies and as general crosschecks to standardized test results. Grade data from two different points in time are more difficult to compare than data from standardized tests because the grades are unlikely to be based on standardized assessment criteria.

Standardized tests have a number of limitations. For example, they can assess only a fraction of the knowledge, skills, and values taught in schools. They are particularly inadequate for assessing the core values and beliefs of groups of students.[1] A major source of these limitations is the narrow range of assessment

---

1. For a discussion of the moral responsibilities of the schools and of teachers, see John I. Goodlad, Roger Soder, and Kenneth A. Sirotnik, eds., *The Moral Dimensions of Teaching* (San Francisco: Jossey-Bass, 1990).

techniques usually used. Most standardized tests rely heavily on multiple choice questions rather than open-ended or essay questions and rarely use non-paper-and-pencil assessment methods.[2]

Apart from these general limitations of standardized tests, cultural differences among racial/ethnic groups can make it difficult for a given test to measure group achievement accurately. The use of a written test in itself may pose an obstacle to the measurement of academic achievement for some groups of students.[3] Students who are not yet proficient in the primary language of the society may find it virtually impossible to demonstrate their true level of competency in many subject areas.[4] Limitations such as these remind one that standardized test and school grade data must be interpreted with caution.

ACHIEVEMENT TRENDS AT THE ELEMENTARY AND SECONDARY SCHOOL LEVELS

In this section I use standardized data from the National Assessment of Educational Progress (NAEP) to assess academic achievement trends. The NAEP testing program was begun in the late 1960s, so trend data are available for about two decades. Although NAEP administers tests in several academic areas, I concentrate on data from the reading and mathematics tests. The achievement score patterns that have emerged on these tests are similar to those on other NAEP subject-area tests, for example, writing and science.

For most of its history, the NAEP has regularly administered subject-area achievement tests to nationally representative samples of public and private school students aged 9, 13, and 17.[5] It is these tests that I use primarily in the analysis of achievement trends because they were designed by NAEP for this purpose.

Some Important Limitations of NAEP Data   An important limitation of the NAEP tests for examining trends in academic achievement by race/ethnicity is that the samples include only youngsters who are in school. Because virtually all 9-year-olds and most 13-year-olds do attend school, this is not a serious limitation for these age groups. However, a considerable number of 17-year-olds drop out of high school, which almost certainly makes it more difficult to interpret the scores of Hispanics because of their especially low high school completion rate.

2. For a recent critique of testing, see *From Gatekeeper to Gateway: Transforming Testing in America* (Chestnut Hill, Mass.: National Commission on Testing and Public Policy/Boston College, 1990).

3. See Ronald Edmonds et al., "A Black Response to Christopher Jencks's *Inequality* and Certain Other Issues," *Harvard Educational Review* 43 (February 1973): 76–91.

4. For example, Hispanic students who are not proficient in English may have difficulty demonstrating their true capacities in mathematics. See Richard P. Duran, "Hispanics' Precollege and Undergraduate Education: Implications for Science and Engineering Studies," in L. S. Dix, ed., *Minorities: Their Underrepresentation and Career Differentials in Science and Engineering* (Washington, D.C.: National Academy Press, 1987), pp. 119–21.

5. Ina V. S. Mullis and Lynn B. Jenkins, *The Reading Report Card, 1971–88* (Princeton, N.J.: The National Assessment of Educational Progress, Educational Testing Service, 1990), pp. 46–48.

A second limitation is that the samples used in the NAEP tests by the late 1980s were much smaller than they had been previously. In the case of the reading test, only 11,439 students were sampled in 1988 compared to 72,407 in 1971 and 70,177 as recently as 1984.[6] The small size of recent samples makes it possible to undertake trend analysis only for whites, African Americans, and Latinos, not for Asians or Native Americans. It also has made it progressively more difficult to identify statistically significant changes in scores for each group, especially for blacks and Hispanics, because their share of each sample has been relatively small to begin with.

Unfortunately, the problem of identifying statistically significant changes is particularly large among the highest scoring students. Only a small percentage of all students sampled have been very high scorers on any of the NAEP tests, but the black and Latino percentages have been especially small. It has become virtually impossible to tell if changes in the percentages of high-scoring African Americans and Hispanics are real or are simply the result of normal variations in sample results.

The NAEP Scoring System for Reading and Mathematics Tests   Each NAEP reading and mathematics test is scored on a 0-to-500 scale. In order to facilitate interpretation, five anchor points for each subject have been established on the scales that describe different levels of competency. The fact that the 500-point scales and the associated anchor points are used with all three age groups makes it possible to compare their performance at each test administration as well as to compare the results achieved by students at successive test administrations over time. Table 3.1 describes the anchor points for the reading and mathematics tests.

Trends in NAEP Reading Scores, 1971–90   Table 3.2 presents trends in average scores for 9- and 17-year-old white, black, and Hispanic students on six administrations of the NAEP reading test between 1971 and 1990. (In order to simplify the analysis, I do not examine test score data for the 13-year-olds.)

As the table shows, there were some large improvements in the reading skills of African American and Latino students. The gains among black 9-year-olds between 1971 and 1980 were followed by large gains among black 17-year-olds by 1984. This suggests that improvements made in reading in the early elementary grades have a good chance of carrying over to the secondary school level. But table 3.2 also gives cause for concern about the likelihood of further reading progress for African Americans, for they indicate that 9-year-olds have not increased their average reading scores since 1980. Indeed, the score for black 9-year-olds was lower in 1990 than in 1980, although the drop was not statistically significant.[7]

6. Ibid., p. 49.

7. Ina V. S. Mullis, John A. Dossey, Mary A. Foertsch, Lee R. Jones, and Claudia A. Gentile, *Trends in Academic Progress: Achievement of U.S. Students in Science, 1969–70 to 1990; Mathematics, 1973 to 1990; Reading, 1971 to 1990; Writing, 1984 to 1990* (Washington, D.C.: Educational Testing Service/U.S. Department of Education, 1991), p. 112. NAEP uses a .05 level test of statistical significance.

Table 3.1
Anchor Points for NAEP Reading and Mathematics Tests

Level	Reading	Mathematics
150	"Rudimentary Skills and Strategies"—Can carry out simple, discrete reading tasks.	"Simple Arithmetic Facts"—Knows some basic addition and subtraction facts.
200	"Basic Skills and Strategies"—Can comprehend specific or sequentially related information.	"Beginning Skills and Understanding"—Can add and subtract two-digit numbers and recognize relationships among coins.
250	"Intermediate Skills and Strategies"—Can search for specific information, interrelate ideas, and make generalizations.	"Basic Operations and Beginning Problem Solving"—Can add, subtract, multiply, and divide using whole numbers.
300	"Adept Skills and Strategies"—Can find, summarize, and explain relatively complicated information.	"Moderately Complex Procedures and Reasoning"—Can compute with decimals, fractions, and percents; recognize geometric figures; and solve simple equations.
350	"Advanced Skills and Strategies"—Can synthesize and learn from specialized reading materials.	"Multi-step Problem Solving and Algebra"—Can solve multi-step problems and use basic algebra.

Source: Arthur N. Applebee, Judith A. Langer, and Ina V. S. Mullis, *Crossroads in American Education* (Princeton, N.J.: National Assessment of Educational Progress, Educational Testing Service, 1989), pp. 20–22, 42–51.

There was no statistically significant change in the average reading scores of Latino 9-year-olds in the 1975–90 period. However, there was a statistically significant increase in average reading scores among 17-year-olds, most of which took place between 1975 and 1984.[8]

There was very little change in the reading scores of whites. The average score for white 9-year-olds was about the same in 1990 as in 1971, while a small, statistically significant gain was registered among white 17-year-olds in this interval.[9]

The NAEP anchor points described in table 3.1 enable one to put these scores into perspective. The average score of white 9-year-olds in 1990 suggests that, as a group, they were reading somewhat above the Basic (200) level (able to

8. Ibid.
9. Ibid., p. 64.

Table 3.2
Average NAEP Reading Scores, by Race/Ethnicity: 1971–90

Group	1971	1975	1980	1984	1988	1990
Age 9:						
White	214	217	221	218	218	217
Black	170	181	189	186	189	182
Hispanic	NA	183	190	187	194	189
Age 17:						
White	291	293	293	295	295	297
Black	239	241	243	264	274	267
Hispanic	NA	252	261	268	271	275

Source: Ina V. S. Mullis, John A. Dossey, Mary A. Foertsch, Lee R. Jones, Claudia A. Gentile, *Trends in Academic Progress: Achievement of U.S. Students in Science, 1969–1970 to 1990; Mathematics, 1973–1990; Reading, 1971 to 1990; Writing, 1984 to 1990* (Washington, D.C.: Educational Testing Service/U.S. Department of Education, U.S. Government Printing Office, 1991), pp. 110, 112, 313, 315.

"comprehend specific or sequentially related information"). In the same year, black 9-year-olds were still reading considerably below the Basic level, although they were further above the Rudimentary (150) level ("can carry out simple, discrete reading tasks") than was the case in 1971. Hispanic 9-year-olds also were still reading between the Rudimentary and Basic levels in 1990, but much closer to the latter.

In 1990, white 17-year-olds had an average score very close to the Adept (300) level ("can find, summarize, and explain relatively complicated information"). In contrast, black 17-year-olds appeared to be reading somewhat closer to the Intermediate (250) level ("can search for specific information, interrelate ideas, and make generalizations"). Still, they had made substantial progress over the two decades. In 1990, Hispanic 17-year-olds seemed to be reading at a level halfway between the Intermediate and the Adept levels, which also represented a substantial improvement over 1975.

An examination of average scores can reveal much about overall changes in each group's reading performance. However, because African Americans and Latinos have historically been overrepresented among low-achievers and underrepresented among high-achieving students, one must look beyond the average scores to see whether there have been significant increases or decreases in the percentages of each group that score at the lowest and highest levels.

Table 3.3 shows the percentages of 9-year-old students from each racial/ethnic group that scored at or above the anchor points. Presenting the data in this way enables one to see whether the reading progress of minority students in this age group has been confined to reducing the number of youngsters with minimal reading skills or has included an expansion in the proportion who are highly proficient readers. Increases in the percentages of black and Hispanic 9-year-olds scoring at or above the Rudimentary (150) and Basic (200) levels can be interpreted as "pulling up the bottom," while increases in the percentages scoring at or above the Intermediate (250) and Adept (300) levels can be interpreted as "building the top." (Virtually no 9-year-olds, regardless of group, score at the 350 level, so it is not included in this analysis.)

Table 3.3

Percentages of Students Performing at Selected NAEP Reading Anchor Points at Age 9, by Race/Ethnicity: 1971–90

Level/Group	1971	1975	1980	1984	1988	1990
≥ 150						
White	94	96	97	95	95	94
Black	70	81	85	81	83	77
Hispanic	NA	81	85	82	86	84
≥ 200						
White	65	69	74	69	68	66
Black	22	32	41	37	39	34
Hispanic	NA	35	42	40	46	41
≥ 250:						
White	18	17	21	21	20	23
Black	2	2	4	5	6	5
Hispanic	NA	3	5	4	9	6
≥ 300						
White	1.1	0.7	0.8	1.2	1.6	2.2
Black	0.0	0.0	0.0	0.1	0.2	0.3
Hispanic	NA	0.0	0.0	0.1	0.4	0.2

Source: Ina V. S. Mullis, John A. Dossey, Mary A. Foertsch, Lee R. Jones, and Claudia A. Gentile, *Trends in Academic Progress: Achievement of U.S. Students in Science, 1969–1970 to 1990; Mathematics, 1973–1990; Reading, 1971–1990; and Writing, 1984–1990* (Washington, D.C.: Educational Testing Service/U.S. Department of Education, U.S. Government Printing Office, 1991), pp. 316–19. The percentages presented for the Rudimentary, Basic, and Intermediate levels are rounded to the nearest whole number. The percentages for the Adept level, however, are rounded to the nearest tenth of a percent because so few 9-year-olds are able to demonstrate reading skills at or above 300 on the NAEP reading scale.

Table 3.3 suggests that improvements were made by African American 9-year-olds at both the bottom and the top of the achievement distribution. For instance, the percentages of black 9-year-olds who scored at or above each of the four anchor points included in the table were higher in 1990 than in 1971. Nevertheless, only 77 percent of the black 9-year-olds scored at or above the Rudimentary (150) level in 1990 compared to 94 percent of the whites. Similarly, 34 percent of African American 9-year-olds scored at or above the Basic (200) level in 1990 compared to 66 percent of the whites. This 2 : 1 ratio of whites to blacks represents an extraordinarily large reading skill gap for blacks in the educationally formative early elementary school years. Still, it is much better than the 3 : 1 ratio in the 1971 NAEP reading assessment.

At the Intermediate (250) and Adept (300) reading levels there was some progress, but on a more limited basis. Between 1971 and 1990, the percentage of blacks reaching the Intermediate level grew from 2 percent to 5 percent, while the comparable percentage for whites grew from 18 percent to 23 percent. This means that the ratio of whites to blacks dropped from 9 : 1 to less than 5 : 1. However, there was little change in the absolute size of the reading gap between whites and blacks at this anchor point. It was still a very substantial 18 percent (23 percent minus 5 percent) in 1990 versus 16 percent (18 percent minus 2 percent) in 1971.

Almost no African American 9-year-olds included in the NAEP samples in 1971, 1975, and 1980 read at the Adept level. Nevertheless, by the mid-1980s, a high-reading-achiever vanguard had begun to emerge among African American children.

The changes in the proportions of Latino 9-year-olds who scored at or above the several NAEP anchor points were relatively small. As a result, white-Hispanic reading score gaps continued to be large at each anchor point in 1990. For example, only 41 percent of Latinos scored at the Basic level compared to 66 percent of whites. Similarly, only 0.2 percent of Hispanics reached the Adept level in 1990 while 2.2 percent of whites did so. Latino 9-year-olds still had extremely serious problems at the highest levels of reading achievement in 1990.

Table 3.4 presents data on the 17-year-olds. Data for the Advanced (350) anchor point are included here because by age 17 a small but significant percentage of the entire student population is able to read at this level. Similarly, data for the Rudimentary level are not included because virtually all students at this age have reading skills at this level or higher.

Table 3.4 tells a generally positive story regarding reading achievement progress among African American 17-year-olds, although large black-white gaps continued to exist at the higher anchor points in 1990. For example, in 1971 only 82 percent of the blacks in the NAEP reading sample compared to 98 percent of the whites read at or above the Basic (200) level. By 1990, this gap had almost been eliminated. Considerable progress was also made at the Intermediate (250) level; the black-white gap in 1990 was still quite substantial, but it was less than half what it had been a generation earlier.

At the Adept (300) anchor point, the percentage of African Americans more than doubled to 20 percent but was still 28 percent below the white rate in 1990. Only 0.4 percent of the blacks in the 1971 sample were able to demonstrate Advanced level reading proficiency ("can synthesize and learn from advanced reading material"), compared to 7.7 percent of the whites. By 1990, 1.5 percent of the blacks and 8.7 percent of the whites had reading scores at the Advanced level.

Owing to the small size of the NAEP reading test samples, one must interpret the African American scores cautiously, especially at the Advanced level. However, it does appear that there has been not only a substantial reduction in the proportion of black 17-year-olds with extremely weak reading skills but also the

Table 3.4
Percentages of Students Performing at Selected NAEP Reading Anchor Points
at Age 17, by Race/Ethnicity: 1971–90

Group	1971	1975	1980	1984	1988	1990
≥ 200						
White	98	99	99	99	99	99
Black	82	82	86	96	98	96
Hispanic	NA	89	93	96	96	96
≥ 250:						
White	84	86	87	88	89	88
Black	40	43	44	66	76	69
Hispanic	NA	53	62	68	72	75
≥ 300:						
White	43	44	43	46	45	48
Black	8	8	7	16	25	20
Hispanic	NA	13	17	21	23	27
≥ 350:						
White	7.7	7.2	6.2	6.9	5.5	8.7
Black	0.4	0.4	0.2	0.9	.4	1.5
Hispanic	NA	1.2	1.3	2.0	1.3	2.4

Source: Ina V. S. Mullis, John A. Dossey, Mary A. Foertsch, Lee R. Jones, and Claudia A. Gentile, *Trends in Academic Progress: Achievement of U.S. Students in Science, 1969–1970 to 1990; Mathematics, 1973–1990; Reading, 1971–1990; and Writing, 1984–1990* (Washington, D.C.: Educational Testing Service/U.S. Department of Education, U.S. Government Printing Office, 1991), pp. 327–30.

recent emergence of a measurable group of black high school students with very strong reading skills.

Still, as I have mentioned, there is reason to be concerned that blacks in this age group will have difficulty making additional improvements. Most of the progress among black 17-year-olds was made in the 1980s, following progress made between 1970 and 1980 by black 9-year-olds, but the reading scores of African American 9-year-olds essentially plateaued in the 1980s.

Table 3.4 also paints a picture of considerable progress among Hispanic 17-year-olds, at least at the lower proficiency levels. Thus, Latinos were largely able to eliminate the gap with whites at the Basic anchor point. They were also able to make very substantial progress at the Intermediate level. At the high-proficiency levels the story was mixed. Between 1975 and 1990 the percentage of Hispanics scoring at or above the Adept anchor doubled, to 27 percent. However, the percentage scoring at or above the Advanced level remained essentially unchanged at 1–2 percent.

The prospects for continued progress among 17-year-old Latinos, as among African Americans, do not appear to be promising. There was no strong upward trend in the NAEP reading scores of Hispanic 9-year-olds in the 1980s.

Trends in NAEP *Mathematics Scores, 1973–90*   Mathematics is an increasingly important subject for all students, but one in which minorities (except Asians) have lagged significantly behind whites in achievement. Table 3.5 presents the average math scores for white, African American, and Latino 9- and 17-year-olds on five NAEP math tests administered during the 1973–90 period.

Table 3.5
Average NAEP Mathematics Scores, by Race/Ethnicity: 1973–90

Group	1973	1978	1982	1986	1990
Age 9:					
White	225	224	224	227	235
Black	190	192	195	202	208
Hispanic	202	203	204	205	214
Age 17:					
White	310	306	304	308	310
Black	270	268	272	279	289
Hispanic	277	276	277	283	284

Source: Ina V. S. Mullis, John A. Dossey, Mary A. Foertsch, Lee R. Jones, and Claudia A. Gentile, *Trends in Academic Progress: Achievement of U.S. Students in Science, 1969–70 to 1990; Mathematics, 1973–1990; Reading, 1971–1990; Writing, 1984–1990* (Washington, D.C.: Educational Testing Service/U.S.Department of Education, U.S. Government Printing Office, 1991), pp. 64, 267, 269. Data for 1973 are extrapolated by NAEP from previous NAEP analyses.

The data indicate that both blacks and Hispanics made important progress. In the case of blacks, improvements were made by 9-year-olds as well as 17-year-olds. However, most of the improvement for both age groups occurred in the 1980s and early 1990s, rather than in the 1970s. Thus, unlike improvements in reading, improvements in math scores at the high school level were not preceded by improvements at the elementary level. Why this should be so is not clear. In any case, the fact that black NAEP math scores did show statistically significant increases in the last half of the 1980s offers reason to hope that additional improvements will be possible in the 1990s.[10]

In the case of Hispanics, of particular importance is the fact that statistically significant improvements in math scores were made among 9-year-old Latinos but not among 17-year-olds. This is just the opposite result found for Hispanics in reading. Moreover, the improvement in NAEP math scores among Hispanic 9-year-olds is a recent phenomenon—it did not really show up until the 1990 assessment.[11]

Improvements in NAEP math scores, especially in recent years, were not confined to African Americans and Latinos. Among white 9-year-olds, the average

10. Ibid., p. 64. The differences in average NAEP math scores for both black 9- and 17-year-olds between 1973 and 1990 were found to be statistically significant.
11. Ibid. The differences between the average math score for Hispanic 9-year-olds in 1990 and the average scores for Hispanic 9-year-olds in 1973, 1978, and 1982 are statistically significant.

math score changed little over the course of the four assessments in the 1973–86 period; however, a substantial, statistically significant increase was recorded in 1990. Among white 17-year-olds, average math scores actually fell between 1973 and 1982 and then increased. As a result, the average math score for whites in this age group was the same in 1990 as in 1973.[12]

The average math score for white 9-year-olds in 1990 was somewhat closer to the Basic Operations and Beginning Problem Solving (250) level than to the Beginning Skills and Understanding (200) level. Blacks and Hispanics were still much closer to the Basic Skills and Understanding level.

Table 3.6 presents data that bear on the question of whether the increase in math score averages for blacks and Hispanics has been limited primarily to pulling up the bottom or has entailed building an academic top. The table includes data for 9-year-olds for the 1978–90 NAEP assessments (data are not available for 1973) for all of the NAEP math anchor points but the Multi-step Problem Solving and Algebra (350) level. This has been excluded because virtually no 9-year-olds are able to score that high.

Table 3.6
Percentages of Students Performing at Selected NAEP Mathematics Anchor Points
at Age 9, by Race/Ethnicity: 1978–90

Level/Group	1978	1982	1986	1990
≥ 150				
White	98	99	99	100
Black	88	90	94	97
Hispanic	93	94	96	98
≥ 200				
White	76	77	80	87
Black	42	46	53	60
Hispanic	54	56	58	68
≥ 250				
White	23	22	25	33
Black	4	4	6	9
Hispanic	9	8	7	11
≥ 300				
White	0.9	0.6	0.8	1.5
Black	0.0	0.0	0.1	0.1
Hispanic	0.2	0.0	0.1	0.2

Source: Ina V. S. Mullis, John A. Dossey, Mary A. Foertsch, Lee R. Jones, and Claudia A. Gentile, *Trends in Academic Progress: Achievement of U.S. Students in Science, 1969–1970 to 1990; Mathematics, 1973–1990; Reading, 1971–1990; and Writing, 1984–1990* (Washington, D.C.: Educational Testing Service/U.S. Department of Education, U.S. Government Printing Office, 1991), pp. 270–73.

12. Ibid. Both the fall and the rise in 17-year-old whites' math scores in the period were found to be statistically significant.

The data suggest that both blacks and Hispanics made more progress in pulling up the bottom than increasing the top, at least among 9-year-olds. Fewer than nine in ten African American 9-year-olds reached the Simple Arithmetic Facts (150) level in 1978, but virtually all did so in 1990. Similarly, between 1978 and 1990, the share of black 9-year-olds able to score at the Beginning Skills and Understanding (200) level increased from 42 percent to 60 percent. However, because white 9-year-olds increased their representation at the 200 level in this period, the black-white gap was reduced only from 24 percent to 17 percent.

The percentage of black 9-year-olds who scored at the Basic Operations and Beginning Problem Solving level doubled to 9 percent between 1978–90, but whites again made large gains as well. At the Moderately Complex Procedures and Reasoning (300) level, black 9-year-olds made no apparent progress in either absolute or relative terms. Virtually no blacks scored at the 300 level throughout the period. Thus, we continue to have a crisis at the top of the math achievement distribution for African American children in the early elementary school years.

Between 1978 and 1990, Latino 9-year-olds were able to reach nearly universal representation at the 150 anchor point. At the 200 level, the percentage of Hispanics increased from 54 percent to 68 percent, but it did not result in closing the Hispanic-white gap at this anchor point because of the increase in the percentage of white 9-year-olds scoring at this level.

At the 250 and 300 levels, progress for Hispanic 9-year-olds was essentially nonexistent; about one in ten scored at the Basic Operations and Beginning Problem Solving anchor point throughout the period. Latinos also began and ended the period with almost no students reaching the Moderately Complex Procedures and Reasoning level. As in the case of blacks, the NAEP math test data suggest that Hispanics entered the 1990s with a crisis in high math achievement in the early elementary school grades.

I want now to examine the trends in the 1978–90 period for African Americans, Latinos, and white 17-year-olds at the 250, 300, and 350 math anchor points (table 3.7). Data for the 150 and 200 levels are excluded because virtually all 17-year-olds in NAEP math test samples are able to reach these anchor points.

Table 3.7 suggests that both black and Hispanic 17-year-olds have made progress in pulling up the bottom and building a top. However, relatively more progress seems to have been made by blacks, whose representation at the Basic Operations and Beginning Problem Solving (250) level grew from 71 percent in 1978 to 92 percent in 1990. The percentage of blacks who reached the Moderately Complex Procedures and Reasoning (300) level doubled to 33 percent by 1990, and the black-white gap at this level was reduced from 41 percent to 30 percent in the period.

At the Multi-step Problem Solving and Algebra (350) level, the data suggest that there may have recently been a surge in high-level math performance

Table 3.7
Percentages of Students Performing at Selected NAEP Mathematics Anchor Points
at Age 17, by Race/Ethnicity: 1978–90

Level/Group	1978	1982	1986	1990
≥ 250:				
White	96	96	98	98
Black	71	76	86	92
Hispanic	78	81	89	86
≥ 300:				
White	58	55	59	63
Black	17	17	21	33
Hispanic	23	22	27	30
≥ 350:				
White	8.5	6.4	7.9	8.3
Black	0.5	0.5	0.2	2.0
Hispanic	1.4	0.7	1.1	1.9

Source: Ina V. S. Mullis, John A. Dossey, Mary A. Foertsch, Lee R. Jones, and Claudia A. Gentile, *Trends in Academic Progress: Achievement of U.S. Students in Science, 1969–1970 to 1990; Mathematics, 1973–1990; Reading, 1971–1990; and Writing, 1984–1990* (Washington, D.C.: Educational Testing Service/U.S. Department of Education, U.S. Government Printing Office, 1991), pp. 282–84.

among blacks. In 1978 and 1982, only 0.5 percent of blacks in the NAEP math test samples reached the 350 level, while only 0.2 percent did so in 1986. Yet in 1990, 2.0 percent of blacks in the sample reached the 350 level. If this is an accurate reflection of the math skills of 17-year-old black students that year, it would constitute a substantial improvement for blacks at the top, both in absolute terms and relative to whites.

Unfortunately, the 1990 results may significantly overestimate the representation of black 17-year-olds at the 350 level. The 2.0 percent figure is not consistent with the 0.2 percent figure achieved by twelfth graders on the 1990 NAEP math test (see table 3.8 below). Although these tests are somewhat different, the 0.2 percent figure is much more consistent with the results of the 1978, 1982, and 1986 NAEP math tests for black 17-year-olds. Further, NAEP math tests of 9- and 13-year-olds prior to 1990 did not produce a sufficient number of high achievers to anticipate an improvement of the kind found among 17-year-olds in 1990. For example, table 3.6 shows that only 4 percent of the black 9-year-olds in the 1982 NAEP math test sample reached the 250 level and 0.0 percent reached the 300 level. Assuming that these results were reasonably representative of blacks in that age group in that year, it is unlikely that the same cohort would have been able to produce a 2 percent representation at the 350 level in 1990. Finally, owing to the small size of the NAEP sample of 17-year-olds for the 1990 math test, the 2.0 percent result is within the range of outcomes that could be expected due to sample variation, even if the "real" percentage for the entire 17-year-old black student population was about the same as in the 1980s.[13]

Given the importance of increasing the proportion of black high school students who are highly proficient in mathematics, the results for black 17-year-olds and twelfth graders on the two 1990 NAEP math tests are strong reminders of the desirability of increasing the size of the NAEP test samples. Until that is done, we will have difficulty determining how much progress is actually being made by African Americans and other racial/ethnic groups at the very top of the achievement distribution in any of the subject areas tested by NAEP.

Hispanic 17-year-olds as a group appear to have made modest progress at the 250 level in the 1978–90 period. However, the data suggest that about one in six Hispanic 17-year-old students in 1990 was not proficient in basic arithmetic.

Progress at higher levels of math achievement also appears to have been quite modest for Hispanics in the 1978–90 period. Only 30 percent of the Latino 17-year-olds in the 1990 NAEP math test sample reached the 300 level, compared to 23 percent in 1978. At the 350 level, the results were about the same in 1990 as they were in 1978. These results give us little reason to believe that there has been a substantial increase in the proportion of high math-achieving Latino 17-year-olds in the past decade or so.

NAEP Test Scores for Asians/Pacific Islanders and Native Americans   Table 3.8 presents fourth- and twelfth-grade data from the 1990 NAEP mathematics test for Asians/Pacific Islanders and Native Americans as well as for whites, blacks, and Hispanics. Data from these two grades are presented because they correspond closely to the data presented earlier on 9- and 17-year-olds.

Like the math test used for students aged 9, 13, and 17, this test uses a 500-point scale. However, NAEP has developed four, rather than five, anchor points for it: Simple Additive Reasoning and Problem Solving with Whole Numbers (level 200); Simple Multiplicative Reasoning and Two-Step Problem Solving (level 250); Reasoning and Problem Solving Involving Fractions, Decimals, Percents, Elementary Geometric Properties, and Simple Algebraic Manipulations (level 300); and Reasoning and Problem Solving Involving Geometric Relationships, Algebraic Equations, and Beginning Statistics and Probability (level 350).[14]

In the top two scoring groups—Asians and whites—the primary differences lie in the percentages of each group that reach the higher anchor points. For example, the highest anchor point that significant numbers of fourth graders are able to meet on this test is level 250. In 1990, 23 percent of the Asians in the sample and only 14 percent of the whites reached this point. Similarly, among

---

13. Ibid., p. 208. The total number of students sampled at all three age levels for the NAEP math test was 17,295 in 1990, 17,000 in 1986, 44,115 in 1982, and 65,717 in 1978. Of the 17,295 in the 1990 sample, only 4,411 were 17-year-olds; the 1978 sample included 26,756 17-year-olds.

14. Ina V. S. Mullis, John A. Dossey, Eugene H. Owen, and Gary W. Phillips, *The State of Mathematics Achievement: NAEP's 1990 Assessment of the Nation and the Trial Assessment of the States* (Washington, D.C.: Educational Testing Service/U.S. Department of Education, U.S. Government Printing Office, 1991), pp. 56–57.

Table 3.8

Table 3.8
Selected Data from the 1990 NAEP Mathematics Assessment of Students
in Grades 4 and 12

| | | Percent Equal to/Greater Than | | | |
Grade/Group	Average Score	Level 200	Level 250	Level 300	Level 350
Grade 4:					
White	223	81	14	0	0
Black	194	41	1	0	0
Hispanic	201	52	3	0	0
Asian/Pacific Islander	228	85	23	0	0
American Indian	211	66	3	0	0
Grade 12:					
White	301	100	95	52	6
Black	270	100	74	16	0
Hispanic	278	100	79	25	1
Asian/Pacific Islander	315	100	97	70	13
American Indian	290	99	92	39	0

Source: Ina V. S. Mullis, John A. Dossey, Eugene H. Owen, and Gary W. Phillips, *The State of Mathematics Achievement: NAEP's 1990 Assessment of the Nation and the Trial Assessment of the States* (Washington, D.C.: Educational Testing Service/U.S. Department of Education, U.S. Government Printing Office, 1991), p. 83.

twelfth graders, 13 percent of the Asians but only 6 percent of the whites scored 350. Moreover, an extraordinary 70 percent of Asian/Pacific Islander twelfth graders reached the 300 level, compared to 52 percent of the whites.

A common denominator among Native Americans, Hispanics, and blacks in the sample is low representation at the higher anchor points in both grade four and grade twelve. Only 3 percent of the American Indians, 3 percent of the Latinos, and 1 percent of the African Americans reached the 250 level in the fourth grade. Only 1 percent of the Hispanics reached the 350 level in the twelfth grade, while 0 percent of the Native Americans and 0 percent of the blacks did so. However, 39 percent of the American Indian twelfth graders in the sample but only 25 percent of the Hispanics and 16 percent of the blacks were able to reach the 300 level.

Of these three groups, American Indians had the most success at the lower anchor points while blacks had the least. It is particularly sobering that only two-fifths of the black fourth graders and half of the Hispanic fourth graders reached the 200 level. By comparison, two-thirds of American Indians reached this anchor point.

It is equally sobering that only 74 percent of the African American twelfth graders and 79 percent of the Hispanics reached the 250 level, suggesting that about a quarter of black high school seniors and a fifth of Latino seniors had not yet developed the minimal mathematics skills that adults need to function effectively in contemporary American society.

If we assume that scores at the 300 level are evidence that test takers possess the math skills necessary to pursue postsecondary education without doing remedial college work in math, then the data in table 3.8 suggest that about seven in ten Asian high school seniors had the requisite skills in 1990 along with one in two whites, two in five Native Americans, one in four Hispanics, and one in six African Americans. If we also assume that scores at the 350 level are evidence that test takers possess the developed capacities in math to pursue quantitatively based majors in college, then table 3.8 indicates that the pool of high school seniors with these skills in 1990 was overwhelmingly Asian or white.

Given the scoring patterns of the fourth graders in the 1990 NAEP math test, we have little reason to believe that the math skill patterns of high school seniors will change dramatically between now and the end of the century. It seems likely that blacks, Latinos, and Native Americans will continue to be considerably underrepresented among the mathematically best prepared students for college in the year 2000.

ACHIEVEMENT TEST SCORE TRENDS FOR THE COLLEGE-BOUND POPULATION

The data I have reviewed so far indicate that non-Asian minorities continue to be significantly underrepresented among high school seniors who are academically very well prepared for college. However, NAEP tests have not been designed to provide much more than very general information related to this issue. Because the SAT has been specifically designed to aid in the admissions decision process, particularly at selective colleges and universities, it is better suited than the NAEP for examining trends in the proportions of different racial/ethnic groups that are well prepared for higher education. Consequently, in this section I look at SAT data.

The SAT includes a verbal and a mathematics section, each scored on a 200–800-point scale. The SAT is not designed to evaluate a student's mastery of a specific college preparatory curriculum. Rather, it measures "developed verbal and mathematical reasoning abilities related to successful performance in college."[15]

From the standpoint of assessing trends in the proportions of racial/ethnic groups that are prepared for college, the SAT has two important limitations: it is not taken by a representative sample of college-bound high school students, and detailed data on test score patterns by race/ethnicity go back only to 1981, although average score data for racial/ethnic groups are available beginning in 1976. For our purposes, the SAT has the advantage of providing information for three Hispanic subpopulations—Mexican Americans, Puerto Ricans, and Other Hispanics.[16] However, subpopulation data are not available on the SAT for any other general racial/ethnic category.

15. College Entrance Examination Board, *College-Bound Seniors: 1990 Profile of SAT and Achievement Test Takers* (New York: College Entrance Examination Board, 1990), p. ii.
16. SAT test takers can choose among the following racial/ethnic categories to describe themselves on the questionnaire that accompanies the test: (a) American Indian or Alaskan native; (b) Asian, Asian American, or Pacific Islander; (c) Black or African American; (d) Mexican American or Chicano; (e) Puerto Rican; (f) Latin American, South American, Central American, or other Hispanic; (g) White; and (h) Other. Test takers are asked to select only one category. See the College

Recent Trends in SAT *Mathematics Test Scores*   Table 3.9 presents selected data on the SAT math results by race/ethnicity for 1981 and 1990. By looking at these two years, we can examine the changes in a decade when the demographics of the under-18 population shifted about 5 percent from the white majority toward minorities. The data in table 3.9 have been selected to show the changes in the number of SAT test takers from each racial/ethnic group, changes in their average scores on the math section of the test, and changes in the representation of each group among high scorers.

With the exception of Asians, minorities began and ended the 1980s with lower average SAT math scores than whites and with extreme underrepresentation relative to whites among high scorers. Yet minorities made very substantial progress in both areas during the period; moreover, they did so in the context of a large increase in the total number of minorities who took the SAT annually over the decade, which is itself a very positive story. In 1990, minorities made up about 25 percent of the SAT test takers who identified themselves as members of a specific racial/ethnic group.[17] In 1981, they had made up only about 15 percent of the test takers.

Blacks, the group that began the period with the lowest average SAT math score, experienced the largest gain—23 points (from 362 to 385). American Indians and Mexican Americans also registered relatively large gains: 12 and 14 points, respectively. Only the 7-point gain by Puerto Ricans was smaller than the 8-point increase by whites. Asians posted a substantial 15-point increase in the period, despite beginning the 1980s with the highest average SAT math score among all groups.

A score of 600 is used as the threshold for measuring progress in expanding representation among high scorers on the math SAT. This score is a good indicator that the test taker is well prepared quantitatively for admission to selective colleges and universities and to pursue quantitatively based majors in college.[18] The groups underrepresented at this level in 1981 made gains in both absolute and proportional terms between 1981 and 1990.

The gains by non-Asian minorities were paralleled by large absolute and proportional gains by both whites and Asians. The number of whites who scored at the 600 level or higher on the math SAT grew 20 percent between 1981 and

---

Entrance Examination Board, *Registration Bulletin 1990–91: SAT and Achievement Tests—New York State Edition* (Princeton, NJ: College Entrance Examination Board, 1990), p. 14. Answering the question is strictly voluntary, but the overwhelming majority of test-takers provide this information.

17. This percentage excludes those who did not identify themselves by race/ethnicity or who selected the "Other" category on the questionnaire. These groups made up less than 8 percent of all test takers in 1990. College Entrance Examination Board, *1990 College Bound Seniors: Ethnic and Gender Profile of SAT and Achievement Test Takers* (New York: College Entrance Examination Board, 1990), p. 9 of each group section.

18. The following were the average SAT math scores for freshmen at a number of the nation's more selective colleges and universities in the early 1990s: Amherst—678; University of Pennsylvania—677; Williams—676; Tufts—673; University of Chicago—670; University of California at Berkeley—644; Oberlin—638; Bryn Mawr—630; University of Illinois at Urbana—611; and Smith—600. Editors of U.S. News and World Report, *America's Best Colleges* (Washington, D.C.: U.S. News and World Report, 1991), pp. 85, 103, 119, 122, 123, 124, 159, 165, 171.

Table 3.9
Selected SAT Math Section Data for 1981 and 1990, by Race/Ethnicity

	American Indian	Asian	Black	Mexican American	Puerto Rican	Other Hispanic	White
No. of Test Takers							
1981	4,655	29,753	75,434	14,405	7,038	NA	719,383
1990	10,466	71,792	94,311	26,073	11,400	23,608	694,976
	+5,811	+42,039	+18,877	+11,668	+4,362	NA	-24,407
% of Test Takers							
1981	0.5	3.5	8.9	1.7	0.8	NA	84.6
1990	1.1	7.7	10.1	2.8	1.2	2.5	74.5
Average Score							
1981	425	513	362	415	398	NA	483
1990	437	528	385	429	405	434	491
	+12	+15	+23	+14	+7	NA	+8
No. ≥ 600							
1981	329	7,946	1,541	770	350	NA	117,000
1990	910	24,171	3,223	1,927	660	2,395	139,916
	+581	+16,225	+1,682	+1,157	+310	NA	+22,916
% ≥ 600							
1981	7.1	26.7	2.0	5.3	5.0	NA	16.3
1990	8.7	33.7	3.4	7.4	5.8	10.1	20.1
No. ≥ 750							
1981	8	633	24	24	9	NA	5,077
1990	30	2,896	79	62	26	86	7,853
	22	+2,263	+55	+38	+17	NA	+2,776
% ≥ 750							
1981	0.2	2.1	0.0	0.2	0.1	NA	0.7
1990	0.3	4.0	0.1	0.2	0.2	0.4	1.1

Sources: Leonard Ramist and Solomon Arbeiter, *Profiles of College-Bound Seniors, 1981* (New York: College Entrance Examination Board, 1982), pp. 32, 41, 51, 60, 70, 79; College Entrance Examination Board, *1990 College-Bound Seniors: Ethnic and Gender Profile of SAT and Achievement Test Takers* (New York: College Entrance Examination Board, 1990), p. 9 in each ethnic group section.

1990, even though the total number of whites who took the SAT dropped over 3 percent during the period (probably owing in part to the smaller post-baby-boom group of white high school students). As a result, the proportion of white SAT test takers who scored at least 600 rose to 20.1 percent in 1990 from 16.3 percent in 1981. The number of Asians scoring at the 600 level tripled. In 1990, an extraordinary 33.7 percent of Asians who took the SAT scored at least 600 on the math section, up from 26.7 percent in 1981.

In 1990, non-Asian minority groups represented about one-quarter of the 18-year-old population but only about 5 percent of those who scored 600 or more on the math section of the SAT. In 1980, blacks, Native Americans, and Latinos had accounted for a little more than 2 percent of the 127,936 SAT test takers who could score 600 or more. This collective 3 percent increase was probably not large enough to keep up with these groups' share of the demographic shift in the under-18 population. Indeed, the actual growth of the Latino component of SAT test takers is almost certainly overstated in these calculations because there was no Other Hispanic category available for students to choose in identifying themselves in 1981. Yet, as table 3.9 shows, the Other Hispanic category accounted for 2,395 of all the test takers from non-Asian minority groups who scored at least 600 on the math SAT in 1990, which was over one-quarter of the 9,115 total for these groups.

Owing to the large increase in the number of non-Asian test takers between 1981 and 1990, the problem of underrepresentation at the 600 level is now as much a function of the lower scoring patterns of these groups as of their underrepresentation among test takers. However, only 7.4 percent of Mexican American test takers, 5.8 percent of Puerto Rican and 10.1 percent of Other Hispanic reached the 600 level on the math section in 1990. These percentages were still far below the Asian and white percentages.

The problem is even more acute for blacks, who made up about 10 percent of the SAT test takers and 15 percent of the under-18 population in 1990. Until we are able to double or triple the 3.4 percent of black test takers who scored at least 600 on the math section in 1990, the underrepresentation of blacks at this level will continue to be extreme.

With 1.1 percent of the SAT test takers who specified their race/ethnicity in 1990 and about 1 percent of the under-18 population that year, virtually all of the Native American underrepresentation among those who could score at least 600 on the SAT math section in 1990 was due to the low proportion (8.7 percent) of test takers from this group who reached this level. (This does not mean that some segments of the Native American community are not still significantly underrepresented among SAT test takers.)

Table 3.9 also presents data on those test takers who scored higher than 750 in 1981 and 1990. These individuals are very highly sought after by the nation's most selective colleges and universities—particularly those that emphasize engineering and the natural sciences.[19] In 1981, there were very few Native Americans, African Americans, and Hispanics who scored 750 or more on the SAT math section. Collectively, these groups accounted for only 65 of the 5,775 SAT test takers who could score at this level.

Over the next decade, the numbers of the underrepresented minority groups

19. In the early 1990s, the average SAT math scores of freshmen were 750 at the California Institute of Technology, 740 at Harvey Mudd College, 735 at the Massachusetts Institute of Technology, and 720 at Cooper Union. See the Editors of U.S. News and World Report, *America's Best Colleges*, pp. 80, 82, 121, 143. Clearly, large proportions of the freshmen at these institutions had scored 750 or more on the SAT.

who could score at the 750 level more than quadrupled, to 283. Yet in absolute and proportional terms, non-Asian minorities were still extremely underrepresented in 1990, partly because the number of white and Asian test takers who scored at least 750 grew 55 percent and 358 percent, respectively.[20] As a result, white and Asian students accounted for 97 percent of those who scored 750. Asians alone accounted for more than one in every four of these students. The increase in the proportion of blacks, Hispanics, and Native Americans who scored over 750 apparently did not keep up with their share of the demographic shift in the 1980s.

The underrepresentation problem at the 750 level remains extremely acute for most of the non-Asian minority groups. Only 0.1 percent of the black test takers, 0.2 percent of the Mexican American test takers, and 0.2 percent of the Puerto Rican test takers reached this level in 1990. The 0.3 percent achieved by Native Americans and 0.4 percent by Other Hispanics were only marginally better. All are far removed from the 1.1 percent of white test takers who reached the 750 level in 1990. Moreover, none of the groups—whites included—is within sight of the Asian performance of 4.0 percent scoring at least 750 on the SAT math section in 1990. This is not only a very high percentage but is nearly twice the proportion of Asians who scored at this level a decade earlier, despite the fact that the number of Asian test takers also grew by 141 percent in the period.

Recent Trends in SAT Verbal Test Scores　　　Table 3.10 presents verbal score data for 1981 and 1990, including data on the average scores of the several racial/ethnic groups as well as on the number and percentage of test takers from each group who scored 600 or higher on this section of the test. However, table 3.10 uses a score of 700 rather than 750 as the break between high and very high scorers because SAT verbal scores tend to average about 50 points lower than SAT math scores.

Table 3.10 suggests that minorities were able to make important gains on the verbal section of the SAT between 1981 and 1990. As in the case of mathematics, however, African Americans, Latinos, and Native Americans were unable to come close in 1990 to achieving parity with whites or Asians on the verbal section of the test. In fact, they made somewhat less progress toward this goal on the verbal section than on the math section.

Again blacks had the largest increase in average verbal SAT scores, 20 points. The pattern of increase for Mexican Americans and Puerto Ricans was also similar to what they had achieved on the math section—7 points and 6 points, respectively. American Indians experienced a small decline (3 points) in their average verbal section score and Asians a 13-point increase, comparable to the

20. The number of whites who scored 750 or more was actually a little higher in 1989 than in 1990 (8,282 versus 7,853). This reflected the fact that more whites took the SAT in 1989 than in 1990—752,257 versus 694,976. The proportion of white test takers who reached the 750 level was the same in both years, 1.1 percent. For the 1989 data, see the College Entrance Examination Board, *1989 College-Bound Seniors: Ethnic and Gender Profile of SAT and Achievement Test Takers* (New York: College Entrance Examination Board, 1989), p. 9 of white section..

Table 3.10
Selected SAT Verbal Section Data for 1981 and 1990, by Race/Ethnicity

	American Indian	Asian	Black	Mexican American	Puerto Rican	Other Hispanic	White
No. of Test Takers							
1981	4,655	29,753	75,434	14,405	7,038	NA	719,383
1990	10,466	71,792	94,311	26,073	11,400	23,608	694,976
	+5,811	+42,039	+18,877	+11,668	+4,362	NA	-24,407
% of Test Takers							
1981	0.5	3.5	8.9	1.7	0.8	NA	84.6
1990	1.1	7.7	10.1	2.8	1.2	2.5	74.5
Average Score							
1981	391	397	332	373	353	NA	442
1990	388	410	352	380	359	383	442
	-3	+13	+20	+7	+6	NA	0
No. ≥ 600							
1981	199	2,140	887	341	173	NA	57,686
1990	261	6,982	1,483	665	246	911	58,709
	+62	+4,842	+596	+324	+73	NA	+1,023
% ≥ 600							
1981	4.3	7.2	1.2	2.4	2.5	NA	8.0
1990	2.5	9.7	1.6	2.6	2.2	3.9	8.4
No. ≥ 700							
1981	28	366	70	40	26	NA	8,239
1990	25	1,174	115	51	24	97	7,659
	-3	+808	+45	+11	-2	NA	-580
% ≥ 700							
1981	0.6	1.2	0.1	0.3	0.4	NA	1.1
1990	0.2	1.6	0.1	0.2	0.2	0.4	1.1

Sources: Leonard Ramist and Solomon Arbeiter, *Profiles of College-Bound Seniors, 1981* (New York: College Entrance Examination Board, 1982), pp. 32, 41, 51, 60, 70, 79; College Entrance Examination Board, *1990 College-Bound Seniors: Ethnic and Gender Profile of SAT and Achievement Test Takers* (New York: College Entrance Examination Board, 1990), p. 9 in each ethnic group section.

15-point increase they had in mathematics. Although whites had the highest average SAT verbal score of any group in both 1981 and 1990, they experienced no change in their score in the period. This means that all groups but Native Americans gained at least some ground on whites during the period.

All groups experienced an increase in the absolute number of students who scored above 600. Among underrepresented minorities, blacks increased their numbers at this level by two-thirds and Mexican Americans came close to doubling their numbers. Gains by American Indians and Puerto Ricans were considerably smaller.

With regard to changes in the percentages of test takers from each group who reached the 600 level, African Americans registered a reasonably substantial increase, from 1.2 percent to 1.6 percent, Mexican Americans, from 2.4 percent to 2.6 percent. The percentages for Puerto Ricans and American Indians fell during the period. The fall was moderate for Puerto Ricans, from 2.5 percent to 2.2 percent, but relatively large for Native Americans, from 4.3 percent to 2.5 percent.

Whites registered a small gain in the absolute number of test takers who scored over 600 and a modest increase (from 8.0 percent to 8.4 percent) in the proportion who scored at the 600 level.

Asians experienced the largest amount of growth of any group at this level, in both absolute and proportional terms, and they ended the period with the highest percentage of test takers of all the groups that reached this threshold. Asians more than tripled their numbers at this level between 1981 and 1990. As a result, although they began the period with 7.2 percent of their test takers scoring at the 600 level, they ended the period with 9.7 percent doing so. This increase is especially impressive in view of the large number of Asian immigrants who arrived in the 1980s. Almost 43 percent of the Asians who took the SAT in 1990 indicated that the first language they had learned to speak was not English; this was more than twice the 20 percent rate for Mexican American SAT test takers in 1990—another group that experienced a high level of immigration to the United States in the 1980s.[21]

Collectively, the number of blacks, Latinos, and American Indians who scored 600 or more on the verbal section of the SAT increased from 1,600 to 3,566. (The 1990 total includes 911 from the Other Hispanic category, which, it will be recalled, was not included on the Student Descriptive Question of the SAT in 1981.) And their collective portion of the 600-level group increased from 2.6 percent to 5.1 percent. Although this increase was substantial, it was less than their share of the demographic shift in the student-age population in the 1980s. In fact, the progress made by Asians alone at the 600 level (from 3.5 percent to 10.1 percent) far outstripped that of all other minority groups combined. Collectively, whites and Asians accounted for 94.9 percent of those who scored over 600 in 1990, down from 97.4 percent in 1981.

At the 700 level, the story is even more mixed. Blacks and Mexican Ameri-

21. College Entrance Examination Board, *1990 College-Bound Seniors: Ethnic and Gender Profile of SAT and Achievement Test Takers*, p. 6.

cans experienced small increases in the number of students scoring at this level between 1981 and 1990, while American Indians and Puerto Ricans had small decreases. As a result, these groups collectively increased the number of test takers who scored at least 700 on the verbal section from 164 in 1981 to 312 in 1990. Whites experienced a decline from 8,239 to 7,659 in the period, but Asians posted another large increase, from 366 to 1,174.

African Americans, Hispanics, and Native Americans increased their collective share of the test takers who scored at least 700 on the verbal section from 1.9 percent to 3.4 percent, which means that the collective white/Asian share fell from 98.1 percent to 96.6 percent. Thus, as was the case at the 600 level, the increase in the black, Hispanic, and American Indian representation at the 700 level was not sufficient to keep pace with the increase in their share of the demographic shift. In contrast, the Asian share of all test takers who scored at least 700 on the verbal section grew from 4.2 percent to 12.8 percent—far in excess of the increase in the Asian share of the student-age population.

The fall in the total number of whites scoring at the 700 level was primarily a result of the lower number of white SAT test takers in 1990. As table 3.10 shows, the actual share of white SAT test takers who scored at this level was 1.1 percent in 1990, the same as it was in 1981.

SAT Scores of Intended Majors in Teacher Education and Engineering in 1990
In chapter 2 I noted that minorities continue to be extremely underrepresented among those who earn bachelor's degrees in education, the natural sciences, the information and computer sciences, and engineering. Given what we have just learned about the continuing large differences in SAT scoring patterns among racial/ethnic groups, it is appropriate to look briefly at these differences from the perspective of the intended college majors of test takers. Table 3.11 shows the number, percentage, and average verbal and math scores in 1990 by racial/ethnic group for individuals who expressed plans to major in education or engineering at the time they took the test.

In 1990, the average verbal and mathematics scores for all students nationally were 424 and 476, respectively, for a combined total of 900.[22] As the table indicates, students who expressed an interest in teaching at the time they took the 1990 SAT had lower verbal and math score averages than the averages for all test takers. The white students expressing an interest in teaching had the highest combined score—867 (416 verbal and 451 math). At 850, the combined score of Asians was close to that of whites. The combined scores of the non-Asian minorities were 787 for American Indians, 767 for Other Hispanics, 757 for Mexican Americans, 736 for Puerto Ricans, and 696 for African Americans.

It is not uncommon for students with a combined SAT score of less than 800 to take at least some remedial/developmental course work once in college.[23] This

22. College Entrance Examination Board, *College-Bound Seniors: National 1990 SAT Profile*, p. iii.
23. An individual with a 900 combined SAT score (the national average for all SAT test takers in 1990) may be generally prepared for college but quite underprepared for highly selective institutions. In contrast, a person with a combined SAT score of less than 700 would probably need to take

Table 3.11

Selected 1990 SAT Information for Planned Education and
Engineering Majors, by Race/Ethnicity

	Education			Engineering		
Group	No. of Test Takers	% of Group	Average Verbal/Math Scores	No. of Test Takers	% of Group	Average Verbal/Math Score
American Indian	778	7.4	374/413	827	7.9	420/508
Asian	1,795	2.5	379/471	11,977	16.7	413/577
Black	4,224	4.5	328/358	9,826	10.4	378/444
Mexican American	1,658	6.4	360/397	3,075	11.8	402/495
Puerto Rican	517	4.5	355/381	1,331	11.7	365/453
Other Hispanic	1,067	4.5	367/400	2,876	12.2	393/492
White	58,003	8.3	416/451	62,519	9.0	475/570

Source: College Entrance Examination Board, *1990 College-Bound Seniors: Ethnic and Gender Profile of SAT and Achievement Test Takers* (New York: College Entrance Examination Board, 1990), p. 8 of each ethnic group section.

suggests that many college-bound students with an interest in teaching—especially those from non-Asian minority groups—need developmental academic assistance if they are to earn a degree.

The data in table 3.11 raise another important issue: relatively few minority test takers are interested in pursuing education as a major in college. Only American Indian test takers, with 7.4 percent stating an interest in majoring in education in 1990, approached the white rate of 8.3 percent. Of course many college-bound minority students with an interest in teaching do not take the SAT or major in a field other than education on the undergraduate level. Nevertheless, the data displayed in table 3.11 are consistent with the education degree data presented in chapter 2 as well as with other data confirming the continuing shortage of minority teachers.[24]

The white test takers who expressed an interest in majoring in engineering when they took the test had a combined average score of 1,045, while the Asians had a combined score of 990. Puerto Ricans had the lowest combined SAT score of the several groups (818), but the combined score for blacks was almost as low

---

remedial/developmental coursework at most colleges. Consistent with these observations, one study found that the cut-off score on the SAT math section used by a large sample of institutions for placement into remedial/developmental mathematics courses ranged from 320 to 525. Ansley A. Abraham, Jr., *A Report on College-Level Remedial/Developmental Programs in SREB States* (Atlanta: Southern Regional Education Board, 1987), p. 42.

24. See American Association of Colleges for Teacher Education, *Recruiting Minority Teachers: A Practical Guide* (Washington, D.C.: American Association of Colleges for Teacher Education, 1989), pp. 1–2; *New Strategies for Recruiting Minority Teachers* (Denver: Education Commission of the States, 1990), pp. 7–8.

(822). With scores of 897 and 885, respectively, neither Mexican Americans nor Other Hispanics were close to the combined scores of whites or Asians. American Indians were in the strongest position of the non-Asian minority groups, with a combined score of 928—but they had the lowest percentage of test takers who expressed an interest in engineering (7.9 percent).

One cannot be certain that those who indicated an interest in an engineering major at the time they took the 1990 SAT actually pursued that major in college. And not all minority high school seniors with an interest in engineering took the SAT. Nonetheless, non-Asian minorities continued to be quite underrepresented among engineering bachelor's degree recipients as the 1990s began. They represented about 7 percent of the recipients of engineering bachelor's degrees in 1989.[25] Moreover, there is considerable evidence that non-Asian minorities who pursue engineering in college collectively have lower high school grades and much lower SAT scores than their white peers—and that these differences are heavily correlated with lower grades and graduation rates in engineering programs.

ACHIEVEMENT SCORES FOR THE GRADUATE-SCHOOL-BOUND POPULATION

Space does not permit a detailed review of minority scoring patterns on the standardized tests used for admissions decisions to various professional and graduate schools. However, I will briefly review some data for those who took the Graduate Record Examinations (GRE) General Test in 1987. The GRE is taken by most students who wish to pursue graduate work in the humanities, the social sciences, and the natural sciences (including engineering). A number of those students who took the GRE in 1987 will be among those who earned a doctoral degree in the first half of the 1990s.

The General Test of the GRE has three sections—verbal, quantitative, and analytical. Each section is scored on a 200–800 point scale. Table 3.12 presents scores only for the verbal and quantitative sections. In the case of the verbal section, the table presents the average score for each group as well as the percentage that scored 600 or more, 700 or more, and the maximum score, 800. The information for the quantitative section is the same except that data are presented for the 750 rather than the 700 level. Data for the 800 level are included for both sections because they show group scoring patterns at the very highest level on the GRE.

With the exception of Asians, who accounted for 2.8 percent of the U.S. citizens who took the GRE in 1987, minorities were extremely underrepresented among the test takers. Blacks, American Indians, and the several Hispanic groups collectively accounted for only 9.5 percent. Whites accounted for the rest.

With regard to the verbal GRE scores, all of the minority groups had significantly lower average scores than whites. Minority groups also were underrep-

25. William H. Freund, *Race/Ethnicity Trends in Degrees Conferred by Institutions of Higher Education: 1978–79 through 1988–89* (Washington, D.C.: Department of Education, U.S. Government Printing Office, 1991), pp. 5–8.

Table 3.12
Selected GRE Verbal section and Quantitative Section Data
for U.S. Citizens (Only) in 1987, by Race/Ethnicity

	American Indian	Asian	Black	Mexican Amer	Puerto Rican	Other Hispanic	White
No. of Test Takers	1,023	4,777	9,324	2,226	1,661	1,902	147,466
% of Total	0.6	2.8	5.5	1.3	1.0	1.1	87.6
Selected Verbal Scores							
Average Score	471	476	386	440	389	469	516
% ≥ 600	15.	18.8	3.5	8.4	4.3	14.4	24.0
% ≥ 700	3.2	5.3	0.6	1.8	1.0	3.3	6.9
% at 800	0.0	0.1	0.0	0.0	0.0	0.2	0.3
Selected Quantitative Scores							
Average Score	473	604	390	456	443	495	541
% ≥ 600	17.8	55.6	6.7	16.8	13.7	25.1	34.3
% ≥ 750	2.7	15.0	0.6	1.6	1.0	4.1	6.2
% at 800	0.5	3.4	0.1	0.3	0.1	0.6	1.1

Source: Educational Testing Service, *A Summary of Data Collected from Graduate Record Examinations Test Takers during 1986–1987 (Data Summary Report # 12)* (Princeton, N.J.: Educational Testing Service, 1988), pp. 81-82. Data exclude about 4 percent of the U.S. citizens who took the 1987 GRE, because they did not respond to the background question on racial/ethnic origin or they marked the "Other" category on that question. The percentages of total test takers represented by the several racial/ethnic groups do not add to 100.0 percent because of rounding. Permission to reprint GRE materials does not constitute review or endorsement by the Educational Testing Service of this publication as a whole or of any other testing information it may contain.

resented among high scorers on the verbal section of the GRE. African Americans and Puerto Ricans had the lowest overall scores by far and were the most extremely underrepresented among the high scorers.

The pattern of average scores on the quantitative section paralleled the pattern produced on the verbal section, but with one important difference: Asians, not whites, had the highest GRE score. Whites performed reasonably well but were still a relatively distant second. Blacks again had the lowest average score.

The other non-Asian minority groups had significantly higher averages than blacks, although none was close to that of whites.

Among high scorers on the quantitative section, Asians set a very impressive standard—almost 55.6 percent scored 600 or more. Whites were a solid but still distant second. With only 6.7 percent of their test takers scoring 600 or more, blacks did least well of any of the groups at this level.

As was the case on the verbal section, the pattern at the 600 level on the quantitative section was repeated at the higher scoring thresholds. The Asian performance was especially strong, with 15.0 percent scoring 750 or more and 3.4 percent receiving 800. Owing to the small percentages of most non-Asian minorities who received the maximum score of 800 on the quantitative section, whites and Asians made up the vast majority of the nearly two thousand individuals who constituted this elite group of test takers in 1987.

Overall, the 1987 GRE data indicate that Asians and whites were significantly better prepared academically for graduate school than the other groups. It is not simply that the non-Asian minorities had lower scores on the GRE; they also tended to be underrepresented among the test taking population. These two factors together help explain why non-Asian minorities continued to be extremely underrepresented among doctoral degree recipients, including those in quantitatively based fields, as the nation entered the 1990s.

RACIAL/ETHNIC GROUP DIFFERENCES IN ELEMENTARY AND SECONDARY
SCHOOL GRADES

Up to now I have focused on differences in standardized achievement test scores among racial/ethnic groups at various levels of education. Here I will shift the focus to the grades students earn in school. The data available for this analysis are much more limited in quality and quantity than are standardized test scores because there is no information source analogous to the NAEP that gathers grade data for nationally representative samples of elementary and secondary school students at regular intervals. As a result, I must select grade data primarily from individual studies, some of which are based on nationally representative samples of students, while others are focused on narrower populations, for example, students who attend a particular school or school district.

Most of the information used in this section has been drawn from the federally funded National Education Longitudinal Study of 1988 (NELS:88). This study, based on a nationally representative sample of students, includes data for all five major racial/ethnic categories—blacks, Hispanics, Native Americans, Asians, and whites. Moreover, the NELS:88 data on students' grades are complemented by standardized test score data for the same youngsters. Thus, the two primary types of academic achievement information can be compared using the same sample of students.

Table 3.13 presents data on school grades and standardized test scores, by race/ethnicity, for the NELS:88 sample of eighth-graders. Part 1 shows the self-reported grades of students from the several groups, on a quartile basis, from

Table 3.13
Selected Data from the National Education Longitudinal Study
of 1988, by Race/Ethnicity

1: Self-reported Grades from Grade Six Until Grade Eight

| | Percent in Each Quartile | | | |
Group	Lowest/ First Quartile	Second Quartile	Third Quartile	Highest/ Fourth Quartile
American Indian	37	28	23	13
Asian/Pacific Islander	17	16	21	46
Black	29	28	26	17
Hispanic	31	25	25	20
White	23	21	24	31

2: Mathematics Test Scores by Proficiency Level

| | Percent at Each Level | | | |
Group	Below Basic	Basic	Intermediate	Advanced
American Indian	32	50	13	5
Asian/Pacific Islander	13	31	21	35
Black	29	49	17	5
Hispanic	28	47	17	9
White	16	38	24	22

Source: Anne Hafner, Steven Ingels, Barbara Schneider, and David Stevenson, *A Profile of the American Eighth Grader: NELS:88 Student Descriptive Summary*, National Longitudinal Study of 1988 (Washington, D.C.: National Center for Education Statistics, U.S. Department of Education, U.S. Government Printing Office, 1990), pp. 29, 34, C-3, C-4. The levels on the math test correspond to the following general capacities: (1) Basic—simple arithmetic and whole numbers; (2) Intermediate—operations with decimals, fractions and roots, including with simple word problems; and (3) Advanced—conceptual understanding and/or development of a solution strategy that may include use of some geometry, algebra, or a logical process.

grade six to grade eight. Part 2 shows the percentages of each group who met various proficiency levels on the standardized mathematics test taken as part of the NELS:88 study.

Part 1 reveals a pattern that has much in common with the standardized test data reviewed earlier. The Asian/Pacific Islanders reported the highest grades, with 46 percent in the highest quartile; Asian eighth-graders were almost twice as likely to be in the top quartile than would be the case if strict proportional representation were the rule. White students had the second strongest grade distribution, with 31 percent in the highest quartile. American Indians, blacks, and Hispanics were all underrepresented in the highest quartile and overrepresented in the bottom quartile. This pattern was most acute for Native Americans—only 13 percent were in the top quartile and 37 percent were in the bottom quartile.

Part 2 shows that the grade patterns of the several racial/ethnic groups are paralleled by their scores on the standardized mathematics test administered to NELS:88 participants. For example, 35 percent of the Asians and 22 percent of the whites were able to score at the Advanced level on the math test (which required at least some mastery of geometry and algebra), while only 5 percent of the American Indians, 5 percent of the blacks, and 9 percent of the Hispanics could do so. In addition, only 13 percent of the Asians and 16 percent of the whites scored below the Basic level (which required mastery of simple arithmetic), while 32 percent of the Native Americans, 29 percent of the African Americans, and 28 percent of the Latinos did so. These patterns are congruent, in the main, with the grade quartile patterns shown in part 1 of table 3.13.

Because the NELS:88 data cover students' grades from the late elementary school period into the middle school years (grades six to eight), we have evidence that differences among racial/ethnic groups develop relatively early in youngsters' school careers. This finding is consistent with the divergences in standardized test score patterns documented for 9-year-olds by the NAEP math and reading data reviewed earlier and also with the results of studies conducted by individual school districts on their elementary and secondary students. For example, a study by the Montgomery County (Maryland) Public Schools (1988) found that racial/ethnic groups develop significant differences in grade patterns in mathematics by the latter half of the elementary school years. Asians and whites had the highest grades in these years, blacks and Hispanics the lowest. These differences in grades were accompanied by similar differences in standardized test scores in math. Moreover, the differences in standardized test score patterns were clearly observable by the second grade.[26]

RACIAL/ETHNIC GROUP DIFFERENCES IN GRADES AMONG THE
COLLEGE-BOUND

Table 3.14 presents the self-reported cumulative grade-point averages of 1990 SAT test takers, broken down by race/ethnicity. The test takers provided this information via a question on the Student Descriptive Questionnaire of the SAT. Their responses were tied to standard letter and point grading systems (A–F and 0–100).

As the table shows, the large majority of SAT test takers in 1990, regardless of race and ethnicity, were above-average students academically as measured by high school grades. However, there were marked differences in the percentages of test takers who reported earning very high grades. Forty percent of the Asians reported grades at the A+, A, and A- levels collectively, followed by 31 percent of the whites, 26 percent of the Mexican Americans, 23 percent of the Other Hispanics, 22 percent of the Puerto Ricans, 17 percent of the American Indians, and 13 percent of the blacks. This pattern was essentially reversed among test

26. Susan Gross, *Participation and Performance of Women and Minorities in Mathematics, Executive Summary* (Rockville, Md.: Montgomery County Public Schools, 1988), pp. E-7 through E-15. See chapter 5 for a more detailed discussion of the emergence of standardized test score gaps among first, second, and third graders.

Table 3.14

Cumulative High School Grade Point Averages of
1990 SAT Test Takers, by Race/Ethnicity

Group	*Percentages at Each Grade Level*					
	A+/ 97–100	A/ 93–96	A-/ 90–92	B/ 80–89	C/ 70–79	D or Less/ Below 70
American Indian	2	6	9	56	26	1
Asian	7	16	17	47	12	1
Black	1	5	7	55	30	1
Mexican American	3	10	13	57	17	0
Puerto Rican	3	9	10	56	21	1
Other Hispanics	3	9	11	57	19	1
White	5	12	14	53	16	0

Source: College Entrance Examination Board, *1990 College-Bound Seniors: Ethnic and Gender Profile of SAT and Achievement Test Takers* (New York: College Entrance Examination Board, 1990), p. 2 of each ethnic group section.

takers who reported having relatively low (C level) grades for college-bound students. For example, 30 percent of the blacks reported having such grades, while 12 percent of the Asians reported grades at the C level.

Predictably, differences in grade patterns were associated with differences in high school class rank patterns, especially at the highest levels. For instance, 29 percent of the Asian SAT test takers in 1990 reported ranking in the top tenth of their class. They were followed by 22 percent of whites, 18 percent of Mexican Americans, 17 percent of Other Hispanics, 15 percent of Puerto Ricans, and 12 percent each of American Indians and African Americans.[27]

RACIAL/ETHNIC DIFFERENCES IN GRADES AT THE UNDERGRADUATE EDUCATION LEVEL

There are no regular sources of information on differences in college grades between nationally representative samples of racial/ethnic groups. However, a range of studies on the grades of undergraduates is available, from small undertakings directed at a portion of the students at a particular institution to relatively large-scale studies involving a sizable sample of students from many colleges and universities. I will present information from three such studies, but my primary focus will be a recent multi-institution survey of minority and majority students' engineering grades. I have chosen this survey in part because engineering is among the most demanding academic majors students can pursue. If non-Asian minorities are to achieve parity with high academic achievers in college as well as with professionals in occupations that require quantitatively based college degrees, they must approach the academic performance levels of whites in such majors as engineering. In addition, a great deal of effort has been expended over the past two decades to increase the representa-

27. College Entrance Examination Board, *1990 College-Bound Seniors: Ethnic and Gender Profile of SAT and Achievement Test Takers*, p. 2 of each ethnic group section.

tion of minorities who earn bachelor's degrees in engineering.[28] It is appropriate, therefore, to assess the progress that has been achieved in this period in the actual academic performance of minority students. And finally, as we have seen, it appears that there are still relatively few non-Asian-minority high school graduates who are academically prepared to perform at the highest levels in the engineering curriculum.

THE ACCREDITATION BOARD FOR ENGINEERING AND TECHNOLOGY STUDY OF ACADEMIC PERFORMANCE IN ENGINEERING

In 1991, Thomas R. Phillips of the Accreditation Board for Engineering and Technology (ABET) completed a study of minority and majority students' grades in engineering. Data were requested from the 281 schools that have programs accredited by ABET, and 89 of these institutions eventually provided information. In 1985, the participating institutions enrolled about 32 percent of all black engineering students and 33 percent of all Hispanic engineering students. In terms of program quality, the participating schools range from nonselective to very selective. In addition to the college transcripts for a random sample of their students (minorities were oversampled), participating institutions provided their high school transcripts and, where available, their SAT and American College Testing (ACT) Assessment Program scores.[29]

The major component of the study was an examination of the academic experiences of twelve hundred engineering majors who entered college in the fall of 1985. Transcripts for each student covered a period of up to five years (through the spring of 1991), depending on whether the student dropped out of the engineering track at some point, received a bachelor's degree in engineering before the end of the period, or was still enrolled in school pursuing an engineering major. This part of the study was designed to assess what happens to a group of students who pursue an engineering major from the beginning of their freshman year.[30]

Table 3.15 presents SAT and high school grade data for the blacks, Hispanics, and whites in the sample of 1985 engineering freshmen. (Asians and Native Americans were not included in the study.) The grade data are based on a standard four-point scale.

28. An early document in the minority engineering movement is Planning Commission for Expanding Minority Opportunities in Engineering, *Minorities in Engineering: A Blueprint for Action* (New York: Alfred P. Sloan Foundation, 1974). For a discussion of the importance of the corporate sector in this effort, see Seymour Lusterman, *Minorities in Engineering: The Corporate Role* (New York: The Conference Board, 1979). And for a recent discussion of the status of the minority engineering movement, see Raymond B. Landis, *Retention by Design: Achieving Excellence in Minority Engineering Education* (New York: National Action Council for Minorities in Engineering, 1991).

29. Thomas R. Phillips, *ABET/Exxon Minority Engineering Student Achievement Profile* (New York: Accreditation Board for Engineering and Technology, 1991), pp. 6–7, and unnumbered pages of the report listing participating institutions.

30. Ibid., pp. 5–7, 10. The second part of the ABET study (not discussed here) examined a group of students who graduated in 1989, regardless of when or where they began their college careers. The results of this segment were generally consistent with the portion of the study that examined the academic experiences of the students who were freshmen in 1985.

Table 3.15
SAT and High School Grade Data for Students in the ABET Engineering Study Who Were College Freshmen in the Fall of 1985, by Race/Ethnicity

| | Combined SAT Score | | | High School GPA | |
Group	Mean	Median	75th Percentile	Mean	Median
White	1,140	1,140	1,260	3.43	3.51
Black	950	940	1,070	3.17	3.27
Hispanic	1,013	1,020	1,150	3.39	3.50

Source: Thomas R. Phillips, *ABET/Exxon Minority Engineering Student Profile* (New York: Accreditation Board for Engineering and Technology, 1991), pp. 7–8.

Earlier in this chapter (table 3.11), I presented data on the average SAT scores of test takers in 1990 who stated an intention to major in engineering at the time they took the test. The SAT data presented in table 3.15 for the ABET sample of 1985 engineering freshmen are directionally consistent with the 1990 SAT data. However the 1,140 mean combined SAT score for whites in the ABET sample is nearly 100 points more than the 1,045 combined average score of the white test takers in 1990,[31] while the African Americans and Latino engineering students in the ABET sample had combined average SAT scores that were 100–200 points higher than the scores of their counterparts among 1990 SAT test takers. This is not surprising, given the very demanding nature of the engineering curriculum.

Nevertheless, the white students in the ABET sample clearly had a large advantage, at least as measured by the SAT. The mean, median, and 75th percentile combined SAT scores for the whites were all nearly 200 points higher than the comparable scores for the blacks and well over 100 points higher than the comparable scores for the Hispanics.

The whites also had a considerable advantage over blacks in terms of mean and median high school grade point averages (GPAs). However, the mean and median GPAs of the whites and Latinos were nearly identical.

On the basis of these data, one would anticipate very large differences in academic achievement levels between the white and black engineering students in the ABET study and somewhat smaller (but still significant) differences between the whites and Hispanics. Table 3.16 presents data on the college GPAs of the students in the ABET sample while they were in the engineering track. A standard four-point scale has been used to calculate the GPAs.

As the table shows, blacks in the study were much less likely than whites to have high GPAs and much more likely to have low GPAs. (About 29 percent of the whites in the sample had a GPA of at least 3.50, compared to only 2 percent of the African Americans. And only 6 percent of the African Americans had a GPA between 3.00 and 3.49 compared to 25 percent of whites.) Thus, to the extent that undergraduate GPA is a good indicator of academic preparation for graduate

31. Ibid., p. 6. A small number of students in each part of the study who had identified themselves as "Other" from a racial/ethnic perspective are included in the white group for purposes of this analysis.

Table 3.16
Grade Point Averages for Students in the ABET Engineering Study
Who Were College Freshmen in the Fall of 1985, by Race/Ethnicity

| Group | Percent in Each GPA Band on Four-Point Scale | | | | | | |
	0.00-0.99	1.00-1.99	2.00-2.49	2.50-2.99	3.00-3.49	3.50-4.00	0.00-4.00
White	6	9	13	19	25	29	100
Black	17	27	25	22	6	2	100
Hispanic	11	14	20	23	21	10	100

Source: Thomas R. Phillips, *ABET/Exxon Minority Engineering Student Profile* (New York: Accreditation Board for Engineering and Technology, 1991), pp. 58, 64. Percentages may not add because of rounding.

work, only 8 percent of the blacks in the sample seemed likely to be reasonably well prepared academically for graduate school in engineering or a related science-based major—and only 2 percent seemed likely to be well prepared to enter a doctoral program in engineering or a related field, particularly at a selective university. In contrast, fully 54 percent of the whites seemed to be progressing academically in ways consistent with pursuing graduate education in engineering or a related field, and 29 percent seemed to have a chance to be well prepared for doctoral studies.

Moreover, 44 percent of the blacks in the sample had less than the 2.00 GPA normally required for graduation from college (regardless of major). Only 15 percent of the whites were in this position.

The situation of the Hispanics in the study was much better, although not nearly as strong as that of whites. Nearly one-third were doing well enough academically to aspire to graduate work in engineering or a related area, and about one-tenth were performing at a level that would enable them to pursue a doctorate in engineering. On the low GPA segment, a quarter of the Latinos were not doing well enough to meet the 2.00 GPA requirement for a college degree in any field.

Given these differences, it is not surprising that Phillips found considerable variation among the groups in the proportion of each group that was able to earn a bachelor's degree in engineering in the five-year period. Of the white students in the sample, 67 percent had earned a bachelor's degree in engineering by the spring of 1991, but this was the case for only 36 percent of the African Americans and 47 percent of the Hispanics. These graduation rates are quite consistent with the rates suggested by national data sets on engineering students and degree recipients. In fact, one recent analysis of the national data found that the proportions of white, black, and Latino freshmen engineering students in the 1980s who eventually earned bachelor's degrees in engineering were 68 percent, 31 percent, and 45 percent, respectively.[32]

32. George W. Campbell, Jr., Ronni Denes, Douglas L. Friedman, and Lynn Miyazaki, "Minority Graduation Rates: Comparative Performance of American Engineering Schools," NACME Research Letter 2 (December 1991), pp. 1, 6. These authors found that the graduation rates of minority freshmen majoring in engineering at historically black colleges and universities—45 percent at

Given the large disparities in GPA distributions for the three groups, one of the most important questions Phillips examined is, "Which students tend to major successfully in engineering and which do not?" The data from the ABET study suggest that academically very well prepared high school graduates generally are much more successful in engineering programs than are high school graduates who are "merely" well prepared for college. This point is demonstrated by the experience of those students in the study who had at least an 1,100 combined SAT verbal and math score and those who had a lower combined score.[33] Table 3.17 presents selected data by race/ethnicity for these two groups of students in the ABET sample of 1985 freshmen.

Table 3.17
Academic Performance of Engineering Students in the ABET Study with a Combined SAT Score of 1100 or More and Those with a Combined Score of less than 1100, by Race/Ethnicity

| | White | | Black | | Hispanic | |
| | < | ≥ | < | ≥ | < | ≥ |
Data Points	1100	1100	1100	1100	1100	1100
Average Combined SAT Score	1017	1258	902	1215	941	1229
Graduation Rate	23%	83%	36%	62%	39%	58%
Median GPA	2.57	3.14	2.04	2.55	2.35	2.80
GPA at 75th Percentile	3.08	3.53	2.42	2.92	2.81	3.21
GPA at 25th Percentile	1.92	2.63	1.41	2.12	1.87	2.41

Source: Thomas R. Phillips, *ABET/Exxon Minority Engineering Student Profile* (New York: Accreditation Board for Engineering and Technology, 1991), pp. 74–76, 81–82.

Tuskegee University, 43 percent at the University of the District of Columbia, 34 percent at North Carolina A&T State University, 33 percent at Howard University, 32 percent at Prairie View A&M University, 28 percent at Southern University, and 19 percent at Tennessee State University—were typically close to the national graduation rate for black engineering freshmen. Although all the historically black institutions with accredited engineering programs were invited to participate in the ABET study, none chose to do so. However, on the basis of the calculations of Campbell and his colleagues, this does not appear to have been a major omission from a graduation-rate perspective.
33. Phillips, *ABET/Exxon Minority Engineering Student Achievement Profile*, pp. 74–75. The actual SAT criteria Phillips used to differentiate these groups were a verbal SAT score of at least 500 and a math SAT score of at least 600. Although students in the "very well prepared" group had to meet both criteria, for convenience, I simply refer to those who had a combined SAT score of 1,100 and to those who did not—which is the approach Phillips used in his text.

For all three racial/ethnic groups, there were very large differences in the average scores of those students who scored at least 1,100 and those who did not. In the case of whites, the difference was 241 points (1,258 - 1,017); for blacks, it was 313 points; and for Hispanics, it was 288 points. These differences in average scores were associated with very substantial differences in the percentages of students who earned a bachelor's degree in engineering. The disparity in graduation rates was largest for whites, at 60 percent (83 percent - 23 percent), second largest for blacks, at 26 percent (62 percent - 36 percent), and smallest for Hispanics, at 19 percent (58 percent - 39 percent).

Consistent with the differences in graduation rates, for each group there were very sizable differences in median GPAs between students with and without a combined SAT score of at least 1,100. For each group the difference was about half a GPA point. The impact of these differences on graduation rates was most acute for blacks with an SAT score of less than 1,100. With a median GPA of 2.04, about half of the African Americans in this group did not have a GPA high enough to earn a degree in any field.

Because the high- and low-achievement issues loom large for both African Americans and Latinos, table 3.17 also includes GPAs at the 75th and 25th percentiles for each group. It shows that the 75th percentile GPA was 3.53 for whites with at least an 1,100 combined SAT score, but only 3.08 for the less-than-1,100 group. This means that the majority of white engineering graduates with very high (3.50+) GPAs came from the group with a combined score of at least 1,100. Similarly, the 25th percentile GPA was 1.92 for whites with less than an 1,100 score but 2.63 for whites who reached the 1,100 threshold. This means that the whites who could not continue in engineering because of low grades were disproportionately drawn from the students with less than an 1,100 combined SAT. This general pattern is repeated for both African Americans and Latinos.

Although the graduation rate and GPA patterns associated with combined SAT scores of over and under 1,100 are directionally similar for all three racial/ethnic groups, table 3.17 shows that there also are large differences among the groups. Most significantly, for both SAT segments, blacks and Hispanics lagged the GPA levels of whites. The black-white gaps were particularly large: among students with less than an 1,100 combined SAT score, the median GPA of the whites was 0.53 higher than that of blacks; among those with a score of 1,100 or higher, the white median GPA was 0.59 higher.

Because the African Americans in the group with less than an 1,100 combined SAT score averaged only 902—115 points lower than the white average of 1,017—it is not surprising that they had a significantly lower median GPA than their white peers. However, this factor seems to be less operative at the 1,100-and-above level. The average SAT score for blacks with a score of at least 1,100 was 1,215—only 43 points lower than the white average of 1,258. It appears that we must look elsewhere for an explanation of the large difference in median GPAs between African Americans and whites with high SAT scores.

Similarly, it is surprising that, with an average combined SAT score of 1,229,

Latinos in the group with at least an 1,100 SAT score have a median GPA 0.34 points lower than that of their white counterparts. Even more surprising are the graduation rates for Latinos. Both those with a combined SAT score of less than 1,100 and those with a higher score had median GPAs that could have translated into much higher graduation rates. The 58 percent graduation rate for the higher-scoring group, with a median GPA of 2.80, seems especially low.

The 23 percent graduation rate for whites with a combined SAT score of less than 1,100 must also be regarded as quite low. Their black and Hispanic counterparts in this SAT stratum had much higher graduation rates. Moreover, the median GPA for the whites in this group was 2.57, almost identical to the 2.55 GPA of blacks in the 1,100 or higher group, who had a 62 percent graduation rate—nearly three times the 23 percent rate of the whites.

Clearly, our standard measures of academic performance, including SAT scores and high school grades, are very helpful in describing, explaining, and predicting the broad contours of the academic performance in college of groups of students. However, the data reviewed here remind us of how much variation can occur between groups, even when most of the students are academically very well prepared for college.

The relatively low college GPAs and graduation rates for black and Hispanic engineering students with high SAT scores demonstrate how costly these inconsistencies can be. The consequences in this case are fewer minority engineers than we might otherwise expect. As we have seen, African Americans and Latinos continue to be significantly underrepresented among high school graduates who are academically very well prepared for college. It is imperative, therefore, that those minority high school graduates who are academically very well prepared maximize the likelihood of their success in college—especially in demanding majors such as engineering.

Other Studies of Grades at the Undergraduate Level   How similar are the findings of the ABET study to those of other studies of the grades of undergraduates? The answer is that they are fairly typical. For example, Walter R. Allen analyzed the transcripts of nearly 31,000 students who enrolled at the University of Michigan between 1975 and 1981. Because of the large sample size, Allen was able to examine the academic results of whites, blacks, Hispanics, Asians, and Native Americans. The Asians and whites in Allen's study had combined SAT scores of 1,076 and 1,064, respectively. In contrast, the average combined scores were 978 for American Indians, 965 for Hispanics, and 866 for blacks.[34]

The pattern is similar with regard to average high school GPAs. Asians led with an average of 3.61, followed closely by whites with 3.50. The other three groups were significantly lower: Native Americans, Hispanics, and African Americans had average GPAs of 3.18, 3.16, and 2.91, respectively.[35]

34. Walter R. Allen, "Black Students in U.S. Higher Education: Toward Improved Access," *Urban Review* 20 (Fall 1988): 170, 173.
35. Ibid.

At the college level, whites and Asians had almost identical average GPAs—3.24 and 3.22, respectively. Native Americans were again third, with an average GPA of 2.75, Hispanics were fourth with 2.65, and blacks were last with only 2.24.[36]

The GPA gaps between Asians and whites, on the one hand, and among non-Asian minorities, on the other, grew between high school and college. At the high school level, the GPA gap for Latinos and American Indians was in the range of .3–.4. It had grown to over a half-point at the college level. For African Americans, the .6–.7-point gap at the high school level had grown to a full point at the college level.

The findings from Allen's analysis are consistent with those of a study undertaken in the 1980s by Michael T. Nettles, A. Robert Thoeny, and Erica J. Gosman. These researchers surveyed over four thousand undergraduates enrolled in thirty universities in ten southern and eastern states. They found that the high school GPAs, SAT scores, and college GPAs of the blacks were significantly lower than those of the whites.[37] The SAT scores of the blacks in the sample actually overpredicted their college GPAs. That is to say, their college GPAs tended to be lower than would have been predicted by their SAT scores.[38] (This, of course, is the opposite of the result that would be expected by those who feel that standardized tests typically underestimate the developed academic skills of minority students.)

The overprediction pattern has also been identified in a number of other studies of the academic performance of black students.[39] Moreover, it is apparently consistent with Phillips's findings for African American engineering students in the ABET study reviewed earlier.

The Limitations and Value of the College GPA Data   It is important that one not overgeneralize from a few studies of the kind cited in this section. The data in the Allen study were drawn from the transcripts of undergraduates from only one university. The data in the Nettles study were collected from a large, diverse group of institutions but used information self-reported by participating students rather than transcripts. The Phillips study was based on transcript information gathered from many institutions, but was confined to a single academic major. The Allen study examined the academic performance patterns of blacks, whites, Hispanics, Asians, and American Indians; the

36. Ibid., 173–74.
37. Michael T. Nettles, A. Robert Thoeny, and Erica J. Gosman, "Comparative and Predictive Analyses of Black and White Students' College Achievement and Experiences," *Journal of Higher Education* 57 (May/June 1986): 293–95, 302–03.
38. Ibid., p. 308.
39. Ibid., p. 291. Also see Robert Klitgaard, *Choosing Elites* (New York: Basic Books, 1985), pp. 160–65. Klitgaard notes that "dozens of technical studies" have identified this phenemonon. "On average," he concludes, "test scores overpredict the later performance of blacks compared to whites, especially at the right tail"—that is, those who earn high scores on standardized tests. He also notes that the overprediction phenomenon for blacks has been found not only with regard to grades in college or graduate/professional school but also with regard to job performance (when job knowledge tests and/or work samples are used as the criteria for work performance).

Nettles study looked at only African Americans and whites; and the Phillips study looked at African Americans, whites, and Latinos. Nevertheless, the GPA patterns for racial/ethnic groups that emerged in these studies are generally quite consistent with one another as well as with the standardized test and grade patterns presented in previous sections of this chapter. And the absolute differences in GPA levels between whites/Asians and non-Asian minorities that are identified by these studies are sizable. For these reasons, we should take these findings very seriously.

RACIAL/ETHNIC DIFFERENCES IN GRADES AT THE GRADUATE SCHOOL LEVEL

Information on the GPA patterns of minority and majority students at the graduate/professional school level is even more limited than that available for undergraduate education. One such study, however, conducted by Michael Nettles, was made of about one thousand doctoral students at four research universities—Florida State, Rutgers, Ohio State, and the University of Maryland at College Park. He selected these universities because they had been among the leaders in awarding doctorates to blacks and Hispanics for a number of years. The individuals in the sample were enrolled doctoral students in the fall of 1986 who had completed at least one year of their programs. Information was gathered via a questionnaire.[40]

The average GPAs for whites, African Americans, and Latinos in the study were 3.76, 3.53, and 3.66, respectively.[41] At first glance, the differences among the groups may seem inconsequential. Nevertheless, they can be important because we would expect GPAs for virtually all second-year doctoral students to fall in the 3.00–4.00 range. When students cluster within one GPA point, seemingly small differences in average GPAs between groups can be quite significant.

This conclusion is supported by other data from the study regarding the percentages of each racial group that earned A (4.00) and A- (3.75–3.99) grades. About 16 percent of the whites in the sample reported 4.00 GPAs, while only 7 percent and 4 percent of the Latinos and African Americans did so. Moreover, 48 percent of the white doctoral candidates had a GPA of 3.75–3.99, while only 38 percent of Hispanics and 28 percent of blacks in the sample had GPAs in that range.[42] Among the very top students in doctoral programs examined by Nettles, blacks and Hispanics were significantly underrepresented relative to whites.

To the degree that high doctoral GPAs are important (directly or indirectly) in securing the most desirable tenure-track academic positions in higher education, Nettles's data suggest that whites have very large advantages over blacks and considerable advantages over Hispanics. Since African Americans and

40. Michael T. Nettles, "Success in Doctoral Programs: Experiences of Minority and White Students," *American Journal of Education* 98 (August 1990): 498–99.
41. Ibid., p. 503.
42. Ibid.

Latinos are significantly underrepresented among doctoral degree recipients in general, the existence of these gaps is particularly unfortunate.

The underrepresentation of African Americans and Latinos at the highest GPA levels is also consistent with the findings of Thomas Phillips. In the ABET engineering student study, 6 percent of the whites but 0 percent of the blacks and Hispanics in the sample who were engineering freshmen in 1985 had 4.00 GPAs while they were in the engineering track.[43]

Like the studies of undergraduate GPAs, the Nettles survey of doctoral candidates must be interpreted with caution. It is only one study in an area in which research is limited. Yet, directionally, the findings of this study are consistent with the overall grade and standardized test score patterns presented over the course of this chapter.

SUMMARY AND CONCLUSIONS

In this chapter I have used standardized test and school grade data to assess the academic achievement patterns of students from the major racial/ethnic groups. My interest in the distribution of the academic skills derives from the recognition that African Americans, Latinos, and Native Americans have historically been significantly overrepresented among low academic achievers and substantially underrepresented among high-achieving students.

I am also concerned about whether the recent progress of non-Asian minorities has been substantial enough to keep up with the demographic shift. Although the white majority has historically had higher academic achievement levels than blacks, Hispanics, and Native Americans, its share of the student-age population is declining rapidly. As a result, American society has a compelling interest in seeing to it that those minority groups, which have long been disadvantaged educationally, increase their academic skills rapidly enough to ensure that, as their share of the population rises, the average skill level of the population as a whole does not decline. This, of course, is a minimum standard. The economic competitiveness, civil rights, and social harmony rationales for accelerating the educational advancement of minorities (reviewed in chapter 1) make a strong collective case that non-Asian minorites need to improve their academic achievement levels at an even higher rate.

On this question, the data reviewed in this chapter send a mixed message. The NAEP reading and math data show some substantial increases in the math scores of black and Hispanic students in the 1971–90 period. However, this progress has not been uniform and may have stopped altogether for some segments of the minority population in some subject areas.

The SAT data for the 1981–90 period show a continuing large underrepresentation of African Americans, Latinos, and Native Americans among the highest scorers on both the verbal and mathematics sections of the test. Despite some clear progress for these groups, the growth in their collective share of stu-

---

43. Phillips, *ABET/Exxon Minority Engineering Student Achievement Profile*, p. 64.

dents with the highest SAT scores does not appear to have been as large as the increase in their collective share of the student-age population in the period.

None of the data on school grades reviewed in this chapter directly contributes to our understanding of academic achievement trends. However, the data do confirm the persistence of large academic achievement gaps at all educational levels. The gaps documented in this chapter are enormously costly for minorities as well as for society as a whole. Effective strategies for eliminating these gaps as quickly as possible, however, are unlikely to be identified unless we have a clear understanding of both their origins and the reasons they persist. In the next chapter, I will begin to develop a preliminary explanation.

CHAPTER FOUR

Opportunity,

Resources, and

Intergenerational Advancement

In this chapter, I develop a framework for understanding the persistence of large educational attainment and academic achievement gaps between whites and Asians, on the one hand, and blacks, Hispanics, and Native Americans, on the other. In subsequent chapters, I use this framework in examining the historical and contemporary causes of these gaps and developing recommendations for eliminating them.

I first review a study conducted in the mid-1960s by the sociologist James S. Coleman and several of his colleagues, one that produced a great deal of information regarding the roles of the family and the school in shaping the academic performance patterns of students. I next examine Coleman's explanation for the findings that, for any single generation of students, the family plays a more powerful role in determining the relative academic success of groups of students than the school does. Drawing on the work of social scientists, educators, and health professionals, I present several categories of resources relevant to school success.

In the third and fourth stages of the analysis, I shift to a dynamic view of education-relevant resource variations among groups by examining the notion of equal educational opportunity and the relationship between the rate of intergenerational educational advancement and the quality of the educational opportunity structure.

I then examine two ways of thinking about the historical and contemporary forces that have produced variations in the education-relevant resources available to children. One of these approaches emphasizes the changes in the family's role in socializing and educating children over the past two hundred years as a result of the nation's shift from an agrarian to a technological/industrial society. The other emphasizes the growing inability of adults with few skills to support their families as a result of recent changes in the job mix of the economy and the concentration of poor minorities in the central cities. Because this approach is especially relevant to variations in educational performance patterns among social classes and racial/ethnic groups, the second half of this chapter discusses it in detail.

FAMILIES, SCHOOLS, AND RACIAL/ETHNIC VARIATIONS IN ACADEMIC
ACHIEVEMENT PATTERNS

Substantial societal interest in identifying, understanding, and attempting to eliminate variations in educational attainment and achievement patterns among racial/ethnic groups is a very recent phenomenon. In fact, the first nationwide study of some of these differences and their underlying causes was an outgrowth of a requirement in the Civil Rights Act of 1964 that the commissioner of education undertake a national survey "concerning the lack of availability of equal educational opportunities for individuals by reason of race, color, religion, or national origin in public educational institutions at all levels in the United States, its territories and possessions, and the District of Columbia."[1] The principal investigator and primary author of the ensuing report for the study was James S. Coleman.

The Coleman Report has proved to be a landmark study. It has contributed to the meaning of equal educational opportunity in American society, stimulated much subsequent research, and influenced efforts to improve schools that serve minorities and other disadvantaged populations.[2] Some of the Coleman Report's most important findings were the following:

1. The average academic achievement levels of white and Asian students (as measured by standardized tests) were significantly higher than those of blacks, Puerto Ricans, Mexican Americans, and American Indians. Moreover, these achievement gaps generally increased between the first and twelfth grades.

2. Differences in standardized test scores among racial/ethnic groups were most strongly correlated with variations in home background, particularly as measured by socioeconomic-status-related characteristics, such as the education levels and occupations of the parents.

3. School characteristics were only modestly related to differences in standardized test scores, but the relationship was somewhat stronger for black and other non-Asian minority students than for whites and Asians.

4. Of those school factors subject to some control by educators and policymakers, variations in the characteristics of teachers were most correlated with group differences in test scores. There was a modest association between differences in teachers' verbal-test scores and differences in students' test scores.

5. Variations in facilities and curricula had little association with differences in the standardized test scores of students from the several racial/ethnic

1. James S. Coleman et al., *Equality of Educational Opportunity* (Washington, D.C.: Office of Education, 1966), p. iii.

2. One of the most significant consequences of the Coleman Report was the strong impetus it gave to efforts to discover schools that successfully educated disadvantaged children (especially those from minority groups) and to document the characteristics that accounted for their success. These and other efforts came to be called the effective schools movement and were intended to demonstrate that good schools could have a more positive impact on student achievement independent of home background than many educators were inclined to believe after reading the Coleman Report. See John I. Goodlad, *Teachers for Our Nation's Schools* (San Francisco: Jossey Bass, 1990), p. 5.

groups. The actual variations in resources among schools tended to be relatively small, and those that did exist were greater on a regional basis (for example, North versus South) than on the basis of the racial/ethnic characteristics of the student bodies.

6. The school factor most correlated with variations in standardized test scores was the composition of the student body. The characteristics of students' peers were more closely associated with variations in students' test scores than differences in teacher characteristics, school facilities, or the curriculum.

7. The study found enormous racial/ethnic segregation in the schools, among both students and teachers. Whites and blacks were found to be the most segregated of the racial/ethnic groups, but segregation was also significant for most of the other groups.[3]

Some of these findings were both unexpected and controversial. For example, among schools within the same region and because of the large disparities that had historically existed in the South between per pupil school expenditures for whites and blacks, it was assumed that there would be extreme differences in financial resources between schools serving primarily white children and those serving primarily minority students—especially African Americans. As recently as 1940, per pupil expenditures in the segregated public schools of the southern states were about three times more for whites than for African Americans. However, by the end of the 1960s, nearly half of all African American students lived outside the South compared to less than a quarter in 1940, and in the country at large expenditure differences had not been so pronounced. Moreover, expenditure differences between southern schools that served largely white or black student populations had narrowed considerably between the 1940s and the 1960s, evidently because of the legal challenges to school segregation.[4]

It was also anticipated that variations in school characteristics would be much more strongly related to differences in students' test scores, independent of the socioeconomic status of the students, than the study found to be the case.

Prior to the Coleman Report there had been general awareness of the strong relationship between the socioeconomic characteristics of families and the academic achievement of their children. But because it was based on a large-scale, national sample of schools and students, the Coleman Report provided powerful, research-grounded support for the existence of this relationship, and in a way that demonstrated its relevance for disadvantaged racial/ethnic minorities.

3. Coleman et al., *Equality of Educational Opportunity*, pp. 3–23, 295–325.

4. Gerald David Jaynes and Robin M. Williams, Jr., eds., *A Common Destiny: Blacks and American Society* (Washington, D.C.: National Academy Press, 1989), pp. 58–61; James P. Comer, "Home, School, and Academic Learning," in *Access to Knowledge: An Agenda for Our Nation's Schools*, John I. Goodlad and Pamela Keating, eds. (New York: College Entrance Examination Board, 1990), p. 34; K. Forbis Jordan and Mary P. McKeown, "Financing the Public Schools in the Post World War II Period: Transmitters, Influencers, Researchers, and Disseminators," *Journal of Education Finance* 12 (Spring 1987): 479; James S. Coleman, "The Evaluation of Equality of Educational Opportunity," in *On Equality of Educational Opportunity: Papers Deriving from the Harvard University Faculty Seminar on the Coleman Report*, Frederick Mosteller and Daniel P. Moynihan, eds. (New York: Random House, 1972), p. 153.

Since the publication of the Coleman Report, numerous studies have confirmed the substantial associations between students' family background/social class characteristics and their standardized test scores. However, these associations have been found to be very strong primarily when students are looked at on a collective rather than on an individual basis. For instance, parent education level is strongly correlated with the achievement test score patterns of groups of students but only modestly associated with the scores of particular individuals.[5]

Numerous studies have also found relatively weak relationships (independent of family background/social class factors) between students' test scores and such school characteristics as expenditures per pupil, curriculum, facilities, teachers' educational attainment levels and standardized test scores, and teachers' (self-reported) classroom practices.[6]

EDUCATION-RELEVANT RESOURCES

Why have family background/social class factors been found to have a strong association with group variations in academic achievement patterns while school factors have only a modest association with these variations? James Coleman has offered the following brief explanation: "The resources devoted by the family to the child's education interact with the resources provided by the school—and there is greater variation in the former resources than in the latter."[7] The idea that the resources of the family vary more than the resources of the school can be regarded, I believe, as a kind of summary of the following points:

1. To ensure their academic success, children must be provided with a substantial quantity of resources by their family or the school.

2. In contemporary America, there are significant differences among families and among schools in the amounts and forms of these resources that are available for the education of children, but the differences among families are much larger than those among schools.

3. Even the best-resourced school under existing arrangements is usually not able to compensate fully for a substantial shortfall on the family side—which means that a child from such a family is not likely to be educated well.

5. For a review of studies of the correlations between social class factors and the academic performance of individuals and groups, see Karl R. White, "The Relationship between Socioeconomic Status and Academic Achievement," *Psychological Bulletin* 91 (1982): 461–81; Robert Klitgaard, *Choosing Elites* (New York: Basic Books, 1985). It is not surprising that socioeconomic characteristics have much more predictive power at the group level. The academic performance pattern of a group typically includes a wide range of performance levels achieved by individual members of the group. Therefore, predicting where a specific individual from the group will come out on that distribution can be difficult. However, at the aggregate level, one would expect that a large sample of children randomly drawn from a particular group (universe) of children would produce a distribution of achievement reasonably close to that group's underlying academic achievement distribution.

6. For a review of the literature, see Eric A. Hanuschek, "The Impact of Differential Expenditures on School Performance," *Educational Researcher* 18 (May 1989): 45–62.

7. James S. Coleman, "Families and Schools," *Educational Researcher* 16 (August-September 1987): 35.

4. Even when there is no resource-quantity problem on either side, there may be an incompatibility of resource forms between the family and the school (for example, language or other cultural differences) that can adversely affect the educational experience of the child.

If Coleman's explanation is to have practical value, we must have an appropriate method for categorizing education-relevant resources. Like Coleman and others, I have borrowed the notion of "capital" from economics; education-relevant resources possessed by families, schools, and other societal institutions are thus described as forms of capital that can be invested in children.[8] The idea of capital implies not only that the successful education of children involves an enormous investment of several types of resources by a number of institutional actors in society but also that these resources are accumulated (or disaccumulated) over time by individuals, groups, and the society as a whole. How successful a nation is in educating a given generation of children depends a great deal on the degree to which it has been able to accumulate appropriate forms and amounts of education-relevant resources over a long period.

There currently is no commonly agreed upon list of education-relevant resources. I shall use five categories of capital to structure the discussion here: (1) human capital; (2) social capital; (3) health capital; (4) financial capital; and (5) polity capital. The terms *human, social,* and *financial capital* will be familiar to many readers. The term *health capital* is largely self-explanatory. *Polity Capital* is a term coined for the purposes of this analysis, and it will be discussed in detail.

Human Capital   In an article entitled "Capital Formation by Education" (1960) the Nobel Prize winner Theodore W. Schultz wrote,

> I propose to treat education as an investment in man and to treat its consequences as a form of capital. Since education becomes a part of the person receiving it, I shall refer to it as human capital. Since it becomes an integral part of a person, it cannot be bought or sold or treated as property under our institutions. Nevertheless, it is a form of capital if it renders a productive service of value to the economy. The principal hypothesis underlying this treatment of education is that some important increases in national income are a consequence of additions to the stock of this form of capital.

As Schultz conceded, the knowledge and skills individuals learn in school and other settings have value far beyond their contribution to economic growth and productivity. From a larger societal perspective, "education serves to develop individuals to become competent and responsible citizens by giving men and

8. James S. Coleman and Thomas Hoffer, *Public and Private High Schools: The Impact of Communities* (New York: Basic Books, 1987), pp. 221–27; Pierre Bourdieu, trans. Richard Nice, "The Forms of Capital," in *Handbook of Theory and Research for the Sociology of Education,* John G. Richardson, ed. (Westport, Conn.: Greenwood, 1986), pp. 241–58. Originally published as "Okonomisches Kapital, kulturelles Kapital, soziales Kapital," in *Soziale Ungleichheiten* (Sociale Welt, Sonderheft 2), Reinhard Kreckel, ed. (Goettingen: Otto Schartz & Co, 1983), pp. 183–98.

women an opportunity to acquire an understanding of the values they hold and appreciation for what they mean in life."[9] It might be argued that a term less strongly associated with economics should be used to describe the formal-education-derived capital that individuals use to participate in society. One such term is *cultural capital*.[10] However, this term can easily be misunderstood in a pluralistic society like the United States because the word *culture* is so intimately tied to notions of race/ethnicity. Another term that has been used is *intellectual capital*.[11] While this term clearly has a school-related dimension, it can be misunderstood as referring to innate rather than developed abilities of the mind. I shall use the term *human capital*, but not in the restricted sense usually meant by economists; rather, it will refer here to the broad range of knowledge and skills that individuals need to function effectively in contemporary American life and that are acquired to a considerable degree via formal schooling.

Extensive access to adults who have large amounts of human capital—including teachers—is essential for most children to become well educated. Without such access, it is difficult to acquire an adequate amount of human capital.

Social Capital   Social capital is concerned with the relationships individuals have with others. In the words of Pierre Bourdieu, one of the people most closely associated with the term, "Social capital is the aggregate of the actual or potential resources which are linked to possession of a durable network of more or less institutionalized relationships of mutual acquaintance and recognition—or in other words, to membership in a group which provides each of its members with the backing of the collectively owned capital, a 'credential' which entitles them to credit in the various senses of the word."[12]

From a child-rearing perspective, James Coleman has defined *social capital* as "the norms, the social networks, the relationships between adults and children that are of value for the children's growing up. Social capital exists within the family, but also outside the family in the community."[13]

From the perspective of schooling, social capital can be helpful when adults with whom children have a close relationship take a strong interest in their academic success, even when the adults have relatively little formal education of their own. For example, parents who value education highly may be able to motivate their children to work hard in school—assuming that both the parents and the children have reason to believe that hard work in school will pay off in terms of academic success and subsequent success in the labor market.[14]

9. Theodore W. Schultz, "Capital Formation by Education," *Journal of Political Economy* 68 (1960): 571, 572.

10. Bourdieu, "The Forms of Capital," pp. 243–48.

11. Torsten Husen and Albert Tuijnman, "The Contribution of Formal Schooling to the Increase in Intellectual Capital," *Educational Researcher* 20 (October 1991): 17–25.

12. Bourdieu, "The Forms of Capital," 248–49.

13. Coleman, "Families and Schools," p. 36. For a more extensive discussion, see James S. Coleman, *Foundations of Social Theory* (Cambridge: Harvard University Press, 1990), pp. 300–21.

14. James Coleman and Thomas Hoffer believe that the academic success of many children of Asian immigrants is due in considerable measure to the large amounts of social capital parents have invested in their education. Coleman and Hoffer, *Public and Private High Schools*, pp. 223. Gener-

Health Capital   For children to succeed academically in school, they generally must be in good health. In industrialized nations with a large middle class and a small poor population, it may not be necessary to single out health as a major resource needed to ensure school success because most children are in good health. But in less developed countries in which the middle class is small and a large majority of the population is poor, improving children's health may be an essential component of an effective strategy for increasing the academic success of students.[15]

Although the United States is an affluent nation, it now has a large number of children with health problems severe enough to undermine their prospects for academic success—and these children are disproportionately members of racial/ethnic minority groups. Consequently, health capital is included here among the resources that must be taken into account when examining variations in family and school resources.

Financial Capital   Financial capital, in the form of high current income or substantial savings, can purchase health capital, human capital, and even social capital for children relevant to their success in school. It can buy health capital in the form of good health care, to prevent and treat health problems that can undermine learning. It can buy human capital through the payment of tuition for a private school, the cost of a home in a community with well-resourced public schools, or the cost of such supplementary educational services as tutoring. It can buy social capital in the form of time for parents to invest in the education of their children, by allowing one or both parents to stay at home full- or part-time. It can also buy social capital in the form of a home in a community in which most of the families are academically oriented.

Because financial capital can often be readily converted into other forms of education-relevant capital, it is an especially valuable resource. As a result, children from economically affluent families have an extremely important advantage over children from economically impoverished families.

Polity Capital   By *polity capital* I am referring to the commitment of the larger society to ensure both the well-being of its members and their capacity to participate effectively in the society. In the educational arena, polity capital refers to the society's commitment that children be educated well. We can

---

ally consistent with this view is recent research on Indochinese families in the United States indicating that the strong support of the parents for their children's schooling is closely associated with these youngsters' academic success. See Nathan Caplan, Marcella H. Choy, and John K. Whitmore, "Indochinese Refugee Families and Academic Achievement," *Scientific American* 266 (February 1992): 36–43. However, I believe that there is much more to this story, especially with regard to the overrepresentation of Asian students among the highest academic achievers. Of great importance is the substantial amount of human capital possessed by many Asian parents in a context in which Asians have experienced much less education-relevant racial prejudice and discrimination in America than some other minority groups (see chapter 9).

15. Marlaine E. Lockheed, "Improving Primary Schools in Developing Countries," *Finance & Development* (March 1990): 26.

hypothesize that the amount of polity capital available to individuals and groups is heavily dependent on their membership status in the society and on the meaning of that membership—the kinds of obligations the larger society has undertaken with regard to its members.

In many contemporary societies those with full membership have the complete set of legal rights that exist in the society. They are typically recognized as able to assume a broad range of valued roles and responsibilities in the society's mainstream. And they are generally accepted by most other members of the society as participants in good standing in the mainstream culture.

People who enjoy full membership in a society are likely to have more polity capital than those who are not full members. They can expect that society will be much more concerned about their well-being than of those who are not full members. Thus children from segments of the population that are secure in their legal rights, that are regarded as having a high national-interest value, and that are part of the mainstream culture are likely to receive relatively large amounts of the education-relevant support available in the society; children from population segments that are poorly positioned on one or more of these membership dimensions often receive relatively small amounts of such support.

In a society that is basically homogeneous in social class and race/ethnicity, most children would be expected to have generally similar amounts of polity capital. In contrast, in a pluralistic society there may be considerable variation in the amount of polity capital possessed by children. Youngsters from racial/ethnic groups and social classes that have historically not enjoyed full membership would typically have less polity capital than children from groups that have historically enjoyed full membership, as would youngsters from new groups that represent racial/cultural minorities.[16]

Polity capital can be very significant educationally in a large-scale technological society because the full, healthy development of children in such a society is dependent not only on the family but on other institutions like the school and the health care system. How much and how well society invests in different groups of children via these nonfamily institutions may be heavily dependent on their membership status in the society.

The amount of polity capital groups possess also depends on the meaning of membership in the society. The distinguished European social scientist Ralf Dahrendorf has argued that democratic, technological societies have typically been concerned with an expansion of the entitlements of citizenship and with expansion of the material and other benefits generated by society that are available for members to enjoy. It is through its efforts in these domains that a society will maximize the life chances of its members.[17]

16. For a discussion of the problem of the acceptance of immigrants by the larger society, see Hans-Joachim Hoffmann-Notwotny, "Social Integration and Cultural Pluralism: Structural and Cultural Problems of Immigration in European Industrial Countries," in *Population in an Interacting World*, William Alonso, ed. (Cambridge: Harvard University Press, 1987), pp. 149–72.

17. Ralf Dahrendorf, *The Modern Social Conflict: An Essay on the Politics of Liberty*, (Berkeley: University of California Press, 1990), pp. 1–24.

In practice most societies have found it difficult to do both tasks equally well. Dahrendorf has argued that the United States has historically been quite effective in generating benefits for citizens, especially of a material/economic nature, but that it has been much more successful in expanding the entitlements of citizenship in some areas than others. For example, he believes that Americans have done better in the political sphere (the right to vote) than in the social sphere (the right to health care, child care, and so forth).[18] The amount of education-relevant polity capital available to children who are full members of American society may be less than is needed to ensure that virtually all are educationally successful. And children who do not enjoy full membership status (many of whom are likely to be from racial/ethnic minority groups) may possess even less of the polity capital needed to ensure their educational success.

EQUAL EDUCATIONAL OPPORTUNITY

One of the most important American myths is that society provides equal opportunity for all its members—that anyone can be what he or she wants to be, given a willingness to work hard. But it is not possible to provide truly equal opportunity to all Americans in all areas; there is too much diversity among individuals and institutions for this. Nevertheless, the equal opportunity myth reminds people that it should be possible for most members of society to share in the rights and benefits of American life to a significant degree. And it should be possible over time for society to provide something close to the same distribution of opportunities in most areas, including education, to the several racial/ethnic groups that make up the population.

Another important American myth is that each generation of children will do better than their parents' generation—be better educated, hold better jobs, have a higher standard of living, be healthier, and have generally more fulfilling lives. In part because of the rapid economic growth and technological change experienced in the United States over the past century, there has in fact been a great deal of progress in a number of areas—education, health, material well-being, and social position. This has given much credence to the myth of intergenerational advancement.

For most of the nation's history, both the myth of equal opportunity and the myth of intergenerational advancement belonged primarily to whites. Few nonwhite minorities could realistically expect to have the same societal opportunities or to experience as much intergenerational improvement as the majority population. However, with the successes of the civil rights movement in the 1950s and 1960s, the two myths finally began to be the property of the nation's minorities as well—even though minorities are still far from being equal beneficiaries.

18. Ibid., pp. 35–41.

The Coleman Report and the Meaning of Equal Educational Opportunity
The Coleman Report helped stimulate debate on the meaning of equal educational opportunity. By collecting information on both standardized test scores and family/school resources, it raised the question of whether it is sufficient to think of equal educational opportunity primarily in terms of providing children from different racial/ethnic groups with equal educational inputs (for example, school curricula) or whether it had become necessary to think in terms of ensuring equal educational outputs (for example, math skills).[19]

Some civil rights leaders had already begun to address this question before the Coleman Report. From their perspective, the ultimate purpose of changing civil rights laws was to gain a full set of societal benefits for African Americans and other minorities.[20] Because blacks have the same range and distribution of intellectual potential and talents as whites, these leaders believed that, if minorities were given truly equal opportunity, the eventual result would be similar patterns of achievement for minorities and the majority in the schools, the workplace, and all other realms of society. By presenting data showing large test-score differences among the racial/ethnic groups, the Coleman Report helped bring this output interpretation of the meaning of equal educational opportunity into sharp focus.

By collecting information on a variety of home and school attributes and assessing their relationship to test score variations among racial/ethnic groups, the Coleman Report also helped to broaden the discussion of education-relevant resources. It pointed to the importance of gaining a better understanding of how family resources influence academic achievement—and of measuring school resources in ways that go beyond per-pupil expenditures and school facilities. And it suggested the need to understand how school and family resources interact to shape academic achievement patterns.

By using standardized tests to measure educational outputs, the Coleman Report helped stimulate a debate about how best to assess the academic performance of students. On one level, it implicitly made a distinction between educational attainment (credentials) and academic achievement (skills). On another level, it raised the question of how well standardized tests measure learning in school. Both questions pointed to the difficulty of measuring educational opportunity from the perspective of results.

Equal Educational Opportunity and Intergenerational Advancement   There is at least one extremely important aspect of the idea of equal opportunity that

19. Coleman and his colleagues designed their study to assess the degree of equality/inequality of educational opportunity among racial/ethnic groups, using several definitions of equal educational opportunity. In particular, they looked at this question from both input and output perspectives; most previous research had been limited primarily to questions about inputs. See James S. Coleman, "The Concept of Equality of Educational Opportunity," *Equal Educational Opportunity* (Cambridge: Harvard University Press, 1969), pp. 9–24; Frederick Mosteller and Daniel P. Moynihan, eds., "A Pathbreaking Report," in *On Equality of Educational Opportunity*, pp. 6–7.

20. See, for example, Bayard Rustin, "From Protest to Politics: The Future of the Civil Rights Movement," *Commentary* (February 1965): 27.

the Coleman Report and similar studies have not fully addressed: the question of how much time it will take to eliminate existing differences among racial/ethnic groups in academic achievement patterns, assuming that very energetic societal efforts are directed toward this objective. As we have seen, there are still very large differences in academic achievement patterns among racial/ethnic groups, and progress in narrowing the gaps has been slow—taking several generations.

Of course, this does not necessarily mean that approximate educational outcome parity cannot be achieved until some very distant point in the future. Yet it does force us to consider whether we can provide completely equal educational results for the several racial/ethnic groups within the next generation or two. A key question here is just how large the current racial/ethnic variations in education-relevant resources are. The larger they are, the more difficult and time consuming the effort to produce equal educational results is likely to be. In this and several subsequent chapters, I examine these resource variations from a variety of perspectives. And in chapter 11, I attempt to quantify them in a way that will allow us to make order-of-magnitude estimates. For present purposes, however, only two general conclusions from that analysis need to be introduced here:

1. Most educationally advantaged students receive several times more education-relevant resources than most educationally disadvantaged students.

2. As Coleman noted, most of this resource advantage is due to variations in family resources rather than school resources.

Another major issue is how much of the variation in resources among racial/ethnic groups can be addressed directly through the schools. Although the school can be a vehicle for investing several types of education-relevant resources in children, it has been designed to provide particular kinds of human capital. Schools are staffed by professional educators who are expected to provide instructional services. Ordinarily teachers can also provide a modest amount of social capital to most students, but the number of children with whom they can develop relatively close relationships is usually limited. Schools can also provide some health services, although few currently have the ability to meet more than a fraction of the health needs of students. Similarly, schools have an extremely limited capacity to provide financial capital to students; some in-kind financial capital can be extended via free or subsidized meals, free child care, and health services. Schools, of course, can also be regarded as a specific institutional expression of polity capital—a means through which society acts on its commitment to educate children.

This summary has the sound of yet another version of the "schools can't make a difference" theme.[21] However, it should be understood that education-rele-

21. Schools can help children learn a great deal that they would not learn otherwise, especially in specialized areas such as mathematics and science, where informal instruction is relatively ineffective. But schools cannot by themselves ensure that every child or group of children learns the same amount and/or achieves the same level of mastery of a subject, skill, or concept. This distinction has not always been made clear in discussions of the Coleman Report or similar research. See Eric A.

vant family resources are in many respects intergenerationally accumulated school resources.[22] In families with a great deal of human capital, one or both parents usually have at least a bachelor's degree. As a result, they are able to make large, direct (but usually informal) human capital investments in their children starting in infancy. These parents also tend to have above-average paying jobs and access to health insurance that enable them to provide large amounts of financial and health capital to their children. Additionally, there is a good chance that these parents will locate their family in a community in which a large proportion of the adults have college degrees, thus providing their children with social capital via a network of like-minded adults (and their children). Finally, because they are well educated and likely to have the associated trappings of the middle-class mainstream of society, their children are likely to enjoy a great deal of polity capital.

If we looked at all the college-educated parents of school-age children in the United States, we would probably find that a majority are the first generation in their families to earn a college degree. That is, most of them had parents who had completed high school (and possibly a few years of college). And if we pushed back further in time, we would find that most parents three or four generations ago had completed only the eighth grade or less. Viewed in this way, group educational advancement can be regarded as an intergenerational phenomenon, whether for a small entity such as a family or a larger entity such as a racial/ethnic group. Equal educational opportunity, defined as similar distributions of educational attainment and academic achievement for all racial/ethnic groups, is something that must be reached through a process of intergenerational educational advancement.[23]

Hanushek and John F. Kain, "On the Value of Equality of Educational Opportunity as a Guide to Public Policy," *On Equality of Educational Opportunity,* p. 116.

22. In support of this view is the well-documented increase in IQ scores in industrialized nations between the 1930s and the 1970s—a period in which the amount of formal schooling provided to children expanded significantly in most societies. That is, successive generations of youngsters attended school for more years than previous generations. There is also evidence that children of a given generation who have many years of formal schooling experience increases in IQ scores that are not shared to the same degree by children who have fewer years of schooling. Neither finding is surprising given that notions of intelligence are culture-bound and that, as Ceci has suggested, "Schooling fosters the development of cognitive processes that underpin performance on most IQ tests." See James R. Flynn, "The Mean IQ of Americans: Massive Gains 1932 to 1978," *Psychological Bulletin* 95 (January 1984): 29–51; and "Massive Gains in IQ Scores in 14 Nations: What IQ Tests Really Measure," *Psychological Bulletin* 17 (1987): 171–91; Husen and Tuijnman, "The Contribution of Formal Schooling to the Increase in Intellectual Capital," pp. 17–25; and Stephen J. Ceci, "How Much Does Schooling Influence General Intelligence and Its Cognitive Components? A Reassessment of the Evidence," *Developmental Psychology* 27 (September 1991): 703–22.

23. Because of data limitations, researchers have rarely been able to examine intergenerational trends over more than three generations. Nevertheless, considerable evidence of intergenerational advancement has been found—although there is little evidence that convergence among groups in virtually all domains can be achieved in as few as three generations. Moreover, Asians and white ethnics seem historically to have enjoyed greater intergenerational advancement, particularly educationally and economically, than blacks and Hispanics. See Timothy L. Smith, "Native Blacks and Foreign Whites: Varying Responses to Educational Opportunity in America, 1880–1950," *Perspectives in American History* 6 (1972): 309–35. See Michael R. Olneck and Marvin Lazerson, "The

Although it is most productive to think of the convergence of educational attainment/academic achievement patterns among racial/ethnic groups in intergenerational terms, there is nothing inevitable about this process. If large differences currently exist among racial/ethnic groups in educational outcomes and in the education-relevant resources available to them, the output gaps are unlikely to be reduced significantly over time unless there are secular forces or institutional mechanisms in place that make it possible to reduce the input gaps substantially. That is, there must be a favorable long-term *opportunity structure*. This term refers to the institutional configurations and societal circumstances that shape the prospects of individuals and groups to share in the benefits of society. In this context, I am defining the educational opportunity structure as the institutional arrangements and societal conditions that heavily influence the ability of groups to acquire and use education-relevant resources to improve their educational performance, both absolutely and relative to other groups, over time.

The many factors that influence the supply of these resources in contemporary America and thus shape the nation's educational opportunity structure are unlikely to have a uniform impact on all racial/ethnic groups, for each group has its own current pattern of achievement and resources and its own distinctive history. Nevertheless, I believe that five factors relevant to all groups stand out:

1. Individuals—and groups—need to have all the legal rights necessary to acquire and use a formal education, including the right to become educated, the right to attend the same schools as other groups on an equal basis, and the right to use what they have learned freely throughout society. Moreover, it must be possible to exercise these rights without facing pervasive, energy-draining extralegal opposition from other, powerfully positioned groups.

School Achievement of Immigrant Children: 1900–1930," *History of Education Quarterly* 14 (Winter 1974): 453–82; Robert M. Hauser and David L. Featherman, "Equality of Schooling: Trends and Prospects," *Sociology of Education* 49 (April 1976): 99–120; Lisa J. Neidert and Reynolds Farley, "Assimilation in the United States: An Analysis of Ethnic and Generation Differences in Status and Achievement," *American Sociological Review* 50 (December 1985): 840–50; Nathan Glazer and Daniel P. Moynihan, *Beyond the Melting Pot* (Cambridge: MIT Press, 1963); Charles Hirschman and Morrison G. Wong, "Socioeconomic Gains of Asian American, Blacks, and Hispanics: 1960–1976," *American Journal of Sociology* 90 (November 1984): 584–609; Gary D. Sandefur and Anup Pahari, "Racial and Ethnic Inequality in Earnings and Educational Attainment," *Social Service Review* (June 1989): 199–221.

The notion of intergenerational advancement is to a considerable degree grounded in a view of industrial society that assumes that there will be a great deal of social mobility over time, owing to the tendency of bureaucratic organizations to award occupational benefits on the basis of ability and performance rather than on the basis of race, ethnicity, class, or other criteria that are not directly relevant to performance issues. Robert Park of the University of Chicago was largely responsible for the early development of this "assimilationist" model of group participation in society. More recently, it has been elaborated by Milton Gordon. See Robert E. Park and Ernest W. Burgess, *Introduction to the Science of Sociology* (Chicago: University of Chicago Press, 1921); Milton Gordon, *Assimilation in American Life: The Role of Race, Religion, and National Origin* (New York: Oxford University Press, 1964).

2. The economy needs to generate enough adequately paying, low-skill jobs to ensure that most adults with little formal education can earn enough to feed, clothe, house, and tend to the health needs of their families, especially the children. If groups have many adults with little education and are facing a growing shortage of adequately paying low-skill jobs, they are not likely to have the necessary economic means to participate successfully in the intergenerational advancement process.

3. The economy also needs to generate significant growth in the number of high-skill, high-paying jobs to ensure that disadvantaged groups are able to increase substantially their representation in these job strata. Because of the large amount of education-relevant family resources associated with high-skill jobs, groups that are already disproportionately represented among such job-holders have a built-in advantage for securing such positions. Their children are likely to do well in school and generally are well positioned to secure such jobs as they become available. This advantage becomes less consequential when the demand for highly educated workers outstrips the supply of academically successful children from occupationally advantaged families. In this situation, children from less educationally advantaged circumstances have greater opportunities to secure such jobs—and greater incentives to do well academically. If these positive conditions prevail, the intergenerational advancement process for disadvantaged groups is strengthened.[24]

4. Parents or their surrogates need to be in a position to be personally supportive of their children's education. The more time parents spend in educationally supportive ways with children, the better the children are likely to do in school. When providing such support to their children, parents often need the backup support of other adults, whether relatives, friends, neighbors, or professional child-care providers. Groups in which parents are able to be strongly and personally supportive of their children's education are much more likely to enjoy solid intergenerational advancement than groups in which the parents are often unable to do so.

5. Appropriately resourced schools need to be available to all children. Note that the phrase used here is "appropriately resourced," not "equally resourced." Student bodies have very different needs. The more the amounts and configurations of school resources can be adjusted to meet the needs of students, the greater the likelihood that disadvantaged populations will enjoy solid school success over time. However, the greater the disparities in home resources among groups of students, the more difficult it will be to adjust school resources sufficiently to provide uniformly high-quality academic results.

24. Historically, individuals with a great deal of formal education have tended to have fewer children than those with little formal education. In recent decades, the fertility rates of highly educated segments have been well below replacement level in most industrial societies, including the United States. The recent demographic shift from whites toward minorities is to a considerable degree a product of differences in fertility rates between the majority population and minority groups that have lower aggregate levels of formal education. See Ellen Jamison, Peter D. Johnson, and Richard A. Engels, *World Population Profile: 1987* (Washington, D.C.: Bureau of the Census, U.S. Government Printing Office, 1987), pp. 7–9.

How are these five factors currently impacting the opportunity structures for the racial/ethnic groups in society that are doing the least well academically—blacks, Hispanics, and Native Americans? I shall review data and research suggesting that educationally disadvantaged minorities are experiencing serious problems with three of the five factors: the supply of low-skill, adequately paying jobs; the capacity of parents (or their surrogates) to provide personal support for the educational advancement of their children; and the ability of schools to adjust the amount of resources they invest in students on the basis of students' needs.

THE FAMILY'S CAPACITY TO SOCIALIZE CHILDREN

James Coleman's work concerning variations in educational performance among students has led him to examine why many parents have apparently become progressively less able to provide their children with the social capital they need to succeed in school. Because schools, under existing arrangements, are poorly equipped to provide large amounts of social capital to students, the erosion of the family's (and the community's) social capital capacities is extremely damaging.

In Coleman's view, the weakening of the social capital capacities of families and communities is an outgrowth of industrialization. Two hundred years ago, most people lived in essentially agrarian societies, and the family was the institutional center. Most children were socialized and educated primarily by their parents, extended family members, and individuals from the immediate community. However, as nations began to industrialize, the site of work for most people gradually shifted away from the home to more distant locations. Initially, it was men who were largely removed from the immediate family environment during the workday. Over the past several decades, however, women have rapidly followed men into the workplace. Consequently, in many families, neither parent is at home during the day.[25]

The movement out of the home during the day has not been confined to adults; it has also included children, primarily as the result of the creation and expansion of a system of universal schooling. Moreover, much of the expansion of the educational system has itself been a result of the industrial/technological revolution: more and more people with specialized knowledge and skills have been needed in the workplace, and these skills have tended to be those that are taught more effectively and efficiently in the school than in the home. As a result of these changes, family members not only are separated from one another during the day but also find themselves segregated by age much of the time. One important result is that children spend much more time primarily in the company of their age peers.[26]

Industrial society has also brought about much more geographic mobility

25. Coleman, "Families and Schools," pp. 32–33.
26. Schultz, "Capital Formation by Education," pp. 571–83; Coleman, "Families and Schools," pp. 32–33, 35.

among families, owing to the emergence of regional and national job markets. This means that family units are now typically nuclear rather than extended; grandparents, aunts, uncles, and cousins are much more likely to live in other towns or cities rather than nearby. Moreover, increases in the divorce rate and in children born to single parents have led to a growth in the percentage of one-parent nuclear families.

The result of all these changes is that the family's capacity to provide support for children is much weaker and more circumscribed than in the past. Parents tend to have less time to spend with their children and to have fewer extended-family members and friends and acquaintances in the community to turn to for assistance in reinforcing the values and attitudes they wish to inculcate in their children—including a strong motivation to do well in school.[27]

Other social scientists have also been concerned about the apparent reduction in the amount of high-quality social capital available to children. In *Two Worlds of Childhood* (1970), Urie Bronfenbrenner examined child-rearing practices in the United States and the former Soviet Union. "Particularly since World War II," he writes, "many changes have occurred in patterns of child rearing in the United States, but their essence may be conveyed in a single sentence: Children used to be brought up by their parents." Some factors are included in Bronfenbrenner's analysis that had not been emphasized by Coleman. For example, he noted that urbanization, not simply industrialization, has made it difficult to maintain strong communities and neighborhoods. He also paid particular attention to the influence of television on children's attitudes, beliefs, and behaviors.[28] Nevertheless, Bronfenbrenner and Coleman clearly share a deep concern that contemporary American society is poorly structured to meet the socialization/social capital needs of children and a belief that this situation is to a considerable extent a product of the weakening of the family's capacities in this area and the inability of other institutions to take up the slack.

The late Margaret Mead argued that the world is now changing so rapidly that there are inherent discontinuities between the experiences of children and adults that make it much more difficult for parents to provide effective guidance into adulthood. One of the implications of her analysis is that parents have much less authority (both experientially and positionally) over their children than they did in the past.[29]

This analysis should not be understood to mean that it is impossible for parents to provide their children with enough social capital to ensure their success in school and a generally healthy transition from childhood to adulthood. But it does suggest that certain characteristics of technological change, industrializa-

27. Coleman and Hoffer, *Public and Private High Schools*, pp. 222–27.

28. Urie Bronfenbrenner, *Two Worlds of Childhood: U.S. and U.S.S.R.* (New York: Russell Sage Foundation, 1970), pp. 95, 109–15. This is not meant to suggest, however, that Coleman does not regard television (or the mass media in general) as a significant factor in socializing children. See Coleman and Hoffer, *Public and Private High Schools*, p. 230.

29. Margaret Mead, *Culture and Commitment: A Study of the Generation Gap* (Garden City, N.Y.: Natural History Press/Doubleday, 1970), pp. 51–76.

tion, and urbanization have made it difficult for them to do so.[30] And to the degree that some groups in America have fewer education-relevant family/community resources of all kinds than other groups, this "generic" social capital problem can be expected to make it even harder for educationally disadvantaged groups to reach substantially higher levels of academic achievement.

THE LABOR MARKET AND THE EROSION OF CAPITAL AMONG THE POOR

Changes in the structure of the labor market in the industrial/technological sectors of the economy have apparently made it difficult for many children to receive the resources they need to do well in school. Given other characteristics of American society, including racial/ethnic pluralism and a history of prejudice and discrimination, these changes appear to account for much of the current variation in education-relevant resources among racial/ethnic groups.

Changes in the Labor Market   During the late nineteenth and early twentieth centuries, the expanding industrial sector of the economy generated millions of jobs that required few skills, most of which were in the cities, especially in the Northeast and Midwest. In the process, a huge job surplus was created that led many Americans in rural areas to seek employment in urban areas and also attracted millions of immigrants from Europe.

Over the course of the twentieth century, economic growth and technological change have dramatically altered both the job mix of the economy and the role of the cities in it. The economy has gradually evolved from one in which most jobs require few skills to one in which a large proportion demands high skill levels. As noted in chapter 2, about half of the new jobs in the years ahead are expected to require at least some postsecondary education.

Technological advances in transportation, communications, production, and distribution have eliminated many of the competitive advantages that cities previously enjoyed in the production and distribution of goods. As the sociologist John D. Kasarda has noted, these advances, "together with growing industrial competition from nonmetropolitan areas and abroad, made our larger, older cities all but obsolete with respect to manufacturing and warehousing. A massive exodus of blue-collar jobs began—and that exodus accelerated during the last decade [the 1970s]."[31] This does not mean that cities have become unimportant to the economy. Rather, their function has changed from producer and

---

30. Those who have been concerned with how the emergence of technological, industrial, urbanized societies has changed relationships between adults and children have not necessarily regarded these forces as the primary source of differences in educational achievement patterns among racial/ethnic groups. Bronfenbrenner has written frequently about the negative consequences of poverty for the healthy development of children, educationally and otherwise. Poverty is a problem that is more acute for several racial/ethnic minority groups than for the white majority. See Bronfenbrenner, "The Changing Family in a Changing World: America First?" *Peabody Journal of Education* 61 (Spring 1984): 62–67; Bronfenbrenner, "Ecology of the Family as a Context for Human Development: Research Perspectives," *Developmental Psychology* 22 (November 1986): 736–38.

31. John D. Kasarda, "Caught in a Web of Change," *Society* 21 (November/December 1983): 41–42.

distributor of goods to provider of administrative, informational, and other professional services. Although old industrial cities have lost huge numbers of low-skill jobs in recent decades, they often have gained large numbers of high-skill jobs.[32]

Even in this new role, central cities have had to share jobs with the suburbs. Kasarda found that the central cities in the six metropolitan areas of Boston, Chicago, Cleveland, Detroit, New York, and Philadelphia lost an aggregate of 985,360 clerical and sales/blue-collar jobs between 1970 and 1980, while the suburbs in these areas gained 796,360 such jobs—a net loss of 189,000 jobs in these low-skill categories. In contrast, both the central cities and their suburban rings in these metropolitan areas gained managerial and professional/technical and administrative support jobs during the same period. However, the suburbs had a collective gain in these job categories over twice as large as the collective gain in the central cities—1,145,020 versus 536,700. More significantly, when the high- and low-skill categories are aggregated, the six central cities had a net loss of 448,660 jobs in the period, and the suburbs had a net gain of 1,941,380 jobs.[33]

For individuals with few skills, finding employment in the six central cities became increasingly difficult in the 1970s, and opportunities in the suburbs were not sufficient to offset the losses in the central cities. For individuals with substantial skills, the six central cities offered considerable opportunity, but the suburbs offered more.

Changes in the Racial/Ethnic Composition of the Cities   By the end of the 1920s, large-scale immigration from Europe had ended, owing to the passage of restrictive immigration legislation and the onset of the Depression. Nevertheless, after 1940, cities continued to attract large numbers of newcomers with few job skills. For the first time, the majority were nonwhite American citizens rather than immigrants. In 1910, about 90 percent of all blacks lived in the South.[34] Net black migration out of the South increased dramatically in the first half of the twentieth century—from 454,000 in the decade 1910–20, equal to about 4 percent of the total black population of 10,463,000 in 1920, to 1,599,000 in 1940–50. The 1940–50 level prevailed until 1970, equal to nearly 11 percent of the total black population of 15,042,000 in 1950.[35]

The proportion of blacks living outside the South had grown to about 23 per-

32. Ibid., p. 41; Kasarda, "Urban Industrial Transition and the Underclass," *Annals of the American Academy of Political and Social Science* 501 (January 1989): 29.

33. Ibid.

34. Gunnar Myrdal, *An American Dilemma: The Negro Problem and Modern Democracy*, Twentieth Anniversary Edition (New York: Harper and Row, 1962), pp. 182, 186; Joseph A. Hill, "Composition of the American Population by Race and Country of Origin," *Annals of the American Academy of Political and Social Science* (November 1936): 178–79.

35. John Reid, "Black America in the 1980s," *Population Bulletin* 37 (December 1982): 19; U.S. Bureau of the Census, *Statistical Abstract of the United States 1991*, 111th Edition (Washington, D.C.: Department of Commerce, U.S. Government Printing Office, 1991), p. 17.

cent in 1940 and reached 47 percent by 1970. About 90 percent of the African Americans in northern and western states in 1940 lived in urban areas, 47 percent of them in just six cities—New York, Chicago, Philadelphia, Detroit, Cleveland, and Pittsburgh. By 1990, 98 percent of all blacks outside the South lived in metropolitan areas and 74 percent in central cities. (By comparison, about 79 percent of the whites in the North and West lived in metropolitan areas and 27 percent in central cities.) In 1990, 72 percent of blacks in the South lived in metropolitan areas and 42 percent in central cities, indicating that blacks in the South also have become more urbanized. (The comparable percentages for whites were 71 percent and 24 percent, respectively.)[36]

By the 1950s, African Americans from the southern states were joined by large numbers of Puerto Ricans.[37] By the 1970s, the great migration of blacks out of the South had ended, but by then, large numbers of immigrants from several Caribbean and Latin American nations were arriving in the United States each year, many settling in northeastern and some southeastern urban areas. In the West and Southwest, non-European newcomers with few job skills have largely come from Mexico and elsewhere in Latin America, although significant numbers of southern blacks have also migrated to that region. Evidence suggests that recent immigrants from Mexico have even less formal education, on average, than did their predecessors of a few decades ago. Large numbers of Asian immigrants and refugees have come to the United States since the late 1960; many of them have settled on the West Coast. In contrast to adult Hispanic immigrants, however, adult Asian immigrants and refugees have generally had at least a high school diploma.[38]

Unemployment, Low Wages, and Poverty among Urban Minorities   In 1990, whites represented about 52 percent of the population of New York City and non-Hispanic whites only about 40 percent.[39] These are remarkably small per-

36. Jaynes and Williams, *A Common Destiny*, p. 60; Myrdal, *An American Dilemma*, p. 183; Claudette E. Bennett, "The Black Population in the United States: March 1990 and 1989," *Current Population Reports, Population Characteristics, Series P-20, No. 448* (Washington, D.C.: Bureau of the Census, U.S. Government Printing Office, 1991), pp. 23–24.

37. Puerto Ricans were the first group of Latinos to arrive in New York City in significant numbers. Their migration to the city, which began after 1910, remained at a relatively low level through 1930, and there was a net migration of Puerto Ricans back to the island during the 1930s owing to the Great Depression. New York did not begin to receive large numbers of Puerto Ricans on a sustained basis until the 1940s. See John H. Burma, *Spanish-Speaking Groups in the U.S.* (Durham: Duke University Press, 1954), 156–59.

38. On black migration from World War I to the 1970s, see Reynolds Farley and Walter R. Allen, *The Color Line and the Quality of Life in America* (New York: Russell Sage Foundation, 1987), pp. 112–18. On the migration of Latinos, see Frank D. Bean and Marta Tienda, *The Hispanic Population of the United States* (New York: Russell Sage Foundation, 1987), pp. 68–70; National Coalition of Advocates for Students, *New Voices: Immigrant Students in the U.S. Public Schools* (Boston: National Coalition of Advocates for Students, 1988), p. 5; Frank D. Bean, Jorge Chapa, Ruth Berg, and Kathryn Sowards, "Educational and Sociodemographic Incorporation among Hispanic Immigrants to the United States," in *Immigration and Ethnicity: The Integration of America's Newest Immigrants*, Barry Edmonston and Jeffrey S. Passel, eds. (Forthcoming).

39. Edward B. Fiske, "New York Growth Is Linked to Immigration," *New York Times*, 22 February 1992, p. B1. The 40 percent figure for non-Hispanic whites is my estimate, based on the

centages in view of the fact that as recently as 1930, about 95 percent of New York's population was European American. Although non-Hispanic whites still represented the largest racial/ethnic group in New York in 1990, blacks accounted for 29 percent of the population that year (up from less than 5 percent in 1930), Hispanics for 24 percent, and Asians for 7 percent.[40] The dramatic changes that have occurred in the racial/ethnic composition of New York's population are illustrative of the demographic shift in most of the nation's largest cities.

Given the extraordinary size, speed, and urban concentration of this demographic shift, it would have taken an extremely positive labor market for the new groups to experience smooth, uniform intergenerational advancement in the economic, educational, social, and political spheres. The mix of jobs generated by the economy in the period would have needed to be generally consistent with the mix of skills possessed by the newcomers. And access to the available jobs would have had to be reasonably good. However, the changing structure of the economy has reduced the supply of adequately paying low-skill jobs relative to the demand, a trend that is expected to persist as the country continues to receive large numbers of new immigrants with little formal education, particularly from Mexico and other Latin American nations. In addition, most of the black migration took place during a period when minorities faced formidable barriers to entry into many segments of the job market owing to racial prejudice and discrimination.

As Gunnar Myrdal wrote in the early 1940s, the beginning of the peak period of black migration to the North and West, "there is no doubt that the overwhelming majority of white Americans desire that there be as few Negroes as possible in America."[41] The so-called white flight that has characterized American cities for several decades clearly attests that most whites in the North and West have been strongly opposed to living in neighborhoods with substantial numbers of African Americans.

With the advantage of hindsight, we can now see that the economic and demographic forces at work in America over most of this century carried the potential for both positive and negative outcomes for the nation's racial/ethnic minorities as well as for the society as a whole. It is possible to list several plausible outcomes that might have been anticipated fifty to seventy-five years ago:

1. The availability of significant numbers of low- and medium-skill jobs would enable a large segment of minority group members to make a reasonably rapid, successful transition from a rural/agrarian to an urban/industrial society.

2. The large long-term surplus of low-skill workers would tend to produce

assumption that half of the Hispanics in New York in 1990 classified themselves as racially white in the decennial census. (This is consistent with the national pattern for Hispanics that year.) Since 24 percent of New Yorkers identified themselves as Hispanic, the white Hispanic population is estimated to have been 12 percent. Subtracting 12 percent from 52 percent produces the 40 percent estimate for the non-Hispanic white population.

40. Ibid; Hill, "Composition of the American Population by Race and Country of Origin," pp. 179–80.

41. Myrdal, *An American Dilemma*, p. 183.

relatively high levels of unemployment among minorities on an ongoing basis unless government was able to pursue effective policies for generating skill-appropriate jobs in the private and public sectors.

3. The surplus of low-skill workers would tend to drive down wages for low-skill jobs, especially in sectors of the economy characterized by strong competitive pressures and cost structures in which wages for low-skill workers are a significant component.

4. Poverty rates among individuals with few job skills and their families would tend to go up because of both high unemployment rates and low wages, unless government was able to establish adequate income-transfer programs and effective job training programs, as well as to help create more jobs.

5. The heavy concentration of minorities in central cities would persist and possibly even intensify, owing to the combination of enduring racial/ethnic prejudice, high poverty rates, and continued movement of minorities to urban areas.

6. The physical separation of whites and minorities, along with the large social-class differences between them, would tend to perpetuate and conceivably increase the real and perceived cultural differences and mistrust between the groups, making it more difficult to develop consensus regarding public policies on employment, education, and other problems confronting minorities.

7. High levels of poverty among minorities would create conditions in which several serious social issues could emerge, such as high crime rates and increased health problems.

8. Virtually all important forms of school-relevant capital would tend to be in short supply for a large portion of poor minority families, which could significantly slow the rate of intergenerational educational/occupational advancement among minorities.

Most of these hypothesized outcomes seem to have come to pass. The widely observed split in the black community between those who have successfully made the transition to the middle class and those who have experienced the ravages of poverty in the urban ghetto is possibly the clearest evidence of the positive and negative consequences of the economic and demographic changes over the past several decades.[42]

A review of unemployment trends since 1940 can help demonstrate the impact of the surplus of low-skill labor over time, despite the generally favorable economic conditions in the United States for most of the past half-century. The decennial census of 1940 found that the national unemployment rates for

---

42. In the mid-1960s, Daniel Patrick Moynihan was among the first to note (from a policy perspective) the splitting of blacks into two groups. Moynihan, *The Negro Family: The Case for National Action* (Washington, D.C.: U.S. Department of Labor, 1965), pp. 5–6, 29. (This report does not actually list an author, but Moynihan is widely recognized as its drafter.) The Business Higher Education Forum has divided African Americans and Latinos into three groups: (1) those who are enjoying at least middle-class incomes; (2) those at the margin of the American economy—that is, the unskilled; and (3) those who are poor. The forum estimates that nearly 40 percent of blacks and Hispanics fall into the first group, 33 percent into the second group, and 30 percent into the third group. See Task Force on Minorities and the Work Force, *Three Realities: Minority Life in the United States* (Washington, D.C.: Business-Higher Education Forum, 1990), pp. 8–10.

whites and nonwhites were 14 percent and 17 percent, respectively. However, among nonwhites living in industrial cities outside the South, the unemployment rate was almost 30 percent—twice the rate for whites.[43] Racial discrimination in favor of whites clearly accounted for a large part of the difference in the rates, and the situation was exacerbated by the continuing shortage of jobs.[44] Also, in 1940 nonwhites had much less formal education than whites, which suggests that skill-level gaps played at least some role in shaping the white and nonwhite unemployment rates at that time. These skill differences were destined to become more important in subsequent decades as racial barriers to workforce participation were lowered.

In the early post–World War II period, favorable economic conditions and a less discriminatory labor market saw unemployment rates for both nonwhites and whites fall dramatically. From 1948 through 1957, the annual national unemployment rate for nonwhites averaged more than 7 percent, as opposed to less than 4 percent for whites. The nonwhite unemployment rate did not reach 10 percent in any of these years. Circumstances changed with the recession of 1958: from 1958 through 1963, the annual unemployment rate averaged over 11 percent for nonwhites, but only about 5 percent for whites. From 1965 through 1971, unemployment rates for nonwhites averaged 8 percent, twice the rate for whites.[45]

Overall, the quarter-century following World War II provided a relatively favorable employment market for minorities, even though they clearly had much higher unemployment rates than whites. Since the early 1970s, however, minorities, especially African Americans, have experienced extraordinarily high unemployment rates. From 1972 through 1991, the unemployment rate for African Americans fell below 10 percent in only one year (9 percent in 1973), with a peak of almost 20 percent in 1983; it averaged nearly 14 percent. In essence, blacks have experienced depression-level unemployment rates for the past generation. The white unemployment rate, however, never reached 9 percent in any single year during that time (despite the deep recession of the early 1980s) and averaged about 6 percent for the period.[46]

Hispanics also have had a generally high unemployment rate since the 1970s: 8 percent in 1979 (compared to 5 percent for whites and 12 percent for blacks that year), and over 10 percent each year in the 1980–86 period, with a peak of nearly 14 percent in 1982 (when the white rate was close to 9 percent and the African American rate was almost 19 percent). Despite substantial economic

43. Moynihan, *The Negro Family*, p. 66.

44. Myrdal, *An American Dilemma*, pp. 293–97, 304–20; Laurence H. Fuchs, *The American Kaleidoscope: Race, Ethnicity, and the Civic Culture* (Hanover, N.H.: Wesleyan University Press/University Press of New England, 1990), pp. 100–09; Bart Landry, *The New Black Middle Class*, (Berkeley: University of California Press), pp. 41–59.

45. Council of Economic Advisors, *Report of the Council of Economic Advisors 1989* (Washington, D.C.: U.S. Government Printing Office, 1989), p. 352.

46. Ibid. Also see Council of Economic Advisors, *Economic Indicators October 1991* (Washington, D.C.: U.S. Government Printing Office, 1991), p. 12; Bureau of Labor Statistics, "Current Labor Statistics," *Monthly Labor Review* 115 (March 1992): 58.

growth in the mid-1980s, the Latino unemployment rate did not return to its 1979 level until 1988. It then averaged about 8 percent in the 1988–90 period (compared to a white average of less than 5 percent and a black average of over 11 percent). In the recession year of 1991, the unemployment rate for Hispanics moved back up to 10 percent while the rates for whites and blacks moved to 6 percent and 12 percent, respectively.[47]

For many years, unemployment among all racial/ethnic groups has tended to be much higher for those with little formal education than for those with a great deal. At each education level, however, the unemployment rates of some minorities have been much higher than the rate for whites. For example, even in 1989 (the last full calendar year of economic growth in the expansive 1980s), African Americans with fewer than four years of high school had an unemployment rate of 16 percent while those with four or more years of college had an unemployment rate of 5 percent; the comparable figures for whites that year were 7 percent and 2 percent, respectively.[48]

Parallel to the higher unemployment rates of the 1970s, 1980s, and early 1990s compared to the 1950s and 1960s has been a much-noted fall in the real earnings of low-skill workers, both absolutely and relative to high-skill workers. According to the Commission on Skills of the American Workforce, "Since 1969, real average weekly earnings in the United States have fallen by more than 12 percent. This burden has been shared unequally. The incomes of our top 30 percent of earners increased while those of the other 70 percent spiraled downward. . . . Over the past decade, earnings of college-educated males age 24 to 34 increased by 10 percent. Earnings of those with only high school diplomas declined by 9 percent. And those in the workforce who do not hold high school diplomas saw their real incomes drop by 12 percent."[49] Because of these educational attainment and achievement gaps with whites, these trends have been most problematic for minorities.

Young adults, particularly those from minority groups, have found it increasingly difficult to earn enough to support a family. For example, as recently as 1973, there were relatively modest differences in the percentages of white, black, and Hispanic 20–24-year-old males who earned enough to support a family of three above the poverty line. By 1986, about 48 percent of white males, 41 percent of the Latinos, and only 24 percent of the African Americans met this criterion.[50]

There were parallel drops between 1974 and 1986 in the percentage of men in this age group who were married. In 1986, only 11 percent of black males in this age group were married, compared to 24 percent of the Latinos and 23 per-

47. Ibid. Also see U.S. Bureau of the Census, *Statistical Abstract of the United States 1987*, 107th Edition (Washington, D.C.: Department of Commerce, U.S. Government Printing Office, 1986), p. 390; and U.S. Bureau of the Census, *Statistical Abstract of the United States 1991*, p. 402.

48. Ibid., p. 403.

49. Commission on the Skills of the American Workforce, *America's Choice: High Skills or Low Wages?* (Rochester, N.Y.: National Center on Education and the Economy, 1990), pp. 1, 20.

50. *The Forgotton Half: Pathways to Success for America's Youth and Young Families* (Washington, D.C.: William T. Grant Foundation, 1988), p. 24.

cent of the whites.[51] There have also been large increases in the proportion of children born to single mothers and children living in single-parent families, most of them headed by females.[52] Table 4.1 presents data charting the increase in the proportion of children living in single-parent families between 1970 and 1989.

Table 4.1
Percentages of Children under Age 18 Living in Various Family Circumstances, by Race/Ethnicity: 1970, 1980, 1989

| Year/Group | Two-Parent | *Family Type* | | |
		Mother Only	Father Only	Other
1970:				
All Children	85	11	1	3
White	90	8	1	2
Black	59	30	2	10
Hispanic	NA	NA	NA	NA
1980:				
All Children	77	18	2	4
White	83	14	2	2
Black	42	44	2	12
Hispanic	75	20	2	3
1989:				
All Children	73	22	3	3
White	80	16	3	2
Black	38	51	3	8
Hispanic	67	28	3	3

Sources: U.S. Bureau of the Census, *Statistical Abstract of the United States: 1991*, 111th ed. (Washington, D.C.: Department of Commerce, U.S. Goverment Printing Office, 1991), p. 53. These data were derived from U.S. Bureau of Census, *Current Population Reports, Series P-20, No. 445*, and earlier reports.

51. Ibid., p. 23. William Julius Wilson has hypothesized that, as the proportion of young males who could support a family dropped, so would their marriage rates. A few recent studies have found that the drop in earnings provides only a partial explanation for the drop in marriage rates. See Wilson, *The Truly Disadvantaged: The Inner City, the Underclass, and Public Policy* (Chicago: University of Chicago Press, 1987), pp. 81–84; "Public Policy Research and *The Truly Disadvantaged*," in *The Urban Underclass*, Christopher Jencks and Paul E. Peterson, eds. (Washington, D.C.: Brookings Intitute, 1991), pp. 467–68.

52. According to the Bureau of the Census, in the July 1989-June 1990 period, 23 percent of the women who gave birth were unmarried. The percentages varied significantly by race/ethnicity: they were 17 percent for whites, 57 percent for blacks, and 23 percent for Hispanics. See Robert Pear, "Larger Number of New Mothers Are Unmarried," *New York Times*, 4 December 1991, p. A20. As recently as 1960, only 5 percent of all births in the United States were to unmarried women. National Commission on Children, *Beyond Rhetoric: A New American Agenda for Children and Families* (Washington, D.C.: National Commission on Children, U.S. Government Printing Office, 1991), p. 19.

As the table makes clear, the trend toward single-parent families has not been confined to minorities; however, the increase has been much larger among blacks and Hispanics than among whites. Between 1970 and 1989, the proportion of black children in two-parent homes dropped from nearly 60 percent to less than 40 percent, continuing a trend that had begun a generation earlier. In the early 1950s, nearly 80 percent of all nonwhite families (the overwhelming majority of whom were black at that time) included both a husband and wife.[53] These data indicate that in only about two generations—1950 to 1989—the proportion of African American children living in two-parent families was essentially cut in half, and the parental burden of this change has largely been born by the mothers. As table 4.1 shows, 50 percent of the black children were in single-parent families headed by the mother in 1989, up from 30 percent in 1970.

Hispanic children are much more likely to live in two-parent families than are black children. However, the shift away from two-parent families was almost 1 percent a year in the Latino community during the 1980s. Only two-thirds of Hispanic children were in two-parent families in 1989, down from three-fourths in 1980.

Owing to rapid, sustained economic growth during the early post–World War II period, the percentage of Americans who lived in poverty declined substantially. In 1939, at the end of a decade dominated by the Great Depression, the poverty rates for whites and blacks were 65 percent and 93 percent, respectively.[54] By 1970, the rate for whites had fallen to 10 percent, while for blacks it was 34 percent, and for Americans as a whole, 13 percent. However, in the less favorable economic environment of the 1970s and 1980s, little additional progress was made as higher unemployment rates, declining incomes for the less skilled, and a reduction in the percentage of two-parent families took their toll. In 1989, the poverty rates for the entire American population and for whites were the same as they had been in 1970, while at 31 percent, the rate for blacks in 1989 was slightly lower. The poverty rate for Latinos in 1989 was 26 percent, and the rate for Asians/Pacific Islanders that year was 14 percent.[55]

Owing in part to the low wages earned by young adults with relatively few skills and the high incidence of female-headed, single-parent families with children, the poverty rate for children has plateaued at a higher rate than for the general population.[56]

The poverty rate for white children under eighteen years old living in families dropped from 20 percent in 1960 to 11 percent in 1970. It then increased to

53. Moynihan, *The Negro Family*, p. 62.

54. Jaynes and Williams, *A Common Destiny*, pp. 277–78.

55. U.S. Bureau of the Census, Statistical Abstract of the United States: 1991, p. 462; Mark S. Littman and Eleanor F. Baugher, "Poverty in the United States: 1988–1989," *Current Population Reports, Consumer Income, Series P-60, No. 171* (Washington, D.C.: Bureau of the Census, U.S. Government Printing Office, 1991, p. 3.

56. Edward J. Welniak, Jr., and Mark S. Littman, "Money Income and Poverty Status in the United States 1989," *Current Population Reports, Consumer Income, Series P-60, No. 168* (Washington, D.C.: Bureau of the Census, U.S. Government Printing Office, 1990), pp. 61–64.

17 percent at the depth of the recession in the early 1980s before declining to 14 percent in 1989. The rate for blacks dropped even more in the 1960s, from 66 percent as the decade began to 42 percent in 1970. In 1989, the poverty rate for black children was 43 percent, the same as it had been two decades earlier. The Latino rate was 33 percent in 1975 and 36 percent in 1989.[57] Clearly, poverty was still an extremely important problem for children—especially minority children—as the nation entered the 1990s.

Job Structure, Culture, and the Ghetto Poor   In the United States, the growing demand for better educated people has constituted an enormous opportunity for economic, educational, and social advancement for all racial/ethnic groups. However, the intersection of the rapidly changing structure of the job market and the large migration of minorities with few skills to our nation's cities has also led to an important downside. It has become increasingly difficult for people with few skills to find employment that will enable them to support their families and, therefore, the educational advancement of their children.

In the early 1940s Gunnar Myrdal noted the difficulties that many African Americans were experiencing in the urban labor markets of that period.[58] When the Coleman Report was published in the mid-1960s, the growing mismatch between the demands of the labor market and the skills of urban blacks was already of concern to a number of social scientists, both black and white.[59] Since the late 1970s, however, one of the most thoughtful, articulate, and influential social scientists concerned with this issue has been William Julius Wilson. On the basis of extensive research and analysis, Wilson has drawn the following key conclusions:

1. In a number of the nation's cities, primarily in the Northeast and Midwest, the proportion of minority poor living in high-poverty neighborhoods has grown over the past quarter century. The higher concentration of minority poor in these areas is a result of the loss of low-skill jobs in the central cities, the increasing ability of middle-class and stably employed working-class blacks to move out of high-poverty neighborhoods, and the relatively limited ability of poor blacks to move away from such neighborhoods or to commute to jobs in the suburbs.[60]

57. U.S. Bureau of the Census, *Statistical Abstract of the United States: 1991*, p. 462; National Center for Educational Statistics, *Digest of Education Statistics 1990* (Washington, D.C.: Department of Education, U.S. Government Printing Office, 1991), p. 27.

58. Myrdal, *An American Dilemma*, pp. 296–97.

59. Kenneth B. Clark, *Dark Ghetto: Dilemmas of Social Power* (New York: Harper & Row, 1965), pp. 34–37; Arnold Rose, "Postscript Twenty Years Later: Social Change and the Negro Problem," in Myrdal, *An American Dilemma* (Twentieth Anniversary Edition), pp. xxix-xxx. Both Clark and Rose had contributed to *An American Dilemma*. Myrdal wrote the foreword to Clark's *Dark Ghetto*.

60. Wilson, *The Truly Disadvantaged*, pp. 29–55, 144; Wilson, "Public Policy Research and the Truly Disadvantaged," pp. 464–65. Most of Wilson's work has focused on the problems facing blacks. For a discussion of the applicability of his ideas (and those of others) to Hispanics, see Joan Moore, *An Assessment of Hispanic Poverty: Is There an Hispanic Underclass?* (San Antonio: Tomas Rivera Center, 1988). For a discussion focused exclusively on Puerto Ricans, see Marta Tienda,

2. The movement of large numbers of middle- and working-class individuals away from high-poverty zones in the central city has eliminated a "social buffer" that might have been able to "deflect the full impact of . . . prolonged and increasing joblessness." The middle class provides a social buffer by ensuring that key community institutions such as the church and the school retain a strong enough base of support to continue to be effective, and second, by ensuring that a sufficient number of individuals with strong ties to the mainstream are available to provide realistic role models to the poor.[61]

3. The increased concentration of poverty and the weakened social buffer in high-poverty neighborhoods have created a group of minority poor who are experiencing profound social isolation, defined as "the lack of contact or of sustained interaction with individuals and institutions that represent mainstream society." The chronically poor have been left behind in high-poverty neighborhoods, where they often lack access to decent jobs and schools. Many have adopted values and behaviors that vary significantly from those of the mainstream, which makes it more difficult for them to take full advantage of the employment and educational opportunities that are available.[62]

In recent years, Wilson's argument has been subjected to a great deal of scrutiny. For example, Mark S. Littman looked at data for census tracts in which the poverty rate is 20 percent or higher and found that nationally there was a modest drop in poverty concentration in metropolitan areas between 1972 and 1989. Nevertheless, the concentration of poverty in central cities remained high in absolute terms; in 1989, about 54 percent of the central city poor lived in neighborhoods with a poverty rate of 20 percent or higher.[63]

Wilson, however, has been most concerned with neighborhoods with poverty rates of 40 percent or higher. Using this threshold, Paul A. Jargowsky and Mary Jo Bane looked at the question of whether ghetto-poverty concentration grew in the 1970–80 period. Their findings tend to support Wilson's conclusion that there has been an increase in poverty concentration in several cities in the Northeast and Midwest. The total number of poor people living in ghetto neighborhoods (census tracts with poverty rates of 40 percent or higher) expanded from 1,891,000 to 2,449,000 between 1970 and 1980, an increase of 30 percent. As a result, about 9 percent of the nation's poor population in 1980 was living in a ghetto-poverty neighborhood. The proportion of poor blacks living in these neighborhoods remained stable at 27–28 percent, while the proportion of poor Hispanics fell from 24 percent to 19 percent. And the percent of non-Hispanic whites living in such areas remained small throughout the period (it was 2 percent in 1980).[64]

"Puerto Ricans and the Underclass Debate," *Annals of the American Academy of Political and Social Science* 501 (January 1989): 105–19.

61. Wilson, *The Truly Disadvantaged*, pp. 56–57.

62. Ibid., pp. 60–61.

63. Mark S. Littman, "Poverty Areas and the 'Underclass': Untangling the Web," *Monthly Labor Review* 114 (March 1991): 19–32.

64. Paul A. Jargowsky and Mary Jo Bane, "Ghetto Poverty in the United States, 1970–1980," in *The Urban Underclass*, pp. 239, 251–53.

Looking beyond these aggregate data, Jargowsky and Bane found that there had actually been very large increases in ghetto poverty in several large cities in the Northeast and Midwest and similarly large decreases in a number of small and medium-sized cities in the South. On the basis of these conflicting trends, they calculated that 49 percent of the nation's ghetto poor were living in just ten metropolitan areas in 1980 (up from 36 percent in 1970). New York City alone accounted for 20 percent of all the ghetto poor in 1980 with nearly 477,000 people; only three cities—New York, Chicago, and Philadelphia—accounted for a third of the ghetto poor that year.[65]

In their examination of four cities (Cleveland, Milwaukee, Philadelphia, and Memphis) in which African Americans are the principal racial/ethnic minority, Jargowsky and Bane found evidence in support of Wilson's position that middle-class blacks have moved away from poor blacks. Increases in ghetto poverty between 1970 and 1980 occurred primarily through a process in which formerly mixed income areas reached ghetto poverty rate levels. The major factor in this shift was usually a net outmigration of nonpoor blacks as well as of significant numbers of whites, both poor and nonpoor. The total number of poor African Americans in these neighborhoods increased, but the data indicate that this was typically of secondary importance.[66]

The Jargowsky and Bane research should not be interpreted as indicating that the movement of nonpoor blacks out of certain sectors of the nation's central cities has led to a dramatic reduction in racial segregation, or that most middle-class African Americans live in neighborhoods or communities that are almost exclusively middle class. To the contrary, a significant body of research shows that housing segregation of blacks and whites has declined only modestly in recent decades and that black-white segregation continues to be severe at all social class levels and is much higher than segregation between whites and Mexican Americans and between whites and Asians.[67] Moreover, although

65. Ibid., pp. 254–57.
66. Ibid., pp. 261–68.
67. Using 1970 and 1980 decennial census data, Massey and Denton found that blacks and whites were highly segregated at all socioeconomic levels in 1970 and that there had been very little reduction in this segregation by 1980. African Americans were particularly segregated in urban areas in the Northeast and North Central regions. Latinos were much less segregated than blacks, and Hispanic segregation from whites tended to vary significantly by social class: poor Latinos, especially recent immigrants, were highly segregated from whites, but middle-class Hispanics were not. The segregation of whites and Asians was generally low, although it increased slightly between 1970 and 1980—a period of substantial Asian immigration. As in the case of Hispanics, the level of white-Asian segregation varied by social class. Importantly, they found that blacks tended to be highly segregated from Hispanics and Asians as well as whites. Within the Hispanic community, Puerto Ricans represented an exception, tending to be relatively highly segregated from whites regardless of social class but only moderately segregated from blacks. Denton and Massey concluded that being black, as opposed to being "just" nonwhite, non-European, or non–middle class, seems to be the most salient factor in the level of residential segregation. They conjecture that Puerto Ricans, because of their substantial African ancestry, have experienced some of the same difficulties in residential integration as have African Americans. Douglas S. Massey and Nancy A. Denton, "Trends in the Residential Segregation of Blacks, Hispanics, and Asians: 1970–1980," *American Sociological Review* 52 (December 1987): 802–25; Douglas S. Massey and Nancy A. Denton, "Residential Segregation of Mexicans, Puerto Ricans, and Cubans in Selected U.S. Metro-

middle-class blacks do not typically live in the highest poverty zones, they are still likely to reside in areas that have substantially higher poverty rates than are typical of middle-class white communities.[68] Consequently, many middle-class black youngsters attend schools that serve significant numbers of black children from low-income families.

A recent study sponsored by the National School Boards Association found that black and Hispanic students continue to experience school segregation in many states, including several of those with large African American and Latino populations, and that school segregation was generally lowest in the South. For example, 86 percent of the Hispanic students in New York were attending schools that were 50 to 100 percent minority. The comparable percentages for other states were 85 percent in Illinois, 84 percent in Texas, 84 percent in New Jersey, and 79 percent in California. With regard to black students, 89 percent were found to be in 50 to 100 percent minority schools in Illinois, 86 percent in New York, 85 percent in Michigan, 80 percent in New Jersey, and 79 percent in California.[69]

One of the most important and controversial aspects of Wilson's work relates to his ideas on social isolation. He has suggested that not only have a significant number of minority poor people in the central city become isolated from the larger society, but that this isolation has led to the emergence of norms and behavior patterns that make it difficult for them to participate effectively in mainstream society. The empirical knowledge base for this view is too limited to support definitive conclusions; however, field research by Elijah Anderson between 1975 and 1989 in two contiguous neighborhoods—one high-poverty/ almost exclusively black and one mainly middle-class/increasingly white—in a large Eastern city has produced findings that generally support Wilson's position.

Specifically, Anderson found that the socioeconomic profile of the black neighborhood had changed dramatically over the last several decades in

politan Areas," *Sociology and Social Research* 73 (January 1989): 73–83; Nancy A. Denton and Douglas S. Massey, "Residential Segregation of Blacks, Hispanics, and Asians by Socioeconomic Status and Generation," *Social Science Quarterly* 69 (1989): 797–817.

A study commissioned by the National Center for Health Statistics found that the percentage of African Americans living in areas less than 10 percent black increased from 10 percent to 12 percent between 1980 and 1990, and the percentage living in areas at least 60 percent black fell from 58 percent to 51 percent. However, the percentage of Hispanics living in areas that were less than 10 percent Latino fell from 15 percent to 11 percent, while those living in mostly Latino areas grew from 30 percent to 34 percent. By contrast, about 48 percent of Asians/Pacific Islanders and 58 percent of Native Americans (most of whom were not living on reservations) resided in areas in which they comprised less than 10 percent of the population in 1990. Peter Schmidt, "Hispanics Found More Segregated in Housing Study," *Education Week*, 25 March 1992, p. 4.

68. Reynolds Farley, "Residential Segregation of Social and Economic Groups among Blacks, 1970–80," in *The Urban Underclass*, pp. 283–91; Douglas S. Massey and Mitchell L. Eggers, "The Ecology of Inequality: Minorities and the Concentration of Poverty, 1970–1980," *American Journal of Sociology* 95 (March 1990): 1153–88. Segregation in the suburbs is also substantial. See Eunice S. Grier and George Grier, *Minorities in Suburbia: A Mid-1980s Update* (Washington, D.C.: The Urban Institute, 1988), pp. 20–23.

69. Karen DeWitt, "The Nation's Schools Learn a 4th R: Resegregation," *New York Times*, 19 January 1992, Section 4, p. 5.

response to the loss of adequately paying low- and moderate-skill industrial jobs and the movement of the black middle class to the suburbs. Most of the current generation of young people in the community were qualified only for low-skill, low-paying jobs, but, owing to their alienation from white society, many of these young people rejected these jobs as part of the legacy of the American race-based caste system and had turned to more financially attractive alternatives in the underground economy—particularly drug dealing. Meanwhile, older citizens in the community had become progressively less able to provide mainstream-oriented leadership. Youngsters tended to reject them as role models in favor of young adults who were doing well in the underground economy. By the late 1980s, Anderson found, the community had developed all the attributes associated with ghetto poverty, including high rates of crime, drug addiction, and teen pregnancy. At the same time many middle-class whites in the adjacent community had developed extremely negative stereotypes of young blacks, especially young black males, primarily as a result of spillover effects that produced higher crime in their neighborhood. Whites tended to distance themselves from blacks on the streets; many were fearful, and some moved to the suburbs.[70]

Wilson's conclusions have thrust him to the center of a long-standing, often intense debate among social scientists and policymakers regarding the relative importance of the structure of the society and the culture of individuals and groups in determining whether people become and stay poor. His position has been especially difficult because he has consistently indicated his belief that there are both structural and behavioral/cultural dimensions of the problem that interact over time.[71] His use of the term *underclass* to describe individuals who face "the dual problem of marginal economic position and social isolation in highly concentrated poverty areas" has probably added to the controversy. Some people tend to define the underclass primarily in terms of its perceived negative behavioral/cultural attributes ("they" are "prone" to violent crime, teen pregnancy, drug abuse, welfare dependency, and so on), giving little recognition to the societal forces that have so heavily shaped their life chances over time. This has led many social scientists and policy analysts to fear that the mere use of the term *underclass* effectively blames the victim for problems that are largely beyond his or her control.[72]

70. Elijah Anderson, *Street Wise: Race, Class, and Change in an Urban Community* (Chicago: University of Chicago Press, 1990), pp. ix, 7, 237–55.

71. Wilson, *The Truly Disadvantaged*, pp. 3–19, 182–83; Alan Wolfe, "The New American Dilemma: Understanding and Misunderstanding Race," *New Republic*, 13 April 1992, 30–37. For some recent comments by Wilson to the education press, see Chris Raymond, "Results from a Chicago Project Lead Social Scientists to a Rethinking of the Urban Underclass," *Chronicle of Higher Education*, 30 October, 1992, pp. A9, A12, A13.

72. Wilson, "Public Policy Research and *The Truly Disadvantaged*," p. 475. Herbert Gans has been one of the most outspoken critics of the use of the term *underclass*. See Gans, "Deconstructing the Underclass: The Term's Danger as a Planning Concept," *Journal of the American Planning Association* 56 (Summer 1990): 271–77. For Wilson's views on the debate, see William Julius Wilson, "Studying Inner-City Social Dislocations: The Challenge of Public Agenda Research," *American Sociological Review* 56 (February 1990): 4–6.

By emphasizing such factors as the changing urban labor market, the limited educational and occupational opportunities of blacks prior to the civil rights movement of the 1950s and 1960s, and the migration of large numbers of blacks with limited skills to industrial cities, Wilson has taken a structural approach to the problem from a public policy standpoint. For example, although he has emphasized that poverty and social isolation have produced nonmainstream attitudes, norms, and behavior patterns that can influence a group's near-term capacity to take advantage of economic and educational opportunities, his public policy recommendations have included such structural approaches as creating more jobs, improving access to available jobs, and providing better schooling, health care, and child care: "The concept social isolation does not mean that cultural traits are irrelevant in understanding behavior in highly concentrated poverty areas; rather, it highlights the fact that culture is a response to social structural constraints and opportunities. From a public policy perspective this would mean shifting the focus from changing subcultural traits . . . to changing the structure of constraints and opportunities."[73]

Recent research has provided support for this approach, particularly in the area of employment. For example, a central question raised by Wilson's analysis is whether a more favorable job market than that currently available would increase the employment rates of young adults who live in central cities and who have relatively little formal education. Richard B. Freeman addressed this issue by examining the labor market experiences of young men who were out of school in the 1980s and who had twelve years or less of education. His study used data from metropolitan areas that had unemployment rates in the 1980s from less than 4 percent to 7 percent. Freeman found that "local labor market shortages greatly improve the employment opportunities of disadvantaged young men, substantially raising the percentage employed and reducing their unemployment rate. Employment of black youths is particularly sensitive to the state of the local labor market." Labor market shortages also increase the hourly earnings of disadvantaged youths, particularly blacks. In the 1980s such an increase was large enough to offset the deterioration in the real and relative earnings of the less skilled.[74]

For Wilson, the unemployment problems of many ghetto poor are a function not simply of the supply and demand for jobs in an area but also of the location of the jobs. Like others (including John Kasarda), he believes that a major obstacle to employment is that many of the available low-skill jobs are now in

73. Wilson, *The Truly Disadvantaged*, pp. 21–29, 56–61, 140–64; "Public Policy Research and *The Truly Disadvantaged*," pp. 476–78; and, Raymond, "Results from a Chicago Project Lead Social Scientists to a Rethinking of the Urban Underclass," pp. A13, 86.

74. Richard B. Freeman, "Employment and Earnings of Disadvantaged Young Men in a Labor Shortage Economy," in *The Urban Underclass*, p. 119. For a summary of research findings regarding the wage and unemployment problems of young blacks as of the mid-1980s, see Richard B. Freeman and Harry Holzer, "Young Blacks and Jobs—What We Now Know," *Public Interest* 78 (Winter 1985): 18–31. Taking a somewhat similar tack, Paul Osterman examined the impact on poverty rates of the extremely strong period of economic growth in the Boston area in the mid to late 1980s. Osterman found that poverty rates dropped significantly in the period for both black and white families and modestly for Hispanic families in Boston. Paul Osterman, "Gains from Growth? The Impact of Full Employment on Poverty in Boston," *The Urban Underclass*, pp. 125–27.

the suburbs rather than in the central city.[75] James Rosenbaum and Susan Popkin looked at the employment rates of female single parents who took part in a program that moved families from public housing in Chicago to private housing elsewhere in the city or in the (mostly white) suburbs in the 1976–88 period. Rosenbaum and Popkin found that those who had been placed in housing in the suburbs had noticeably higher employment rates after the move than their counterparts who had been assigned housing in the city. Those housed in the suburbs also indicated that they found it easier to locate and accept a job, partly because they found the suburbs safer and therefore were more willing to leave their children to go to work. The positive impact of the program was not uniform, however. For example, mothers who had been on welfare for five or more years prior to moving to the suburbs were less likely to find employment than mothers who were not long-term welfare recipients.[76]

Rosenbaum and his colleagues also looked at how children from a sample of the families assigned to the suburbs performed in school and how their parents assessed their experiences with the schools. They compared these results to those of a control group of families assigned housing in the city. The results were more ambiguous than those relating to employment. Parents whose children attended the suburban schools indicated that the academic standards were much higher than in the city schools, that suburban teachers generally provided more assistance to their children than they had received in the city schools, but that their children had experienced racial discrimination from other students; evidently such discrimination had been permitted by some teachers. The black students in the suburban schools were more likely to have been placed in special education classes than the group that remained in the city schools, and they received grades that were about the same as those received by the control group in the city schools. Assuming that academic standards in the suburban schools were somewhat higher than those in the city schools (reflecting the middle-class constituency), this can be viewed as a positive result.[77]

These findings suggest that access to favorable labor markets does result in relatively quick and significant economic improvements for many poor families. But developing strategies that will provide favorable conditions on an ongoing basis is not likely to be easy. Over the past quarter-century, the U.S. economy has been unable to produce enough jobs to reduce unemployment rates to 4 percent or 5 percent.[78] The primary value of this research may be to remind us of just how costly the shortage of jobs in industrialized societies really is.

75. See Kasarda, "Urban Industrial Transition and the Underclass," pp. 36–42. Kasarda clearly believes that the "spatial" (job location) issue is important, along with such matters as differences in education levels between blacks and whites and racial discrimination in employment. He is particularly interested in "race and space, including their interaction, rather than race versus space."

76. James E. Rosenbaum and Susan J. Popkin, "Employment and Earnings of Low-Income Blacks Who Move to Middle-Class Suburbs," The Urban Underclass, pp. 347–53.

77. James E. Rosenbaum, Marilyn J. Kulieke, and Leonard S. Rubinowits, "Low-Income Black Children in White Suburban Schools: A Study of School and Student Responses," Journal of Negro Education 56 (Winter 1987): 35–43.

78. As Ralf Dahrendorf has noted, several West European nations have experienced extremely high unemployment rates—often about 10 percent—for their entire populations since the 1970s.

Similarly, the research showing mixed educational results for children of the ghetto poor who are able to move to the suburbs reminds us that the gap in education-relevant resources noted by James Coleman is unlikely to be closed quickly simply by increasing the access of poor minority children to the schools of the white middle class (or to schools resourced at middle-class levels) or by reducing the unemployment rates of their parents.

Job Structure, Culture, and Education-Relevant Resources   Both structural and cultural factors shape the life chances of families, and in later chapters I shall examine research bearing on the important differences in these factors. At this point, however, it is sufficient to note that the changing structure of the U.S. economy in combination with the migration of minorities with few skills to the central cities has contributed immensely to the variations in education-relevant family resources available to children, both within and among racial/ethnic groups, and that these differences now include cultural dimensions.[79]

It is reasonable to conclude that these variations in resources are likely to exist in all five forms of education-relevant capital. For example, children from poor families typically have much less human, social, health, financial, and polity capital available to them than children from middle-class families.

Some connections between poverty and the limited social and polity capital available to many minority children deserve special mention here. As discussed earlier, James Coleman believes that changes in the institutional position of the family have reduced the education-relevant social capital available to children from all social classes and, therefore, from most racial/ethnic groups. William Julius Wilson and Loic J. D. Wacquant have concluded that structural changes in the job market and other forces resulting in the social isolation of many of the minority ghetto poor have produced an enormous loss of social capital within this population in particular. Wilson and Wacquant found in 1986–87 that in areas of Chicago in which at least 40 percent of the population is poor, three in five adults were not working, one in three held working-class jobs, and only about one in twenty had a middle-class occupation. In areas in which the poverty rate was 20–30 percent (close to the average poverty rate for Chicago at that time, but still high by national standards) one in three was unemployed, well over half held working-class jobs, and about one in ten had a middle-class

---

None of these nations has yet found an answer to the question of how to lower unemployment rates to the 4–5 percent level on a long-term basis. See Dahrendorf, *The Modern Social Conflict*, pp. 141–49.

79. Despite much debate over whether the current problems confronting the ghetto poor are primarily structural or cultural in origin, there is an increasing tendency for social scientists and policy analysts to develop explanations that draw on both perspectives and to emphasize essentially structural solutions. In this sense, William Julius Wilson has been particularly influential. Recent books by Lawrence Mead and Mickey Kaus are illustrative of this. Mead believes that significantly more low-wage jobs are available to the nonworking poor in inner cities than is generally acknowledged. At the same time, the ghetto poor "do harbor attitudes that discourage work . . . but the origin of most of these feelings lies mainly in the difficult histories of the most disadvantaged ethnic

position. Adults in the extreme poverty areas were also less likely to have a spouse or permanent partner, and their partners and best friends were also less likely to have a high school education or to be steadily employed.[80]

Summarizing their findings, Wilson and Wacquant stated, "Our data indicate that not only do residents of extreme-poverty areas have fewer social ties, but also that they tend to have ties of lesser social worth, as measured by the social position of their partners, parents, siblings, and best friends, for instance. In short, they possess lower volumes of social capital."[81]

Turning to polity capital, one can cite ample evidence that many whites continue to hold negative views of minorities, especially blacks. Of notable importance from an educational perspective, many whites apparently continue to believe that African Americans are intellectually inferior to whites for innate or cultural reasons. Moreover, the poverty being experienced by large numbers of poor African Americans in the inner city may actually reinforce these negative stereotypes, which, in turn, may lead many whites (and others) to be less supportive of societal efforts to address the educational, economic, and social needs of the minority poor.[82] If this is the case, it is reasonable to infer that the structural forces that have produced high levels of minority poverty may also have made it more difficult for polity capital to be accumulated in the amounts necessary to accelerate the educational advancement of many minority children.

---

groups." Mead is a strong proponent of expanding societal efforts to improve employment opportunities for the nonworking poor and to require that they work. Specifically, he advocates "workfare" programs, which tie welfare benefits to work. Kaus, on the other hand, is inclined to accept the line of analysis that structural changes in the economy have resulted in a shortage of jobs available to the urban poor. Nevertheless, he has also stated that many of the ghetto poor are now members of a "culture of poverty." His major recommendation is to replace the existing welfare system with a government-guaranteed program that would provide jobs for all able-bodied persons, including single mothers of young children. See Lawrence M. Mead, *The New Politics of Poverty: The Nonworking Poor in America* (New York: Basic Books, 1992), pp. 99–109, 133–34, 159–84; Mickey Kaus, *The End of Equality* (New York: New Republic/Basic Books, 1992), pp. 108, 116–19, 121–35.

80. Loic J. D. Wacquant and William Julius Wilson, "The Cost of Racial and Class Exclusion in the Inner City," *The Annals of the American Association of Political and Social Science* 501 (January 1989): 10, 16–17, 23.

81. Ibid., pp. 22–23.

82. There is very little opinion research on how minority groups view one another (see chapter 8). However, we can glimpse these views from various sources. For example, in the aftermath of the tragic riot in Los Angeles in late April 1992, a Korean American was quoted in the *New York Times* as saying, "I think the black people are jealous of the Koreans. . . . They're lazy; we are working hard. They're not making money; we are making money." Later in the same article, another Korean was quoted as being "pretty disappointed" when none of the police officers in four nearby patrol cars protected him and other Koreans during the armed attacks of looters. He said that the officers (most of whom presumably were white) "ran away in half a second." One wonders what impact such an event has on Koreans' views of the white majority—and governmental institutions. Seth Mydans, "A Target of Rioters, Koreatown Is Bitter, Armed and Determined," *New York Times*, 3 May 1992, p. A1, A22. These, of course, are the words of individuals under great stress (the homes and businesses of many Koreans had been destroyed in the riot, many Koreans had been injured, and some had been killed). Yet it is unlikely that they are isolated views, given the complex intersections among race/ethnicity, social class, and immigrant-versus-native-born in urban America. Not only do we not know the extent of these views, we have little feel for how they are linked to attitudes on public policy options to address the needs of the ghetto poor.

The Ghetto Poor and the Academic Achievement of the Minority Middle Class
Understandably, Wilson and other social scientists and policy analysts have
been preoccupied with the dismal conditions and prospects of extremely disadvantaged minorities. Also understandably, they have paid a great deal of
attention to the potential negative impact of the isolation many of these individuals may be experiencing as a result of lack of access to mainstream institutions or to people with close ties to the mainstream.

There is reason to believe, however, that we need to pay attention not only to
how the lack of mainstream ties may undermine the prospects of the ghetto
poor but also to how the existence of direct and indirect ties to the ghetto poor
may negatively impact some segments of the minority middle class and the
stable working class. As discussed in chapter 6, many middle-class minority students are not performing nearly as well academically as middle-class white and
Asian students. This appears to be a serious problem for other minority students, including Puerto Ricans, Mexican Americans, and Native Americans.
One factor that seems to be contributing to this phenomenon is the low level of
academic aspiration of many poor minority youngsters, particularly blacks, due
in part to their real and perceived bleak prospects for enjoying the benefits of
mainstream society. There is reason to believe that this negative academic
achievement orientation may be undermining the educational performance of
many middle-class African American youngsters. In a race-conscious society, in
which many whites continue to have low expectations for the intellectual performance of blacks, whether poor or middle class, it is hard to imagine that it
could be otherwise.

I shall examine this issue in some depth in chapter 9, using the research of
the Nigerian-born anthropologist John U. Ogbu and others. The relevant point
to be made here, however, is that this phenomenon seems to be producing
undesirable variations in school-relevant social capital for some middle-class
minority students. That is, the quality of the education-relevant social capital of
middle-class minority students may be eroded if they identify with the academic outlook of the most alienated poor minorities or if the negative stereotypes of disadvantaged populations are applied to them by influential adults in the
school, community, or workplace because of their minority status. Such erosion
suggests that a largely unrecognized cost of society's continued inability to meet
the needs of ghetto minority poor may be lower academic achievement among
middle-class minority students. It also suggests that an unrecognized (indirect)
benefit of investing more of society's resources in disadvantaged minority children might be stronger academic performance by middle-class minorities.

SUMMARY AND CONCLUSIONS

In this chapter, I have developed a framework that helps one understand why
substantial differences persist in educational attainment and academic achievement patterns among racial/ethnic groups in the United States. The discussion
began with a review of the Coleman Report (1966), which found a close associ-

ation between variations in family attributes related to social class (such as parent education level) and variations in standardized test scores among students from different racial/ethnic groups. In the decades since publication of the Coleman Report, researchers have consistently found that social-class factors are powerful predictors of the academic performance patterns of groups of students, while school factors are relatively weak predictors.

Coleman's explanation for these findings is that the variations in education-relevant family resources are greater than the variations in school resources. I went on to discuss five types of resources that are extremely important to the education of children and that can vary substantially in the amount and quality available to different groups of students: human, social, health, financial, and polity capital.

The next step in this analysis was to develop a realistic, policy-relevant definition of equal educational opportunity for our racially/ethnically pluralistic society. Society has come to define equal educational opportunity primarily in terms of outputs, not inputs, particularly for racial/ethnic groups. The objective now is to produce similar results for the groups in terms of both educational attainment and academic achievement.

Nevertheless, because the largest variations in education-relevant resources are on the family side rather than the school side, it is difficult to understand how similar educational results can be achieved for a single generation of children. This led to a linkage of the concept of equal educational opportunity for groups and the notion of intergenerational advancement. Since the most educationally successful groups in contemporary America have typically taken several generations to reach their present levels of performance, it seems inevitable that the groups currently having the least educational success will require a number of generations to reach full parity.

Although this conclusion may be frustrating, it reflects the reality that the variations in school-relevant resources among families and groups can properly be regarded as variations in the amounts of intergenerationally accumulated resources they possess, which in turn reflect differences in the educational opportunities families have had over several generations. This perspective allows one to restate Coleman's explanation of the differences in group attainment/achievement patterns: The variations in home-based, formal-schooling-derived resources that have been intergenerationally accumulated by families are greater than the variations in education-relevant resources that society is investing in the current generation of children directly through the schools.

There is nothing inevitable about the particular educational performance trajectories of groups over time. These trajectories will be influenced by the specific configurations of education-relevant factors in the groups' environments from generation to generation. I referred to the societal conditions and institutional arrangements that bear on these trajectories as the educational opportunity structure and specified what racial/ethnic groups with little formal education seem likely to need in order to experience relatively rapid, sustained intergenerational educational advancement: (1) a full set of legal rights to acquire and use formal education; (2) a supply of adequately paying, low-skill jobs, so that the majority of parents will be able to support their children materially; (3) a growing supply of high-skill, higher-paying jobs so that educationally disadvantaged groups can obtain genuine occupational payoffs from raising their education levels from generation to generation; (4) circumstances in which parents and other key adults are available in sufficient numbers and for sufficient amounts of time to provide emotional, intellectual, and other nonmaterial forms of support necessary for children to do well in school; and (5) appropriately resourced schools for the children they serve.

I reviewed two lines of analysis that identify important opportunity structure problems in contemporary America. The first is a concern that the industrial/technological society in the United States has contributed to a dramatic reduction in the amount and quality of nonmaterial parental and other adult support for children. The most important consequence is a significant drop in the amount of social capital available to children through the family and the community.

Because this is a problem that cuts across social class lines, the second line of analysis looks for opportunity structure problems that tend to vary in impact by social class. It examines how the evolution of the urban and national job markets away from low-skill jobs toward high-skill jobs interacted with the large-scale migration of southern blacks with little formal education into northern and midwestern industrial cities from 1910 to 1970, and the large-scale migration of other unskilled minorities to urban centers in the post–World War II period. This phenomenon continues in the 1990s.

So far I have discussed the relationship between social class and academic achievement patterns in very general terms. However, if this relationship is as powerful as it appears to be, and some of our educationally least successful minority groups are disproportionately the victims of poverty, it is important that a more precise understanding of this relationship be gained. In chapter 5 I return to some of the standardized test data sets that were reviewed in chapter 3, but this time to look at how test-score patterns vary by social class rather than race/ethnicity.

CHAPTER FIVE

Educational Achievement

and

Socioeconomic Status

Since the publication of the Coleman Report, the strong relationship between social class and the educational outcomes of students has been confirmed by many studies. Consequently, it is now common to collect socioeconomic information on students as part of the standardized testing process.

In this chapter I review some of the available information on this relationship. First I shall briefly discuss how the socioeconomic status (SES) of students is generally measured. I then review standardized achievement score data, broken down by two of the most common measures of social class, parent education and family income level. In the third stage, I review the findings from an analysis of the association between variations in the intensity of the poverty experience and variations in academic-achievement patterns. I shall then review research on two poverty-related problems that appear to be of growing importance—the high rates of student turnover (mobility) in many central city schools and the high rates of preventable health conditions among children that can impair their ability to learn. Although these factors are not limited to poor or minority children, they are quite common among such youngsters and thus tend to have a disproportionate impact on minority children.

MEASURES OF SOCIAL CLASS

In the standardized testing process, information is usually gathered primarily through questionnaires filled out voluntarily. Most items are designed to be answered easily and quickly, and only a few questions can typically be directed to any single topic. In most cases, therefore, the social-class information gathered on test takers is of a fairly general nature, for example, families' or parents' current incomes, education levels (often expressed in terms of the highest degree earned), and occupations.[1] It is rarely possible to obtain relatively nuanced information on, for example, parents' net financial worth, their work histories, details of their education, or the social-class characteristics of their

1. For an example of such a questionnaire, see College Entrance Examination Board, *Registration Bulletin 1990–91: SAT and Achievement Tests—New York State Edition* (Princeton, N.J.: College Entrance Examination Board, 1990).

friends and colleagues. For parents who are college graduates, it is unlikely that information will be sought about academic majors, GPAs, or the selectivity of the institutions they attended, or about the education levels of *their* parents.

Sometimes questions are asked about the types of books and periodicals available in the home and the range of cultural/educational activities engaged in by the family on a regular basis; such questions represent an attempt to measure home atmosphere attributes that are associated with successful academic performance.[2] It seems likely that these are more direct measures than social class of education-relevant family resources (or the inclination and capacity to use these resources). Even though information of this kind is often easiest to gather in a one-of-a-kind study, some ongoing standardized testing programs collect such information.[3]

My interest in this chapter is in understanding variations in academic-achievement patterns associated with relatively standard measures of social class. Therefore, I shall focus on variations in test-score patterns among groups of test takers who have different parent/family income and parent education levels.

VARIATIONS IN STANDARDIZED TEST SCORES BY PARENT EDUCATION AND PARENT/FAMILY INCOME LEVEL

In this section I use three sources of information—the National Education Longitudinal Study of 1988 (NELS:88), which examined the academic performance of a nationally representative sample of eighth graders; the National Assessment of Educational Progress (NAEP) reading and math test trend data over the past two decades for 9- and 17-year-olds; and 1990 Scholastic Aptitude Test (SAT) data for college-bound seniors.

Variations in NELS:88 Test Scores by Parent Education and Family Income Level Table 5.1 presents data on the relationship between parent education level and achievement test scores for a recent large, nationally representative sample of eighth graders, and table 5.2 provides similar information on the relationship between family income and test scores.

As table 5.1 indicates, in 1988 substantial differences among eighth graders in the education levels of their parents were associated with dramatically different likelihoods that students would be among the highest or lowest scorers on the standardized tests used in NELS:88. Fully 56 percent of the eighth graders with a parent who had a graduate degree were in the top achievement test score quartile, and only 7 percent of this group were in the bottom quartile. The situ-

2. Karl R. White,"Relation between Socioeconomic Status and Academic Achievement," *Psychological Bulletin* 91 (1982): 466, 470.

3. For example, for the 1984 NAEP writing test, participants were asked about the amount and types of reading materials in the home, whether there was a computer in the home, and whether they used the computer for writing. See Arthur N. Applebee, Judith A. Langer, and Ina V. S. Mullis, *The Writing Report Card: Writing Achievement in American Schools* (Princeton, N.J.: Educational Testing Service, 1986), pp. 106–07.

Table 5.1
Parent Education and Eighth-Grade Student Achievement Patterns
in the National Education Longitudinal Study of 1988

	<High School	High School Graduate	Parent Education Some College	College Graduate	Graduate Degree	Total
% of All Students at Each Parent Education Level:	11	21	42	14	12	100
% of Students, by Parent Education Level, in Each Test Quartile:						
Lowest Quartile	21	27	41	7	4	100
>25–50%	12	24	47	11	7	100
>50–75%	7	21	46	16	11	100
Highest Quartile	2	11	36	23	28	100
% of Students, within Each Parent Education Category, in Each Test Quartile:						
Lowest Quartile	51	33	24	12	7	—
>25–50%	28	29	28	20	13	—
>50–75%	16	25	27	27	23	—
Highest Quartile	5	13	21	41	56	—
Total	100	100	100	100	100	—
% of Racial/Ethnic Groups at Each Level of Parent Education:						
Asian/Pacific Islander	9	13	33	23	22	100
Hispanic	33	18	36	7	6	100
Black	16	24	47	8	6	100
White	6	21	42	16	14	100
American Indian/ Alaskan Native	15	24	45	11	6	100

Source: Anne Hafner, Steven Ingels, Barbara Schneider, and David Stevenson, A Profile of the American Eighth Grader: NELS:88 Student Descriptive Summary, National Education Longitudinal Study of 1988 (Washington, D.C.: Department of Education, U.S. Government Printing Office, 1990), p. 3. Percentages may not add to 100 because of rounding.

ation was virtually reversed for eighth graders who had parents with relatively little formal education. About 51 percent had test scores in the bottom quartile, while only 5 percent scored in the top quartile. Only among students who had one or two parents with some college was the distribution by quartiles close to equal.

Asian and white eighth graders were much more likely to have well-educated parents and much less likely to have poorly educated parents than the African

American, Latino, and Native American students. On the basis of these data alone, one would predict significant underrepresentation among high academic achievers and substantial overrepresentation among low achievers for blacks, Hispanics, and Native Americans, with the opposite pattern for whites and Asians.

As table 5.2 indicates, there was also considerable variation in family income

Table 5.2
Family Income and Eighth-Grade Student Achievement Patterns
in the National Education Longitudinal Study of 1988

| | *Family Income* | | | |
	<$15,000	$15,000–$50,000	>$50,000	Total
% of All Students at Each Income Level:	21	58	21	100
% of Students, by Family Income Level, in Each Test Quartile:				
Lowest Quartile	37	53	10	100
>25–50%	25	59	16	100
>50–75%	15	62	23	100
Highest Quartile	8	55	37	100
% of Students, within Each Family Income Category, in Each Test Quartile:				
Lowest Quartile	44	23	11	—
>25–50%	30	26	19	—
>50–75%	18	27	27	—
Highest Quartile	9	24	43	—
Total	100	100	100	—
% of Racial/Ethnic Groups at Each Level of Parent Education:				
Asian/Pacific Islander	18	51	31	100
Hispanic	38	53	10	100
Black	47	44	9	100
White	14	61	25	100
American Indian/ Alaskan Native	42	49	9	100

Source: Anne Hafner, Steven Ingels, Barbara Schneider, and David Stevenson, *A Profile of the American Eighth Grader: NELS:88 Student Descriptive Summary*, National Education Longitudinal Study of 1988, (Washington, D.C.: Department of Education, U.S. Government Printing Office, 1990), p. 3. Percentages may not add to 100 because of rounding.

levels among the eighth graders in the NELS:88 study, which was linked to very different likelihoods that students would be high or low scorers on the NELS:88 standardized tests. High family income was associated with high test scores and vice versa. Whites and Asians were much more likely than African Americans, Latinos, and American Indians to be from high-income families and much less likely to be from low-income families. Consequently, on the basis of the family income data, one would predict substantial underrepresentation among high achievers and significant overrepresentation among low achievers for blacks, Hispanics, and Native Americans, with the opposite pattern for Asians and whites.

Clearly, the NELS:88 study suggests that a substantial portion of the large educational achievement gaps between whites and Asians, on the one hand, and African Americans, Latinos, and American Indians, on the other hand, is related to differences in parent education and family income levels.

Trends in NAEP Scores by Parent Education Level   The NELS:88 data, useful as they are, have at least two inherent limitations from the perspective of understanding the relationship between social class and educational achievement patterns. First, they concern the academic performance of students in only one of their middle school years, so that it is not possible to use the NELS:88 data to examine whether there were changes in the relationship between social class and academic achievement over the course of their formative educational years.[4] And second, the NELS:88 data pertain to only one group of students; no information is provided regarding how academic performance patterns may be changing on a social-class basis for several successive cohorts of children over a long period of time.

The specific NELS:88 data presented so far also have a third limitation: they provide information on the relative ranking of students on the standardized tests used in the study but not on the absolute differences among students in the academic skills they were able to demonstrate on the tests.

A review of trend data from the NAEP reading and math test programs permits one to address the second and third of these limitations. In the case of the reading-trend data, there are six data points going back two decades (1971-90). In the case of the math data, there are four data points spanning more than a decade (1978-90). There are data available on students' average scores on both the reading and math tests as well as on the percentages of students that exceeded each of the several NAEP anchor points on the tests. Consequently, one is able to look at students' scores from the perspective of demonstrated skill differences.

The most important limitation of the NAEP data from a social-class analysis perspective is that information is available only on the education levels of the test takers' parents. In the case of the reading test, there is the added limitation that the scores of test takers with at least one parent who graduated from college

4. Future follow-ups on the NELS:88 sample will rectify this situation, at least with regard to the post-eighth-grade years.

and those who had at least one parent who attended college but did not earn a bachelor's degree are lumped together in the Some Post High School Education category. The NAEP math data, however, present information on parents in both this category and a Graduated College category. For neither test is there a separate category for test takers who had one or more parents with a graduate degree. These individuals are included in the Graduated College category in the case of the math data and in the Some Post High School Education category in the case of the reading data.

With these limitations in mind, I turn to table 5.3, which provides information on the average NAEP reading scores over time for 9- and 17-year-olds by parent education level. As the table shows, there was little movement in the average scores of 9-year-olds over the 1971-90 period when viewed from the perspective of parent education level. None of the changes that did occur was statistically significant. The difference in average scores between test takers with no parent with a high school degree and those with a parent with some college remained large throughout the period, although it did decline somewhat over the years. This gap was 25 points in 1990 (193 vs. 218). To put it in terms of NAEP anchor points, 9-year-olds with no parent with a high school degree read somewhat below the 200/Basic Skills level ("can comprehend specific or sequentially related information") throughout the period, and those with a parent with some college consistently scored considerably above this level.

Table 5.3 shows a parallel pattern for 17-year-olds. There were no statistically significant differences for this age group between their 1971 and 1990 average reading scores from a parent education level perspective. In 1990, there was a 30-point difference between 17-year-olds with no parent with a high school diploma and those with a parent with some college. In 1990, the average 17-year-old without a parent with a high school degree was reading about halfway between the 250/Intermediate Skills level ("can search for specific information, interrelate ideas, and make generalizations") and the 300/Adept Skills level ("can find, summarize, and explain relatively complicated information"). In contrast, the average 17-year-old with a parent with some college was reading at the 300 level.

A shifting of the analysis from comparisons of average scores to comparisons of percentages that exceed anchor points generally produces similar results. Large gaps existed throughout the period among test takers with parents with different levels of education. The gaps are especially noteworthy for both 9- and 17-year-olds at the high NAEP anchor points. For example, 24 percent of the 9-year-olds with a parent with some college read at the 250 level in 1990, while the comparable figures were 17 percent for those with a parent with a high school degree and only 9 percent for those with no parent who had graduated from high school. At the 300 level (the highest level that a significant number of 9-year-olds are able to reach), the respective percentages were 2.7 percent, 1.3 percent, and 0.5 percent.[5]

5. Ina V. S. Mullis, John A. Dossey, Mary A. Foertsch, Lee R. Jones, and Claudia A. Gentile, *Trends in Academic Progress: Achievement of U.S. Students in Science, 1969–1970 to 1990; Mathe-*

Table 5.3
Average NAEP Reading Scores for 9- and 17-Year-Olds,
by Parent Education Level: 1971–90

Level of Parent Education	1971	1975	1980	1984	1988	1990
Age 9:						
Did Not Finish High School	189	190	194	195	193	193
Graduated from High School	208	211	213	209	211	209
Some Post High School Education	224	222	226	223	220	218
Age 17:						
Did Not Finish High School	261	263	262	269	267	270
Graduated from High School	283	281	278	281	282	283
Some Post High School Education	302	301	299	301	300	300

Source: Ina V. S. Mullis, John A. Dossey, Mary A. Foertsch, Lee R. Jones, Claudia A. Gentile, *Trends in Academic Progress: Achievement of U.S. Students in Science, 1969–1970 to 1990; Mathematics, 1973–1990; Reading, 1971 to 1990; Writing, 1984 to 1990* (Washington, D.C.: Educational Testing Service/U.S. Department of Education, U.S. Government Printing Office, 1991), pp. 117, 313, 315.

Among 17-year-olds in 1990, 90 percent of test takers with a parent with some college reached the 250 level, while 81 percent of those with a parent with a high school degree and 71 percent of those with no parent with a high school diploma did so. At the 300 level, the percentages were 51 percent, 32 percent, and 20 percent, respectively. At the highest NAEP reading anchor point, the 350/Advanced Skills level ("can synthesize and learn from specialized reading materials"), the percentages were 9.8 percent, 3.9 percent, and 1.8 percent, respectively, in 1990.[6]

Because a score at the 300 level is roughly the minimum required to be prepared for postsecondary education, the 1990 data suggest that, from a reading skills perspective, about half of the test takers with a parent with some college, about one-third of those with a parent who had graduated from high school, and

matics, 1973–1990; Reading, 1971 to 1990; Writing, 1984 to 1990 (Washington, D.C.: Educational Testing Service/U.S. Department of Education, U.S. Government Printing Office, 1991), pp. 318–19.

6. Ibid., pp. 328–30.

about one-fifth of those with no parent with a high school degree were prepared to go on to college. Using a score at the 350 level as a measure of reading skill preparation for higher education produces even greater relative differences among the groups of test takers.

The NAEP math trend data from a parent education level perspective are presented in table 5.4.

The data for 9-year-olds reveals that scores changed little during the 1978-90 period except for a moderate increase in average math scores between the 1986 and 1990 NAEP tests. More important, since the increase between 1986 and 1990 was shared by test takers at all parent education levels, the between-group score gaps were essentially constant throughout the period. In 1990, there was

Table 5.4
Average NAEP Mathematics Scores for 9- and 17-Year-Olds,
by Parent Education Level: 1978–90

Level of Parent Education	1978	1982	1986	1990
Age 9:				
Did Not Finish High School	200	199	201	210
Graduated from High School	219	218	218	226
Some Post High School Education	230	225	229	236
Graduated from College	231	229	231	238
Age 17:				
Did Not Finish High School	280	279	279	285
Graduated from High School	294	293	293	294
Some Post High School Education	305	304	305	308
Graduated from College	317	312	314	316

Source: Ina V. S. Mullis, John A. Dossey, Mary A. Foertsch, Lee R. Jones, Claudia A. Gentile, *Trends in Academic Progress: Achievement of U.S. Students in Science, 1969–1970 to 1990; Mathematics, 1973–1990; Reading, 1971 to 1990; Writing, 1984 to 1990* (Washington, D.C.: Educational Testing Service/U.S. Department of Education, U.S. Government Printing Office, 1991), pp. 70, 267, 269.

a 28-point difference between test takers with a parent with a college degree and test takers with no parent with a high school diploma. The former group demonstrated math skills relatively close to the 250/Basic Operations and Beginning Problem Solving level ("can add, subtract, multiply, and divide using whole numbers"), while the latter demonstrated math skills relatively close to the 200/Beginning Skills and Understanding level ("can add and subtract two-digit numbers and recognize relationships among coins").

Table 5.4 also shows very little change in average NAEP math scores for 17-year-olds at all four parent education levels. It also shows that the gap between 17-year-olds with high levels of parent education and those with low levels was generally similar to the one experienced by 9-year-olds. There was a 31-point difference in 1990 between the average score of 17-year-old test takers with a parent with a college degree and those with no parent who had graduated from high school. The test takers with relatively well educated parents tended to have math skills somewhat above the 300/Moderately Complex Procedures and Reasoning level ("can compute with decimals, fractions, and percents; recognize geometric figures; and solve simple equations"), while the test takers with relatively less well educated parents tended to have skills below this level.

As was the case in reading, an anchor-point analysis of math score patterns for test takers with different levels of parent education reveals substantial variations, particularly at the higher anchor points. Among 9-year-olds, 37 percent of the test takers with a parent with a college degree in 1990 exceeded the 250 level; the comparable percentages were 35 percent for those with a parent with some college, 24 percent for those with a parent with a high school degree, and only 10 percent for those with no parent who had completed high school. At the 300 level, the respective percentages were 2.1 percent, 1.4 percent, 0.4 percent, and 0.0 percent.[7]

Among 17-year-olds in 1990, 99 percent of the test takers with a parent with a college degree reached the 250 level. About 99 percent of those with a parent with some college also reached this level, while 94 percent of those with a parent with a high school degree and 91 percent of those with no parent with a high school diploma did so. At the 300 level, the percentages were 71 percent, 61 percent, 42 percent, and 30 percent, respectively. At the highest NAEP math anchor point, the 350/Multi-step Problem Solving and Algebra level ("can solve multi-step problems and use basic algebra"), the percentages were 12.5 percent, 6.7 percent, 2.4 percent, and 1.2 percent, respectively.[8]

The 300 level represents the minimum math skills that college-bound individuals must possess. The 350 level represents an even more appropriate level, particularly for those who pursue studies that have a significant quantitative dimension. Using either of these thresholds, in 1990 test takers with a parent with a college degree and those with a parent with some college were far more likely to be prepared for college than those with a parent with a high school degree and those with no parent with a high school diploma.

7. Ibid., pp. 272–73.
8. Ibid., pp. 282–84.

Variations in SAT Scores by Parent Education and Income Level   Although the NAEP anchor points can be used to estimate the percentages of 17-year-olds who have the reading or math skills necessary to pursue some form of postsecondary education, the test is not well designed to estimate the proportion of students who are well prepared for selective colleges and universities. For this purpose, the SAT probably provides a better source of information, even though it is not based on a random sample of students. The SAT has the added advantage of collecting both parent education and parent income information from test takers.

Table 5.5 presents average verbal, math, and combined SAT scores for 1990 SAT test takers, by parent education and parent income level.

Table 5.5
Average Verbal, Mathematics, and Combined SAT Scores for 1990,
by Parent Education and Parent Income Levels

1: Average Scores by Parent Education Level

Highest Level of Parent Education	% of Test Takers	Average SAT Scores		
		Verbal	Mathematics	Combined
No High School Degree	5	342	412	754
High School Degree	38	397	445	842
Associate Degree	7	409	457	866
Bachelor's Degree	27	443	498	941
Graduate Degree	24	476	529	1005

2: Average Scores by Parent Income Level

Parent Income Level	% of Test Takers	Average SAT Scores		
		Verbal	Mathematics	Combined
Less than $10,000	5	357	419	776
$10,000–$20,000	12	383	437	820
$20,000–$30,000	16	407	457	864
$30,000–$40,000	19	420	469	889
$40,000–$50,000	14	434	484	918
$50,000–$60,000	11	443	495	938
$60,000–$70,000	7	450	503	953
$70,000 or more	17	468	527	995

Source: College Entrance Examination Board, *1990 College-Bound Seniors: Ethnic and Gender Profile of SAT and Achievement Test Takers* (New York: College Entrance Examination Board, 1990), National section pp. 7–8.

As part 1 of the table shows, there were very large variations in average SAT scores in 1990 among test takers with parents who had different education levels. The score gaps were substantial on both the verbal and the mathematics sections of the test as well as on a combined score basis. On a combined basis, there was a 251-point difference in average scores between test takers with at least one parent with a graduate degree and those with no parent with a high school diploma (1005 vs. 754). These scores suggest that, on average, members of the former group were very well prepared academically for college, while members of the latter group were underprepared, with many in need of remediation.

Significantly, test takers with a parent with a graduate degree had average SAT scores considerably higher than the scores of all other groups. The combined SAT score difference between this group and the test takers for whom the highest level of parent education was a bachelor's degree was 64 points.

Part 2 of table 5.5 indicates that the average 1990 SAT score patterns, broken down by parent income levels, are very similar to those based on parent education. These data suggest that test takers with high-income parents tend to be well prepared for college while the opposite tends to be true for those with low-income parents. The gap between the segments with parents who earned $70,000 or more and those who earned less than $10,000 in 1990 was 219 points.

POVERTY AND STUDENT ACHIEVEMENT

As noted, low-income/poverty is an important predictor of below-average educational achievement. But there may be much more to the story as it pertains to explaining the difference in achievement patterns among racial/ethnic groups. As William Julius Wilson has argued, the concentration of poverty among minorities in our nation's central cities is accompanied by social isolation, and this combination creates a more extreme form of poverty than is typically experienced by poor whites. If Wilson is correct, we have reason to believe that the NELS:88 and similar data do not describe the full impact of poverty on the academic achievement of the ghetto poor.

The Intensity of Poverty and Academic Achievement Patterns　　Do more intense forms of poverty have greater negative impact on student achievement than less intense forms? Are minorities much more likely than whites to experience intense forms of poverty? These were among the questions addressed by Mary M. Kennedy, Richard K. Jung, Martin E. Orland, and several colleagues in a report written in 1986 that was part of an assessment of the federal government's Chapter 1 program for disadvantaged children. Kennedy and her colleagues measured the degree of a family's poverty on the basis of the length of time the family had been in poverty and the proportion of the student population of the school the children attended who were poor.

There are no national trend data available on the impact of the duration of poverty on student achievement. It is not known therefore whether youngsters born in, say, 1960 experienced more or less long-term childhood poverty than did children born in 1970 or 1980. Kennedy and her colleagues, however, were able to draw on data from a national sample of children born in the mid- to late 1960s who had been tracked into the 1980s as part of a study of family income and labor-market participation patterns. Thus, we do have longitudinal data on a national sample of children who were growing up during a period when the poverty rate leveled off after a long decline. These data show that 78 percent of black youngsters in the sample experienced at least some poverty during childhood, compared to 25 percent of the whites. More important, 46 percent of the black children but only 5 percent of the white children were poor for five or more years.[9]

On average, the black children experienced five years of poverty during the fifteen-year period from 1968 to 1983 while the nonblack children were poor for an average of one year. Moreover, these different averages were not simply a product of differences in the proportions of the two groups that experienced conditions heavily associated with poverty. For example, single-parent family status has a relatively strong correlation with poverty among children, and higher proportions of black children than of nonblack children are in single-parent homes. However, nonblack youngsters in the sample who were members of a single-parent family throughout childhood were poor for an average of three years, while the black children in such families were poor for an average of seven years.[10]

Kennedy and her colleagues were able to estimate the impact of the duration of poverty on students' academic progress as measured by whether they were enrolled in the modal grade for their age as teenagers. They found that the longer the duration of poverty, the greater the likelihood that 16-year-olds in the sample were at least one grade below the modal level (tenth grade) for their age. About 22 percent of all students in the sample who did not experience poverty during their childhood were at least one grade level below the tenth. In contrast, 42 percent of the students who were poor for eight or more years during childhood were below their modal grade.[11]

The researchers also looked at the impact of the intensity of poverty on the academic performance of children in school, relying on the Sustaining Effects (SE) Study data base for information on elementary school students in the mid- to late 1970s and the High School and Beyond (HS&B) data base for information on high school sophomores and seniors in the early 1980s. Both studies were large-scale, federally funded enterprises. Because the large achievement gaps among students from different social classes (and racial/ethnic groups) tend to emerge in the early elementary school years, my discussion will focus on the SE-based portion of the Kennedy, Jung, and Orland analysis.

Table 5.6 presents information on selected student characteristics of schools in the SE sample that were categorized as having low-, medium-, and high-poverty concentrations. In low-poverty schools, fewer than 7 percent of the stu-

9. Mary M. Kennedy, Richard K. Jung, Martin E. Orland et al., *Poverty, Achievement and the Distribution of Compensatory Education Services* (Washington, D.C.: Department of Education, U.S. Government Printing Office, 1986), pp. 15–20, 42–50; Gregory J. Duncan and Willard L. Rogers, "A Demographic Analysis of Childhood Poverty," unpublished paper, University of Michigan Institute for Social Research, cited in ibid., p. 45.

10. Kennedy et al., *Poverty, Achievement and the Distribution of Compensatory Education Services*, p. 46.

11. Ibid., p. D6.

dents were from low-income families. In medium-poverty schools between 7 percent and 24 percent of the students were from poor families. And high-poverty schools had more than 24 percent of the student population from families with low incomes.

Table 5.6
Selected Characteristics of Low, Medium, and
High Poverty Concentration Elementary Schools

(Percentages)

Student Characteristic	*Poverty Concentration*		
	(<7% Poor) Low	(7–24% Poor) Medium	(>24% Poor) High
White	95	82	53
Black	3	9	32
Hispanic	1	6	12
Free/Reduced Lunch	11	22	52
Language other than English	6	11	19
Mobility Rate	14	22	23

Source: David E. Myers, "The Relationship between School Poverty Concentration and Students' Reading and Math Achievement and Learning" (Appendix D), in Mary M. Kennedy, Richard K. Jung, Martin E. Orland et al., *Poverty, Achievement and the Distribution of Compensatory Education Services* (Washington, D.C.: Department of Education, U.S. Government Printing Office, 1986), pp. D47–48.

Table 5.6 shows that the low-poverty schools in the study were overwhelmingly white, while the high-poverty schools were disproportionately black and Hispanic. About 52 percent of the children in the high-poverty schools compared to 11 percent in the low-poverty schools qualified for the free or reduced lunch program, and the high-poverty schools had a much higher percentage of children who did not speak English as a first language. Finally, the rate of turnover among students during the academic year (the student mobility rate) was much higher in the high-poverty schools.

Table 5.7 shows how these differences among schools in student clienteles translated to divergent student academic achievement patterns.

The data on the percentages of elementary school students scoring in the bottom quartile in all schools in the SE sample are quite consistent with the achievement-score patterns by family income for the national sample of eighth graders in the NELS:88 study. Table 5.7 shows that 47 percent of the poor students in all elementary schools in the sample scored in the bottom quartile, nearly twice as many as the 25 percent that would be anticipated had poor children performed on the achievement tests in the same fashion as the student population as a whole. Recall that table 5.2 shows that about 44 percent of the eighth graders in the NELS:88 study who were from families with incomes of less than $15,000 per year scored in the bottom quartile. In contrast, less than 19 percent of the nonpoor students scored in the bottom quartile on the

Table 5.7
Selected Student Achievement Data for Low, Medium, and
High Poverty Concentration Elementary Schools

	Poverty Concentration			All
	(<7% Poor) Low	(7–24% Poor) Medium	(>24% Poor) High	All Schools
% of Students with Achievement Scores below the 25th Percentile:				
Nonpoor	11	21	37	19
Poor	28	39	56	47
All Students	12	24	48	25
Mean Reading Achievement Scores for Entire School:				
Grade 1 (Fall)	354	347	339	—
Grade 1 (Spring)	426	413	392	—
Grade 2 (Fall)	446	423	398	—
Grade 2 (Spring)	492	466	446	—
Grade 3 (Fall)	491	463	442	—
Grade 3 (Spring)	531	501	475	—
Grade 6 (Spring)	606	590	555	—

Source: Mary M. Kennedy, Richard K. Jung, Martin E. Orland et al., *Poverty, Achievement and the Distribution of Compensatory Education Services* (Washington, D.C.: Department of Education, U.S. Government Printing Office, 1986), pp. 21, D47–48.

achievement tests in the SE sample. There is no identical category of students in the NELS:88 study, but a roughly equivalent one can be created from the available information. Table 5.2 shows that 23 percent of the students from families earning $15,000–$50,000 per year and 12 percent of those from families earning more than $50,000 per year scored in the bottom quartile. Averaging these two percentages on the basis of the relative representation of middle- and upper-income students in the entire NELS:88 sample (58 percent and 21 percent, respectively) indicates that about 20 percent of the nonpoor students in the NELS:88 study scored in the bottom quartile—which is very close to the 19 percent nonpoor figure in the SE sample.

Further, table 5.7 indicates that there were large variations among low-, medium-, and high-poverty schools in the percentages of both poor and nonpoor students who scored in the bottom quartile on the achievement tests used in the SE project. In the high-poverty schools, 56 percent of the poor children were in the bottom quartile compared to 28 percent of the poor children in the low-poverty schools. Almost 37 percent of the nonpoor students in the high-poverty schools but only 11 percent in the low-poverty schools had bottom-quartile scores. Thus, a nonpoor student in a high-poverty school was more likely to be in the bottom quartile than a poor student in a low-poverty school.

As Kennedy and her colleagues point out, this finding may reflect nothing other than "differences already associated with individual family backgrounds." For example, many of the nonpoor children in the high-poverty-concentration schools may have been from families with relatively low incomes, while many of the nonpoor students in the low-poverty schools may have been from relatively high-income families. (These seem likely to be common patterns in high-poverty schools in the central cities and in low-poverty schools in the suburbs.) However, after statistically adjusting for such differences, a school-based "poverty concentration effect" was found to exist.[12]

Because of limitations in the data available from the SE sample it was not possible for Kennedy and her colleagues to determine what specific underlying factors contributed to the poverty-concentration effect of schools on student achievement. Nevertheless, this conclusion is generally consistent with the Coleman Report's finding that variations in the composition of the student bodies of schools were more strongly associated with variations in students' standardized test scores than any other school-based factor. In any case, Kennedy, Jung, and Orland's finding is not surprising because schools with large proportions of poor children tend to have much greater demands on their resources than schools with small proportions of poor children. Therefore, many high-poverty schools could be expected to find it difficult to meet the academic needs of both poor and nonpoor students.

Early Learning Patterns of Children in High- and Low-Poverty Schools The SE data also provide a glimpse into the formation of group achievement patterns in the early elementary years. This is an extremely important feature because available evidence indicates that these patterns change relatively little after the middle elementary school years for most age cohorts of students, regardless of social class or race/ethnicity.[13] The SE sample is able to provide this kind of information because of the design of the project. Reading and math achievement tests were administered to participating students in both the fall and the spring of each school year over a three-year period, a total of six times. This approach provides information regarding learning gains (and losses) during both the school year and the summer vacation. For first graders at the start of the study, this means that longitudinal data are available on their reading and math achievement scores up to the third grade, the crucial midpoint of the elementary school years, when age-cohort achievement patterns have largely locked in.

Table 5.7 presents average first- through third-grade reading achievement scores for students in the low-, medium-, and high-poverty schools. It is immediately clear that the children in the high-poverty schools began the first grade

12. Ibid., pp. 24–25.
13. For example, the NAEP data presented in chapter 3 show that the reading score patterns of nine-year-olds generally anticipate the reading score patterns of seventeen-year-olds. The NAEP data are cross-sectional rather than longitudinal; that is, the seventeen-year-olds tested eight years after a particular group of nine-year-olds are not the same students. But in each case, those tested are representative national samples of the students in their age groups.

at a significant disadvantage in reading preparation relative to students in low-poverty schools: a 15-point difference in average reading test scores in the fall of the first grade. This gap is not surprising, given the high proportion of children from economically disadvantaged circumstances in the high-poverty schools.

Second, the achievement gap grew substantially during the school year and continued to grow rapidly over the summer. By the beginning of the second grade, the reading achievement score gap between the children in the high-poverty schools and those in the low-poverty schools had risen to almost 48 points. By the spring of the third grade, the gap had grown to 56 points, which was slightly higher than the 51-point gap between the average reading scores of sixth graders in the high- and low-poverty schools. A similar score-gap growth tendency was found on the math achievement test.[14] These data suggest that if the nation wishes to use schools to reduce achievement differences among groups, it must maximize its efforts in the early years. By the third grade, the problem appears to be less a matter of preventing large achievement gaps from developing than of finding ways to recover lost ground.

A close look at table 5.7 reveals that 32 of the 56-point reading achievement score gap between students in high- and low-poverty schools by the end of the third grade had developed while the students were not attending school: about 15 points emerged prior to the first grade, about 14 during the summer between the first and second grades, and about 3 points in the summer between the second and third grades. It can be argued that the non-school-based portion of the gap is somewhat less than 32 points. Barbara Heynes has pointed out that the SE data underestimate the school-year contribution to student learning because of the timing of the achievement tests: the fall test was typically given three or four weeks after school had started, and the spring test about five weeks before the end of the school year. This means that about two months of school-based learning each year was included in the difference between the fall and spring test scores.[15] And the gap found at the beginning of the first grade could be attributable to learning differences that took form during kindergarten and preschool.

Heynes nevertheless believes that the SE data set makes a strong case that a large portion of the differences in achievement levels between middle-class and poor students (and, therefore, between majority and minority students) is the product of different summer learning (or learning-loss) rates. In Heynes's view, this is further evidence of the strong role played by the family in shaping the academic performance of children. When school is not in session, learning opportunities for children continue (and education-relevant resources continue to be invested in them), but these opportunities and resources are greater for middle-class children than for disadvantaged children.[16]

Heynes has concluded that the school is much more successful than many

14. Ibid., p. D 48.
15. Barbara Heynes, "Schooling and Cognitive Development: Is There a Season for Learning?" *Child Development* 58 (October 1987): 1153.
16. Ibid., pp. 1151–60.

people believe in closing the educational opportunity gaps among children that are associated with variations in the socioeconomic attributes of families and communities. Further, she believes that we should be exploring ways to make much more effective educational use of the summer months for disadvantaged children. Effective systems would not necessarily involve simple extensions of the standard school year.[17] Heynes's point is consistent with Coleman's observation that differences in achievement patterns among groups are ultimately explained by the fact that variations in education-relevant family resources are much greater than variations in school resources. Expanding formal education for disadvantaged children to include the summer months would entail a large increase in the educational resources society invests in these youngsters.

STUDENT MOBILITY, PREVENTABLE HEALTH CONDITIONS, AND ACADEMIC ACHIEVEMENT

Two problems that are disproportionately experienced by economically disadvantaged youngsters appear to have important consequences for their educational prospects—high rates of student mobility and high rates of preventable health conditions that can impair children's ability to learn.

Educational Consequences of High Student Mobility   The high-poverty schools in the SE sample had a much higher student mobility rate than the low-poverty schools—23 percent versus 14 percent. Unfortunately, student mobility has not been a focus of sustained attention by educational policymakers or researchers, so little is known about it. There are no trend data available to indicate whether mobility rates have changed over the past ten or twenty years and no longitudinal studies of large samples of students to determine who moves, where they move, why, with what frequency, and with what impact on achievement patterns. There is little information about what strategies school systems or individual schools employ to reduce mobility rates, with what results.

Nevertheless, the problem of student mobility is a matter of concern among principals and teachers in central city schools. They believe that mobile students do less well academically than nonmobile students and that high mobility rates reduce a school's ability to meet the educational needs of both groups of students.[18]

As an outgrowth of a state-funded program, thirty-three elementary schools in Milwaukee, Racine, Beloit, and Kenosha, Wisconsin, have produced substantial information regarding the extent of student mobility in central city schools, its educational consequences, and some possible solutions to the

17. Ibid.
18. L. Scott Miller, Mark Fredisdorf, and Daniel C. Humphrey, *Student Mobility and School Reform* (New York: Council for Aid to Education, 1992), p. 4; Colin Lacey and Dudley Blane, "Geographic Mobility and School Attainment—The Confounding Variables," *Educational Research* 21 (June 1979): 200–06.

problem.[19] The information generated to date indicates that the student mobility rate in these schools is over 40 percent per year in most cases, and that there is general correlation between high mobility rates in the schools and high student body poverty rates. On average, 76 percent of the students in the thirty-three schools qualify for the free or reduced-cost lunch program. There is also a high correlation between student mobility and minority status in these schools, since large proportions of the student populations are minority. Although no data have yet been reported on the factors contributing to these high mobility rates, many of the possible causes are poverty-related—unemployment, a shortage of low-cost housing, substance abuse, and domestic violence.

The schools have begun to experiment with a busing strategy to respond to the student mobility problem. Parents who move to nearby areas have been given the option of having their children bused back to their original schools. Owing to resource limitations, only a portion of the families who have moved away have been given this opportunity to date, and most of them have taken advantage of it.[20]

The Wisconsin schools are also collecting information on the achievement test scores of the nonmobile students, the mobile students who have been bused back to their original schools, and the mobile students who have not been bused back. Evaluations of the busing program's first year of operation have not established clearly whether the program is producing academic benefits for the participating children.[21] More research, in which participating students are tracked for several years, will be required.

The busing strategy has produced two important problems of its own. First, it is expensive, costing several hundred dollars a year for each participating student. Second, it has created overcrowding in several schools as new students have moved into their areas from other communities while many of those who have moved out have been bused back.

The Educational Consequences of Preventable Health Conditions   In 1990, Lucile Newman and Stephen L. Buka estimated that about 12 percent of young American children suffer from one or more preventable health conditions that can undermine their ability to learn by the time they enter school. This amounts to about 450,000 of each age-cohort of young children. Newman and Buka excluded infants and young children who die or who suffer from mental retardation; thus, their estimate "included only those children still within the normal range of intelligence but whose learning capacities have been so compromised that they are at risk of school failure." The researchers used the following categories of preventable health conditions to develop their estimate: low birthweight; prenatal exposure to tobacco, alcohol, or drugs; lead

19. Wisconsin Department of Public Instruction, *Working Together for Wisconsin Youth* (March 1990), pp. 18–19.
20. Miller, Fredisdorf, and Humphrey, *Student Mobility and School Reform*, pp. 1, 5, 6.
21. See, for example, Sammis B. White and M. Marc Thomas, "Busing for Stability and Student Achievement in P-5 Program Milwaukee Public Schools," Paper, July 3, 1991.

poisoning; malnutrition; and child abuse and neglect. Among the many serious education-related consequences of these conditions are delayed speech, hyperactivity, cognitive and attention deficit disorders, depression, aggression, apathy, social withdrawal, and low IQ.[22]

Poor children are much more likely to be victims of malnutrition, low birthweight, and lead poisoning than are middle-class children, and, because they make up a disproportionate share of the poor, minority children are much more likely than white children to be afflicted with these conditions.[23] For example, African American children have been found to be much more likely to have blood lead levels high enough to be linked to significant physical damage, including damage to the central nervous system. Urban black children from low-income families have been found to be especially likely to have elevated lead levels, reflecting in part the fact that many such children live in substandard houses or apartments with peeling lead-based paint.[24]

Remediation of learning and other problems associated with some of these health conditions appears to be possible but is not necessarily easy to undertake on a large-scale basis. For instance, recent research has found that well-planned and well-executed intervention programs directed at low-birthweight infants and their parents during the first several years of the children's lives (from infancy to age three or four) can produce cognitive and behavorial gains.[25] But it has not yet been established that these early gains will generally be translated into equivalent improvements in academic performance in elementary and secondary school. Moreover, still ahead is the difficult step of institutionalizing these interventions in such a way that large numbers of needy children and parents around the country receive the necessary services at high levels of program quality over the years. Finally, in some areas there has been little progress in developing effective remedial strategies. Lead poisoning is again a case in point. As I note in chapter 13, effective strategies to prevent lead poisoning are available, but our society has not been willing to pay the financial cost necessary to exploit them fully and quickly.

The impact of the major preventable health conditions on poor children is exacerbated by the large number who are not covered by health insurance—estimated at more than eight million youngsters in 1991. About half of these

22. Lucile Newman and Stephen L. Buka, *Every Child a Learner: Reducing Risks of Learning Impairment during Pregnancy and Infancy* (Denver: Education Commission of the States, 1990), pp. 1–2, 4–5, 8, 10–13, 16, 18.

23. National Commission on Children, *Beyond Rhetoric: A New American Agenda for Children and Families* (Washington, D.C: National Commission on Children, U.S. Government Printing Office, 1991), pp. 119, 121, 124.

24. Kathryn R. Mahaffey et al., "National Estimates of Blood Levels: United States, 1976–80: Association with Selected Demographic And Socioeconomic Factors," *New England Journal of Medicine* 307 (2 September 1982): 573–79; Herbert L. Needleman et al., "The Long-term Effects of Exposure to Low Doses of Lead in Childhood: An 11-year Follow-up Report," *New England Journal of Medicine* 322 (11 January 1990): 83–88.

25. The Infant Health and Development Program, "Enhancing the Outcomes of Low-Birth-Weight, Premature Infants," *Journal of the American Medical Association* 263 (13 June 1990): 3035–42; Virginia A. Rauh et al., "Minimizing Adverse Effects of Low Birthwight: Four-Year Results of an Early Intervention Program," *Child Development* 59 (June 1988): 544–53.

children were from families with incomes below the poverty line, and two-thirds were from families with incomes of less than 200 percent of the poverty line. Uninsured children are less likely to receive regular health care, including immunization against such diseases as measles, mumps, and rubella. Lack of routine health care is also associated with other common medical problems (ear infections, vision problems that can be corrected with glasses, and so forth).[26] Left untreated, such health problems can lead to missed days of school and low academic achievement.

The percentage of children who are at risk of experiencing consequential learning problems as a result of a major preventable health condition could be somewhat higher than the 12 percent estimated by Newman and Buka. Their estimate is based on the proportion of children who are experiencing one or more of these conditions to the point that they are at risk of doing very poorly in school. It does not explicitly include those children who, having experienced one of these conditions, are likely to perform within the acceptable range academically but are at risk of doing less well than they would have if they had been able to avoid the condition. The numbers of these children could be significant. Some of the preventable health conditions in question—for example, prenatal smoking and lead poisoning—appear to produce negative impacts in children that range from the very small to very large; and the degree of their impact seems to be heavily dependent on the extent of exposure to them. Small losses in academic performance are hard to identify and measure but are potentially very important for blacks, Hispanics, and Native Americans because of their substantial underrepresentation among high academic achievers.[27]

There are no trend data on the overall incidence of preventable health problems among children that correspond to the single-point estimate generated by Newman and Buka. However, there is little reason to believe that these problems collectively will be less severe over the next several years. To the extent that child abuse and neglect are associated with poor economic conditions, the recent economic recession and subsequent slow recovery suggest that this problem is unlikely to become markedly less severe in the near term.[28] The widespread use of crack in the 1980s suggests that over the next few years the number of school-age children with that form of prenatal drug exposure will

26. National Commission on Children, *Beyond Rhetoric: A New American Agenda for Children and Families*, pp. 119–21, 125, 136–38.

27. Newman and Buka, *Every Child a Learner*, pp. 6–7; Paul Mushak et al., "Prenatal and Postnatal Effects of Low-Level Lead Exposure: Integrated Summary of a Report to the U.S. Congress on Childhood Lead Poisoning," *Environmental Research* 50 (October 1989): 1–36. Some of the negative academic consequences for children of smoking by their mothers during pregnancy are difficulties in reading and problem solving, assignment to special education classes, and the need to repeat a grade. A reduction in the number of high academic achievers, of course, is also associated with heavy exposure to these conditions. However, because heavy exposure is often likely to produce outright school failure, one can lose sight of the fact that, in the absence of these health conditions, the afflicted children would have collectively produced something approaching a full distribution of academic achievement.

28. For a discussion of the relationship between economic conditions and child abuse, see Laurence D. Steinberg, Ralph Catalano, and David Dooley, "Economic Antecedents of Child Abuse and Neglect," *Child Development* 52 (September 1981): 975–85.

continue to grow.[29] It is likely to take years to eliminate most of the major sources of lead poisoning, for example, the lead-based paint in the older housing stock of our inner cities. Finally, there is little reason to believe that large, rapid drops in smoking and drinking among men and women are imminent.

SUMMARY AND CONCLUSIONS

In this chapter I have reviewed data on the relationship between variations in socioeconomic attributes of the family and school and variations in the academic achievement patterns of students. High-academic achievers are much more likely to come from high-income families and to have parents with a great deal of formal education, and low-academic achievers are much more likely to come from low-income families and to have parents with little or modest amounts of formal education. (These patterns are very consistent with the general findings of research on the relationship of social class and academic achievement patterns discussed in chapter 4.) Because of the large differences in parent education and family income levels between whites and Asians, on the one side, and African Americans, Latinos, and Native Americans, on the other, the social-class-related variations in academic achievement appear to account for a substantial proportion of the variations in academic achievement patterns among racial/ethnic groups.

The SAT math and verbal test score data for 1990 also suggest that the best-prepared students for selective colleges and universities are disproportionately drawn from those whose parents have graduate and bachelor's degrees and high incomes.

My review of the NAEP reading and math trend data suggests that there have been few changes in the school's capacity to serve children from different social classes over the past two decades. I examined the results of an analysis of the relationship between students' academic achievement patterns and the intensity of poverty. The data suggest that the longer children are poor, the greater the likelihood that they will be in a lower grade than would be expected for their age. These data also indicate that black children are much more likely to experience long-term poverty than white children. In addition, there is a relationship between the level of concentration of poor children in a school and the academic performance of the student body as a whole. High-poverty concentration was found to be associated with low levels of academic performance for both poor and nonpoor children, and vice versa. This is potentially a very important finding, given Wilson's general concern about the negative consequences of poverty concentration for the ghetto poor.

Additional analysis of SE data shows that the academic achievement gaps between students in high- and low-poverty concentration schools develop rapidly in the early elementary school years and are a combined result of edu-

29. Susan Chira, "Crack Babies Turn 5, and Schools Brace," *New York Times,* 25 May 1990, pp. A1, B5.

cational gaps that existed between poor and nonpoor children prior to entering the first grade, differences in rates of academic progress during the early elementary school years, and differences in learning gain/loss rates when the school is not in session.

Two obstacles to student learning that are strongly associated with poverty are the high student-mobility rates in many inner city schools and the high incidence of preventable health problems that can seriously impair youngsters' capacities to learn. Because minority children are experiencing the highest poverty rates among children, they are disproportionately impacted by these problems.

The standardized test data presented in this chapter are concerned exclusively with the relationship between social class and academic achievement for the American population as a whole. No test data have been presented that look simultaneously at social class and race/ethnicity. Nevertheless, a major question that remains to be examined is whether our standard measures of social class have essentially the same relationships with variations in academic achievement for each of the major racial/ethnic groups in America. In chapter 6, I shall review data relevant to this question.

CHAPTER SIX

An Analysis of

Academic Achievement Patterns

by Race/Ethnicity

and Social Class

Over the past twenty years, the collecting of socioeconomic and racial/ ethnic information about test takers has become a common practice. Consequently, large amounts of such information are now available from several testing programs and for many individual federally funded educational studies. Published analyses of data from these sources have typically included discussions of variations in achievement test score patterns among students from different social classes and different racial/ethnic groups. Normally, however, social class and racial/ethnic data are analyzed and reported separately. For example, the analyses often look at differences in achievement patterns between all poor children and all middle-class children or between all black children and all white children, but do not ordinarily examine differences in achievement patterns between segments of racial/ethnic groups in the same socioeconomic stratum (for example, middle-class Asians and middle-class Latinos) or between social classes within a single racial/group (for example, poor and middle-class blacks). As a result, it has been difficult to determine whether variations in achievement test score patterns among the several racial/ethnic groups can be accounted for mainly by such broad measures of socioeconomic status as family income level and parent education level.

There is, however, a modest body of data available that bears on this question. In this chapter, I review some of it, looking first at data from two studies that permit comparisons among students grouped on the basis of both race/ethnicity and socioeconomic characteristics. I then attempt to ascertain whether within-social-class differences have changed in size over the past two decades. Finally, I look at how these differences are manifested in the college-bound segments of several major racial/ethnic groups.

RACIAL/ETHNIC VARIATIONS IN STANDARDIZED TEST SCORE PATTERNS
AMONG STUDENTS WITH SIMILAR SOCIOECONOMIC CHARACTERISTICS

One of the principal findings of the Coleman Report was that variations in standardized test scores among students from different racial/ethnic groups were strongly associated with variations in social-class-related characteristics, for example, parent education level. In the late 1960s, some staff members of the U.S. Office of Education (the predecessor of the U.S. Department of Education) broke down the verbal test score data for the sixth graders, ninth graders, and twelfth graders in the sample of students used in the Coleman Report, assigning test takers to one of three social-class/socioeconomic-status (SES) categories on the basis of the education level of their mothers and fathers and the occupational levels of their fathers. To facilitate comparisons, the average verbal test score for each segment of students was converted into a Grade Level Equivalent (GLE).[1]

Analyzed in this way, the data show that there were substantial between-social-class differences in verbal test score averages, expressed in GLEs, for each racial/ethnic group at all three school grades. Moreover, these differences were in the expected direction: within each racial/ethnic group, test takers in the high-SES category had a higher GLE than test takers in the medium-SES category, who consistently had a higher GLE than those in the low- SES category. For example, among Puerto Rican ninth graders, the high-SES segment had an average verbal GLE of 8.4, the medium-SES segment 7.2, and the low-SES segment 6.6.[2]

The analysis also revealed substantial within-social-class differences in GLE among racial/ethnic groups at each grade level. Significantly, whites and Asians in each social class consistently had GLEs higher than those of their black, Puerto Rican, Mexican American, and American Indian counterparts. In many cases, the gaps were quite large. For example, there was a two-point GLE score difference—7.3 vs. 5.3—between high-SES whites and high-SES African Americans in the sixth grade. High-SES black sixth graders were somewhat below grade level on the verbal test and two full grade levels behind their high SES white counterparts. The 5.3 GLE for high-SES black sixth graders was slightly lower than the 5.6 GLE of low-SES white sixth graders.[3]

Similar gaps existed in the ninth and twelfth grades. High-SES black ninth graders had a GLE of only 8.4 vs. 11.4 for their high-SES white counterparts. In the twelfth grade, the respective GLEs were 10.7 and 14.0. This suggests that as recently as the mid-1960s, the most advantaged black ninth graders were collectively below grade level and three years behind high-SES whites. In the twelfth grade, high SES blacks had a verbal test average well below the average for all twelfth graders, while their white counterparts had a verbal test score average similar to that of college students. The pattern of low GLE scores relative to whites and Asians was most pronounced for African American and Puerto Rican students, less pronounced for Mexican Americans, and least pronounced for American Indians.[4]

1. Tetsuo Okada, Wallace M. Cohen, and George W. Mayeske, "Growth in Achievement for Different Racial, Regional, and Socio-economic Groupings of Students," Paper, U.S. Office of Education, 1969, cited in Frederick Mosteller and Daniel P. Moynihan, "A Pathbreaking Report," in *On Equality of Educational Opportunity: Papers Deriving from the Harvard University Faculty Seminar on the Coleman Report,* Frederick Mosteller and Daniel P. Moynihan, eds. (New York: Random House, 1972), pp. 22–24.
2. Ibid., p. 23.
3. Ibid.
4. Ibid.

An obvious question is whether these results are typical of those produced by other standardized tests. The answer is yes. For example, reading and math achievement test data from NELS:88 show large within-social-class differences among racial/ethnic groups. Asian, white, black, and Hispanic students in the sample were divided into four social-class quartiles on the basis of the education levels, occupations, and incomes of their parents.[5] The data presented in table 6.1 are for students in the top and bottom SES quartiles.

Table 6.1
Selected Reading and Mathematics Proficiency Data for High and
Low Socioeconomic Status Eighth Graders from Each Racial/Ethnic Group
in the National Education Longitudinal Study of 1988

1: Percent of Eighth Graders in Low and High Social Classes Who Failed to Show Basic Reading Skills

Racial/Ethnic Group	Top SES Quartile	Bottom SES Quartile
Asian	5	26
White	5	17
Hispanic	11	26
Black	14	30

2: Percent of Eighth Graders in Low and High Social Classes Who Were Proficient in Advanced Mathematics

Racial/Ethnic Group	Top SES Quartile	Bottom SES Quartile
Asian	54	18
White	40	7
Hispanic	25	4
Black	21	2

Source: Anne Hafner, Steven Ingels, Barbara Schneider, and David Stevenson, *A Profile of the American Eighth Grader: NELS:88 Student Descriptive Summary,* National Education Longitudinal Study of 1988 (Washington, D.C.: National Center for Education Statistics, U.S. Department of Education, U.S. Government Printing Office, 1990), pp. 32–33, C3–C5. The NELS:88 reading test scale has two competency levels: (1) Basic—competence in simple reading comprehension; and (2) Advanced—ability to make inferences beyond main points and/or to understand and evaluate relatively abstract concepts. The NELS:88 math test has three competency levels: (1) Basic—simple arithmetic and whole numbers; (2) Intermediate—operations with decimals, fractions, and roots; and (3) Advanced—conceptual understanding and/or development of a solution strategy that may include use of some geometry, algebra, or logical process.

Part 1 of the table shows that within each racial/ethnic group, bottom SES quartile students were much more likely to be low reading achievers than were top SES quartile students. However, African American and Latino students in

5. Anne Hafner, Steven Ingels, Barbara Schneider, and David Stevenson, *A Profile of the American Eighth Grader: NELS:88 Student Descriptive Summary, National Education Longitudinal Study of 1988* (Washington, D.C.: National Center for Education Statistics, U.S. Department of Education, U.S. Government Printing Office, 1990), p. B9.

both the top and the bottom SES quartiles were much more likely than their white counterparts to read below the basic level (defined as competence in simple reading comprehension). Asians had a reading pattern in between those of whites and of African Americans and Latinos.

Part 2 of table 6.1 shows that within each racial/ethnic group, top SES quartile students were significantly more likely to be high math achievers than were bottom SES quartile students. Nonetheless, black and Hispanic students from both the top and bottom SES quartiles were much less likely than Asians and whites to have math scores at the advanced level (defined as conceptual understanding and/or development of a solution strategy that may include use of some geometry, algebra, or logical process).

Although these data indicate that within-social-class differences among racial/ethnic groups were substantial in both the mid-1960s and the late 1980s, we cannot use these data sets to determine whether the size of the gaps has changed in this period. I want to turn to this question, using NAEP reading and mathematics trend data.

RACIAL/ETHNIC TRENDS IN STANDARDIZED TEST SCORES AMONG
STUDENTS WITH PARENTS AT SIMILAR EDUCATION LEVELS

Traditionally, NAEP trend analyses that examine test scores for students categorized simultaneously by race/ethnicity and social class (parent education level) have not been available. Recently, however, Bernice Taylor Anderson of the Educational Testing Service has concluded analyses of NAEP reading and mathematics scores that took race/ethnicity and parent education level into account simultaneously. Anderson's analyses focused on scores of 9-year-olds and 13-year-olds in reading for the 1971–88 period and in mathematics for the 1978–90 period.[6] I shall draw on Anderson's analyses to review trends in average reading and math scores for whites, African Americans, and Latinos at three parent education levels: test takers who had no parent with a high school degree, test takers who had at least one parent with a high school diploma (but no postsecondary education), and test takers who had at least one parent with some college education. These data must be interpreted with great caution, owing to sample size limitations. Nevertheless, Anderson's data provide some important preliminary insights into the question of whether within-social-class score gaps among racial/ethnic groups have been narrowing since the publication of the Coleman Report.

NAEP Reading Trends by Race/Ethnicity and Parent Education Level   Table 6.2 presents the average NAEP reading scores for 9-year-olds in 1971–88 by race/ethnicity and parent education level.

6. Bernice Taylor Anderson, "Reading Proficiency of Minority Students, 1971–1988: A Descriptive Analysis of Trend Data for Ages Nine and Thirteen by Background Factors," Paper, Educational Testing Service, 1990; Bernice Taylor Anderson, "Mathematics Proficiency of Minority Students, 1978–1990: A Descriptive Analysis of Trend Data for Ages Nine and Thirteen by Background Factors," Paper, Educational Testing Service, 1991.

Table 6.2
Average NAEP Reading Scores for 9-Year-Olds, by Race/Ethnicity
and Parent Education Level: 1971–88

Parent Education Level and Racial/Ethnic Group	1971	1975	1980	1984	1988
Did Not Finish High School:					
White	195	198	204	204	197
Black	160	169	181	171	186
Hispanic	NA	173	178	186	190
Graduated from High School:					
White	214	217	219	215	216
Black	173	182	190	186	193
Hispanic	NA	190	188	189	190
Some Post High School Education:					
White	228	227	231	218	219
Black	182	190	197	183	191
Hispanic	NA	188	203	198	194

Source: Bernice Taylor Anderson, *Reading Proficiency of Minority Students, 1971–1988: A Descriptive Analysis of Trend Data for Ages Nine and Thirteen by Background Factors* (Unpublished paper, Educational Testing Service, 1990).

The data tell a complex story, some parts of which are very encouraging and some quite troubling. Looking first at the data for students with no parent with a high school degree, we see that there were large increases in average reading scores for 9-year-old African Americans and Latinos in the NAEP samples, while the average score for whites in the samples remained virtually unchanged. As a result, there was considerable convergence in the average scores for these three groups by 1988: the white-black score gap was only 11 points, down from 35 points in 1971, and the white-Hispanic gap only 7 points, down from 25 points in 1975.

Turning to 9-year-olds with at least one parent with a high school diploma, we see that African Americans again enjoyed substantial gains in the period, although little progress was made after 1980. The scores for both Latinos and whites remained essentially unchanged. Overall, large white-black and white-Hispanic gaps remained in 1988.

Looking now at the data for 9-year-olds with one or both parents with some college, we find yet another pattern. Both blacks and Hispanics in the samples experienced a moderate increase in average reading scores, while whites experienced a moderate drop. However, there was little change in the average score for African Americans after 1975, and there was considerable volatility in the average score for Latinos throughout the 1975–88 period (possibly owing to the relatively small number of Latinos included in these samples). On the basis of these data, there is reason to believe that there was significant narrowing of the white-black and white-Hispanic score gaps among 9-year-olds with at least one parent with some college. Again, however, the absolute size of these gaps remained large in 1988.

Among the critical aspects of the data is the similarity in the average scores of blacks and Hispanics by 1988 when viewed from a parent education perspective. At each parent education level, the black-Hispanic gap had been reduced to 3 or 4 points by 1988. Moreover, the difference in the average scores of students with no parent with a high school degree and those with at least one parent with some college was only 4 or 5 points. The positive interpretation of this convergence of sample results is that it suggests a greater uniformity of reading experience among students from these groups. The negative interpretation is that the overall reading levels of African American and Latino 9-year-olds were still below those of their white counterparts in 1988—especially at the two highest parent education levels.

Complex reading-score trend patterns also existed among 13-year-olds in the NAEP samples. Table 6.3 tells this story.

Table 6.3
Average NAEP Reading Scores for 13-Year-Olds, by Race/Ethnicity
and Parent Education Level: 1971–88

Parent Education Level and Racial/Ethnic Group	1971	1975	1980	1984	1988
Did Not Finish High School:					
White	246	246	245	245	250
Black	215	217	220	228	238
Hispanic	NA	227	232	233	233
Graduated High School:					
White	260	259	258	258	255
Black	226	228	232	235	242
Hispanic	NA	241	240	241	246
Some Post High School Education:					
White	273	273	275	270	270
Black	238	239	243	245	248
Hispanic	NA	252	255	250	248

Source: Bernice Taylor Anderson, *Reading Proficiency of Minority Students, 1971–1988: A Descriptive Analysis of Trend Data for Ages Nine and Thirteen by Background Factors* (Unpublished paper, Educational Testing Service, 1990).

Looking first at the average reading scores for 13-year-olds with no parent with a high school degree, we see that African Americans were the only group that experienced a large score increase in the period. In 1988, whites in the sample had a 12-point average score advantage over blacks, less than half of the 31-point gap in 1971. In contrast, the white-Hispanic gap of 17 points in 1988 had changed little from the 19-point gap that existed in 1975.

A similar pattern prevailed among 13-year-olds with at least one parent with a high school diploma. Only African Americans had a substantial increase in average score in the period. Latinos had a small increase while whites had a small decrease. As a result, the black average score in the 1988 sample was only 13 points lower than the white average that year; this gap had been 34 points in 1971. In 1988 the white-Hispanic gap was only 9 points, half of the 18-point gap that had existed in the 1975 sample.

The least positive story for African Americans and Latinos was among 13-year-olds with at least one parent with some college. The average score for blacks increased moderately in the period, while those for both Hispanics and whites fell slightly. The net result of these changes was that very substantial 22-point gaps still existed both between whites and African Americans and between whites and Latinos in the 1988 sample.

NAEP Mathematics Trends by Race/Ethnicity and Parent Education Level
Table 6.4 presents average mathematics score data for 9-year-olds in the 1978-90 period.

As was the case in reading, some of the largest increases for African American and Latino 9-year-olds were achieved by youngsters who did not have a parent with a high school diploma. Since the average score for whites changed little in this period, the white-black gap was much smaller in 1990 than it had been in 1978 and was substantially smaller for whites and Hispanics.

The story was considerably different among students who had at least one parent with a high school degree. All three groups had small to moderate increases in average scores during the period. This meant that the white-black score gap remained very large throughout the period, while the white-Hispanic gap remained moderate in size.

The story was more positive for African American and Latino 13-year-olds with at least one parent with some college. Both groups enjoyed reasonably large increases in the period, while the white score changed little. Consequently, both African Americans and Latinos ended the period with an average score 16 points below the white average. Although this gap was still substantial, it was much less than the 34-point white-black gap in the 1978 sample and the 30-point white-Hispanic gap.

Table 6.5 presents average NAEP math scores for 13-year-old whites, blacks, and Hispanics by parent education level.

Both African Americans and Latinos with no parent with a high school degree enjoyed moderate increases in their average scores. However, since whites also enjoyed a small to moderate increase, there were only small reductions in the

Table 6.4
Average NAEP Mathematics Scores for 9-Year-Olds, by Race/Ethnicity and Parent Education Level: 1978–90

Parent Education Level and Racial/Ethnic Group	1978	1982	1986	1990
Did Not Finish High School:				
White	208	204	202	212
Black	180	178	192	203
Hispanic	194	201	212	206
Graduated from High School:				
White	225	223	224	232
Black	194	197	198	206
Hispanic	216	204	199	219
Some Post High School Education:				
White	236	233	233	233
Black	202	202	206	217
Hispanic	206	209	212	217

Source: Bernice Taylor Anderson, *Mathematics Proficiency of Minority Students, 1978–1990: A Descriptive Analysis of Trend Data for Ages Nine and Thirteen by Background Factors* (Unpublished paper, Educational Testing Service, 1991).

white-black and white-Hispanic score gaps. The white-black gap was a still-substantial 25 points in 1990, down from 30 points in the 1978 sample. The white-Hispanic gap was only 9 points in 1990, in comparison to 14 points in 1978.

Among 13-year-olds with at least one parent with a high school diploma, the patterns were somewhat different. African Americans and Latinos again enjoyed moderate increases in their average scores, but the score for whites changed little. As a result, while the white-black gap in the 1990 sample was a still-large 19 points, it was less than half the 37-point gap that existed in 1978. The white-Hispanic gap in 1990 had closed to 13 points, down from 25 points in 1978.

Among 13-year-olds with at least one parent with some college, African Americans and Latinos enjoyed relatively large increases in average math scores while whites experienced a small drop. Consequently, the white-black gap dropped from 40 points in the 1978 sample to only 16 points in the 1990 sample. The white-Hispanic gap dropped from 26 points in 1978 to 7 points in 1990.

Interpreting the NAEP Trend Data   Over the years, NAEP's primary mission has been to measure changes in the academic performance of the nation's ele-

Table 6.5
Average NAEP Mathematics Scores for 13-Year-Olds, by Race/Ethnicity and Parent
Education Level: 1978–90

Parent Education Level and Racial/Ethnic Group	1978	1982	1986	1990
Did Not Finish High School:				
White	252	257	256	259
Black	222	232	240	234
Hispanic	238	248	248	250
Graduated from High School:				
White	269	267	266	266
Black	232	242	246	247
Hispanic	244	250	252	253
Some Post High School Education:				
White	284	285	277	280
Black	244	247	255	264
Hispanic	258	267	266	273

Source: Bernice Taylor Anderson, *Mathematics Proficiency of Minority Students, 1978–1990: A Descriptive Analysis of Trend Data for Ages Nine and Thirteen by Background Factors* (Unpublished paper, Educational Testing Service, 1991).

mentary and secondary school population in very broad terms. Its capacity to monitor subpopulation trends is fairly limited. Sample sizes, in particular, have been determined by NAEP's broad monitoring requirements, not by extensive subpopulation tracking.

Historically, this limitation has been much larger for racial/ethnic minorities than for whites. The numbers of black and Hispanic students included in typical NAEP test samples have usually not been large enough to make precise estimates of the academic performance of many subpopulations of African American or Latino students, including those defined in terms of parent education level. (Not enough Asians or Native Americans have been included in NAEP samples to provide trend data for these groups on an aggregate basis, much less to provide trend data for their social-class-related subpopulations.)

Beginning in the mid-1980s, the problem of small sample sizes became more acute as the NAEP began to test (separately) on the basis of age and grade level. Prior to that time, NAEP tests were geared to 9-, 13-, and 17-year-olds. Subsequently, NAEP has also regularly administered tests to large samples of fourth, eighth, and twelfth graders, evidently reflecting the desire for a relatively detailed understanding of what students are able to do academically at these grade levels, regardless of age. The age-group samples were essentially reduced to the smallest numbers required for broad trend analysis. This point is illustrated in table 6.6, which presents the size of the samples of 9- and 13-year-old white, black, and Hispanic students used in the NAEP tests analyzed by Anderson.

Table 6.6
NAEP Reading and Mathematics Test Sample Sizes for
9- and 13-Year-Olds, by Race/Ethnicity

1: Reading Test Sample Sizes

Year of Test	White		Black		Hispanic	
	Age 9	Age 13	Age 9	Age 13	Age 9	Age 13
1971	18,755	20,907	3,899	4,254	NA	NA
1975	16,882	16,963	3,610	3,208	855	900
1980	16,146	17,366	3,081	3,180	1,570	1,475
1984	16,169	16,862	3,713	3,416	1,746	1,863
1988	2,509	3,087	788	594	360	215

2: Mathematics Test Sample Sizes

Year of Test	White		Black		Hispanic	
	Age 9	Age 13	Age 9	Age 13	Age 9	Age 13
1978	11,078	18,559	2,646	3,983	794	1,447
1982	8,726	11,795	2,238	2,300	815	1,195
1986	5,098	4,038	1,041	1,442	554	561
1990	4,358	4,991	1,073	751	541	603

Sources: Bernice Taylor Anderson, *Reading Proficiency of Minority Students, 1971–1988: A Descriptive Analysis of Trend Data for Ages Nine and Thirteen by Background Factors* (Unpublished paper, Educational Testing Service, 1990); Bernice Taylor Anderson, *Mathematics Proficiency of Minority Students, 1978–1990: A Descriptive Analysis of Trend Data for Ages Nine and Thirteen by Background Factors* (Unpublished paper, Educational Testing Service, 1991).

Part 1 of the table shows that the numbers of students sampled in the NAEP reading test were much smaller in 1988 than they were in 1984. Part 2 shows a similar phenomenon for mathematics, although the most significant changes in sample size took place between the 1982 and 1986 tests. Both the reading and the math sample data show that this problem has been especially acute for Latinos. In 1988, only 360 Hispanic 9-year-olds and 215 13-year-olds were included in the reading sample, and only 541 and 603 Latino test takers in these two age groups, respectively, were included in the 1990 math sample. The numbers of African Americans sampled for the reading and math tests were only moderately larger.

As Anderson discovered, the actual pools of NAEP test takers that could be used in calculations of the average reading and mathematics test scores for groups defined in part by parent education level were even smaller in several instances than the sample-size data in table 6.6 would suggest. Information on parent education levels is provided by NAEP participants on a voluntary basis, and some test takers choose not to answer the question. And many test takers are unable to respond to this question because they evidently do not know the educational attainment levels of their parents.

Owing to these two problems, Anderson's calculations were often based on very small numbers of test takers. For example, for her average reading score calculations for 9-year-olds (see table 6.2), the pool of Latino test takers in 1988 included only 33 with no parent with a high school degree, only 46 with at least one parent with a high school diploma, and only 17 with at least one parent with some postsecondary education. Obviously, it is difficult to draw conclusions on the basis of the performance of so few test takers. Variations in scores associated with such small numbers of individuals are typically very large. Under such circumstances, the statistical techniques available for assessing the likelihood that changes in test scores over time are due to actual changes in skills, rather than to sampling variations, are of little practical help. With the exception of cases in which changes in test score averages are very large, these techniques will consistently tell us that the observed differences are not statistically significant (whether or not the differences are to some degree "real").

Nevertheless, because several standardized test-data sets over the years have found substantial within-social-class test score differences between racial/ethnic groups, it is important to get as good a feel as possible for trends in this area. To that end, table 6.7 presents the NAEP reading- and math-trend data, by race/ethnicity and parent education level, for the 1971-88 and 1978-90 periods in a slightly different format. Rather than focus on the specific scores for each subpopulation, the table shows the net increases and decreases in these scores that took place in the periods in question.

Among whites, the most distinctive aspect of the changes in reading and math scores is that they were generally quite small for both 9- and 13-year-olds at each of the three parent education levels. The largest increases were 7 points, while the largest decrease was 9 points. Most of the increases and decreases were in the 2-4-point range. Half of the twelve score changes for whites were increases and half were decreases.

Among blacks all twelve changes in scores were increases, and all were either moderate or large. Five of the increases were 20 points or more; only one was less than 10 points. Given this pattern as well as the previously discussed pattern for whites, the data in the table are consistent with the view that there have been reductions in the within-social-class test score gaps between blacks and whites since the early 1970s. The sample size limitations of the NAEP reading and math tests, however, make it hard to judge both the magnitude of the improvements in the scores of African Americans at every parent education level and the size of the reduction in black-white gaps at each of these levels. The degree of uncertainty on this point is underscored by the substantial variations Anderson found in the score changes of black 9- and 13-year-olds that took place from test to test in the 1984-90 interval, the period during which the NAEP sample sizes were getting much smaller (see tables 6.2-6.5). These changes

Table 6.7
Absolute Changes in Average NAEP Reading Scores, 1971–88,
and in Average NAEP Mathematics Scores, 1978–90, for 9- and 13-Year-Olds,
by Race/Ethnicity and Parent Education Level

Parent Education Level and Racial/Ethnic Group	Changes in Average Reading Scores		Changes in Average Mathematics Scores	
	Age 9	Age 13	Age 9	Age 13
Did Not Finish High School:				
White	+2	+4	+4	+7
Black	+26	+23	+23	+12
Hispanic	+17	+6	+12	+12
Graduated from High School:				
White	+2	-5	+7	-3
Black	+20	+16	+12	+15
Hispanic	0	+5	+3	+9
Some Post High School Education:				
White	-9	-3	-3	-4
Black	+9	+10	+15	+20
Hispanic	+6	-4	+11	+15

Source: Calculated from data presented in tables 6.2 and 6.3 (reading) and in tables 6.4 and 6.5 (math). The Hispanic numbers for reading are based on the 1975–88 period.

ranged from a decrease of 6 points in the average math score of black 13-year-olds with no parent with a high school degree to an increase of 15 points in the average reading score of black 9-year-olds with no parent with a high school diploma.

The degree of uncertainty is further underscored by some of the results of the 1990 NAEP reading test, although they were not available to Anderson at the time she undertook her analysis. As we saw in table 3.2, the average NAEP reading score for all black 9-year-olds in 1990 was 182, 7 points lower than the average score for their counterparts in 1988 and only 1 point higher than in 1975.

The score pattern for Hispanics falls between those of whites and blacks. Ten of the twelve changes were positive, and a number were moderate to large. But several were small. Overall, one gets a sense that there has been some narrowing of the within-social-class reading and mathematics test score gaps between whites and Latinos, but possibly less than occurred between whites and blacks. Again, there is uncertainty about the amount of narrowing that has taken place, and again, this uncertainty is reinforced by the results of the 1990 NAEP reading test. Table 3.2 shows that the average score for all Latino 9-year-olds on the 1990 reading test was 189, 5 points lower than the comparable score in 1988 and 1 point lower than the comparable score in 1980.

RACIAL/ETHNIC VARIATIONS IN STANDARDIZED TEST SCORE PATTERNS AMONG COLLEGE-BOUND STUDENTS WITH SIMILAR PARENT EDUCATION OR INCOME CHARACTERISTICS

By examining the differences in average verbal and mathematics SAT scores for college-bound students for 1990 by race/ethnicity and parent education level as well as by race/ethnicity and parent income level one can assess the size of the within-social-class differences in academic preparation for college that existed among racial/ethnic groups at the beginning of the 1990s; and one can do so using two standard social-class measures.

Table 6.8 presents average 1990 SAT scores by race/ethnicity and two very different parent education levels: test takers with no parent with a high school degree and test takers with at least one parent with a graduate degree. This approach allows one to examine the within-parent-education level differences among racial/ethnic groups at both very high and very low parent educational attainment levels.

The 1990 SAT data shown in table 6.8 are generally consistent with the data from other sources presented earlier in this chapter. The average 1990 verbal, math, and combined SAT scores of test takers with at least one parent with a graduate degree were much higher than those with no parent with a high school diploma. But at both parent education levels, the average scores varied considerably among the racial/ethnic groups. Asians and whites tended to have significantly higher average SAT scores in 1990 than the other racial/ethnic groups. Blacks and Puerto Ricans had the lowest average verbal, math, and combined SAT scores. Native Americans, Mexican Americans, and Other Hispanics had average scores at both education levels that generally fell between those of whites and Asians, on one side, and African Americans and Puerto Ricans, on the other.

One of the most troubling aspects of the data shown in table 6.8 is that the average 1990 SAT score gaps among racial/ethnic groups were often larger among test takers with at least one parent with a graduate degree than among those with no parent with a high school education. For example, there was a 127-point difference between the average combined 1990 SAT scores of Asians and Puerto Ricans with no parent with a high school degree, but a 215-point gap between Asians and Puerto Ricans with at least one parent with a graduate degree. Similarly, there was a 58-point gap between whites and Mexican Americans with no parent with a high school degree, but a 109-point gap between whites and Mexican Americans with at least one parent with a graduate degree.

Another troubling aspect of the data is how low the average verbal, math, and combined SAT scores were in 1990 for blacks and Puerto Ricans with at least one parent with a graduate degree. For example, African Americans with one parent with a graduate degree had a combined average SAT score of 830, which was only 25 and 28 points higher, respectively, than the combined average scores of Asians and whites with no parent with a high school degree. Puerto Ricans were only marginally better off than their black counterparts. The

Table 6.8
Average 1990 Verbal, Math, and Combined SAT Scores, by Race/Ethnicity and Selected Parent Education Levels

1: Average Verbal Scores
Parent Education Level

Group	No Parent Has High School Degree	At Least One Parent Has Graduate Degree	Increase in Average Score with More Parent Education
American Indian	334	421	+87
Asian	326	477	+151
Black	310	402	+92
Mexican American	342	434	+92
Puerto Rican	318	391	+73
Other Hispanic	324	428	+104
White	377	484	+107

2: Average Math Scores
Parent Education Level

Group	No Parent Has High School Degree	At Least One Parent Has Graduate Degree	Increase in Average Score with More Parent Education
American Indian	382	470	+88
Asian	479	576	+97
Black	352	428	+76
Mexican American	402	475	+73
Puerto Rican	360	447	+87
Other Hispanic	380	486	+106
White	425	534	+109

3: Average Combined Scores
Parent Education Level

Group	No Parent Has High School Degree	At Least One Parent Has Graduate Degree	Increase in Average Score with More Parent Education
American Indian	716	891	+175
Asian	805	1053	+248
Black	662	830	+168
Mexican American	744	909	+165
Puerto Rican	678	838	+160
Other Hispanic	704	914	+210
White	802	1018	+216

Source: College Entrance Examination Board, *1990 College-Bound Seniors: Ethnic and Gender Profile of SAT and Achievement Test Takers* (New York: College Entrance Examination Board, 1990), p. 8 of each ethnic group section.

average math SAT score of 428 for blacks with one parent with a college degree was only 3 points higher than the average score of whites with no parent with a high school degree—and 51 points lower than the average score for Asians with no parent with a high school degree. The average verbal score for Puerto Ricans with at least one parent with a graduate degree was just 14 points higher than the average score of whites with no parent with a high school degree.

I now turn to SAT score differences in 1990 between racial/ethnic groups at both very high and very low parent income levels.

Table 6.9

Average 1990 Verbal, Math, and Combined SAT Scores, by Race/Ethnicity and Selected Parent Income Levels

	1: Average Verbal Scores		
	Parent Income Level		Increase in
	<$10,000	>$70,000	Average Score with
Group	per Year	per Year	More Parent Income
American Indian	358	414	+56
Asian	339	479	+140
Black	323	411	+88
Mexican American	342	433	+91
Puerto Rican	316	429	+113
Other Hispanic	325	448	+123
White	411	471	+60

	2: Average Math Scores		
	Parent Income Level		Increase in
	<$10,000	>$70,000	Average Score with
Group	per Year	per Year	More Parent Income
American Indian	406	467	+61
Asian	483	587	+104
Black	360	443	+83
Mexican American	398	479	+81
Puerto Rican	363	480	+117
Other Hispanic	382	502	+120
White	455	527	+72

	3: Average Combined Scores		
	Parent Income Level		Increase in
	<$10,000	>$70,000	Average Score with
Group	per Year	per Year	More Parent Income
American Indian	764	881	+117
Asian	822	1066	+244
Black	683	854	+171
Mexican American	740	912	+172
Puerto Rican	679	909	+230
Other Hispanic	707	950	+243
White	866	998	+132

Source: College Entrance Examination Board, 1990 College-Bound Seniors: Ethnic and Gender Profile of SAT and Achievement Test Takers (New York: College Entrance Examination Board, 1990), p. 7 of each ethnic group section.

The data in table 6.9 have two patterns that are now quite familiar. First, for each racial/ethnic group in 1990, the average verbal, math, and combined SAT scores of test takers with parent incomes greater than $70,000 were much higher than those of test takers with parent incomes of less than $10,000 per year. Second, at both of these parent education levels, there were substantial differences in scores among test takers from the several racial/ethnic groups.

The within-parent-income level SAT score differences between racial/ethnic groups in 1990 also had some very familiar patterns: whites and Asians tended to have higher scores at both parent income levels than the other racial/ethnic groups, and blacks again tended to have the lowest scores. Puerto Ricans had average SAT scores that were about the same as blacks in the case of test takers with parents with less than $10,000 per year. But Puerto Ricans whose parents had incomes of over $70,000 per year had SAT scores that were much closer to those of some other groups, notably Mexican Americans and Native Americans.

Possibly the most notable way in which the within-parent-income-level SAT score pattern differs from the within-parent-education-level pattern is that the score gaps between several of the educationally disadvantaged racial/ethnic groups and whites were smaller at the high-income level than at the low-income level. For example, the combined SAT score gap between whites and African Americans was 126 points at the below $10,000 parent income level (866 vs. 740), but fell to 86 points at the above $70,000 parent income level. None of the disadvantaged groups, however, had a smaller score gap with Asians at the over $70,000 parent income level than at the below $10,000 level.

Overall, the relative performance of test takers from high-income families was very weak for some minority groups. The average verbal score of 411 for African Americans was the same as that of whites whose parents had incomes of less than $10,000 per year, and their math score of 443 was actually 12 points lower than the 455 registered by low-income whites. The situation for Native Americans was only moderately better.

Substantial between-social-class and within-social-class SAT score gaps are also present in narrower ranges of parent education and parent income levels. For example, the average combined SAT scores for African Americans who had at least one parent with a high school diploma was 709 in 1990, while it was 780 for African Americans with at least one parent with a bachelor's degree; the comparable scores for whites were 872 and 959, respectively.[7] Thus, the average SAT score in 1990 for blacks with one parent with a bachelor's degree was 179 points lower than the score for comparable whites and 92 points lower than that of whites with a parent with only a high school education.

SUMMARY AND CONCLUSIONS

In this chapter I have examined whether variations in standardized test scores among racial/ethnic groups are a function of education-relevant resource differences that can be largely summarized by broad measures of social class, such as parent education and family income level. I began the exploration of this question by reviewing data derived from the Coleman Report and from NELS:88,

7. College Entrance Examination Board, *1990 College-Bound Seniors: Ethnic and Gender Profile of SAT and Achievement Test Takers* (New York: College Entrance Examination Board, 1990), p. 8 of each ethnic group section.

which allowed one to look at test-score patterns simultaneously from the perspective of race/ethnicity and social class. Although standard social-class measures do seem to account for a major portion of the differences in test scores between racial/ethnic groups, a large component remains unexplained. More specifically, each racial/ethnic group's standardized test scores tend to go up with increases in social class and down with decreases in social class. This is consistent with the research literature and data on the strong relationship between social class and academic performance (when students are viewed on an aggregate basis) examined in chapters 4 and 5. At the same time, the Coleman Report and NELS:88 data revealed large differences in standardized test scores among segments of racial/ethnic groups that fall into similar social class categories. Thus, these data suggest that variations in standardized test scores among racial/ethnic groups have both between and within-social-class dimensions, at least as social class is typically measured.

I then turned to the question of whether this component seems to have changed in size over the past few decades. There is reason to believe that the within-social-class component has grown smaller over time, at least with regard to test-score gaps between whites and blacks and between whites and Hispanics. However, owing to the sample-size limitations of the NAEP data, it is difficult to estimate with any precision how substantial the reductions in within-social-class gaps have been.

In the final stage of the analysis, I used SAT data to examine between- and within-social-class differences in the test scores of a large segment of the college-bound population. Average verbal, mathematics, and combined SAT scores in 1990, broken down by race/ethnicity and parent education level as well as by race/ethnicity and parent income level, reveal that within-social-class gaps tend to be largest between Asians and whites, on the one hand, and blacks and Puerto Ricans, on the other. However, significant gaps vis-à-vis whites and Asians were found to exist for Native Americans, Mexican Americans, and Other Hispanics.

The existence of large within-social-class differences in test scores among racial/ethnic groups both complicates and informs analysis of education-relevant resource variations among them. It indicates that, in effect, standard socioeconomic categories "mismeasure" one or more of the important education-relevant resources available to some racial/ethnic groups. At the same time, it makes clear that as a nation Americans must be concerned with improving the educational prospects not only of those living in poverty and those whose parents have little education but also of those who are middle-class minority students.

In the next chapter, I shall examine some of the reasons this mismeasurement problem exists. I shall look closely at the human capital available to minority children, including a substantial number who are growing up in what most of us would regard as middle-class circumstances.

CHAPTER SEVEN

Standard Social Class Categories

and the

Mismeasurement of

Education-Relevant Resources

The large within-social-class differences in the test scores of students from several racial/ethnic groups suggest that parent education level, family income level, and other commonly used social-class categories are unable to identify some important variations among these groups in the amounts of education-relevant resources they possess. In this chapter I wish to reach a better understanding of why this mismeasurement problem exists by exploring the limitations of one of the most frequently used social-class categories, parent education level, in identifying racial/ethnic variations in human capital. I focus on this specific combination of social-class category and education-relevant resource because a central purpose of schooling in America—and of the support parents provide for their children's formal education—is the development of human-capital-type knowledge and skills in students.

I first review an important limitation in the use of parent education level to assess human capital: the fact that it is a measure of educational attainment, not academic achievement. Using standardized test data, I then examine variations in developed academic skills among adults from different racial/ethnic groups who are likely to be parents of pre-/school-age children. Finally, I explore how these variations in parent-held human capital may have originated, focusing on the variations in school investments that have been available to different racial/ethnic groups over several generations.

DIFFICULTIES IN MEASURING THE HUMAN CAPITAL POSSESSED BY PARENTS

Consistent with the general trend toward collecting social-class-related information about individuals who take standardized tests, it is now common to ask several background questions on the education levels of their parents. For instance, item 41 on the background questionnaire for the 1990–91 SAT was, "Indicate the highest level of education completed by your father (or male guardian) and your mother (or female guardian) by filling in the appropriate oval in each column." Nine alternative responses were supplied, from grade school to graduate or professional degree.[1]

---

1. College Entrance Examination Board, *Registration Bulletin 1990–91: SAT and Achievement Tests—New York State Edition* (Princeton, N.J.: College Entrance Examination Board, 1990), p. 14.

Responses to questions like this are susceptible to some fairly obvious sources of error or distortion. For instance, some test takers may not know how much formal education their parents have had. Some may not wish to disclose it. Others may wish to misrepresent it for some reason. The degree of inaccuracy these factors introduce into the pattern of responses is probably greatest for young students because they are the least likely to know their parents' education levels. Nevertheless, we have no reason to believe that children from some racial/ethnic groups are significantly more or less accurate than others in answering parent-education-level questions. These sources of inaccuracy are unlikely to explain the large within-parent-education level differences in standardized test scores among racial/ethnic groups.

This is not the case for two other limitations of parent-education-level questions associated with standardized tests. The first is that test takers are not typically asked for information on the academic majors or curricular content of their parents' degrees. Yet there can be enormous variations in this area. For example, as I pointed out in chapter 2, some minority groups are still significantly underrepresented among individuals who earn college degrees in the natural sciences, the computer/information sciences, and engineering, fields that are highly important in a technological society. To the extent that these fields provide greater human-capital development opportunities of certain kinds (for example, in math and science) than other fields, one might expect differences in college majors to be associated with human-capital gaps among parents from different racial/ethnic groups, even when these parents have the same educational attainment/degree level.

The second important limitation of typical parent-education-level questions is that they ask for information about the parents' general educational attainment, not their academic achievement. For example, the SAT background questionnaire for 1990–91 requested information on the highest degree earned by test takers' parents but sought no information about the parents' academic performance, for example, their grades in various subject areas or their scores on standardized tests. (It would no doubt be difficult to gather such information at a reasonable cost.) Nevertheless, as I noted in chapter 3, substantial differences in test score and grade patterns among students from different racial/ethnic groups appear at all levels of the educational system. It is reasonable to assume that these differences are associated with human-capital gaps among parents from the several racial/ethnic groups, including parents who have similar attainment and degree levels.

THE PARENT-EDUCATION-LEVEL MISMEASUREMENT PROBLEM: SOME
RELEVANT DATA

One of the most direct ways to answer the question of whether there are large differences in academic skill levels among categories of parents from the several racial/ethnic groups would be to administer standardized tests not simply to children but to their parents as well. Such data are not currently available.

An alternative approach is to examine standardized test score data for national samples of adults who are likely to have pre-school- and school-age children, samples large enough to be analyzed simultaneously on the basis of race/ethnicity and educational attainment level. Somewhat surprisingly, data of this kind have not been regularly collected over the years. Nevertheless, there are a few studies in which standardized tests were administered to representative samples of some relevant segments of the parent-age population. In this section, I examine information from a NAEP project undertaken in the mid-1980s that assessed the literacy skills of a large national sample of young adults and from the National Longitudinal Study of Youth (1980), which administered the Armed Forces Qualification Test to a national sample of young adult men.

The National Assessment of Educational Progress Literacy Study   In 1985, NAEP conducted a study of the literacy skills of the 21–25-year-old population, drawing on a national sample of 3,600 young adults. This study was extremely valuable, in part because of the sophisticated, contemporary view of literacy that informed it. Rather than define literacy in relatively traditional terms (such as being able to read at a particular grade level), the designers of the study viewed it as "a set of complex information-processing skills that go beyond decoding and comprehending textual materials" and that people use "at work, at home, at school, and in their communities." "Simulation tasks" were designed to assess three types of literacy. Prose literacy was defined as "the knowledge and skills needed to understand and use information from texts that include editorials, news stories, poems, and the like"; document literacy was defined as "the knowledge and skills required to locate and use information contained in job applications or payroll forms, bus schedules, maps, tables, indexes, and so forth"; and quantitative literacy was defined as "the knowledge and skills needed to apply arithmetic operations, either alone or sequentially, that are embedded in printed materials, such as in balancing a checkbook, figuring out a tip, completing an order form, or determining the amount of interest from a loan advertisement." The study was also designed to assess general reading skills in the young adult population in ways that were consistent with NAEP reading tests given to 9-, 13-, and 17-year-olds.[2]

The scores on the several sections of the literacy study were presented on 0–500 scales. To facilitate interpretation, traditional NAEP-style anchor points were used to describe various proficiency levels on these scales. In addition, specific tasks included in the assessment were given numerical values so that they could be clearly related to the anchor points. For example, being able to "follow directions to travel from one location to another using a map" was given a score of 300 on the document literacy scale.[3]

Table 7.1 presents average score and anchor-point and proficiency-level data in reading for the young adults (21–25-year-olds) in the 1985 literacy sample

2. Irwin S. Kirsch and Ann Jungeblut, *Literacy: Profiles of America's Young Adults* (Princeton, N.J.: Educational Testing Service, 1986), pp. 2–4, 38–41.
3. Ibid., pp. 7–8, 28.

and for the 17-year-olds in the 1980 reading test sample. (See table 3.1 for a summary of the NAEP reading test anchor points.) The results for the latter group are used as the basis for comparison with the results for the young adults in 1985 because the 1980 group would have reached age 22 by 1985 and therefore would have been included in the target population for the literacy study. The 21–25-year-olds were representative of the entire national population in that age bracket in 1985, while the 17-year-olds were representative only of those who were in school in 1980.

Table 7.1

Average NAEP Reading Scores and Reading Anchor Point Percentages for Young Adults in 1985 and In-School 17-Year-Olds in 1980

| Group | Average Score | *Percent at or above Proficiency Level* | | | | |
		150	200	250	300	350
White:						
Young Adults	314	100	98	89	61	25
17-year-olds	293	100	99	87	43	6
Black:						
Young Adults	263	99	90	61	25	4
17-year-olds	243	99	86	44	7	0
Hispanic						
Young Adults	287	100	96	76	41	10
17-year-olds	261	100	93	62	17	1

Sources: Irwin S. Kirsch and Ann Jungeblut, *Literacy: Profiles of America's Young Adults* (Princeton, N.J.: Educational Testing Service, 1986), p. 39; Richard L. Venezky, Carl F. Kaestle, and Andrew M. Sum, *The Subtle Danger: Reflections on the Literacy Abilities of America's Young Adults* (Princeton, N.J.: Educational Testing Service, 1987), p. 31; Ina V. S. Mullis, John A. Dossey, Mary A. Foertsch, Lee R. Jones, and Claudia A. Gentile, *Trends in Academic Progress: Achievement of U.S. Students in Science, 1969–1970 to 1990; Mathematics 1973–1990; Reading, 1971–1990; and Writing, 1984–1990* (Washington, D.C.: Educational Testing Service/U.S. Department of Education, U.S. Government Printing Office, 1991), pp. 315, 326–30.

For all three racial/ethnic groups the average scores for the young adults were significantly higher than the scores for the 17-year-olds. Moreover, the differences between the two age cohorts in average scores for the three racial/ethnic groups were roughly similar in size: 21 points for whites, 20 for blacks, and 26 for Hispanics. This pattern of higher scores for the young adults than for the 17-year-olds is not surprising because many young people from each group go on to some form of postsecondary education after high school. Moreover, some of those who drop out of high school at some point return to high school, and many others complete a Graduation Equivalency Diploma (GED) program.[4]

4. Ibid., pp. 47–49. About 15 percent of all of the young adults sampled in the literacy study reported that they had dropped out of school before receiving their high school diploma. About 13

In spite of these general similarities, the young white adults in 1985 clearly had substantial reading skill advantages over their African American and Latino counterparts. The white-black gap in average scores was 51 points, while the white-Hispanic gap was 27 points. Essentially, the young white adults were reading somewhat above the Adept (300) level ("can find, summarize, and explain relatively complicated information"), the Latinos were reading somewhat below the 300 level, and the African Americans were reading somewhat above the Intermediate (250) level ("can search for specific information, interrelate ideas, and make generalizations").

The anchor-point percentages in table 7.1 indicate that the primary difference in scoring patterns between the young adults and the 17-year-olds within each racial/ethnic group concerned the proportions of individuals with medium- to high-level reading skills. All of the young adults and 17-year-olds from each of the groups were able to read at the Rudimentary (150) level ("can carry out simple, discrete reading tasks"), and almost all were able to read at the Basic (200) level ("can comprehend specific or sequentially related information"). However, in most cases there were much larger percentages of young adults who could read at the Intermediate (250) level, the Adept (300) level, and the Advanced (350) level ("can synthesize and learn from specialized reading materials").

It was also at the 250, 300, and 350 anchor points that young white adults had the largest reading skill advantages over their African American and Latino counterparts. Importantly, 25 percent of the whites reached the Advanced (350) level, while only 4 percent of the African Americans and 10 percent of the Latinos did so. These data suggest that the whites in this group of young adults in 1985 had much more reading-based human capital available to invest in children (when they become parents) than did their black and Hispanic peers. This is a matter of current significance because the young adults sampled by NAEP for the 1985 literacy study are now in their late twenties and early thirties. Many are now parents of children currently enrolled in school.

So far, I have used data from the NAEP literacy study to discuss the broad patterns of reading skills among the young adults sampled in 1985. Now I want to review some data from this study that show how literacy skills varied among segments of the three racial/ethnic groups in which the individuals had similar educational attainment levels.

In the prose section, the young adults in the sample were given exercises that tested their ability to understand and to use information in various kinds of textual material. Essentially, these exercises entailed three types of reading tasks: (1) locating information in a text; (2) producing responses to or interpretations of

---

percent of the whites, 23 percent of the African Americans, and 24 percent of the Latinos reported dropping out. At the same time, about half of all the dropouts reported studying for a GED, but only two in five of these reported that they had received a GED. African American dropouts had a somewhat higher enrollment rate in GED programs than did white and Latino dropouts. However, blacks had much lower GED completion rates than either whites or Hispanics. The enrollment rates were 56 percent for African Americans, 46 percent for whites, and 43 percent for Latinos. The GED success rates were 23 percent for blacks, 44 percent for whites, and 45 percent for Hispanics.

information in a text; and (3) developing a theme or organizing principle from information in a text.[5]

There were substantial differences in average scores on the prose section produced by whites, blacks, and Hispanics with similar educational attainment levels. The largest differences were between blacks and whites. For example, the average prose score for young white adults with a high school degree was 48 points higher than that of their African American counterparts (301 vs. 253). Similarly, the average prose score gap between young white and black adults with a bachelor's degree was 36 points (345 vs. 309). The gap was 54 points between whites and blacks with an eighth-grade education or less (251 vs. 197).[6] The average prose score of white high school graduates was only 8 points lower than the average score of African Americans with a four-year college degree.

The gaps between whites and Latinos were small to moderate in some cases. For instance, among high school graduates, the white-Hispanic gap was only 15 points (301 vs. 286), and among those with a bachelor's degree, it was only 4 points (345 vs. 341). The gaps were considerably larger between whites and Latinos with little formal education; and between those with an eighth-grade education or less it was 38 points (251 vs. 213). Among young adults with a four-year college degree, whites had an average prose literacy score that ranked at about the 83d percentile, Latinos at about the 80th percentile, and African Americans at about the 56th percentile. Among those with a high school degree (but no postsecondary education), whites' average literacy score ranked at about the 49th percentile, Hispanics at about the 37th percentile, and blacks at about the 18th percentile.[7]

The results for the three racial/ethnic groups on the prose literacy-scale were generally similar to those that they achieved on the document and quantitative scales. Of special concern are the uniformly low average scores and percentile rankings of Africans Americans at all education levels. For example, on the document and quantitative scales, blacks with a four-year college degree scored at the 50th and 51st percentiles, respectively; and blacks with a high school degree scored at the 20th percentile on both of these scales.[8]

The intergenerational significance of these data looms large when one considers that many 21–25-year-olds in 1985 are currently parents of school-age children. Among other things, the data suggest that the average black college graduates in this cohort can make home-based, literacy-skill-type human-capital investments in their children that are about the same as those that can be made by the average white high school graduates in their children. And because so many Latino adults do not have even a high school diploma, these data also suggest that a very large portion of the Hispanic parents in this age group have

5. Ibid., pp. 8–9.
6. Richard L. Venezky, Carl F. Kaestle, and Andrew M. Sum, *The Subtle Danger: Reflections on the Literacy Abilities of America's Young Adults* (Princeton, N.J.: Educational Testing Services, 1987), p. 32
7. Ibid., pp. 32, 35.
8. Ibid., pp. 31, 35.

extremely low levels of literacy skills (in English or Spanish) to draw upon in furthering the educational development of their children.

The differences in literacy-skill scores can be given more concrete meaning by summarizing some of the tasks associated with specific skill levels. For example, on the prose-skill scale, those with 200-level skills were able to write a brief description of a job they would like to have or to find a single fact in a newspaper article. Those with 275-level skills could draft a letter explaining an error in a bill or use the instructions in an appliance warranty to categorize what was wrong with the product. Those with 325-level skills could locate information in a long newspaper article or summarize the primary argument of a lengthy news column. And those with 375-level skills could explain orally the primary differences between two employee fringe benefits or develop an unfamiliar theme from a short poem.[9]

The National Longitudinal Survey of Youth (1980)   How generalizable are the NAEP literacy findings for describing variations in the human-capital resources of young white, black, and Hispanic adults with similar educational attainment levels? Owing to a lack of large-scale data sets of this kind, it is not possible to reach a firm conclusion. Nevertheless, some confirmation that large academic-skill gaps continue to exist between young white and black adults with similar amounts of formal schooling is provided by data from the National Longitudinal Survey of Youth (NLSY). In this study, the Armed Forces Qualification Test (AFQT) was given to a nationally representative sample of young adult males. The AFQT is a verbal and mathematics achievement test used to assess the educational preparation of individuals for military service.

June O'Neill examined AFQT score data, broken down by educational attainment level, for the 19–21-year-old blacks and whites included in the NLSY. She found within-social-class differences between blacks and whites that parallel those found in the NAEP literacy test discussed above. For example, 19–21-year-old whites with three to four years of college scored at the 80th percentile on the AFQT, while their black counterparts scored at the 50th percentile. Whites in the NLSY study who had three to four years of high school scored at the 47th percentile and blacks at the 19th percentile.[10]

ORIGINS OF BETWEEN- AND WITHIN-SOCIAL-CLASS HUMAN CAPITAL GAPS

Clearly, the data suggest not only that there are still enormous variations in human capital among parents of pre-school- and school-age children from the different racial/ethnic groups, but that these variations exist on both a between-social-class and a within-social-class basis (using educational attainment level as the marker for social class). What are the origins of these gaps?

Much of the answer seems to lie in variations in access to formal education

9. Kirsch and Jungeblut, *Literacy: Profiles of America's Young Adults*, pp. 8–18.
10. June O'Neill, "The Role of Human Capital in Earnings Differences between Black and White Men," *Journal of Economic Perspectives* 4 (Fall 1990): 33.

over a long period of time. In chapter 2, I noted that early in this century there were very large educational attainment gaps at all levels of formal schooling between young adults in the majority and minority populations, but that some of these gaps (especially at the elementary and secondary school levels) had been virtually closed by the end of the 1980s. In chapter 4, I summarized the Coleman Report's finding in the mid-1960s that the amounts of resources invested in schools attended by children from different racial/ethnic groups did not differ greatly.[11] Here, I consider variations in the quantity and quality of schooling from a third perspective: the history of the resources available to schools attended by minority and majority children. This is important because the convergence of school resources documented by the Coleman Report was a recent phenomenon; the evidence is that before the 1950s there were substantial differences in the resources invested in schools serving primarily white and minority children.[12]

Because they have been the largest minority group for most of our history, more trend data are available for blacks than for the other racial/ethnic minorities regarding the resources invested in the schools they attended. My discussion will therefore focus on a comparison of the school resources available to black and white students over time. These comparisons are relatively easy to make because the vast majority of African Americans lived in the South until the post–World War II period (90 percent in 1910, 77 percent in 1940),[13] and virtually all African Americans in the South were required to attend racially segregated schools until recent decades.

In the first several decades of the twentieth century, the southern states' annual educational expenditures per pupil were several times larger for white children than for African American children.[14] Indeed, as recently as 1940, there was a three-to-one expenditure ratio in favor of white students, although there was considerable variation among the southern states. For example, in the 1939–40 school year, Mississippi spent over seven times as much on the education of white pupils as on blacks, while North Carolina spent less than twice as much on white students.[15]

These large differences in per-pupil expenditures on black and white children translated into substantial differences in key school characteristics during this period. For instance, the first half of this century saw extraordinary expansion in the number of days students spent in school each year. Nevertheless, until midcentury whites enjoyed much longer school years than African Americans. The average annual number of days attended by pupils enrolled in all

11. Current variations in school resources are examined in chapter 11.
12. Meyer Weinberg, *A Chance to Learn: The History of Race and Education in the United States* (New York: Cambridge University Press, 1977), p. 5.
13. Gerald David Jaynes and Robin M. Williams, Jr., eds., *A Common Destiny: Blacks and American Society* (Washington, D.C.: National Academy Press, 1989), p. 60; Gunnar Myrdal, *An American Dilemma: The Negro Problem and Modern Democracy*, Twentieth Anniversary Edition (New York: Harper and Row, 1962), p. 183.
14. Weinberg, *A Chance to Learn*, p. 57.
15. Jaynes and Williams, *A Common Destiny*, pp. 58–59.

schools was 121 days in the 1919–20 academic year; yet the comparable figure for black schools was only 80—a 41-day gap. The figure for all schools had grown to 152 days by the 1939–40 school year, yet the average attendance in the black schools was only 126 days per year—26 days less than the all-school average and only modestly higher than the per-pupil average for all schools a generation earlier. However, by the 1953–54 school year—the eve of the Supreme Court's landmark school desegregation decision—the gap between all schools and black schools had been reduced to only 8 days (159 vs. 151).[16]

A similar pattern existed with regard to the ratio of pupils per classroom teacher. In the 1919–20 school year, the ratio for all schools was about 32 children per teacher, while it was 56 per teacher in the black schools. By the 1953–54 school year, however, the 24-students-per-teacher difference had been reduced to about 5: the ratio for all schools was about 28 students per teacher, while it was about 33 in the black schools.[17]

These data recognize the existence of dramatic differences in educational opportunity between students who attended black schools and those who attended mostly white schools during the first half of the twentieth century. For instance, we can see that on average, students attending all-black schools between 1910 and 1920 spent many fewer days in school, with much less opportunity for contact with teachers, than did their white counterparts, even when they attended school for the same number of years. As a result, even the few African Americans who graduated from all-black high schools at the end of that period accumulated much less human capital than white high school graduates. This means that, when they became parents, that generation of African Americans almost certainly had much less human capital to invest in their children. Thus, it can be inferred that these human-resources gaps between blacks and whites would have continued into the next generation because of the persistence of large differences in the school resources available to black and white children in the 1920s and 1930s and the large differences in the amount of human capital available to them from their parents.

The fact that some of the major gaps in school resources had been largely eliminated by the 1950s and 1960s no doubt improved the relative educational prospects for the children of the African Americans who went to underresourced, racially segregated schools in the 1930s and much of the 1940s. But the schools were hardly designed to make up within a single generation the very substantial and cumulative differences in human capital between blacks and whites that were to a considerable degree a product of differences in educational opportunity in the first half of the twentieth century (and in the preceding centuries as well). At best the schools were much closer to being able to provide the educational opportunities for African Americans necessary to eliminate the academic achievement gap over a period of several more generations. That is to say, through the intergenerational educational advancement process, the varia-

16. James P. Smith and Finis R. Welch, *Closing the Gap: Forty Years of Economic Progress for Blacks* (Santa Monica, Cal.: Rand Corporation, 1986), p. 38.
17. *Brown vs. the Board of Education of Topeka, Kansas,* 347 U.S. 483 (1954).

tions in human-capital resources between black and white parents could be expected to diminish gradually, assuming that the school resources available to white and black children—as well as the quality of other dimensions of the educational opportunity structure, for example, access to both the high- and low-skill segments of the labor market—continued to converge.

Although the data reviewed here tell a powerful story about intergenerational variations in the quantity of school resources available to African American and white children, they do not address resource quality questions, such as whether there were differences in the curricula available to the two groups of children or in the academic skill levels of their teachers. Available evidence, however, indicates that there were great differences in resource quality in these areas as well as others, such as the quality of school libraries and science laboratories.[18] Thus the net intergenerational variations in school resources available to black and white children were very large whether viewed from a quality or a quantity perspective.

A considerable amount of information shows school-resource disparities throughout much of the twentieth century (and earlier) between whites and Latinos and between whites and Native Americans. Mexican Americans, for example, faced many of the problems that have confronted blacks. Across the Southwest, Mexican American children were frequently required to attend segregated schools that were almost always much less well funded than those of their white counterparts. The Mexican American schools often operated on a much shorter school year and with much higher teacher-pupil ratios than the white schools. Education was limited primarily to the elementary and junior high levels; few Mexican American students had the opportunity to attend high school in the first half of this century. Similarly for Native Americans and Puerto Ricans, the past was one of an extreme lack of educational opportunity, both in absolute terms and relative to white children.[19]

Intergenerational Variations in School Resources and Other Dimensions of the Educational Opportunity Structure   My discussion thus far has emphasized the intergenerational impact of variations in the school resources available to racial/ethnic groups in the twentieth century. It has not considered differences in other dimensions of the educational opportunity structure experienced by successive generations of these racial/ethnic groups and the consequences of these differences for the accumulation of human capital. But it is important to recognize that changes in the school segment of the educational opportunity structure have been paralleled by changes in other segments and that these changes have no doubt interacted in ways that have significantly influenced the human-capital accumulation patterns of the several racial/ethnic groups. For example, the differences in school resources available to blacks and whites in the first half of the twentieth century were largely a function of the very

18. See James D. Anderson, *The Education of Blacks in the South, 1860–1935* (Chapel Hill: University of North Carolina Press, 1988), pp. 110–237.
19. Weinberg, *A Chance to Learn*, pp. 140–259.

limited legal rights accorded to African Americans by the racially prejudiced white majority (see chapters 8 and 9). Whites controlled government expenditures on public schools so that fewer school resources were invested in the education of black children than of white children.[20] The civil rights movement eventually produced dramatic improvements in the legal sphere for blacks and other racial/ethnic minorities, and these improvements have contributed to a reduction in (but not an elimination of) school resource disparities in ways that support more robust intergenerational advancement of minorities.

The intergenerational accumulation of human capital by some minority groups has also been affected by the supply of adequately paying low-skill jobs. The growing shortage of such jobs has contributed to the extremely high rates of unemployment and poverty among blacks and Hispanics in many urban areas. Communities with high concentrations of economically disadvantaged minorities (and low concentrations of middle-class residents, majority or minority) have fewer resources available locally to invest in their schools. Yet they experience greater demands on those resources that are available.

SUMMARY AND CONCLUSIONS

This chapter has explored some of the reasons for the apparently limited utility of standard social class categories for summarizing variations in the education-relevant resources available to children from different racial/ethnic groups. The primary motivation for examining this question is the finding (chapter 6) that standardized test data consistently show large within-social-class variations among students from the several racial/ethnic groups.

In order to simplify the analysis, I have focused on one specific social class category, parent education level, as used to measure the variations in one particular education-relevant resource, human capital. An examination of the primary method of measuring parent education level in the standardized testing process reveals that the information gathered is generally concerned with the parents' educational attainment (years of school attended or degrees earned) rather than with their academic achievement (standardized test scores). This is a serious shortcoming when it comes to measuring human capital.

I then examined some NAEP literacy and AFQT test data on the young adult population broken down simultaneously on the basis of race/ethnicity and educational attainment levels. These data support the view that there are currently very consequential differences in the amounts of human capital possessed by young white adults and their African American and Latino counterparts and that these variations exist at most educational attainment levels.

Concerning the origins of these gaps, a review of data on the variations in school resources invested in several successive generations of white and African American children supported the conclusion that the current variations in

20. Anderson, *The Education of Blacks in the South, 1860–1935,* pp. 148–237.

human capital are largely due to very different opportunities over time for whites and African Americans to accumulate school (human capital) resources in their families.

The 1985 NAEP literacy study data and AFQT data shed little direct light on how large within-social-class human-capital gaps may be in the next generation of parents. However, the NAEP reading and math score data for 9- and 13-year-olds presented in chapter 6 indicate that the within-parent-education-level gaps between white and black students and between white and Hispanic students narrowed somewhat in the 1971–90 period. This suggests that when they become adults, the 9- and 13-year-olds sampled in the most recent NAEP reading and math tests will have smaller within-parent-education-level human-capital gaps than their predecessors. However, those same data as well as data from other sources also suggest that, in absolute terms, some of these gaps will still be quite large in the next generation of parents.

The data on trends in the quantity of resources invested in schools attended primarily by African Americans and by whites introduced the powerful role that racial/ethnic prejudice and discrimination have played historically in shaping the differences in educational attainment and academic achievement among racial/ethnic groups. In the next two chapters I want to consider the role currently played by racial/ethnic discrimination and prejudice in perpetuating the tendency for black, Hispanic, and Native American students, regardless of socioeconomic level, to do less well academically than whites. In chapter 8, I review the origins, evolution, and current dimensions of prejudiced attitudes and beliefs. In chapter 9, I examine some of the ways in which these beliefs seem to be influencing the academic achievement patterns of minorities in contemporary America.

CHAPTER EIGHT

The Origins, Evolution,

and

Contemporary Dimensions

of Racial/Ethnic Prejudice

The long-standing belief that some racial/ethnic groups are not as intelligent as whites is grounded in theories that these groups have less innate intellectual potential than whites or are unable for cultural reasons to develop their capacities as fully as whites. These notions can be stressful to discuss, but they must be clearly understood if one is to devise more effective strategies for promoting the educational advancement of minorities.

In this chapter I first review the origins and evolution of racial/ethnic prejudice in the United States. Next, I examine the extent to which some white Americans continue to believe in the innate and cultural inferiority of blacks, relying on the results of research conducted by social psychologists on the formation of group stereotypes and on the findings of opinion research on racial/ethnic groups' beliefs about one another. I then review survey research on how the intellectual capacities of racial/ethnic groups are viewed by experts on the nature of intelligence and the use of standardized tests, including those commonly called intelligence or IQ tests and more recent research on the roles played by heredity and environment in producing racial/ethnic differences in scores on IQ tests. Finally, I offer some thoughts on why many whites apparently continue to believe in the intellectual or cultural inferiority of minorities, in spite of empirical evidence to the contrary.

A HISTORICAL PERSPECTIVE

Throughout most of its history, the United States has been a nation in which nonwhite minorities were the victims of a government-sanctioned and government-enforced system of racial stratification that relegated them to subordinate positions relative to the white majority. This subordination pervaded the political, economic, and social realms and kept most nonwhites permanently on the bottom rungs of society, regardless of their talents and abilities.[1] Institutional-

---

1. Both class and caste are concerned with the grouping of individuals in society on a hierarchical basis. A key distinction between the concepts is that there is usually at least some potential for upward (and downward) mobility of individuals between classes, but essentially none between castes. For a discussion of the American caste system as it applied to blacks for much of U.S. history

ized racism in American life was most obvious with regard to blacks, but it also existed for Hispanics, Native Americans, and Asians, although not necessarily in the same form or always to the same extent.[2]

The institution of black slavery in America was established in colonial law and subsequently confirmed by the Constitution. Only a tenth of the black population was free at the time of the first decennial census in 1790, and this segment of African Americans faced severely restricted opportunities in both the North and the South.[3] With the Emancipation Proclamation in 1863 and the victory of the North in the Civil War in 1865, blacks soon gained what appeared to be a relatively full set of constitutional rights.[4] There was reason to hope that America's race-based caste system was ending. But within a few decades, the passage of Jim Crow laws throughout the South—establishing separate public facilities for blacks and whites and effectively denying blacks the right to vote—created a rigidly segregated world that excluded blacks from the political, economic, and social mainstream. Since the vast majority of blacks lived in the South until after World War II, these laws ensured the continuation of America's racial caste system. Moreover, although legal and other restrictions on the rights and opportunities of blacks tended to be more limited elsewhere in the country, they were still strong enough to keep African Americans in a subordinate position to whites in those regions as well.[5]

It was not until the civil rights movement of the 1950s and 1960s that the legal basis for the systematic segregation and subordination of blacks was dismantled through a series of legislative and judicial actions. Thus, many black adults living today have clear memories of a time when African Americans were the victims of a government-enforced racial caste system.

The victories of the civil rights movement also marked the end of many legal barriers to broader participation in society that had been experienced by other minority groups. For example, almost immediately after the end of the Mexican American War in 1848, the white majority began to take steps to restrict political, social, and economic opportunities for Mexican Americans.[6]

see Gunnar Myrdal, *An American Dilemma: The Negro Problem and Modern Democracy*, (New York: Harper and Row, 1962), pp. 667–88.

2. See Michael Omi and Howard Winant, *Racial Formation in the United States from the 1960s to the 1980s* (New York and London: Routledge & Kegan Paul, 1986), pp. 70–86.

3. See Reynolds Farley and Walter R. Allen, *The Color Line and the Quality of Life in America* (New York: Russell Sage Foundation, 1987), p. 8.

4. The Thirteenth Amendment to the Constitution, ratified in 1865, outlawed slavery. The Fourteenth Amendment, ratified in 1868, provided citizenship to all persons born or naturalized in the United States. It also contained the controversial clause that no state could "deny to any person within its jurisdiction the equal protection of the laws." The Fifteenth Amendment, ratified in 1870, provided that citizens could not be denied the right to vote by the federal or state governments "on account of race, color, or previous conditions of servitude."

5. George M. Fredrickson, *The Arrogance of Race: Historical Perspectives on Slavery, Racism, and Social Inequality* (Middletown, Conn.: Wesleyan University Press, 1988), pp. 254–69.

6. Thomas F. Pettigrew, George M. Fredrickson, Dale T. Knobel, Nathan Glazer, and Reed Ueda, *Prejudice* (Cambridge: The Belknap Press of Harvard University Press, 1982), pp. 57–60. For a strong attack on the treatment of Mexican Americans by Anglos during much of the nation's history, see Rodolfo Acuna, *Occupied America: A History of Chicanos*, 3d ed. (New York: Harper & Row, 1988).

Native Americans experienced direct conflict with whites from virtually the beginning of European settlement. Large-scale loss of life and territory was an immediate consequence of European colonization and continued after the United States became an independent nation. Throughout the nineteenth century, the U.S. Army was used to remove Indian tribes from most of their historic lands as white settlers pushed west. In the twentieth century, many American Indians have lived on or near reservations that were established as a result of treaties between the federal government and many of the tribes. For most of this century, the federal government (through the Bureau of Indian Affairs) has exercised a great deal of control over the lives of Native Americans—in some ways, much more than it has been able to exercise over whites within the framework of the nation's system of federal, state, and local government.[7]

Given the recency of the legal reforms undertaken in response to the civil rights movement, it would be surprising if there were not dimensions of this racist past that continue to plague American life. These dimensions are no longer centered primarily in institutional or legal arrangements designed to perpetuate castelike hierarchies. Rather, they are heavily grounded in the negative attitudes and beliefs that racial/ethnic groups have about one another. These views influence the nature of intergroup contact and the way group members perceive and respond to one another's needs. Consequently, they can have profound impact in both the public and private spheres.

Prejudicial Attitudes and Beliefs   The legal subordination of blacks and other minorities reflected the view of most whites that they were superior to minorities. Many believed that white (European-derived) culture was much more advanced than the cultures of blacks, Native Americans, many Hispanics, and Asians. And many held the view that whites were innately superior to blacks. From the perspective of modern social science, these views can be regarded as examples of racial/ethnic prejudice—"irrationally based negative attitudes against certain ethnic groups and their members."[8]

Both theories of white supremacy included an educational and intellectual dimension. Native American cultures, for example, were regarded in the main as producing children who were neither as well prepared to learn in school nor as interested in formal education as white children were.[9] Black children were typically regarded as not having as much innate physical capacity to learn as whites. These cultural and genetic notions of inferiority were applied, in varying degrees, to most minority groups. However, the genetic theory was most commonly and persistently applied to blacks.[10]

7. On the history of white discrimination against Native Americans and of the power exercised by the federal government over the lives of the Indians, see Pettigrew et al., *Prejudice*, pp. 33–40; Angie Debo, *A History of the Indians of the United States* (Norman: University of Oklahoma Press, 1970).

8. Pettigrew et al., *Prejudice*, p. 2.

9. Meyer Weinberg, *A Chance to Learn: A History of Race and Education in the United States* (New York: Cambridge University Press, 1977), pp. 182–84, 189–91, 202–07, 227–29.

10. Pettigrew et al., *Prejudice*, pp. 86–87.

These two theories not only were used to help justify laws that denied minorities a full set of rights but led to two other kinds of action by whites that have been extremely damaging to the educational advancement of minorities. First, they provided an important rationale for the decision not to invest as much in the education of minority children as in white children. During the period of slavery, southern states passed laws that actually made it illegal for slaves to be educated: in other words, they passed *compulsory ignorance laws*.[11] Even free blacks were typically denied access to public schools in both the North and the South in the period when slavery was legal.[12] With the end of slavery, it became necessary for government to provide public education for African American children. But, as I noted in chapter 7, extremely large variations in black/white school investment patterns existed until the 1950s. (And, as we shall see in chapter 11, some important resource gaps persist in many places.)

Second, both the cultural and innate inferiority theories were used by whites to support decisions that emphasized vocational education for minority groups at the expense of providing them with a liberal education, especially at the college level. Liberal education was viewed by many whites as the province of people who, by virtue of native biological endowment and/or cultural experience and predisposition, were able to be educated for leadership and other positions in society that required well-developed intellectual capacities. Because blacks, Hispanics, and Native Americans were regarded as not possessing these attributes, whites concluded that it was better to teach them a trade, so that they could lead productive lives and meet the responsibilities of the (lower) stations of society for which they appeared to be suited.[13]

Of the two theories of white superiority, the more damaging has probably been the notion that some nonwhites are innately inferior intellectually. Culture can be changed over time, but not one's genetic inheritance.[14] Thus, a genetic theory of group inferiority could potentially provide a more powerful basis for legally mandated or sanctioned racial discrimination than a theory based on a belief in cultural inferiority. Since the genetic theory has been applied most consistently and extensively to blacks, there is reason to believe that they have suffered more educationally from this aspect of white racism than any other minority group. This does not mean, however, that the notion of cultural inferiority has not done immense damage to African Americans as well as to other minorities; and it does not

11. Meyer Weinberg believes that the first use of this term with regard to American blacks was by James Simpson of the Society of Friends in England in 1865. Subsequently, W. E. B. Du Bois also used it, evidently independently of Simpson. See Weinberg, *A Chance to Learn*, pp. 11–15, 368.

12. Ibid., pp. 15–26.

13. James D. Anderson, *The Education of Blacks in the South, 1860–1935* (Chapel Hill: University of North Carolina Press, 1988), pp. 33–109; Weinberg, *A Chance to Learn*, pp. 199, 269; Estelle Fuchs and Robert J. Havighurst, *To Live on This Earth: American Indian Education* (Garden City, N.Y.: Doubleday, 1972), pp. 8–9; and Ricardo Romo, *East Los Angeles: History of a Barrio* (Austin: University of Texas Press, 1983), pp. 139–41.

14. Jeff Howard and Ray Hammond, "Rumors of Inferiority," *New Republic*, 9 September 1985, p. 19.

mean that other groups have not suffered from being branded as innately less intelligent by some whites.[15]

Historical Origins of the Belief in Racial Differences in Intellectual Capacities
Evidence of a belief in the inferiority of minorities can be found from the colonial period to the present. In fact, before the English established colonies in North America, at the beginning of the seventeenth century, they already held negative views of (black) Africans and their cultures. As the historian George M. Fredrickson has written, "As a result of early contacts with Africa, Englishmen tended to associate blackness with savagery, heathenism, and general failure to conform to European standards of civilization and propriety. Contributing to this predisposition to look upon Negroes with disfavor were the conscious and unconscious connotations of the color black. The association of black with evil was of course deeply rooted in Western and Christian mythology."[16] This view was based on very limited contact with black Africans before the seventeenth century. Indeed, blacks residing in England (as slaves or free persons) were a rarity until that time.[17]

In spite of these early negative views, the English and other Europeans had not yet developed a racist doctrine that explicitly asserted the inborn inferiority of blacks. On the basis of a review of the historical record, Fredrickson has concluded that this doctrine developed gradually, over a long period of time. Consequently, the notion that blacks were innately inferior was not widely held until the early nineteenth century.[18]

A major reason for this delay, Fredrickson believes, is that a theory of inherent black inferiority was simply not needed until the abolitionist movement had begun in earnest. Since a rationale for the American republic was that "all men are created equal," the southern slave system required a powerful justification to defend the "peculiar institution." The theory that blacks were innately inferior intellectually provided one. Fredrickson has noted that an added reason for the emergence of such a theory at that point was the growing scientific conception of man as a biological creature with a variety of physical characteristics. And, of course, because whites already had a long-standing belief in the cultural inferiority of blacks, it was only a short step to conclude that blacks were innately

15. For a discussion of these views with regard to some Latino groups, see the *Hispanic Journal of Behavioral Sciences* 10 (September 1988).

16. Fredrickson, *The Arrogance of Race*, p. 191. In addition to the many negative connotations of *blackness* in Western history and culture, there are also numerous positive connotations of *whiteness*. For example, blackness is associated with death and evil, whiteness with peace (the white dove of peace) and with messengers from God (white-garbed angels). These connotations frequently surface in the regular use of the English language. Thus, Ali Mazrui is concerned about the problems they pose for the growing number of black speakers of English in Africa and elsewhere in the world. See Mazrui, "The Afro-Saxons," in *Ethnicity in an International Context*, Abdul Said and Luiz R. Simmons, eds. (New Brunswick, N.J.: Transaction Books, 1976), pp. 208–12.

17. William D. Phillips, Jr., *Slavery from Roman Times to the Early Transatlantic Trade* (Minneapolis, MN: University of Minnesota Press, 1985), p. 155.

18. Fredrickson, *The Arrogance of Race*, pp. 201–02.

intellectually inferior as well.[19] Interestingly, some African American leaders in the nineteenth century, for example, Alexander Crummell, apparently reached a conclusion in agreement with Fredrickson's interpretation. Crummell believed that whites' denial that blacks were intelligent "was an afterthought."[20]

A similar line of analysis may help explain why whites generally did not come to embrace a theory of the innate intellectual inferiority of Native Americans. From the perspective of whites, a belief in the cultural inferiority of American Indians was sufficient to seize their lands and remove them to distant sites. Once the Native Americans were "out of view" there was no need for further explanations.[21]

The larger historical record of slavery in Europe, the Middle East, and Africa is also consistent with the belief that the English and other Europeans who came to the American colonies did not initially believe in the innate inferiority of blacks. From at least the time of the Romans, slavery had been a common aspect of life. Conquered (alien) people were routinely enslaved. After Roman times, slavery in Europe was slowly replaced by serfdom. But vestiges of slavery remained, especially in Spain and Italy. A major reason for this was the strong linkages these countries had (given their location on the Mediterranean) with the Islamic world. By the beginning of the colonial period, slavery had been practiced by Moslems for hundreds of years (and continued to be practiced until well into the nineteenth century). The Moslems' major source of slaves was sub-Saharan Africa.[22]

Given this historical precedent, Europeans did not need a rationale for the enslavement of blacks in the Americas. They simply required a strong economic incentive to use large amounts of slave labor, a supply of alien peoples who could profitably be enslaved, and the military power and transportation system necessary to tap this supply effectively. With the European "discovery" of the Americas, all these factors fell into place. The labor requirements of the sugar plantations that were quickly established in the Americas provided the economic need. Sub-Saharan Africans had already been identified as a source of alien people "available" for enslavement. And the Europeans also possessed the military power in the form of guns and the transportation system in the form of ships that could reliably cross the Atlantic to make the transatlantic slave trade a reality.[23]

19. Ibid., pp. 201–04.

20. Alexander Crummell, *The Attitude of the American Mind toward the negro Intellect*, The American Negro Academy Occasional Papers, No. 3 (Washington, D.C.: Academy Press, 1898), p. 12.

21. Pettigrew et al., *Prejudice*, pp. 35–38.

22. Phillips, *Slavery from Roman Times to the Early Transatlantic Trade*, pp. 66–87. Of course, slavery has been practiced in varying forms and degrees by societies all over the world throughout history. See Orlando Patterson, *Slavery and Social Death: A Comparative Study* (Cambridge: Harvard University Press, 1982).

23. Ibid., pp. 171–217. Had there been an indigenous labor supply available in the Americas large enough to meet demand, it seems unlikely that the transatlantic slave system would have developed. However, owing in no small measure to the extraordinarily high death rates of Native Americans as a result of exposure to Old World diseases, European attempts to enslave Indians on a large scale were not successful. See William H. McNeill, *The Rise of the West: A History of the Human Community, with a Retrospective Essay* (1963; repr. Chicago: University of Chicago Press, 1991), pp. 600–01.

One of the most vital sources of information about the belief by whites in the innate or cultural inferiority of racial/ethnic minorities is the work of social psychologists on the stereotypes individuals hold of different racial and ethnic groups. For purposes of this analysis, *stereotype* will be defined as "The set of traits that is used to explain and predict the behavior of members of a socially defined group."[24] Under this definition, stereotypes may include positive, negative, and neutral attributes and characteristics, some of which may be largely accurate and some completely inaccurate.

A number of studies and analyses of stereotypes that whites and blacks have held of each other have been conducted since the mid-1930s. On the basis of their review of these studies, Walter Stephan and David Rosenfield found that blacks listed only two traits of whites that most people would regard as generally positive—intelligent and industrious. However, they had a long list of negative traits, including deceitful, sly, treacherous, dirty, lazy, cruel, selfish, nervous, and conceited.[25] Given the history of racially discriminatory behavior of whites, it is understandable that African Americans might ascribe these negative traits to them.

In whites' perceptions of blacks, the pattern is repeated. Stephan and Rosenfield found that whites listed only a few attributes of blacks that most would regard as positive—musical, peace-loving, and very religious. In contrast, the list of negative attributes is much longer—lazy, superstitious, ignorant, loud, materialistic, stupid, dirty, and militant. (Several of the traits on the whites' list of black attributes, poor, happy-go-lucky, and proud, for example, can be viewed as positive or negative, depending on the perspective.)[26] What is particularly important about the negative attributes that whites ascribe to blacks is that several are consistent with both the innate and cultural theories of black inferiority. Stupidity can be regarded as an innate trait, while laziness, superstitiousness, ignorance, loudness, and dirtiness can be thought of as culturally derived.

Blacks and whites alike have generally positive images of themselves. For example, blacks view themselves as being intelligent and sportsmanlike, while whites see themselves as intelligent and progressive. (However, each group does acknowledge the existence of a negative attribute or two in themselves: for example, African Americans evidently think that many of their group are lazy, and whites apparently think that many of their group are materialistic.)[27]

Given the heavy weighting toward negative qualities associated with the stereotypes whites and blacks have had of one another, an important question is whether these and other racial/ethnic stereotypes are changing. Since my main

24. Walter G. Stephan and David Rosenfield, "Racial and Ethnic Stereotypes," in *The Eye of the Beholder: Contemporary Issues in Stereotyping*, Arthur G. Miller, ed. (New York: Praeger, 1982), p. 92.
25. Ibid., p. 100.
26. Ibid.
27. Ibid.

interest is in assessing the current impact of white racism on the academic performance and educational prospects of minorities, I focus the examination primarily on evidence of possible changes in the stereotypes that whites have of blacks and other minorities.

Trend Data on Whites' Views   Survey researchers have been exploring the attitudes and beliefs whites hold about racial/ethnic issues, especially those concerning blacks, for over fifty years. The first survey of a national sample of Americans to provide information on this question was undertaken by the Roper organization in 1939 for *Fortune* magazine. More than five thousand Americans nationally were asked, "Do you think Negroes now generally have higher intelligence than white people, lower, or about the same?" About 71 percent of those interviewed indicated that they thought blacks were less intelligent than whites, 22 percent indicated that they thought that blacks and whites had about the same intelligence, less than 1 percent indicated that blacks were more intelligent than whites, and 6 percent indicated that they did not know.[28]

The respondents who said they thought blacks were less intelligent than whites were asked, "Do you think this is because: (1) they have lacked opportunities, or (2) they are born less intelligent, or (3) both?" About 44 percent said it was because blacks were born less intelligent, 22 percent said it was due to a combination of lack of opportunity and differences in intelligence at birth, 32 percent indicated that lack of opportunty alone was to blame, and 3 percent had no opinion.[29] The Roper study data suggest that about 47 percent of the entire national sample of Americans held the view that blacks are innately less intelligent than whites (44 percent + 22 percent = 66 percent; 66 percent x 71 percent = 47 percent). They also suggest that about 45 percent of the total sample did not believe that there were innate differences in intelligence between blacks and whites (32 percent x 71 percent = 23 percent; 23 percent + 22 percent = 45 percent).

In 1942, the National Opinion Research Center (NORC) at the University of Chicago conducted a national survey of the attitudes of whites toward blacks. It was funded by the Office of War Information. The following question was included: "In general, do you think Negroes are as intelligent as white people— that is, can they learn just as well if they are given the same education?" Although worded very differently from both of the intelligence-related questions in the Roper survey, the NORC question can be read as asking respondents whether there are differences between blacks and whites in innate intellectual ability, that is, in the potential to learn. The responses the question elicited tend to confirm this interpretation. For example, about 42 percent of the whites indicated that they thought blacks were as intelligent as whites, which is about the same as the 45 percent that (effectively) expressed this view in the Roper study a few years earlier.[30]

28. Eugene L. Horowitz, "'Race' Attitudes," in *Characteristics of the American Negro*, ed. Otto Klineberg (New York: Harper & Row, 1944; J. & J. Harper Edition, 1969), pp. 196–97.

29. These percentages were derived from data in ibid, pp. 198–99.

30. Mildred A. Schwartz, *Trends in White Attitudes toward Negroes* (Chicago: National Opinion Research Center, University of Chicago, 1967), pp. 2, 8, 19. One way to interpret the data from

NORC went on to ask its question on intelligence in surveys conducted in the 1940s, 1950s, and 1960s. The responses over time provide trend data on this issue during a period of enormous change in the position of blacks in American life. Most of the blacks who migrated from the South to urban areas in the North, Midwest, and West did so in this period. And the 1950s and 1960s brought both the post–World War II economic boom and the civil rights movement—and the attendant sea changes in the economic and legal status of African Americans.

The changes in responses to the NORC question on intelligence were quite substantial—even dramatic. By 1956, 78 percent of the whites indicated that they thought African Americans and whites were of equal intelligence, and only about 20 percent indicated that they thought that blacks were less intelligent than whites.[31] This response pattern remained stable through the late 1960s. (The last year NORC asked this particular question was 1968.) In these years, about three quarters of the whites continued to say that African Americans and whites were equally intelligent, while one-fifth to one-quarter indicated that they believed blacks were less intelligent than whites.[32]

Although the NORC trend data stop in the late 1960s, since 1963, Louis Harris has been regularly asking national samples of white Americans whether they agree or disagree with the following statement: "Blacks have less native intelligence than whites." In 1963, 39 percent of whites indicated that they agreed with that statement, while 46 percent agreed with it in 1967. Thus, in the 1960s, Harris was getting responses from whites that were very similar to those that Roper and NORC obtained in the 1939–42 period. Nonetheless, between the early 1970s and early 1990s, the response of whites to the Harris question followed a trajectory similar to what NORC experienced in the 1940s and 1950s. By 1976, only 28 percent of whites indicated that they believed that blacks had less native intelligence than whites; by 1991 this percentage had fallen to 11 percent.[33]

It is difficult to explain why the findings of the NORC and Harris surveys in the 1960s differed so much. It is not uncommon for differently worded survey questions addressing the same issue to elicit considerably different response

these two studies is that, as recently as a half-century ago, between two-thirds and three-quarters of Americans thought that blacks had fewer developed capacities than whites of the kind that can be thought of as evidence of "intelligence" in our society—and about half of all Americans thought that these differences were due at least in part to differences in innate intellectual potential between the two races.

31. Ibid., p. 9. Also see Gerald David Jaynes and Robin M. Williams, Jr., eds., *A Common Destiny: Blacks and American Society* (Washington, D.C.: National Research Council, National Academy Press, 1989), pp. 118–19.

32. H. H. Hyman and P. B. Sheatsley, "Attitudes toward Desegregation," *Scientific American* 211 (July 1964): 16–23. Also see Howard Schuman, Charlotte Steeh, and Lawrence Bobo, *Racial Attitudes in America: Trends and Interpretations* (Cambridge: Harvard University Press, 1985), pp. 198–99; Schwartz, *Trends in White Attitudes toward Negroes*, pp. 19–22, 131; and Jaynes and Williams, *A Common Destiny*, pp. 122–23.

33. Louis Harris, Remarks at the annual meeting of the Education Commission of the States, Denver, 19 July 1991, p. 2.

patterns. In any case, it is probably more important to consider the trend that the two data sets, taken together, suggest: Over the past half-century, the view that blacks are innately less intelligent than whites seems to have become much less widely held within the general white adult population.

There are several reasons for this change. First, beginning in the 1920s and 1930s, some scholars had begun to marshal evidence against theories of racial differences—and their arguments apparently made many converts in academic circles.[34] Second, the rise of Nazism and the systematic killing of Jews during World War II provided a vivid example of the horrible consequences for humanity that theories of racial supremacy can have.[35] Third, during the 1940s and 1950s, a much larger percentage of whites completed high school and college than ever before—and individuals with relatively large amounts of education are more inclined to hold racially tolerant views than individuals with relatively little education.[36] Fourth, by the mid-1960s, the civil rights movement had succeeded in raising public awareness of the grave racial injustices to which blacks were being subjected. (In the 1963–65 period, the Gallup Poll consistently found that about half of all Americans regarded civil rights as the "most important problem facing the country.")[37] Fifth, beginning with President Truman, several presidents had taken strong action in support of expanded civil rights for blacks. And sixth, over the past several decades, blacks have become increasingly numerous and visible in managerial and professional positions—positions that require substantial amounts of formal education.

Yet there is reason to believe that the NORC and Harris surveys have recorded a somewhat larger shift in whites' views on the innate intellectual ability of blacks than may have actually taken place. Given the pervasiveness of legally sanctioned segregation prior to World War II, whites did not have to be concerned about expressing what racist views they may have held at that time. However, by the 1960s and 1970s it had become much less socially acceptable to express racist beliefs publicly. Consequently, since that time a growing number of people may have become inclined to avoid expressing such opinions in most contexts. This may have led a significant number to adjust their responses to survey researchers' questions regarding the relative intelligence of racial/ethnic groups.[38]

Additional Survey Data   A number of surveys since the late 1960s have examined how whites view the intelligence of blacks and, in some cases, other

34. Otto Klineberg's *Race Differences* (New York: Harper & Bros, 1935) is an example of a book that argued strongly against the validity of genetic theories of racial differences.

35. Lawrence Bobo noted that U.S. propaganda in World War II calling attention to the "inherently antidemocratic" nature of Nazism may also have helped erode Americans' belief in theories of biological differences between races. Lawrence Bobo, "Group Conflict, Prejudice, and the Paradox of Contemporary Racial Attitudes," in *Eliminating Racism: Profiles in Controversy*, Phyllis A. Katz and Dalmas A. Taylor, eds. (New York: Plenum Press, 1988), p. 94.

36. Tom W. Smith and Paul B. Sheatsley, "American Attitudes toward Race Relations," *Public Opinion* 6 (October/November 1984): 51–52.

37. Jaynes and Williams, *Common Destiny*, pp. 223–24.

38. Ibid., p. 120.

racial/ethnic groups. One of the more valuable studies, by Mary R. Jackman and Mary Scheuer Senter, surveyed a nationally representative sample of about nineteen hundred American adults in 1975 about the applicability of intelligence, dependability, and laziness—among other things—to blacks and whites. The question about each trait took the following form: "How many whites would you say are intelligent?" Respondents were asked to rate each group on a scale from 0 to 8. Respondents provided their answers to the questions via a self-administered booklet and did not have to respond orally to an interviewer.[39] Some 57 percent of whites in their sample indicated that they believed whites were to some degree more intelligent than African Americans, which was double the percentages of whites in the 1976 Harris survey who held this view. However, respondents in the Jackman-Senter survey were not asked to explain whether they thought differences in intelligence were due to innate or other factors. Therefore, the 57 percent and 28 percent figures should probably not be viewed as associated with comparable questions.

Only 2 percent of the whites in the Jackman-Senter study appeared to think that the differences in intelligence between the two races were large; about 35 percent believed them to be of moderate size, and 20 percent believed them to be small. Disturbingly, about 18 percent of the *blacks* in the sample indicated that they felt that whites were at least somewhat more intelligent than blacks.[40]

Jackman and Senter found that 37 percent of whites believed that African Americans were more likely to be lazy than whites, and 51 percent of whites believed that blacks were less dependable. Moreover, about 90 percent of the whites who believed that African Americans were lazy also indicated that they disliked blacks to some degree. (Whites who said that African Americans were less intelligent or less dependable than whites did not evidence a tendency to dislike blacks.)[41]

In 1990, James R. Kluegel undertook a synthesis of relevant data from the General Social Survey (GSS), an annual survey by NORC. One of the questions that appeared on the GSS in some years in the 1970s and 1980s concerns the degree to which some whites believe that blacks are innately or culturally inferior to whites:

On average, blacks have worse jobs, income and housing than white people. Do you think these differences are . . .

a. Mainly due to *discrimination*.
b. Because most blacks have less *in-born ability* to learn.
c. Because most blacks don't have the *chance for education* that it takes to rise out of poverty.

39. Mary R. Jackman and Mary Scheuer Senter, "Different, Therefore Unequal: Beliefs about Trait Differences between Groups of Unequal Status," in *Research in Social Stratification and Mobility*, Donald J. Treiman and Robert V. Robinson, eds. (Greenwich, Conn.: JAI Press, 1983), pp. 316–17.
40. Ibid., pp. 318–19.
41. Ibid., pp. 316, 317, 318, 319, 324, and 325.

d. Because most blacks just don't have the *motivation* to pull themselves out of poverty.[42]

Respondents were asked to answer yes or no to each of the four parts (a through d) of the question. Thus, they could attribute the differences to more than one cause. Kluegel aggregated the data for the late 1980s and compared them to responses given in 1977. He found that significant percentages of whites at both times believed that differences in white-black socioeconomic circumstances were due at least in part to differences in innate intelligence. However, the percentage of whites holding this genetic view fell from 27 percent in 1977 to 21 percent in 1988–89.[43] Interestingly, the percentages for both years are generally consistent with the responses to the comparable question in the NORC surveys from the mid-1950s through the late 1960s and also with the responses to the comparable question in the Harris surveys from 1976 through 1991.

Kluegel also found that more than two in five whites believed that lack of motivation was entirely or partially responsible for poverty among blacks. Moreover, the percentage of whites who held this view remained essentially unchanged between 1977 and 1988–89 (41 percent vs. 44 percent).[44] Motivation, of course, can be described as a cultural attribute, and a lack of motivation to work in American society is generally regarded as a negative trait. Thus, the belief that many African Americans lack the motivation to pull themselves out of poverty can be viewed as evidence that whites regard blacks as culturally inferior in this important area.

The GSS data indicate that a total of 30 percent relied exclusively on a combination of genetic and cultural theories of inferiority to explain why blacks were doing less well than whites in 1988–89. Similarly, 30 percent of whites regarded these differences to be grounded exclusively in racial discrimination and lack of educational opportunity. About 65 percent of whites relied on the genetic and cultural theories in combination with discrimination and lack of educational opportunity to explain this phenomenon.[45]

It would be encouraging to report that the GSS data analyzed by Kluegel are balanced by other data showing a different pattern of white opinion. However, that is not the case. In fact, a new "ethnic images" module of questions for the GSS was administered for the first time in 1990 and produced very similar (negative) findings regarding beliefs about the cultural attributes and intellectual abilities of blacks and Hispanics.[46]

In this survey, respondents were asked about the applicability of certain attributes to several groups—whites as a whole, southern whites, Jews, African Americans, Hispanics, and Asians. In his analysis of the data, Tom W. Smith

42. James R. Kluegel, "Trends in Whites' Explanations of the Black-White GAP in Socioeconomic Status, 1977–1989," *American Sociological Review* 55 (August 1990): 514.
43. Ibid., pp. 514–15, 517.
44. Ibid.
45. Ibid.
46. Tom W. Smith, *Ethnic Images*, GSS Topical Report No. 19 (National Opinion Research Center, University of Chicago, December 1990).

found that blacks and Hispanics clearly had the most negative images relative to whites. For instance, 53 percent of all respondents viewed both blacks and Hispanics as less intelligent than whites. Disturbingly, about 30 percent of the *black* respondents said that African Americans as a group are less intelligent than whites, while 35 percent of the *Hispanic* respondents thought that Latinos as a group are less intelligent than whites.[47]

However, the question on intelligence in this survey did not explicitly ask respondents for their opinion on the innate intelligence of groups. (The question was, "Do people in these groups tend to be unintelligent or tend to be intelligent?")[48] As in the survey findings over the past half-century, the percentage of whites who indicate that they believe there are differences in intelligence between racial/ethnic groups tends to be significantly smaller when the question specifies innate intelligence than when it does not. I shall return to this phenomenon at the end of this subsection.

Several of the ethnic-images questions in the 1990 GSS also produced responses consistent with the belief that some minority groups are culturally inferior to whites in important respects. For example, about 62 percent of respondents thought that African Americans are lazier than whites, and 54 percent held this view of Latinos. About 56 percent believed that blacks are more prone to violence than whites, while 50 percent had this opinion of Hispanics. And about 78 percent said they thought African Americans were more likely than whites to prefer to live on welfare, while about 72 percent believed this of Latinos. Many of these beliefs appear to be closely related to certain positions on other racial/ethnic issues. For example, Smith found that those who believed that African Americans are lazier and more disposed to live on welfare than whites were less supportive of affirmative action programs and additional government spending for blacks. Those who believed that blacks are less intelligent and more violence-prone than whites expressed less willingness to send their children to integrated schools.[49]

Smith also found that respondents' beliefs regarding these issues were clearly "related to the social distance that people wish to maintain between themselves and other racial/ethnic groups." As respondents' overall image of a group moved from positive to negative, as measured by their views on all of the image characteristics taken together (with the exception of rich/poor), they were less likely to favor living in a neighborhood in which half of the residents were from the other group or less likely to approve of having a close relative marry an individual from the other group.[50]

Responses to the ethnic-images questions reveal considerable variation. Jews were, on average, viewed slightly more favorably than whites as a whole. For example, they were regarded as richer, more hard-working, less prone to violence, and more likely to prefer being self-supporting than

47. Ibid., p. 6
48. Ibid., p. 16.
49. Ibid., pp. 7, 9.
50. Ibid., p. 7.

whites. They were regarded as having about the same level of intelligence. Only with regard to patriotism were they held in a slightly less positive light than whites.[51]

Asians were regarded as less prone to violence than whites and about as hard-working. Surprisingly, they were viewed as slightly less intelligent than whites, despite the widely reported academic success of many Asian students. Asians, however, were viewed as markedly less patriotic than whites. Since many Asians are recent immigrants, this may reflect a belief that they are more foreign.[52]

Interestingly, the data show that the images of southern whites are much more negative than those of whites as a whole. From a cultural perspective, southern whites were viewed as much lazier, somewhat more prone to violence, and much more likely to prefer living off welfare than the overall white community. Curiously, 38 percent of the respondents believed that southern whites are less intelligent than whites as a whole.[53] It seems extremely unlikely that these respondents believed that southern whites are genetically different from the white population nationally; a plausible explanation, therefore, is that most did not view the question about intelligence to concern primarily inborn intellectual potential. Instead, they may have tended to read it as a question about differences in developed ability.

If this is how the ethnic-images question on intelligence was generally interpreted, then the very negative views expressed about the intelligence of blacks and Hispanics probably should also be interpreted in that light. This suggests that significantly fewer respondents believed that African Americans and Latinos are innately less intelligent than whites than a simple reading of the ethnic-images data might imply, while considerable percentages believed that there are differences in their intellectual capacities that have origins other than genetic endowment.

Using results from several of the most recent surveys, one is able to develop rough estimates of the percentage of whites who currently believe that blacks have intellectual capacities that are less developed, on average, than whites; the percentages who believe that these differences are grounded in differences in innate intellectual potential; and the percentages who believe that these differences are due exclusively to other factors. (We do not have sufficient data to develop similar estimates for Latinos.) About 57 percent of all *nonblacks* in the 1990 GSS indicated a belief that blacks are less intelligent than whites.[54] This is the same percentage found to hold this view in the Jackman-Senter survey of 1975. On the basis of these two results, we can estimate that 50–60 percent of whites held this view as the 1990s began.

I previously noted that, in a 1991 Harris survey, about one in ten whites indicated a belief that blacks are innately less intelligent than whites. Kluegel's analysis of the 1988–89 GSS question on intelligence found that about one in

51. Ibid., p. 9.
52. Ibid., pp. 4, 9.
53. Ibid., p. 9.
54. Ibid., p. 6.

five whites subscribed to this notion. Because the Harris question is worded in such a direct fashion, at least some of the respondents who believed in the inherent intellectual inferiority of blacks may have refrained from saying it. This suggests that more weight should be given to the 1988–89 GSS data than to the recent Harris data. Thus, a reasonable estimate is that about 20 percent of whites currently believe that blacks are innately less intelligent than whites.[55] Subtracting 20 percent from 55 percent yields 35 percent, our estimate of the portion of whites who currently believe that blacks have less developed intellectual ability than whites for nongenetic reasons.

An obvious question, of course, is, "What are these reasons?" Although available survey data cannot provide definitive answers, they can offer directional insights. The survey questions reviewed in this section basically asked respondents about two other kinds of causes of the perceived differences in intelligence between whites and blacks: (1) those associated with the quality of the overall opportunity structure in America, for example, racial discrimination and lack of educational opportunity; and (2) those centered in the culture of the group, for example, motivation and willingness to work. To date, no national survey has asked questions that would simultaneously produce estimates of the percentages of each racial/ethnic group that believe there are differences in developed intellectual capacities among various groups; the percentages who believe such differences originate in innate, opportunity-structure, or cultural differences; and the grounds on which respondents base their beliefs.[56] Such information might be extremely valuable as one contemplates the steps necessary to accelerate the educational advancement of minorities in the 1990s.

SOME CONTEMPORARY VIEWS ON INTELLIGENCE DIFFERENCES

In 1984, Mark Snyderman and Stanley Rothman surveyed a random sample of 1,020 individuals regarded as experts on the nature of intelligence and the characteristics, uses, and value of IQ tests. These individuals included technical experts on testing as well as psychologists and educational specialists. A total of 661 (65 percent) responded to the survey. Most were faculty at colleges or universities, a majority were currently engaged in research on testing or intelli-

55. About 21 percent of white adults of all ages indicated in the 1988–89 GSS that they believed blacks had less innate intelligence than whites. However, Kluegel found substantial differences among white adults who held these views based on age. For example, only 15 percent of the 18–28-year-old whites held this view, as did 15 percent of the 29–39-year-olds; but about 35 percent of those over 73 years of age held this view, as did 32 percent of the 62–73-year-olds. This suggests that in the years ahead cohort replacement may lower the percentage of the white adult population that believes blacks are innately less intelligent than whites. Among those who had doubts about blacks' motivation—44 percent of the entire white adult population—there was very little variation by age level. "Trends in Whites' Explanations of the Black-White Gap in Socioeconomic Status, 1977–1989," p. 517.

56. James Kluegel, among others, distinguishes between "individualist" and "structuralist" explanations for differences in the economic circumstances of whites and blacks. On the individualist side, he makes a further distinction between "traditional" and "motivational" explanations (ibid., pp. 512–13). I prefer to use the three-category approach outlined here: biogenetic, cultural, and opportunity-structure rationales.

gence, and the average respondent had written eleven articles on matters related to testing.[57] Given the racial/ethnic profile of college and university professors in America, one can assume that a large majority were white.

The group was asked to answer a number of questions regarding the nature and heritability of intelligence, differences among groups in intelligence, and the use of IQ tests. Importantly for our purposes, respondents were asked how they explained differences in IQ test scores between blacks and whites. Only 1 percent said they believed that the differences were due exclusively to innate attributes, 45 percent believed they were due to a combination of genetic and environmental factors, and 15 percent said the differences were due solely to variations in the environment. (Another 24 percent felt that there was not sufficient evidence to reach a conclusion, and 14 percent did not respond to the question.)[58]

It is striking that 46 percent of a mid-1980s sample of individuals with extensive professional experience in testing or test-related areas expressed the belief that African Americans are, on average, at least somewhat less innately intelligent than whites (45 percent + 1 percent = 46 percent). This is almost the same percentage the Roper survey found among the general white population over half a century ago, and probably more than twice the percentage of the white population that currently holds this view (assuming that the 1988–89 GSS data analyzed by Kluegel are reasonably accurate). It must be recognized, however, that large numbers of academics have espoused some variety of this view since the beginning of the intelligence testing movement. For example, Lewis Terman of Stanford University, the developer of the Stanford-Binet intelligence test, believed that blacks, Mexicans, and Native Americans were disproportionately represented among individuals with low innate intelligence. Moreover, he apparently believed this before his intelligence test was published—and, therefore, before there were any IQ test data available on racial/ethnic differences.[59]

At the time Snyderman and Rothman published the results of their survey, Snyderman was a postdoctoral fellow at Harvard and Rothman was a professor at Smith. Thus, they were presenting their findings from seats at elite institutions. However, unlike Terman, the individuals they polled were in a position to draw on an enormous amount of test data and research findings generated over a long period of time. Also unlike Terman, Snyderman and Rothman published the results of their survey after a twenty-year period of extensive scholarly research, discussion, and debate over both the nature of intelligence and the possible variations among racial groups and social classes. This was also a period in which the use of IQ test results in student placement and other educational

57. Mark Snyderman and Stanley Rothman, "Survey of Expert Opinion on Intelligence and Aptitude Testing," *American Psychologist* 42 (February 1987): 138–39; Mark Snyderman and Stanley Rothman, "Science, Politics, and the IQ Controversy," *The Public Interest* 83 (Spring 1986): 85.

58. Snyderman and Rothman, "Survey of Expert Opinion on Intelligence and Aptitude Testing," p. 141.

59. Leon J. Kamin, "The Politics of IQ," in *The Myth of Measurability*, Paul L. Houts, ed. (New York: Hart, 1977), p. 47.

decisions had come under sustained attack by minorities and others who regarded them as culturally biased.[60]

At the core of this recent scholarly activity is the old debate regarding the relative importance of nature and nurture in shaping human capacities and behavior. If a single event triggered the renewal of scholarly debate on this question, especially as it pertained to intelligence, it was the publication of Arthur R. Jensen's article "How Much Can We Boost IQ and Scholastic Achievement?" in the the *Harvard Educational Review* (Winter 1969). Jensen presented his personal synthesis and interpretation of the accumulated research findings regarding the nature of intelligence, what IQ tests measure, the complex relationship between genes and environment in shaping developed intellectual capacities, the variations in intelligence that might exist among individuals and among groups, the impact of these possible variations on their academic and occupational success, and the prospects for using educational interventions to raise children's IQs and their academic achievement.[61]

When discussing intelligence, Jensen indicated that he was referring to the ability of humans "to see the differences between things which seem similar and to see the similarities between things which seem different"; these, he said, "are essentially the processes of abstraction and conceptualization." He made it clear that he believed these capacities represent a narrow range of human abilities. However, he argued, they are capacities that technological/industrial societies have increasingly needed, valued, and rewarded, especially when they take the form of verbal and quantitative reasoning skills. Schools have been designed to nurture these capacities in students, and intelligence and achievement tests have been designed to measure (albeit imperfectly) the capacities of individuals in these areas.[62]

Jensen went on to say that he believed the best available evidence supported the conclusion that, on average, variations in intelligence among individuals were 80 percent due to variations in genetic makeup and 20 percent due to variations in environment. This conclusion was particularly important in light of the data on black-white differences in IQ test scores that Jensen reported on in some detail. He summarized the results of many studies that collectively indicated that the average IQ test score for blacks was 15 points lower than the average score for whites. Adjusting for broad variations in socioeconomic status, Jensen stated that the difference was about 11 points.[63]

A difference of even 11 points in IQ test score averages is extremely large. IQ tests have typically been normed with 100 as the mean score, with scores dis-

60. For a history of the debate over "nature versus nurture" in the twentieth century, see Carl N. Degler, *In Search of Human Nature: The Decline and Revival of Darwinism in American Social Thought* (New York: Oxford University Press, 1991). For a discussion of the history of the public debate on IQ tests, see Lee J. Cronbach, "Five Decades of Public Controversy over Mental Testing," *American Psychologist* 30 (January 1975): 1–14.

61. Arthur R. Jensen, "How Much Can We Boost IQ and Scholastic Achievement?" *Harvard Educational Review* 39 (Winter 1969): 1–123.

62. Ibid., pp. 5–16.

63. Ibid., pp. 42, 81.

tributed in a manner generally consistent with the so-called normal (bell-shaped) curve. About 68 percent of all individuals have usually scored within +15 points of 100, and about 96 percent of all individuals have scored within ±30 points of 100.[64] But with an average IQ score of 85 rather than 100, blacks in the late 1960s were extremely underrepresented among high scorers and extremely overrepresented among low scorers on IQ tests. Based on the typical distribution of IQ scores, only about 2 percent of African Americans could be expected to score over 115, vs. 16 percent of whites. A fraction of 1 percent of blacks could be expected to score over 130, vs. 2 percent of whites. In contrast, 50 percent of blacks could be expected to score less than 85 on an IQ test, while only 16 percent of whites were likely to score below that level. And about 16 percent of blacks could be expected to score less than 70, vs. only 2 percent of whites.

The data on IQ score averages plus the conclusion that intelligence is overwhelmingly the product of inherited factors made Jensen's article explosive. Written by a scholar at an elite research university (Berkeley), detailed in its analysis, generally reserved in its prose style, and published in a major journal, the article could be read as providing powerful support for those who believed in the innate intellectual inferiority of blacks. Worse, the evidence presented could be interpreted as indicating that these disadvantages were so large that it would be virtually impossible for blacks to become well represented in positions that required large amounts of higher education.[65]

Similarly, the data could be interpreted as providing support for the conclusion that relatively little can be done to improve the academic performance of black children whose parents have had little formal education and low incomes. This potential conclusion was especially potent because those academics who believed in a large hereditary component for intelligence also tended to believe that differences in IQ scores between children from different social classes (regardless of race/ethnicity) could be explained to a considerable extent by differences in innate intelligence.[66] Conceivably, such interpretations could be used to support the conclusion that racism is not the primary cause of blacks' current educational and economic difficulties.

The impact of Jenson's article was probably magnified by the fact that the Coleman Report had been published only about three years earlier. In his article, Jensen noted that the differences in test-score averages reported by Coleman and his colleagues were consistent with those that would have been

64. J. D. Matarazzo and D. R. Denver, "Intelligence Measures," in *Encyclopedia of Psychology,* vol. 2, Raymond J. Corsini, ed. (New York: Wiley, 1984), p. 233.

65. Researchers have estimated that the average IQ score for people who earn a Ph.D. or M.D. degree is about 125, while the average IQ score for people who earn a bachelor's degree is about 115 (ibid., p. 232).

66. This view continues to be very widely held. In their 1984 survey of test experts, Snyderman and Rothman reported that 55 percent believed that social class differences in IQ scores were due to a combination of genetic and environmental factors. Only 12 percent attributed these differences solely to the environment. Of the remaining respondents, 18 percent did not feel there was enough information to answer the question, and 15 percent did not respond to it. Snyderman and Rothman, "Survey of Expert Opinion on Intelligence and Aptitude Testing," p. 141.

predicted by the IQ score difference typically found to exist between the two groups.[67] Jensen's statement was particularly ironic because Coleman, as we have seen, had concluded that differences in test scores between racial/ethnic groups were the result of environmental factors heavily associated with variations in the family and community resources necessary for school success in American society. In fact, Coleman's emphasis on the importance of differences in social capital in producing variations in student achievement is far removed from the debate regarding the relative roles of heredity and environment in shaping intelligence.[68]

Over the past twenty years, research by behavioral geneticists and others has produced a great deal of additional information on the complex interplay between genes and the environment. Robert Plomin has noted that recent research suggests that genes and the environment have, on average, roughly equal impact on variations in intelligence among individuals.[69] (Intelligence is this context refers to developed intellectual capacities that are regarded as evidence of intelligence in mainstream society—and that can be sampled to a reasonable degree by IQ tests.) Interestingly, Snyderman and Rothman were not able to get a consensus response to a question on this topic from the experts in their sample, even though 94 percent indicated their belief that intelligence is a product of both hereditary and environmental factors. When they were asked to estimate the relative roles of genes and the environment on the IQ scores of white Americans, 21 percent said they were not qualified to answer, and 40 percent said there was not enough evidence to provide an answer. Of the 39 percent who did respond, the response pattern was generally consistent with Plomin's interpretation of recent research, a mean estimate of 60 percent heredity and 40 percent environment.[70]

Clearly, neither Plomin nor the respondents in the Snyderman-Rothman survey offered support for the 80 percent-20 percent division suggested by Jensen in the late 1960s. Apart from the apparent concern that available research does not lend itself to precise estimates in this area, this situation appears to reflect considerable agreement that those developed capacities that tend to be categorized as intelligence are subject to a great deal of malleability in response to environmental changes.[71] Consistent with this view, Edward

67. Jensen, "How Much Can We Boost IQ and Scholastic Achievement?" pp. 81–82.

68. The national sample of students tested by Coleman and his colleagues took both "achievement" tests and "ability" (intelligence) tests. Interestingly, Coleman and his associates viewed ability tests as "simply broader and more general measures of education" and achievement tests as "narrower measures directed to a restricted subject area"—that is, both measure developed intellectual capacities. They found that scores on ability tests were "affected by school differences" at least as much as scores on achievement tests. See James S. Coleman et al., *Equality of Educational Opportunity* (Washington, D.C.: Office of Education, U.S. Government Printing Office, 1966), pp. 292–93.

69. Robert Plomin, "Environment and Genes: Determinants of Behavior," *American Psychologist* 44 (February 1989): 105–06, 108; Robert Plomin, *Development, Genetics, and Psychology* (Hillsdale, N.J.: Lawrence Erlbaum Associates, 1986).

70. Snyderman and Rothman, "Survey of Expert Opinion on Intelligence and Aptitude Testing," p. 140.

71. Sandra Scarr, "Toward a More Biological Psychology," in *Science and the Question of Human*

Zigler, a leading early childhood expert, believes that environmental variations can produce IQ score variations of as much as 20–25 points.[72] This degree of malleability is, of course, much larger than the difference in average IQ scores for whites and blacks reported by Jensen in the late 1960s.

The view among many researchers that both heredity and the environment have substantial impact on variations in intelligence requires elaboration. First, the relative influence of the environment on intelligence is largely a function of the degree to which the environment tends toward heterogeneity or homogeneity. The more individuals tend to experience very similar environments, the greater the relative impact of genes on variations in intelligence. Conversely, the more individuals tend to experience very different environments, the less the impact of genes. An estimate that about half of the current variation in intelligence can be explained by the environment suggests that, on average, contemporary America is somewhere toward the middle of the homogeneity-heterogeneity continuum.[73]

Second, environment has both physical-organic and social-cultural dimensions. For example, differences in health habits and access to regular health care

---

Equality, Margaret S. Collins, Irving W. Wainer, and Theodore A. Bremner, eds. (Boulder, Col.: Westview Press, 1981), pp. 73–74.

72. E. Zigler and V. Seitz, "Social Policy and Intelligence," in *Handbook of Human Intelligence,* Robert J. Sternberg, ed. (New York: Cambridge University Press, 1982), pp. 586–641.

73. Of course, it is not possible to provide truly identical or equivalent environments to all individuals. Even siblings have a significant amount of "nonshared environmental influences." This means that, in concert with hereditary differences, environmental differences will continue to play a significant role in shaping variations in intelligence and other human behaviors. Plomin, "Environment and Genes: Determinants of Behavior," p. 109. Parents who have more than one child are well aware that differences in personality, interests, etc. among members of the family produce very substantial variations in parent-child and family-child interactions. Differences between the children also contribute to differences in the environments they experience outside the home, beginning with their friendship networks.

In a related vein, clearly some environmental factors in people's lives exist largely independent of genes while others are heavily shaped by them. Some behavioral geneticists have theorized that people who are born into "normal" circumstances tend to have a great deal of opportunity to "construct" their own environments over time—and that the decisions they make are to a considerable degree a function of their genetic inheritances. For instance, people who find that they have strong interests and aptitudes in mathematics may seek out contexts in which those attributes can be developed and emphasized. The key notion here is normal. The normal range of opportunities these researchers are referring to is that which applies to most whites in U.S. society. That is to say, although white children born to parents who have little education, extremely low income, and serious emotional problems would typically not be regarded as having opportunities that fall within the normal range, white children in middle-class and skilled working-class homes usually do have such opportunities. Owing to cultural differences, poverty, and discrimination, many more minority children have opportunities that fall outside the normal range. For a discussion of this perspective, see Sandra Scarr, "Developmental Theories for the 1990s: Development and Individual Differences," *Child Development* 63 (1992): 1–19; Richard Q. Bell, "A Reinterpretation of the Direction of Effects in Studies of Socialization," *Psychological Review* 75 (March 1968): 81–95. That individuals can shape their environments to a considerable degree calls attention to the fact that genes and environment interact in complex ways that make it very hard to estimate the environment's role in shaping variations in behavior. For a discussion of the general difficulty of estimating the relative contributions of genes and environment to variations in human behavior, see Christopher Jencks, "Heredity, Environment, and Public Policy Reconsidered," *American Sociological Review* 45 (October 1980): 723–36.

among pregnant women can produce a range of fetal experiences that have organic consequences associated with variations in intelligence among children.[74] Similarly, differences in child-rearing practices between well-educated and less-well-educated parents can produce culturally based variations in intelligence among youngsters.[75] The relative importance of the organic and cultural dimensions varies with the circumstances.

Third, available research suggests that there is much more homogeneity among whites in contemporary America regarding environment-related conditions that shape intellectual development than there is among other racial/ethnic groups. This means that, although heredity may now explain about 50 percent of the variation in white children's intelligence-test scores, it probably explains much less than 50 percent of the variation among blacks and some other minority groups.[76]

On the basis of research, Sandra Scarr believes that heredity accounts for 20–50 percent of the variation in IQ test scores among African Americans and for 40–70 percent among whites.[77] Regarding this point, our discussion of the differences in socioeconomic circumstances between blacks and whites attests to the fact that, on average, African American children grow up in environments much less favorable for developing intellectually in ways that are valued in the mainstream of our society.

Many minority youngsters grow up in environments that are culturally quite different from those typically experienced by whites, so that the kinds of intellectual skills that are developed and rewarded within some segments of the black community are quite different from those developed and rewarded in most segments of the white community—and very different from those measured by IQ tests (see chapter 10 for a fuller discussion).

Given these circumstances, the question becomes, Are the differences in physical-organic and social-cultural environments experienced by blacks and whites large enough to produce the observed difference in average IQ scores between the two groups?

RESEARCH ON THE ROLE OF ENVIRONMENTAL FACTORS

The results of a number of studies from the 1970s and 1980s strongly suggest that differences in the environments commonly experienced by black and white Americans are large enough to produce the differences in IQ test score averages that have been found to exist between the two groups. Before reviewing

74. Lucile Newman and Stephen L. Buka, *Every Child a Learner: Reducing Risks of Learning Impairment during Pregnancy and Infancy* (Denver: Education Commission of the States, 1990).

75. Zena Smith Blau, *Black Children/White Children: Competence, Socialization, and Social Structure* (New York: Free Press, 1981).

76. Ibid.; Sandra Scarr and Richard A. Weinberg, "The Influence of 'Family Background' on Intellectual Attainment," *American Sociological Review* 43 (October 1978): 674–92.

77. Sandra Scarr, *Race, Social Class, and Individual Differences in I.Q.* (Hillsdale, N.J.: Lawrence Erlbaum, 1981), p. 458. This reference is from Part IV.2, "From Evolution to Larry P., or What Shall We Do about IQ Tests?" It was originally published in *Intelligence* 2 (1978): 325–42.

these findings, however, I want to describe the major kinds of research strategies used to study a question of this kind. Behavioral geneticists have two primary approaches. First, they can study pairs of identical and fraternal twins to measure variations in behavior between the two types of twins. Second, they can study adopted children—that is, unrelated individuals raised together and related individuals raised apart.[78] Twin and adoption-study strategies can be pursued separately or in combination. Using a variety of statistical techniques, social scientists can also compare samples of children from different socioeconomic or cultural circumstances within each racial/ethnic group.

The Scarr-Weinberg Adoption Study   During the 1970s, Sandra Scarr and Richard Weinberg undertook a large-scale adoption study to answer the question of whether black and white children's average IQ test scores converge when they experience similar environments. More precisely, the study was designed to test the hypothesis that "black and interracial children reared by white families (the culture of the tests and the schools) would perform on IQ tests and school achievement measures as well as other adopted children." All adoptive parents in the study were white, well educated, with above-average incomes and occupational status. The 101 families who participated had 321 children above the age of four. (Intelligence tests do not provide reliable results for children under four years old, so such children are typically not included in studies of this kind.) Of these, 145 were biological children and 176 were adopted. Of the adopted children, 130 were socially classified as black and 25 as white; the remaining 21 adopted children were classified as members of other racial/ethnic groups. Many of the children classified as black actually had one biological parent socially classified as white and one as black. This allowed Scarr and Weinberg to compare the IQ scores of white, interracial, and black children.[79]

The results of the study support the conclusion that the differences between African American and white IQ scores are due to differences in environmental circumstances, not to genes. In the North Central region of the country, the average black IQ score in the mid-1970s was around 90—about 10 points below the white average nationally. However, the black children in the study averaged over 106. Moreover, the average score for the black children who had the most favorable adoption circumstances (such as being adopted very early in life) was 110, which compared favorably with that of white children adopted by high-SES white families. Moreover, it implied an average environmentally induced malleability of as much as 20 IQ points (110 - 90 = 20).[80] This is generally consistent with Zigler's estimate of IQ score malleability as well as with Plomin's con-

---

78. Plomin, "Environment and Genes: Determinants of Behavior," p. 105.

79. Sandra Scarr and Richard A. Weinberg, "IQ Test Performance of Black Children Adopted by White Families," *American Psychologist* 31 (October 1976): 726–39; "The Minnesota Adoption Studies: Genetic Differences and Malleability," *Child Development* 54 (April 1983): 261.

80. Scarr and Weinberg, "IQ Test Performance of Black Children Adopted by White Families," pp. 732, 734–39.

clusion that, on average, heredity and the environment each contribute about 50 percent to the variance in IQ scores among individuals.

Within the group of youngsters who were socially classified as African American, the interracial children had an average IQ score of 109, while the children with two black parents averaged about 97. Scarr and Weinberg found significant differences in the backgrounds of the two groups that accounted for these score differences. For example, the children with two black birthparents had been adopted on average at older ages than the interracial children, and their birthmothers had less education than the mothers of the interracial children.[81]

The Smith Cultural-Socioeconomic Study   In 1968, Zena Smith Blau initiated a large-scale study directed at "identifying the social processes that influence the development of intellectual competence in black children and white children." At the center of the study were interviews with 579 African American and 523 white mothers who had children in the fifth and sixth grades in one of three communities in the Chicago area. Information was gathered on the current socioeconomic status, family structure, and child-rearing practices of the parents; the characteristics of the families in which the parents grew up; and the parents' close friends. Extensive academic information on the children was also collected from school records. The sample was made up almost exclusively of middle- and working-class families.[82]

Using a number of statistical techniques, Blau analyzed how variations in social characteristics among the families influenced variations in their children's IQ and achievement test scores. In her sample the average IQ scores of African American and white students differed by about 10 points. However, after taking into account differences in broad social class measures (such as parent education level) and much more subtle differences in family characteristics (such as child-rearing practices), she was able to account for all but 3 points of the difference.

Because this gap is small in the context of the imperfect tools available for estimating the average intelligence of individuals and groups, Blau regarded her analysis as providing strong evidence that the differences in measured intellectual ability between blacks and whites is not genetic in origin. This conclusion is made more persuasive by the fact that although many studies, including Blau's, have found that white girls score somewhat higher than white boys in the late elementary school years, she found virtually no difference in the average IQ scores of the African American girls and boys in her sample (97 vs. 96).[83] This suggests that environmental factors were suppressing the IQ scores of both African American boys and girls.

Blau focused on only one of the two dimensions in which differences in environment can influence variations in intellectual ability among both individuals and groups. That is to say, she explored variations in social class and cultural

81. Ibid.
82. Blau, *Black Children/White Children*, pp. 188, 198.
83. Ibid., pp. xv, 147.

attributes of the blacks and whites in her sample; she did not examine the possibility of (environmentally induced) physical or organic differences between the groups. Because the families in her study were drawn from the working and middle classes, her decision to focus on social class and cultural differences rather than physical or organic differences was appropriate. Nonetheless, when examining the backgrounds of the black parents, Blau found that most of those who were members of the middle class had themselves grown up in working-class circumstances, and many of those who were working class had grown up in low-income families.[84] In recent years, researchers have found evidence that first-generation working-class and middle-class African American adults often have health habits that are more similar to those of impoverished blacks than to those of working-class and middle-class whites. For example, they have poorer nutritional habits and are less likely to consult a doctor on other than an emergency basis.[85] This suggests that the children born to the African Americans in Blau's sample had been exposed to prenatal and postnatal health risks that could undermine intellectual development more than was the case for the white children in her study.

Finally, Blau's study was not able to assess the impact of racism on the performance of the black children on IQ (or other) tests. As we will see, there is reason to believe that historic and contemporary racism continues to take a toll on the academic development and performance of African American youngsters.

The Moore Adoption Study   In the 1980s, Elsie G. J. Moore undertook a study of African American children adopted by middle-class black and white families.[86] The study provided an opportunity to test the malleability of black children's IQ scores when the children were exposed to a high-SES-family setting. It also offered a chance to see whether there are differences in African American and white middle-class family circumstances that contribute to different intellectual development trajectories for black and white children. The first of these objectives was consistent with the Scarr-Weinberg research, the second with the Blau research. Indeed, Moore was especially interested in exploring some of the differences in family characteristics previously examined by Blau (such as variations in parenting strategies and friendship networks) that seem to influence IQ test scores and overall academic achievement in school.

Moore's study included a sample of 46 children socially classified as black. Half of these children had been adopted by white families and half by African American families. Twenty of the children were actually interracial—one of

84. Ibid., pp. 19–22.

85. Richard A. Davis, "The Legacy of Poverty: A Study in the Persistence of Penurious Attitudes and Behaviors in the Black Middle Class," *Western Journal of Black Studies* 13 (Winter 1989): 208–16.

86. Elsie G. J. Moore, "Family Socialization and the IQ Test Performance of Traditionally and Transracially Adopted Black Children," *Developmental Psychology* 22 (May 1988): 317–26; and Elsie G. J. Moore, "Ethnic Social Milieu and Black Children's Intelligence Test Achievement," *Journal of Negro Education* 56 (Winter 1987): 44–52.

their biological parents was black and the other white. Fourteen of the interracial children had been adopted by whites and six by blacks. All of the children had been adopted before they were two years old and had been with their adoptive families for at least five years at the time of the study. They ranged in age from seven to ten when the data were collected. Both the black and the white adoptive mothers had an average of 16.0 years of education. The white fathers had an average of 17.3 years of education, the black fathers an average of 15.6. All of the families had middle-class occupational status, although the white families had a somewhat higher occupational status average than the African American families. Moore found that the adopted black children in the African American families had an average IQ score of almost 104, while the adopted black children in the white families had an average IQ score of about 117.[87] Thus, in both cases the children had average IQ scores well above the national average for African American children of about 85. The differences in scores between these and the national average were fully consistent with the level of environmentally induced malleability in intelligence scores suggested by Zigler and Plomin and were generally consistent with the increases found by Scarr and Weinberg.

The 13-point difference in average scores between the African American children being raised in white homes and those being raised in black homes (117 - 104 = 13) meant that the former group had IQ scores near the national average of 100 for all youngsters in the United States, while those in the white homes had an average IQ score above the level (115) achieved by only the top one-sixth of all children nationally.

Unlike Scarr and Weinberg, Moore did not find a difference in average scores between the children with two biological black parents and those who were interracial. In the African American homes, the interracial children had a slightly higher average IQ score than the black children (106 vs. 103). But in the white homes the pattern was reversed (116 for the interracial children vs. 118). In neither case were these differences statistically significant.[88]

The IQ tests were administered to the children in their homes. In addition, the children were asked to perform a demanding cognitive task with the help of their mother. Moore found that the adopted children in the white and black homes had very different response styles and that the ways in which the mothers assisted their children with the cognitive task were very different. The children in the white homes were much more apt to demonstrate an assertive approach to the test questions, to offer voluntary elaborations of their answers, and to attempt to solve a difficult problem, even when they were likely to be wrong. And they seemed to enjoy the test process more than their adoptive peers in the African American homes. In contrast, the black children in African American homes were much more likely not to respond to test questions.

87. Moore, "Ethnic Social Milieu and Black Children's Intelligence Test Achievement," pp. 47–48, 49.
88. Moore, "Family Socialization and the IQ Test Performance of Traditionally and Transracially Adopted Black Children," p. 320.

Moore found that the white mothers typically adopted very encouraging and supportive demeanors in their interactions with their children. They smiled, joked, offered suggestions (usually in the form of hints), and indicated that it was all right for their children to be wrong. In contrast, the black mothers were more likely to scowl, to offer negative evaluations of how the children were doing, and to offer very specific instructions about what to do. Overall, they were less supportive of child-initiated problem-solving approaches than the white mothers were.[89]

Moore concluded that these observed differences in child-rearing approaches probably contributed to the differences in the test behavior (and scores) of the children. Generally, she concluded that "the ethnicity of the rearing environment, not just socioeconomic status and maternal education level, exerts a significant influence on children's styles of responding to standardized intelligence tests and their test achievement."[90] To put it slightly differently, she found cultural differences that were not necessarily predicted by standard measures of social class but were associated with differences in the children's intellectual development patterns.

Moore also found critical differences in the social milieus of the families, as defined by such things as the neighborhoods in which they lived and the friendship networks they had established. For example, the children in the white families were much more likely to live in predominantly white or ethnically mixed neighborhoods, while the children in African American homes were much more likely to live in predominately black neighborhoods. The black children in white homes were much more likely to have close friends who were all white or equally divided between blacks and whites, while those in the African American homes were more likely to have all black friends. Moore also found that the school peers of the children in white homes had higher average reading levels than the school peers of the children in black homes. Moore's analysis showed that the composition of the children's neighborhoods and the racial composition of their friendship networks were significantly correlated with the IQ scores of the African American children in the black homes.[91]

Moore concluded that her data were consistent with Blau's findings on the role that differences in the social context and cultural attributes of families play in generating differences in average IQ scores between groups of children, including blacks and whites.[92] Both researchers' findings are consistent with those of the Coleman Report.

SOME REASONS FOR THE RESILIENCY OF RACIAL/ETHNIC STEREOTYPES

Over the years, African American children have consistently tended to score much less well than whites, on average, on IQ tests. Yet, as a review of the

89. Ibid., pp. 318–25.
90. Ibid., p. 325.
91. Moore, "Ethnic Social Milieu and Black Children's Intelligence Test Achievement," pp. 48–52.
92. Ibid., pp. 50–52.

Scarr-Weinberg, Blau, and Moore studies indicates, there is now considerable empirical evidence that variations in environmental circumstances, not differences in innate intellectual potential, account for the large differences in average IQ scores between blacks and whites. These studies indicate that, given similar environmental circumstances, the IQ scores of African American children will converge with those of white children.[93]

In view of these findings, is there reason to believe that the doubts expressed by many whites about the educational prospects of blacks and other minorities will be reduced in the near future? Although a definitive answer is not possible, further examination of the nature of stereotypes can shed light on the question.

One of the reasons that stereotypes are established in the first place is that there usually are a number of differences among groups that must be explained.[94] Stereotypes can contribute (accurately or inaccurately) to the development of these explanations. For example, it is a fact that, at the present time in the United States, much higher percentages of blacks and Hispanics than of whites are living in poverty (as defined by the federal governement). It is also true that African Americans and Latinos have higher rates of unemployment, lower average incomes, lower rates of educational attainment, and lower average levels of academic achievement than whites. Many people seek comprehensible explanations for these differences. But what is comprehensible can vary considerably, depending on the information available—and on whether one is black, white, Hispanic, Asian, or Native American.

The explanation for such differences put forward by members of a racial/ethnic group can be shaped by the stereotype they have of themselves.

93. In view of the importance of this subject, it would be helpful if we had many studies to call upon to strengthen the case against the claim that there are innate differences in intelligence between whites and blacks. Unfortunately, there have been only a few such studies. Two of the most notable were undertaken under the leadership of Sandra Scarr. One examined whether variations in intellectual skills among children socially classified as black were associated with variations in their degree of African ancestry. The idea was that, if there *were* differences in innate intelligence between blacks and whites, those children with large amounts of white ancestry should do significantly better on IQ tests. Scarr and her colleagues found no support for this hypothesis when they studied a large sample of black and white twins. See Sandra Scarr, Andrew J. Pakstis, Solomon H. Katz, and William B. Barker, "Absence of a Relationship between Degree of White Ancestry and Intellectual Skills within a Black Population," *Human Genetics* 39 (1977): 69–86.

The second study, which drew upon the same twin sample, tested the hypothesis that African Americans do less well than whites on IQ and other tests of intellectual skills because the black children are less familiar, from a cultural perspective, with the kinds of skills and types of materials necessary to do well on such tests. The results of this study were interpreted as being generally supportive of the cultural-difference hypothesis. See Scarr, *Race, Social Class, and Individual Differences in I.Q.*, pp. 261–315. Scarr has been a pivotal figure in the generation of empirical evidence strongly contradicting the notion that blacks are innately less intelligent than whites. However, she and Richard Weinberg have also produced evidence that they believe supports the conclusion that differences in average IQ scores between white children from working- and upper-middle-class families reflect, at least in part, genetic differences between the groups. Their explanation for this finding is that there has been significant upward and downward social mobility within the white population from generation to generation for a relatively long period of time, and that this mobility has been to some extent a function of variations in abilities that are partly heritable. See ibid., pp. 526–28; Scarr and Weinberg, "The Influence of 'Family Background' on Intellectual Attainment," pp. 674–92.

94. Stephan and Rosenfield, "Racial and Ethnic Stereotypes," p. 104.

That is, members of one group will often attempt to explain the behavior of another group on the basis of attributes and traits consistent with those they use to explain their own behavior. For example, if whites regard themselves as industrious (as research suggests they do), they might explain the extent of poverty among blacks by saying that they are not as hardworking as whites.[95] In fact, many whites might simply conclude that blacks are lazy. Similarly, if whites tend to believe that high academic achievement among white children is due in large part to innate intelligence, they might believe that a plausible explanation for the low academic achievement of blacks is that they have limited innate intellectual ability.[96]

In contemporary America, most racial/ethnic groups already have stereotypes of the other groups that have been in place for a long time.[97] Research suggests that once a stereotype is formed, individuals are likely to note and regard information that seems to support the stereotype as confirmation of its validity and to ignore or discard information that is not consistent with the stereotype rather than change the stereotype in a significant way.[98] These tendencies make the persistence of the historic white stereotype of black inferiority understandable. The current high poverty and welfare rates among African Americans, along with their lower levels of educational attainment and academic achievement, may feed preexisting beliefs in their innate or cultural inferiority. Over the past several decades, the number of African Americans who objectively do not have any of the attributes predicted by this stereotype has risen rapidly, but large numbers of whites may still be ignoring them on the grounds that they are the exceptions that prove the rule.

95. Ibid., pp. 95–97, 99–100, 104–06.

96. In general, American parents have been found to explain the math performances of their own children largely in terms of their perceptions of the children's innate math ability. See Harold W. Stevenson, Shin-Ying Lee and James W. Stigler, "Mathematics Achievement of Chinese, Japanese, and American Children," *Science* (14 February 1986): 74.

97. For a discussion of the stereotypes that exist for several racial/ethnic groups in America, see William B. Helmreich, *The Things They Say Behind Your Back* (Garden City, N.Y.: Doubleday, 1982).

98. Stephan and Rosenfield, "Racial and Ethnic Stereotypes," pp. 116–20. These information processing tendencies are likely to be at work among many populations, including, for example, the academic experts on intelligence and testing sampled in the Snyderman and Rothman study. Many of these individuals no doubt receive a great deal of information that could be regarded as confirming the impact of heredity on the differences in developed intellectual abilities between blacks and whites. A primary source of such information is the continuing stream of standardized test data showing that African American students still perform much less well than whites, even after adjusting for social class (see chapter 6). In contrast, "disconfirming" evidence is available primarily from the relatively few studies of the types undertaken by Scarr and Weinberg, Blau, and Moore. Moreover, owing to the nature of such studies, it is relatively easy to identify methodological problems with them or to interpret their data differently. Thus, probably many reject such evidence in favor of the view they already hold.

The findings of Snyderman and Rothman probably reflect a pattern of beliefs that had been held by this population for some time. Prior to starting their research program in the 1970s, Scarr and Weinberg asked about twenty psychologists what they thought would be found. Much to their surprise, the consensus was that they would find evidence in support of at least a partial genetic interpretation of differences in average IQ test scores between blacks and whites. See Scarr, *Race, Social Class, and Individual Differences in I.Q.*, p. 525.

Although it is very difficult to modify stereotypes, it is not impossible. For example, change can be the product of high-quality contact between groups. Stephan and Rosenfield believe that research has identified four essential conditions for constructive contact. First, individuals from different groups must be able to come into close, substantive contact in a variety of circumstances; such contact allows them to identify genuine misperceptions they have about each other. Superficial contact, in contrast, merely reinforces stereotypes. Second, the contact must be between individuals who are equal in status. For example, if equally well-educated blacks and whites are brought into close contact, there may be a real prospect that many of the whites will discard the general belief in the intellectual or cultural inferiority of blacks. However, if well-educated whites are paired with poorly educated African Americans, there is a high risk that the negative stereotype will be perpetuated. Third, the contact between individuals should be of a cooperative nature. If, instead, it is competitive, it may simply reinforce negative views. And fourth, the contact must have the clear support of leaders with genuine authority over the individuals in the situation.[99] A president of the United States taking steps to integrate the armed forces is an example of authoritative leadership that can attack racial stereotypes. A governor blocking the door to a public schoolhouse to a group of African American children who wish to enter offers an example of such leadership applied to perpetuating negative racial stereotypes. The problem is not primarily to identify the general conditions that must be satisfied in order to reduce negative racial/ethnic images. Instead, it is to find implementable strategies that satisfy these conditions.[100]

SUMMARY AND CONCLUSIONS

Over the past several decades, the nation's government-sanctioned system of racial subordination has been essentially dismantled. It is no longer the law of the land.

As the legal foundations of the race-based caste system were swept away, it was tempting to assume that massive changes had also taken place in the attitudes and beliefs of whites, changes that had provided a rationale for these societal arrangements. Certainly important changes have occurred. However, survey research data suggest that much less change has taken place than was hoped. The core notion of black inferiority seems still to be widely credited. Other minority groups, notably Hispanics, also seem to be the victims of this

99. Stephan and Rosenfield, "Racial and Ethnic Stereotypes," p. 121.

100. The problem of group stereotypes is complicated by the fact that children tend to develop images of racial/ethnic groups at a relatively early age (between ages four and seven). Moreover, these images often have negative dimensions. However, the initial development of prejudiced views by young children is not necessarily a product of the prejudiced views of their parents or other key adults. Indeed, young children seem perfectly capable of developing negative views toward other groups even when their parents do not have racial/ethnic prejudice. For a review and interpretation of the research on prejudice among children, see Frances Aboud, *Children and Prejudice* (Oxford, England: Basil Blackwell, 1988).

stereotype. Moreover, while it is true that stereotypes can be transformed, if circumstances are favorable, it is not clear that such circumstances are at hand.

As I noted in chapter 4, the changing structure of the U.S. economy has made it increasingly difficult for many minority group members to avoid poverty and unemployment. Many of them continue to be physically and socially isolated from the mainstream as a result of their concentration in inner cities. Many minority children growing up in these circumstances continue to face enormous obstacles to doing well in school. On the positive side, there has been considerable growth in the size of the minority middle class. Yet, many middle-class African American and other minority students are still performing much less well academically than their white counterparts. These circumstances collectively may be providing powerful "confirmation" of beliefs in the inferiority of blacks that many whites still hold. Studies like those by Scarr and Weinberg, Blau, and Moore, which provide strong evidence that differences in academic performance are based on environmental factors, are too few in number and too inaccessible to the general public to be a meaningful source of disconfirming information for these negative stereotypes.

In retrospect, one should not be surprised by the resiliency of notions of the inferiority of African Americans and other minority groups. The civil rights movement focused on securing legal rights for minorities. But the concept of legal equality does not require groups to see each other as social, cultural, or biological equals. It does not require an understanding that there may be real and important differences among groups in environmentally grounded capacities that bear heavily on how fully each group is able to participate in society at a given time. Finally, it does not require recognition of the reality that racial/ethnic groups (worldwide) routinely draw large, enduring distinctions between themselves and other groups, even when there are few objective bases for them.

This last point is especially salient given the recent large-scale immigration to the United States from Latin America and Asia. It is reasonable to conjecture that the structure of racial/ethnic stereotypes in America is more complex now than when the civil rights movement began in the 1950s and that it will become even more complex in the decades ahead.

All this suggests that it may now be necessary to make it a national priority to improve the condition of minorities in a way that will expand both the reality and the perception that common ground is growing among the diverse racial/ethnic groups. These policies will have to take into account what we know about the current intergroup stereotypes and about the essential conditions for changing them. But the question of immediate interest is, What are the current educational consequences for minorities of historical and contemporary racism in America? I address this question in the following chapter.

CHAPTER NINE

The Educational Impact

of Racial/Ethnic Prejudice

and

Discrimination

In this chapter, I review the research findings of social scientists and educators, many of them members of minority groups, regarding the influence of racial/ethnic prejudice and discrimination on the academic performance and educational prospects of minority students. I first look at the recent reactions of some African American educators and scholars to the continuing belief by many whites in the intellectual inferiority of blacks. I then review research on how the limitations historically imposed by racial/ethnic prejudice and discrimination on the educational and occupational opportunities available to African Americans have undermined the academic motivation of some black students; I also consider whether historical prejudice and discrimination have had similar consequences for other minority groups. I then explore how contemporary prejudice is affecting the economic opportunity structure available to minorities and thus possibly undermining their educational prospects. Following this, I examine how racial/ethnic prejudice works to undermine minority educational aspirations and performance directly through the school via the low expectations of teachers, administrators, and others for minority students.

THE IMPACT OF WHITES' BELIEF IN THE INTELLECTUAL INFERIORITY OF
AFRICAN AMERICANS

So far I have talked about the inclination of whites to embrace the notion of black inferiority; now I want to look at the reaction of African Americans to this belief. One of the most compelling statements in this regard was made by Jeff Howard, a social psychologist, and Ray Hammond, a physician and ordained minister, in 1985. They were keenly aware of data indicating that black students at all socioeconomic levels tend, on average, to perform less well on standardized tests than whites and Asians. For example, they noted that "Asian-Americans consistently produce a median SAT score 140 to 150 points higher than blacks with the same family income" and that, in the mid-1980s, only 1.6 percent of the African American police officers who took the sergeants' examination in New York City were able to pass the test compared to 10.6 percent of the whites who sat for the exam, in spite of the fact that the test had been revised on court order to ensure that its content "was job-related and nondiscriminatory."[1] Howard and Hammond believe that this educational performance gap is grounded in the historical and contemporary influence of the belief by whites that blacks have innately inferior mental abilities:

> The performance gap is largely a behavioral problem. It is the result of a remediable tendency to avoid intellectual engagement and competition. Avoidance is rooted in the fears and self-doubt engendered by a major legacy of American racism: the strong negative stereotypes about black intellectual capabilities. Avoidance of intellectual competition is manifested most obviously in the attitudes of many black youths toward academic work, but is not limited to children. It affects the intellectual performance of black people of all ages and feeds public doubts about black intellectual ability.[2]

There is ample reason to believe that a significant number of whites are still convinced of the inferiority of blacks (see chapter 8). Howard and Hammond link the persistence of this belief to the impact of the academic debate about black intellectual ability that emerged in the late 1960s: "For 15 years news magazines and television talk shows have enthusiastically taken up the topic of black intellectual endowment. We have watched authors and critics debate the proposition that blacks are genetically inferior to whites in intellectual capability." If the academic performance gap between blacks and other groups is to be closed, Howard and Hammond argue, the African American community must make intellectual development and competition a primary objective, and the white community must abandon its low expectations for the academic achievement of blacks and become unambiguously supportive of their educational progress.[3]

Howard and Hammond are not alone in the black community in their concern about the "rumor of inferiority." In 1989, the Joint Center for Political Studies (JCPS), a nonprofit research and public policy institution concerned with issues of importance to African Americans, published *Visions of a Better Way: A Black Appraisal of Public Schooling*, which stated,

> We hold this truth to be self-evident: all black children are capable of learning and achieving. Others who have hesitated, equivocated, or denied this fact have assumed that black children could not master their schoolwork or have cautioned that blacks were not "academically oriented." As a result, they have perpetuated a myth of intellectual inferiority, perhaps genetically based. These falsehoods prop up an inequitable social hierarchy with blacks disproportionately represented at the bottom, and they

---

1. Jeff Howard and Ray Hammond, "Rumors of Inferiority," *New Republic* 72, 9 September 1985, p. 18.
2. Ibid.
3. Ibid., pp. 19, 21.

absolve schools of their fundamental responsibility to educate all children, no matter how deprived.[4]

Those responsible for developing this report included several of the nation's most highly respected black scholars and educators. The historian John Hope Franklin, emeritus professor of history at Duke University, chaired the committee that prepared the report, and Sarah Lawrence Lightfoot, of the Harvard Graduate School of Education, was the principal author. The committee also included, among others, the child psychiatrist and school reformer James P. Comer of Yale University and the sociologist William Julius Wilson of the University of Chicago.

In the late 1980s and early 1990s, the rumor of inferiority problem was presented separately to national audiences by twin (African American) brothers Claude M. Steele of Stanford University and Shelby Steele of San Jose State University. In *The Content of Our Character: A New Vision of Race in America* (1990), Shelby Steele emphasized the self-doubt that he believes many African Americans feel regarding their ability to compete academically as a result of whites' historical view that blacks are inferior to whites.[5] In an article that appeared in the *Atlantic Monthly*, Claude Steele discussed the tendency of many African Americans to "disidentify" with academic achievement and thus avoid competing for high grades. He took the position that the disidentification process is heavily associated with a deep-seated worry that if blacks do not do well in school this will confirm whites' belief that blacks in general are intellectuallly inferior.[6]

The concerns of Howard and Hammond, the Steeles, and others have emphasized the psychological costs that this belief imposes on African American students through self-doubt and aversion to academic competition. Another approach to this issue has emphasized the disincentives to academic achievement posed by the truncated opportunity structure that initially emerged as a result of the nation's race-based caste system. These disincentives are believed to have contributed to a substantial lowering of the academic motivation and, therefore, the performance of many black students.

PREJUDICE AND DISCRIMINATION, THE OPPORTUNITY STRUCTURE, AND ACADEMIC ACHIEVEMENT ORIENTATION

For more than two decades, John U. Ogbu, a Nigerian-born anthropologist at Berkeley, has been concerned with discovering why some minority groups have done well academically in American schools while others have done poorly. Ogbu observed that the more academically successful groups have usually been

4. Committee on Policy for Racial Justice, *Visions of a Better Way* (Washington, D.C.: Joint Center for Political Studies Press, 1989), p. 1.

5. Shelby Steele, *The Content of Our Character: A New Vision of Race in America* (New York: St. Martin's Press, 1990), pp. 37–55.

6. Claude M. Steele, "Race and the Schooling of Black Americans," *Atlantic Monthly* (April 1992): 68–78.

voluntary minorities—those who immigrated to the United States in the hope of improving their life circumstances. In contrast, the less academically successful groups have typically been involuntary minorities, people who originally did not want to be a part of the American population. Those who came from eastern and southern Europe in the late nineteenth and early twentieth centuries are obvious examples of voluntary immigrant groups that have successfully joined the American mainstream. Africans brought to this country in bondage, as well as Hispanics and Native Americans who were incorporated into the U.S. population through territorial conquest and expansion, are among the primary examples of involuntary minorities.[7]

Ogbu believes that voluntary minorities have typically been reasonably well prepared to cope with at least some problems in their new country associated with being considered foreigners: they anticipated some degree of prejudice and discrimination against them as an inevitable cost of coming to America. Many could take this perspective because they were able to compare the United States with their country of origin in terms of the quality of life it offered. In most cases, Ogbu believes, the comparison was probably in favor of the U.S. experience. In contrast, groups that were involuntarily incorporated into the United States were more likely to be preoccupied with what they had lost.

Probably more important over the long term has been the quality of the opportunity structure. Ogbu points out that the voluntary immigrants from Europe were subjected to much less discrimination on the basis of race/ethnicity than were the involuntary immigrants.[8] For example, although most immigrants from eastern and southern Europe at the turn of the century had little formal education, they had ready access to low-skilled industrial jobs that paid enough to support their families, and their children were able to take advantage of the public schools available in northeastern cities.[9] By the time these children reached adulthood, they were collectively much better educated and generally more acculturated than their parents.[10] Because they were white, they were able to use these advantages to secure better jobs and higher social positions than their immigrant parents had. This process of intergenerational advancement repeated itself in subsequent generations, with the result that the present-day descendants of turn-of-the-century European immigrants are now basically full members of mainstream society.[11]

7. John U. Ogbu, "Diversity and Equity in Public Education: Community Forces and Minority School Adjustment and Performance," in *Policies for America's Schools: Teachers, Equity, and Indicators,* Ron Haskins and Duncan MacRae, eds. (Norwood, N.J.: Ablex, 1988), pp. 141–42.

8. Ibid., pp. 141–43.

9. John D. Kasarda, "Caught in a Web of Change," *Society* 22 (November/December 1983): 42.

10. Michael R. Olneck and Marvin Lazerson, "The School Achievement of Immigrant Children: 1900–1930," *History of Education Quarterly* 14 (Winter 1974): 453–82. As the authors point out, while the various European immigrant groups enjoyed substantial intergenerational educational advancement, the rates of advancement varied among the groups: e.g., Russian Jews progressed more rapidly than Southern Italians.

11. Lisa J. Neidert and Reynolds Farley, "Assimilation in the United States: An Analysis of Ethnic and Generation Differences in Status and Achievement," *American Sociological Review* 50 (December 1985): 840–50.

Most involuntary minorities confronted a much greater barrier to the mainstream than a low level of formal education: difference in racial status. African Americans were enslaved for well over two centuries and subsequently subjected to another hundred years of pervasive race-based subordination. And until recent decades, those blacks who did succeed in obtaining a substantial amount of formal education were usually prevented from seeking employment consistent with their education in white-dominated institutional settings.[12]

Ogbu believes that, having been blocked from access to mainstream society, many members of America's involuntary minorities eventually developed definitions of themselves that were oppositional to the majority culture: that is, they developed a dislike of whites so great that they did not want to take on attributes they identified with white culture, especially attributes that whites had actively prevented them from cultivating.[13] The cost of rejecting some aspects of white culture (European classical music, for example) was often inconsequential for involuntary minorities, but it has been extraordinarily high for other aspects, including education. Ogbu believes that the severe truncation of the educational and occupational opportunity structure blacks experienced eventually led many of them to define substantial amounts of formal education and the jobs it led to (such as scientist or university professor) as "white," not "black." Some blacks developed extremely low academic motivation because there was little prospect of gaining a high occupational return on their efforts.[14]

The development of this oppositional orientation toward education is probably relatively recent. Long before the end of slavery, free blacks in the North pursued educational advancement with remarkable dedication despite the obstacles erected by the white community. Newly freed slaves in the South manifested a similar passion for education. In 1910, in many northern cities a higher percentage of black children were enrolled in school than of American-born children of European immigrants. This continued to be true in many cities as late as 1930, in spite of the large migration of rural southern blacks, most of whom had relatively little formal education.[15]

With the successes of the civil rights movement in the 1950s and 1960s, most of the legal obstacles to educational and occupational advancement for African Americans and other involuntary minorities were removed, but great damage

12. Bart Landry, *The New Black Middle Class* (Berkeley: University of California Press, 1987), pp. 18–57; Timothy L. Smith, "Native Blacks and Foreign Whites: Varying Responses to Educational Opportunity in America, 1880–1950," *Perspectives in American History* 6 (1972): 332–34.

13. Ogbu, "Diversity and Equity in Public Education," pp. 147–48. Similar to this notion of oppositional orientation is the idea that there are reactionary elements to black culture—attributes that developed in reaction to slavery and other forms of subordination. See James M. Jones, "Racism in Black and White," in *Eliminating Racism: Profiles in Controversy*, Phyllis A. Katz and Dalmas A. Taylor, eds. (New York: Plenum Press, 1988), pp. 120–21.

14. John U. Ogbu, "Overcoming Racial Barriers to Equal Access," in *Access to Knowledge: An Agenda for Our Nation's Schools*, John I. Goodlad and Pamela Keating, eds. (New York: The College Board, 1990), pp. 65–84.

15. See Meyer Weinberg, *A Chance to Learn: The History of Race and Education in the United States* (New York: Cambridge University Press, 1977), pp. 21–57; James D. Anderson, *The Education of Blacks in the South, 1860–1935* (Chapel Hill: University of North Carolina Press, 1988); Smith, "Native Blacks and Foreign Whites," pp. 309–35.

had already been done. Poverty rates among southern blacks continued to be high, and large numbers of northern blacks had been confined to poverty in central cities for two generations. Such researchers as William Julius Wilson and John Kasarda have shown that poverty among urban blacks in the North has been heavily associated with a shortage of low-skill, adequately paying jobs. However, African Americans were made even more vulnerable to these structural problems in the economy by the institutionalized racism that characterized the period before the civil rights movement. In the job market, this discrimination took two forms. First, blacks were blocked artificially from gaining access to most professional and skilled jobs in the mainstream of the economy. (This is what Ogbu and others have referred to as the "job ceiling.")[16] Second, in those areas in which blacks could seek employment, whites were usually hired first. This overt job market discrimination took an especially heavy toll in bad economic times; during the depths of the depression in the 1930s, "unemployment among Chicago Blacks in professional, proprietary, and managerial jobs had grown at five times the rate prevailing among whites, three times that of whites in clerical, skilled, and semiskilled positions, and twice that of whites even in unskilled and service occupations."[17]

Much of Ogbu's line of analysis is grounded in field work conducted with African American, Mexican American, and Asian American youngsters in California in the late 1960s and early 1970s. Subsequently, Ogbu and Signithia Fordham explored academic attitudes and behaviors among students in a mostly black high school in Washington, D.C. They found that the peer culture of the African American students strongly rejected behaviors that could be construed as "acting white"; among these were speaking standard English, visiting the Smithsonian Institution, reading or writing poetry, studying hard to get good grades, and actually getting high grades. (African American students who received good grades were labeled by their peers as "brainiacs.") Some students reduced their academic effort as a means of avoiding peer harassment. Others attempted to hide the fact that they were studying hard by not speaking in class, acting like the class clown, and participating extensively in athletic programs.[18]

There is some evidence that pressures against academic achievement experienced by black students do not originate exclusively with their peers; they also come from some adults in the African American community, including some parents.[19] This should not be surprising, for many African American adults have

16. Ogbu, "Overcoming Racial Barriers to Equal Access," pp. 65–67.
17. Smith, "Native Blacks and Foreign Whites," p. 333.
18. Signithia Fordham and John U. Ogbu, "Black Students' School Success: Coping with the Burden of 'Acting White'," *Urban Review* 18:3 (1986): 10–11, 13–23. For a discussion of the strategies employed by high-achieving black students to avoid being labeled brainiacs, see Signithia Fordham, "Racelessness as a Factor in Black Students' School Success: Pragmatic Strategy or Pyrrhic Victory?" in *Facing Racism in Education*, Nitza M. Hidalgo, Ceasar L. McDowell, and Emilie V. Siddle, eds. (Cambridge: *Harvard Educational Review*, Reprint Series No. 21, 1990), pp. 232–62.
19. Ogbu, "Overcoming Racial Barriers to Equal Access," pp. 77–78; Ogbu, "Diversity and Equity in Public Education," p. 158; Sophronia Scott Gregory, "The Hidden Hurdle," *Time*, 16 March 1992, p. 45.

had extensive experience with the lack of economic opportunity. Moreover, blacks' stereotypes of whites suggest profound distrust (see chapter 8). Survey researchers have repeatedly found that many African Americans are alienated from whites and mistrustful of mainstream institutions,[20] including schools and white teachers and school administrators. (Much of James Comer's work in elementary schools in New Haven has directly addressed the question of how school personnel can win the trust of minority students and their parents.)[21] This oppositional orientation is centered in the most economically disadvantaged segments of the black community, but Ogbu believes that even some middle-class black children are under peer pressure not to act white academically.[22]

Ogbu's general line of analysis has been challenged from a number of perspectives, especially because many studies, beginning with the Coleman Report in 1966, have found that black students from all socioeconomic levels verbally express high educational aspirations.[23] Three questions in particular stand out: (1) Do peers really have a significant impact on the academic motivation and achievement of students? (2) Do black students generally have lower academic motivation than white students? (3) Are middle-class black students as well as poor blacks likely to have lower academic motivation than whites?

It will be recalled that the Coleman Report concluded that a student's school peers were the most important school factor in predicting his or her academic achievement. (Family factors, however, were found to be much more significant predictors than were school factors in general.) Consistent with this conclusion, Kennedy, Jung, and Orland found that both poor and nonpoor students in schools with high proportions of poor students did less well than students in low-poverty-concentration schools (see chapter 5). Over the years, many other studies have found evidence that peers can, indeed, have an impact on student achievement. In a review of these studies in 1981, Judith K. Ide and her colleagues concluded that there was a modest but consistent relationship between peer influence and students' standardized test scores, course grades, educational aspirations, and occupational aspirations. Moreover, they found that peer influences were strongest in urban areas, which, of course, are locations with disproportionate numbers of economically disadvantaged minority students.[24]

20. For a recent analysis of this problem, using data collected in 1987 by the National Opinion Research Center, see Robert C. Smith and Richard Seltzer, *Race, Class, and Culture: A Study in Afro-American Mass Opinion* (Albany: SUNY Press, 1992). For a general summary of research on this topic, see Gerald David Jaynes and Robin M. Williams, Jr., eds., *A Common Destiny: Blacks and American Society* (Washington, D.C.: National Research Council, National Academy Press, 1989), pp. 131–36.

21. James P. Comer, "Educating Poor Minority Children," *Scientific American* 259 (November 1988): 42–48; John U. Ogbu, "Variability in Minority School Performance: A Problem in Search of an Explanation," *Anthropology and Education Quarterly* 18 (December 1987): 325–26, 332–33.

22. Ogbu, "Overcoming Racial Barriers to Equal Access," p. 80.

23. Roslyn Arlin Mickelson, "The Attitude-Achievement Paradox among Black Adolescents," *Sociology of Education* 63 (January 1990): 44.

24. Judith K. Ide, JoAnn Parkerson, Geneva D. Haertel, and Herbert J. Walberg, "Peer Group Influence and Educational Outcomes: A Quantitative Synthesis," *Journal of Educational Psychology* 73 (August 1981): 472–84.

A large study of American high school students conducted by Laurence Steinberg and others in the late 1980s substantially supports this conclusion. This study included fifteen thousand students from nine high schools, selected to provide diversity in race/ethnicity, social class, and location (rural, suburban, central city). It found that African American students often had difficulty becoming members of a peer group in which academic achievement was encouraged. The problem was so acute that many high-achieving black students reported that they "eschew contact with other African-American students and affiliate primarily with students from other ethnic groups."[25]

Roslyn Arlin Mickelson has undertaken a study designed to test Ogbu's theory that black students' negative perceptions of the opportunity structure are a source of their generally lower academic motivation and school achievement. Although her study has not produced results that prove or disprove Ogbu's theory, it has provided information responsive to our second and third questions—whether African American students in fact tend to have lower educational motivation than whites and, if so, whether this is a problem for middle-class as well as poor blacks. Mickelson administered a questionnaire to 1,193 seniors in eight public high schools to determine whether there were differences between the abstract and concrete attitudes of students toward education. An abstract attitude was defined as one reflecting society's general belief in the importance of education; a concrete attitude was one reflecting the student's empirical experiences with the economic/occupational value of education. Abstract attitudes were measured by whether students agreed with such statements as "Education is the key to success in the future" and "The way for poor people to become middle class is for them to get a good education." Concrete attitudes were measured by such statements as "Based on their experiences, my parents say people like us are not always paid or promoted according to our education," "Although my parents tell me to get a good education in order to get a good job, they face barriers to job success," and "When our teachers give us homework, my friends never think of doing it."[26]

Mickelson hypothesized that most black students in her sample would hold an abstract attitude toward education similar to the one generally held by the mainstream (white) population: that education is the key to success. She also hypothesized that many African American students (but relatively few whites) would have a concrete attitude toward education that was much more negative than their abstract attitude: that education frequently does not produce good economic/occupational opportunities for black people such as themselves. Finally, she hypothesized that most black students would have school grades reflecting their concrete, not their abstract, attitude toward education. The findings were consistent with these hypotheses: black and white students from middle-class as well as working-class families were in general agreement, in the

25. Laurence Steinberg, Sanford M. Dornbusch, and B. Bradford Brown, "Ethnic Differences in Adolescent Achievement: An Ecological Perspective," *American Psychologist* 47 (June 1992): 728. See also chapter 10 below.
26. Mickelson, "The Attitude-Achievement Paradox among Black Adolescents," pp. 44, 49, 51.

abstract, about the high value of education. However, the concrete aspirations of black students were much lower than both their own abstract aspirations and the concrete aspirations of white students. In contrast, the abstract and concrete attitudes of white middle-class students were very similar. The concrete aspirations of working-class whites were somewhat lower than their abstract aspirations but were actually higher than the concrete aspirations of middle-class blacks. Finally, the concrete attitudes of black students toward education, but not their abstract attitudes, were closely associated with their grades and standardized test scores. For the African American students in Mickelson's study, low concrete attitudes toward the value of education and poor academic performance went hand in hand.[27]

The recent study of high school students by Steinberg and his colleagues also supports Ogbu's view that students' academic performance is influenced by their perception of the relationship between academic achievement and access to jobs. The researchers found that "the more students believe that doing well in school pays off, the more effort they exert in school and the better they perform there." They also found, however, that "the extent to which students believe that there are negative consequences of school failure is a better predictor of their school performance than the extent to which they believe that there are positive consequences of school success. That is, across ethnic groups, the more youngsters believe that not getting a good education hurts their chances, the better they do in school." They found that Asian Americans, the group of students who performed best academically, were the most likely to believe that poor academic performance would make it difficult to secure the kinds of jobs to which they aspired. Blacks and Hispanics, on the other hand, were the most optimistic about getting the kinds of jobs they wanted, even if they did poorly in school.[28]

It may be difficult to accept the finding that some African Americans are now opposed to the majority culture to such a degree that they reject the pursuit of high academic achievement. However, the research by Mickelson as well as by Steinberg and his colleagues suggests that a poor opportunity structure may produce a range of responses that can have a negative impact on academic performance. Some black students may reject high academic achievement because they consider it to be a white attribute. Some may simply lower their effort when it has become difficult for them to perform well academically or when they perceive that good academic performance is unlikely to translate into significantly improved life chances. Black students may also be unable to assess the level of academic performance it takes to prepare for good jobs or to avoid bad jobs, possibly in part because the students know few adults who have excellent educations and the associated desirable jobs. And it is often extremely difficult for black students to become members of peer groups that are supportive of academic achievement.

27. Ibid., pp. 52–60. It is not possible, of course, to determine from correlation analysis whether low concrete attitudes toward the value of education helped "cause" low grades, whether low grades helped "cause" low attitudes, or whether they were mutually reinforcing phenomena.

28. Steinberg, Dornbusch, and Brown, "Ethnic Differences in Adolescent Achievement" p. 726.

What applicability does Ogbu's line of analysis have to the academic performance patterns of students from other minority groups? In particular, why have some nonwhite minorities, including Chinese Americans and Japanese Americans, generally done well academically while many Hispanics and Native Americans have done significantly less well than the white majority?[29] In the mid-1980s, Ogbu and Maria Eugenia Matute-Bianchi explored these questions using Chinese Americans and Mexican Americans as case studies. They found that Chinese students have generally benefited from a long-standing cultural tradition that places a very high value on learning and education and family norms that establish strong educational "duties" for both parents and children. Parents are expected to encourage their children's academic advancement and to make appropriate sacrifices to ensure their success, and children are obliged to reciprocate by making whatever personal effort is necessary to be successful in their studies.[30]

Ogbu and Matute-Bianchi believe that the academic success of the Chinese has been a product of another important advantage: The occupational opportunity structure in the United States improved somewhat sooner for the Chinese than for blacks, allowing them to penetrate professional occupations in significant numbers by the 1940s—a generation before African Americans were able to do so, especially in the South.[31]

Research by others suggests several additional factors were at work. For example, because large numbers of Chinese immigrants did not arrive in the United States until around 1850, the total period of time in which the Chinese experienced an extremely negative opportunity structure was much shorter than was the case for blacks—about a century. The Chinese were also a very small minority throughout this period, which meant that they could seek out occupational niches such as laborers in agriculture and workers in domestic or personal services, which minimized the job market conflict with the white community.[32] There were, as well, few Chinese children in the United States during this period, owing primarily to a shortage of Chinese women for the men to

29. See Ronald Takaki, *Strangers from a Different Shore: A History of Asian Americans* (Boston: Little, Brown, 1989), Penguin Books edition, 1990).

30. John U. Ogbu and Maria Eugenia Matute-Bianchi, "Understanding Sociocultural Factors: Knowledge, Identity, and School Adjustment," in *Beyond Language: Social and Cultural Factors in Schooling Language Minority Students* (Sacramento: Bilingual Education Office, California State Department of Education, 1986), pp.73–142; Nathan Caplan, Marcella H. Choy, and John K. Whitmore, "Indochinese Refugee Families and Academic Achievement," *Scientific American* 266 (February 1992): 36–42; Barbara Schneider and Yongsook Lee, "A Model for Academic Success: The School and Home Environment of East Asian Students," *Anthropology and Education Quarterly* 21 (December 1990): 358–75.

31. Ogbu and Matute-Bianchi, "Understanding Sociocultural Factors," pp. 100–02, 105–06.

32. Everett S. Lee and Xue-lan Rong, "The Educational and Economic Achievement of Asian Americans," *Elementary School Journal* 88 (May 1988): 545–60. Between 1850 and 1940, the Chinese population in the United States never exceeded 120,000. Robert W. Gardner, Bryant Robey, and Peter C. Smith, "Asian Americans: Growth, Change, and Diversity," *Population Bulletin* 40 (October 1985): 11.

marry.[33] And finally, Chinese children were never viewed by large numbers of whites as being intellectually inferior (for either cultural or innate reasons), possibly because they were obviously doing very well in school as early as the 1860s.[34]

These factors suggest that the historical experience of Chinese Americans as a subordinate group to whites was vastly different from that of African Americans. Although the Chinese confronted extensive opportunity structure constraints, these were neither as pervasive nor, importantly, as long-lasting as those experienced by blacks. Consequently, the Chinese were less vulnerable to the emergence of an oppositional orientation toward whites and, in any case, were unlikely to view high academic achievement as an exclusively white attribute. Indeed, some researchers have suggested that, given the opportunity structure they encountered, Asian immigrants had a strong incentive to pursue high academic achievement as a means of reducing their vulnerability to discrimination in the labor market. For example, by the 1940s, when many sectors of the economy were still closed to them (including unionized semiskilled jobs, politics, sports, entertainment), opportunities began to open up in technical and scientific areas. Thus, Chinese parents could realistically urge their children to do as well as possible in school as a means of minimizing employment discrimination.[35]

The experience of Japanese Americans was in some respects similar to that of the Chinese. Japanese students have also benefited from a tradition of strong cultural and familial support for education. Because Japanese immigrants did not arrive in the United States in sizable numbers until the start of the twentieth century, their subordination to whites lasted only two to three generations. As a small minority, the Japanese were able to pursue a niche strategy in the job market, concentrating initially in farm labor and domestic and personal service work.[36] Finally, Japanese students also experienced virtually immediate academic success in American schools, so that whites did not develop negative stereotypes of their intellectual capacities. Indeed, researchers in the 1920s found that Japanese high school students earned better grades than students from other groups and performed about as well as white students on IQ tests.[37] Relative to most other nonwhite groups, including the Chinese, the Japanese had a high educational level among the immigrant generation. At the turn of the century, the average Japanese immigrant had about an eighth-grade education and a literacy rate somewhat

33. In 1890, there were twenty-seven Chinese men in the United States for every Chinese female; the ratio of men to women did not fall below two to one until the middle of the twentieth century. Lee and Rong, "The Educational and Economic Achievement of Asian-Americans," p. 51.

34. Jayjia Hsia, Asian Americans in Higher Education and at Work (Hillsdale, N.J.: Lawrence Erlbaum Associates, 1988), p. 11.

35. Stanley Sue and Sumie Okazaki, "Asian-American Educational Achievements: A Phenomenon in Search of an Explanation," American Psychologist 45 (August 1990): 917–19.

36. Lee and Rong, "The Educational and Economic Achievement of Asian Americans," p. 551. There were only about 285,000 Japanese in the United States as late as 1940. Gardner, Robey, and Smith, "Asian Americans: Growth, Change, and Diversity," p. 11.

37. Hsia, Asian Americans in Higher Education and at Work, p. 13.

higher than that of European immigrants. In contrast, many Chinese immigrants had relatively little formal education.[38]

Turning to Mexican Americans, one finds parallels to the experiences of African Americans in the period between the end of slavery and the beginning of the civil rights movement. For example, Mexican Americans in the Southwest were subjected to occupational discrimination, including a job ceiling that tended to restrict their employment to low-skill jobs. Their children were often sent to segregated schools, and many whites considered them to be culturally inferior (although not necessarily innately inferior). Consistent with this history, there has been a pattern of low academic performance and motivation among economically disadvantaged Mexican Americans.[39]

These parallels notwithstanding, Ogbu and Matute-Bianchi believe that, until recently, Mexican Americans have generally been more ambivalent than oppositional in their orientation to the Anglo majority. They suggest that this has been due, in part, to their descent from both Spaniards and Indians, which they believe led many Mexican Americans to identify with whites to a considerable degree, even when they were subjected to discrimination. This tendency may have been reinforced by the large number of Mexican Americans who have faced few or no physical appearance obstacles to becoming integrated into the white community.[40] Furthermore, many Mexican Americans are either immigrants or the children of immigrants. Indeed, many arrived in this country after the legal changes brought about by the civil rights movement in the 1950s and 1960s. These constitute a voluntary minority group, in Ogbu's terms, and have not experienced living under a legally enforced or sanctioned caste system.

The lack of an oppositional orientation among Mexican Americans may also be a product of the generally favorable labor market for low-skill workers that existed in the Southwest in the decades following World War II (especially in comparison to the Northeast). Mexican Americans have typically had a lower unemployment rate than blacks (although a higher one than whites).[41] The find-

38. Takaki, *Strangers from a Different Shore: A History of Asian Americans*, pp. 31–36, 45–46, 48. Many of the Chinese immigrants were peasants with little formal education, although a sizable number were merchants with considerable literacy skills. Among the Japanese immigrants the women as well as the men tended to have a significant amount of formal education for that period, reflecting the fact that, beginning in the early 1870s, the Japanese government had required the education of females as well as males. Also see Ogbu and Matute-Bianchi, "Understanding Sociocultural Factors: Knowledge, Identity, and School Adjustment," p. 103.

39. Ibid., pp. 111–34; Maria Eugenia Matute-Bianchi, "Ethnic Identity and Patterns of School Success and Failure among Mexican-Descent and Japanese-American Students in a California High School: An Enthnographic Analysis," *American Journal of Education* 95 (November 1986): 233–55. Also see chapter 6 above.

40. Ogbu and Matute-Bianchi, "Understanding Sociocultural Factors," pp. 118–19. Mexican Americans tend to vary in physical appearance, from those who look essentially like southwestern American Indians to those who look like whites. See David E. Hayes-Bautista, "On Comparing Studies of Different Raza Populations," *American Journal of Public Health* 73 (March 1983): 274–76.

41. The unemployment rate for Latinos in general has typically fallen between those of whites and African Americans (see chapter 4). The rate for Mexican Americans has generally followed the Hispanic pattern. For example, unemployment rates in 1989 were less than 5 percent for whites, about 8 percent for Hispanics, and over 11 percent for blacks. The rate for Mexican Americans was 8–9 percent. See Council of Economic Advisors, *Economic Indicators July 1992* (Washington, D.C.:

ings of a study by the Rand Corporation in the mid-1980s indicate that there was strong educational and occupational intergenerational advancement among Mexican Americans in California between 1950 and 1980, even though the immigrant generation usually had little formal education upon arrival in the United States. Significantly, the Rand researchers found that second- and third-generation (U.S.-born) Mexican Americans who completed their schooling in the 1970s had high school graduation rates close to the 80+ percent statewide average for all adult Californians, and the third generation had a college graduation rate about two-thirds of the statewide average. These cohorts had been largely able to move out of the low-skill job sector into middle-level craft, sales, and clerical positions — and a significant number into managerial and professional occupations.[42]

The outmarriage percentages also suggest that much of the Hispanic community, Mexican Americans included, is now in a qualitatively different position vis-à-vis the white majority than are African Americans. In the 1980–87 period, 16–17 percent of married Latinos had a non-Hispanic spouse; in contrast, less than 3 percent of married blacks had a nonblack spouse.[43] These outmarriage percentages look even more robust when the large-scale immigration from Latin America of the 1970s and 1980s is taken into account. Some studies have found that middle-class, native-born Mexican Americans have outmarriage rates about twice as high as the average outmarriage rate for Mexican Americans as a whole.[44]

U.S. Government Printing Office, July 1992), p. 12; Deborah J. Carter and Reginald Wilson, *Ninth Annual Status Report on Minorities in Higher Education* (Washington, D.C.: American Council on Education, 1991), p. 40.

42. Kevin F. McCarthy and R. Burciaga Valdez, *Current and Future Effects of Mexican Immigration in California, Executive Summary* (Santa Monica, Cal.: Rand Corp., 1985), pp. 28–32.

43. Bureau of the Census, Marital Characteristics, 1980 Census of Population, vol. 2, Subject Reports, PC80–2–4C (Washington, D.C.: U.S. Government Printing Office, 1985), p. 175; Dr. William P. O'Hare, Assimilation and Socioeconomic Advancement of Hispanics in the U.S., Staff Working Paper (Washington, D.C.: Population Reference Bureau, April 1989), pp. 58–59. Since the outmarriage percentage for blacks was less than 1 percent as recently as 1940, the 3 percent outmarriage figure in the 1980s can be regarded as evidence of some reduction in racial/ethnic barriers. But this figure is about what the outmarriage rate was for the immigrant generation of Japanese in the 1920s. About 30 percent of all married Japanese Americans in 1980 had a non-Japanese spouse. See Paul R. Spickard, *Mixed Blood: Intermarriage and Ethnic Identity in Twentieth-Century America* (Madison: University of Wisconsin Press, 1989), pp. 344–45; Bureau of the Census, *Marital Characteristics, 1980 Census of Population*, p. 175; John N. Tinker, "Intermarriage and Assimilation in Plural Society: Japanese-Americans in the United States," *Marriage and Family Review* 5 (Spring 1982): 62–64. On contemporary attitudes of whites and African Americans toward intermarriage, see Isabel Wilkerson, "Black-White Marriages Rise, But Couples Still Face Scorn," *New York Times*, 2 December 1991, pp. A1, B6; Orde Coombs, "Black Men and White Women," *Essence* 14 (May 1983): 81–82, 137–38, 143–44; Ernest Porterfield, "Black-American Intermarriage in the United States," *Marriage and Family Review* 5 (Spring 1982): 17–34; Gary A. Cretser and Joseph J. Leon, "Intermarriage in the U.S.: An Overview of Theory and Research," *Marriage and Family Review* 5 (Spring 1982): 3–15; Delores P. Aldridge, "Interracial Marriages: Empirical and Theoretical Considerations," *Journal of Black Studies* 8 (March 1978): 355–68; Thomas P. Monahan, "The Occupational Class of Couples Entering into Interracial Marriages," *Journal of Comparative Family Studies* 7 (Summer 1976): 175–92.

44. See Edward Murguia, *Chicano Intermarriage: A Theoretical and Empirical Study* (San Antonio: Trinity University Press, 1982); Avelardo Valdez, "Recent Increases in Intermarriage by Mexican American Males: Bexar County, Texas, from 1971 to 1980," *Social Science Quarterly* 64 (March 1983): 136–44.

Overall, there are a number of indications that racial/ethnic discrimination had been substantially reduced for many Mexican Americans by the 1980s. Why, then, is it reasonable to surmise that an oppositional orientation may be developing among Mexican Americans? Ogbu and Matute-Bianchi pointed out that many Mexican Americans continue to live in barrios segregated from the mainstream of society, and that the concentration of Mexican Americans has increased owing to recent large-scale immigration. They believe that this is taking place in a context in which many Mexican Americans still experience a great deal of discrimination in employment, housing, and education.[45]

Importantly, many of the barrios have been experiencing economic stress owing in part to the shortage of adequately paying low-skill jobs for a number of years.[46] This appears to be an increasingly serious problem for Mexican Americans as well as other Latinos because recent Mexican immigrants have much less formal education than those who came to the United States a few decades ago. On average, Mexican immigrants since 1985 have had less than a sixth-grade education, while those in the early 1960s typically had more than an eighth-grade education.[47]

Further, it has been estimated that 65 percent of the young Hispanic adults in the 1980s were either high school dropouts or low-skill high school graduates — findings that do not bode well for the next generation of Latino students. Many will be children of adults who do not have the education and skills necessary to secure jobs that can keep their families out of poverty.[48] In several major cities, median earnings of Latinos not only have continued to be much lower than those of either whites or blacks but also have fallen as a percentage of white earnings.[49]

Because so many of the children of economically disadvantaged Mexican Americans continue to do poorly in school, it is plausible that a significant number of them will become increasingly estranged from the mainstream of society in the years ahead. For this reason, it is very disturbing that some recent research suggests a tailing off in the rate of intergenerational educational advancement among the children and grandchildren of Mexican immigrants — something that might be expected to occur in a context in which economic prospects are deteriorating and many young people from disadvantaged families begin to lose hope of making progress toward the mainstream.[50]

45. Ogbu and Matute-Bianchi, "Understanding Sociocultural Factors; Knowledge, Identity, and School Adjustment," pp. 124–26.

46. Roberto Suro, "Mexicans Come to Work, But Find Dead Ends," New York Times, 19 January 1992, pp. A1, A20.

47. Frank D. Bean, Jorge Chapa, Ruth Berg, and Kathryn Sowards, "Educational and Sociodemographic Incorporation among Hispanic Immigrants to the United States," in Immigration and Ethnicity: The Integration of America's Newest Immigrants, Barry Edmonston and Jeffrey S. Passel, eds. (Forthcoming).

48. "Children and Parents: The Two-Generation Approach," Research Bulletin, Hispanic Policy Development Project, 1 (Fall 1989): 3–9.

49. A More Perfect Union: Achieving Hispanic Parity by the Year 2000 (New York: The Hispanic Policy Development Project, 1990).

50. See Roberto Suro, "Generational Chasm Leads to Cultural Turmoil for Young Mexicans in

Given the diversity of the Latino population in the United States, an obvious question is whether Ogbu's line of analysis is relevant to other segments of the Hispanic community. There are several reasons to believe that it may be applicable to portions of the Puerto Rican community. First, many Puerto Ricans have substantial African ancestry, so that they may be viewed as black (as well as Latino) by many non-Hispanic whites and subjected to the prevailing negative white stereotypes of blacks.[51] (Puerto Ricans have historically experienced a degree of residential segregation from whites similar to that experienced by African Americans.)[52] Second, Puerto Ricans on the mainland are concentrated in northeastern cities that have long had extensive structural unemployment and underemployment problems.[53] Third, there is a long-standing pattern of extremely low academic achievement among some Puerto Rican students, particularly those from economically disadvantaged circumstances (see chapters 3, 6). And finally, poverty and unemployment rates for Puerto Ricans have tended to be extremely high—considerably higher even than those for Mexican Americans. For example, in 1989, the unemployment rate for Puerto Ricans was 12 percent compared to about 8 percent for Mexican Americans. That year the poverty rate was 34 percent for all Puerto Ricans and 49 percent for Puerto Ricans under 18. The corresponding rates for Mexican Americans were, respectively, 29 percent and 38 percent.[54] Given these circumstances, it would not be surprising if large numbers of Puerto Rican students saw little hope of escaping poverty by working hard in school and did not feel estranged from the white community.

Ogbu has suggested that his line of analysis is also likely to be relevant to understanding the educational achievement patterns of Native Americans.[55] Relatively little relevant research is available for this diverse segment of the U.S. population, but in a recent review of data on dropout rates among American Indian high school students, Susan Ledlow has suggested that long-standing opportunity structure problems, which have their origins largely in the treat-

---

U.S.," *New York Times*, 20 January 1992, p. A16; Bean, Chapa, Berg, and Sowards, "Educational and Sociodemographic Incorporation among Hispanic Immigrants to the United States." It cannot be said that historical white prejudice and discrimination are a primary cause of the labor market problems confronting many recent Mexican immigrants with little formal education. However, the contemporary racial/ethnic prejudices of some whites may be making it more difficult to establish social policies designed to address their circumstances.

51. Apparently very few Puerto Ricans classify themselves as black. A recent analysis of 1980 census data revealed that 44 percent of the Puerto Ricans in New York City that year classified themselves as white; 4 percent as black; 48 percent as other while also writing in a Spanish descriptor such as Hispanic or Boricua; and 4 percent as other without using an additional descriptive term. Clara E. Rodriguez, "Racial Classification among Puerto Rican Men and Women in New York," *Hispanic Journal of Behavioral Sciences* 12 (November 1990): 369–70.

52. Douglas S. Massey and Nancy A. Denton, "Residential Segregation of Mexicans, Puerto Ricans, and Cubans in Selected U.S. Metropolitan Areas," *Sociology and Social Research* 73 (January 1989): 73–83.

53. See Marta Tienda, "Puerto Ricans and the Underclass Debate," *Annals of the American Academy of Political and Social Science* 501 (January 1989): 105–19.

54. Carter and Wilson, *Ninth Annual Status Report on Minorities in Higher Education*, p. 40.

55. Ogbu, "Overcoming Racial Barriers to Equal Access," pp. 63–65.

ment of American Indians by the white majority, seem to have contributed to the emergence of attitudes, beliefs, and behaviors among Native Americans that are consistent with Ogbu's theories.[56]

One of the primary sources of evidence for Ledlow's case is a study by Donna Deyhle of Navajo, Ute, and white youth in a border reservation community. Some of her subjects lived in a traditional community on the Navajo reservation, some on the Ute reservation, and some in a town at the edge of the Navajo reservation. The population was split between those who attended a Navajo high school with few white students and those who attended a high school in the border community, with a student body that was more than 50 percent white.[57]

Deyhle found that a chronic problem facing the Navajo and Ute young people was an inadequate supply of jobs in the area requiring a high school diploma or postsecondary education. Their employment prospects were made even worse by the fact that Navajos and Utes have historically not fared well in competition with whites for the middle- and high-skill positions that do exist (owing to a considerable extent, in her view, to discrimination). Regardless of whether they had earned a high school diploma, Dehyle found that most of the employed Navajos and Utes had low-skill occupations: cook, janitor, bus driver, seamstress, and so on. Consequently, many of the young people she studied did not have strong occupational incentives to stay in school or to do high quality academic work. Of those who did graduate from high school, 31 percent had jobs, 28 percent were students, 21 percent were unemployed, and 20 percent had an unknown status; among those who did not graduate, 38 percent were unemployed, 11 percent had jobs, 9 percent were students, and 42 percent had an unknown status. Deyhle estimated that only 1 percent of the Navajo young people in the area earn four-year college degrees and 2 percent earn two-year degrees.[58]

A large number of the Navajo and Ute youth, particularly those who attended the border community high school, expressed distrust of the school. Deyhle documented that academically oriented Navajo and Ute students were subjected to negative academic pressure from both their Indian peers and adults, in part because high academic achievement is considered a white attribute. Successful Indian students who aspired to attend college were especially vulnerable to this charge because they had to leave the area to attend college and probably would be unable to return to the reservation after graduation if they wanted a job that made full use of their higher education. She also found evidence that those who go away to college tend to feel they are rejecting their cultural identity because they must leave their families and tribe.[59]

56. Susan Ledlow, "Is Cultural Discontinuity an Adequate Explanation for Dropping Out?" *Journal of American Indian Education* 31 (May 1992): 21–36.
57. Donna Deyhle, "Constructing Failure and Maintaining Cultural Identity: Navajo and Ute School Leavers," *Journal of American Indian Education* 31 (January 1992): 24–27, 45.
58. Ibid., pp. 37–39.
59. Ibid., pp. 40–41, 44.

High poverty rates, high unemployment rates, and lack of access to jobs near or on reservations requiring substantial amounts of formal education are problems that exist not only for the Navajos and Utes, but for a number of other tribes.[60] Moreover, the high school dropout rate for Navajos, which has been recently estimated to be 31 percent, is similar to that of the Native American population as a whole.[61]

THE IMPACT OF CONTEMPORARY PREJUDICE ON THE OPPORTUNITY STRUCTURE FOR MINORITIES

The discussion so far has focused on how historical racial/ethnic prejudice and discrimination have contributed to the emergence of a negative educational and occupational opportunity structure for some minorities and, as a consequence, may have helped undermine the academic motivation of students from these groups. An equally important issue is, What relationship, if any, is there between contemporary racial/ethnic prejudice and the quality of the opportunity structure being experienced by minority youngsters?

Some of the survey research data presented in chapter 8 shed light on this matter. A case can be made that their belief in the cultural or innate inferiority of some minorities contributes to the unwillingness of some whites to support government policies to improve the circumstances of economically disadvantaged segments of these racial/ethnic groups. In this way, contemporary prejudice may play a crucial (albeit indirect) role in perpetuating academic motivation and achievement problems among economically disadvantaged minority students.

In chapter 8, I described James Kluegel's analysis of General Social Survey data from 1977 and 1988–89 regarding the explanations whites give for the differences between whites and blacks in socioeconomic circumstances. Kluegel explored the relationship between these explanations and the degree of support whites expressed for government efforts to help African Americans. Responses to two GSS questions about government's responsibilities to blacks provided data for this exploration. One question was concerned with whether the government was spending enough money to improve the conditions of African Americans. The second probed whether whites believed government had a responsibility to help blacks improve their standard of living, owing to the nation's history of discrimination.

Kluegel found that of those whites who said that the poor socioeconomic conditions experienced by blacks were due essentially to their lack of innate ability to learn, fewer than 9 percent felt that government was spending too little

60. Harold L. Hodgkinson, *The Demographics of American Indians: One Percent of the People, Fifty Percent of the Diversity* (Washington, D.C.: Institute for Educational Leadership, 1990); Peter T. Kilborn, "Sad Distinction for the Sioux: Homeland Is No. 1 in Poverty," *New York Times*, 20 September 1992, pp. A1, A32.

61. Karen Swisher and Michelle Hoisch, "Dropping Out among American Indians and Alaska Natives: A Review of the Studies," *Journal of American Indian Education* 31 (January 1992): 3–23.

money on blacks; about 52 percent said that government was spending too much. Similarly, among those who ascribed the difference in socioeconomic conditions to a lack of motivation on the part of African Americans, about 9 percent said that too little money was being spent on blacks, and 48 percent said that too much was being spent. In contrast, of those whites who said that the socioeconomic differences between blacks and whites were due exclusively to discrimination, about 48 percent said that government was spending too little on African Americans, and 7 percent said it was spending too much. Among other respondents, there was no strong tendency to believe that too much or too little money was being spent by government on African Americans. This was generally the case even for those who ascribed the differences in socioeconomic conditions solely to a lack of educational opportunity for African Americans; only about 14 percent of this group thought that the government was spending too much money on blacks, while 27 percent said it was spending too little.[62]

Relatively few whites expressed the opinion that government had a special obligation to improve the standard of living of African Americans owing to the nation's history of discrimination. With the exception of those whites who said they thought that the socioeconomic gaps between whites and blacks were due exclusively to discrimination, an absolute majority of whites disagreed with the notion that the government has such an obligation.

In the case of whites who hold negative cultural views of blacks, however, other survey data suggest that their attitudes may be even less sympathetic than the GSS data analyzed by Kluegel imply. For example, Mary Jackman and Mary Scheuer Senter found in a national survey in the mid-1970s not only that 37 percent of the whites in the sample believed blacks were lazy, but that over 90 percent of those who held this belief admitted that they disliked blacks. And about 90 percent of those who said they disliked blacks indicated that their dislike was strong rather than mild. Thus, about 30 percent of all whites in this national sample felt that African Americans were lazy (culturally inferior with regard to the work ethic) and had a strong dislike for blacks (37 percent × 90 percent × 90 percent = 30 percent).[63]

The GSS data of 1990 analyzed by Tom Smith showed that the negative racial/ethnic views held by some whites are not confined to African Americans but also extend to at least some Latinos (chapter 8). Smith's analysis indicates that 53 percent of all the respondents to the survey believed that blacks and Hispanics are less intelligent than whites; about 62 percent believed African Americans are lazier than whites, while 54 percent believed that about Latinos; about 78 percent believed African Americans are more likely than whites to prefer to be on welfare rather than to be self-supporting, while 72 percent

62. James R. Kluegel, "Trends in Whites' Explanations of the Black-White Gap in Socioeconomic Status, 1977–1989," *American Sociological Review* 55 (August 1990): 521.

63. Mary R. Jackman and Mary Scheuer Senter, "Different, Therefore Unequal: Beliefs about Trait Differences between Groups of Unequal Status," in *Research in Social Stratification and Mobility*, Donald J. Treiman and Robert J. Robinson, eds. (Greenwich, Conn.: JAI Press, 1983), pp. 316–23.

believed that of Hispanics; and 62 percent believed that blacks are more prone to violence than whites, while 50 percent believed that of Hispanics. This last finding touches on another important aspect of many whites' attitude toward African Americans and Latinos: fear.[64] Significantly, these attitudes are consistent with the actual behaviors of large numbers of whites. This is particularly true regarding whites' apparent desire to separate themselves spacially and socially from African Americans. Currently most whites live in neighborhoods with few African Americans and send their children to schools in which few blacks are enrolled. In metropolitan areas, whites also increasingly work, not simply live, in the suburbs.[65]

It is possible, of course, to interpret these data much differently. For example, the residential patterns of whites may reflect a preference to live among those who are culturally similar to themselves, not negative views of racial/ethnic minorities. The increasing tendency of white suburbanites to work in the suburbs rather than commute to jobs in central cities can be interpreted as primarily a response to the long-term structural shift of jobs from inner cities to the suburbs or as a general preference for short commutes. Similarly, the tendency not to support an expansion of minority-oriented government spending programs or to oppose affirmative action programs may reflect a concern that federal budget deficits have grown too large, a strong belief in the American tradition of individual responsibility, a belief in the associated idea that one should be awarded benefits on the basis of his or her demonstrated merits (accomplishments), or a belief that affirmative action programs are not an effective means of helping minorities develop the capacities necessary to compete on equal terms with whites in the labor market.[66]

Moreover, even when whites' views on some of these questions actually have racial/ethnic dimensions, they might be grounded more in intergroup conflict

64. There is more than a small amount of irony in this finding, since, historically, whites used both violence and the threat of violence to help maintain the race-based caste system that existed for so long in this country. For example, the lynching of black males was a common feature of the Jim Crow period. A frequent justification was that rape had been committed against a white woman, although the available evidence suggests that rapes of white women by black men rarely occurred. Robert L. Zangrando, *The NAACP Crusade against Lynching, 1909–1950* (Philadelphia, 1980), pp. 6–7; William Cohen, *At Freedom's Edge: Black Mobility and the Southern White Quest for Racial Control, 1861–1915* (Baton Rouge: Louisiana State University Press, 1991), pp. 210–13; George C. Wright, *Racial Violence in Kentucky, 1865–1940: Lynchings, Mob Rule, and "Legal Lynchings"* (Baton Rouge: Louisiana State University Press, 1990).

65. See Jaynes and Williams, *A Common Destiny*, pp. 76–80, 144–46; Lawrence Bobo, "Group Conflict, Prejudice, and the Paradox of Contemporary Racial Attitudes," in *Eliminating Racism: Profiles in Controversy*, Phyllis A. Katz and Dalmas A. Taylor, eds. (New York: Plenum Press, 1988), pp. 92–93; Harold L. Hodgkinson, *The Same Client: The Demographics of Education and Service Delivery Systems* (Washington, D.C.: Institute for Educational Leadership, 1989), pp. 9–11.

66. Some survey researchers believe that racial prejudice is being confounded by traditional American values related to the work ethic and individual responsibility. For example, the conclusion that blacks are lazy may reflect the use of a traditional work ethic to interpret the motives of an individual's or a group's behavior. Moreover, people who embrace traditional values may be opposed as a matter of principle to government social policies that transfer income from one group to another. This would make racial questions irrelevant to their opposition to more government spending on blacks. See Donald R. Kinder, "The Continuing American Dilemma: White Resistance to Racial Change 40 Years after Myrdal," *Journal of Social Issues* 42 (1986): 151–71.

over the allocation of scarce resources than in prejudice. Affirmative action is a case in point. The opposition of many whites may be based largely on a perception that it is a policy that tends to increase competition for good jobs.[67]

Again, white flight from inner cities may be interpreted primarily as a social class rather than a racial/ethnic phenomenon. As the economist Thomas Sowell has pointed out, wealthy and middle-class people have attempted to live apart from the poor throughout U.S history. For example, middle-class whites moved away from poor white ethnic immigrants in New York City and Boston in the nineteenth century. Sowell has pointed out that in the nineteenth century some blacks in Detroit and New York moved away from Italian and Polish immigrants as well as the Irish.[68] And, as I mentioned in chapter 4, William Julius Wilson believes that much of the social isolation of poor blacks in inner cities is due to the movement of middle-class African Americans to the suburbs.

In a related vein, whites' belief that blacks are prone to violence may reflect pragmatic social class observations rather than racially prejudiced views. There is more violence among the extremely poor than among other social classes, regardless of race/ethnicity. Since African Americans are disproportionately represented among the poor, these whites may have concluded that blacks are more likely to be violent than groups experiencing much less poverty.

Each of these is a plausible explanation of our current circumstances. But to acknowledge this is not to deny that the negative stereotypes whites hold of blacks and some other minorities have been enduring and consequential. Ample reason exists to conclude that these negative racial/ethnic stereotypes help to explain why many whites currently believe that little can be done to reduce poverty, unemployment, and low education levels among disadvantaged minority populations. To the extent that such beliefs place limitations on societal efforts to alleviate these circumstances, contemporary racial/ethnic prejudice contributes to the academic motivation and achievement problems of minorities.

Such a situation is both tragic and ironic. As George Fredrickson has pointed out, a full-blown theory of black inferiority was not the original cause of the race-based caste system in America but a delayed justification for it.[69] Although the nation's historical caste system has been largely dismantled and its legal foundations swept away, the negative stereotypes that were used by whites to justify the system live on with sufficient vigor to weaken the contemporary societal response to the pressing problems of poverty, unemployment, and under-education; that these problems are in many respects legacies of that system seems to have been forgotten.

67. See Bobo, "Group Conflict, Prejudice, and the Paradox of Contemporary Racial Attitudes," pp. 85–114.

68. Thomas Sowell, *Ethnic America: A History* (New York: Basic Books, 1981), p. 277.

69. George M. Fredrickson, *The Arrogance of Race: Historical Perspectives on Slavery, Racism, and Social Inequality* (Middletown, Conn.: Wesleyan University Press, 1988), pp. 3, 205.

Prejudice and discrimination influence not only the academic motivation and performance of minority students through the creation or maintenance of a negative economic opportunity structure, but also the opportunities for learning within the school itself.

The historical record gives good reason to examine the school from this perspective. For example, prior to the defeat of the Confederacy in the Civil War it was literally against the law in the southern states to educate slaves, and free blacks in the North were commonly denied access to public schools. During the Jim Crow era, schools in the South (and in other regions of the country) were segregated by race. There were also enormous differences in per pupil expenditures for black and white students for decades. Moreover, in the North and South, opportunities for African Americans to pursue a college preparatory program in high school and to attend college were extremely limited. Thus, until very recently, America's race-based caste system and the prejudiced attitudes and beliefs associated with it were deeply reflected in the practices of the educational system.

Although empirical data are not available, there is reason to believe that white educators have been as likely to hold negative racial/ethnic stereotypes as the white population as a whole. For example, in his book *The Mis-Education of the Negro* (1933), the eminent African American historian and educator Carter G. Woodson told the following anecdote:

> At a Negro summer school two years ago, a white instructor gave a course on the Negro, using for his text a work which teaches that whites are superior to the blacks. When asked by one of the students why he used such a textbook the instructor replied that he wanted them to get that point of view. Even schools for Negroes, then, are places where they must be convinced of their inferiority. The thought of the inferiority of the Negro is drilled into him in almost every class he enters and in almost every book he studies.[70]

Three decades later, another African American, the social scientist Kenneth B. Clark, wrote,

> In the late 1950s a number of teachers in the New York public school system told white student interviewers assigned by the author that Negro children are inherently inferior in intelligence and therefore cannot be expected to learn as much or as readily as white children; and that all one would do, if one tried to teach them as if they could learn, would be to develop in them serious emotional disturbances, frustrations and anxieties.[71]

70. Carter G. Woodson, *The Mis-Education of the American Negro* (Washington, D.C.: Associated Publishers, 1933; Trenton, NJ: African World Press Edition, 1990), p. 2.
71. Kenneth B. Clark, *Dark Ghetto: Dilemmas of Social Power* (New York: Harper & Row, 1965), p. 127.

A quarter-century later, yet another black American, the Yale law school professor Stephen L. Carter, told the following personal anecdote:

Particularly vivid is my memory of moving from a mostly black elementary
school to a mostly white junior high school, where I was not allowed to
enroll in even a basic Spanish class, despite three years' study of the language, because, my mother was told, the limited spaces were all allocated
to graduates of a particular elementary school—which happened to be all
white. I was assigned to vocational education instead. And when I moved
on to high school, carrying with me an A average in mathematics and excellent test scores, not only was I prevented from enrolling in the highest
math section—I was not even told that it existed![72]

Carter was born in 1954—the year of the Supreme Court decision declaring
racially segregated public schools unconstitutional. Even though he was both
an excellent student and the child of well-educated parents (his mother was a
college graduate and his father a lawyer who has both practiced the law and
taught it at Cornell), he was unable to avoid the rumor of inferiority. Moreover,
Carter believes that relatively little has changed since he was a student. In his
view, many whites continue to believe that the most intelligent African Americans are not as able as the most intelligent whites. He even has a name for this
phenomenon—"the best black syndrome." As he noted, "All black people who
have done well in school are familiar with it. We are measured by a different
yardstick: first black, only black, best black."[73]

Although Carter recognizes that many white educators continue to expect
that few blacks will perform as well academically as the best-performing whites,
he also is aware of an enormous obstacle to changing this expectation: at all
levels of the educational system, African Americans continue to be underrepresented among students who score highly on standardized tests and who earn
high grades.[74] Even though African Americans and some other minorities have
made considerable academic progress over the past twenty years, they remain
quite underrepresented among high-academic achievers and very overrepresented among low-academic achievers, a problem that exists at all social class
levels.

Clearly, schools in America have offered many fewer educational opportunities to minority groups than to whites. And it is reasonable to assume that some
white educators still do not expect African American students and students from
some other minority groups to do as well in school, on average, as white students. Still, it is difficult to assess how great a role these views currently play in
creating obstacles to the educational advancement of minorities. Do large numbers of teachers and administrators interact differently with minority students

72. Stephen L. Carter, *Reflections of an Affirmative Action Baby* (New York: Basic Books, 1991),
p. 49.
73. Ibid., p. 50.
74. Ibid., pp. 52–54.

than with majority students in ways that are detrimental to the educational prospects of the minority youngsters? If so, is this a product of racial/ethnic prejudice? Similarly, are minority students still being tracked into low-content academic programs in disproportionate numbers? If so, is this phenomenon a product of prejudice?

Teacher Expectations, Teacher-Student Interactions, and Academic Performance Patterns   In the late 1940s, the sociologist Robert Merton coined the term *self-fulfilling prophecy*, something that happens when "a false definition of the situation evokes a new behavior which makes the original false conception come true."[75] According to Kenneth Clark, assumptions that whites make about the inferiority of blacks are self-fulfilling prophecies:

> Once one organizes an educational system where children are placed in tracks or where certain judgments about their ability determine what is done for them or how much they are taught or not taught, the horror is that the results seem to justify the assumptions. . . . Children who are treated as if they are uneducable almost invariably become uneducable. This is educational atrophy. It is generally known that if an arm or a leg is bound so that it cannot be used, eventually it becomes unusable. The same is true of intelligence.[76]

In terms of the academic achievement of children, the notion that what you get is what you expect quickly became influential in educational circles as a result of two independent lines of research: that of identifying attributes of schools that are instructionally effective with disadvantaged children and that of understanding whether and how teachers' perceptions of their students' capacities ultimately influence how pupils perform. Both led specifically to an interest in the role educators' expectations play in shaping students' academic achievement patterns. The search for "effective schools" was stimulated by the Coleman Report. Although Coleman and his colleagues found that differences in the education-relevant resources of families were the primary cause of racial/ethnic differences in test score patterns, some educators and researchers believed that some schools must be exceptions to this rule. If the characteristics of these schools could be identified, they reasoned, it should be possible to adapt them successfully to other schools. Among the first to undertake the search for instructionally effective schools for disadvantaged urban children was George Weber, associate director of the Council for Basic Education.[77]

Weber, Ronald Edmonds, and other leading researchers found that a primary attribute of instructionally effective schools is that the teachers and administrators have high expectations for all students. In Edmonds's words, these schools

75. Robert K. Merton, *Social Theory and Social Structure* (New York: Free Press, 1957), p. 423.
76. Clark, *Dark Ghetto*, pp. 127, 128.
77. George Weber, *Inner-City Children Can Be Taught to Read: Four Successful Schools*, Occasional Papers No. 18 (Washington, D.C.: Council for Basic Education, 1971).

"have a climate of expectation in which no children are permitted to fall below minimum but efficacious levels of achievement."[78]

This conclusion has been underscored by a second line of research. In 1964, Robert Rosenthal, a psychologist, and Lenore Jacobson, an elementary school principal, began an experiment to determine whether the generally poor academic performance of disadvantaged children is due in part to the low expectations of teachers—expectations that tend to produce self-fulfilling prophecies. Teachers in Jacobson's school were asked to administer to their students the so-called Harvard Test of Inflected Intelligence. They were told that the test was part of a study by researchers at Harvard. The following fall, the teachers were informed that the test had identified some children who were "potential academic spurters," likely to do well in school; in reality, these children had been selected at random.

During the school year, teachers readministered the test in the middle of the year and again at the end. The year-end administration produced score patterns that Rosenthal and Jacobson regarded as strong evidence of an expectancy effect on students' intellectual development. The scores of the first- and second-grade "spurters" were much higher than those of the control group, although there was no clear pattern for the third through sixth graders. The teachers were asked at the end of the school year to describe how their pupils had conducted themselves in class. In the words of the researchers, "The children from whom intellectual growth had been expected were described as having a better chance of being successful in later life and as being happier, more curious and more interesting than the other children. There was also a tendency for the designated children to be seen as more appealing, better adjusted and more affectionate, and as less in need of social approval."[79]

The study was subjected to extensive scrutiny by the educational research community, owing to concerns about its methodology and to the failure of replications to produce similar results.[80] Nevertheless, it stimulated numerous studies designed to shed light on (1) the nature and variety of teachers' expectations for their students, (2) the basis on which their expectations are initially formed, (3) the factors that seem to influence whether teachers' expectations change over time, (4) the extent to which teachers' expectations vary among students from different groups (for example, males and females, members of different racial/ethnic groups, or members of different social classes), (5) the extent to which variations in teachers' expectations are associated with variations in how they treat students, (6) students' perceptions of teachers' expectations of

78. Ronald Edmonds, "Effective Schools for the Urban Poor," *Educational Leadership* 37 (October 1979): 16, 22.

79. Robert Rosenthal and Leonore F. Jacobson, "Teacher Expectations for the Disadvantaged," *Scientific American* 218 (April 1968): 19–23. In 1968, Rosenthal and Jacobson reported their findings in their book *Pygmalion in the Classroom: Teacher Expectation and Pupils' Intellectual Development* (New York: Holt, Rinehart & Winston, 1968).

80. For a history of some of these criticisms, see Samuel S. Wineburg, "The Self-Fulfillment of the Self-Fulfilling Prophecy," *Educational Researcher* 16 (December 1987): 28–37. For a summary of one early critic's views, see Lee J. Cronbach, "Five Decades of Public Controversy over Mental Testing," *American Psychologist* 30 (January 1975): 6–7.

them and of other students, and (7) the impact of teachers' expectations on students' academic performance and classroom conduct.

Although these studies have generated a variety of conflicting results, a number of general findings have emerged. First, teachers *do* typically form perceptions and beliefs about the academic ability, prospects, and other school-relevant attributes of each of their students. Importantly, they regard some students as having more academic ability than others and as likely to perform better academically in the future.[81]

Second, research suggests that teachers tend to rely primarily on school records (test scores, grades), conversations with other teachers, and their classroom experiences with their students to develop their initial impressions of the academic prospects and needs of each pupil. Teachers also tend to have accurate perceptions of school records for each student and to make accurate assessments of each student's academic prospects on the basis of the information available to them. And most teachers are willing to modify their expectations in response to new information and experiences, but usually not to a single new piece of information (such as a standardized test score provided by a researcher).[82]

Third, teachers do treat students differently because of differences in their expectations, and these differences can add up to fewer opportunities to learn for low-expectation students than for high-expectation students. The ways in which teachers have been found to treat low-expectation students differently include (1) calling on them less often to answer questions, (2) giving them less time to answer questions when they are called on, (3) giving them the answers to questions more frequently rather than spending time helping them to improve their responses, (4) criticizing them more often when they fail at a task, (5) praising them less frequently when they do succeed, (6) placing fewer academic demands on them, (7) paying less overall attention to them, (8) exercising greater supervision and control over them, (9) interacting with them in private more than publicly, (10) giving them less benefit of the doubt when grading tests and assignments, (11) generally giving them less information when providing feedback to their questions, (12) interacting with them less warmly (for example, smiling less often), (13) providing them with less opportunity to work independently, and (14) using fewer time-intensive instructional strategies with them.[83]

Fourth, students do become aware of their teachers' expectations for them and other students as well as of variations in teacher-student interactions based on those expectations. Both first graders and fifth graders are aware of differences in how teachers treat high- and low-achievers; however, younger students are less likely to feel that they have received negative treatment from their

81. See Thomas L. Good, "Teacher Expectations and Student Perceptions: A Decade of Research," *Educational Leadership* 38 (February 1981): 415–21; Jerome B. Dusek and Gail Joseph, "The Bases of Teacher Expectancies: A Meta-Analysis," *Journal of Educational Psychology* 75 (June 1983): 327–46.

82. Jere E. Brophy, "Research on the Self-Fulfilling Prophecy and Teacher Expectations," *Journal of Educational Psychology* 75 (October 1983): 636.

83. Ibid., pp. 641–42.

teachers, to regard how they are treated as related to their teachers' expectations, or to assess accurately their teachers' expectations for them personally. Older elementary school students tend to have expectations for themselves that are very similar to those held of them by their teachers.[84]

Finally, teachers' expectations do appear to influence their students' academic performance. Research indicates that low teacher expectations tend to lower students' academic performance and high expectations tend to raise it. However, the impact of teachers' expectations on students' performance tends to be small to moderate, suggesting that changes in expectations alone are unlikely to lead to large changes in academic achievement patterns. For example, Jere E. Brophy has concluded from his research and his synthesis of the findings of others that, on average, a student's academic performance is lowered or raised 5–10 percent as a result of the teacher's expectations.[85]

Brophy believes that the most common cases of self-fulfilling prophesies based on teacher expectations are those in which inappropriately low (rather than high) expectations lead to reductions in students' academic achievement. The largest expectancy effects identified through research seem to have been produced by the few teachers classified as overreactive, high bias, or dogmatic—those who are inclined to form pronounced and inflexible stereotypes of their students. Low expectations formed by these teachers can have a negative impact on the academic achievement of students. Brophy and his colleague Thomas L. Good found that most teachers tend to be reactive—open to adjusting their expectations to new information received from others or through their ongoing experiences with their students. They suggested that there is a third type of teacher, whom they describe as proactive. Such teachers tend to shape their expectations on the basis of what they want their students to achieve academically much more than on their students' actual performance. This group is the most likely to produce positive academic outcomes for students, including low academic performers.[86]

Although according to Brophy the average effect of teacher expectancy is small in absolute terms, it can loom large for the academic fortunes of many students. For instance, a 5 percent decrease in a student's score on a major test in a subject could be the difference between making an A or a B or

84. Rhona S. Weinstein, Hermine H. Marshall, Lee Sharp, and Meryl Botkin, "Pygmalion and the Student: Age and Classroom Differences in Children's Awareness of Teacher Expectations," *Child Development* 58 (August 1987): 1090–91; Elisha Babad, "Measuring and Changing Teachers' Differential Behavior as Perceived by Students and Teachers," *Journal of Educational Psychology* 82 (December 1990): 683–90; Karen A. Brattesani, Rhona S. Weinstein, and Hermine H. Marshall, "Student Perceptions of Differential Teacher Treatment as Moderators of Teacher Expectation Effects," *Journal of Educational Psychology* 76 (April 1984): 236–47.

85. Brophy, "Research on the Self-Fulfilling Prophecy and Teacher Expectations," pp. 633–35. Walberg has reached a similar conclusion: "High teacher expectations for student performance also have a moderate effect" on student learning. Herbert J. Walberg, "Improving the Productivity of America's Schools," *Education Leadership* 41 (May 1984): 23.

86. Brophy, "Research on the Self-Fulfilling Prophecy and Teacher Expectations," pp. 645, 647; Jere E. Brophy and Thomas L. Good, *Teacher-Student Relationships: Causes and Consequences* (New York: Holt Rinehart & Winston, 1974).

between being regarded by teachers as a student with above average versus average potential.[87]

A related finding is that variations in teachers' expectations about their pupils do not seem to have the same impact in all academic areas. Mary Lee Smith concluded that "reading and other achievement (e.g., language arts, social studies, number of concepts learned in a lesson) were influenced more than math achievement and grades. Pupil participation and social competence were affected by teacher expectation, but not other affective variables [such as creativity]." Smith also found that variations in teacher expectations usually had relatively little impact on variations in students' scores on IQ tests, and others have reached generally similar conclusions.[88]

Much of the research on teacher expectancy has focused on variations in teacher expectations and treatment of students from different racial/ethnic groups. In a review of these studies, Jacqueline Jordan Irvine concluded that "teachers, particularly white teachers, have more negative expectations for black students than for white students" and that teachers have more negative opinions of black students with regard to "personality traits and characteristics, ability, language, behavior, and potential."[89] Similarly, Jerome B. Dusek and Gail Joseph found that "black students and Mexican students are expected to perform less well than white students." However, the differences in expectations were fairly small. Aggregating data from twenty studies, they calculated that "approximately 54 percent of the white students were expected to outperform the average black student."[90]

The evidence is less clear whether teachers treat minority students differently as a result of their different expectations. Irvine found that most studies concerned with the character of interactions between teachers and black and white students have produced evidence that African American students receive less positive feedback and more negative feedback than white students; yet some studies have found no differences in feedback patterns on the basis of race. In her own classroom-based study, Irvine did not find large differences in teachers' responses to black and white students.[91]

Data from the NELS:88 national sample of eighth graders (table 9.1) are consistent with the conclusion that most teachers try to be genuinely responsive to the needs of students, regardless of their race/ethnicity, social class, or gender.

87. Robert Rosenthal is among those researchers who has made this point. See Rosenthal, "Pygmalion Effects: Existence, Magnitude, and Social Importance," *Educational Researcher* 16 (December 1987): 37–41; Monica J. Harris and Robert Rosenthal, "Mediation of Interpersonal Expectancy Effects: 31 Meta-Analyses," *Psychological Bulletin* 97 (May 1984): 363–86.

88. Mary Lee Smith, "Teacher Expectations," *Evaluation in Education* 4, no. 1 (1980): 52; Stephen W. Raudenbush, "Magnitude of Teacher Expectancy Effects on Pupil IQ as a Function of the Credibility of the Expectancy Induction: A Synthesis of Findings for Eighteen Experiments," *Journal of Educational Psychology* 76 (February 1984): 85–97.

89. Jacqueline Jordan Irvine, *Black Students and School Failure: Policies, Practices, and Prescriptions* (Westport, Conn.: Greenwood, 1990), pp. 56, 57.

90. Dusek and Joseph, "The Bases of Teacher Expectancies: A Meta-Analysis," p. 336; Theresa E. McCormick and Tino Noriega, "Low Versus High Expectations: A Review of Teacher Expectations Effects on Minority Students," *Journal of Equity and Leadership* 6 (Fall 1986): 224–34.

91. Irvine, *Black Students and School Failure*, pp. 57–59, 63, 66, 81.

Table 9.1
Agreement of NELS:88 Eighth Graders with Various Statements about Their Relationships with Their Teachers and Schools, by Race/Ethnicity, Social Class, Gender, and Grades

	Students and teachers get along	Discipline is fair	The teaching is good	Teachers are interested in students	Teachers praise my effort	Teachers really listen to me
All Students	67	69	80	75	63	68
Racial/ Ethnic Group						
Asian	73	73	83	79	71	75
Hispanic	66	71	81	77	71	71
Black	61	65	80	77	72	73
White	68	70	80	75	60	67
Native American	65	64	77	69	63	62
SES Quartile						
1st (bottom)	64	67	79	74	67	69
2nd	66	68	79	74	62	67
3rd	67	69	80	75	61	67
4th (top)	72	73	83	77	63	71
Gender						
Male	68	67	79	75	63	67
Female	67	71	82	76	64	70
Grade Quartile						
1st (bottom)	57	61	72	67	56	58
2nd	64	67	79	73	62	66
3rd	70	72	83	77	65	71
4th (top)	75	76	86	83	69	77

Source: Anne Hafner, Steven Ingels, Barbara Schneider, and David Stevenson, *A Profile of the American Eighth Grader: NELS:88 Student Descriptive Summary, National Education Longitudinal Study of 1988* (Washington, D.C.: Department of Education, U.S. Government Printing Office, 1990), p. 43

Looking first at the data for all students, we see that the response pattern was generally very positive. In just one case did fewer than two-thirds of the students indicate agreement with a statement about their teachers and schools: "only" 63 percent agreed that "teachers praise my effort."

The Asian American eighth graders were generally the most positive about their teachers. This response pattern is consistent with findings that teachers tend to have higher expectations for Asian students as well as generally more favorable views of their academic and classroom performance.[92]

Native American eighth graders had the least favorable overall response pattern. They had the lowest percentage in agreement with four of the six statements, including "teachers really listen to me" and "teachers are interested in students." This is consistent with the research. As I have noted, the school dropout rate is very high among American Indians. Like school-leavers in general, Native American students who drop out of school indicate that one of the factors that influenced their decision was their conviction that teachers did not care about them.[93]

The African American eighth graders had the most mixed response pattern. Only 61 percent agreed that "students and teachers get along," the smallest percentage of any group. However, 80 percent agreed that "the teaching is good," and 72 percent that "teachers praise my effort." The percentage on the last statement was the highest for any of the groups.

In terms of consistency of positive responses, Latinos were probably second only to Asians. About 81 percent agreed that the "teaching is good" and 71 percent "teachers praise my effort," that "teachers really listen to me," and "the discipline is fair."

In view of the hypothesis that teachers' expectations are lower for minority than for majority students, it is noteworthy that lower percentages of the white eighth graders than of the blacks and Latinos agreed that "teachers are interested in students," that "teachers really listen to me," and that "teachers praise my efforts."

How can these response patterns be explained? One possibility is that they reflect the fact that the students were not asked to estimate how much praise they received relative to children from other groups. Note also that the statements used in the NELS:88 sought students' perceptions of teachers' behaviors and teacher-student interactions but not their opinions about teachers' underlying attitudes toward them personally. Such questions might have produced less positive response patterns from minorities.

Another possibility is that the response patterns reflect the fact that the majority of eighth graders in the sample, regardless of race/ethnicity, were per-

92. See, for example, George Farkas, Robert P. Grobe, Daniel Sheehan, and Yuan Shuan, "Cultural Resources and School Success: Gender, Ethnicity, and Poverty Groups within an Urban School District," *American Sociological Review* 55 (February 1990): 127–42; Morrison G. Wong, "Model Students? Teachers' Perceptions and Expectations of Their Asian and White Students," *Sociology of Education* 53 (October 1980): 236–46.

93. Dehyle, "Constructing Failure and Maintaining Cultural Identity: Navajo and Ute School Leavers," pp. 27–32.

forming reasonably well in school, as measured by grades. Support for this interpretation can be inferred from the response patterns for students in the bottom and top quartiles by grades. Table 9.1 shows that, for all six statements, much lower percentages of students in the bottom quartile than of students in the top quartile expressed agreement. Moreover, both second- and third-quartile students were in general considerably more positive in their responses than the bottom-quartile students.

Support for this interpretation can also be inferred from the NELS:88 grade data by race/ethnicity (see table 3.13), which found Asians and whites to be underrepresented in the bottom quartile on grades and blacks, Hispanics, and Native Americans to be overrepresented. However, the overrepresentation was extreme only for the American Indian students. All racial/ethnic groups had reasonably close to proportional representation in the second and third quartiles. In the top quartile, Asians and whites were overrepresented, while the other three groups were underrepresented—with the underrepresentation again reaching an extreme level only for American Indians. Thus, in terms of academic success, *as measured by grades*, most students in the survey, regardless of race/ethnicity, had reason to be generally positive about their relationships with their teachers.

Teacher Expectations, Curriculum Content and Instruction, and Academic Performance Patterns   Variations in teachers' expectations may contribute to decisions that produce differences in the curricula and in the instructional strategies and materials provided to pupils from diverse groups. Differences in the content of the education provided to whites and to minorities have historically been among the most important sources of variations in academic achievement. For example, many whites long believed that schooling for blacks, Hispanics, and Native Americans should be limited primarily to vocational education (especially the manual arts and industrial education versions, which stressed preparation for very low-skill, physical-labor-intensive work). Rigorous academic programs were regarded as inappropriate for minorities.[94] This tendency to offer a substantially different educational program to whites than to some minority groups has been part of a general pattern of grouping children (including whites) on the basis of their perceived academic ability at the elementary school level and subsequently tracking them into varying curricula at the secondary school level. Young children are commonly assigned to high, medium, and low groups on the basis of assessments of their school readiness or early school performance. At the secondary level, it has been standard practice to steer students thought to have the most academic potential into the academic/college preparatory track and to guide those regarded as having less potential into the vocational or so-called general tracks.[95]

94. See James D. Anderson, *The Education of Blacks in the South, 1860–1935* (Chapel Hill: University of North Carolina Press, 1988.)

95. On grouping in elementary schools, see Robert E. Slavin, "Grouping for Instruction," *Equity and Excellence* 23 (Spring 1987): 31–36; in secondary schools, see Jeannie Oakes, *Keeping Track:*

Over the course of the twentieth century, grouping and tracking have been justified variously on the grounds that differences in intellectual potential are largely a function of innate capacities and that children learn best in homogeneous ability groups; that the proportion of children with substantial academic ability is relatively small and only the more academically able can profit intellectually from exposure to rigorous schooling in math, science, and so forth; that there are large differences in the academic potential of children from different racial/ethnic groups; and that the American economy requires relatively few people with advanced education. Given these views, the grouping of children during their school careers could be regarded as an efficient, humane method of educating a diverse population. In the first several decades of this century, the rapidly expanding secondary education system, in particular, could be viewed as an effective means of meeting the small but growing demand for college-trained individuals to fill leadership and professional positions in business and government, socializing (that is, Americanizing) immigrants, and providing most young people with the low- to middle-level skills required for most work in the society.[96]

Although grouping and tracking have been firm institutional features of the American educational landscape, their merits have been periodically debated. Many believe that most children are capable of mastering a demanding school curriculum. Others embrace the traditional view that democracy cannot function effectively unless all citizens are educated well. Along with the economy's increasing educational requirements, the growing strength of these two perspectives may have influenced the nation's efforts after World War II to make secondary education universal and to expand substantially the proportion of high school graduates who go on to college.[97] By the 1980s, increasing international economic competition, the findings of educational research, and the changing racial/ethnic demographics of the United States all contributed to a reemergence of concern about grouping and tracking practices.

The authors of *A Nation at Risk*, published in 1983, were deeply concerned that America's technological and economic leadership position in the world was eroding rapidly, in part because some other nations had begun to surpass the

How Schools Structure Inequality (New Haven: Yale University Press, 1985), pp. 2–3, 40–60; Ernest Boyer, *High School: A Report on Secondary Education in America* (New York: Harper & Row, 1983), pp. 79–80. For a summary of grouping practices in a large sample of elementary and secondary schools, see John I. Goodlad, *A Place Called School: Prospects for the Future* (New York: McGraw-Hill, 1984), pp. 130–66.

96. On the rationale for tracking, see Goodlad, *A Place Called School,* pp. 138–57; Oakes, *Keeping Track,* pp. 6–39.

97. The Educational Policies Commission of the National Education Association and the American Association of School Administrators recommended in its 1944 report, *Education for All American Youth,* that the legal age of compulsory education be extended to eighteen as part of an effort to increase the high school graduation rate. And the Commission on Higher Education argued in its 1948 report, *Higher Education for American Democracy,* that at least 49 percent of the U.S. population has the intellectual potential to complete at least fourteen years of formal schooling and at least 32 percent has the potential to complete a bachelor's or a professional degree. See Lawrence A. Cremin, *Popular Education and Its Discontents* (New York: Harper & Row, 1990), p. 15.

United States educationally. Although they did not call for an end to all grouping and tracking, the authors did strongly urge that academic standards be raised for all students and that all high school students take a demanding set of academic courses. Specifically, they proposed that all high school graduates have a total of 13.5 years of study in the "new basics"—four years of English, three years of math, three years of science, three years of social studies, and one-half year of computer science. They also recommended that all college-bound high school graduates take two years of a foreign language in addition, for a minimum of 15.5 years of academic coursework.[98]

Educational researchers have produced empirical information on grouping and tracking practices and outcomes that has been extremely valuable to school reformers and educational policymakers. One of the most influential sources of information has been *A Study of Schooling*, undertaken by a team of researchers led by John I. Goodlad, which examined conditions in more than one thousand classrooms in thirty-eight elementary and secondary schools across the country. The Goodlad study produced a large body of information on the nature and extent of grouping and tracking, the variations in classroom practices (particularly with regard to curriculum and instruction), and the demographics of grouping and tracking (which students tend to be assigned to which groups and tracks). It found that grouping and tracking typically led to much heavier academic demands being placed on high-achieving than on low-achieving students. And it showed that poor and minority students continued to be heavily overrepresented in groups and tracks for low achievers and significantly underrepresented in groups and tracks for high achievers. Goodlad's book *A Place Called School* (1984), discussed the overall results of the study. In 1985, Jeannie Oakes's *Keeping Track: How Schools Structure Inequality* offered a detailed analysis of the findings regarding tracking at the secondary level.

The work of Goodlad and Oakes heightened awareness of the serious inequalities in access to knowledge that continue to exist in the nation's schools among students from different social classes and racial/ethnic groups. And it did so at a time when the rapidly changing demographics of the student-age population was increasing interest in finding ways to improve the academic achievement of minority groups.

No long-term trend data are available on national grouping and tracking patterns. However, information from a number of sources can shed light on the extent to which students from different racial/ethnic groups have experienced tracking at the secondary level over the past decade. For example, the High School and Beyond (HS&B) longitudinal study of a national sample of high school seniors and sophomores offers a general picture of secondary school tracking patterns just prior to the beginning of the current period of educational reform. Among the students in the sample who were sophomores in 1980, only 29 percent, 23 percent, and 23 percent, respectively, of the blacks, Hispanics,

98. National Commission on Excellence in Education, *A Nation at Risk: The Imperative for Educational Reform* (Washington, D.C.: Department of Education, U.S. Government Printing Office, 1983), p. 24.

and American Indians were in the college preparatory track, compared to 47 percent of the Asians and 37 percent of the whites. These variations in track-enrollment patterns were not associated with substantial variations in the total number of credits earned, on average, by students from each racial/ethnic group; they were all clustered in the 21–23-credit range. (A credit is defined as one year's study of a subject.) However, they were associated with fairly large differences in the average number of credits in the new basics earned by students from each group. Asians again led the way with an average of 14.7 new basic credits, followed by whites with 13.2, African Americans with 11.9, Latinos with 11.7, and Native Americans with 11.2.[99] Only the Asians came close, on average, to meeting the 15.5-credit new basic standard for college bound students set forth by the authors of *Nation at Risk* and exceeded the 13.5 credit new basic standard for all students.

Table 9.2 presents data on the percentages of high school seniors in 1982 and 1987 who took college preparatory math and science courses. Math and science constitute excellent college preparation for all students, and many of the courses in the table are essential for several quantitative or science majors.

The table shows, first, that blacks and Hispanics lagged substantially behind whites in all the math and science courses except Algebra I and Biology in both 1982 and 1987. In these subjects, African Americans and Latinos approached parity with whites in 1987, having made substantial progress in absolute terms since 1982. Higher percentages were taking each of the math and science courses in 1987 than in 1982. However, whites were also making advances. In fact, the absolute increases in course-taking percentages were larger for whites in several courses, including trigonometry, precalculus, and physics, than for African Americans and Latinos. And in several cases, whites, blacks, and Hispanics all lost ground to Asians, especially in such courses as trigonometry, precalculus, calculus, chemistry, and physics, which provide important preparation for quantitative or science majors. By 1987, the percentages of Asians who had taken these courses had become enormous. In only one course did Asians have course-taking percentages in 1982 and 1987 that lagged behind the other groups—Algebra I. The reason is probably that large numbers of Asians had taken first-year algebra in junior high rather than high school.[100]

Course-taking patterns of comparable samples of high school seniors are not currently available for the post-1987 period. However, data for this period are available for the subset of the college-bound population that takes the SAT. Table 9.3 presents information regarding the percentages of SAT test takers in 1987 and 1992 from several racial/ethnic groups who took at least 20 credits in six college-preparatory subject areas (English, mathematics, natural sciences, social

99. Samuel S. Peng, Jeffrey A. Owings, and William B. Fetters, *School Experiences and Performance of Asian American High School Students,* paper presented at the annual meeting of the American Educational Research Association in New Orleans, April 1984.

100. Policy Information Center, *What Americans Study* (Princeton, N.J.: Educational Testing Service, 1989), p. 6.

Table 9.2
Percentages of 1982 and 1987 High School Graduates
Who Took Selected Math and Science Courses

Course/Year	Asian	White	Black	Hispanic
Algebra I				
1982	66	68	58	55
1987	66	78	71	77
Geometry:				
1982	64	51	29	26
1987	82	64	44	44
Algebra II:				
1982	56	39	24	21
1987	68	51	32	33
Trigonometry				
1982	28	14	6	6
1987	47	22	12	12
Pre-calculus				
1982	14	7	2	3
1987	41	13	5	8
Calculus:				
1982	13	6	1	2
1987	33	6	2	4
Biology				
1982	82	77	71	67
1987	93	91	85	86
Chemistry:				
1982	51	34	21	15
1987	72	48	30	32
Physics				
1982	34	16	7	6
1987	50	21	11	11

Source: Policy Information Center, *What Americans Study* (Princeton, N.J.: Educational Testing
Service, 1989), p. 20. The original sources for the data were the High School and Beyond Study
for 1982 and the 1987 High School Transcript Study.

science and history, foreign and classical languages, and arts and music). Those
who have 20 or more academic years of study in these areas tend to be among
the most academically prepared students for college (as measured by SAT test
score averages).

Several interesting patterns can be found in the data: (1) in both 1987 and
1992, more Asian and white test takers took 20 or more college preparatory
courses; (2) for all the groups, the percentage of test takers who accumulated at
least 20 academic credits increased substantially between 1987 and 1992; (3)

Table 9.3

Table 9.3
Selected SAT Data for 1987 and 1992, by Race/Ethnicity

| | Test Takers with ≥ 20 Credits/Years' Study in Academic Subjects | | | | Combined Average Mathematics and Verbal SAT Score All Test Takers | |
| | % of All Test Takers | | Combined Average Mathematics and Verbal SAT Score | | | |
Group	1987	1992	1987	1992	1987	1992
American Indian	23	31	918	928	825	837
Asian	38	46	1048	1049	926	945
Black	22	27	833	832	728	737
Mexican American	16	23	917	901	803	797
Puerto Rican	32	38	855	859	760	772
Other Hispanic	32	38	921	914	819	816
White	35	44	1032	1012	936	933

Sources: College Entrance Examination Board, *1987 College-Bound Seniors: Ethnic and Gender Profile of SAT and Achievement Test Takers* (New York: College Entrance Examination Board, 1987), p. 2 of each ethnic group section; College Entrance Examination Board, "College Board Reports Rise in SAT Scores for Class of 1992, but Many Urban, Rural, and Minority Students Being Left Behind," *News from the College Board* (press release materials), 27 August 1992, pp. 9–10.

the gaps between whites and Asians, on the one hand, and the several other groups, on the other hand, did not grow smaller in the period: in some cases, they actually grew larger; (4) the increases in the percentages of test takers who took 20 academic courses were not always associated with increases in combined verbal and math SAT scores: the scores went up substantially (10 points) for American Indians and modestly (4 points) for Puerto Ricans, were essentially unchanged for Asians and blacks, and were down moderately (7 points) for Other Hispanics, substantially (16 points) for Mexican Americans, and even more substantially (20 points) for whites.

For each of the racial/ethnic groups, the average combined SAT score was much higher for those who had 20 or more academic courses than for all test takers from the group. However, there were large between-group differences in average scores in both cases. Among test takers with 20 or more academic courses in both 1987 and 1992, large differences in scores existed between Asians and whites, on the one hand, and American Indians, blacks, Mexican Americans, Puerto Ricans, and Other Hispanics, on the other hand. In several instances, these gaps did grow smaller during the period, often as the result of the large drop in the average score for whites in this segment.

The Current Situation   Research indicates that teacher expectations and grouping/tracking practices continue to contribute to differences in academic achievement among students from different racial/ethnic groups. However, it is difficult to estimate from the available data how much of these differences is due to these factors. It is even more difficult to assess trends in this area or to estimate the degree to which racial/ethnic prejudice influences either teacher expectations or grouping/tracking practices. Nonetheless, it is possible to offer some plausible conclusions.

It seems likely that prejudice is playing a less substantial role in shaping teacher expectations and grouping/tracking practices than was the case several decades ago. The proportion of white Americans who believe in the inferiority of minorities has become considerably smaller over the past half-century. There should have been a corresponding drop in the proportion of white teachers who regard minorities as inferior, which in turn should have led to a significant reduction in the role racial/ethnic prejudice plays in shaping teacher expectations and grouping/tracking patterns. However, if teachers tend to have the same pattern of views on race/ethnicity as the population as a whole, about one in five white teachers may still believe that blacks are innately somewhat less intelligent than whites, and about half may hold some negative cultural views of African Americans and other minorities, including Latinos.

Another important reason that racial/ethnic prejudice may be playing a smaller role today than previously is that achieving equality of educational results for all children has emerged over the past quarter-century as a major objective of schooling. The Coleman Report was interpreted by some to mean that schools could not make a difference in the education of poor and minority students (even though this was not what Coleman and his colleagues had said). The meaning of the term *equal education opportunity* was undergoing a change during that period. Increasingly, the focus was on achieving similar educational results for children, not simply providing them with equal school inputs. Given the tension between the schools-can't-make-a difference interpretation of the Coleman Report and the emerging view of equal opportunity, it is not surprising that some educators responded to the Coleman Report as if it were a challenge to find instructionally effective schools—schools that did close a meaningful part of the academic achievement gap between poor and middle-class students as well as between whites and minorities, by strategies that other schools could learn to use.

A distinguishing feature of the current period of educational reform, which began in the early 1980s, is the commitment of many to improving the educational performance of all students—and, in the process, closing the academic achievement gaps between majority and minority youngsters.[101] In addition,

---

101. I have noted that *A Nation at Risk* (1983) called for higher academic standards and performance for all students and that *A Place Called School* (1984) and *Keeping Track* (1985) called attention to the enormous differences in access to knowledge for different student populations as a result of grouping and tracking. As early as 1982, the philosopher Mortimer J. Adler called for a high-quality common education for all children in *The Paideia Proposal* (New York: Macmillan, 1982). In 1983, Ernest L. Boyer, president of the Carnegie Foundation for the Advancement of Teaching and former U.S. Commissioner of Education, called for a core academic program for all high school students in *High School: A Report on Secondary Education in America*. In 1984, Theodore R. Sizer, former dean of the Harvard Graduate School of Education, called for, among other things, a common academic-oriented curriculum for all high school students in *Horace's Compromise: The Dilemma of the American High School* (New York: Houghton Mifflin, 1984).

The needs of minority students were addressed in several influential books and reports in the early years of the educational reform movement but were typically not their central focus. How-

several school reform initiatives launched over the past decade have emphasized improving the schooling of minority and poor children. For example, the Coalition of Essential Schools, a consortium of high schools dedicated to implementing school reform principles developed by Theodore Sizer of Brown University, has among its members a large number of urban high schools attended primarily by minority students.[102] The Accelerated Schools Project, launched by Henry M. Levin of Stanford University, is concerned with helping elementary schools learn to serve disadvantaged children in ways that will enable all such youngsters to emerge from elementary school academically well prepared for secondary education.[103] The College Board's Equity 2000 initiative is concerned with helping middle schools and high schools to increase the number of poor and minority students who are academically prepared to succeed in college, with emphasis on improving their preparation in mathematics.[104]

Older initiatives that have focused primarily on disadvantaged and/or minority youngsters have also gained in prominence during the current period of educational reform. One of the most notable examples is the School Development Program, headed by the child psychiatrist James P. Comer of Yale, which for a quarter century has been developing an approach to elementary school improvement that stresses increasing the capacity of school professionals to work effectively with students and their parents.[105] The Central Park East elementary schools in East Harlem, New York, have also received a great deal of attention. For nearly two decades, these small "public schools of choice," under the leadership of Deborah Meier and several of her colleagues, have successfully offered largely disadvantaged minority student populations academically rich programs, using a variation of the progressive education philosophy and practices employed by independent schools serving advantaged student popu-

---

ever, the need to raise the academic performance of minority students had become a prominent concern of many reform-oriented reports published in the late 1980s and early 1990s; among the documents published were the following: Research and Policy Committee, *Children in Need: Investment Strategies for the Educationally Disadvantaged* (New York: Committee for Economic Development, 1987); Commission on Minority Participation in Education and American Life, *One-Third of a Nation* (Washington, D.C.: American Council on Education/Education Commission of the States, 1988); *An Imperiled Generation: Saving Urban Schools* (Princeton, N.J.: Carnegie Foundation for the Advancement of Teaching, 1988); Quality Education for Minorities Project, *Education that Works: An Action Plan for the Education of Minorities* (Cambridge: MIT, 1990).

102. By mid-1991, about two hundred high schools were participating in the Coalition of Essential Schools or in an associated initiative, Re:Learning, launched by the Education Commission of the States. The Coalition of Essential Schools has nine common principles, calling for a "less is more" curriculum, making the student the "worker" and personalizing instruction. See Theodore R. Sizer, *Horace's School: Redesigning the American High School* (Boston: Houghton Mifflin, 1992), pp. 207–09, 214–21.

103. Ron Brandt, "On Building Learning Communities: A Conversation with Hank Levin," *Educational Leadership* 50 (September 1992): 19–23.

104. For a brief discussion of this initiative, see "Equity 2000 Fosters Systemic Change," *College Board News*, September 1992, p. 3.

105. Comer, "Educating Poor Minority Children," pp. 42–48, Council of Chief State School Officers, *Voices from Successful Schools: Elements of Improved Schools Serving At-Risk Students and How State Educational Agencies Can Support More Local School Improvement* (Washington, D.C.: Council of Chief State School Officers, 1990).

lations.[106] Meier has gone on to develop a secondary school that combines some of the principles employed at the elementary level, for example, choice, school-based management, and small size, with those of the Coalition of Essential Schools.

Educational researchers also seem to have increased their efforts to clarify the impact of grouping and tracking on students as well as the circumstances under which grouping or tracking may be appropriate or inappropriate.[107] Attention is being paid to the grouping and tracking practices of other industrialized nations.[108] And efforts are being made to synthesize and disseminate information on the most effective instructional practices for disadvantaged and minority students.[109]

From the perspective of raising educators' expectations for the academic performance of minority children, one of the most important changes in the past two decades has been the increase in the number of minority educators who head large public school systems or hold other relevant leadership positions. For example, the College Board has been headed by an African American, Donald Stewart, for several years, and it was under Stewart's leadership that the

106. David Bensman, *Quality Education in the Inner City: The Story of the Central Park East Schools* (New York: Kramer Communications/Central Park East School, 1987). A Central Park East School is profiled in Council of Chief State School Officers, *Voices from Successful Schools*.

107. For syntheses of research on grouping and tracking, see *Educational Leadership* 48 (March 1991); *Equity and Excellence* 23 (Spring 1987); *Review of Educational Research* 57, 60 (Fall 1987, Fall 1990). Examples of recent studies of ability grouping/tracking include Adam Gamoran, "Access to Excellence: Assignment to Honors English Classes in the Transition from Middle to High School," *Educational Evaluation and Policy Analysis* 14 (Fall 1992): 185–204; Thomas B. Hoffer, "Middle School Ability Grouping and Student Achievement in Science and Mathematics," *Educational Evaluation and Policy Analysis* (Fall 1992): 205–27; Sally B. Kilgore, "The Organizational Context of Tracking in Schools," *American Sociological Review* 56 (April 1991): 189–203. Gamoran found that previous (high) academic performance was generally predictive of being assigned to an honors English class, but that, for average performers, students from high-SES families had a better chance of being admitted to an honors class than those from average-SES families. Hoffer found that in both science and math, "students in the high groups learn somewhat more and students in the low groups learn less than comparable students in nongrouped schools." Kilgore found no significant evidence of arbitrary high school tracking policies and decisions, but she did find that a number of organizational characteristics of high schools were related to tracking patterns. For example, strong student demand for the academic track was associated with the practice of excluding some students from that track. In contrast, inclusion of more students in the academic track was associated with teachers' control over the school tracking policies.

108. Virtually all industrialized nations eventually place students into different academic tracks, but they vary considerably in the ages at which tracking begins. Japan, for instance, has a very competitive system at the secondary school level that entails extensive tracking of students based on academic performance. However, the Japanese do not use tracking or ability grouping at the elementary school level, and neither do China and Taiwan. See Harold W. Stevenson and James W. Stigler, *The Learning Gap* (New York: Summit Books, 1992), pp. 151–52.

109. SRI International and Policy Studies Associates, *Better Schooling for the Children of Poverty: Alternatives to the Conventional Wisdom*, vols. 1, 2 (Washington, D.C.: Department of Education, 1990). Although there is a substantial amount of research on how to improve instruction for disadvantaged students, relatively little of it has been developed in ungrouped/untracked classrooms and schools. Thus, developing effective educational strategies for "detracked" schools is regarded as a high priority by some researchers and school reformers. See Jeannie Oakes, "Can Tracking Research Inform Practice? Technical, Normative, and Political Considerations," *Educational Researcher* 21 (May 1992): 12–21.

Equity 2000 initiative was launched.[110] A recent director of the National Science Foundation, Walter Massey, is an African American. Under Massey's leadership, the foundation launched a major grants program concerned with systemic reform of elementary and secondary school mathematics and science education. Greater emphasis has also been placed on increasing the number of minority students who become well prepared to pursue engineering and science majors in college.[111]

This review is not intended to suggest that the problems of low expectations and restricted curricular options have been eliminated from schools serving disadvantaged student populations. Rather, it suggests that efforts to improve schooling for these populations have been growing over many years, and in a context in which racial/ethnic prejudice among educators is probably a less pervasive problem than it was a few decades ago.

The Beginning School Study (BSS), a longitudinal project initiated in the Baltimore public elementary schools in 1982 by Doris R. Entwisle and Karl L. Alexander of Johns Hopkins University, has produced data that are generally consistent with this interpretation. For example, Entwisle and Alexander found that during the first two years of elementary school, the increase in math test-score differences between poor and nonpoor children occurred during the summer months, when the school was not in session. The schools were able to help disadvantaged students make up some of the summer learning gaps during the academic year.[112] Their conclusion, that "schools seem to be doing a better job than they have been given credit for," is in general agreement with researchers' findings from the Sustaining Effects Study of elementary school students (see chapter 5) and with James Coleman's conclusion that differences in academic achievement patterns are due primarily to variations in the education-relevant family resources available to children.

Entwisle and Alexander reached a much more mixed conclusion regarding how teachers assessed the school potential of minority (black) children. Many teachers had high expectations for all students, but a significant number tended to view African American children as less mature than white children in ways that are relevant to becoming a good student and less likely to do well academically. The primary predictor of whether a teacher held positive or negative

110. The College Board has long been committed to increasing the number of high school graduates, particularly minorities, who are well prepared academically to be successful in college. Under Stewart's tenure, this interest has continued and become more visible. See, for example, Sol H. Pelavin and Michael Kane, *Changing the Odds: Factors Increasing Access to College* (New York: College Entrance Examination Board, 1990). On the board's growing commitments in this area, see Jean Evangelauf, "College Board to Put New Emphasis on Academic Matters," *Chronicle of Philanthropy*, 28 October 1992.

111. Peter West, "N.S.F. Awards $75 Million for 'Systemic' Reforms," *Education Week* (22 May 1991), p. 4. National Science Foundation, *Career Access Opportunities in Science and Technology: Program Announcement and Guidelines* (Washington, D.C.: National Science Foundation, 1990). A vital figure in the development and implementation of the NSF's efforts in this area is assistant director Luther Williams, who is also an African American.

112. Doris R. Entwisle and Karl L. Alexander, "Summer Setback: Race, Poverty, School Composition, and Mathematics Achievement in the First Two Years of School," *American Sociological Review* 57 (February 1992): 82.

views of African American students was the teacher's own social class background. Those who grew up in lower-middle to middle-class homes were most likely to hold negative views; those who grew up in working-class to poor circumstances were most likely to hold positive views of these youngsters. This pattern held for both black and white teachers. In fact, in some respects African American teachers with middle-class origins were less likely to see black students in a positive light than were white teachers with middle-class origins. (The white teachers' low expectations were related primarily to black students' conduct, while the African American teachers' were broader-based, extending to academic achievement.) Black students' academic achievement did appear to suffer somewhat in the classrooms of teachers with middle-class origins, but not in those of teachers with lower-class origins. And this pattern of low expectations and low performance seems to apply to African American students regardless of their own social class, as measured by the educational level of their parents. Thus, this was not simply a problem of high-SES teachers doing less well with low-SES students, some of whom were black.[113]

SUMMARY AND CONCLUSIONS

In this chapter, I have explored a number of ways in which racial/ethnic prejudice and discrimination may be undermining the educational progress of minorities. Some African American educators believe that widespread doubt among black students about their ability to do high-quality academic work leads many of them to avoid academic competition. This self-doubt is considered to be a response to the long-standing belief among many whites that blacks are intellectually inferior.

A second explanation focuses on the interconnections among racial/ethnic prejudice and discrimination, the quality of the economic opportunity structure, and students' motivation to do well academically. This line of analysis posits that America's historical race-based caste system produced a truncated opportunity structure for blacks and some other minority groups and that over time it tended to undermine their motivation to do well in school. Although the caste system has been largely eliminated, minorities continue to face an unfavorable economic opportunity structure, especially in cities with large concentrations of African Americans and Latinos with few job skills. In extreme cases, some minority youngsters are now inclined to reject high academic achievement as a supposed white attribute.

Although this problem has its origins in historical racial/ethnic prejudice and discrimination, contemporary prejudice may be contributing to its perpetuation. Many whites continue to hold negative views of blacks and some other minority groups. These views—which include notions of the innate intellectual inferiority of blacks and the cultural inferiority of African Ameri-

113. Karl L. Alexander, Doris R. Entwisle, and Maxine S. Thompson, "School Performance, Status Relations, and the Structure of Sentiment: Bringing the Teacher Back In," *American Sociological Review* 52 (October 1987): 670–81.

cans and Latinos—seem to be associated with a lack of interest in or opposition to the addressing of critical economic, health, and educational needs of urban minorities.

Although whites have historically tended to have very low academic expectations for minority students and have made it extremely difficult for them to pursue demanding academic programs, that attitude seems to have improved. In all likelihood some teachers still have low academic expectations for minority youngsters, but many probably do not. Most seem to be working hard to help all their students succeed academically.

Grouping and tracking continue to represent serious obstacles to the academic progress of some minority youngsters, but the percentages of minority high school students who are pursuing demanding college preparatory programs have been increasing. Grouping and tracking issues are being addressed energetically by many school reformers. Indeed, a major focus of the current school reform movement is to increase minority students' access to knowledge.

Both this chapter and chapter 8 treat primarily the educational consequences of racial/ethnic prejudice and discrimination for minorities. Let me recast this issue in terms of an important education-relevant resource, polity capital—that is, the commitment that individuals and groups have from the larger society to ensure both their well-being and their capacity to participate effectively in the society. In the educational arena it refers to the society's commitment to see to it that individual children and groups of children will be educated well. Hypothetically, the amount of polity capital individuals and groups receive is heavily dependent on their membership status in the society and on the meaning of membership in the society—the kinds of obligations the larger society has undertaken with regard to its members. Full membership in many contemporary societies has at least three dimensions—legal, national interest, and cultural. From a legal perspective, those with full membership have a complete set of the legal rights that exist in the society. From a national interest perspective, those with full membership are typically recognized as able to assume a broad range of valued roles and responsibilities that exist in the society's mainstream. From a cultural perspective, those with full membership are generally accepted by most other members as participants in good standing in the mainstream culture.

Deep racial/ethnic divisions in a society can present formidable polity capital problems to some or all of the population. This has certainly been the case in the United States, where full or even (substantial) partial membership was not possible for individuals from several racial/ethnic groups for most of our nation's history. Minorities had few legal rights until very recently. They were generally regarded by whites as suitable only for marginal political, economic, and social roles in American life. And they were believed by many whites to be culturally and innately inferior.

Thanks especially to the civil rights movement, the legal rights necessary for full membership are now largely available to all groups. And minorities are now exercising their legal rights in most realms of society, including education.

Recent changes in the structure of the economy have made it increasingly clear that it is in America's national interest for all people to have full membership. Each of us must be able to play a productive role in society. Yet, ironically, these same changes in the economy have made it more difficult for minorities (and whites) with little education to join the mainstream of society. If John Ogbu is correct, these conditions may be undermining the desire of many to become full members of the society. By trapping many minority group members in poverty, these economic conditions feed the old sterotypes that blacks and other minorities are innately and culturally inferior. Under these circumstances, it becomes more difficult for whites to overcome their prejudices and embrace minorities as full members of society in the cultural sense. On the positive side, my review of survey research suggests that substantially fewer whites hold these negative views than was the case a half-century ago. Yet this remains an extremely important polity capital issue for all Americans. Indeed, if recent economic and demographic trends continue, a combination of an increasingly limited supply of adequately paying, low-skill jobs and growing numbers of minority group members with too few skills for better jobs could raise the polity capital problems confronting American society to genuine crisis proportions.

In the next chapter, I shall consider the extent to which significant cultural differences, on average, between the white majority and minorities contribute to variations in their academic performance patterns. An exploration of cultural differences is in part an exploration of the cultural continuities and discontinuities between the home and the school experienced by different groups of students.

CHAPTER TEN

Education-Relevant

Cultural Differences

Associated with

Race/Ethnicity and Social Class

Schools in America generally reflect the mainstream of society. In America, most nonwhites and members of low socioeconomic strata have some cultural characteristics that are similar to those of the mainstream and some that are different. Awareness of these similarities and differences is essential for understanding existing variations in educational achievement patterns and for designing strategies to accelerate the educational advancement of minorities.

In my discussion of cultural differences, I first present some ways of describing the mainstream culture of American society, and I examine attributes of school and nonschool learning that are consistent with crucial characteristics of the cultural mainstream. I then review research on ways in which the cultures of various racial/ethnic groups differ from mainstream culture in general and the school in particular and on ways in which education-relevant knowledge, skills, beliefs, and behaviors vary by social class. Finally, I consider the current capacity of schools to respond to cultural differences among children.

MAINSTREAM CULTURE, "INTELLIGENT" BEHAVIOR, AND SCHOOLING

In the broadest sense, culture is everything that has been made by humans,[1] including attitudes, beliefs, and behaviors regarding child rearing and the types and characteristics of a society's institutions, especially those that are heavily concerned with the socialization of the young (for example, the family and school) and those that are settings in which individuals spend much of their adult life (for example, the corporation).

The terms one uses to describe something as diverse and complex as American culture depend heavily on the dimensions being explained. The dimension of political organization and governance, for example, might call for such terms as *representative democracy, constitutional democracy,* or *federalist system;* for economic dimensions, *market economy, industrial/postindustrial economy,* and *capitalist system.* Some of the most frequently used terms, especially in the

---

1. Melville J. Herskovits, *Man and His Works: The Science of Cultural Anthropology* (New York: Alfred A. Knopf, 1948), p. 17.

cross-cultural/comparative sense, are *industrial, Western,* and *modern*.[2] A common denominator of these terms is the role science and technology play in defining the nature of American life. The generation of new scientific knowledge and the use of that knowledge via technology are central aspects of American culture. As a result, contemporary life in the United States places high value on symbol manipulation and abstract thinking of the kinds associated with science and technology. These skills are important in both the verbal and quantitative realms; adults who possess them in abundance tend to have jobs that are highly rewarded in social status and in economic benefits. Schools have been organized to help develop these capacities in students.

The kinds of intelligence valued in American society, however, are culturally defined; they are not necessarily characteristics of other societies. Moreover, even the skills that are rewarded in American schools represent only a segment of the intelligent behaviors that individuals need to function effectively in society and that are actually developed by schools and other institutions.[3]

School and Nonschool Learning   Anthropologists often make a distinction between informal and formal education. Informal education, which can be described as learning that occurs when one watches what others do and then imitates their actions, tends to take place in the context in which what is being learned is usually done. It relies on natural demonstration, and those responsible for ensuring that learning takes place often have a personal relationship with the individual learner. In contrast, formal education relies heavily on learning through the use of language—that is, through being told what to do or reading what to do and then applying this information. Typically it is organized exclusively for the purpose of enabling individuals to learn. And the persons with instructional responsibilities have been given these duties by the larger society. As a result, they are unlikely to have close personal relationships with most of the learners.[4]

In societies such as the United States, which have extensive, complex, interrelated language and numeracy systems, great emphasis is placed on learning through formal educational processes, although much learning takes place through informal education as well. The school has been explicitly designed to help large numbers of individuals gain knowledge and skills that they would usually have difficulty acquiring through other means, either informal or formal.

The attributes of American elementary and secondary schools include the following:

1. Schools are staffed by professional educators. The professionals at the school-building level have a great deal of control over the educational processes

2. Marshall H. Segall, Pierre R. Dasen, John W. Berry, and Ype H. Poortinga, *Human Behavior in Global Perspective* (New York: Pergamon, 1990), pp. 293–310.

3. For a brief summary of concepts of intelligence, see Douglass R. Price-Williams, *Explorations in Cross-Cultural Psychology* (San Francisco: Chandler & Sharp, 1975), pp. 51–57.

4. Silvia Scribner and Michael Cole, "Cognitive Consequences of Formal and Informal Education," *Science* 182 (9 November 1973): 554–56.

of the school, including the content of the curriculum and the instructional strategies used.

2. The delivery of the school's educational program is largely the responsibility of teachers, who practice their profession primarily on an individual rather than a collective (team) basis.

3. Teachers are expected not only to be literate and numerate but also to possess a good general education. Many must have extensive specialized knowledge in a subject area. All are expected to have appropriate professional skills, including those related to pedagogy. They also tend to be fully acculturated to the traditional ways of formal education in American schools—they tend to teach in the ways they were taught.[5]

4. On the basis of their education and income, teachers are generally members of the middle class. They also are disproportionately native-born white Americans who speak standard (American) English.[6]

5. Teachers are the primary authority figures in the classroom.

6. The curriculum of the schools is heavily weighted toward academic learning. In addition to ensuring that all youngsters develop the minimal literacy and numeracy skills required to function effectively in society, the schools are expected to nurture advanced skills in a substantial proportion of students.

7. Because most of the learning opportunities associated with the formal curriculum of the school are based on language rather than observation, many of these opportunities are decontextualized. Students are often expected to learn in a manner that is not similar to the way in which the knowledge acquired was originally developed and not presented in formats like those in which it will be used most frequently outside the school.[7]

8. Students' mastery of what is to be learned is often judged by national and, increasingly, international standards. They are also evaluated on a competitive basis that often has important consequences for their future schooling and occupational opportunities.[8]

9. Students typically are expected to learn through individual effort, with relatively little opportunity for collaborative learning with their peers in the classroom.[9]

5. For an overview of contemporary teaching practices based on classroom observations in a large sample of schools and classrooms, see John I. Goodlad, *A Place Called School: Prospects for the Future* (New York: McGraw Hill, 1984), pp. 93–129.

6. In 1987, only about 10 percent of elementary and secondary school teachers were minority members. See American Association of Colleges for Teacher Education, *Recruiting Minority Teachers: A Practical Guide* (Washington, D.C.: American Association of Colleges for Teacher Education, 1989), p. 1.

7. See Goodlad, *A Place Called School*, pp. 93–129; Scribner and Cole, "Cognitive Consequences of Formal and Informal Education," pp. 556–57.

8. The use of scores from standardized achievement tests in decisions regarding college admissions is one of the major ways in which national standards are being applied to individual students.

9. In recent years, interest in cooperative learning techniques seems to have increased. For a review of research on cooperative learning strategies, especially at the elementary level, see, for example, Robert E. Slavin, *Cooperative Learning: Theory, Research, and Practice* (Englewood Cliffs, N.J.: Prentice-Hall, 1990).

10. Teachers use a fairly narrow range of techniques and strategies to facilitate learning. Much class time is devoted to lectures by teachers and to class discussion, which teachers guide by directing questions to individual students. Written exercises tend to have preformulated questions in which the objective is to find a single right answer. Most specific learning opportunities are designed to take very little time in class or at home; rarely does learning take place through long-term projects.[10]

Non-school-based learning opportunities are both formal and informal. For example, large corporations often provide formal education to their employees through company-sponsored classes on topics of importance to their work. These non-school-based opportunities are most plentiful for those who have had the most formal schooling—those with bachelor's or graduate/professional degrees. These are the persons, of course, who are likely to be members of the upper and middle classes and to hold managerial and professional jobs.[11] According to one estimate, American employers have been spending about $30 billion annually on formal training, about two-thirds of it on the college-educated portion of the work force.[12] Corporations also provide extensive informal education through on-the-job training, which can be a virtually career-long affair for many managers and professionals, especially if their work involves a technical area in which the knowledge base is growing rapidly or if they take on new job responsibilities.

Although the formal education provided by a corporation may have many of the attributes of classroom learning, on-the-job training differs from formal schooling in many respects. For example, it is contextualized; learning will occur by doing the real work of the business. Opportunities for observation of and consultation with experts may frequently be available. Extensive collaboration and cooperative learning may be involved because the individual employee is commonly a member of a group of people engaged in a particular task. Inter-

10. Goodlad, *A Place Called School,* pp. 93–129. Increasing teachers' range of instructional techniques and strategies, of course, has been an objective of the current school reform movement. See, for example, Theodore R. Sizer, *Horace's School: Redesigning the American High School* (Boston: Houghton Mifflin, 1992).

11. See for example, Thomas Amirault, "Training to Qualify for Jobs and Improve Skills, 1991," *Monthly Labor Review* 115 (September 1992): 31–40. Companies that require well-educated employees are finding it necessary to increase their educational expenditures for virtually all employee segments, from the manufacturing floor to the research lab. However, such efforts are still typically weighted toward managers and professionals. Moreover, much of the effort directed toward nonprofessional/nonmanagerial workers is concerned with upgrading basic skills. Nonetheless, helping manufacturing workers to reach true high-school-level math and verbal skills in an employment environment in which they actually use these skills over time could pay important intergenerational dividends by giving them more human capital to invest in their children. For a description of the educational programs of one high-technology company, see William Wiggenhorn, "Motorola U: When Training Becomes an Education," *Harvard Business Review* 90 (July-August 1990): 71–83.

12. Commission on the Skills of the American Workforce, *America's Choice: High Skills or Low Wages* (Rochester, N.Y.: National Center on Education and the Economy, 1990), p. 49. For a discussion of the economic factors that influence corporate investment in employees, see Jacob Mincer, "Human Capital and the Labor Market: A Review of Current Research," *Educational Researcher* 18 (May 1989): 27–34.

personal skills are often as important as the analytical skills related to the specific topic.[13]

On-the-job learning in the corporate environment, of course, typically draws on knowledge and skills originally developed during formal schooling. For example, managers' and professionals' core literacy and numeracy skills are grounded in their elementary and secondary school experiences, while their sophisticated technical knowledge and skills (in engineering, finance, and so on) are platformed on their years of higher education. Nevertheless, almost certainly they will use these skills in ways that are quite different from those that regularly prevailed when they were in school.[14]

Although I have focused on the corporate sector, one could just as easily have referred to the government, the military, or other sectors of society. As in the corporate world, the greatest opportunities for continuing formal and informal learning in these institutional settings are likely to be available to those in positions that require substantial amounts of higher education. Thus, over the years well-educated individuals are likely to continue to accumulate large additional increments of human capital—and other education-relevant resources—upon which they can draw in their role as parents.

DIFFERENCES BETWEEN THE CULTURE OF THE SCHOOL AND THE CULTURES
OF SEVERAL RACIAL/ETHNIC GROUPS

Children from some racial/ethnic groups tend to be more successful academically in school than children from other groups. Those groups that have been least successful are disproportionately likely to confront problems of poverty and prejudice. In addition, they have cultural attributes that are different from and can be incompatible with aspects of the school's culture. These cultural attributes are not necessarily inherent obstacles to academic learning. To the contrary, many are potential resources for achieving academic success, if only the school was better positioned to capitalize on them.

Over the past generation, research has been conducted on ways in which the cultures of some racial/ethnic groups (and social classes) may be incompatible with the culture of the schools and on ways of modifying school practices to take

13. For a discussion of the collaborative, on-the-job learning opportunities at a preeminent Japanese industrial corporation, see Neil Gross, "Inside Hitachi," *Business Week*, 28 September 1992, pp. 92–95, 98–100.

14. Consider, for example, the work of a cross-functional new product development team. The specific issues the team will address over a period of years (beginning with identifying the appropriate features of a potential new product and moving on through the development, manufacturing, and sales phases) will be only partially formulated by others. The market research, design, report writing, etc. will commonly be undertaken by several members working together. Along the way, there will be few unambiguously right answers to questions raised by their work. The actual answers and solutions will be heavily dependent on decision criteria selected by the team (or others). Moreover, these criteria may change quickly, reflecting advances in technology, dynamic market conditions, etc. By the standards of formal schooling, the key tasks undertaken by team members during this effort will often take a great deal of time. See Charles H. House and Raymond L. Price, "The Return Map: Tracking Product Teams," *Harvard Business Review* 61 (January-February 1991): 92–100.

account of this disparity. Roland G. Tharp has been one of the most productive researchers in developing and evaluating strategies for helping schools meet the educational needs of minority children more effectively. In 1970, Tharp and some of his colleagues began the Kamehameha Early Education Program (KEEP), a long-term, research-based, school-improvement program for Native Hawaiian primary-grade students. Early on, KEEP began to focus on academic learning problems that seemed to originate in incompatibilities between the culture of the home and that of the school.[15] The result has been the development of a highly regarded reading program for the target population as well as efforts to adapt KEEP classroom strategies for students from other minority groups.[16]

In Tharp's view, the KEEP staff, along with many other researchers, has produced significant advances in four areas in which America's classrooms tend to have attributes that are at variance with the cultures of many minority youngsters: social organization, sociolinguistics, cognition, and motivation.[17] Advances have also been made in a fifth area: primary language differences between the school and minority students and their parents.

Social Organization   To most Americans, a school is a building that has several classrooms, each with a desk for the teacher and twenty to thirty chairs for the students, arranged in rows. The school day is broken into several periods, most of equal duration. During many of these periods, a single teacher in each classroom spends much of the time delivering a lecture to the entire group. If students have an opportunity to interact with a teacher in the classroom, it usually is through responding on request to a question raised by the teacher. Assignments undertaken in class are usually written exercises that are completed by each student individually. Students are discouraged from communicating directly with one another during class.

Not all classrooms are organized in this fashion, of course. Nevertheless, educational research tends to confirm the general validity of this description, in which the teacher, not the student, is the primary actor.[18] Research also shows that school organization of this kind is not optimal for many students. There is now much evidence that it can be especially inappropriate for children from a number of minority groups. For example, Native Hawaiian culture has historically been characterized by groups (largely based on kin) that share resources and work together on tasks. At an early age, many Hawaiian children learn these values and behaviors by working with their peers and siblings on tasks in their

15. Cathie Jordan, "Translating Culture: From Ethnographic Information to Educational Program," *Anthropology and Education Quarterly* 16 (Summer 1985): 107–08.

16. Lynn A. Vogt, Cathie Jordan, and Roland G. Tharp, "Explaining School Failure, Producing School Success: Two Cases" *Anthropology and Education Quarterly* 18 (December 1987): 283–86.

17. Roland G. Tharp, "Psychocultural Variables and Constants: Effects on Teaching and Learning in Schools," *American Psychologist* 44 (February 1989): 350.

18. See, for example, Goodlad, *A Place Called School*. Much of the current interest in "restructuring" schools is directed at ways to make the student the worker and to provide the student with a wider variety of academic tasks. See Theodore R. Sizer, *Horace's Compromise: The Dilemma of the American High School* (Boston: Houghton Mifflin, 1984), pp. 222–37.

homes and communities, seeking advice as required from those who are older and more experienced. This makes for a strongly peer-oriented group of children and means that Hawaiian adults do not have to teach and supervise their children as closely as, say, Chinese or middle-class white adults normally have to.[19]

In their observations of Native Hawaiian primary-grade students, Tharp and his colleagues found that, consistent with this home pattern, the children spent about half their time in school in peer interactions.[20] Moreover, in many instructional contexts they tended to take direction from their peers rather than from the teacher.[21] This led KEEP to make a number of changes in classroom organization, including the use of a small-group instructional strategy. Groups of four or five students are organized for various instructional tasks. While one group works intensively with the teacher, the others work independently.[22]

An effort to adapt KEEP for use with Navajo children illustrates how much modification may be required to make the use of this familiar concept compatible with a particular group's culture. Initially the KEEP small-group approach produced little interaction among the Navajo children. Most of them simply worked independently when the teacher was not working with their group and rarely offered or asked for help from their peers. Anthropologists reported that Navajo have a great deal of experience working independently, beginning in childhood; a six-year-old, for example, may be expected to tend a herd of sheep. Moreover, starting at about the age of eight, girls and boys are encouraged to play primarily with children of their own sex. After some experimentation, the KEEP program for Navajos was organized into single-sex groups of two or three children.[23]

Research on black children also bears on the social organization of the classroom. For example, Harry Morgan, in a study of African American and white middle-school students in a "community of moderate to low income," found that the black students were more socially active and peer-oriented in the sense that they were more likely to initiate contact with a peer. Other researchers have found that African American students are more physically active in the classroom, leading A. Wade Boykin to suggest that many black students may need a classroom environment that offers frequent changes in task.[24]

Sociolinguistics   The formal educational processes of the school rely heavily on the use of spoken and written language. Teachers control the rules of oral

19. Roland G. Tharp, "The Effective Instruction of Comprehension," *Reading Research Quarterly* 17, no. 4 (1982): 506–07.
20. Jordan, "Translating Culture," p. 111.
21. Vogt et al, " Explaining School Failure, Producing School Success," p. 280.
22. Tharp, "Psychocultural Variables and Constants," p. 351.
23. Ibid.; Vogt et al, "Explaining School Failure, Producing School Success," pp. 283–84.
24. Harry Morgan, "Assessment of Students' Behavioral Interactions during On-Task Classroom Activities" *Perceptual and Motor Skills* 70 (April 1990): 566–67; A. Wade Boykin, "Task Variability and the Performance of Black and White Children: Vervistic Explorations," *Journal of Black Studies* 12 (June 1982): 480–83.

discourse and expression in the classroom. The standard approach is teacher-approved turn-taking. That is, students are usually expected to speak only when they have permission to do so, and only one person is expected to speak at a time. When asking a question, teachers tend to wait a relatively short amount of time for the student to begin to answer before calling on another student. Depending on the situation, teachers usually will address a question to a specific student or choose among volunteers.[25]

The degree of cultural fit this sociolinguistic environment has with different racial/ethnic groups varies considerably. For many middle-class white children, the fit is very good; Shirley Brice Heath has found that middle-class white parents socialize their children, beginning very early in life, to a question-and-answer style similar to that of the school. However, it is a very poor fit with traditional Native Hawaiian linguistic behaviors. Hawaiian youngsters' interactions with adults are usually in a peer-group context; one-on-one adult-to-child questioning of the kind that takes place in a standard school environment is not the norm. Moreover, Hawaiian children are socialized into a distinctive linguistic process called a talk-story, which "is characterized by overlapping speech, voluntary turn-taking, co-narration and joint construction of a story."[26] Together, these two attributes produced a counterproductive result in a standard teacher-student questioning process but provided the basis for an effective departure from this process. Hawaiian children were generally unresponsive to direct questions by teachers. However, a rich pattern of student responsiveness was elicited through daily small-group discussions of a written text. Instead of calling on a child and requiring one student to speak at a time, teachers directed their questions to the whole group; any or all of the students could respond. According to Tharp, this approach produced "rapid fire responses, liveliness, mutual participation, interruptions, overlapping volunteered speech, and joint narration," which in turn have resulted in better academic performance.[27]

Asking questions of the entire group rather than of individual children proved as effective with the Navajo children as it was with the Native Hawaiians. However, teachers of the Navajo students had to discard the response pattern that entailed several children answering a question in overlapping fashion in favor of one that supported individual turn-taking in which each student spoke without

25. This questioning pattern is so pervasive that it has become the subject of a great deal of educational research. For example, researchers have examined whether teachers tend to: (1) call on some types of students more than others (e.g., boys versus girls, middle class versus poor, high academic achievers versus low achievers, majority versus minority); (2) wait longer for some types of students to give their responses than others; and (3) have feedback patterns that vary by type of students. Much of the "teacher expectations" research has been concerned with these matters. See, for example, Jere E. Brophy, "Research on the Self-Fulfilling Prophecy and Teacher Expectations," *Journal of Educational Psychology* 75 (October 1983): 640–42.

26. Shirley Brice Heath, "Questioning at Home and at School: A Comparative Study," in *Doing the Ethnography of Schooling: Educational Anthropology in Action*, George Spindler, ed. (New York: Holt, Rinehart and Winston, 1982), pp. 102–31; Jordan, "Translating Culture," pp. 113–14; Vogt et al., "Explaining School Failure, Producing School Success," p. 280.

27. Jordan, "Translating Culture," pp. 113–15; Vogt et al., "Explaining School Failure, Producing School Success," p. 280; Tharp, "Psychocultural Variables and Constants," p. 352.

interruption, a pattern that Tharp believes is consistent with the conversational style of the powwow.[28]

Several studies have found sociolinguistic similarities to this Navajo pattern among children from several other tribes, as well as large sociolinguistic differences between Native American and white children in talk/silence patterns, voice loudness/tone patterns, and view/gaze patterns. According to Paul E. Greenbaum and Susan D. Greenbaum, Native American children tend to talk less and to tolerate longer periods of silence in the classroom. They are also much quieter than white children, more inclined to speak in low voice tones, and less likely to look directly at someone (including the teacher) with whom they are in conversation; but they tend to gaze for longer periods of time at subjects when not in conversation.[29]

In their review of the literature, the Greenbaums found little research on whether these cultural differences have a negative impact on the academic performance of Native American children. They believe, however, that they could be obstacles to academic success in schools in which the teachers use a white cultural frame of reference to guide both their instructional practices and their interpretations of Native American children's actions. Similarly, they also could increase the likelihood of misinterpretation of the teacher's conduct by the children and vice versa. For instance, a white middle-class teacher might interpret a Native American child's tendency to look away while in conversation as sullen or evasive behavior. Alternatively, Native American children might regard the teacher's tendency to speak more loudly than Native American adults as evidence that the teacher is mean.[30]

Many black children also have distinctive sociolinguistic characteristics. In a study of a working-class African American community in the South, Heath found that the language environment stressed storytelling by adults. Children were allowed to join in but had to take the initiative; adults did not so much ask children to join the conversation as allow them to participate. Adults expressed approval of storytelling and conversation by black children that was imaginative in content and dramatic in verbal and nonverbal (physical) expression. Heath also found that the questioning style of working-class black adults was considerably different from that of middle-class whites. African American children were not expected to provide specific, detailed answers to questions. And black adults tended to ask their children "what is this like" (analogy) questions, whereas white middle-class adults tended to ask about the specific names and attributes of objects and places.[31]

Similarly, Barbara J. Shade found that when black children speak, they have a much more "varied range of pitch and intensity" in their voices than whites (or

28. Vogt et al., "Explaining School Failure, Producing School Success," p. 284; Tharp, "Psychocultural Variables and Constants," p. 352.

29. Paul E. Greenbaum and Susan D. Greenbaum, "Cultural Differences, Nonverbal Regulation, and Classroom Interaction: Sociolinguistic Interference in American Indian Education," *Peabody Journal of Education* 61 (Fall 1983): 26–28.

30. Ibid., pp. 28–30.

31. Heath, "Questioning at Home and at School," pp. 109–20.

Native Americans) do, and they are more vocally dramatic. She also found a distinctive African-American way of viewing/gazing—when speaking, blacks tend to look directly at an individual, but while listening they tend to look away. This is essentially the opposite of the viewing pattern used by many whites in a conversation.[32] Shade has suggested that, to the degree that African American children have these attributes, they may need a classroom environment in which the teacher promotes warm, interpersonal contact with an emphasis on group instructional strategies that allow for active, verbally demonstrative activities.[33] Boykin's previously mentioned suggestion that black children might benefit from more varied learning tasks in some contexts also seems persuasive from a sociolinguistic standpoint.

Research indicates that children from many Mexican immigrant families also have distinctive sociolinguistic characteristics (apart from the fact that Spanish is usually their first language). In general, these children may not be engaged in conversation by their parents or other adults during their preschool years as regularly as is the case among Anglos. Mexican American children learn that they are not to interrupt adult conversations. Adults do provide children with verbal instructions on task performance but tend to do so primarily as needed because the assumption is that children will learn through observing the actions of others in particular task situations.[34] To the degree that learning opportunities in the classroom take place primarily through verbal (oral/written) means, with considerably less use of visual/observational modes, these youngsters may be at a significant academic disadvantage. Lily Wong Fillmore and Susan Britsch have suggested that these experiences lead many Mexican children in U.S. schools to be reluctant to initiate questions in the classroom.[35]

Cognition Like culture, cognition can be difficult to define.[36] A modest variation on the definition of *cognition* in the *American Heritage Dictionary* is "the mental processes or faculties by which knowledge is acquired and used."[37] The fact that notions of intelligence vary from culture to culture suggests that people from different cultures have developed different cognitive patterns, that is, different mental techniques for gathering, processing, interpreting, and using information. Thus, to the degree that U.S. racial/ethnic minorities differ

32. Barbara J. Shade, "The Influence of Perceptual Development on Cognitive Style: Cross Ethnic Comparisons," *Early Child Development and Care* 51 (October 1989): 146–47.

33. Barbara J. Shade, "Afro-American Cognitive Style: A Variable in School Success?" *Review of Educational Research* 52 (Summer 1982): 237–38.

34. Guadalupe Valdes, "Brothers and Sisters: A Closer Look at the Development of 'Cooperative' Social Orientations in Mexican-American Children," paper presented at the Thirty-Seventh Annual Convention of the California Association of School Psychologists, 1986.

35. Lily Wong Fillmore and Susan Britsch, "Early Education for Children from Linguistic and Cultural Minority Families," paper prepared for the Early Education Task Force of the National Association of State Boards of Education, June 1988, p. 12.

36. For a discussion of some of the difficulties associated with defining *cognition*, see Thomas J. Ciborowski, "Cross-Cultural Aspects of Cognitive Functioning: Culture and Knowledge," in *Perspectives on Cross Cultural Psychology*, Anthony J. Marsella, Roland G. Tharp, and Thomas J. Ciborowski, eds. (New York: Academic Press, 1979), pp. 103–08.

37. *American Heritage Dictionary*, 2d College Edition, s.v. "cognition."

culturally from the white majority, as well as from each other, they may have distinctive cognitive attributes or styles that have educational consequences. This does not mean that all members of a particular racial/ethnic group have identical cognitive styles or that the differences among the groups are always large. There are doubtless both commonality and diversity within groups as well as between groups.

Barbara Shade has suggested that the most academically successful students in our schools typically have the following cognitive characteristics:

(1) an attention style that focuses on the task itself, rather than on the people in the situation; (2) an abstraction ability that separates ideas and concepts into parts and reweaves them into a unified whole; (3) a perceptual style that leads to the abstraction of both obvious and nonobvious attributes that seemingly link things, ideas, or principles; (4) a perceptual style that facilitates the extraction of important information embedded in distracting influences; (5) a long attention span with prolonged concentrating ability; (6) an attending preference for verbal cues rather than nonverbal cues; (7) a reflective rather than an impulsive response style in problem solving; (8) a highly differentiated or analytic thinking style that leads to abstract and logical reasoning.[38]

Collectively these attributes are consistent with the language-based, decontextualized environment of much formal schooling—as well as with many of the intellectual needs of a contemporary technological society. The emphasis on analytical/abstract thought seems especially appropriate. But for our purposes, the question is whether the list helps us to identify and to understand variations in cognitive style among racial/ethnic groups.

One of the most interesting ways to differentiate among groups has been to examine the degree to which they are inclined toward analytic or holistic thought. Analytical thinking here refers to a tendency to break things down into component parts, holistic thinking to a tendency to look at things in their totality (items 2 and 8 on Shade's list). It has also been useful to examine the degree to which groups are inclined toward verbal or nonverbal learning (item 6). Verbal learning is language based, while nonverbal learning may be observational. Verbal learning in the schools frequently combines the oral and the written—in a focused way, it marries auditory and visual components of texts, lectures, and so forth, which are introducing knowledge in a decontextualized (abstracted) way. Learning tasks in the schools often entail using language to break things down into component parts. Whites are usually thought to be inclined toward a verbal/analytical mode, while minority groups that do less well academically than whites under current schooling arrangements are thought to emphasize nonverbal/holistic cognitive patterns.[39]

38. Shade, "Afro-American Cognitive Style," p. 232.
39. Tharp, "Psychocultural Variables and Constants," p. 353.

Cross-cultural researchers have found that such cognitive-style preferences tend to be associated with the extent to which an individual or group has had formal schooling experiences that emphasized verbal/analytical learning. A nonverbal/holistic cognitive style is often found among those who have had little or no schooling of this kind, whereas a verbal/analytic cognitive style is more often seen among those who have had a significant amount of such schooling.[40] This pattern may be seen most vividly in nations that have only recently begun to establish large numbers of schools with Western characteristics. For example, John Ogbu believes that "current developments in many Third World countries appear to illustrate both the cross-cultural variation in cognitive skills and changes which occur in these skills as a result of social change. Under the impact of Western technology, economy, emergent bureaucracy, urbanization and formal schooling, various African peoples and others appear to be undergoing a kind of cognitive acculturation. They are increasingly acquiring Western-type cognitive skills."[41]

In their home environment, Native Hawaiian children often learn by watching an experienced individual perform a task or by participating in the effort with verbalized guidance. This kind of learning has dimensions that might be described as contextual and observational. Applying this knowledge, the KEEP researchers redesigned the reading program to emphasize comprehension of stories. All instruction was in small groups. Efforts were made to focus on major themes and characters and to relate them to the children's lives. Technical reading skills such as phonics in a decontextualized fashion were deemphasized. This approach produced a marked improvement in the students' reading performance as well as much higher scores on standardized reading tests.[42]

Unlike the Native Hawaiian children, Lynn Vogt and her colleagues write, "Navajo children . . . seemed uncomfortable with chopping a story into small segments, discussing each segment separately, and putting the pieces together at the end. They preferred to read and discuss the stories as complete units, rather than in an event-by-event, linear way."[43] Tharp believes this is evidence of preference for a holistic, visual cognitive style and is consistent with traditional community storytelling among the Navajo.[44]

Shade and others have concluded from available research that black children tend to be comfortable with both verbal and nonverbal types of communication

40. Scribner and Cole, "Cognitive Consequences of Formal and Informal Education," p. 554.
41. John U. Ogbu, "Social Stratification in the United States," in *Dimensions of Social Life: Essays in Honor of David Mandelbaum*, P. Stockting, ed. (The Hague: Mouton, 1987), p. 584.
42. Tharp, "The Effective Instruction of Comprehension," pp. 508–21.
43. Vogt et al, "Explaining School Failure, Producing School Success," p. 284.
44. Tharp, "Psychocultural Variables and Constants," p. 353. From her examination of the literature, Shade also concluded that American Indian children tend to be visual/holistic learners and that they preferred working in small groups. Shade, "The Influence of Perceptual Development on Cognitive Style," p. 150. Arthur J. More has interpreted the research on the learning/cognitive styles of native peoples in the United States and Canada in a generally similar fashion. See Arthur J. More, "Native Indian Learning Styles: A Review for Researchers and Teachers," *Journal of American Indian Education*, special issue (August 1989): 15–28.

during learning and tend to prefer holistic problem solving approaches. They also tend to prefer socially oriented/people-oriented learning approaches to object-oriented approaches.[45] Earlier I noted Heath's finding that African Americans in a working-class community in the South had a linguistic pattern that emphasized storytelling. The African American linguistic tradition tends to be characterized by a broad variety of oral and written forms, including "Afro-American rhymes, stories, music, sermons, and joking."[46] Another aspect of this tradition is its focus on people rather than on things.[47] This cultural tradition is consistent with the conclusions of some researchers that blacks tend to exhibit a high degree of interpersonal intelligence (an ability to read the emotions, preferences, and motives of others), in contrast to abstract/logical intelligence of the kind given developmental priority in the school.[48]

A problem-solving course for New York City high school students designed by Edmund W. Gordon offers an example of how several dimensions of African American youngsters' cognitive style can be drawn upon for instructional purposes. Gordon and his colleagues developed problems that were contextual (for example, using a cooking example to develop a particular quantitative reasoning skill). Students were divided into small groups to work on the problems and were given relative freedom of expression as they went about their tasks. As a result, "their discussions of the problems were animated, and they expressed themselves with exclamations of delight and a shared camaraderie as they solved one problem after another. They slapped hands, joked, touched, laughed, encouraged, and supported each other as they explained to each other the intricacies of the problems they were solving."[49]

There has been relatively little research on the cognitive styles of the various Hispanic populations. However, it is reasonable to assume that many Latinos have some cognitive-style similarities to other minority groups that historically

45. Shade, "The Influence of Perceptual Development on Cognitive Style," pp. 150–51; Madge Gill Willis, *The Journal of Black Psychology* 16 (Fall 1989): 54–55. Some researchers have taken different approaches to the examination of cognitive differences between African Americans and whites. For example, some have looked at this question from an information-processing perspective. One study of this kind found differences in metacognitive patterns between elementary-school-age black and white working-class children who lived in a small town in Michigan. The researchers attributed their findings to differences in early learning environments experienced by the African American and white youngsters. See John G. Borkowski and Audrey Krause, "Racial Differences in Intelligence: The Importance of the Executive System," *Intelligence* 7 (December 1983): 379–95.

46. Shirley Brice Heath, "Oral and Literate Traditions among Black Americans Living in Poverty," *American Psychologist* 44 (February 1989): 367.

47. This is an orientation that has been found among (black) Africans, not simply American blacks. See Beverly M. Gordon, "Towards a Theory of Knowledge Acquisition for Black Children," *Journal of Education* 164 (Winter 1982): 95–99.

48. Serge Madhere, "Models of Intelligence and the Black Intellect," *Journal of Negro Education* 58 (Spring 1989): 200.

49. Ernest D. Washington, Edmund W. Gordon, and Eleanor Armour-Thomas, "Family, School, Metacognition and Achievement in Afro-American Students," in *Improving Life Chances for Young Children*, Robert L. Egbert, ed. (Lincoln, Neb.: Bureau of Education Research, Services and Policy Studies and the Center for Curriculum and Instruction, Teachers College, University of Nebraska-Lincoln, 1989), p. 103.

have had relatively little access to formal schooling.[50] Jaime Escalante, a math teacher who has received national recognition for his success in helping Latino high school students pass the advanced placement calculus course, has employed several strategies that relate to the issue of cognitive style (as well as to social organization and sociolinguistics). For example, Escalante has used an instructional approach that stresses contextualization of learning by presenting specific math problems and concepts in terms that are culturally and experientially relevant to his students. He has also used the small-group format extensively and promoted a socially oriented, expressive environment.[51] This approach appears to be similar to the one used by Gordon and his colleagues with African American high school students.

Research on the cognitive style of most groups of Asian Americans is also scarce. Tharp has interpreted the results of an international comparison of math and reading achievement of Japanese, Taiwanese Chinese, and white American elementary students as suggesting that many Asian groups have cognitive-style attributes that are similar to those of whites.[52] Indeed, by the fifth grade students from all three countries had similar scores on cognitive-task questions.[53] Ogbu has noted research showing that at least some Asian students in the United States seem able to succeed even though they have come from cultural circumstances that are not consistent with the cognitive attributes of American schools. For example, some Punjabi immigrant students are relatively successful in American schools, apparently more as a result of their high academic motivation than because their early childhood experiences prepared them for the cognitive tasks of the school.[54]

Motivation   Over the long term, a crucial factor in determining a racial/ethnic group's motivation to succeed in school are the benefits its members receive from education. If most members of a group believe that education will open the door to good economic and occupational opportunities, children from the group may be more motivated to succeed academically than if they believe that the opposite is true. Over time, one would expect the group members' perceptions of their economic opportunities to reflect their actual opportunities. As their real opportunity structure changes, so will their perceptions, but probably with some time lag.

50. For a discussion that is generally consistent with this interpretation, see Manuel Ramirez III, "A Bicognitive-Multicultural Model for a Pluralistic Education," *Early Child Development and Care* 51 (October 1989): 129–36.

51. Jaime Escalante and Jack Dirmann, "The Jaime Escalante Math Program," *Journal of Negro Education* (Summer 1990): 413–14.

52. Tharp, "Psychocultural Variables and Constants," 352–53.

53. Harold W. Stevenson, James W. Stigler, Shin-ying Lee, and G. William Lucker, "Cognitive Performance and Academic Achievement of Japanese, Chinese, and American Children," *Child Development* 56 (June 1985): 733–34.

54. John U. Ogbu and Maria Eugenia Matute-Bianchi, "Understanding Sociocultural Factors: Knowledge, Identity, and School Adjustment," in *Beyond Language: Social and Cultural Factors in Schooling Language Minority Students* (Los Angeles: Evaluation, Dissemination and Assessment Center, California State University, 1986), p. 76.

As I pointed out in chapter 9, substantial variations in academic motivation patterns evidently exist among racial/ethnic groups. Many black children and youth apparently believe that their chances of securing a good job are very low, regardless of education, whereas many recent Asian immigrants believe that their prospects are generally positive if they get a good education but relatively poor if they do not.[55] The school's role in shaping the overall opportunity structure for a group is limited, especially if the society has artificially restricted the occupational and social mobility of that group, as was the case for U.S. blacks until recently. However, if the opportunity structure has been changing rapidly in some positive way, the school may be able to help bring the group's perceptions into line with the new reality. This is an important role for the school with regard to economically disadvantaged minority children, especially in the central cities. The job opportunities available to many adults in their communities may be limited by a shortage of low-skill, adequately paying positions, yet good jobs that require higher levels of education than their parents possess may exist elsewhere. If the schools can help these youngsters to see these opportunities, they may be able to accelerate the (positive) perceptual adjustment process. The result should be greater (reality-based) motivation to succeed in school.

The school can also provide learning opportunities that are motivating in their own right. Most children enjoy learning; the issues for the school are what they are asked to learn and how they are asked to learn it. The more difficult it is for disadvantaged students to see positive things in the economic opportunity structure, the more important a genuinely engaging learning environment becomes for their academic success.[56] Moreover, the younger children are, the more important it is for the school to be intrinsically rewarding to them. In the early school years, the extrinsic rewards of education may be too far in the future to motivate many children to do schoolwork that lacks meaning to them.

It is on this "micromotivational" level that the cultural compatibility of home and school often becomes especially salient. For example, a common way for teachers to motivate students is to praise them individually for doing good work (or to criticize them individually for poor work). The KEEP researchers found, however, that with Native Hawaiian students it was more effective to praise the group as a whole. A combination of warmth and firmness improved the children's motivation to learn. In contrast, with Navajo children, when responding to specific misconduct in the classroom, it often proved more effective to call on the group to meet appropriate standards than to comment directly on the individual's unacceptable behavior.[57]

Similarly, Jaime Escalante has relied on a combination of high demands and personal warmth to motivate the Hispanic high school students in his math

55. See Jayjia Hsia, *Asian Americans in Higher Education and at Work* (Hillsdale, N.J.: Lawrence Erlbaum Associates, 1988), pp. 166–203, for a discussion of the relationships between education and occupation/income for Asians.

56. John D'Amato, "'Acting': Hawaiian Children's Resistance to Teachers," *The Elementary School Journal* 88 (May 1988): 540–43.

57. Vogt et al., "Explaining School Failure, Producing School Success," pp. 281–83.

classes. Students are expected to do the work, with no excuses, and Escalante has provided tutoring or other assistance as required. Yet Escalante has also used the "macromotivational" strategy of bringing his students into contact with individuals of similar backgrounds to their own who hold good jobs that require well-developed mathematics skills. For example, he has arranged for former students working in science and technology to speak to the class. He has also taken his students on trips to industrial sites.[58]

Motivation can be regarded as both a source and a product of student achievement. Academically successful students are likely to be highly motivated, and highly motivated students are likely to be academically successful. Consequently, motivational strategies undertaken by school professionals to ensure greater compatibility between the culture of the school/classroom and the cultures of their students cannot be separated easily from actions they take in other areas, including social organization, the sociolinguistic environment, and cognitive task selection.

Language   Standard English, as spoken and written by most Americans, is the primary language of the major institutions of society, including the school. But the United States has always been a multidialect and multilingual society. In the past hundred years, for example, America has experienced two distinct phases of increased multilingualism as a result of the large-scale immigration from southern and eastern Europe in the early decades of this century and of the substantial immigration from Asia and Latin America that began in the late 1960s and continues today. The current increase in multilingualism is presenting a much more complex challenge for the schools (and for society as a whole), in many respects:

1. Both the number and the diversity of the languages spoken by the current wave of immigrants are much greater than at the turn of the century. Most of the earlier immigrants spoke a European language; the languages of today's immigrants include several of European origin (notably Spanish), but also many Asian.[59]

2. Students who enter school today with limited English proficiency (LEP) need more and better formal education than was the case with the earlier immigrants. Society's legal obligations toward such students are also much greater today. For example, the Supreme Court decision in *Lau v. Nichols* in 1975 provided school remedies to meet the academic needs of language minority children.[60]

3. Many of the new immigrants have not had the benefit of extensive formal

58. Escalante and Dirmann, "The Jaime Escalante Math Program," pp. 411, 412, 417, 418.
59. Joan McCarty First and John Willshire Carrera, *New Voices: Immigrant Students in U.S. Public Schools* (Boston: National Coalition of Advocates for Students, 1988), p. 6.
60. Courtney B. Cazden and Ellen L. Leggett, "Culturally Responsive Education: Recommendations for Achieving Lau Remedies II," in *Culture and the Bilingual Classroom: Studies in Classroom Ethnography*, Henry T. Trueba, Grace P. Guthrie, and Kathryn H. Au, eds. (Rowley, Mass.: Newbury House Publishing, 1981), pp. 69–85.

education. This was, of course, true of many of the southern and eastern European immigrants early in the century. But the gap between the immigrants' formal education and the amount required for full participation in the mainstream is probably much larger now.[61]

4. The current period of large-scale immigration, already a quarter-century old, could last much longer than the previous period. The schools need to be prepared to serve large numbers of linguistically diverse LEP students for the indefinite future.

5. Many of the new immigrants are from places much closer to us geographically than was true of the earlier immigrants. Indeed, our largest single source of new immigrants—Mexico—shares a long border with the United States. This helps maintain the vitality of the Spanish language on the U.S. side of the border.[62]

Owing to the rapidly changing demographics of the United States, there is no firm count of language minority children or of those youngsters who cannot pursue their studies effectively in a traditional English-only classroom environment. One estimate suggests that there were about 6.2 million language minority children of school age in the late 1980s, of whom about 3.5 million were thought to have limited English proficiency.[63] In the 1987–89 period, enrollment in U.S. public and private schools averaged about 45.6 million per year.[64] Thus, LEP students represented close to 8 percent of the total. The educational challenge posed for the schools is more than this 8 percent share might suggest because LEP children are concentrated in a relatively few states and cities. For example, in the 1987–88 school year California's 613,000 LEP students represented more than 12 percent of the state's student-age population. Nearly 50 percent of the students in Los Angeles County were LEP.[65]

How can Americans as a society ensure that the growing number of language-minority students become proficient in English, the primary language of the institutional mainstream, as quickly as possible? To what extent should public policy promote or discourage the maintenance of the primary language of lan-

61. The fact that Mexican immigrants since 1985 have averaged less than a sixth-grade education, compared to the more than an eighth-grade education averaged by Mexican immigrants in the early 1960s provides support for this conclusion. See Frank D. Bean, Jorge Chapa, Ruth Berg, and Kathryn Sowards, "Educational and Sociodemographic Incorporation among Hispanic Immigrants to the United States," in *Immigration and Ethnicity: The Integration of America's Newest Immigrants*, Barry Edmonston and Jeffrey S. Passel, eds. (Forthcoming).

62. Joseph O. Prewitt Diaz, "Assessment of Puerto Rican Children in Bilingual Education Programs in the United States: A Critique of Lloyd M. Dunn's Monograph," *Hispanic Journal of Behavioral Sciences* 10 (September 1988): 239.

63. Estimates of the LEP student population in the latter part of the 1980s have ranged from 1.2 million to 5.5 million. Council of Chief State of School Officers, *School Success for Limited English Proficient Students: The Challenge and State Response* (Washington, D.C.: Council of Chief State School Officers, 1990), p. 15.

64. National Center for Education Statistics, U.S. Department of Education, *Digest of Education Statistics, 1990* (Washington, D.C.: U.S. Government Printing Office, 1991), p. 11.

65. Council of Chief State School Officers, *School Success for Limited English Proficient Students*, p. 16.

guage minority students, even as they learn English?[66] And what educational approaches seem most likely to maximize the overall academic success of LEP students?

A distinction must be drawn between proficiency in conversational language, "the language used for informal, interpersonal communication," and the academic language used in the school "for learning and discussing abstract ideas."[67] Research suggests that children may reach conversational proficiency in a second language within two years, but academic proficiency can take up to a half-dozen years to develop.[68]

The design of effective educational programs for language minority students must take into account that these students must not simply learn English; they must also make normal progress in several academic subjects. Further, many language minority youngsters enter school with relatively few literacy skills in their primary language. This is to a considerable degree a social class issue, for these children are disproportionately from homes in which the parents have little formal education, and their preschool educational opportunities are not sufficient for them to develop literacy skills in either their primary language or English comparable to those of children with relatively well educated parents.[69]

These twin problems have led many bilingual educators and researchers to endorse early childhood education programs in which instruction is almost exclusively in the children's primary language, on the theory that it is easier to develop literacy skills initially in the primary language and that these basic literacy skills, once learned, are readily transferable to a second language.[70] On the basis of his review of the research, Richard Duran has noted, "If an individual has literate skills appropriate for schooling in a first language, then acquisition of literate skills for schooling in a second language may be facilitated."[71]

Early childhood programs that use the children's primary language also ensure that the youngsters do not lose their capacity to speak their primary lan-

66. Mary McGroarty, "The Societal Context of Bilingual Education," *Educational Researcher* 21 (March 1992): 7–9. Some have called this issue a conflict between assimilationists and cultural pluralists.

67. Stephen Krashen and Douglas Biber, *On Course: Bilingual Education's Success in California* (Sacramento: California Association for Bilingual Education, 1988), p. 19.

68. Lily Wong Fillmore, "Research Currents: Equity or Excellence?" *Language Arts* 63 (September 1986): 475–76.

69. See Luis C. Moll, "Bilingual Classroom Studies and Community Analysis: Some Recent Trends," *Educational Researcher* 21 (March 1992): 20; Luis M. Laosa, "School, Occupation, Culture, and Family: The Impact of Parental Schooling on the Parent-Child Relationship," *Journal of Educational Psychology* 74 (December 1982): 791–827. Limited formal education among parents is a problem for many of the new immigrant groups. However, owing to the large proportion of Mexican immigrant adults with little formal education, it is an issue of special salience for students from this population. For example, 41 percent of the Mexican American eighth graders in the NELS:88 study reported having no parent with a high school diploma. Children's Defense Fund, *The State of America's Children 1991* (Washington, D.C.: Children's Defense Fund, 1991), p. 79.

70. Kenji Hakuta and Eugene E. Garcia, "Bilingualism and Education," *American Psychologist* 44 (February 1989): 375.

71. Richard P. Duran, "Factors Affecting Development of Second Language Literacy," in *Becoming Literate in English as a Second Language*, Susan R. Goldman and Henry T. Trueba, eds. (Norwood, N.J.: Ablex, 1987), p. 35.

guage—which is likely to be the language of the home. It is essential that efforts to develop the children's mastery of English not undermine their capacity to communicate with their parents, who may speak little English.[72]

Many bilingual educators have concluded that, at the elementary school level, the preferred approach is for LEP students to be taught academic subjects in their primary language for the first few years, with English taught as a second language. As the students develop their academic English skills over time, instruction in academic subjects is gradually shifted to English. Students are not mainstreamed into an all-English classroom until the seventh grade. This approach has the virtue of allowing LEP students to accumulate subject-area knowledge via their primary language, while they undertake the long process of acquiring proficiency in English. The shift to English can ordinarily come in math before social studies because math requires less verbal facility for effective learning.[73]

This approach is a so-called late-exit version of a transitional bilingual education (TBE) program. However, most TBE programs are of the early-exit variety, in which students receive instruction in their primary language for only two or three years, often for as little as an hour a day.[74] The late-exit TBE approach, it is thought, not only ensures that language minority students keep up with the majority in the acquisition of content knowledge but also facilitates their mastery of academic English. Like most kinds of learning, the acquiring of a second language benefits from contextualization. The acquisition of subject-area competence is a kind of contextualization for the learning of English; it becomes easier to learn a second language when one already possesses considerable content knowledge that can be tapped when learning the second language in a subject-area-specific context.[75]

In 1990, a major government-funded evaluation of early-exit TBE, late-exit

72. Lily Wong Fillmore, "Now or Later? Issues Related to the Early Education of Minority-Group Children," in *Early Childhood and Family Education: Analysis and Recommendations of the Council of Chief State School Officers* (Orlando, Fla.: Harcourt Brace Jovanovich, 1990), pp. 134–39; Roberto Rodriquez, "Non-English Speaking Preschoolers Stymied by English Instruction," *Black Issues in Higher Education*, 31 January 1991, p. 5. There is at least some disagreement on this point among educators. For example, some believe that available evidence suggests that well-designed early childhood education programs can prepare LEP preschoolers to do well in English-based elementary school programs without undermining the children's capacity to communicate with their parents in their first language. For an exchange of views on this question, see Rosalie Pedalino Porter, "The False Alarm over Early English Acquisition," *Education Week*, 5 June 1991, pp. 36, 29; Lily Wong Fillmore, "A Question for Early-Childhood Programs: English First or Families First?" *Education Week*, 19 June 1991, pp. 32, 34.

73. Krashen and Biber, *On Course: Bilingual Education's Success in California*, pp. 25–28.

74. J. David Ramirez, "Comparing Structured English Immersion and Bilingual Education: First-Year Results of a National Study," *American Journal of Education* 95 (November 1986): 124. Another name for programs that offer extensive amounts of instruction in the primary language throughout the elementary school years is additive maintenance bilingual education (MBE). See Marcello Medina, Jr., and Kathy Escamilla, "English Acquisition by Fluent- and Limited-Spanish-Proficient Mexican Americans in a 3-Year Maintenance Bilingual Program," *Hispanic Journal of Behavioral Sciences* 14 (May 1992): 253.

75. Gary A. Cziko, "The Evaluation of Bilingual Education: From Necessity and Probability to Possibility," *Educational Researcher* 21 (March 1992): 12.

TBE, and English-immersion programs (approaches in which students receive virtually all instruction in the new language) for Spanish-speaking LEP elementary school students provided support for late-exit programs. The researchers found essentially no differences in the academic achievement patterns of students in English immersion and early-exit TBE programs. But those in late-exit programs that provided ample opportunities to maintain and develop Spanish skills and shifted to English for subject-area instruction over several years showed significantly greater progress in reading and other English-language skills and in mathematics than students in the other programs.[76]

However, given the size and diversity of the language minority population, it is difficult to institute this approach for all LEP students. Currently, there are shortages of qualified bilingual teachers for most languages, and in some states these shortages have become acute.[77] For example, California, with an estimated 861,000 LEP students in 1991, needed more than 22,000 bilingual teachers; there were only about 8,000 credentialed bilingual teachers statewide that year.[78]

Further, in some schools and school districts several languages are spoken, yet not enough LEP students speak any one language to make a TBE program economically or logistically feasible.[79] In these circumstances, schools must rely on some version of the immersion approach, perhaps offering subject-area instruction in English to LEP students for 80–90 percent of the school day and allocating the remaining time to formal English language instruction.[80]

Finally, many people are concerned that late-exit TBE programs are obstacles to learning English. This fear reflects a belief that the existence of large numbers of non-English-fluent citizens threatens the linguistic coherence of the society.[81] Those who argue for English immersion point out that some groups of

76. J. David Ramirez et al., *Executive Summary Final Report: Longitudinal Study of Immersion Strategy, Early-Exit and Late-Exit Transitional Bilingual Education Programs for Language-Minority Children* (San Mateo, Cal.: Aguirre International, submitted to the U.S. Department of Education, 1990). These findings are generally consistent with the results of a meta-analysis conducted in the middle 1980s of a number of studies of bilingual education programs. See Ann C. Willig, "A Meta-Analysis of Selected Studies on the Effectiveness of Bilingual Education," *Review of Educational Research* 55 (Fall 1985): 269–317.

77. Reynaldo F. Macias, *Bilingual Teacher Supply and Demand in the United States* (University of Southern California Center for Multilingual, Multicultural Research and The Tomas Rivera Center, 1989), pp. 19–26.

78. Peter Schmidt, "California Is Short 14,000 Bilingual Teachers, Panel Finds," *Education Week*, 19 June, 1991, p. 14.

79. In the spring of 1992, P.S. 19, an elementary school in Queens (New York City) had two thousand pupils who came from forty-seven nations and spoke twenty-seven languages. In one fourth-grade math class, the thirty-five students were from fifteen nations and spoke seven languages. See James Dao, "At P.S. 19, Bilingual Is Not Enough," *New York Times*, 25 May 1992, p. B1. This is less likely to be a problem for students who speak Spanish as a first language because of their large numbers. Spanish is the primary language for about four out of five LEP students. For this reason, some believe that all but 20–25 percent of the LEP students in most schools are present in sufficient numbers to make instruction in the students' primary language possible. See Council of Chief State School Officers, *School Success for Limited English Proficient Students*, pp. 16–17.

80. Christine H. Rossell, "The Research on Bilingual Education," *Equity and Choice* (Winter 1990): 29.

81. First and Carrera, *New Voices: Immigrant Students in U.S. Public Schools*, p. 18.

students—usually Asians—seem able to master English much more quickly than other groups. If the Asians can do it, they believe, other groups can too.[82] Ironically, on closer inspection the Asian immigrant experience may provide some of the best evidence in favor of late-exit TBE programs. Asian students with a primary language other than English are quite likely to have well-educated parents with relatively strong literacy skills.[83] Thus, these students benefit from both literacy-skill transferability and the ability to use content knowledge to facilitate learning in the second language.

The success of the Asian students has been greatest in math and science—subject areas that require the least well developed academic English skills.[84] Even Asian college graduates who have good grades may have inadequate English-language skills. One explanation is that many Asian students become adept in choosing courses that require minimal English skills, even when the courses are apparently in language arts. For example, they may take humanities or social science courses in which few papers are required and most tests are multiple choice rather than essay in format. If students like these were able to benefit from the more protracted process for mastering English that characterizes well-designed late-exit TBE programs, they might emerge from their years of formal education with much better balanced development in verbally and quantitatively based academic areas.[85]

Language diversity is one of the major aspects of the cultural-differences challenge facing our schools as a result of changing demographics. Much higher priority must be given to ensuring that LEP students have academic programs designed to promote academic-English proficiency and subject-area competence simultaneously. Late-exit TBE programs seem to be the most promising approach to these goals for many LEP students—especially for those whose parents have little formal education.[86]

Racial/Ethnic-Based Cultural Differences: Some Limitations of the Knowledge Base   This brief review of some of the cultural differences among racial/ethnic groups that may have educational consequences has necessarily been much more suggestive than definitive. At this point, few research findings seem immune to challenge. For example, T. L. McCarty and his colleagues have recently called for a reassessment of evidence that many Native Americans tend toward holistic and nonverbal cognitive styles. These researchers have found

82. Hakuta and Garcia, "Bilingualism and Education," p. 377; Jim Cummins, "Empowering Minority Students: A Framework for Intervention," in Nitza M. Hidalgo, Ceasar L. McDowell, and Emilie V. Siddle, *Facing Racism in Education* (Cambridge: Harvard Educational Review, 1990), p. 52.

83. Jayjia Hsia and Marsha Hirano-Nakanishi, "The Demographics of Diversity: Asian Americans and Higher Education," *Change* (November/December 1989): 23–25.

84. Krashen and Biber, *On Course: Bilingual Education's Success in California*, p. 26.

85. Ray Lou, "Model Minority? Getting Behind the Veil," *Change* (November/December 1989): 16–17.

86. Krashen and Biber, *On Course: Bilingual Education's Success in California*, pp. 29–56; Peter Schmidt, "Three Types of Bilingual Education Effective, E.D. Study Concludes," *Education Week*, 20 February 1991, p. 23.

that "in classrooms where talk is shared between teachers and students, where the expression of the students' ideas is sought and clearly valued, where students' social environment is meaningfully incorporated into curricular content, and where students are encouraged to use their cultural and linguistic resources to solve new problems, Native American students respond eagerly and quite verbally to questioning, even in their second language. . . . this occurred in the context of instruction that explicitly emphasized inductive/analytical learning processes."[87]

Most racial/ethnic groups also have substantial within-group cultural differences, associated with differences in social class—and especially in parent education levels. Many middle-class African Americans, for example, may display relatively few of the sociolinguistic attributes Heath identified in her research on working-class blacks in the South. And many may have cognitive patterns that are generally more like those of middle-class whites than of working-class or disadvantaged African Americans.[88] Substantial within-group differences (related in part to variations in access to formal education) evidently exist in segments of the Latino population.[89]

The application of the existing cultural-difference knowledge base to improve school practices for minority students is still in its infancy. The success of programs such as KEEP suggests that efforts to adapt school practices to the cultural attributes of a particular group of children can be educationally very rewarding. Yet the reading strategies developed by the KEEP team were many years in the making. Moreover, these researchers do not claim to have produced results as good as those achieved by typical middle-class white children.[90] Finally, there is not as yet a comprehensive KEEP strategy for all subject areas or for all of the elementary school years. Certainly, there is no K-12 KEEP "system."[91]

87. T. L. McCarty, Regina Hadley Lynch, Stephen Wallace, and AnCita Benally, "Classroom Inquiry and Navajo Learning Styles: A Call for Reassessment," *Anthropology and Education Quarterly* 22 (March 1991): 53.

88. For example, a study of deductive reasoning strategies employed by a group of black undergraduate business majors at Florida A&M University in the late 1980s described as being "from privileged socioeconomic backgrounds" produced results similar to those that other researchers have previously found for whites. See Wilbur I. Smith and Saundra T. Drumming, "On Strategies That Blacks Employ in Deductive Reasoning," *Journal of Black Psychology* 16 (Fall 1989): 1–22.

89. Much of these findings also have pertained to variations in parenting behavior that are associated with differences in parent education level. See, for example, Estella A. Martinez, "Child Behavior in Mexican American/Chicano Families: Maternal Teaching and Child-Rearing Practices," *Family Relations* 37 (July 1988): 275–80; Luis M. Laosa, "Maternal Teaching Strategies in Chicano and Anglo-American Families: The Influence of Culture and Education on Maternal Behavior," *Child Development* 51 (September 1980): 759–65.

90. The KEEP researchers have evaluated their program by comparing Native Hawaiian children who participated in the program with control groups who did not. Because their focus was on Native Hawaiian children who retained much of the traditional culture, these youngsters have usually come from low-SES families. The control groups were selected to have similar characteristics. Consistent with this situation, when evaluating the KEEP program, middle-class students in KEEP were excluded from the analysis. See Tharp, "The Effective Instruction of Comprehension," p. 511.

91. The substantial research and development effort that characterized KEEP in the 1970s and early 1980s has been cut back, along with staff development for the program, evidently because a new generation of administrators concluded that they were too costly. Tharp and Gallimore view these changes as an example of how hard it is to build the capacity to learn and change into the edu-

Many social class differences of educational importance can justifiably be regarded as cultural—differences in kinds of knowledge, beliefs, and behavior. Consequently, the reexamining of social class differences from a cultural perspective can be revealing.

Before beginning this review, I want to recall just how large some of the educational gaps are among groups of children from different social classes, as measured by parent education level. Table 5.1 shows that children with at least one parent with a graduate degree had a 56 percent chance of being in the top quartile on standardized achievement tests used in the NELS:88 study and a 7 percent chance of being in the bottom quartile. In contrast, children with no parent with a high school degree had a 5 percent chance of being in the top quartile and a 51 percent chance of being in the bottom quartile. About 12 percent of all students in the study had at least one parent with a graduate degree, while nearly 11 percent had no parent with a high school diploma. However, these percentages varied considerably by race/ethnicity. For example, 22 percent of the Asians and 14 percent of the whites had at least one parent with a graduate degree, compared to 6 percent each for Latinos, African Americans, and Native Americans. Only 6 percent of the whites and 9 percent of the Asians had no parent with a high school diploma, compared to 33 percent of the Hispanics, 16 percent of the blacks, and 15 percent of the American Indians.

Much of the education-relevant research on social-class-related cultural differences focuses on differences in family characteristics. Relatively little of this research is directly concerned with differences between the culture of the school and the cultural patterns of different social classes. Thus, the research tends to emphasize class variations in education-relevant interactions between parents and children rather than in interactions between school professionals and children or between school professionals and parents. Further, there is relatively little social-class-oriented cultural difference research that looks simultaneously at race/ethnicity. This is unfortunate given the large within-class differences in academic achievement among racial/ethnic groups (see chapter 6). Nevertheless, there is a modest amount of research of this kind; it offers some important preliminary glimpses into cultural differences that have both social-class and racial/ethnic dimensions.

The discussion that follows reviews research on the amount of time parents from different social classes spend with their children in education-relevant ways; how parents perform the role of teacher to their children; the relationship between differences in parenting styles and children's academic success; varia-

---

cational system. See Roland G. Tharp and Ronald Gallimore, *Rousing Minds to Life: Teaching, Learning, and Schooling in Social Context* (Cambridge: Cambridge University Press, 1988), pp. 269–70. John Goodlad has also written about this general problem: the inability of the schools to be "renewing" institutions. See Goodlad, *A Place Called School*, pp. 256–57. The rapidly changing demographics of the student-age population has made this historic shortcoming of the educational system increasingly costly.

tions in how parents from different social classes and racial/ethnic groups interact with their children; and how parents from different social classes interact with the school on behalf of their children.

The Investments of Time Parents Make in Their Children   Available evidence suggests that there are substantial variations in the amount of time parents, particularly mothers, have available to invest in their children, and that these variations have social class dimensions. For example, high-SES parents are often in a position to invest more time in their children than are low-SES parents because they can afford to have the mother spend full time at home rather than hold a job. Similarly, mothers with a great deal of formal education may be able to invest more time in each of their children because they tend to have fewer children than mothers with little formal education.[92]

A national survey of families conducted in the mid-1970s by C. Russell Hill and Frank P. Stafford provided a valuable opportunity to develop estimates of social class differences in parents' investments of time in their children and to quantify the amount of time the mothers spent in several activities thought to have educational consequences. The heart of the research was a set of diaries that respondents filled out over several days, recording what they did and how much time they spent doing it. The major finding was that "more educated women spend more time playing with children, helping with the teaching of children, and in child-related travel."[93]

This difference in mothers' time investment patterns held for both younger and older children, but the gaps between classes were largest for young children. For example, mothers with at least some college reported spending about two hours more per week in caring for children under three years of age and an hour more per week with high school age youngsters than did mothers with only an eighth-grade education. (The parent time gap for high school age youngsters, although smaller in size, may have been just as important because mothers with an eighth-grade education or less reported spending very little child-care time with their children in this age group.)[94]

Most studies have centered on active as opposed to passive investments of parents' time. Yet when parents are present but not actively engaged with their children, the children may be able to learn from observing their behavior in an informal way. To the extent that high-SES families are more likely to have a parent in the home on a full- or part-time basis, the opportunities for passive parental investment are much larger for their children than for low-SES children. But because research has generally focused on the parents' active investments of time in their youngsters, social class variations in passive time investments cannot be quantified.

92. See Arleen Leibowitz, "Parental Inputs and Children's Achievement," *The Journal of Human Resources* 12 (Spring 1977): 242–51; Arleen Leibowitz, "Home Investments in Children," *Journal of Political Economy* 82 (March/April 1974): S111–31.
93. C. Russell Hill and Frank P. Stafford, "Parental Care of Children: Time Diary Estimates of Quantity, Predictability, and Variety," *The Journal of Human Resources* 15 (Spring 1980): 219–39.
94. Ibid., pp. 226, 238.

A slightly different way to think about this topic is to look at variations in indirect rather than direct time investments. Some of the most important indirect investments parents make are through their influence on the amount of time their children spend in "constructive learning activity" outside of school. This can be heavily related to the norms, standards, and guidance parents provide. Reginald M. Clark estimates that academically successful students spend twenty to thirty-five hours a week in constructive learning activities.[95] He believes

> this would consist of 4 or 5 hours of discussion with knowledgeable adults or peers, 4 or 5 hours of leisure reading, 1 or 2 hours of writing of various types (whether writing grocery lists, writing a diary, taking messages on the telephone, or writing letters), 5 or 6 hours of homework, several hours devoted to hobbies, 2 or 3 hours of chores, 4 or 5 hours of games (certain kinds of games in particular, like Monopoly and Scrabble and Dominoes, that require the player to read, spell, write, compute, solve problems, make decisions, and use other cognitive skills and talents transferable to school lessons). This constructive learning activity also includes exposure to cultural activities, theater, movies, and sports.[96]

Clark's focus on activities undertaken outside of school that are consistent with the school's academic program can be viewed as ensuring that the activities supported by the culture of the home are a good fit with the culture of the school. Parents who are most familiar with the culture of the school are in the best position to guide their children's use of time in ways consistent with their formal educational development. Those who have a great deal of formal education are most likely to be in this position. In social class terms, these are high-SES parents.[97]

Parents as Teachers   As Barbara Rogoff has observed, "Children's learning frequently occurs in social contexts that permit adults or more experienced peers to guide the young learner. . . . Cognitive skills such as reading are first practiced in social interaction with a more experienced person. This leads to internalization of the skill so that a child is able to carry it out independently. Adults or competent peers can support children's performance so that they can extend their activity beyond what could be accomplished independently."[98]

To maximize learning, the child must be able to provide feedback, so that the adult can offer appropriate supplementary information as needed. And adults

95. Reginald M. Clark, *Critical Factors in Why Disadvantaged Students Succeed or Fail in School* (Washington, D.C.: Academy for Educational Development, 1988), p. 4.
96. Ibid., pp. 4–5.
97. However, as Clark has found through his research, some low-SES parents are very effective nurturers of high-academic-achieving students. Reginald M. Clark, *Family Life and School Achievement: Why Poor Black Children Succeed or Fail* (Chicago: University of Chicago Press, 1983).
98. Barbara Rogoff, "Adult Assistance of Children's Learning," in *The Contexts of School-Based Literacy,* Taffy E. Raphael, ed. (New York: Random House, 1986), pp. 27.

have to be able to adjust their instruction to the child's competency level. The general process through which an adult attempts to promote learning among children in a structured, interactive process has been called guided participation.[99] Rogoff and William. P. Gardner have identified five aspects of this process that mothers commonly use in helping children master both home and school tasks. In their view, guided participation

1. Provides a bridge between familiar skills or information and those needed to solve a new problem.
2. Provides structure for problem solving.
3. Involves the transfer of responsibility for management of problem solving [from the parent to the child].
4. Involves active participation by the child as well as the adult.
5. May be tacit as well as explicit in the everyday arrangements and interactions between adults and children.[100]

Parents are not only their children's first teachers, but also their teachers for a much longer period of time than any other individuals. Parents who have had a great deal of formal schooling are well positioned to develop capacities of academic value in their youngsters. This helps to explain many of the advantages with which high-SES children enter school and why they are often able to maintain these advantages over time. For instance, parenting behaviors correlated with children's cognitive development and school success have been found to include the creation of a stimulating language environment for the children, beginning in infancy.[101] Researchers have further identified a number of attributes of the linguistic environment, especially with regard to parent-child verbal interaction, that are associated with school success. Collectively, these attributes might be regarded as constituting a democratic, or inquiry-oriented, approach, in which parents and children exchange a great deal of information verbally and are on relatively equal footing. The children can initiate conversation, interrupt their parents, ask questions, and disagree with what their parents are saying. For their part, the parents may frequently state why they hold a belief or have reached a conclusion and may help the children reach conclusions through a process of asking questions rather than simply volunteering the answer.[102]

99. Ibid., pp. 27, 31, 33, 34; Barbara Rogoff, Shari Ellis, and William Gardner, "Adjustment of Adult-Child Instruction according to Child's Age Task," *Developmental Psychology* 20 (March 1984): 193–99.
100. Rogoff, "Adult Assistance of Children's Learning" p. 32.
101. Laosa, "School, Occupation, Culture, and Family," pp. 792–94, 823–24; Robert H. Bradley and Bettye M. Caldwell, "The Relation of Infants' Home Environments to Achievement Test Performance in First Grade: A Follow-up Study," *Child Development* 55 (June 1984): 803.
102. See Pedro R. Portes, "Longitudinal Effects of Early-Age Intervention on Family Behavior: Understanding the Role of Social Class and Ethnicity on Adolescent Scholastic Achievement," paper presented at the Annual Meeting of the American Educational Research Association, New Orleans, Louisiana, April 1984, pp. 15–25; Linda Datcher-Loury, "Family Background and School Achievement among Low Income Blacks," *The Journal of Human Resources* 24 (Summer 1989): 529–30; Robert D. Hess, Susan D. Holloway, W. Patrick Dickson, and Gary G. Price, "Maternal Variables as

In Rogoff's terms, this approach might be regarded as a form of guided participation, tailored to verbally based learning of a kind consistent with the more cognitively demanding learning tasks students undertake in school. That is to say, parents give general direction to the children's verbally grounded problem solving behavior instead of providing specific answers. And they often do so through a logical, mutual question-and-response process that has much in common with discussion pedagogies used in school seminars. Pedro R. Portes has hypothesized that this style of parent-child verbal interaction is beneficial in part because "a greater degree of verbal participation and involvement could expose the child to more information and information-processing skills." It could also prepare the child for the kind of language use often required in an intellectually demanding classroom.[103]

Parenting Styles and the Academic Success of Children   An important theme of the research on interactions between parents and children is the relationship between parenting styles and children's school success. Eleanor E. Maccoby and John A. Martin discuss four types of parenting patterns: authoritarian-autocratic, indulgent-permissive, indifferent-uninvolved, and authoritative-reciprocal. These parenting styles vary in the degree of their demandingness of and responsiveness to children.[104] Differences in parenting styles are thought to contribute to differences between children in social and cognitive development.[105]

Authoritarian parents place high demands on their children, are determined to control their children's behavior, and tend to rely on their power as parents to get the children to comply with their wishes. At the same time, they tend to be relatively unresponsive to the wishes and needs the children express. Diana Baumrind has found that authoritarian parents tend to adopt absolute standards that their children are expected to meet, emphasize obedience and respect for authority, and discourage conversational give-and-take.[106]

Indulgent parents tend to place few demands on their children and make

Predictors of Children's School Readiness and Later Achievement in Vocabulary and Mathematics in Sixth Grade," *Child Development* 55 (October 1984): 1909–11; Paul R. Amato and Gay Ochiltree, "Family Resources and the Development of Child Competence," *Journal of Marriage and the Family* 48 (February 1986): 48, 49, 54.

103. Portes, "Longitudinal Effects of Early-Age Intervention on Family Behavior," p. 24. As Edmund W. Gordon has observed, "learning to use 'elaborated' language is critical in school and in scientific and technological fields." See Edmund W. Gordon, "Educating More Minority Engineers," *Technology Review* (July 1988): 70.

104. Eleanor E. Maccoby and John A. Martin, "Socialization in the Context of the Family: Parent-Child Interaction," in *Handbook of Child Psychology*, 4th ed., vol. 4, Paul H. Mussen, ed. (New York: John Wiley and Sons, 1983), p. 39.

105. Sanford M. Dornbusch et al., "The Relationship of Parenting Style to Adolescent School Performance," *Child Development* 58 (October 1987): 1244.

106. Maccoby and Martin, "Socialization in the Context of the Family," pp. 39–46; Diana Baumrind, "Current Patterns of Parental Authority," *Developmental Psychology Monograph* 4 (1971): 1–103. Also see Diana Baumrind, "The Development of Instrumental Competence through Socialization," in *Minnesota Symposium on Child Psychology*, vol. 7, ed. A. D. Pick (Minneapolis: University of Minnesota Press, 1973), pp. 3–46.

little effort to control the youngsters' behavior. They are inclined to be highly accepting of what the children say and do and tend not to punish their children for misbehavior.[107]

Indifferent parents tend to demonstrate a limited commitment to their role and responsibilities as parents. In general, they seem interested in minimizing the work they put into parenting and the interactions they have with their children. They tend to make few demands of their children and are less likely to be responsive to their wants and needs. In the extreme, such parents can be neglectful and even physically or psychologically abusive of their children.[108]

Authoritative parents tend to make high demands of their children and to exercise a great deal of control over their behavior. Yet they also are very responsive to the children's expressed wants and needs. Baumrind has suggested that authoritative parents set clear standards for their children and expect them to behave maturely; consistently enforce the standards and rules they have established; encourage the children to be independent and to develop their individual attributes; use a conversational style with their children characterized by open give-and-take; and make it clear that both children and parents have rights.[109]

A substantial body of research suggests that the authoritative parenting style is more likely than the others to promote academic success among children, at least under existing U.S. schooling arrangements.[110] Laurence Steinberg, Julie D. Elmen, and Nina S. Mounts claim that "adolescents who describe their parents as treating them warmly, democratically, and firmly are more likely than their peers to develop positive attitudes toward, and beliefs about, their achievement, and as a consequence, they are more likely to do better in school." Put in different terms, they noted that an authoritative parenting style seems to promote mature behavior by children, including a stronger work orientation, particularly with regard to school. And working hard in school evidently contributes to good grades.[111]

A great deal of the research on parenting has focused on variations in responsiveness to children in the first years of their lives and the associated variations in developmental paths. On the basis of a long-term study, Robert H. Bradley, Bettye M. Caldwell, and Stephen L. Rock have suggested that "having a respon-

107. Maccoby and Martin, "Socialization in the Context of the Family," pp. 44–46.

108. Ibid., pp. 39, 48–51.

109. This parenting style is associated with a reciprocal pattern in which children are responsive to parents and parents are responsive to children. Ibid., pp. 39, 46–48; Baumrind, "Current Patterns of Parental Authority," pp. 1–103.

110. See Susie D. Lamborn et al., "Patterns of Competence and Adjustment among Adolescents from Authoritative, Authoritarian, Indulgent, and Neglectful Homes," *Child Development* 62 (October 1992): 1057–58; Dornbusch et al., "The Relationship of Parenting Style to Adolescent School Performance," pp. 1248–57; Laurence Steinberg, Julie D. Elmen, and Nina S. Mounts, "Authoritative Parenting, Psychosocial Maturity, and Academic Success among Adolescents, *Child Development* 60 (December 1989): 1428–35; Hess et al., "Maternal Variables as Predictors of Children's School Readiness and Later Achievement in Vocabulary and Mathematics in Sixth Grade," pp. 1907–11.

111. Steinberg, Elmen, and Mounts, "Authoritative Parenting, Psychosocial Maturity, and Academic Success among Adolescents," pp. 1431–33.

sive early social environment may start a child on a developmental trajectory that enables [him or her] to feel more comfortable and to act more responsively in situations encountered later in childhood." Parents' responsiveness in the children's early years is associated with the youngsters' cognitive development as preschoolers and their capacity to behave considerately in elementary school.[112] Other researchers have found that positive emotional relationships between parents and their children during the early childhood years were correlated with higher vocabulary and mathematics achievement test scores in the sixth grade.[113]

The stability of the parent-child relationship is also very important for children's school success, as is the current quality of the relationship for children's academic performance at any given point in time.[114]

Variations in Parent-Child Interactions   Although examples of most types of parent-child interaction can be found in every social class, there are clear class differences in the patterns of these relationships. For example, Steven R. Tulkin found that middle-class mothers typically spend much more time in reciprocal verbal interaction with their infants than mothers in working-class families. He also found that middle-class infants vocalized more than working-class infants and that this difference was partly associated with their greater verbal interaction with their mothers.[115]

Research has also found that middle-class parents tend to rely less on authoritarian approaches to their children, both younger and older, and more on authoritative strategies than working-class parents do.[116] Middle-class parents are more responsive to their children in other respects associated with later

112. Robert H. Bradley, Bettye M. Caldwell, and Stephen L. Rock, "Home Environment and School Performance: A Ten-Year Follow-up and Examination of Three Models of Environmental Action," *Child Development* 59 (August 1988): 857, 864; Bradley and Caldwell, "The Relation of Infants' Home Environments to Achievement Test Performance in First Grade: A Follow-up Study," p. 808.

113. Hess et al., "Maternal Variables as Predictors of Children's School Readiness and Later Achievement in Vocabulary and Mathematics in Sixth Grade," pp. 1906, 1907, 1909.

114. See Bradley, Caldwell, and Rock, "Home Environment and School Performance: A Ten-Year Follow-up and Examination of Three Models of Environmental Action," pp. 863–65; Edward Zigler and Karen Anderson, "An Idea Whose Time Had Come: The Intellectual and Political Climate for Head Start," in *Project Head Start: A Legacy of the War on Poverty*, Edward Zigler and Jeanette Valentine, eds. (New York: The Free Press, 1979): pp. 6–9, 13.

115. Steven R. Tulkin, "Social Class Differences in Maternal and Infant Behavior," in *Culture and Infancy: Variations in the Human Experience*, P. Herbert Lederman, Steven R. Tulkin, and Anne Rosenfeld, eds. (New York: Academic Press, 1977): pp. 502, 504.

116. Zena Smith Blau, *Black Children/White Children: Competence, Socialization, and Social Structure* (New York: Free Press, 1981), p. 202; Tulkin, "Social Class Differences in Maternal and Infant Behavior," p. 50. Even though there are differences in parent-child interaction patterns between social classes, there also can be considerable overlap in these patterns. For example, in a study of low-SES Mexican American families in the Midwest, Estella A. Martinez found that about half of the mothers used an authoritarian parenting style and about half used an authoritative style. On average, these mothers had a tenth-grade education. However, they were generally well acculturated to American life: They were third and fourth generation Americans living in predominantly white neighborhoods who spoke English fluently. See Martinez, "Child Behavior in Mexican American/Chicano Families: Maternal Teaching and Child-Rearing Practices," pp. 275–80.

school success; for example, Tulkin found that they were more likely to respond to vocalizations initiated by their infants, including spontaneous frets.[117] Because educationally disadvantaged minorities—blacks, Hispanics, and Native Americans—are underrepresented among high-SES families and over-represented among low-SES families, these social-class variations in parent-child interaction patterns are potentially quite significant. It is not always clear, however, if the research findings are generalizable to racial/ethnic groups other than whites, owing to the nature of the samples used in many studies.[118]

In a series of studies of white and Mexican American mothers, Luis Laosa found that "the Anglo-American mothers used inquiry and praise as teaching strategies more frequently than the Chicano mothers. On the other hand, the Chicano mothers used modeling, visual cue, directive, and negative physical control more frequently than the Anglo-Americans. The mothers in the two cultural groups did not differ in their use of negative verbal feedback or disapproval, positive physical control, and physical affection." The white mothers in the sample had an average of 13.2 years of education, the Mexican American mothers only 8.8 years. This proved to be a crucial factor: "The cultural group differences in maternal teaching behavior disappeared entirely when the mothers' or the fathers' schooling levels were held constant. In contrast, holding constant the mothers' or fathers' occupational statuses did not erase the cultural group differences in maternal teaching behavior."[119]

The teaching strategies used by the more highly educated mothers, white or Mexican American, were quite consistent with those typically used in school. Thus, Laosa's research supports the conclusion that the culture of the school and that of the middle class are educationally compatible and also that differences between racial/ethnic groups in maternal teaching strategies seem to be significantly related to differences in access to formal schooling.[120]

Such an inference does not mean, of course, that increases in formal education levels among minorities would (or should) eliminate parenting differences between whites and minorities. However, all other things being equal, one might expect a gradual convergence in many areas over a period of time. For

117. Tulkin, "Social Class Differences in Maternal and Infant Behavior," p. 502.
118. The samples of parents and children in studies range widely in their racial/ethnic and social-class mixes. Tulkin's study, for example, included only white middle-class and working-class families; the research of Bradley, Caldwell, and Rock is based on a sample of families and children that is disproportionately black. See also Jere Edward Brophy, "Mothers as Teachers of Their Own Preschool Children: The Influence of Socioeconomic Status and Task Structure on Teaching Specificity," *Child Development* 41 (March 1970): 79–94 (this has an all-black sample, mixed in terms of SES); Cynthia T. Garcia Coll, Joel Hoffman, and William Oh, "The Social Ecology and Early Parenting of Caucasian Adolescent Mothers," *Child Development* 58 (August 1987): 955–63 (this has an all-white sample of mixed SES); James V. Wertsch et al., "The Adult-Child Dyad as a Problem-Solving System," *Child Development* 51 (December 1980): 1215–21 (this has a sample of middle-class mothers and children); and Langdon E. Longstreth et al., "Separation of Home Intellectual Environment and Maternal IQ as Determinants of Child IQ," *Developmental Psychology* 17 (September 1981): 532–41 (this has a sample that is mostly white and mixed in SES.)
119. Laosa, "Maternal Teaching Strategies in Chicano and Anglo-American Families: The Influence of Culture and Education on Maternal Behavior," pp. 763–65.
120. Ibid., p. 765.

example, Portes and his colleagues found that African Americans at each socioeconomic level are more likely than whites to use punitive disciplinary styles.[121] These within-social-class differences seem to have more to do with mismeasurement of class than with true differences. As Zena Smith Blau has observed, a disproportionate number of middle-class African American parents have been raised in working-class circumstances, and therefore, as first-generation members of the middle class, they can be expected to have parenting strategies similar to the working-class approaches they themselves experienced as children. As more blacks become second- and third-generation middle class, it seems plausible that they will tend to converge on many middle-class parenting strategies, including those concerned with child discipline.[122]

A study of American high school students conducted by Laurence Steinberg, Sanford M. Dornbusch, and B. Bradford Brown has produced important insights into whether and how racial/ethnic variations in parenting styles are associated with: (1) schooling outcomes (academic performance, educational aspirations and expectations, time invested in school-related activities, and school-related attitudes and beliefs); (2) psychosocial adjustment (self-esteem, work-orientation, self-reliance, and personal and social competence); (3) behavior problems (delinquency, vulnerability to antisocial peer pressure, alcohol and drug abuse, and school misconduct); and (4) psychological distress (depression, anxiety, and psychosomatic distress). One insight into authoritative parenting was that white high school students reported experiencing that type of parenting more frequently than blacks, Hispanics, or Asians. Asian American students were the least likely to experience an authoritative parenting style, an interesting finding because the Asian students in the sample had higher grades than any other group, including whites, while the African Americans had the lowest grades. Another insight was that in all racial/ethnic groups, "youngsters from authoritative homes fared better than their counterparts from nonauthoritative homes" on all the non-school-related factors (psychosocial adjustment, behavior problems, and psychological distress). And a third was that authoritative parenting was associated with higher grades for white and Latino high school students, but not for African Americans and Asians.[123]

121. Portes, Dunham, and Williams, "Assessing Child-Rearing Style in Ecological Settings: Its Relation to Culture, Social Class, Early Age Intervention and Scholastic Achievement," p. 73. Evidence of a greater tendency for African American than white parents to use authoritarian parenting strategies, including physical punishment, has been found in a number of studies. See Jewelle Taylor Gibbs, "Developing Intervention Models for Black Families: Linking Theory and Research," in *Black Families: Interdisciplinary Perspectives*, Harold E. Cheatham and James B. Stewart, eds. (New Brunswick, N.J.: Transaction Publishers, 1990), p. 335.

122. Blau, *Black Children/White Children*, pp. 191–92. There is some evidence that differences in parenting behavior between Anglos and Latinos also continue to exist in some cases after initial convergence in educational attainment levels. For example, Robert P. Moreno has developed preliminary evidence (via a very small sample) that Anglo mothers use more "perceptual" questions (What is that? Where does it go?) with their children than Mexican American mothers use with their children, despite having generally similar attainment levels. See Moreno, "Maternal Teaching of Preschool Children in Minority and Low-Status Familes: A Critical Review," *Early Childhood Research Quarterly* 6 (1991): 395–410.

123. Laurence Steinberg, Sanford M. Dornbusch, and B. Bradford Brown, "Ethnic Differences

Steinberg, Dornbusch, and Brown derive much of the explanation for these findings from the combinations of family and peer relations experienced by each group. They found that among all racial/ethnic groups, students whose academic achievement is supported by both friends and parents perform better than those who receive support from only one of these sources; and the latter youngsters, in turn, perform better than those who receive support from neither friends nor parents. However, the "congruence of parent and peer support is greater for white and Asian-American youngsters than for African-American and Hispanic adolescents."[124]

A consistency was observed between the friendship networks of whites (especially middle-class whites) and the parenting styles they experienced: Whites with authoritative parents were likely to have academically oriented friends. But no such relationship was found for Asians or blacks. In the case of Asians, large numbers of students were found to be academically oriented. Given their tendency to socialize with youngsters from the same racial/ethnic group, the likelihood was high that a particular Asian student would be part of an academically oriented friendship network. Similarly, the fact that relatively few of the black students were academically oriented reduced the chances that an individual black student would have academically oriented friends. Like African Americans, Latino students in the study also tended to have lower grades than whites, although this deficit seemed to be due to a combination of the lower percentages of Hispanics with authoritative parents and academically oriented peers—the opposite of the pattern experienced by whites.[125]

Steinberg, Dornbusch, and Brown also found that academically successful students worked harder at school than less successful students. The Asian students, for example, spent more time studying than other students and were most likely to attribute school success to hard work.[126] Steinberg and two of his colleagues, Julie Elmen and Nina Mounts, found that authoritative parenting seemed to influence student achievement by promoting a more mature behavior pattern, which included a greater propensity to work hard in school. It seems, however, that there are other parenting-related factors that can either encourage youngsters to work hard in school or discourage them from doing so.

The discussion of the impact of prejudice on minority students' academic achievement patterns (see chapter 9) suggests how the academic work ethic of students might be strengthened or weakened in ways unrelated to parenting style. The negative economic and educational opportunity structure that confronted African Americans for a long time persists for many, in part owing to

---

in Adolescent Achievement: An Ecological Perspective," *American Psychologist* 47 (June 1992): 723–72. Asian high school students have been found to be substantially more likely than whites to experience authoritarian parenting. Dornbusch et al., "The Relationship of Parenting Style to Adolescent School Performance," p. 1248.

124. Steinberg, Dornbusch, and Brown, "Ethnic Differences in Adolescent Achievement: An Ecological Perspective," p. 727.

125. Ibid., pp. 727–728.

126. Ibid., p. 726.

changes in the nation's economy in recent decades. Moreover, this negative economic environment has been linked to lower levels of academic achievement motivation, even an anti-academic-achievement orientation, among many disadvantaged black youngsters.

In their research on the achievement patterns and experiences of students in the United States, Japan, China, and Taiwan, Harold W. Stevenson, James W. Stigler, and their colleagues found substantial differences among these national groups in the degree to which parents attributed the academic prospects of their children to native ability versus their willingness to work hard in school. American mothers placed relatively large emphasis on native ability, while the Asian mothers tended to emphasize the role of hard work. The ability-versus-work orientation of each group of mothers seems to be grounded in the cultural attributes and traditions of their respective countries. This suggests that, all other things being equal, East Asian immigrants have probably inculcated a stronger work orientation to schooling in their children than have white Americans. Further, Steinberg, Dornbusch, and Brown found that "social supports for help with academics—studying together, explaining difficult assignments, and so on—are quite pervasive among Asian-American students." This suggests that the peer network of a great many Asian high school students not only supports the value of high academic achievement and of working hard to do well but also provides collective support for the actual content of schoolwork that is extremely helpful in achieving academic success.[127]

This is not an isolated finding. In the mid-1970s, Philip Uri Treisman learned that 60 percent of the African American students who took freshman calculus at Berkeley did not pass, while only 12 percent of the Chinese students failed this subject. Subsequently, he studied twenty black students and twenty Chinese students enrolled in freshman calculus and found that only two of the black students ever studied together while thirteen of the Chinese students had begun to study with other (Chinese) students regularly by the middle of the first term. Moreover, this pattern for the Chinese students extended well beyond work for the calculus course; most of them formed what they referred to as study gangs and in general had "organized their lives around common classes and common academic goals."[128]

Recent research by Nathan Caplan, Marcella H. Choy, and John K. Whitmore on two hundred Southeast Asian immigrant families suggests that many Asian students learn group-study skills in the home. In the families in this study, which included students from kindergarten through twelfth grade, the parents saw to it that the time after dinner on weeknights was usually dedicated to homework. Moreover, the typical pattern was for all the children, regardless

127. Harold W. Stevenson and James W. Stigler, *The Learning Gap: Why Our Schools Are Failing and What We Can Learn from Japanese and Chinese Education* (New York: Summit Books, 1992), pp. 94–112; Steinberg, Dornbusch, and Brown, "Ethnic Differences in Adolescent Achievement: An Ecological Perspective," p. 728.

128. Beverly T. Watkins, "Berkeley Mathematician Strives 'to Help People Get Moving,'" *The Chronicle of Higher Education*, 14 June 1989, p. A16.

of age, to study at the dinner table. In this situation, older children were frequently observed helping their young siblings with their homework. According to the researchers, the older children seemed "to learn as much from teaching as from being taught."[129]

Robert D. Hess and Hiroshi Azuma have noted that Japanese parents and educators seem to be interested in encouraging preschool children to develop perseverance, patience, diligence, compliance, cooperativeness, and concern for others, attributes that collectively have proved to be of great value in adapting to the culture of the school and doing well academically. They believe that American parents and educators are more interested in encouraging verbal assertiveness, independence and self-reliance, and tolerance of diversity, attributes that have much general value but are not necessarily helpful in adjusting successfully to the demands of school.[130]

Hess and Azuma found differences in problem-solving approaches between Japanese and American four-year-olds; these suggest that the children tend to develop not only their respective society's preferred mix of attributes but its distinctive behaviorial and performance patterns as well. For example, the Japanese children took more time to solve problems and made fewer errors than the American children. Not surprisingly, differences in parenting strategies seem to be associated with these results. For example, Hess and Azuma have noted that, in direct teaching situations, American mothers are more likely to ask questions that produce prompt responses from their children, while Japanese mothers ask questions that lead their children to take their time in formulating answers.[131]

There is evidence that many Japanese American students have a mix of attributes that has much in common with their native Japanese counterparts. Maria Eugenia Matute-Bianchi concluded from her research that "belief in diligence, persistence, and hard work—as opposed to inherent ability—as the keys to academic success is the single most commonly shared perception among the Japanese-descent students. Moreover, they believe in these values as being absolutely essential to becoming successful as adults."[132]

The adoption study by Elsie Moore examined in chapter 8, which sought an explanation for differences in IQ test scores between blacks and whites, is of interest to this discussion because it included an examination of parent-child interactions in testing and learning contexts and gathered information on the socioeconomic status of the parents and on the children's current friendship networks. The participants were a group of black children adopted by middle-class white and black couples. Moore observed the children as the IQ test was

129. Nathan Caplan, Marcella H. Choy, and John K. Whitmore, "Indochinese Refugee Families and Academic Achievement," *Scientific American* 266 (February 1992): 39–40.

130. Robert D. Hess and Hiroshi Azuma, "Cultural Support for Schooling: Contrasts between Japan and the United States," *Educational Researcher* 20 (December 1991): 3.

131. Ibid., pp. 4–5.

132. Maria Eugenia Matute-Bianchi, "Ethnic Identities and Patterns of School Success and Failure among Mexican-Descent and Japanese-American Students in a California High School: An Ethnographic Analysis," *American Journal of Education* 95 (November 1986): 247.

administered and watched the interactions between the mothers and their children while the mothers were helping with a demanding cognitive task. She found that the children reared in white homes had substantially higher IQ scores, on average. However, she also found variations in the children's response patterns and in the mothers' parenting strategies that are quite consistent with the social-class-oriented research I have reviewed. For example, the white mothers tended to use an approach with their children that is similar to what researchers have often documented for middle-class families in general, while the black mothers tended to use a style more typical of working-class parents. Specifically, the white mothers usually took an encouraging approach to their children's efforts: they smiled, joked, and offered suggestions for how to think about the problem (but without providing specific answers). In contrast, the black mothers were more likely to offer specific instructions about what the child should do. They were also more likely to scowl and to offer negative evaluations of their children's efforts. Interestingly, the children from white homes seemed to enjoy the testing process more than those from black homes. They were also more inclined to take an assertive approach in their answers, to volunteer elaborations, and to attempt to solve difficult problems when they were likely to be wrong.

Finally, Moore found that the children from white homes tended to have friendship networks that were mainly white, while those from African American homes tended to have primarily black friends. Further, the racial composition of the friendship networks of the children from black homes was correlated with their IQ score patterns.

Thus, this study documents differences among children in (1) developed cognitive capacities of the types that are nurtured and valued in American schools; (2) parent-child interactions of the kinds associated with social-class-based variations in children's academic performance; (3) social-class-related behaviors in learning and testing situations that appear to be relevant to academic success; and (4) peer networks similar to those associated with variations in academic achievement patterns between blacks and whites.[133]

Because Moore's parent sample was made up of blacks and whites with comparable amounts of education (the mothers in both groups averaged sixteen years of schooling), her study also sheds light on within-social-class differences between racial/ethnic groups in standardized test scores. In chapter 6 I noted that the standardized test scores of African American students continue to be lower than those of white students even when they have parents with similar educational attainment levels. Moreover, these gaps are quite large. In chapter 7, I suggested that part of the explanation for this phenomenon is that African Americans and whites have had different opportunities for intergenerational accumulation of human capital. In this chapter, I have reviewed research indi-

133. Although Moore's study is not able to establish firmly that these differences in parent-child interaction patterns and child friendship networks are major sources of the differences in academic achievement levels between African American and white students, it makes the research base in these areas very difficult to ignore from an educational policy perspective.

cating that people use what they learn in school in their parental roles in ways that can be very important for their children's success in school. On the basis of the analysis in chapter 7, however, I would hypothesize the presence of large differences in school-relevant parenting behaviors, on average, between black and white parents who have considerable amounts of higher education. Moore's study provides empirical support for this hypothesis.

Recent research by Shirley Brice Heath focused on the verbal interactions between young black mothers and their children in a disadvantaged urban context. Her findings lend support to William Julius Wilson's conclusion that extreme poverty and social isolation are undermining the capacity of some minority families in central cities to support their children's academic and social development. In her previous research on a working-class black community in the South Heath found that children born into that community typically had strong extended families and ample opportunity to interact with many adults and other children in a positive fashion. As a result, they were able to develop substantial verbal communication and reasoning skills (even though these were not always entirely compatible with the culture of the school or the mainstream of the society). But Heath found that

> young mothers, isolated in small apartments with their children, and often separated by the expense and trouble of cross-town public transportation from family members, watch television, talk on the phone, or carry out household and caregiving chores with few opportunities to tease or challenge their youngsters verbally. No caring, familiar, and ready audience of young and old is there to appreciate the negotiated performance. Playmates and spectators are scarce, as are toys and scenes for play. The mother's girlfriends, the older children of neighbors, visits to the grocery store, welfare office, and laundromat, and the usually traumatic visits to the health clinic may represent the only breaks in daily life in the apartment.[134]

Heath arranged for a mother in the project to record her exchanges with her children during a two-year period. She has summarized these interactions as follows:

> Within approximately 500 hours of tape and over 1,000 lines of notes, she initiated talk to one of her three preschool children (other than to give them a brief directive or query their actions or intentions) in only 18 instances. On 12 occasions, she talked to the children as a result of introducing some written artifact to them. In the 14 exchanges that contained more than four turns between mother and child, 12 took place when someone else was in the room. Written artifacts, as well as friends or family

134. Shirley Brice Heath, "Oral and Literate Traditions among Black Americans Living in Poverty," p. 36. See chapter 4 for a discussion of Wilson's views.

members anxious to listen to talk about the children's antics, stimulated the mother's talk to her preschoolers.[135]

Clearly, the circumstances Heath found among at least some single-parent families in an inner city housing project are far removed from those that research suggests are developmentally desirable for any young children. Even more important, these circumstances seem to be virtually inevitable products of a tragically distorted opportunity structure generated over a long period of time by forces well beyond the control of the black community. (For example, blacks did not make the public policy decisions that created high-density public housing projects for poor minorities in urban areas.)[136] It seems likely that in the process the original social and linguistic resources of many black southerners who migrated to the cities have been eroded or altered in unintended ways. Only a minority of black children are growing up in such extreme circumstances. Nonetheless, Heath's research may be an all-too-accurate description of some of the profoundly negative consequences for the unlucky youngsters trapped by a confluence of historical forces in the highest poverty zones of urban America.[137]

But what a negative opportunity structure has wrought, a positive opportunity structure can undo. These problems did not develop in a day and will not disappear overnight. But real change can occur if the larger society chooses to provide genuine economic and educational opportunity to the urban minority poor on a sustained basis.

Variations in Parent-School Interactions   An important, albeit limited, research literature looks at the interaction of parents with the school from a social class perspective. David P. Baker and David L. Stevenson have pointed out that one of the most important ways parents can support their children academically is by helping to manage their school careers as the youngsters move through the educational system. The school system presents many academic hurdles that must be jumped and educational decisions that must be made in order to maximize a child's learning and secure the most favorable educational opportunities. Baker and Stevenson believe that for parents to be good man-

135. Ibid., pp. 369–70.
136. Chicago is a case in point. Robert R. Taylor, the first African American to head the Chicago Housing Authority, proposed in 1949 that a large number of (federally funded) public housing units be built on several vacant sites located primarily in white neighborhoods in that city. In 1950, however, the (white-controlled) City Council declined his proposal and decided to locate all the units in neighborhoods that were mostly black. This led to the construction of a series of high-rise/high density projects in those neighborhoods. Ironically, the largest of these projects in Chicago (and in the nation) was eventually named the Robert Taylor Homes. Made up of some forty-three hundred apartments, it housed twenty-five thousand people. See Nicholas Lehmann, "Four Generations in the Projects," *New York Times Magazine*, 13 January 1991, pp. 17–21.
137. A recent extensive review of relevant research lends substantial support to this conclusion. See Vonnie C. McLoyd, "The Impact of Economic Hardship on Black Families and Children: Psychological Distress, Parenting, and Socioemotional Development," *Child Development* 61 (1990): 311–46.

agers of their children's school careers they must be familiar with the demands of the school and the academic performance of their children and know how to use their resources effectively on the children's behalf.[138]

Baker and Stevenson have taken a close look at how social class differences seem to influence variations in mothers' capacity to manage their children's school careers. (Like many researchers, they have used the education level of the mother as the measure of social class because it usually has more predictive force than other SES variables.)[139] They found that in general high-SES mothers are more likely than low-SES mothers to have accurate knowledge about their children's school performance, including academic problems and to have been in contact with school personnel to help resolve the problems. They also found that high-SES mothers are more likely to take an active role in shaping their children's high school academic experience. Specifically, mothers with a college degree were much more likely to choose college preparatory courses for their children, regardless of the children's GPA in the eighth grade. Thus, the studies by Baker and Stevenson (as well as those by other researchers) indicate that children from high-SES families have important home resources related to academic career management that are frequently not shared by low-SES children.[140]

Social-Class-Based Cultural Differences: Some Important Education-Relevant Themes   That parents with a great deal of formal education typically interact with their children in ways that are more consistent with the culture of the school and the mainstream of society than do parents with relatively little schooling is not surprising. After all, a primary objective of schooling is to develop the minds of the young in ways that will shape their behavior as adults. It should be expected, even desired, that individuals will use much of what they learned in school in their parental roles. Nonetheless, when there are substantial variations in the amount of formal education possessed by a given generation of parents, some children in the next generation will have very large home-based resource advantages that are likely to enable them to be much more successful academically than other youngsters. In turn, these differences in educational outcomes can be expected to have important reverberations in the next generation because of the variations in education-relevant parental resources they will represent. If the nation is to accelerate the educational advancement of minority groups, therefore, the school must be made into a much more powerful educational institution for minority students, and ways must be devised to equalize the education-relevant resources available to both minority and majority parents.

138. David P. Baker and David L. Stevenson, "Mothers' Strategies for Children's School Achievement: Managing the Transition to High School," *Sociology of Education* 59 (July 1986): 156–57.

139. David L. Stevenson and David P. Baker, "The Family-School Relation and the Child's School Performance," *Child Development* 58 (October 1987): 1349.

140. Baker and Stevenson, "Mothers' Strategies for Children's School Achievement," pp. 163, 165; Adam Gamoran, "Access to Excellence: Assignment to Honors English Classes in the Transition from Middle to High School," *Educational Evaluation and Policy Analysis* 14 (Fall 1991): 201–02.

Discussion of the differences between Asian and white parenting practices calls attention to the fact that there is more than one combination of parenting strategies that can prepare children to succeed academically. This should inform all thinking directed at the improvement of the educational fortunes of disadvantaged minorities in the United States.

THE CAPACITY OF SCHOOLS TO MEET THE NEEDS OF CHILDREN FROM DIFFERENT CULTURAL CIRCUMSTANCES

Much of the discussion prior to this chapter has been guided by a modified version of James Coleman's dictum about family and school resources: the variations in home-based, formal-schooling-derived resources that have been intergenerationally accumulated by families are greater than the variations in the resources that society is investing in the current generation of children directly through the schools. This formulation emphasizes variations in the quantity (and quality) of education-relevant resources available to different groups of children over time. However, research reviewed in this chapter indicates that there may also be incompatibility between the resources of the home and of the school, especially for youngsters from racial/ethnic minorities and from the lower socioeconomic rungs of society. As a result, Coleman's dictum can be restated in yet another way: The variations in school-culture-compatible resources available to families are greater than the variations in family-culture-compatible resources available to schools. This version recognizes that the quality of the match between family and school resources can be as important as the quantity of educational resources the two institutions collectively invest in the education of the child. The rapidly changing demographics of the student-age population and the associated cultural and socioeconomic pluralization of families and children seem to require societal actions that aggressively address the issues of family/school resource compatibility as well as the general resource quantity problem.

Linkages can also be made between the cultural difference research base and the discussion in earlier chapters of the impact of the economic opportunity structure on the educational aspirations of minority students. As we saw in chapter 4, William Julius Wilson and others have argued that the high poverty rate of inner city blacks and other minorities is to a considerable degree a result of structural factors in the economy that have led to a shortage of adequately paying low-skill jobs. African Americans have been especially vulnerable to this situation because of the race-based caste system that prevented them from pursuing educational and occupational advancement for most of the nation's history and because of contemporary racial/ethnic prejudice. In chapter 9, I noted that John Ogbu has suggested that over time many blacks have responded to this situation by lowering their educational aspirations to a level consistent with what they perceive as their truncated occupational opportunities. Finding ways to reach out to extremely disadvantaged students is a major responsibility of the schools that serve them. Yet if these schools have substantive cultural incompatibilities with many minority students, the situation is made even more complex and challenging for educators.

On the basis of research concerning the relationship between minority children's academic performance and the educational and occupational opportunity structures, Frederick Erickson has suggested that in order to be successful in school children must trust their teachers and the school as an institution. They must also eventually trust society's commitment to provide them with real economic opportunity. To the degree that students trust both the school and the society, they will put forth effort to learn; to the degree that they lack trust, they will resist becoming educated. Culturally attuned classroom curricula and pedagogies offer an important basis for establishing trust in the school by respecting the culture of the children and providing the bridges required for them to develop the capacities to succeed in the mainstream. The absence of such culturally attuned educational practices increases the likelihood of school failure and alienation.[141]

Erickson believes that trust in the school is crucial for young children, while trust in society becomes increasingly important for children as they get older.[142] In this connection, the child psychiatrist James Comer has observed that many young minority children are already distrustful of the school when they enter it for the first time. That is, even before they begin their formal education, these children have absorbed their parents' mistrust of school and of society as a whole, a reflection of their own long-standing lack of economic, educational, and social opportunity.[143] For this reason, the use of culturally attuned classroom practices is one strategy for building a relationship of trust and legitimacy between teachers and minority students and between the school and minority parents. Another way to improve their performance, however, does not rely on promoting cultural compatibility per se. Rather it emphasizes helping teachers, administrators, parents, and children develop a strong common view of the purposes of schooling. In Erickson's opinion, many students in such a school can do reasonably well even if the academic program is not always well matched to the culture of their homes.[144]

The work of Comer and his colleagues over the past twenty years, initially in two elementary schools in New Haven, Connecticut, and subsequently in other

141. Frederick Erickson, "Transformation and School Success: The Politics and Culture of Educational Achievement," *Anthropology and Education Quarterly* 18 (December 1987): 344–45, 350–51, 354–55.

142. Ibid., p. 351.

143. James P. Comer, "Educating Poor Minority Children," *Scientific American* 259 (November 1988): 45–46.

144. Erickson, "Transformation and School Success," p. 35. This situation has evidently occurred in some schools serving large numbers of immigrant children from Asia and Central America. Many Central American immigrant children are apparently quite academically oriented, in a range of school settings and a variety of family circumstances. See Steven P. Wallace, "The New Urban Latinos: Central Americans in a Mexican Immigrant Environment," *Urban Affairs Quarterly* 25 (December 1989): 239–63; Marcelo M. Suarez-Orozco, "'Becoming Somebody': Central American Immigrants in U.S. Inner-City Schools," *Anthropology and Education Quarterly* 18 (December 1987): 287–99.

communities around the country, supports the view that making the school and the classroom more culturally compatible with the students is not the only method of raising their academic achievement. Comer's objective has been "to promote psychological development in students, which encourages bonding to the school" through strategies designed to foster "positive interaction between parents and school staff." A vital element has been the creation of a governance and management team for the school that includes the principal, teachers, parents, and a mental-health professional. The team attempts to make consensus decisions in areas ranging from the academic program to school rules and procedures. Comer's approach also stresses the use of social events to improve home/school relationships and relies heavily on the use of mental health professionals to minimize school-prompted emotional and behavioral problems among students.[145]

The evidence suggests that this approach has been successful. Students in schools that use Comer's strategies have consistently performed better on standardized tests, behavioral problems of students have been reduced, and home-school relations have been much improved.[146] Interestingly, the achievement test score data for students in the Comer schools and those in the KEEP schools look very similar: test score averages have typically been higher than those usually attained by comparable minority students in regular schools, but they have continued to be considerably below the average scores of most white middle-class students in suburban schools. That is, neither approach by itself has helped disadvantaged minority populations reach the academic performance levels of the white middle class. Given the intergenerational school investment advantages that middle-class children typically enjoy through the home, this is not really surprising; indeed, it makes the performance of the Comer and KEEP schools all the more impressive. Nevertheless, it also raises the question of what might be achieved if a home-school-relations strategy were to be combined with a research-based, classroom-cultural-compatibility approach throughout the elementary and secondary school years.

At this juncture, the capacity of educators to meet the needs of a culturally different group of students may be limited or compromised by one or more of the following conditions: (1) incongruities between the culture of the school and that of the group of students, (2) teachers' failure to recognize these cultural differences, (3) the lack of proven strategies for altering school practices to accommodate certain cultural differences; (4) the lack of consensus that specific practices should be implemented in the school to address cultural differences, (5) the lack of training for teachers and administrators in the relevant knowledge base for addressing cultural differences, (6) insufficient financial resources to

145. Comer, "Educating Poor Minority Children," pp. 45–48.
146. Ibid.; Comer et al., "Yale Child Study Center School Development Program: Developmental History and Long Term Effects" (New Haven: Yale University Child Study Center, 1987), pp. 14–23; Comer et al., "Academic and Affective Gains from the School Development Program: A Model for School Improvement," paper presented at the Annual Meeting of the American Psychological Association, Washington, D.C., August 1986, pp. 21–46.

implement available strategies, and (7) the absence of humane social and economic conditions and associated public policies that are crucial to the academic success of the children.

The KEEP project illustrates some of these problems as well as the potential for addressing them sucessfully. As the program got under way in the early 1970s, those involved had high expectations. However, the Native Hawaiian students did not do well in the beginning, evidently in part because the reading-instruction approach used was not responsive to their social organization, sociolinguistic, cognitive, and motivational differences from the white youngsters for whom the schools were originally designed. Moreover, initially the KEEP researchers and educators were neither fully aware of these cultural differences nor equipped with educational strategies for addressing them.[147] Only through a rigorous long-term research and development program were these knowledge-base problems resolved. Unfortunately, support for continuing research and development through KEEP eroded in the 1980s.[148]

SUMMARY AND CONCLUSIONS

In this chapter, I have explored the role of cultural differences in generating and maintaining differences in academic achievement patterns among racial/ethnic groups and social classes. I noted that American schools, as institutional servants of the mainstream culture, have as one of their central missions to nurture in children the skills and attributes necessary for them to function effectively as adults in that culture. I then explored a number of ways in which students from minority groups tend to be culturally different from the mainstream and, consequently, from the culture of the school. For example, minority children often exhibit cultural incompatibility with such basic characteristics of the classroom as how teachers organize their students for instructional purposes. Many minority children have culturally based verbal and nonverbal interaction patterns and preferred learning styles that differ from those of most majority children and are often inconsistent with the modes of learning emphasized in the classroom. From the perspective of academic motivation, many minority children may respond differently from most majority children to the classroom practices of many teachers. Growing numbers of language minority students enter school without having reached the level of proficiency in English necessary to succeed academically in an English-language-only instructional environment.

I next examined education-relevant cultural differences between social classes. Research suggests that high-SES/well-educated parents tend to have more time to spend with their children for educational purposes than low-SES/less-well-educated parents and, moreover, are more likely to ensure that their children spend a great deal of their time on school-relevant activities. Par-

147. Vogt, Jordan, and Tharp, "Explaining School Failure, Producing School Success," pp. 277–82; Jordan, "Translating Culture," pp. 108–09.
148. See footnote 91.

ents with a great deal of formal education tend to use teaching strategies consistent with those used by the school, while this is much less commonly the case for parents with little formal education. A linguistically rich, inquiry-oriented home environment has been found to be correlated with children's academic success.

All other things being equal, an authoritative parenting style is more likely to be associated with academic success than other parenting styles, possibly because it helps children mature in ways that lead them to work hard in school. Middle-class parents, especially those with a great deal of formal education, are the most likely to interact with their children in ways that are associated with academic success. Authoritative parenting is not consistently predictive of higher academic achievement across all racial/ethnic groups. However, the exceptions to the pattern may be due largely to cultural factors (especially for Asians) or to opportunity structure obstacles (notably for African Americans).

Within-social-class differences in academic achievement between some groups (for example, blacks and whites) are associated in part with differences in parenting patterns, which in turn appear to be related to variations in the quality of schooling historically available to the groups. There also is evidence that conditions of chronic poverty and social isolation are strongly associated with parent-child interaction patterns unconducive to academic success. These conditions, of course, are most likely to be experienced by non-Asian minorities.

Some parents, particularly high-SES mothers, are much more effective than others in working with the school in ways that promote their children's academic success. Individuals use what they learned in school in a variety of contexts, including their role as parents. Thus, there is much more social-class-based cultural compatibility, on average, between the school and high-SES homes than between the school and low-SES homes. If the United States is to accelerate the educational advancement of minorities, it will be necessary to strengthen the educational capacities of the schools and find ways to increase the education-relevant resources available to minority families directly.

Finally, I reflected on the capacity of schools to meet the needs of children from different cultural circumstances. I introduced a variation on James Coleman's dictum on family and school resources: The variations in school-culture-compatible resources available to families are greater than the variations in family-culture-compatible resources available to schools. The KEEP experience demonstrates that a high-quality research and development effort can produce significant increases in the family-culture-compatible resources of the school—increases that produce higher academic achievement among students. Similarly, the Comer school effort shows that schools can overcome limitations in their family-culture-compatible resources to some extent by building strength in other areas, such as home-school trust. Nonetheless, cultural incompatibility between the home and the school remains a pressing problem for which even more effective educational strategies need to be developed.

So far, my examination of family and school resource variations has been qualitative. In the next chapter, we will develop some quantitative estimates of these variations.

CHAPTER ELEVEN

Estimating

Current School and Family Resource

Variations

In several preceding chapters, I have examined variations in the school resources and education-relevant family resources available to children from different racial/ethnic groups and social classes. In this chapter, I shall quantify these variations by placing a monetary value on a range of family and school resource combinations. The intention is not to produce precise, dollar-based calculations; that is not really possible. Instead, it is to develop order-of-magnitude estimates.

I first review data on variations in school expenditure patterns per student between and within states and then review data and research concerning the relationship between variations in the amount of school resources available to students and variations in their academic performance. Next, I quantify the differences in education-relevant family resources available to children. I then compare our school and family resource variation estimates and make some observations about the implications of these patterns for efforts to accelerate the educational advancement of minorities.

The distinction between school- and education-relevant family resources is somewhat artificial because the knowledge, skills, and attitudes toward learning that parents in American society possess are typically heavily grounded in their own schooling experiences (and, often those of their parents and grandparents). What they learned in school (and at home) as children is available to be passed on to their own youngsters through the parenting process. Moreover, to the degree that the parents have jobs requiring substantial educational credentials or skills grounded in things they learned in school, the financial resources they have to invest in their children are also a product of their formal education. Thus, education-relevant parent resources can be regarded, to a considerable degree, as intergenerationally accumulated school resources. Many families have a large amount of this "formal education capital," while others possess little of it.

ESTIMATING VARIATIONS IN SCHOOL RESOURCES

A standard method of examining educational investments at the elementary and secondary levels is to look at current expenditures per pupil as opposed to long-term/capital expenditures. Current expenditures are typically associated directly with providing instructional and related services.[1] Therefore, comparing current expenditure per pupil averages for groups of youngsters is a useful way to assess the differences in the school investments being made in those groups.

In this section, we will examine differences in current expenditure per pupil averages among states and among school districts within states. In each case, we will consider the relationship between the per pupil expenditure level and the racial/ethnic composition of the student population.

Variations among the States   Table 11.1 presents data on current expenditure per pupil averages for the fifty states and the District of Columbia for the 1988–89 school year. The expenditure data are presented on two bases—adjusted and unadjusted for cost of living (COL) differences among the states.[2] Table 11.1 also gives information on the racial/ethnic composition of the student enrollment in the public elementary and secondary schools in each state and the District of Columbia. The 1988–89 data provide a good picture of the expenditure pattern that has existed for a number of years, as changes take place relatively slowly.[3] The table shows that the District of Columbia and Utah, respectively, had the highest and lowest per pupil expenditure averages (unadjusted for COL) in the 1988–89 academic year. The current expenditure per pupil average of $7,850 for the district was three times greater than the $2,579 figure for Utah. (The data also show that the expenditure range was influenced little by the inclusion of the District of Columbia [a large city] in the analysis.) Alaska and New York also had current expenditure per pupil averages about three times that of Utah.

Information is also provided on the degree of concentration of current expenditure per pupil averages around the national average. For example, the table indicates that the majority of states were clustered fairly closely around the national average of $4,639: thirty-one states (61 percent) had a current expenditure per pupil average that was within 20 percent of the national average. Fifteen states (29 percent) were within 10 percent of the national average. In addition to the District of Columbia, just three states—Alaska, New York, and New Jersey—had current averages more than 50 percent higher than the national average.[4]

After taking differences in the cost of living into account, the variation among

1. See National Center for Education Statistics, U.S. Department of Education, *Digest of Education Statistics 1990* (Washington, D.C.: U.S. Government Printing Office, 1991), p. 154; Paul E. Barton, Richard J. Coley, and Margaret E. Goertz, *The State of Inequality* (Princeton, N.J.: Policy Information Center, Educational Testing Service, 1991), p. 28.

2. The current adjusted expenditure per pupil averages for the 1988–89 school year were calculated by applying an interstate cost-of-living index developed by F. Howard Nelson to the 1988–89 data. For a discussion of the index, see Nelson, "An Interstate Cost of Living Index," *Educational Evaluation and Policy Analysis* 13 (Spring 1991): 103–11.

3. National Center for Education Statistics, U.S. Department of Education, *Digest of Education Statistics 1991* (Washington, D.C.: U.S. Government Printing Office, 1991), p. 157.

4. Ibid.

Table 11.1
Current Expenditure per Pupil Averages in 1988–89 and the Racial/Ethnic Composition of the Public School Population in the Fall of 1989, by State

State	1988–89 Current Expenditure Per Pupil Average Unadjusted Amount	Rank	Cost of Living Adjusted Amount	Rank	White	Black	His-panic	Asian	Nat. Amer.
						% of School Enrollment by Race/Ethnicity, Fall 1989				
Nation	$4,639	—	$4,639	—	70	16	9	3	1
Alabama	3,197	48	3,479	46	63	36	0	1	1
Alaska	7,716	2	—	—	68	5	2	4	22
Arizona	3,902	34	3,871	38	64	4	24	2	7
Arkansas	3,273	47	3,601	44	75	24	0	1	0
California	4,121	31	3,891	51	47	9	33	10	1
Colorado	4,408	24	4,417	29	76	5	16	2	1
Connecticut	6,857	5	5,451	10	76	13	10	2	0
Delaware	5,422	11	5,254	12	69	27	3	2	0
District of Columbia	7,850	1	6,488	2	4	91	5	1	0
Florida	4,563	21	4,690	22	63	24	12	1	0
Georgia	3,852	38	4,094	34	61	38	1	1	0
Hawaii	4,121	31	—	—	23	3	2	72	0
Idaho	2,838	50	3,108	48	93	0	5	1	1
Illinois	4,906	16	5,037	15	66	22	9	3	0
Indiana	4,284	29	4,611	24	87	11	2	1	0
Iowa	4,285	28	4,578	26	95	3	1	1	0
Kansas	4,443	23	4,845	19	85	8	4	1	1
Kentucky	3,347	45	3,634	43	90	9	0	0	0
Louisiana	3,317	46	3,551	45	53	44	1	1	0
Maine	4,744	19	5,156	14	98	1	0	1	0
Maryland	5,758	8	5,197	13	62	33	2	3	0
Massachusetts	5,979	6	4,909	17	82	8	7	3	0
Michigan	5,116	15	5,363	11	78	18	2	1	1
Minnesota	4,755	18	4,974	16	91	3	1	3	2
Mississippi	2,874	49	3,183	47	49	51	0	0	0
Missouri	4,263	30	4,589	25	83	15	1	1	0
Montana	4,293	27	4,712	20	93	0	1	1	6
Nebraska	4,360	25	4,693	21	90	5	2	1	1
Nevada	3,791	39	3,864	40	76	9	10	3	2
New Hampshire	4,807	17	4,455	28	97	1	1	1	0
New Jersey	7,549	4	6,001	3	66	19	11	4	0
New Mexico	3,473	43	3,738	41	43	2	45	1	0
New York	7,663	3	6,769	1	62	21	13	4	0
North Carolina	3,874	37	4,139	32	67	30	1	1	2
North Dakota	3,952	33	4,286	30	92	1	1	1	6
Ohio	4,649	20	4,853	18	84	14	1	1	0
Oklahoma	3,379	44	3,653	42	75	10	3	1	11
Oregon	5,182	14	5,501	9	89	2	4	3	2
Pennsylvania	5,609	9	5,537	7	83	13	3	2	0
Rhode Island	5,976	7	5,596	6	84	6	6	3	0
South Carolina	3,736	40	4,034	35	58	41	0	1	0
South Dakota	3,581	41	3,909	36	91	1	1	1	8
Tennessee	3,491	42	3,750	39	77	22	0	1	0
Texas	3,877	36	4,120	33	50	15	33	2	0

Table 11.1 (continued)
Current Expenditure per Pupil Averages in 1988–89 and the Racial/Ethnic Composition of the Public School Population in the Fall of 1989, by State

| State | 1988–89 Current Expenditure Per Pupil Average | | | | % of School Enrollment by Race/Ethnicity, Fall 1989 | | | | |
| | Unadjusted | | Cost of Living Adjusted | | | | | | |
	Amount	Rank	Amount	Rank	White	Black	His-panic	Asian	Nat. Amer.
Utah	2,579	51	2,776	49	93	1	4	2	1
Vermont	5,481	10	5,837	4	98	0	0	1	1
Virginia	4,539	22	4,675	23	73	24	1	3	1
Washington	4,352	21	4,487	27	83	4	5	5	2
West Virginia	3,883	35	4,225	31	96	4	0	0	0
Wisconsin	5,266	3	5,520	8	87	9	2	2	1
Wyoming	5,375	12	5,755	5	91	1	6	1	2

Sources: National Center for Education Statistics, U.S. Department of Education, *Digest of Education Statistics 1991* (Washington, D.C.: U.S. Government Printing Office, 1991), pp. 58 and 156; F. Howard Nelson, "An Interstate Cost-of-Living Index," *Educational Evaluation and Policy Analysis* 13 (Spring 1991): 107. Current per pupil expenditure data are based on average daily attendance in public elementary and secondary schools in the 1988–89 school year. Owing to unique climatic-and transportation-related conditions, adjusted current per pupil data are not available for Alaska and Hawaii. The racial/ethnic enrollment percentages for the nation as a whole, and for the states of Georgia, Idaho, Maine, Missouri, Montana, South Dakota, Virginia, and Wyoming are for the fall of 1986 rather than the fall of 1989.

the states and the District of Columbia in current expenditure per pupil averages grows smaller. On a COL-adjusted basis, the lowest per pupil expenditure average in 1988–89 was the $2,776 spent in Utah, while the highest was $6,769 in New York State—2.4 times that of Utah. More significantly, on a COL-adjusted basis, thirty-five (71 percent) of the states and the district (excluding Alaska and Hawaii) were within 20 percent of the national current expenditure average, and seventeen (35 percent) were within 10 percent of it.

Table 11.1 shows that the highest and lowest current per pupil expenditure averages did not tie closely with the racial/ethnic profiles of the student populations of the states. For example, Vermont had one of the highest percentages (98 percent) of white students enrolled in public schools and had an unadjusted current expenditure per pupil average about 18 percent above the national average. In contrast, Utah had a very high percentage (93 percent) of white students but had the lowest per pupil expenditure average among the states, about 44 percent below the national average. Mississippi had an unadjusted per pupil expenditure average in 1988–89 almost as low as Utah's. Excluding the District of Columbia, Mississippi had the highest percentage (51 percent) of black students. The district, with its high percentage (91 percent) of African American students, had a current expenditure per pupil average 69 percent above the national average.

Among the four states with the highest unadjusted current expenditure per pupil averages, three—Alaska, New York, and New Jersey—had slightly lower white student percentages than did the United States as a whole. Both New Jersey and New York had black and Latino student percentages that were modestly above the national average. Alaska had the highest percentage of Native American/Alaskan Native students of any state. The Asian student percentage in each of these three states was modestly above the national average.

Within-State Variations　　Since disadvantaged minority students are disproportionately concentrated in central cities, comparisons of the per pupil averages of major cities with the statewide averages for the states in which they are located can reveal variations in city-versus-noncity school resources. In the late 1980s, Robert Berne compared the current expenditure per pupil averages for twenty-three of the nation's twenty-six largest cities to the statewide per pupil average for the states in which these cities are located, using 1983–84 school year data. Only four of the twenty-three cities had averages that were lower than those for their states as a whole; one was equal to the statewide average and eighteen exceeded the statewide average. More significantly, the percentage difference in most cases was relatively small. For example, of the four cities that had lower current expenditure averages than their states, Baltimore had the largest negative gap. Its current expenditure per pupil average was $2,863, which was about 88 percent of the Maryland statewide average of $3,262. In contrast, Cleveland had the largest positive gap. Its current expenditure per pupil average was $4,433, or about 152 percent of the statewide average for Ohio of $2,922. Thirteen of the eighteen cities had a current expenditure per pupil average that was less than 125 percent of the statewide average in their state.[5]

A different way of looking at within-state variations is to examine the expenditure averages of districts throughout each state. Using data from the 1984–85 school year, Myron Schwartz and Jay Moskowitz undertook an analysis of this kind.[6] They found a pattern of variations in within-state expenditure averages that is generally similar to the among-state pattern shown in table 11.1. In order to avoid distortions created by "outlier" districts, Schwartz and Moskowitz excluded the districts in each state that were in the top 5 percent and bottom 5 percent in terms of per pupil expenditure averages. With these districts excluded, the expenditure average for districts in the 95th percentile in an average state was found to be 65 percent above the average for districts in the 5th percentile. Moreover, the districts in the 5th percentile were found to have a per pupil expenditure average equal to about 91 percent of the expenditure average for the median student in their state.[7]

5. Robert Berne, "Education," in *The Two New Yorks: State-City Relations in the Changing Federal System,* C. Breecher and G. Benjamin, eds. (New York: Russell Sage Foundation, 1988), pp. 309–13.

6. Myron Schwartz and Jay Moskowitz, *Fiscal Equity in the United States, 1984–85* (Washington, D.C.: Decision Resources Corporation, 1988).

7. Ibid., pp. 7–8.

By excluding outlier districts, the Schwartz/Moskowitz analysis tends to underestimate the full range of per pupil expenditure averages among districts within most states. That is, the highest spending district in a typical state may spend from two to four times as much per student as the lowest spending district. For example, in Pennsylvania in the mid-1980s, the highest spending district in the state spent $6,200 per student, while the lowest spending district spent $2,009 per student.[8]

When analyzing differences in spending, it is common to focus on the extremes because the highest spending districts tend to be in affluent communities and the lowest in economically disadvantaged communities.[9] However, as the discussion in this subsection has suggested, endpoint/outlier analysis tends to overlook the modest variation in spending among most districts. For this reason, the decision of Schwartz and Moskowitz to exclude the top and bottom 5 percent of districts from their analysis seems warranted.

The question of whether to exclude outlier districts also crops up when the analysis shifts to comparisons between a central city school district (which, as we have seen, is likely to be fairly close to the statewide per pupil expenditure average) and suburban districts in the metropolitan region (which in a number of cases may be considerably higher than the statewide average). For example, during the 1989–90 school year, the average per pupil operating cost for the Milwaukee public schools was $5,742, while the highest spending district in the metropolitan area spent $7,556 per student—a $1,814 per pupil per year difference. This is a substantial gap. However, for the thirty-one districts in the Milwaukee metropolitan area, the average was $5,871 per pupil, only $129 (2 percent) more than was being spent by the Milwaukee public schools. Of the thirty-one districts in the area, twenty-one (68 percent) had average per pupil expenditures within 10 percent ($587) of the average for the group as a whole.[10] In this metropolitan region, it is the concentration, rather than the range, of per pupil expenditure averages that is noteworthy.

The racial composition of the student population did not strongly predict extremely high or extremely low average per pupil expenditures in districts within the Milwaukee metropolitan area, even though this area includes a number of relatively affluent suburban communities. For example, the highest spending district had a 22 percent minority enrollment, and the fourth, fifth, and sixth highest spending districts had 23 percent, 19 percent, and 16 percent minority enrollments, respectively. In contrast, the lowest spending district in the area ($4,892 per pupil) had a minority enrollment of less than 3 percent. Many of the suburban-Milwaukee districts, however, had a relatively high

8. William T. Hartman, "District Spending Disparities: What Do the Dollars Buy?" *Journal of Education Finance* 13 (Spring 1988): 436.

9. Arthur E. Wise and Tamar Gendler, "Rich Schools, Poor Schools: The Persistence of Unequal Education," *College Board Review* (Spring 1989): 12, 14.

10. Public Policy Forum, *Public Schooling in the Milwaukee Metropolitan Area 1990: Demographics, Enrollments, Finances* (Milwaukee: Public Policy Forum, 1990), p. 27.

minority enrollment owing to a busing program. Without busing, there would have been more of a relationship between the composition of the student population of a district in the metropolitan region and its per pupil expenditure average.[11]

VARIATIONS IN PER PUPIL EXPENDITURES AND IN OUTCOMES

The preceding discussion reviews information on the variations in school investments in groups of children. Consistent with James Coleman's conclusion that resource variations among schools are relatively small, the data suggest reasonably modest variations in school expenditures, whether these are viewed in terms of differences among states or among districts within states. Moreover, differences in the racial/ethnic composition of student populations do not seem to be strongly related to high or low spending patterns per student from a national perspective.

These findings are important because ever since the Coleman Report of 1966 researchers have found little relationship between differences in academic outcomes for racial/ethnic groups and the variations in school resources available to them (see chapter 4). Indeed, numerous studies over the past twenty-five years have generally confirmed the Coleman Report's conclusions on this point, including those that have looked explicitly at how variations in current expenditures per pupil may relate to educational outcomes of students.[12]

Studies on this topic can be relatively complex. However, it is possible to demonstrate the general basis for these findings by looking at per pupil expenditure averages at the state level relative to such educational outcome measures as high school dropout rates, high school graduation rates, and standardized test scores.

State-Level Variations in Expenditure Averages and in High School Completion and Dropout Rates   Table 11.2 presents high school completion, high school dropout, and current expenditure per pupil data (both adjusted and unadjusted for COL differences) for the fourteen states that had at least a 90 percent white enrollment in their public schools in the late 1980s. Similar data are provided for the nation as a whole as well as for the District of Columbia, which had a mostly black public school student population at the end of the 1980s. These locations are highlighted because they demonstrate that variations in educational performance (as measured by high school graduation and dropout rates) tend not to track variations in school resources (as measured by expenditures per pupil).

The fourteen states as a group had a 93 percent white student population in

11. Ibid., pp. 14, 27.
12. For example, see T. Stephen Childs and Carol Shakeshaft, "A Meta-Analysis of Research on the Relationship between Educational Expenditures and Student Achievement," *Journal of Education Finance* 12 (Fall 1986): 249–63; Eric A. Hanushek, "The Impact of Differential Expenditures on School Performance," *Educational Researcher* 18 (May 1989): 45–62.

Table 11.2
Selected Student Demographic, School Expenditure, High School Completion, and
High School Dropout Data for Fourteen States

State	Racial Composition of Public Schools in the Late 1980s, in % White	Black	1988–89 Current Expenditure Per Pupil Average Unadusted	Cost of Living Adjusted	% of 19-20-Year-Olds in 1990 with a High School Degree	% of 16-19-Year-Olds in 1990 Who Were Dropouts
Idaho	93	0	$2,838	$3,108	86	10
Iowa	95	3	4,285	4,578	93	7
Kentucky	90	9	3,347	3,634	82	13
Maine	98	1	4,744	5,156	90	8
Minnesota	91	3	4,755	4,974	92	6
Montana	93	0	4,293	4,712	89	7
Nebraska	90	5	4,360	4,693	92	7
New Hampshire	97	1	4,807	4,455	87	10
North Dakota	92	1	3,952	4,286	95	4
South Dakota	91	1	3,581	3,909	91	7
Utah	93	1	2,579	2,776	87	8
Vermont	98	0	5,481	5,837	90	9
West Virginia	96	4	3,883	4,225	85	11
Wyoming	91	1	5,375	5,755	90	6
14-State Ave.	93	2	$4,163	$4,436	89	8
District of Columbia	4	91	$7,850	$6,488	83	19
Nation	70	16	$4,639	$4,639	83	11

Sources: National Center for Education Statistics, U.S. Department of Education, *Digest of Education Statistics 1991* (Washington, D.C.: U.S. Government Printing Office, 1991), pp. 58, 156; Phillip Kaufman, Marilyn M. McMillen, and Denise Bradby, *Dropout Rates in the United States 1991* (Washington, D.C.: National Center for Education Statistics, U.S. Government Printing Office, 1992), p. 13; National Education Goals Panel, *The National Education Goals Report 1992: Building a Nation of Learners* (Washington, D.C.: U.S. Government Printing Office, 1992), pp. 143–255; Robert Kominski, "Educational Attainment in the United States: March 1989 and 1988," *Current Population Reports: Population Characteristics, Series P-20, No. 451* (Washington, D.C.: Bureau of the Census, U.S. Government Printing Office, 1991), p. 21; F. Howard Nelson, "An Interstate Cost-of-Living Index," *Educational Evaluation and Policy Analysis* 13 (Spring 1991): 107. The high school completion percentage for the nation is for 20-year-olds only, for 1989.

their public schools in the late 1980s, well above the 70 percent for the nation.[13] These states tended to spend slightly less per pupil than was the case nationally, whether one uses current expenditure data adjusted or unadjusted for amongst-state COL differences. For example, the adjusted average for the fourteen states was about 4 percent less than the national average of $4,639 in 1988–89, while the unadjusted average for the group was about 10 percent below the national average. At the same time, the fourteen states taken together had a somewhat

13. The averages for the fourteen states have not been weighted to reflect the relative sizes of their student populations.

higher high school completion rate for their 19–20-year-old population in 1990 than the nation. Their dropout average among 16–19-year-olds was also lower than the national average in 1990.[14]

The differences among the fourteen states collectively and the District of Columbia were even more pronounced. The district, which had a public school population that was about 91 percent African American in the late 1980s, had much higher unadjusted and adjusted current expenditure per pupil averages in 1988–89 than did the fourteen states taken together. Yet the district had a somewhat lower high school graduation rate, and its dropout rate was over twice as high as that of the fourteen states.

Among the fourteen states there were substantial differences in current expenditures per pupil, high school completion rates, and dropout rates, but states that were similar in one area were not necessarily similar in all three. For example, the state with both the highest graduation rate (95 percent) and the lowest dropout rate (4 percent) in the group (and among all fifty states) in 1990, North Dakota, had unadjusted and adjusted current expenditure per pupil averages that were lower than those of eight of the fourteen states—and modestly lower than those of the nation as a whole. In contrast, West Virginia, a state with both adjusted and unadjusted current expenditure averages that were almost the same as those of North Dakota, had the second lowest high school completion rate (85 percent) among the fourteen and the second highest dropout rate (11 percent). Utah, the state whose unadjusted and adjusted current expenditure per pupil averages in 1988–89 were the lowest among the fourteen states (and among all fifty states as well), had high school graduation and dropout rates that were similar to the group average and about the same as such states as Montana and New Hampshire, which spent $1,700–$2,000 per pupil more on an adjusted basis. And Iowa, Nebraska, and South Dakota, which had average to somewhat below average per pupil expenditures on both an unadjusted and adjusted basis, had graduation and dropout rates that were generally equal (and in some ways superior) to those of high-spending states such as Vermont and Wyoming.

State-Level Variations in Expenditure Averages and Standardized Achievement Test Scores   In 1991, the U.S. Department of Education released the results of the first effort to compare the academic performance of students from different states on a National Assessment of Educational Progress (NAEP) test. Representative samples of eighth graders in thirty-seven states, the District of Columbia, and two U.S. territories (the Virgin Islands and Guam) took a NAEP math test. Table 11.3 presents the average-score data for each of the participating government units.

The states are listed in rank order, based on the average scores for all students in each state on the NAEP 1990 Trial State Assessment.

14. Dropouts are defined as 16–19-year-olds who are not enrolled in school and who have not earned a high school diploma. Phillip Kaufman, Marilyn M. McMillen, and Denise Bradby, *Dropout Rates in the United States: 1991* (Washington, D.C.: National Center for Education Statistics, U.S. Government Printing Office, 1992), pp. 12, 111–12.

Table 11.3
Average Math Scores of Eighth Graders in the NAEP 1990 Trial State Assessment

State/Territory	All	White	Black	Hispanic	Asian/Pacific Islander	American Indian
Nation	261	269	236	243	280	246
North Dakota	281	284	*	251	*	242
Montana	280	284	*	263	*	256
Iowa	278	280	*	257	*	*
Nebraska	276	279	236	253	*	*
Minnesota	276	278	239	240	266	*
Wisconsin	274	279	236	251	*	*
New Hampshire	273	274	*	254	*	*
Wyoming	272	275	*	254	*	257
Idaho	272	274	*	249	*	254
Oregon	271	274	*	253	278	254
Connecticut	270	278	241	236	*	*
New Jersey	269	279	241	244	297	*
Colorado	267	274	237	247	*	*
Indiana	267	271	241	246	*	*
Pennsylvania	266	272	238	230	*	
Michigan	264	271	230	243	*	*
Virginia	264	271	241	243	296	*
Ohio	264	269	233	239	*	*
Oklahoma	263	268	236	246	*	255
New York	261	273	236	237	279	*
Delaware	261	268	242	241	*	*
Maryland	260	273	237	238	291	*
Illinois	260	271	233	235	279	*
Rhode Island	260	265	225	228	*	*
Arizona	259	271	246	242	*	235
Georgia	258	271	239	231	*	*
Texas	258	273	234	245	*	*
Kentucky	256	260	240	227	*	*
California	256	271	233	236	271	*
New Mexico	256	272	*	247	*	237
Arkansas	256	265	230	232	*	*
West Virginia	256	257	233	231	*	*
Florida	255	265	231	246	273	*
Alabama	252	263	233	225	*	*
Hawaii	251	262	*	230	252	*
North Carolina	250	261	232	220	*	235
Louisiana	246	258	229	226	*	*
Guam	231	256	*	209	235	*
District of Columbia	231	*	229	219	*	*
Virgin Islands	218	*	220	208	*	*

*: The sample size was too small to reliably estimate the average score for this group.

Source: Ina V. S. Mullis, John A. Dossey, Eugene H. Owen, and Gary W. Phillips, *The State of Mathematics Achievement: NAEP's 1990 Assessment of the Nation and the Trial Assessment of the States* (Washington, D.C.: Educational Testing Service/U.S. Department of Education, U.S. Government Printing Office, 1991), pp. 239, 240, 266.

When the achievement score data in table 11.3 are combined with the current expenditure per pupil data in table 11.1, the relationship between expenditures and achievement scores appears to be relatively weak. For example, North Dakota, Montana, Iowa, Nebraska, and Minnesota had the highest average scores for all students, yet ranked 33th, 27th, 28th, 25th, and 18th, respectively, among the states in unadjusted current expenditure per pupil averages in 1988–89. Similarly, excluding Guam and the Virgin Islands, the lowest math score averages for all students were turned in by Alabama, Hawaii, North Carolina, Louisiana, and the District of Columbia, which ranked 48th, 31st, 37th, 46th, and 1st respectively, in current expenditure per pupil averages in 1988–89. Moreover, the District of Columbia's average score was far below that of any of the thirty-seven participating states. In fact, among all forty participating political jurisdictions, only the Virgin Islands had a lower average score than the District of Columbia—even though the district had unadjusted and adjusted current expenditure per pupil averages in 1988–89 well above the national average. Moreover, significant amounts of money were being spent on the students in Guam (which had the same average score as the District of Columbia) and the Virgin Islands in the late 1980s: $4,067 and $5,281, respectively, in 1988–89.[15]

The fact that Alabama, Hawaii, North Carolina, and Louisiana ranked in the bottom two-fifths of the states in per pupil expenditure averages in 1988–89 might be regarded as evidence of a fairly consistent relationship between low math score averages and low per pupil expenditures. However, this is not the case. For each of these states, there are others that spent a similar amount per pupil, yet achieved much higher average math scores for all students. For example, although low-scoring Alabama ranked 48th in unadjusted per pupil expenditures in 1988–89, Idaho, which ranked 50th in unadjusted per pupil expenditures, was 9th among the participating states in average math scores.

The point is not that variations in school expenditures have no impact on variations in student academic performance. Rather, it is that existing variations in school resources are evidently too small to account for more than a fraction of the observed differences in the average math scores for all students among the states. The data also are consistent with the related hypothesis that variations in education-relevant resources available to children through their families and communities are a principal source of the observed differences in average NAEP math scores.

The average scores in each state for students from the major racial ethnic/groups provide some additional basis for these conclusions. For example, the table shows that there were very large differences in average scores among the racial/ethnic groups in virtually all states for which scores are available. For example, with an overall average score for all students of 276, Minnesota was one of the top five states in the NAEP Trial State Assessment. However, the

---

15. National Center for Education Statistics, *Digest of Education Statistics 1991*, p. 156.

average score for whites was 278, while the average scores for blacks, Hispanics, and Asians in the state were 239, 240, and 266, respectively.

In contrast, Louisiana, with one of the lowest average scores for all students (246), also showed considerable score differences among racial/ethnic groups. The white average was 258, while the averages for African Americans and Latinos were 229 and 226, respectively. None of these three groups did nearly as well as their counterparts in Minnesota, but Louisiana whites had an average score that was much higher than Minnesota blacks and Hispanics (but not as high as Minnesota Asians).

Another example, the state of Connecticut, with an average score of 270 for all students, was above the national average of 261 but not in the top ten states. However, whites in Connecticut had an average score of 278—the same as whites in Minnesota. With scores of 241 and 236, respectively, Connecticut African Americans and Latinos also had scores that were close to those of their counterparts in Minnesota.

The data for Minnesota, Louisiana, and Connecticut raise three questions. First, why was there considerable variability in average scores within most racial/ethnic groups? Second, why were there large differences in average scores among racial/ethnic groups? And third, how could two states in which the average scores for most racial/ethnic groups were quite similar (Minnesota and Connecticut) produce different average scores (276 versus 270) for all students? Answers to these questions can be inferred from the line of analysis presented in previous chapters. Different academic performance patterns of children from different social classes are due in large measure to differences in their access to family and community resources relevant to education (see chapters 4, 5, 10). But children from different racial/ethnic groups also have substantially different academic performance patterns, even when they appear to be from the same socioeconomic segments (see chapter 6). This situation is no doubt a product of several factors, including (1) our standard methods of measuring socioeconomic status tend to overestimate the social-class-related family resources of many children from a number of racial/ethnic groups (see chapter 7); (2) historical and contemporary racial/ethnic prejudice evidently undermines the academic achievement of many minority students from all social classes (see chapters 8, 9); and (3) racial/ethnic- and social/class-based cultural differences can produce incompatibilities with the culture of the school (see chapter 10).

A substantial portion of the variation among the states in average NAEP math scores, then, is evidently a product of differences among the states in the demographic profiles of the student populations. For example, in the late 1980s, Minnesota's public school population was about 91 percent white while Connecticut's was only 76 percent white. This difference accounts for much of the difference between these states in average scores for all students—not differences in the quality of schooling or in the amounts of money spent on schooling. In fact, Connecticut had an adjusted current expenditure per pupil average of $5,451 in 1988–89, about $477 more than the Minnesota average. But this modest expenditure advantage did not translate into significantly higher NAEP math performance for majority or minority students in Connecticut relative to Minnesota.

Similarly, 28 percent of the students in Louisiana who took the NAEP test reported having a parent with a college degree while 13 percent reported that neither parent had a high school diploma. In contrast, 42 percent of the children tested in Minnesota indicated that they had a parent who had graduated from college while only 4 percent said that neither parent had a high school degree. Nationally, the students in the NAEP Trial Assessment who had a parent with a college degree had an average score of 274, while those who did not have a parent with a high school diploma had an average score of 243.[16] Given the large differences in the parent education levels of the students in the two states, one would expect substantial differences in their NAEP scores, regardless of their school expenditure patterns.[17]

There are also substantial differences in the racial/ethnic compositions of the student populations of Minnesota and Louisiana (see table 11.1). Among Minnesota students tested in the Trial Assessment, 90 percent were white and 2 percent were black, while in Louisiana 55 percent were white and 38 percent were black.[18] Thus, on the basis of the between- and within-social-class achievement test score differences among racial/ethnic groups discussed in chapter 6, one can hypothesize that the differences in overall average scores on the Trial Assessment for Minnesota and Louisiana are associated with both racial/ethnic and parent education level factors. Unfortunately, scores from the Trial State Assessment have not yet been published for subpopulations that are defined in terms of both parent education level and race/ethnicity. It is possible, however, to look at these factors together on a de facto basis by comparing North Dakota, West Virginia, and the District of Columbia. This is the case because whites make up the majority of students in North Dakota and West Virginia, and African Americans make up a large majority of the students in the District of Columbia. Table 11.4 presents the racial/ethnic and parent education level breakdowns for students in these two states, the District of Columbia, and the nation as a whole.

As can be seen from table 11.4, 91 percent and 90 percent of the students in the Trial Assessment samples in North Dakota and West Virginia, respectively, were white. This means that the parent education level percentages for these students should be close to the percentages for the white students in the respective samples. Similarly, since 84 percent of the students in the sample in the District of Columbia were black, the parent education percentages for the students should be reasonably close to those of African American students in the sample in the district.[19]

16. Ina V. S. Mullis, John A. Dossey, Eugene H. Owen, and Gary W. Phillips, *The State of Mathematics Achievement: NAEP's 1990 Assessment of the Nation and the Trial Assessment of the States* (Washington, D.C.: Educational Testing Service/Department of Education, U.S. Government Printing Office, 1991), p. 282.

17. In 1988–89, Louisiana had an adjusted current expenditure average per pupil of $3,551 compared to Minnesota's average of $4,974—the reverse of the Connecticut/Minnesota situation.

18. Mullis et al., *The State of Mathematics Achievement*, p. 266.

19. The fact that 10 percent of the students in the District of Columbia sample were Hispanic adds to the reasonableness of this assumption, because the average scores for blacks and Latinos in the district were within 10 points of each other.

Table 11.4
The Composition of the National, District of Columbia, North Dakota, and West Virginia Student Samples for the NAEP Trial State Assessment, by Race/Ethnicity and Parent Education Level

1: Race/Ethnicity of Students

| | % of Student Sample, by Race/Ethnicity | | | | |
	White	Black	Hispanic	Asian/Pacific Islander	American Indian
Nation	70	16	10	2	2
District of Columbia	3	84	10	1	2
North Dakota	91	1	3	1	5
West Virginia	90	3	4	1	2

2: Parent Education Level of Students

| | % of Student Sample, by Parent Education Level | | | |
	Did Not Finish High School	Graduated from High School	Some Education after High School	Graduated from College
Nation	10	25	17	39
District of Columbia	8	31	17	34
North Dakota	4	24	19	49
West Virginia	12	38	17	27

Source: Ina V. S. Mullis, John A. Dossey, Eugene H. Owen, and Gary W. Phillips, *The State of Mathematics Achievement: NAEP's 1990 Assessment of the Nation and the Trial Assessment of the States* (Washington, D.C.: Educational Testing Service/U.S. Department of Education, U.S. Government Printing, 1991), pp. 430–431. The parent-education-level percentages do not add to 100%, because not all students knew the education level of their parents.

The fact that both North Dakota and West Virginia have very high percentages of whites in their student populations is particularly interesting because North Dakota (along with Montana) had the highest white student average math score among the thirty-seven states that participated in the Trial Assessment and West Virginia had the lowest. The District of Columbia is of interest because its heavily black/minority student population is similar to that of a number of major cities. (Disproportionate numbers of African American and Latino children currently attend public elementary and secondary schools in the nation's central cities.)[20]

Two key measures of performance on the Trial State Assessment are the average math score that groups of students attained on the test and the percentage of students in each group that scored over 300. The latter is important because it suggests what proportion of a group is reasonably well prepared for the college preparatory math curriculum in high school. Table 11.5 presents data on these measures by parent education level for the District of Columbia, North Dakota, West Virginia, and the nation.

---

20. *Education That Works: An Action Plan for the Education of Minorities* (Cambridge: Quality Education for Minorities Project/Massachusetts Institute of Technology, 1990), p. 98.

Table 11.5

Selected Math Performance Data for the Nation, The District of Columbia, North Dakota, and West Virginia for the NAEP Trial State Assessment, by Parent Education Level

	Parent Education Level			
	Did Not Finish High School	Graduated from High School	Some Education After High School	Graduated from College
Average Math Score				
Nation	243	254	266	274
District of Columbia	225	224	237	238
North Dakota	255	273	283	288
West Virginia	240	250	263	270
% above 300				
Nation	1	5	12	21
District of Columbia	0	0	1	6
North Dakota	2	14	25	32
West Virginia	1	2	11	16

Source: Ina V. S. Mullis, John A. Dossey, Eugene H. Owen, and Gary W. Phillips, *The State of Mathematics Achievement: NAEP's 1990 Assessment of the Nation and the Trial Assessment of the States* (Washington, D.C.: Educational Testing Service/U.S. Department of Education, U.S. Government Printing Office, 1991), pp. 282, 284.

There are substantial differences in the scores attained by students from different social classes as measured by parent education level. Nationally, the difference in average scores between students who had at least one parent with a bachelor's degree and those who had no parent with a high school diploma was 31 points (274 minus 243). This pattern held for students in North Dakota and West Virginia, but with important variations. There was a much weaker overall pattern for students from the District of Columbia.

In the case of North Dakota, the difference in average scores between these two groups of students was 33 points, almost identical to the national difference. However, at each parent education level in the North Dakota sample, the average scores were higher than for the comparable group nationally. For example, North Dakota students who had at least one parent with a college degree averaged 14 points more than their counterparts nationally.

In contrast to the significantly above-average performance of North Dakota students at each parent education level, students in West Virginia tended to score slightly below the national averages at each parent level. For instance, the gap was 4 points for West Virginia students with a parent with a bachelor's degree.

In the case of the District of Columbia, the picture is disturbingly different. The average scores for students at all parent education levels were much lower than the national averages. For example, D.C. students who had at least one parent with a college degree averaged only 238, that is, 36 points below the national average for this group, 50 points below the average for such students in North Dakota, and 32 points below the average in West Virginia. In fact, D.C. students who had a parent with a college degree had a lower average score than West Virginia students who had no parent with a high school degree (238 versus 240). Further, the average score spread between students with high and low levels of parent education was much smaller in the District of Columbia than it was nationally or in North Dakota or West Virginia: in the district there was only a 13-point difference in average scores between students who had at least one parent with a college degree and those who had no parent with a high school diploma, compared to the 31-point spread nationally.

This pattern of lower scores is quite similar to the one I presented for the SAT. As noted in chapter 6, the average scores of black students on the 1990 SAT math section were much lower than those of whites regardless of parent education level and the white-black SAT score gap was actually much larger among students who had at least one parent with a graduate degree than among students who did not have a parent with a high school diploma. The same pattern appears in the NAEP math data shown in table 11.5, but this time for eighth graders rather than college-bound seniors.

Students in the District of Columbia were also dramatically underrepresented among high scorers on the test relative to their counterparts nationally and in North Dakota and West Virginia. For example, only 6 percent of the D.C. students with at least one parent with a college degree scored 300 or more on the test, while 21 percent, 32 percent, and 16 percent of the students nationally, in North Dakota, and in West Virginia, respectively, did so.

To the degree that the performance of District of Columbia students on the Trial Assessment is similar to that of students in other major cities with large minority populations, one must be deeply concerned about the current rate of true intergenerational educational advancement among large segments of the nation's historically disadvantaged groups. Moreover, although published reports on the NAEP Trial Assessment do not provide information regarding how representative the District of Columbia's results are of other large American cities, we have reason to believe that they are fairly typical, particularly for African Americans. First, as table 11.3 shows, the national average for African Americans in the Trial Assessment was only moderately higher than the average for the district—236 versus 229. Second, there was little variation among participating states in the scoring patterns for blacks. For example, the difference between the highest and lowest average math score for African Americans among the thirty-seven states and the District of Columbia was only 17 points. Third, several states with large cities had average scores for blacks that were close to the district's average. For example, the African American average was only 233 in Illinois, California, and Ohio (which include Chicago, Los Angeles, and Cleveland, respectively); it was only 231 in Florida (which includes Miami); 230 in Michigan (which includes Detroit). And fourth, like the District of Columbia, several of the nation's largest cities have extremely high dropout rates among 16–19-year-olds. In 1990, when the dropout rate for the district was 19 percent, the rate was 22 percent in Los Angeles, 19 percent in Miami, 16 percent in Atlanta, 19 percent in Detroit, 16 percent in Philadelphia, and 18 percent in Houston.[21]

School and Family Resources and the 1990 NAEP Trial State Assessment Table 11.6 presents information drawn from the Trial Assessment and other sources about school-based resources available to students in the District of Columbia, in North Dakota, in West Virginia, and nationally. The table reminds us that both the unadjusted and the adjusted current expenditure per pupil averages for 1988–89 were different from what one might have expected on the basis of the pattern of scores that emerged on the NAEP Trial State Assessment—assuming that there was a relatively strong, direct relationship between educational expenditures and student achievement patterns. But table 11.6 also reminds us that there are substantial variations in the cost of specific school resources, including teachers, among regions of the country. Significantly, the average unadjusted salary for a teacher in the District of Columbia was $36,290 in the 1988–89 school year, 63 percent higher than the $22,249 average for North Dakota, 66 percent higher than in West Virginia, and 23 percent higher than for the nation. Even after adjusting for COL differences, the district was still paying its teachers more than the national average that year and considerably more than the North Dakota and West Virginia averages. The higher cost of teachers in the District of Columbia is one reason for its above-average per pupil expenditures.

In recent years, however, the District of Columbia has enjoyed a slightly lower pupil/teacher ratio than have North Dakota, West Virginia, and the country in general. Its 14.3 : 1 ratio in the fall of 1988 ranked fifth in the nation.[22] Nonetheless, it is difficult to conclude that the 15.4 and 15.1 : 1 ratios of North Dakota and West Virginia, or the 17.3 : 1 ratio for the nation, were enough higher than the D.C. ratio to produce an educational (classroom) resource advantage for D.C. students. However, it does represent an additional cost of serving students that was not being incurred by North Dakota and West Virginia.

As table 11.6 shows, most students in the District of Columbia, North Dakota, and West Virginia had math teachers from their own racial/ethnic group. To the degree that having a teacher of the same race/ethnicity is important to student achievement, this was not a resource limitation for most students in this case. Similarly, the table suggests that variations in the academic majors of teachers did not account for differences in students' math scores on the Trial State Assessment. About 64 percent of the students in the district who participated in the Trial Assessment had a math teacher who majored in mathematics

21. Kaufman, McMillen, and Bradby, *Dropout Rates in the United States: 1991*, pp. 149–51.
22. With a ratio of 13.0 : 1, Connecticut had the most favorable pupil/teacher ratio in 1988–89, followed by New Jersey and Vermont, each with a 13.6 : 1 ratio, Massachusetts with 13.7, and the District of Columbia with 14.3. See National Center for Education Statistics, *Digest of Educational Statistics 1991*, p. 72.

Table 11.6

Selected School Resource Data for the District of Columbia, North Dakota, West Virginia, and the Nation

Resource	District of Columbia	North Dakota	West Virginia	Nation
Current Expenditures per Pupil 1988–89:				
1. Unadjusted	$7,850	$3,952	$3,883	$4,639
2. Adjusted	$6,488	$4,286	$4,225	$4,639
Average Teacher Salary 1988–89:				
1. Unadjusted	$36,290	$22,249	$21,904	$29,570
2. Adjusted	$29,992	$24,131	$23,835	$29,570
Pupils per Teacher Fall 1988	14.3	15.4	15.1	17.3
% of Trial Assessment Students with a:				
1. White Teacher	8	99	97	90
2. Black Teacher	84	0	2	7
% of Trial Assessment Students Who Had a Teacher with an Undergraduate Math Major	64	61	46	43
% of Trial Assessment Students Taking a Course in:				
1. Eighth-Grade Math	57	73	63	62
2. Pre-Algebra	10	17	19	19
3. Algebra	32	8	16	15

Sources: Ina V. S. Mullis, John A. Dossey, Eugene H. Owen, and Gary W. Phillips, *The State of Mathematics Achievement: NAEP's 1990 Assessment of the Nation and the Trial Assessment of the States* (Washington, D.C.: Educational Testing Service/U.S. Department of Education, U.S. Government Printing Office, 1991), pp. 358, 393, 397; National Center for Education Statistics, U.S. Department of Education, *Digest of Education Statistics 1991* (Washington D.C.: U.S. Government Printing Office, 1991), pp. 72, 82, 156; F. Howard Nelson, "An Interstate Cost-of-Living Index," Educational Evaluation and Policy Analysis 13 (Spring 1991): 107.

as an undergraduate. The comparable percentages for North Dakota, West Virginia, and the nation were 61 percent, 46 percent, and 43 percent, respectively. Ironically, North Dakota and the District of Columbia, the highest and lowest scoring participants in the Trial Assessment (excluding Guam and the Virgin Islands), had similar percentages of students with teachers who had undergraduate math majors.

Finally, table 11.6 shows that there were substantial variations in the types of math courses in which students in these three cases were enrolled. However, the differences were not necessarily in the direction that might have been predicted, given their scoring patterns on the NAEP math test. Among the three, the district had the highest percentage of students taking an algebra course and the lowest percentage taking a general eighth-grade math course; the opposite was true for North Dakota. Such a pattern might have been expected to be a great advantage for the district students. This does not mean that having an opportunity to take algebra is of little value, but it is no panacea. The D.C. students who took algebra averaged 253 on the Trial Assessment versus 241 for those who were enrolled in a pre-algebra course and 217 for those in a general eighth-grade math course. The comparable averages for North Dakota students were 307, 289, and 277, respectively; and for the students in West Virginia they were 291, 267, and 244.[23] Among the largely white student populations in the states with the highest and lowest overall average scores for white students on the Trial Assessment, only those West Virginia students enrolled in a general eighth-grade math course scored lower than black students in the District of Columbia who were taking an algebra course. (Importantly, other standardized test data sets tend to show similar patterns.)[24]

By a number of measures, the variations in school resources among the District of Columbia, North Dakota, and West Virginia were relatively small, while, at least on paper, the uses to which the district's resources had been put to promote math achievement were generally appropriate: most of the teachers were racially/ethnically like their students; most of the students had teachers with apparently solid math credentials; relatively large numbers of students were assigned to a college preparatory math course. These data suggest that good educational practices applied within the confines of existing school and family resource variations are not sufficient to produce the needed improvements in minority student math achievement.

With this in mind, let us look at some of the family resource differences

23. Mullis et al., *The State of Mathematics Achievement*, p. 358.
24. For example, data from the SAT show that within each racial/ethnic group, math test scores increase with additional college prep math coursework. However, at each level of coursework, there tend to be large score gaps among racial/ethnic groups. For example, in 1990, the average math section scores for students who had completed only one year of algebra were 440 for American Indians, 525 for Asians, 387 for blacks, 429 for Mexican Americans, 407 for Puerto Ricans, 436 for Other Hispanics, and 491 for whites. Among those who took calculus, the average scores were 559 for American Indians, 619 for Asians, 504 for blacks, 542 for Mexican Americans, 530 for Puerto Ricans, 546 for Other Hispanics, and 608 for whites. See College Entrance Examination Board, *1990 College-Bound Seniors: Ethnic and Gender Profiles of SAT and Achievement Test Takers* (New York: College Entrance Examination Board, 1990), p. 5 in each racial/ethnic group section.

Table 11.7
Selected Family-Resource-Related Data for the District of Columbia, North Dakota,
West Virginia, and the Nation

Resource	District of Columbia	North Dakota	West Virginia	Nation
Estimated Median Income of 4-Person Families, 1991:				
1. Unadjusted	$38,562	$31,346	$29,743	$39,051
2. Adjusted	$31,869	$33,998	$32,365	$39,051
Estimated Average Child Poverty Rate, 1983–87	31	16	30	21
% of Mothers with Late or No Prenatal Care, 1988	11	3	6	6
% of Babies that Were Low Birthweight, 1988	14	5	6	7
School Attendance of Trial Assessment Students:				
1. % not Absent in Month Prior to Assessment	33	50	40	45
2. % Absent Three or More Days Prior to Assessment	37	14	25	23
Living Arrangements of Trial Assessment Students:				
1. % with both Parents	47	85	82	75
2. % with One Parent	45	13	16	22
3. % with No Parent	7	1	2	3
% of 1990 Trial Assessment Students with Parent with:				
1. No High School Degree	8	4	12	10
2. High School Degree	31	24	38	25
3. Some Post High School	17	19	17	17
4. Graduated from College	34	49	27	39
Pages Read Each Day by Trial Assessment Students for School and Homework for All Subjects:				
1. % Reading More Than Ten Pages	24	41	36	35
2. % Reading Five or Fewer Pages	49	28	34	37

Table 11.7 (continued)
Selected Family-Resource-Related Data for the District of Columbia, North Dakota,
West Virginia, and the Nation

Resource	District of Columbia	North Dakota	West Virginia	Nation
Trial Assessment Students' Television Viewing Habits				
1. % Watching Less than One Hour per Day	8	14	9	12
2. % Watching Six Hours or More per Day	33	6	16	16
Types of Reading Materials in Trial Assessment Students' Homes				
1. % with Four Types	42	60	47	48
2. % with Two or Fewer Types	24	10	20	21

Sources: Children's Defense Fund, *The State of America's Children 1991* (Washington, D.C.: Children's Defense Fund, 1991), pp. 151, 154, 155; Ina V. S. Mullis, John A. Dossey, Eugene H. Owen, and Gary W. Phillips, *The State of Mathematics Achievement: NAEP's 1990 Assessment of the Nation and the Trial Assessment of the States* (Washington, D.C.: Educational Testing Service/U.S. Department of Education, U.S. Government Printing Office, 1991), pp. 417, 420, 421, 423, 425, 431; F. Howard Nelson, "An Interstate Cost-of-Living Index," *Educational Evaluation and Policy Analysis* 13 (Spring 1991): 107.

among the District of Columbia, North Dakota, and West Virginia. Table 11.7 presents selected family resource data.

The table presents estimates of the median income of four-person families in 1991 and the average child poverty rates for 1983–87. Among the fifty states and the District of Columbia, the district ranked 20th in median family income, North Dakota 46th, and West Virginia 48th (unadjusted for COL).[25] If COL differences are adjusted, North Dakota had a somewhat higher mean family income than either West Virginia or the District of Columbia. However, all three were well below the national average in 1991.

The child poverty data present a somewhat different picture. The district's 31 percent rate for the 1983–87 period was nearly double North Dakota's 16 percent rate but only slightly higher than the 30 percent rate for West Virginia. The district ranked 49th in poverty rate, while North Dakota ranked 18th and West Virginia 47th.[26]

Interpreting these data, one can hypothesize that the large percentage of North Dakota students who were solid scorers on the Trial Assessment did not owe much of their performance to their parents' ability to spend large amounts of money on their education. It appears to have been sufficient that they were from families that typically had adequate financial resources and lived in com-

25. Children's Defense Fund, *The State of America's Children 1991* (Washington, D.C.: Children's Defense Fund, 1991), p. 151.
26. Ibid.

munities in which relatively few students were experiencing poverty, especially intense, long-term poverty.

It can also be hypothesized that, in spite of the similarity in overall child poverty rates between the District of Columbia and West Virginia, a larger percentage of poor students in the district has experienced long-term poverty. In chapter 5, I reviewed research that found blacks much more likely than whites to experience long-term poverty—it is long-term poverty that is associated with less academic success.

One might expect substantial differences in poverty rates (especially long-term rates) to lead to differences in access to health care, which would have serious consequences for many children. Data in table 11.7 support such a conclusion. For example, 11 percent of new mothers in the District of Columbia in 1988 received late or no prenatal care. The comparable percentages for West Virginia and North Dakota were 6 percent and 3 percent, respectively. The district ranked 49th in mothers experiencing late or no prenatal care; West Virginia ranked 36th and North Dakota 4th. Similarly, 14 percent of the babies born in the District of Columbia in 1988 were low birthweight, compared to 6 percent in West Virginia and 5 percent in North Dakota, respectively. The rankings were 51st (that is, last) for the district, 21st for West Virginia, and 2d for North Dakota.[27] In chapter 7, I discussed the impact of preventable health problems on students' academic achievement. The District of Columbia is at a clear disadvantage in this area.

As the table shows, D.C. students who took the NAEP Trial State Assessment were much less likely than test-taking students from North Dakota to report missing no days of school in the month prior to taking the math test and much more likely to report missing three or more days of school during that period. It is reasonable to hypothesize that this poorer attendance record for district students is due in part to health-related factors. As I pointed out in chapter 5, another aspect of the health care problems of poor children is their inability to get ongoing preventive care or timely treatment of illness. This could lead to more missed days of school and, therefore, lower academic achievement.

There are very large differences in the relative proportions of two-parent and single-parent families in the district and in North Dakota and West Virginia. The higher incidence of single-parent families no doubt contributes to the high poverty rate among the District of Columbia's children.

Table 11.7 also presents the parent education profiles for Trial Assessment students nationally as well as for the three areas under discussion. Looking only at these data, one might expect many students in the district to perform close to the national average for the Trial Assessment math test, because the district had a parent education profile generally similar to the national pattern. To be sure, given the high poverty rate in the district, one might expect significantly below-average scores from the students who had no parent with a high school degree or even from many of those who had at least one parent with a high school diploma. But it is difficult to use poverty as a primary explanation for the very low scores produced by D.C. students who had at least one parent with a college degree.

27. Ibid., pp. 154–55.

It is not possible to provide a definitive explanation for the low scores of this (or any other) segment of the district's student population. However, judging from my discussion of the contemporary impact of racial prejudice (see chapter 9), one might hypothesize that one element would be the lower academic motivation that racial/ethnic prejudice has helped to produce in a number of African American youngsters.[28]

From the review in chapters 2 and 10 of educational attainment trend data and research on social-class-based cultural differences, one also might hypothesize that many college-educated black parents in the District of Columbia are the first in their families to earn a college degree or even to complete a few years of higher education. As noted in chapter 10, many first-generation college graduate, middle-class parents tend to rely more heavily on the working-class parenting strategies that they experienced as children than on middle-class strategies that have been found to correlate with high academic performance.

Some of the data presented in table 11.3 support these hypotheses. For instance, only 24 percent of the D.C. students reported that they read ten or more pages a day in school or for homework, while 41 percent of the North Dakota and 36 percent of the West Virginia students reported doing so. Similarly, 33 percent of the district students in the Trial Assessment reported that they watched six or more hours of television per day, compared to only 6 percent of North Dakota's students and 16 percent of West Virginia's. Finally, only 42 percent of D.C. students said they had four types of reading materials in their homes (a daily newspaper, books, magazines, and reference works) compared to 60 percent of the students in North Dakota.

If, as a result of the contemporary impact of prejudice, a significant number of students were less motivated to achieve academically or felt peer pressure not to do well in school, one would expect to see these factors influence their academic behavior. Doing little reading for school and watching a great deal of television are two ways in which this lack of academic emphasis might manifest itself among some students.

If, as a result of growing up in economically and educationally disadvantaged circumstances, many first-generation middle-class parents were relatively unaware of the importance of supervising their children's schoolwork closely or of effective methods of doing so, one might expect to see this lack of knowledge show up in the form of such behaviors as allowing their children to do relatively little school-connected reading or to watch a great deal of television. For some parents, the relative scarcity of reading materials in their homes could also be a reflection of their non-middle-class origins.

And if many of these same adults were single parents, they might not have the time to supervise their children's academic life to the degree that is necessary. Ironically, these same parents might need to provide more supervision of their children than middle-class parents in suburban circumstances because the

28. It was in a Washington, D.C., public high school that Signithia Fordham and John Ogbu documented a strong anti-academic-achievement orientation in a group of black students, which evidently made it difficult for them to pursue high academic achievement in a visible way.

forces that lead children away from academic work are typically stronger in the inner city.

It is apparent from this analysis that the very large differences in academic performance among groups (as measured by scores on an NAEP eighth-grade math test) were accompanied by large differences in family resources. It is also plausible to conclude that the variations in school resources were neither as large as the family resource variations nor as likely to move consistently in the same direction as the variations in academic achievement patterns among groups.

ESTIMATING VARIATIONS IN FAMILY RESOURCES

In chapter 5, I noted that the substantial variations among groups of students in the amounts of family income and parent education available to them are strongly correlated with the large variations in academic performance among these groups. Family income level and parent educational attainment level are two measures of the education-relevant resources that families have available to help their children succeed academically in school. In this section, I present estimates of the variation in family resources available to groups of children by considering five hypothetical families, differentiated on the basis of the income and education levels of the parents. These examples are designed to describe the range and distribution of education-relevant family resources available to children.

In chapter 4, I discussed five types of education-relevant resources: human, social, health, financial, and polity capital. Family income and parent-education levels are most obviously related to financial and human capital. The analysis that follows reflects this reality. However, the analysis will also make connections between family and parent-education levels and the other three forms of education-relevant resources.

Estimating Variations in Family Income among Five Hypothetical Families
Table 11.8 presents the incomes available to five hypothetical families expressed in after-tax dollars because they provide a better picture of the relative purchasing power available to the families. They are also consistent with the current expenditure per pupil data used to measure the variation in school resources available to educate children.

For simplicity's sake, each of the hypothetical families has two children, and all but one have two parents in the home. The family with the lowest after-tax income has a single (female) parent as the head of the household, a common situation among poor families with children. (Twenty percent of the hypothetical families were headed by a single parent; about 22 percent of the eighth graders in the NELS:88 study were living with one parent.)[29] In accord with contempo-

29. Anne Hafner, Steven Ingels, Barbara Schneider et al., *National Longitudinal Study of 1988, A Profile of the American Eighth Grader: NELS:88 Student Descriptive Summary* (Washington, D.C.: Department of Education, U.S. Government Printing Office, 1990), p. 6.

rary employment patterns in the United States, most of the adults in the hypothetical families work outside the home on a full- or part-time basis. The only unemployed parent is the father in Family A, who is not living with his children and their mother.

Table 11.8
Hypothetical After-Tax Family Income Examples

Family	Total Annual Family $ Income	Annual per Capita $ Income	Per Capita $ Income, Birth to Age 18
A. Single Parent/Two Children (Mother employed full-time and part-time [second job], father unemployed and not living with family)	11,000	3,667	66,006
B. Two Parents/Two Children (Father employed full-time, mother part-time)	18,000	4,500	81,000
C. Two Parents/Two Children (Father employed full-time, mother part-time)	26,000	6,500	117,000
D. Two Parents/Two Children (Father employed full-time, mother not employed outside home)	37,000	9,250	166,500
E. Two Parents/Two Children (Both father and mother employed full-time)	60,000	15,000	270,000
Five-Family Average	30,400	7,783	144,001

As table 11.8 shows, the per capita after-tax income of Family A is $3,667 per year ($11,000 divided by three), while that of Family E is $15,000 ($60,000 divided by four), more than four times larger. If one assumes a constant family income over time, a child in Family E would have a cumulative after-tax income from the time of birth until age eighteen of $270,000 ($15,000 × 18 = $270,000), while a child in Family A would have $66,006.

Most people would consider Family E to be affluent but not wealthy. To put this in perspective, 10 percent of U.S. families with children under age 18 in 1989 had an annual income of $75,000 or more—the before-tax equivalent, give or take a few thousand dollars, of Family E's $60,000—depending on such things as the state/local income tax structure and the cost of home ownership. Similarly, although it has a low income, Family A is not among the very poorest in the country. In 1989, about 12 percent of families with children under age 18 had an annual before-tax income of less than $10,000. Family A's after-tax income of $11,000 is equivalent to a before-tax income of about $12,000, which is modestly higher than the official poverty threshold for 1990 ($10,560 for a family of three).[30]

It is useful to compare the family income range shown in table 11.8 with the current expenditure per pupil range among the states (see table 11.1). The $5,084 difference between New York State's 1988–89 (unadjusted) current expenditure per pupil average of $7,663 and Utah's $2,579 amounts to only about 45 percent of the $11,333 gap between the per capita incomes of our high- and low-income hypothetical families. On a COL-adjusted basis, the difference in per pupil expenditure averages between New York State and Utah is only $3,993, or 35 percent of the income gap between the families. This is additional evidence in support of Coleman's view that the variations in family resources are greater, in absolute terms, than the variations in school resources.

It can be argued, of course, that only a small portion of the per capita income of most families is dedicated directly to educational pursuits. This is true—but the impact of family income on student achievement is often indirect. For example, high-income families are in a much better position to provide high-quality medical care (health capital) for their children, which is essential for ensuring that the children are physically able to learn. High-income families are also able to purchase housing in communities that are largely populated by families with equally high SES status. Thus, they are able to provide their children with a group of peers (a form of social capital), which is associated with doing well academically (see chapters 5, 10). Poor families often do not have this option. In fact, as we saw from the data reviewed in chapter 4 regarding the increasing concentration of poor (minority) families in several central cities, the housing available to these families may all too often contribute to the formation of the kind of peer groups for their children correlated with low academic achievement.[31]

Ironically, by purchasing or renting homes in a high-SES community, high-income families are able to take advantage of whatever variation in per pupil expenditures exists among public schools in their area. Because suburban communities tend to spend more per capita on students than most other communities, it is high-income rather than low-income families who benefit most from the variations in school resources. In a related vein, because there are typically few economically disadvantaged students in high-SES communities, the children of high-income families also may benefit from having comparatively little

30. Edward J. Welniak, Jr., and Mark S. Littman, "Money Income and Poverty Status in the U.S. 1989," *Current Population Reports*, Series P-60, No. 168 (Washington, D.C.: Bureau of the Census, U.S. Government Printing Office, 1990), p. 37. Children's Defense Fund, *The State of America's Children 1991*, p. 22. For the assumptions used in calculating equivalent income before and after taxes, see note 48 below.

31. By making the point that high-income families tend to segregate themselves along social class—and often racial—lines, I am not condoning the practice but simply observing that under existing educational and social arrangements, some academic achievement benefits for the children of such families do seem to result from it. The parallel de facto heavy segregation of low-SES families, of course, may contribute to negative academic results for many poor children.

of their school's resources used for special-needs youngsters. High-income families are also better positioned to purchase supplementary educational services. Finally, because high-income families are likely to have savings, they are usually in a better position to weather economic disruptions, unemployment, for example.[32]

It is not simply the highest income family in this hypothetical group that enjoys favorable indirect educational benefits, both in absolute terms and relative to the poorest family in the group. Family D has a family income of $37,000 after taxes, or a disposable per capita income of $9,250—that is, $5,583 more than the per capita average for Family A. Judiciously used, Family D's resources can purchase a significant amount of health care and school peer-group advantages for their children. Furthermore, the $5,583 per capita income advantage that Family D has over Family A is much larger than the $3,993 difference in the adjusted current expenditure per pupil averages between New York and Utah in 1988–89.

Family C, with $26,000 after-tax income, also enjoys some valuable advantages over Family A. Its after-tax per capita income of $6,500 is $2,833 more than the per capita average of the poorest family. This should translate into an ability to provide reasonably good health care and to purchase housing in a community that does not have an extremely high concentration of poor children. The per capita income advantage for Family C is equivalent to 71 percent of the $3,993 difference in the adjusted current expenditure per pupil averages of New York and Utah.

In contrast to the three highest income families, Family B, with $18,000 after-tax family income, has a limited capacity to provide the financially grounded dimensions of high-quality educational opportunity for its children. Its per capita after-tax income of $4,500 is only $823 higher than the $3,667 per capita income of Family A, but this additional amount of resources, if managed very carefully, may enable the parents to provide their children with minimally adequate health care. However, access to such care may hinge on having favorable job-related health insurance benefits or unusually low living expenses (possibly due to low housing costs)—conditions that many families in this income bracket are unlikely to enjoy. Indeed, if the parents' jobs are in the central city, it may be very difficult for Family B to secure housing outside the poorest areas of the city at an affordable price. If they do end up living in a high-poverty zone, their children are likely to attend schools that have high concentrations of disadvantaged children. As discussed in chapter 5, under existing schooling arrangements this could put their children at some additional risk of school failure. The relatively fragile economic circumstances of Family B can be further demonstrated by the fact that the $823 per capita income advantage they enjoy over Family A is only about 21 percent of the $3,993 difference in the adjusted current expenditure per pupil averages of New York and Utah.

32. Robert Pear, "Rich Got Richer in 80s; Others Held Even," *New York Times*, 11 January, 1991, pp. A1, A20.

Although the examples in this discussion are hypothetical, they are generally consistent with available evidence regarding the current income distribution of families with school-age children. About 21 percent of the students in the NELS:88 national sample of eighth graders reported family incomes of less than $15,000; about 58 percent reported incomes of $15,000–$50,000; and the remaining 21 percent reported family incomes over $50,000.[33] Of the five hypothetical family examples, one (20 percent) is in the below-$15,000 category; three (60 percent) are in the $15,000–$50,000 category; and one (20 percent) is in the over-$50,000 category. Although these incomes are in after-tax dollars and the NELS:88 income data are in before-tax dollars, if they were grossed-up to before-tax dollars, the incomes of the hypothetical families would be consistent in most circumstances with the NELS:88 family income data.

Estimating the Value of Parent Education Resources   Table 11.9 presents the education levels of the parents in the five hypothetical families. For each parent, the education level is described in terms of both educational attainment (degree) and achievement (test scores) because, as chapters 6 and 7 suggest, there may be substantial differences in developed academic capacities between individuals and groups with similar educational attainment levels. Further, developed academic-based skills (not simply credentials) are important parent education resources from the perspective of children's success in school. As the review of the racial/ethnic and social-class cultural differences revealed (see chapter 10), parents who possess a great deal of academic knowledge and skills are in a much better position to help their children succeed academically. To make good estimates of the hypothetical families' parent education resources, therefore, one must make realistic assumptions about both the parents' educational attainment and their achievement levels. The academic achievement of the parents is expressed in terms of proficiency levels on the National Assessment for Educational Progress reading and mathematics tests, discussed in chapter 3. This allows us to tie their reading and math skills to a well-developed method of measuring reading and mathematics proficiency levels.

In the NELS:88 survey, 11 percent of the students in the sample reported that the highest level of parent education in their family was less than a high school degree; 21 percent stated that it was a high school diploma; 42 percent indicated that it was some college; 14 percent reported that it was a bachelor's degree; and 12 percent stated that it was a graduate or professional degree.[34] Having one family (20 percent) in each of these five parent-education-level categories, the group of hypothetical families described in table 11.9 is reasonably consistent with the NELS:88 experience.

33. Hafner et al., *National Education Longitudinal Study of 1988, A Profile of the American Eighth-Grader,* p. 3.

34. Ibid. For a more detailed description of the parent-education-level profile of the NELS:88 families, see Laura Horn and Jerry West, *National Education Longitudinal Study of 1988: A Profile of Parents of Eighth Graders* (Washington, D.C.: Department of Education, U.S. overnment Printing Office, 1992): pp. 4–5.

Table 11.9

Education Levels of Parents in Hypothetical Families

Family/ Parents	Educational Attainment Level	Educational Achievement (NAEP) Level	Occupation/ Employment Status
A. Mother	11th grade	255 reading score and 260 math score	Full-time day care aide; and part-time cleaning person
Father	11th grade	260 reading score and 255 math score	Unemployed
B. Mother	High school graduate	285 reading score and 280 math score	Part-time receptionist
Father	High school graduate	275 reading score and 275 math score	Full-time maintenance worker
C. Mother	High school graduate	310 reading score and 295 math score	Part-time secretary
Father	Two years of college	320 reading score and 315 math score	Full-time insurance agent
D. Mother	Three years of college	345 reading score and 330 math score	Not in work force
Father	Bachelor's degree	355 reading score and 375 math score	Full-time engineer
E. Mother	Ph.D.	375 reading score and 350 math score	Full-time professor of history
Father	Bachelor's degree	355 reading score and 340 math score	Full-time newspaper editor

More meaningful than the specific assumptions about parent educational attainment levels for the hypothetical families, however, are one's assumptions about their academic achievement levels. Unfortunately, the NELS:88 and similar data sources cannot provide information on the achievement level patterns of parents, so that the assumptions made about the reading and math achievement levels of the parents in the hypothetical families must be regarded as illustrative of the range of academic knowledge and skills among parents rather than as representative of the actual distribution of these capacities.

The head of Family A, as noted, is a single (female) parent. She dropped out of high school at the end of the eleventh grade to have a baby. Subsequently, she and the father, also a high school dropout, had a second child. For a few years, the family lived with the father's mother in her apartment and were therefore able to meet their expenses with his earnings at a low-skill job. However, two years ago, the father was laid off from his job, and since then he has been unemployed. Last year the couple separated, and the mother moved out with the two children.

The mother had been a below-average student before she dropped out of school. Currently her reading skills are the equivalent of about a 255 score on the NAEP reading test—just above the Intermediate Level (250) on the NAEP proficiency scale. She "can search for specific information, interrelate ideas, and make generalizations" from written material but is not able to summarize or synthesize information from relatively complicated written material of the kind individuals routinely handle in higher education and in many jobs. About 84 percent of the 17-year-olds in the 1990 NAEP reading test sample and a similar percentage of a national sample of 21–25-year-olds scored at the Intermediate Level or higher.[35] The mother's skills are equivalent to a NAEP math score of 260, which is modestly above the Basic Operations and Beginning Problem Solving Level (250). She is able to "add, subtract, multiply, and divide using whole numbers"—essentially skills that students are expected to master by the end of elementary school years. About 96 percent of the 17-year-olds who took the 1990 NAEP math test scored at Level 250 or higher.[36]

Having such limited academic skills, the mother has had difficulty finding employment that pays enough to support herself and the children at a level above the poverty line. Recently, she started a full-time job as an aide in a day care center. A hard worker, she has also taken a part-time job cleaning the offices of a local business on weekends.[37] Even with two jobs, she is having difficulty making ends meet. (The father of the children is unable to provide child support, owing to his unemployment.) Because one of her tasks at the day care center is to read to the children, she is involved in school-oriented activities regularly for the first time since she dropped out of high school. She is hoping to begin working toward her GED.

The mother in Family A lives with her two children in a small apartment in

35. Ina V. S. Mullis, John A. Dossey, Mary A. Foertsch, Lee R. Jones, and Claudia A. Gentile, *Trends in Academic Progress: Achievement of U.S. Students in Science, 1969–70 to 1990; Mathematics, 1973 to 1990; Reading, 1971–1990; and Writing, 1984–1990* (Washington, D.C.: Educational Testing Service/U.S. Department of Education, U.S Government Printing Office, 1991), p. 124; Irwin S. Kirsch and Ann Jungeblut, *Literacy: Profiles of America's Young Adults* (Princeton, N.J.: Educational Testing Service, 1986), p. 39.

36. Mullis et al., *Trends in Academic Progress: Achievement of U.S. Students in Science, 1969–1990 to 1990; Mathematics, 1973 to 1990; Reading, 1971 to 1990; and Writing, 1984 to 1990,* p. 77.

37. In 1989, 7.2 million people held two jobs or more, which represented over 6 percent of all employed persons that year. Moreover, multiple jobholding increased substantially in the 1980s. It was up 26 percent between 1985 and 1989 and up 52 percent between 1980 and 1989. Women accounted for almost two-thirds of the growth in multiple jobholders in the latter half of the 1980s. See John F. Stinson, Jr., "Multiple Jobholding Up Sharply in the 1980s," *Monthly Labor Review* 113 (July 1990): 3.

one of the poorest sections of the central city. The elementary school the children attend serves a student population drawn primarily from families who live in a nearby public housing project and the contiguous area. Over 90 percent of the children qualify for the free or reduced lunch program at the school.

In Family B, both parents are high school graduates; neither has had any postsecondary education. The mother has been working part-time as a receptionist for the past few years. The couple's older child is in the third grade and the younger one is in kindergarten. When the younger child enters the first grade, the mother plans to work full-time.

Both parents were average students at a large inner city high school. The mother was in the general education track, which did not prepare her for college upon graduation. (The prospect of having to enroll in several remedial courses at the local community college is one reason she did not consider pursuing postsecondary education.) The father was in the vocational track in high school. His current job as a maintenance worker in an office building does not require extensive use of such schooling-derived skills as reading. The mother's responsibilities as a receptionist also require relatively limited skills. Both parents read a newspaper a few times a week as well as an occasional magazine or book. Having reading skills equivalent to a NAEP score of 285, the mother is reasonably close to NAEP's Adept Level of 300 ("can find, summarize, and explain relatively complicated information"), a reading skill level that is required for postsecondary education. Possessing reading skills equivalent to a NAEP score of 275, the father is halfway between the Intermediate and Adept Levels of the NAEP. About 41 percent of the 17-year-olds who took the 1990 NAEP reading test reached the Adept Level or higher, while about 54 percent of the national sample of young adults in the mid-1980s scored at this level.[38]

The math skills of the parents in Family B are equivalent to NAEP math scores of 280 and 275, respectively. Thus, each parent is about halfway between Level 250, Basic Operations and Beginning Problem Solving, and Level 300, Moderately Complex Procedures and Reasoning. Individuals at Level 300 "can compute with decimals, fractions, and percents, recognize geometric figures, and solve simple equations." Most of these skills are taught initially no later than the middle school for most students. In 1990, about 56 percent of the 17-year-olds had math skills equal to or greater than Level 300.[39]

Family B lives in a modest apartment in a three-family dwelling on the fringe of a relatively poor area of the central city. About 35 percent of the students in the elementary school their children attend are from families with incomes below the poverty line.

The mother in Family C is a high school graduate, and the father has completed two years of college. (He dropped out of college just before the birth of

38. Kirsch and Jungeblut, *Literacy: Profiles of America's Young Adults*, p. 39. Mullis et al., *Trends in Academic Progress: Achievement of U.S. Students in Science, 1969–1970 to 1990; Mathematics, 1973 to 1990; Reading, 1971 to 1990; and Writing, 1984–1990*, p. 124.

39. Mullis et al., *Trends in Academic Progress: Achievement of U.S. Students in Science, 1969–1970; Mathematics, 1973 to 1990; Reading, 1971 to 1990; and Writing, 1984–1990*, p. 77.

the couple's first child.) The mother has been working as a secretary part-time for a local business. The father is an insurance agent in his uncle's independent insurance agency.

The mother was in the general education track in high school, but did above-average work academically. The father was in the college prep track and did average academic work. Both parents have needed to use a considerable amount of their academic skills in their jobs and have continued to learn new skills that are closely tied to what they learned in school. For example, the mother has learned to use a word processing program and has had to become familiar with her employer's lines of merchandise, which has entailed substantial reading. She talks frequently with both customers and suppliers about product matters. The father has had to become knowledgeable about several kinds of insurance (auto, homeowners, life) from several companies. This has involved extensive use of both verbal and quantitative skills. The job requires a modest amount of writing, often in the form of short letters.

The mother has a NAEP reading proficiency of 310, while her husband has the equivalent of a 320. Thus, both parents are reading above the Adept Level, in the father's case by a considerable amount. The mother's math skills are equivalent to a NAEP score of 295, the father's about 315. Consequently, both parents are fairly close to the Moderately Complex Procedures and Reasoning Level in math.

The family owns their own home, a small house in a lower-middle-class suburb. Their older child is in the seventh grade and the younger is in the fourth. The children attend schools that serve primarily families with socioeconomic profiles similar to theirs. A cross-district school busing program to promote racial integration, however, has resulted in an increase in the number of economically disadvantaged students. About 18 percent of the school's students are eligible for the free or reduced lunch program, up from about 10 percent prior to the implementation of the busing program.

In Family D, both parents have attended college. The father earned a bachelor's degree in engineering at the state university. The mother dropped out of college at the end of her junior year, when her husband, who was a year ahead of her in school, received a job offer from a company headquartered elsewhere in the state. When the couple's first child was born, within a year of the husband's graduation, the mother decided to stay at home full-time while the children were preschool-age. Their second child was born two years after the first. The older child recently started the first grade. As a result, the mother has begun making plans to attend a nearby campus of the state university to complete her degree in elementary education.

The father was an above-average engineering student and has been progressing well in his career. He recently became the leader of a small project team. In his new position, he will have to use his verbal skills in conjunction with his quantitative skills more extensively than was the case in his first few job assignments. For example, he will now have to prepare written reports frequently and occasionally make brief oral presentations to management.

The mother's reading proficiency is the equivalent of a 345 NAEP reading score. The father's is the equivalent of 355. Thus, her reading skills are a little below the Advanced Level (350) on the NAEP, while his are a little above it. Only 7 percent of the 17-year-olds scored at the Advanced Level on the NAEP reading test in 1990, and about 21 percent of the national sample of young adults in the mid-1980s reached this level.[40]

The mother's math skills are equal to a score of about 330 on the NAEP, the father's to a score of about 375, well above the Multistep Problem Solving and Algebra Level (350), which is a threshold only 7 percent of the 17-year-olds reached on the 1990 NAEP math test.[41] Indeed, because the father completed the demanding quantitative coursework of an engineering major and continues to use mathematics in an applied (engineering) context, his NAEP math score equivalent probably underestimates his developed math capacities. (The NAEP, for example, does not include questions on calculus.) In contrast, the mother has math skills that place her a little more than halfway between Level 300 and Level 350.

Family D resides in a suburban community inhabited largely by middle- and moderately upper-middle-class families. The public schools reflect the socioeconomic profile of the community. Only about 5 percent of the students in their older child's elementary school are eligible for the free lunch program.

Among the five hypothetical families, the parents in Family E have completed the most higher education. The mother has a Ph.D. in history and the father has a bachelor's degree in journalism. Both parents have held full-time jobs in their professional fields for a number of years. The mother is an associate professor at a private liberal arts college, and the father is an editor with the local newspaper.

The mother has a reading proficiency that is the equivalent of a 375 NAEP reading score, well above the Advanced Level; the father's proficiency is the equivalent of a 355 score, modestly above it. Because of her well-developed research and writing skills in the humanities, the mother's NAEP reading score probably underestimates her developed verbal reasoning and communication capacities.

The mother has math skills equal to a NAEP score of about 350, while the father's are equal to a 340. Thus, the mother is at the Multistep Problem Solving and Algebra Level, while the father is reasonably close to it.

Family E lives in an upper-middle-class community. One of their children is a sophomore in high school; the other is in the eighth grade. They attend schools serving only students from their community. Hence, virtually all of their peers are children from families in which one or both parents is a manager or professional. Students from families with incomes below the poverty line are a rarity in these schools.

These brief contextualized profiles of the five hypothetical families make it

40. Ibid., p. 124; Kirsch and Jungeblut, *Literacy: Profiles of America's Young Adults*, p. 39.
41. Mullis et al., *Trends in Academic Progress: Achievement of U.S. Students in Science, 1969–70 to 1990; Mathematics, 1973 to 1990; Reading, 1971 to 1990; and Writing, 1984 to 1990*, p. 77.

clear that the academic (human capital) skills the parents have available to invest in their children vary enormously—and also that these variations do not "lock in" at the end of formal education. Education-related capacities continue to change through time as a function of both the level of developed skills individuals have when they leave school and the subsequent opportunity structures (in the form of jobs, friendship networks, and so forth) they have developed over the years.[42]

Among the five families, the parents in Family A and Family E represent the extremes of the formal education, skills proficiency distribution, both in terms of their developed academic abilities at the conclusion of formal schooling and in the opportunity structures available to them for continued intellectual growth. The parents in Family B appear to be relatively close to the Family A parents in regard to developed skills and opportunity structures for further learning, while those in Family D are very close to Family E in these areas. The parents in Family C are somewhere in the middle.

Estimating the Dollar Value of Parent Education Resources   A descriptive overview of the formal-education-derived resources parents have available to invest in their children is one thing, quantifying their value is quite another. Our approach involves, first, developing estimates of the amount of time that the parents have to invest in their children and then putting a dollar value on this time.

This approach has some limitations. For the most part, it does not consider the quality of the time parents invest in their children or variations in their motivation to use the time with their children for educational purposes. It does not adjust for differences in personality and interests between parents and children, which may influence the quality of the parents' time investments, and it does not take into account the educational resource investments that might be made by other members of the family or friends. Finally, it ignores imperfections in the market's ability to assess the monetary value of parents' formal-education-derived knowledge and skills.

In spite of these and other limitations, the proposed methodology is adequate for my purposes. The primary objective is to make not fine distinctions but order-of-magnitude estimates of variations in the value of the education-relevant resources that parents invest in their youngsters.

The academic achievement patterns of groups tend to be established no later than the middle of the elementary school years.[43] Paralleling this is the fact that parents spend more time with their children when the children are very young than when they are older.[44] Thus, one should be particularly interested in devel-

42. For a discussion of the intellectual gains associated with college attendance, see Ernest T. Pascarella and Patrick T. Terenzini, *How College Affects Students: Findings and Insights from Twenty Years of Research* (San Francisco: Jossey-Bass, 1991), pp. 62–161.

43. See the discussion of the Sustaining Effects Study data in chapter 5 as well as the review of NAEP reading and math test scores in chapter 3.

44. C. Russell Hill and Frank P. Stafford, "Parental Care of Children: Time Diary Estimates of Quantity, Predictability, and Variety," *Journal of Human Resources* 12 (Spring 1977); 226, 228.

oping estimates of parents' education-relevant investments of time in their children from infancy until age nine or ten.

Robert L. Egbert has estimated the amount of time that children spend in school versus the amount of time they spend under the supervision of their parents or other child care providers up to their ninth birthday. He concluded that children spend less than 10 percent of their waking hours in school in their first nine years of life.[45] Even in later years, children spend a relatively small fraction of their time in school—probably about 20 percent of their waking hours from age nine through age eighteen.[46] Consequently, the question of how and with whom children spend their nonschool time continues to be very important to their academic success.

Given the diversity among families regarding both the parents' work outside the home and their inclination to spend their nonwork time in the company of their children, it is difficult to make more than very general estimates of the amount of time that parents spend with their children. It can be just as difficult to determine how much of this time contributes to the children's academic success. Most of us would agree that there is educational value in parents' spending time reading to their preschoolers, helping their second graders with homework, taking their middle schoolers to a science museum, or advising their tenth graders on course selection. But what about time spent shopping for clothes? Does discussing the quality of clothing relative to cost have educational value? What about time spent showing a child how to follow the directions for assembling a model airplane or baking a cake? or used for conversation among parents and children regarding the planning of a logistically complex vacation? or devoted to helping an aged family member weigh alternative treatment strategies for a serious health problem? The children might be able to observe the parent's effort or discuss it with him or her after the fact.

Upon reflection, these and many other parent-child interactions entail what I have called active or passive instruction. Each of the examples might well involve the parents' modeling or coaching certain ways of thinking and behaving. If the parents have had a great deal of formal education, one might expect them to adapt many of the problem-solving skills they learned in school to these situations, as suggested by the research on differences in parenting strategies among different social classes reviewed in chapter 10.

It is reasonable to believe that the more parents use intellectual and behavioral tools derived from their formal education in their interactions with their

---

45. Robert L. Egbert, "Improving Life Chances for Young Children," in *Improving Life Chances for Young Children*, Robert L. Egbert, ed. (Lincoln: Bureau of Education Research, Services and Policy Studies and the Center for Curriculum and Instruction, Teachers College, University of Nebraska-Lincoln, 1989), pp. 9–17.

46. Assuming that children average eight hours of sleep from age nine to eighteen, they will be awake 52,560 hours (16 [hours] × 365 [days] × 9 [years]). Assuming a 6.5-hour school day and a 180-day school year, they will be in school 10,530 hours during these years, or 20 percent of their waking hours. This calculation ignores the difference between time spent at school and time actually spent on school tasks. It also ignores time spent in school after the end of the school day on educationally valuable extracurricular activities and time spent on homework.

children, the more supportive they will be of their youngsters' academic progress in school. Parents with a great deal of formal education will be in a much better position than parents with little formal education to use such tools for this purpose.

This line of thinking suggests that much of the time parents spend with their children has significant educational investment dimensions. For this analysis, however, I shall use conservative assumptions about the amount of time the parents in the five hypothetical families spend in this fashion. I shall assume that parents in each of the families spend a total of two hours a day in educational investment activities with their children from the time their children are born until their sixth birthday, an average of one hour a day in such activities from the time the children are six years old until their twelfth birthday, and a half-hour a day from the time their children are twelve until their eighteenth birthday. These assumptions represent total parental time per day for each of the five families regardless of whether the parents are in the work force in some capacity. They are based on a 365-day year in order to average across school days, weekends, holidays, and vacation time. They also are adjusted for the age of the children, reflecting the fact that the largest amount of parental time will be invested in the early years. Under these assumptions, each child will receive the same average amount of parental time each day. Implicit in this last point is the additional assumption that during much of the time parents invest in their children the family is together as a group. That is to say, time investments often perform double duty—the parents work with more than one of their children simultaneously.

Table 11.10 translates these assumptions into total hours invested by the parents from the time their children are born until they reach their eighteenth birthday. As the table indicates, I am estimating that in each hypothetical family the parents will have spent, on average, a total of 7,665 hours personally investing education-relevant resources in their youngsters by the time the children are eighteen. In contrast, most children will spend more than 15,000 hours in school from the time they enter preschool at age four until they graduate from high school fourteen years later.[47]

I noted earlier that parents in the five families have accumulated diverse amounts of knowledge and levels of skills, in large measure owing to differences in their formal education. It is reasonable to assume that the quality of the educational resource investments the parents make in their children will vary a great deal as a result of these differences in the parents' educations. The question is how to quantify these differences in a meaningful way.

Since (in economists' terms) it is human capital the parents are investing, the

47. The 15,000-hour estimate is based on several assumptions: that the school year is 180 days long from preschool through twelfth grade; that the school day is 6.5 hours long from the first through the twelfth grades; that children attend one year of half-day preschool and one year of half-day kindergarten; and that all time spent in school is educational, whether in class, lunch, etc. Thus, we get 6.5 (hours) × 180 (days) × 12 (years) = 14,040 hours, and 3.25 (hours) × 180 (days) × 2 (years) = 1,170 hours, for a total of 15,210 hours.

Table 11.10
Estimates of the Time Parents Spend Making
Educational Investments in Their Children

Period of Children's Lives	Parental Time Calculation	Total Hours of Educational Resource Investment by Parents in Their Children
1: Birth to 6th birthday	2 hours × 365 (days) × 6 years =	4,380 hours
2: 6th birthday to 12th birthday	1 hour × 365 (days) × 6 (years) =	2,190 hours
3: 12th birthday to 18th birthday	1/2 hour × 365 (days) × 6 (years) =	<u>1,095 hours</u>
4: Birth to 18th birthday		7,665 hours

most obvious way to undertake these measurements is to use a labor market approach. Employers attach a monetary value to human capital via the wage structure for different jobs, which in turn is heavily influenced by the supply and demand for individuals who possess the knowledge and skills necessary to perform the various jobs effectively. We can use the parents' respective wage rates to value their education-relevant time investments in their children.

In the five hypothetical families there are nine parents currently living in the home, eight of whom are employed either full- or part-time. Only one (the mother in Family D) is not employed outside the home, but we have information about the job (elementary school teaching) for which she is almost prepared. Table 11.11 uses this information to present monetary values for the human capital the parents invest in their children. Since four of the families have two parents in the home, this requires some method of developing a combined parental human-capital investment value. This is done in this example by assuming that in two-parent families two-thirds of the educational resource investment is made by the mother and one-third by the father, reflecting the fact that, in contemporary America, the mother typically has a disproportionate amount of the direct child-rearing responsibilities. But it is also designed to reflect the fact that many fathers do play a very significant educational investment role in the lives of their children, especially when the modeling of behavior is factored into the equation. In the case of the single-parent family, I shall use the mother's wage rate to value the entire parent investment in the children.[48]

48. The data in table 11.11 are consistent with the after-tax income figures presented in table 11.8 for the five hypothetical families. These figures were calculated by using the 1990 federal income tax and New Jersey gross income rate schedules. In the case of the three hypothetical families that own their homes, assumptions also were made regarding mortgage interest and property

Table 11.11
Monetary Value of the Educational Resource Investments that Parents
in the Hypothetical Families Make in Their Children

Family	Individual Hourly $ Wage Rate	Average Hourly Parent $ Wage Rate	Total Parent Educational Resource $ Investment per Child
A	4.93 (mother)	4.93	37,788
B	5.77 (mother) 7.21 (father)	6.25	47,906
C	6.54 (mother) 11.54 (father)	8.21	62,930
D	11.90 (mother) 21.15 (father)	14.98	114,822
E	24.06 (mother) 18.27 (father)	22.13	169,626
Five-Family Average		11.30	86,614

Note: In the case of the two-parent families, the average hourly parent wage rate is calculated by adding two-thirds of the mother's before-tax hourly wage rate to one-third of the father's before-tax hourly wage rate. The total parental educational resource investment is calculated by multiplying the average before-tax parental wage rate by the 7,665 hours of parenting time calculated in table 11.10. A before-tax wage rate is used because the parents would have to pay a before-tax wage to a third party if they wanted to duplicate the investment. See note 48 of this chapter for further details regarding the development of the data for this table.

tax payments. The before-tax family incomes that were developed for the analysis are $12,300 for Family A; $21,000 for Family B; $30,800 for Family C; $44,000 for Family D; and $76,500 for Family E. In order to calculate the educational resource investment values for the hypothetical families, the before-tax incomes must be used because our objective is to establish a market value for these investments. The market cost is a before-tax wage rate in that it is the wage rate the parents would have to pay if they purchased the services from others instead of providing them to their children personally.

In the case of Family A, there is only one parent (the mother) in the home. Her average wage rate is calculated by dividing her before-tax income by the number of hours she works each year. Since she holds both full- and part-time jobs, it is assumed that she is working 48 hours a week, 52 weeks a year, a total of 2,496 hours a year. Dividing $12,300 by 2,496 produces an hourly wage rate of $4.93. Because she is the only employed adult in the home, this is also the average wage rate for the family. Multiplying $4.93 by 7,665 hours produces a total parent education resource investment in each of the children of $37,788.

The calculation for Family B is based on the assumption that the mother is working half-time (20 hours a week over a 52-week year, for a total of 1,040 hours) and earns $6,000 a year. Dividing $6,000 by 1,040 produces a wage rate of $5.77. The father is assumed to work 40 hours a week over a 52-week year, or 2,080 hours, and earns $15,000—an hourly wage rate of $7.21. The average parent hourly wage rate is calculated by adding two-thirds of the mother's wage rate to one-third of the father's wage rate. The resulting average rate of $6.25 is then multiplied by 7,665 hours to produce a total parent education resource investment in each of their children of $47,906.

The calculation for Family C is based on the assumption that the mother's annual income for her half-time job is $6,800 and the father's annual income for his full-time job is $24,000. The mother's

The dollar value of the educational resource investment that the parents in Family E make in each of their children is $131,838, or 4.5 times larger ($169,626 - $37,788) than the amount invested by the parent in Family A. The investment per child made by the parent in Family A is 56 percent below the five-family average of $86,615. The investment per child made by the parents in Family E is 96 percent above the average.

Family B is only slightly better off than Family A. The parents' $47,906 human-capital investment per child is $10,118 larger than that of Family A but $121,720 less than that of Family E. In terms of multiples, Family E's educational resources investment per child is 3.5 times that of Family B.

Even Family C has a substantial disadvantage relative to Family E, whose human-capital investment per child is $106,696 larger than that of Family C. In terms of multiples, Family E's educational resource investment per child is 2.7 times as large as that of Family C.

Only the parents in Family D appear to be making a human-capital investment that is even reasonably close to that of Family E. Their $114,822 investment per child is $54,804, or 32 percent less than that of Family E. Although this may seem to be a large gap, not only is it small in comparison to the gaps experienced by the other three families, but it may be overstated to a significant extent. The father in Family D is an engineer. If he takes a strong interest in the academic progress of his children, he may be able to provide more support for their development in mathematics and the physical sciences than any of the other parents will be able to provide to their youngsters. Owing to the weaknesses of many schools in math and science, this may be extremely valuable for his children. In addition, the educational resource contribution of the mother in Family D may be understated. Because she has been in the home full-time during her children's early years, the conservative approach taken here is especially likely to underestimate her (time) contribution. And because she is planning to become a teacher, to the extent that teachers' salaries lag behind those of some other professions the value of her educational resource investment in her children is underestimated.

---

hourly wage rate is $6.54 and the father's is $11.54. The average parent wage rate is $8.21, and the total parent investment in each of the children is $62,930.

The calculation for Family D is slightly more complicated because the mother does not work outside the home. Because she has completed three years of college and plans to be an elementary teacher, it is assumed that she is paid in the home the equivalent of a starting salary for a new elementary teacher. In the late 1980s, the average starting salary for a new teacher was $19,598 for an approximately 42-week school year (National Center for Education Statistics, Digest of Education Statistics 1990, p. 85). Thus, her hourly wage rate is calculated by dividing 1,680 hours (40-hour work weeks x 42 weeks) into $20,000. This results in $11.90 per hour. The father's wage rate is calculated by dividing his $44,000 salary by 2,080 hours, which produces a figure of $21.15. Two thirds of $11.90 plus one-third of $21.15 produces an average parent hourly wage rate of $14.98, for a total parent education resource investment of $114,822 per child.

In Family E, both parents have full-time jobs. It is assumed that the mother earns $38,500 for the 40-week academic year and the father $38,000 for a 52-week year. The mother's hourly wage is $24.06 and the father's $18.27. Together these figures produce an average parent hourly wage rate of $22.13, resulting in a total parent education resource investment in each child of $169,626.

So far in this chapter we have looked separately at variations in school resources, in family/parent financial resources, and in family/parent educational resources. In this section I shall bring these three threads of analysis together to assess the overall magnitude of the variations in resources available for the education of children in the United States, particularly those from different racial/ethnic groups. Drawing upon data presented in tables 11.8 and 11.11, I present in table 11.12 a consolidated picture of the financial and educational resources of the five families as well as per pupil school resources for five different school expenditure cases: Low, Medium, High, Very High, and Extremely High.

Table 11.12
Comparisons of School Resources with Family Resources

1: Estimated Family Resources Invested by the Parents in the Hypothetical Families in Each of Their Children, from Birth to Age 18

Family	Family Resource Investment in $		
	Financial	Educational	Total
A	66,006	37,788	103,794
B	81,000	47,906	128,906
C	117,000	62,930	179,930
D	166,500	114,822	281,322
E	270,000	169,626	439,626
Five-Family Average	140,001	86,614	226,715

2: Estimated School Investment per Student from Preschool through Twelfth Grade in the Low, Medium, High, Very High, and Extremely High Expenditure Cases

Expenditure Case	$
Low (50% of National Average)	35,000
Medium (100% of National Average)	70,000
High (150% of National Average)	105,000
Very High (200% of National Average)	140,000
Extremely High (300% of National Average)	210,000

Note: The national current per pupil expenditure average is assumed to be $5,000 per year.

Because it combines both financial and educational resource dimensions, part 1 of table 11.12 puts the extremely large variations in resources among the five hypothetical families into sharp focus, showing the total education-related investment per child made by the parents in each family from the birth of a child until his or her eighteenth birthday in absolute terms and also relative to the other families. Part 2 of the table shows the total cumulative investment that schools make in an individual child over a fourteen-year period, from preschool through the twelfth grade. The cases hypothesized here assume that the national average of current expenditures per pupil was about $5,000 per year in the early 1990s and that the current expenditure is the same at each level of education.[49] The Medium case presented in table 11.12 assumes that the per pupil expenditure average is equal to the national average. Over fourteen years, this represents a total investment of $70,000 ($5,000 × 14). The family resource investment per child exceeds this amount in all five hypothetical families. Family E's resource investment is 6.3 times the school resource investment.

Part 2 also makes it clear that the variations in school investments are much smaller, in absolute terms, than the variations in family investments. The Low case assumes that the annual current expenditure per pupil average is only $2,500—50 percent below the national average. This translates into a $35,000 per pupil school investment over the fourteen-year period. The High case assumes that the current per pupil average is $7,500—50 percent more than the national average—and produces a fourteen-year school investment per student of $105,000. As will be recalled from the earlier discussion of expenditure variations among the states in 1988–89, none of the states had per pupil expenditures that year that were as much as 50 percent below the national average, while only three states and the District of Columbia had per pupil expenditures that were more than 50 percent above the national average. This means that the Low case and the High case together account for most of the variation in current per pupil expenditure averages among the states. Over the fourteen-year period, there is a school resource investment difference between the two cases of $70,000 ($105,000 - $35,000 = $70,000). This compares to the $335,832 difference in family resource investment per child between Family E and Family A, the highest and lowest resourced hypothetical families. Thus, the difference between Family E's and Family A's resources is 4.8 times larger, in absolute terms, than the difference in school resources in the High and Low cases.

As noted above, some affluent suburban school districts tend to spend considerably more per pupil than the average for their state or for the nation. Reflecting this fact, the Very High case assumes a current school expenditure per pupil average of $10,000 per year, twice the national average. Over fourteen years, annual spending at this level produces a school investment per student of $140,000—that is, $105,000 more than the Low case. Nonetheless, the $335,832 gap between Family A and Family E in family resource expenditures

49. The current expenditure per pupil average for the nation was $5,097 for the 1991–92 school year. See "How Your State Compares," *Teacher Magazine* (May/June 1992), p. 49.

per child is 3.2 times as large as the $105,000 gap in the Low and Very High school expenditure cases.

Even the Extremely High case, which assumes a $15,000 current expenditure per pupil average, does not produce a school investment gap with the Low case as large as the gap between Family A and Family E. Under the Extremely High case, $210,000 per pupil is spent through the schools over fourteen years, which is $175,000 more than in the Low case. However, the $335,832 family resource gap between Family A and Family E is 1.9 times the school expenditure gap in the Extremely High and Low cases.

The discussion so far has looked at variations in family and school resources from a birth-to-age-18 perspective. Yet early investments in children are crucial for getting them off to a good start academically. In our example, no formal school investments are made until the children in the hypothetical families enter a preschool program at age four.[50] However, by that time the parents have already invested family resources in them for four years. For Family A, the per child investment during these important early years is a relatively modest $29,064. For Family E, however, the investment is $124,620 per child—a very substantial investment of resources.[51] Clearly, the school investments for children in the hypothetical families do not begin until very different amounts of education-relevant family resources have been invested in them in the earliest childhood years.

For many youngsters the education-relevant family and school resource investments do not end at age 18 (that is, at the age at which most graduate from high school); many will go on to some form of postsecondary education. At that point, the children of Family E are much more likely than the children of Family A to receive large education-related investments from both the family and the school (college/university). These youngsters are likely to have done well enough academically in high school to be accepted by selective postsecondary institutions. (See the social-class-related standardized test data in chapter 5.) These tend to be expensive places, especially if they are private. However, their parents are likely to have the resources to ensure that they will be able to attend a quality institution. In contrast, the youngsters in Family A may not even graduate from high school. If they do, they are likely to be underprepared for col-

---

50. Although some children begin preschool at age three and have a two-year preschool experience, many begin at age four and have only one year. Moreover, poor children are generally less likely to attend preschool than middle-class chilen. Finally, some preschools are half-day programs and others full-day. For this analysis, one year of half-day preschool is assumed for all children.

51. The total family-resource investment in each of the children during their first four years of life would be $29,064 in Family A and $124,628 in Family E. Each family's investments would have financial and educational resource components. In the case of Family A, the financial investment per child would be $14,668 over the four-year period ($3,667 × 4). For Family E, the per child financial investment would be $60,000 over the four years ($15,000 × 4). In the case of Family A, the education-resource investment would be $14,396 (2 hours a day of parent time × 365 days × 4 = 2,920 hours in the first four years; 2,920 hours × the parent educational resource hourly rate of $4.93 = $14,396.) For Family E, the per child education-resource investment of the parents would be $64,620 (2,920 hours × the parent educational resource hourly rate of $22.13). See tables 11.8, 11.10, and 11.11 for underlying data for these calculations.

lege, which may lead them to enroll in a local community college. Their parent (mother) is unlikely to be able to provide much financial assistance, and the community college is unlikely to be able to invest as much in them as a selective four-year institution would.

Cultural and Racial/Ethnic Dimensions of Comparative Family and School Resources   Up to this point, estimates of family and school resources have been presented without reference to cultural or racial/ethnic differences among students. Instead, they have fundamentally reflected a social class perspective—family resources have been estimated via assumptions about differences in the income and education levels of the parents in the hypothetical families. Nonetheless, the assumed social class attributes of these hypothetical families are consistent with differences in socioeconomic patterns that actually exist among racial ethnic groups in the United States. For instance, from earlier chapters we know that whites and Asians are overrepresented among American families that are similar to Family D and Family E and underrepresented among those like Family A and Family B. The opposite is true for African Americans, Latinos, and Native Americans.[52]

There are also important cultural differences among the groups that are not easily captured through socioeconomic measures. As discussed in chapter 10, such differences raise the question of the cultural compatibility of family and school resources. A family whose primary language is English, for example, may have a different level of resource compatibility with a school in the United States than a family whose primary language is Spanish. All other things being equal, the children of the English-speaking family would be better able to tap the instructional capacities of a U.S. school than would the children of the Spanish-speaking family.

It is extremely difficult to take cultural differences of this kind into account when developing dollar estimates of family and school resources. Rather than attempt to do so, I will simply point out that, because such differences among families have probably been growing as a result of the rapidly changing demographics of the nation, the variations in family resources are probably considerably larger than the data for the five hypothetical families suggest.

It is even more difficult to take racial/ethnic prejudice directly into account in making dollar estimates of family and school resource variations. Based on the analysis in chapters 8 and 9, it is reasonable to assume that prejudice is a significant source of variation in both family and school resources.

SOME IMPLICATIONS OF RESOURCE VARIATIONS FOR THE EDUCATIONAL ADVANCEMENT OF MINORITIES

In this discussion of variations in school resources, I have focused primarily on differences in the amount of financial resources available per student rather

52. Welniak and Littman, "Money Income and Poverty Status in the U.S. 1989," pp. 35–36.

than on differences in how the funds are spent by the schools. It is important to know whether school dollars tend to be invested differently on the basis of the socioeconomic or racial/ethnic status of students because such variations in the deployment of school resources, if they exist, could be a source of differences in group achievement patterns.

Tracking is one of the most obvious mechanisms through which variations result in the way school resources are invested in students. Many educators have become increasingly concerned about the underrepresentation of the children of the poor and several minority groups in the college preparatory track in secondary school and their overrepresentation in the vocational and general education tracks. Similar preoccupations have been voiced about grouping and tracking patterns for these student populations at the elementary school level. It is believed that, partly as a result of tracking and ability grouping, many poor and minority students receive a diluted academic program, which virtually guarantees that they will fall ever further behind their white middle-class counterparts (see chapter 9).

Whether, when, and how tracking and ability grouping should be used in the schools are among the most crucial questions confronting educators. For present purposes, however, another question is in order: Is there reason to believe that misallocation of school resources in the form of too much tracking or ability grouping is a greater source of group achievement differences than are variations in the amount of school resources? This is a difficult question. However, one can shed some light on this issue by describing several examples of ways in which educators have learned to use school resources differently for minority and disadvantaged children.

In chapter 10, I discussed the Kamehameha Early Education Program (KEEP), which has developed a culturally attuned primary grade reading program for Native Hawaiian children, and Dr. James Comer's School Development Program, which has emphasized improving the quality of home-school relationships for low-income minority children in elementary schools in several cities. Each of these approaches has produced marked improvements in the academic performance of disadvantaged minority youngsters, but neither has come close to producing the academic results typically seen from white and Asian high-SES children. Moreover, KEEP has focused only on the reading components of the curriculum.

To take another example, in the mid-1960s Congress passed the Elementary and Secondary Education Act. Title I of that legislation (now called Chapter 1) provided federal aid to elementary and secondary schools for the purpose of improving the educational opportunities of disadvantaged children. Monies made available through this legislation have usually been used to fund supplementary remedial services for children who were not mastering basic skills in the regular classroom. Typically, these students have been pulled out of their classrooms for a part of the day to receive special instruction.[53] The cost of ser-

53. Robert E. Slavin, "Chapter 1: A Vision for the Next Quarter Century," *Phi Delta Kappan* 72 (April 1991): 587.

vices along these lines was about $500 a year in the late 1980s. Research has found that most of these efforts produce small improvements in the academic performance of participating students—gains of one to three percentile points on standarized achievement tests.[54]

Over the past several years some new approaches to the use of Chapter 1 funds have been developed. One of these is the Success for All program developed by Robert E. Slavin and his colleagues. Success for All uses Chapter 1 monies to redesign the elementary schooling experience for disadvantaged children. It is therefore concerned primarily with using school resources differently rather than with spending Chapter 1 dollars for supplementary services. The Success for All program has several components, including (1) reading tutors to provide one-on-one help to students as soon as they have difficulties; (2) reduced class size during the daily ninety-minute reading period; (3) homogeneous grouping of students during the reading period based on reading skill levels; (4) frequent (eight-week) reading assessments to monitor students' progress closely; (5) a family-support team to involve parents in their children's schoolwork; (6) a program facilitator at the school; and (7) in-service training for participating teachers. The cost of the program at the best-funded participating schools is about $800 per student.[55]

Success for All has produced results comparable to those achieved by the KEEP and Comer models: participating students were found to read on average at the 46th percentile, while the control group read at the 30th percentile.[56] Although promising, these results are well below middle-class and upper-middle-class performance norms.[57] Moreover, they are limited to reading. Extension of the program to other academic subjects, including math, is still under development.[58]

In view of the limited investment being made in the education of disadvan-

54. Robert E. Slavin, "Making Chapter 1 Make a Difference," *Phi Delta Kappan* 68 (October 1987): 110.

55. Nancy A. Madden, Robert E. Slavin, Nancy L. Karweit, Lawrence Dolan, and Barbara A. Wasik, "Success for All," *Phi Delta Kappan* 72 (April 1991): 594–96, 598.

56. Nancy A. Madden, Robert E. Slavin, Nancy L. Karweit, Barbara J. Liverman, and Lawrence Dolan, *Success for All: First-Year Effects of a Comprehensive Plan for Reforming Urban Education,* Report No. 30 (Baltimore: Center for Research on Elementary & Middle Schools, The Johns Hopkins University, 1989), p. 11.

57. For example, in Montclair, N.J., in 1988, the mean percentiles on the reading section of the Iowa Test of Basic Skills ranged from the high 70s to the middle 80s among white students from first through eighth grade. Their mean math percentiles ranged from the low 80s to the low 90s. White students in Montclair are disproportionately from high-SES families. See Beatriz C. Clewell and Myra F. Joy, *Choice in Montclair, New Jersey* (Princeton, N.J.: Policy Information Center, Educational Testing Service, 1990), pp. 5 and 14. This pattern also can be found in public school systems of major cities that have a mostly minority population. For example, in Community School District 26 in New York City, 80 percent of the students read above grade level in 1992 and 90 percent had math scores that exceeded grade level. This compared to 46 percent and 58 percent for the city as a whole. District 26 is one of the few in New York City that still has a large proportion of white students, many of them from high-SES families. See Joseph Berger, "Test Scores Drop in Math and Reading," *New York Times,* 12 June 1992, pp. B1 and B4.

58. Madden et al., *Success for All: First-Year Effects of a Comprehensive Plan for Reforming Urban Education,* p. 16.

taged students with Chapter 1 dollars, one should not be surprised that even the best-designed programs funded with these monies have not produced more dramatic results. Instead, one should regard it as extremely encouraging that modest additional funds—well invested—can help produce substantial gains.

So far I have mentioned only elementary school interventions. At the high school level, one of the most interesting efforts is a highly regarded program developed and funded by the Macy Foundation for preparing minority and economically disadvantaged high school students for postsecondary education focused on health-related academic majors. Students in participating high schools take a demanding college preparatory course sequence, especially in math and science. Honors and advanced placement courses are emphasized. Among the other attributes of the program are small class sizes, academic and personal support and guidance services, tutoring services, and teacher training. Summer academic programs are also available for many participating students.[59]

The results of the Macy program have been encouraging: Graduates have taken more math and science in high school than have students nationally, and a higher percentage of Macy high school graduates than high school graduates nationally are majoring in health-related fields, math, and the physical and biological sciences in college.[60] Participants have also performed relatively well on such standardized measures of academic performance as the SAT. A sample of Macy program students in 1989 had a combined verbal and math SAT score average of 848, which was fairly close to the 903 national average for all students who took the SAT that year. Possibly more significant, the African American students in the Macy sample had a combined SAT score average of 840, which was 103 points above the 737 national average for blacks in 1989. And the Puerto Rican students had a combined SAT score average of 858, or 92 points above the 766 national average for Puerto Ricans.[61] However, the combined SAT score averages for black and Puerto Rican students were still well below the combined verbal and math SAT score averages for all white and all Asian students in 1989 (937 and 934, respectively) and even further below the average combined scores for the white and Asian students who took a full college preparatory academic program (1021 and 1042, respectively).[62] Thus, even a four-year high school program that addresses the tracking issue directly by ensuring that students take an extensive college preparatory curriculum and

59. Janis L. Cromer and Elizabeth D. Steinberger, *Expanding Horizons: A Vision for Our High Schools* (New York: Josiah Macy, Jr. Foundation/The McKenzie Group, 1990), pp. 14–16, 90–92.
60. Ibid., pp. 16, 17.
61. Ibid., pp. 75–76; College Entrance Examination Board, *College-Bound Seniors: 1989 Profile of SAT and Achievement Test Takers* (New York: College Entrance Examination Board, 1989), p. iv.
62. The Macy sample of students did score at about the same levels as African American and Puerto Rican students nationally who took a full college preparatory program. The national averages in 1989 for these subpopulations were 838 and 859, respectively. College Entrance Examination Board, *College-Bound Seniors: 1989 Profile of SAT and Achievement Test Takers*, p. iv; *1989 College-Bound Seniors: Ethnic and Gender Profile of SAT and Achievement Test Takers* (New York: College Entrance Examination Board, 1989), p. 2 of each racial/ethnic group section. These combined average scores are for students who took twenty or more school years' worth of coursework in academic subjects—e.g., four years of math, four of science, etc.

that provides high-quality student support services and curricular/teaching improvements is not able to bring black and Puerto Rican students close to white and Asian academic achievement norms, at least as measured by the SAT.

This may seem both surprising and discouraging. Yet given my analysis of the differences in family and school resources, it should have been expected. The Macy program operates primarily within the budgetary constraints of participating high schools. By the standards of foundation investments, Macy has provided a significant amount of supplementary resources—about $300–$400 per participating student each year. Nonetheless, this is a modest investment compared to the large family resource investments that high-SES parents routinely make in their children.

Further, Macy has found it necessary to target its program at students who are reasonably well prepared for high school. Prior to entering high school, participating students have achieved at levels that typically fall within the 50th to 75th percentiles of all students.[63] Thus, they are above-average (but not top) students in terms of previous performance. Macy has not demonstrated that it can achieve similar results with students who are far below average in academic preparation for high school.

The programs discussed here have involved only modest additional expenditures. Unfortunately, there has not been a comparable set of initiatives mounted to assess the value of making societal investments in poor and minority children that approach in magnitude the investments high-SES families generally make in their youngsters. Thus, little is known about what could be gained from such efforts.

Indeed, even apparently substantial school investments in disadvantaged children often turn out to be small relative to the investments being made by high-SES families. For example, quality early childhood education programs for disadvantaged children—like those patterned after the High Scope/Perry School preschool model—cost about $5,000 per year per student, a large amount by school-resource standards.[64] Yet the parents in the hypothetical high-SES Family E invested $124,620 per child during the first four years of their children's lives—$95,556 more than the $29,064 per child invested by the hypothetical low-SES Family A. A $5,000 investment for one year of preschool represents only about 5 percent of the family resource gap between these families. From this perspective, it is small wonder that preschool programs have been able to close only a fraction of the academic achievement gap between high- and low-SES children.[65]

This brief review leads to two conclusions. First, how money is spent does make a difference. Some strategies for investing school resources in disadvan-

63. Cromer and Steinberger, *Expanding Horizons: A Vision for Our High Schools*, p. 25.

64. David P. Weikart, *Quality Preschool Programs: A Long-Term Social Investment*, Occasional Paper Number Five, Ford Foundation Project on Social Welfare and the American Future (New York: Ford Foundation, 1989), p. 11.

65. Ibid., pp. 2–7; Ron Haskins, "Beyond Metaphor: The Efficacy of Early Childhood Education," *American Psychologist* 44 (February 1989): 274–82.

taged children are substantially more productive than others. Second, there is little evidence that any existing strategy can close more than a fraction of the overall achievement gap between high- and low-SES children.

If, as I have argued, education-relevant family resources are to a considerable extent intergenerationally accumulated school resources, it becomes much easier to recognize that providing nearly equal school resources for all children, even when these resources are spent as wisely as possible by educators, cannot produce equal academic results among children from families with very different levels of formal education. Some children will have the additional benefit of large amounts of intergenerationally accumulated formal education capital within their families, while other children will not.

In *Savage Inequalities: Children in America's Schools,* Jonathan Kozol compellingly describes the reality that minority children in some of the most racially isolated and economically distressed urban areas in the nation receive far too few school resources to succeed academically—and vastly less than upper-middle-class white students in affluent suburbs typically receive. At the same time, he does not argue that merely providing equal school resources, as measured in terms of dollars spent or the quality of teachers and facilities, would produce equal educational results. Acknowledging the non-school-based advantages of upper-middle-class children, he points out that in order to achieve educational equality society should be spending much more on the education of our most disadvantaged children than on advantaged youngsters.[66]

With this point in mind, I want to look at the combined family and school resources available to the children in Family A and Family E. Assume for the moment that the inner city school attended by the children in Family A spends close to the national average per pupil. This is my Medium Case, $5,000 per year, in table 11.12. Also assume that the suburban school attended by the children in Family E spends close to the level in the Very High Case, $10,000 per year per pupil. Table 11.13 presents the combined school and education-relevant family resources invested in these children to age eighteen.

As the data show, the combined family/school resource investment in the children is $579,626 in Family E but only $173,794 in Family A—a difference of $405,832. On a combined family/school basis, 3.3 times more education-relevant resources are being invested in the children in Family E. These are sobering numbers.

To acknowledge the existence of extremely large differences in education-relevant family resources in a context in which disadvantaged students can usually

66. See Jonathan Kozol, *Savage Inequalities: Children in America's Schools* (New York: Crown, 1991), p. 54. There has been a growing recognition that disadvantaged children need not just equal school resources but, in many cases, more resources than middle-class children. And this recognition is being reflected in the recent resurgence of school finance court cases. See, for example, Robert K. Goertz and Margaret E. Goertz, "The Quality Education Act of 1990: New Jersey Responds to Abbott v. Burke," *Journal of Education Finance* 16 (Summer 1990): 104–14; Richard L. Henderson "An Analysis of Selected School Finance Litigation and Its Impact upon State Education Legislation," *Journal of Education Finance* 17 (Fall 1991): 193–214; Allan Odden, "School Finance in the 1990s," *Phi Delta Kappan* 73 (February 1992): 455–61.

Table 11.13
Combined School and Education-Relevant Family Resource Investments in the Children in Hypothetical Family A and Family E, from Birth to Age 18

Children	School Resources	Education-Relevant Family Resources	Total Educational Resources
In Family A	$70,000	$103,794	$173,794
In Family E	$140,000	$439,626	$579,626
Difference in favor of Children in Family E	$70,000	$335,832	$405,832

Note: It is assumed that the children in Family A attend a school that spends at the Medium case level in table 11.12, while the children in Family E attend a school that spends at the Very High case level.

expect fewer school resources to be invested in them than in many of the most advantaged students does not mean that existing academic achievement gaps between racial/ethnic groups (and social classes) are acceptable or immutable. But how to close these educational gaps as quickly as possible is by no means obvious. It is to this question that I turn in the next chapter.

SUMMARY AND CONCLUSIONS

My primary concern in this chapter has been to estimate the variations in education-relevant family and school resources available to children in contemporary America. My underlying purpose has been to assess the general validity of James Coleman's view that differences in the academic performance of groups of children reflect to a considerable degree the fact that the variations in education-relevant family resources are greater than the variations in school resources. Although family and school resources have been expressed in dollar terms, my object has been to develop order-of-magnitude estimates of these resource variations.

I first reviewed data on how school expenditures per pupil vary both among and within states. Although the range of school resources is broad, most states are reasonably close to the average per pupil expenditure level among the states. There was also substantial clustering around the average among districts within states.

I then looked at data and research on the relationship between the variations in school resources available to students and the variations in their academic performance. Data from the NAEP 1990 Trial State Assessment in mathematics suggest that the between-state differences in eighth-grade math scores were not strongly related to existing variations in school resources. This finding is consistent with a long line of studies, beginning with the Coleman Report in 1966, that have found a very limited relationship between the achievement patterns of groups of students and school investment levels.

In the third section, I examined a set of hypothetical families with widely varying social class characteristics, as measured by parent income level (financial capital) and parent education level (human capital). These hypothetical families clearly illustrate that very large differences exist in education-relevant family resources available to children from low- and high-SES families.

Next, I compared the absolute size of the differences in the family resources of the highest and lowest SES families with the difference between the highest and lowest school-resource cases. The family-resources difference was much larger than the school-resources difference. This finding is consistent with Coleman's view that the variations in family resources are much greater than the variations in school resources.

In the final section, I looked at some of the implications of these findings. One major conclusion was that it is possible to improve the educational opportunities provided to disadvantaged populations through the use of various strategies designed to make more effective use of available school resources. However, more effective use of available school resources alone cannot be expected to close more than a fraction of the academic achievement gap between advantaged and disadvantaged students. If the nation is to accelerate the educational advancement of minorities more resources will be required. And since much of the educational resource gap between advantaged and disadvantaged students is located outside the school, one must look carefully at where and how these additional investments should be made in minority youngsters.

CHAPTER TWELVE

Principles

and Recommendations

for Action

At least ten major findings from the preceding analysis can enhance our understanding of the educational advancement patterns and trends of several racial/ethnic groups in the United States, as well as their underlying causes:

1. The proportion of the student-age population made up of minority children has been growing rapidly—0.5 percent per year. About 75–80 percent of this growth has been among Latinos, African Americans, and Native Americans; the remaining growth has been primarily among Asians.

2. Over the course of the twentieth century all minorities have made marked progress in educational attainment (degree levels), both absolutely and relative to the white majority, but only Asians have generally reached or surpassed the attainment levels of whites. Large gaps remain between non-Asian minorities and the white majority.

3. Minorities also have made considerable progress in educational achievement (developed academic skills), as measured by standardized test scores— but again large differences remain. Blacks, Hispanics, and American Indians are still quite overrepresented among low-achieving students and very underrepresented among high achievers.

4. As a group, children from high-SES families, as measured by parent education and family income, do much better in school than low-SES children. These differences are most pronounced at the tails of the academic achievement distribution: high-SES children tend to be heavily overrepresented among high achievers and substantially underrepresented among low achievers; the reverse is true for low-SES children.

5. The differences in academic achievement patterns between high- and low-SES children are due in large measure to the fact that the differences in education-relevant family resources between these groups are too large for schools to overcome under existing arrangements. Until the nation can find a way to increase markedly the education-relevant family resources available to low-SES children and the school resources invested in them, similar educational results are unlikely to be produced for high- and low-SES youngsters.

6. A major reason that African Americans, Latinos, and Native Americans tend to do less well academically than whites is that these groups are overrepresented among low-SES families and underrepresented among high-SES families.

7. Variations among social classes do not fully account for racial/ethnic differences in academic achievement patterns; there are also large within-social-class differences in academic achievement patterns among groups. At each social class level, whites and Asians tend to do much better academically than blacks, Hispanics, and American Indians.

8. One explanation for the within-social-class differences in racial/ethnic achievement patterns is that standard methods of measuring social class tend to overestimate the education-relevant resources available to many non-Asian minority students and their families. Parent education level is usually measured by degrees earned or years spent in school rather than by standardized test scores or grades. However, available data suggest that, at each attainment level, minority parents on average have less well developed formal-education-derived knowledge and skills (human capital) than their white counterparts.

9. Both within- and between-social-class differences in achievement patterns are in part a function of historical and contemporary racial/ethnic prejudice and discrimination. Although America's race-based caste system has been essentially dismantled, many minority group members entered the new era with little education and consequently were concentrated in low-skill occupations. Thus, a principal legacy of historical racism has been to make minorities especially vulnerable to the growing shortage of adequately paying low-skill jobs. Contemporary racial prejudice has complicated these circumstances. The continuing belief of many whites in the intellectual or cultural deficiencies of minorities helps explain their lack of support for social policies that might help disadvantaged minority families pull themselves into the economic mainstream. Racism too has over time taken a heavy toll on minority students directly through the schools via low expectations and tracking.

10. Within- and between-social-class variations in academic achievement patterns also are largely explained by ethnic- and social-class-based cultural differences. Racial/ethnic groups differ substantially in their experience with the kind of formal education typically provided in industrialized, technology-based societies; in their notions of what constitutes "intelligent" behavior; and in their preferred modes of learning in the home, the community, and the school. These differences are often compounded by language differences between the home and the school. Cultural dissimilarities also account in part for the diversity of parenting strategies and parent-school relations associated with variations in student achievement patterns.

Over the course of this analysis, three concepts emerged that can draw on these findings in the development of more effective strategies for improving minority educational performance:

1. As James Coleman has noted, differences in academic achievement patterns among racial/ethnic groups reflect the fact that the variation in family

resources is greater than the variation in school resources.[1] My quantification of the education-related resources available to children from different social classes confirms that most high-SES students receive several times more resources than most low-SES students and that most of the resource gap is due to variations in family rather than school resources. Moreover, owing to the social class mismeasurement phenomenon I have identified for some racial/ethnic groups, the resource gap for many minority youngsters is much greater than the calculations suggest.

2. Group educational advancement is an intergenerational process. The knowledge and skills a group of youngsters acquire as a result of formal schooling and home experiences are generally put to use in most realms of their lives during adulthood, including work and interactions with their own children. Viewed from this perspective, education-relevant family resources are school resources that have been accumulated across two or more generations. On average, investments in the current generation of African American, Latino, and American Indian children in the form of intergenerationally accumulated education-relevant family resources are much less than comparable investments in white and Asian children.

3. Educational advancement is heavily dependent on the quality of the education-relevant opportunity structure over a long period of time. When several generations of children are able to attend good schools and their parents are able to secure adequately paying jobs, it is likely that the group will advance educationally and occupationally (as well as politically and socially) at a relatively rapid rate. When the opposite conditions prevail, the group's advancement rate is likely to be slow. The legal successes of the civil rights movement, coupled with the positive economic conditions that prevailed in the United States from the 1940s through the early 1970s, engendered a favorable opportunity structure for minority group members for the first time. For those who had the skills necessary to get stable, decently paying jobs, the intergenerational advancement process gathered momentum. Their descendants now enjoy a promising long-term outlook, although some important problems remain. For those who had limited skills at the beginning of the period, the ensuing shortage of adequately paying jobs often counteracted the benefits associated with improved civil rights. Research by William Julius Wilson and others suggests that many of their descendants face an even more restricted opportunity structure.

These three concepts are intertwined. Current variations in education-relevant family resources are heavily a function of variations in the historical opportunity structure experienced by generations of racial/ethnic groups. At the same time, the quality of the contemporary opportunity structure is crucial to the further evolution of family resource variation patterns. The nation's ability to accelerate the intergenerational advancement process for minorities

1. James S. Coleman, "Families and Schools," *Educational Researcher* 16 (August-September 1987): p. 35.

may be decisively shaped by its capacity to engineer a much more favorable opportunity structure for them in the years ahead as well as to supplement family and school resources for these groups at a level commensurate with their actual needs.

PRINCIPLES FOR DEVELOPING RECOMMENDATIONS FOR ACTION

There is no shortage of recommendations for how to improve the educational prospects of minority students. Many of these have been directly concerned with improving the educational system; others have focused on the alleviation of a broader set of economic and social problems, unemployment, for example, that are associated with poor academic performance. A partial listing of these proposals (some of which have been implemented) includes expanding early childhood education programs for poor children; expanding low-cost child care services, especially for the poor and working class; increasing funding for central city school districts or for schools with high concentrations of poor children; increasing financial aid for minority college students; improving and expanding support services for academically underprepared college students; creating multicultural elementary and secondary school curricula; developing an effective health insurance program for the working and nonworking poor; introducing school choice for public or both public and private schools; improving and expanding parent education and teacher education programs; increasing the number of minority teachers at all levels; introducing school-based management; improving the coordination of social services to poor families; eliminating tracking in elementary and secondary schools; expanding publicly funded low-income housing; expanding (or ending) school busing to achieve racially integrated schools; expanding late-exit transitional bilingual education programs; expanding English-immersion programs; establishing a generous income supplement program for the working poor; expanding job training programs for the unemployed; creating public sector jobs for the chronically unemployed; expanding drug treatment programs; establishing separate schools for black males; developing special schools for non-English-proficient immigrant children; expanding programs designed to increase the number of minority students in selected academic areas in college (for example, engineering); decreasing the use of academic evaluation systems (like standardized tests), believed by many to discriminate against minority students, or increasing the use of these systems; and developing new academic evaluation systems.

Some strategies are more likely to produce good results than others, and in any case the scarcity of resources (money, people, time, public attention) means that priorities must be established. On the basis of the previous analysis of minority education issues, I propose nine principles to be used in making choices:

1. The collective effort should be designed to produce a full distribution of academic achievement for minorities as soon as possible. A successful strategy

must effectively address the twin problems of the overrepresentation of non-Asian minorities among low academic achievers and their underrepresentation among high achievers.

2. The collective effort should capitalize on the reality that group advancement is a cumulative process that takes place over several generations. Our analysis suggests that there may be no feasible strategy to enable the present generation of extremely poor children to produce a distribution of academic achievement as strong as that produced by the present generation of middle-class white children. But it also suggests that minority educational advancement can be accelerated if support to groups of minority children is tailored to where they happen to be in the intergenerational educational advancement process. The strategies for advancing extremely disadvantaged minority children should be different in some respects from those pursued on behalf of middle-class minority children.

3. The approach should invest in several institutions, not simply the school, to achieve the intended results. At a given level of resources, a school may be effective for some individuals but not for others. Adding to or reconfiguring the school's resources may expand its "effectiveness range" to some extent, but even a well-resourced school will have serious limitations. A good strategy for improving minority educational performance, therefore, will entail increasing the effectiveness range of other institutions as well, for example, the health care system and the family.

4. The collective effort should improve our capacity to evaluate progress. As we have seen, available trend data supply relatively little information about the interplay of social class and minority status. Information linking these trends to specific resource variations among groups is also limited. And little of the educational data can be related directly to the changing demographics of the student-age population. As a result, the ability to monitor and assess progress is much more limited than the situation warrants.

5. The collective effort should be designed to close important gaps in the knowledge base for educating minority children over the next few decades. For example, the research base on the educational dimensions of cultural differences is still modest. Limitations of the knowledge base represent an important constraint on the educational progress that we can expect minorities to make in the short to medium term.

6. The collective effort to meet the educational needs of minorities should be very large and long-term. To overcome the huge resource gaps between minorities and the majority, much more of society's resources must be committed to the educational and other needs of minorities than is now the case. And owing to the intergenerational nature of the educational advancement of groups, these additional resources must be invested on a sustained basis for several decades—probably for several generations.

7. The collective effort should be designed to produce broad public support. Many whites (and some minority group members) have low expectations regarding the educational potential of blacks and Hispanics. This presents a

serious obstacle to efforts to increase the resources invested by society to improve the educational and other conditions of minorities.

8. The collective effort should maximize institutional redundancy. In order to increase the probability of achieving an important objective, it is desirable to have duplicate or backup capacity so that in the event a primary system fails, the secondary system is available to do the job. Two-parent families, for example, represent a form of within-institution child-rearing redundancy. There also can be between-institution redundancy, as when both schools and parents are in a position to support the education of children.

9. The collective effort should maximize institutional complementarity. Achieving an important objective often requires that essential tasks be undertaken by different parties or institutions. In a two-parent family, for example, one parent may have strong math skills that can be brought to bear in support of their children's education, and the other parent may have strong language arts skills. This is a form of within-institution complementarity. An example of between-institution complementarity is the use of the school system as a primary means of educating children and the use of the health care system as a primary means of maintaining children's health.

The first seven of these principles are minority specific; the final two are generic. Together, they offer not a blueprint but qualitative guidance for the development of an effective strategy to promote minority educational advancement; they can help us to identify combinations of approaches that seem more plausible than others.[2] In the next section, I offer a mix of plausible recommendations for action.

RECOMMENDATIONS FOR ACCELERATING THE EDUCATIONAL
ADVANCEMENT OF MINORITIES

The sets of recommendations discussed below focus, respectively, on mobilizing society's resources on behalf of the most economically disadvantaged minority youngsters, addressing the needs of middle-class minority children and youth and those of high-achieving minority students, establishing a more substantial research and development effort directed at minority-related education issues; and establishing more sophisticated information systems for monitoring minority educational progress. Most of these proposals have been advanced by others over the years. What distinctive aspects there are lie mainly in the mix of actions and in the size and scope of the effort suggested. The separate proposals for poor and middle-class minority group segments reflect an effort to respond to the intergenerational nature of group advancement.

Recommendation 1: Pursue "Social Policy Mobilization" to Promote the Educational Advancement of the Minority Poor

Because the poverty rate among minority families continues to be very high and the most disadvantaged families tend to have several acute education-rele-

2. Donald T. Campbell, "Can We Be Scientific in Applied Social Science?" *Evaluation Studies Review Annual* 9 (1984): 28.

vant resource problems, I believe that the educational advancement of poor minority youngsters requires the aggressive use of a broad range of government policies to address their economic, social, health, and schooling needs. Yet a broad-based social policy effort must contend with resource constraints. The challenge is to try to identify an affordable mix of actions that will increase family and school resources in ways that improve their combined educational effectiveness for poor children. Priority should be given to policies that expand the family resources available to poor youngsters. Only if this is done can the nation expect increases in school resources to pay large dividends.

Increasing the Financial and Health Capital Available to the Poor   From the standpoint of quickly increasing family resources, it is probably easiest to provide poor families with more financial capital; government can literally send checks to families (if it has adequate support from the public to do so).

It is somewhat more difficult to increase their health capital rapidly. Ironically, improvement is possible in part because not all Americans are covered by health insurance. If low-cost coverage were extended to poor families, many more poor parents would see to it that their children got good health care.[3]

The technical ease with which financial capital can be distributed to individuals and families has been a major reason that governments in many industrial societies have frequently resorted to financial investment strategies to increase the amount of resources the poor possess. These strategies have often been successful in reducing poverty, but usually only when the financial capital transfers have been large.

It is important to recognize, moreover, that it has not been possible for governments to meet all the needs of poor families for living productive lives simply through financial transfer programs. Investments in such key institutions as the health care and education systems have also been crucial. Variations in the effectiveness with which governments have pursued improvements in these areas help explain why some societies have succeeded more than others in addressing the problem of poverty.

3. It is likely to be very hard to engineer a large, rapid increase in the stock of human capital that many poor families possess. Most parents who have accumulated a great deal of human capital did so primarily by attending school for many years and by having a reasonable amount of human capital available to them from their parents. Sending large numbers of extremely undereducated adults with family responsibilities back to school would be very expensive and time consuming; many would probably need several years of high-quality education to reach the desired skill levels. It is also likely to be difficult to increase rapidly the stock of social capital of many poor families because ways would have to be found to help the parents establish strong work and friendship networks with other individuals (or families) who have large amounts of human capital or who identify with mainstream institutions. Adding to the poor minority families' social capital is made even more complex by the extensive racial/ethnic segregation in the United States, which contributes to the economic and social isolation of some minorities, especially African Americans (Douglas S. Massey and Mitchell L. Eggers, "The Ecology of Inequality: Minorities and the Concentration of Poverty, 1970–1980," *American Journal of Sociology* 95 [March 1990]: 1170–84). It is probably most difficult to generate large, rapid increases in the stock of polity capital available to minorities, for attitudes and beliefs about racial/ethnic groups tend to be heavily shaped by history and can be very hard to change. Ironically, the paucity of polity capital available to minorities can make it difficult for government to mount efforts designed to help minorities accumulate the other types of education-relevant capital.

Such disparities can be seen by examining how the United States has used financial transfer and health care/nutrition strategies to meet the needs of two population segments that have consistently been among the most vulnerable to poverty in industrial societies: the elderly and children. Over the past several decades, the responses of government to the needs of these two groups have been very different. As a result, by the late 1980s, the poverty rate for the elderly was about 12 percent, while it was about 20 percent for children.[4]

The elderly have benefited from a relatively generous combination of government social insurance and means-tested income transfer programs. Social Security and Medicare are social insurance programs available to most of the elderly because they or their spouses were employed during most of their working years. Supplementary Security Income, Medicaid, and food stamps are means-tested programs available to those elderly who have few financial resources of their own and are not eligible for Social Security or Medicare. Although many elderly persons have sizable savings or private pensions or both, the majority relies on one or more government programs to avoid poverty.[5] The value of these programs is demonstrated by the fact that as recently as the mid-1960s over 28 percent of those aged sixty-five or older were poor.[6]

In contrast to the elderly, children in the United States can look to government primarily for Medicare, food stamps, and Aid to Families with Dependent Children (AFDC)—all means-tested income transfer programs—to alleviate poverty (although some are eligible for social insurance programs). AFDC has long been the core government program concerned with child poverty, providing cash income to qualifying poor families with children on an ongoing basis. However, AFDC benefits in most states are much too low to lift a family with no other income above the poverty line. For example, the median monthly AFDC payment for a three-person family in mid-1990 was $367 per month, or $4,404 per year—less than half of the $10,560 annual income defined as the poverty line for a family of three in 1990. Even with the addition of food stamps, such a family would have had an income less than three-quarters of the poverty line that year.[7]

In addition, AFDC was designed originally to meet the income needs of children who were members of very low income families with a single mother (usually a widow) or a disabled father. It was not designed to provide ongoing income support to two-parent families with a father who was able to work or for working-poor families, in which one or both parents held a low-wage job. As a

4. Mary Jo Bane and David T. Ellwood, "One Fifth of the Nation's Children: Why Are They Poor?" *Science*, 8 September 1989, p. 1047.

5. About one-third of retirees receive income from a private pension. Ford Foundation Project on Social Welfare and the American Future, *The Common Good: Social Welfare and the American Future* (New York: Ford Foundation, 1989), p. 70.

6. Sheldon H. Danziger, Robert H. Haveman, and Robert Plotnick, "Antipoverty Policy: Effects on the Poor and the Nonpoor," in *Fighting Poverty: What Works and What Doesn't*, Sheldon H. Danziger and Daniel H. Weinberg, eds. (Cambridge: Harvard University Press, 1986), p. 56.

7. Children's Defense Fund, *The State of America's Children 1991* (Washington, D.C.: Children's Defense Fund, 1991), pp. 22, 26.

result of the rapid increase in single-parent families headed by females, AFDC has become a program that de facto targets poor, female-headed families with children in which the mother is unemployed.[8] Modifications of AFDC guidelines as a result of the Family Support Act of 1988 broaden the circumstances under which two-parent poor families can be eligible for AFDC benefits, but the basic female-headed family profile of AFDC recipients is expected to change little in the next few years.[9]

By the late 1980s, the inability of government financial support programs to reduce poverty among children had become abundantly clear. Up to half of all poor children were living in two-parent homes, in part because two million adults were working full-time at jobs that did not pay enough to keep a family above the poverty line. But given the rules of AFDC, most of these children could not be reached by AFDC.[10]

Further, many working-poor families are neither covered by private health insurance nor eligible for Medicaid, the federal health insurance program for the poor. Of the eight million children who did not have health insurance in the early 1990s, most were from low-income families.[11]

The (posttransfer) child poverty rate in America is not only much higher than the rate among the elderly, but also higher than the rate among children in many other industrialized nations. In some countries (Germany and Switzerland, for instance), the lower posttransfer child poverty rate might reflect their much lower pretransfer rate. However, that does not explain why the posttransfer child poverty rate in Canada is much lower than that of United States; pretransfer rates in the two countries have been similar over time.[12]

How have Canada and other industrialized nations been able to achieve lower posttransfer child poverty rates? The answer is straightfoward: by providing more extensive financial, health, and (sometimes) human-capital transfer programs to poor and nonpoor families with children. The benefits available through specific programs are often higher in these countries; they also typically represent a combination of social insurance and means-tested income programs that are much more generous than those in the United States.

To put the answer slightly differently, in a number of other technological/indus-

8. Judith M. Gueron, *Reforming Welfare with Work* (New York: Ford Foundation, 1987), pp. 5–6.

9. See Mark Rom, "The Family Support Act of 1988: Federalism, Developmental Policy, and Welfare Reform," *Journal of Federalism* 19 (Summer 1989): 69–71; Children's Defense Fund, *The State of America's Children 1991*, p. 31.

10. Bane and Ellwood, "One Fifth of the Nation's Children," p. 1049; Ford Foundation Project, *The Common Good*, p. 54. Children's Defense Fund, *The State of America's Children 1991*, p. 27.

11. National Commission on Children, *Beyond Rhetoric: A New American Agenda for Children and Families* (Washington, D.C.: U.S. Government Printing Office, 1991), p. 137. The number may be even higher; see Ellen Flax, "Business Implored to Ensure Health Care for Children," *Education Week*, 6 May 1992, p. 8.

12. Timothy Smeeding, Barbara Boyle Torrey, and Martin Rein, "Patterns of Income and Poverty: The Economic Status of Children and the Elderly in Eight Countries," in John L. Palmer, Timothy Smeeding, and Barbara Boyle Torrey, eds., *The Vulnerable: America's Young and Old in the Industrial World* (Washington, D.C.: Urban Institute Press, 1988), pp. 91–99, 113. Rebecca M. Blank, "Testimony before the Joint Economic Committee," paper delivered at the Hearings on the Current State of Poverty in the U.S., 25 July 1991, pp. 8–12.

trial societies, social policy was mobilized long ago to minimize poverty among children and to provide support systems that are universally available to poor and nonpoor families alike. Moreover, these systems are increasingly recognized as being crucial for managing stable family life in societies with high levels of work force participation among both mothers and fathers and growing numbers of single-parent families. France's expansive, highly subsidized child care/early childhood education system and Canada's government-funded health care system are examples of universal systems that are extremely valuable to virtually all families with children in these nations.[13]

Accessible high-quality, low-cost health care and child care are only two of the pressing needs of poor families in the United States (and many middle-class families as well). Many poor families need additional income to pay for life's essentials—housing, for example. But policymakers have been reluctant to expand the benefits of AFDC, partly for fear of undermining the work ethic of adult recipients.[14]

Some industrialized nations have sidestepped the issue of work incentives by developing a system of financial allowances for families with children.[15] The Canadian approach is instructive. In addition to having national health insurance for all citizens and an AFDC-like program that provides somewhat higher benefits on average to poor families than is the case in the United States, Canada has two income-transfer programs directed specifically at families with children: a refundable tax credit program for all low-income families, regardless of whether the parents are employed; and a family allowance program under which all families with children regardless of income level receive checks from the government. To a poor family with two children, the combined value of these programs is currently about $1,500 per year.[16] For a working-poor family in Canada with earnings in the $8,000–$12,000 range, the combination of national health insurance and the $1,500 makes a vital difference in the ability of parents to meet their children's needs.

Currently, the United States does have a refundable tax credit program—the Earned Income Tax Credit—but it is limited to low-income working parents.[17]

13. See Gail Richardson and Elisabeth Marx, *A Welcome for Every Child, How France Achieves Quality in Child Care: Practical Ideas for the United States* (New York: French-American Foundation, 1989); and Julie Kosterlitz, "Taking Care of Canada," *National Journal,* 15 July 1989, pp. 1792–97.

14. See Leslie Lenkowsky, *Politics, Economics, and Welfare Reform: The Failure of the Negative Income Tax in Britain and the United States* (Lanham, Md.: American Enterprise Institute/University Press of America, 1986), pp. 83–114; Frank P. Stafford, "Income-Maintenance Policy and the Work Effort: Learning from Experiments and Labor-Market Studies," in Jerry A. Hausman and David A. Wise, eds., *Social Experimentation* (Chicago: University of Chicago Press, 1985), pp. 95–143.

15. See Sheila B. Kamerman and Alfred J. Kahn, "What Europe Does for Single-Parent Families," *The Public Interest* 93 (Fall 1988): 70–86; and Kamerman and Kahn, "Notes on Policy Practice: Income Transfers and Mother-Only Families in Eight Countries," *Social Service Review* 57 (September 1983): 448–64.

16. Blank, "Testimony before the Joint Economic Committee," p. 11.

17. See Steven D. Gold, "Replacing an Impossible Dream," *State Legislatures* (February 1991): 24; National Commission on Children, *Beyond Rhetoric*, pp. 87–89.

It does not yet have a family allowance program or a national health insurance strategy that makes quality health care available to all Americans. If the nation is serious about meeting the needs of poor children, it must devise an American variation on the social policy mobilization that Canada and several other industrialized nations have undertaken. By addressing the health insurance problems of the poor, especially the working poor, and increasing significantly direct financial support for families with children, with emphasis on the poor (regardless of work force status), the nation can expand the effectiveness range of working-poor families and support greater intergenerational educational advancement.

But even these changes will be insufficient for the apparently growing number of extremely disadvantaged minority children. For example, many of these children are not simply victims of poverty but also have preventable health problems (lead poisoning, prenatal exposure to drugs, child abuse) that themselves can make it difficult to succeed in school. The developing of effective responses to these problems entails far more than increasing the availability of affordable health insurance. Often both preventive and remedial health care services must be brought to the poor via community health centers and other vehicles that can work on a proactive as well as a reactive basis. Home visitations may be required in many cases to ensure that parents and children receive the necessary services. The knowledge base in this area is relatively large, and effective government programs directed at some of these problems already exist—for example, the Special Supplemental Food Program for Women, Infants, and Children (WIC), which provides poor pregnant women and their young children with health screening, advice on nutrition, and food supplements.[18] Thus, an important question in this area is, What mix of programs has the most promise in terms of broad impact and cost-effectiveness?

It is easiest to recommend expansion of such proven programs as WIC, which do not require unusually large additional financial outlays. Yet an all-out attack on several of the most important education-relevant health problems will require a substantial investment, at least initially. For example, a major effort directed at rapidly removing or neutralizing the sources of lead poisoning for the urban poor would be costly.[19] Much more will have to be done for parents who have substance abuse problems.

18. On the community health center experience of the federal government, see Paul Starr, "Health Care for the Poor: The Past Twenty Years," in Danziger and Weinberg, eds., *Fighting Poverty* (Cambridge: Harvard University Press, 1986), pp. 112–13. On making health clinics more readily available to poor families, see Ernest L. Boyer, *Ready to Learn: A Mandate for the Nation* (Princeton, N.J.: Carnegie Foundation for the Advancement of Teaching/Princeton University Press, 1991), pp. 24–31. On home visitations in the delivery of health and educational services, see David A. Hamburg, *A Decent Start: Promoting Healthy Child Development in the First Three Years of Life* (New York: Carnegie Corporation of New York, 1990), pp. 11–12; and Lisbeth B. Schorr with Daniel Schorr, *Within Our Reach: Breaking the Cycle of Disadvantage* (New York: Anchor Press, 1988), pp. 64–214. On the value of WIC, see Starr, "Health Care for the Poor," p. 120; and Ford Foundation Project, *The Common Good,* pp. 15–16.

19. An estimate of the cost of expanding WIC to reach most women and small children who could benefit from it is $1.25 billion per year. See Committee for Economic Development, *The Unfinished Agenda: A New Vision for Child Development and Education* (New York: Committee for Economic

It may be necessary to offer many of the parents who attend these programs a genuine prospect of becoming productive citizens, including the opportunity to work. As long as their opportunity structure remains extremely negative, the value of participation in high-quality treatment programs for many individuals will be marginal. This leads to the potentially expensive option of a large guaranteed employment program, a topic that I shall address after discussing strategies for improving schools.

Increasing the School Resources and Educational/Child Care Systems Available to the Disadvantaged   Assuming that the nation takes separate non-school-based actions to increase the financial and health capital available to poor minority families, what steps are most likely to produce substantial increases in the educational system's capacity to address the human-capital and social-capital development needs of disadvantaged minority children? A good school is a true learning community—a group of teachers, parents, and children working together to meet the educational needs of the youngsters. If the school is to have a chance of becoming a learning community for disadvantaged children and youth, it must have a small student enrollment, the student and teacher populations must be stable, and the students must be physically healthy. It has become less and less likely that all (or even one) of these conditions will exist in urban schools with heavily poor and minority student populations. Consequently, I regard them as the minimum conditions for educational reform in urban America.

With regard to the problem of school size, the average enrollment in the 816 public high schools studied by James S. Coleman and Thomas Hoffer in the 1980s was 1,381 students. Moreover, the average size of public high schools in urban areas tends to be even larger than this sample suggests. For instance, public high schools in New York City have typically had enrollments in the 2,000–5,000 student range, and public elementary schools often have enrollments of 800–1,000 students.[20]

One proponent of small schools as an effective school reform strategy is Deborah Meier, founder of the Central Park East Elementary School (CPEES) and the Central Park East Secondary School (CPESS) in District 4 in East Harlem in New York City. Enrollment in CPEES is about 250 students, while enrollment in CPESS is about 450.[21] John Goodlad also recommends that secondary schools

Development, 1991), p. 14. About 3.8 million residences with children have serious lead paint health hazards. Annual testing of 500,000 homes and remediation of 190,000 would cost $1.9–$2.4 billion. Philip J. Hilts, "U.S. Opens a Drive to Wipe Out Lead Poisoning among Children," *New York Times*, 20 December, 1990, pp. A1, B20.

20. James S. Coleman and Thomas Hoffer, *Public and Private High Schools: The Impact of Communities* (New York: Basic Books, 1987), p. 38. Joan Griffin McCabe and Diana Oxley, *Making Big High Schools Smaller: A Review of the Implementation of the House Plan in New York City's Most Troubled High Schools* (New York: The Public Education Association, 1989), p. 1. The high school in New York City with the largest enrollment in the early 1990s had 4,660 students. See Joseph Berger, "Cutting the Big High School Down to Size," *New York Times*, 7 August 1992, p. B3.

21. Deborah W. Meier, "Choice Can Save Public Education," *The Nation*, 4 March 1991, pp. 253, 266, 268, 270–71. Author's conversation with Deborah Meier, 18 November 1991.

have enrollments of 600–800 students.[22] Interestingly, the Catholic high schools included in the Coleman and Hoffer study had an average enrollment of 797 students, and the other private schools in their sample had an average enrollment of 533.[23] Among the things that parents usually purchase when they send their children to a private school is small size.

It is difficult for educators to influence directly either low student-mobility rates between schools or good student health. These conditions must be addressed through other means, including the direct investment of financial and health capital in poor families. Educators do have considerable control over school size, although they face some important obstacles even in this area. One is that many school buildings were designed to accommodate a large number of students, so that a move toward small schools will require that more than one school be housed in a single building (the "schools within schools" model). This has been the approach used in District 4 to establish a large number of small elementary and middle schools. It is also part of a plan in the New York City public school system to create 30 new small high schools (each with 300–1,000 students) in the next few years.[24]

A variation on the school-within-school theme is the house system, in which students take all or some of their courses with the same group of students under the guidance of a team of teachers. This approach has been used in large high schools in a number of cities in recent years.[25] The house system can be applied at the elementary school level by assigning groups of students to a single teacher or to a team of teachers for more than one year.

The idea of having a group of students stay with a team of teachers for several years leads to the fact that the student stability/mobility issue has both horizontal and vertical dimensions. When students move from school to school, they are horizontally mobile. When they change teachers each year within the same school, they are vertically mobile. Athough educators have little influence on horizontal mobility rates, they have a great deal of control over vertical ones. Low vertical and horizontal mobility rates are crucial in the creation of an effective learning community for disadvantaged minority children. Teachers need time to come to know the students and their parents. Yet under standard arrangements, educators forfeit much of the benefit that can accrue from a horizontally stable student population because of the built-in vertical mobility within the school. For minority students, many of whom are from cultures that are quite different from the culture of the school and have few social networks

22. John I. Goodlad, *A Place Called School: Prospects for the Future* (New York: McGraw-Hill, 1984), p. 330.

23. Coleman and Hoffer, *Public and Private High Schools*, p. 37.

24. Meier, "Choice Can Save Public Education," pp. 266, 268; Joseph Berger, "Plan Seeks Small Schools with Themes," *New York Times*, 6 August 1992, pp. B1, B3. Nevertheless, there are opportunities to create small school buildings in a cost-effective fashion via new construction and renovation. See Diane Dolinsky, *Small Schools and Savings: Affordable New Construction, Renovation and Remodeling* (New York: Public Education Association, 1992); and Susan E. Heinbuch, *Small Schools' Operating Costs: Reversing Assumptions about Economies of Scale* (New York: Public Education Association, 1992).

25. McCabe and Oxley, *Making Big High Schools Smaller*, p. 5.

that include people from the mainstream of society, the cost of vertical mobility may be very high.

In contrast, if an elementary school team consists of three teachers, for example, the probability that a student (and parent) will have at least one good relationship with a teacher at any given time is three times higher than in a system of vertical mobility. If the team works well together, the collegial process may enable the teachers to help each other raise their overall effectiveness with students and parents. In general, this approach can be expected to offer redundancy and complementarity in teacher-pupil and teacher-parent relationships.

This vertical stability approach should be heavily emphasized in attempts to improve schools for extremely disadvantaged children, especially at the elementary school level, because academic achievement patterns are established in the early grades.[26]

The establishing of small schools characterized by team-teaching is not inherently costly. However, two other important changes that should be made, increasing the number of teachers and the length of the educational year in schools with high percentages of poor minority children, would carry a considerable price tag

For many years to come, poor minority children will collectively have some important educational needs that are different in kind or degree from those of middle-class white children. Some of these needs are related to cultural differences: having a primary language other than English, for example. Others are in the area of learning disabilities, especially those associated with preventable health problems.[27] In inner city schools in high poverty neighborhoods, we often find that several children in a class have at least one preventable health condition that makes learning difficult for them. Lowering the pupil/teacher ratio is one way to address this situation in the short to medium term. (Over the long term, U.S. society must find ways to reduce the incidence of preventable learning problems among children.)[28] Although it is not clear how pervasive this problem will be in the years ahead or what an appropriate pupil/teacher ratio is for these circumstances, one should assume that a great many classrooms and schools serving poor minority youngsters in the 1990s could usefully be "overstaffed."[29]

26. Some schools in Germany have adopted a version of this approach for a cultural minority in that country—Turkish children. Groups of students are kept with teams of teachers from the fifth grade through the end of secondary school (six years). See Debra Viadero, "L.A. School Embraces a West German Import," *Education Week*, 1 November 1989, pp. 1, 10; Committee for Economic Development, *The Unfinished Agenda*, p. 54. John Goodlad specifically recommended a vertical stability/team teaching approach for the primary grades in *A Place Called School*. Goodlad, *A Place Called School*, p. 329.

27. Many white children, including some who are middle class, also have learning problems grounded in preventable health conditions. Linda J. Stevens and Marianne Price, "Meeting the Challenge of Educating Children at Risk," *Phi Delta Kappan* 74 (September 1992): 19.

28. The businessman and philanthropist Irving B. Harris has pressed for preventive strategies, beginning with prenatal care, to reduce the number of children who have health-related and other "readiness" problems. Irving B. Harris, "Education—Does It Make Any Difference When You Start?," speech delivered to the Forum of the City Club of Cleveland, 15 December 1989.

29. Students with serious learning problems are likely to be assigned to special education classes, while those with small problems tend to remain in regular classrooms. There probably will be a

The general case for more favorable pupil/teacher ratios for minority students has been difficult to make because of the mixed results of studies of the relationship between pupil/teacher ratios and academic performance. However, large-scale initiatives in Indiana and Tennessee in the 1980s have yielded evidence that pupil/teacher ratios in the 13 : 1 to 18 : 1 range in the primary grades are associated with significant improvements in students' academic performance. The improvements were found to be especially notable for minority students.[30]

Turning to the question of an extended school year, I want to reiterate that a sizable portion of the academic achievement gap that emerges between middle class and poor children by the end of the primary grades develops when school is not in session—that is, in the summer months. This suggests that a year-round educational strategy for disadvantaged children could generate substantial academic performance benefits for these youngsters.

If this road is taken, it will require more than offering a basic-skills-oriented summer school to disadvantaged first and second graders. The challenge will be to develop an integrated set of school and non-school-based experiences that extend over a much longer period of time than the current 180-day school year. The most disadvantaged children may need to experience an array of intellectual and social development opportunities equivalent to the combined home and school experiences of advantaged children during the primary school years.[31]

Other changes that appear to have merit for improving the educational opportunities of disadvantaged minority children include developing more culturally attuned curricula and associated pedagogical strategies for minorities, increasing the supply of bilingual teachers, introducing school-based management, and introducing some form of public school choice. All these changes will take time to make.

Because the cultural-difference knowledge base is modest in size, there currently is not a large inventory of proven educational strategies in this area. Over the next decade or two, this situation could be improved considerably through an appropriate research and development effort.[32] (This will be discussed further in Recommendation 3.)

---

need for more special education teachers as well as for more regular teachers (to reduce class size) in schools serving large numbers/proportions of disadvantaged youngsters.

30. M. Edith Rasell and Eileen Appelbaum, *Investment in Learning: An Assessment of the Economic Return* (Washington, D.C.: Investment 21, 1992), p. 26; Jennifer McGiverin, David Gilman, and Chris Tillitski, "A Meta-Analysis of the Relation between Class Size and Achievement," *The Elementary School Journal* 90 (September 1989): 47–56.

31. Three interdenominational elementary schools with 240-day school years recently opened in Detroit for disadvantaged students. Mark Walsh, "Motor City Miracle: 3 Interfaith Schools Open Doors," *Education Week*, 4 September 1991, pp. 1, 24–25.

32. It is increasingly recognized that minority and/or disadvantaged youngsters must have opportunities to develop "higher order thinking skills," not simply basic skills. On some emerging approaches in this area, see Barbara Means, Carol Chelemer, and Michael S. Knapp, eds., *Teaching Advanced Skills to At-Risk Students: Views from Research and Practice* (San Francisco: Jossey-Bass, 1991).

Expanding the supply of bilingual teachers, potentially a move of great value, has been especially slow and difficult. The situation is complicated by the large shortage of minority high school graduates who are academically well prepared for college. Further, few majority high school graduates with an interest in teaching are pursuing extensive second language studies at the college level. For these and other reasons, the percentage of aspiring teachers, regardless of race/ethnicity, who are proficient in more than one language remains very small—about 3 percent, according to a recent sample of teacher education majors engaged in student teaching.[33] The nation needs a national strategy (and associated financial investment) for increasing the supply of bilingual teachers that takes these realities into account. Unfortunately, the immediate prospects for establishing one seem slim.[34]

Highly touted as a key ingredient in school restructuring, school-based management is difficult to implement.[35] Although the basic idea is simple enough—principals and teachers are given a great deal of control over decisions pertaining to curriculum and instruction—it entails the bureaucratically daunting task of changing the way in which state education departments and the central offices of school systems regulate the schools. It also requires that principals, teachers, and (often) parents learn to work together in a much more collegial fashion than they do now. The attractiveness of school-based management is that it offers a potential means for schools to become more flexible and much more responsive to instructional and other needs of students. It is hard to imagine, however, that it can be made to work in schools with large student enrollments, geographically mobile student populations, or high turnover rates among teachers and administrators. Still, should these problems be brought under control, the possibilities for school-based management become much more interesting, especially if a vertical-stability/team-teaching strategy is also widely adopted. The capacity of the teams of teachers to make productive decisions for the children could be enhanced by the expanded educational authority of the building-level professionals.

School choice is one of the most controversial proposals in the current period of educational reform.[36] The notion that parents and children should be able to

33. About 92 percent of this 1989 sample also was white. Mark S. Lewis, "AACTE RATE Study Finds Enrollment Increase," *American Association of Colleges for Teacher Education Briefs* 11 (April 1990): 1.

34. Some efforts are being made to change this situation. For several years, the Tomas Rivera Center, a policy organization concerned with Latino issues in the Southwest, has had a substantial initiative concerned with increasing the number of Hispanic teachers. See Raymond E. Castro and Yolanda Rodriquez Ingle, eds., *Reshaping Teacher Education in the Southwest, A Forum: A Response to the Needs of Latino Students and Teachers* (Claremont, Calif.: Tomas Rivera Center, 1993).

35. See Diana W. Rigden, *School Restructuring: Designing Schools for Better Student Learning* (New York: Council for Aid to Education, 1990); William H. Clune and Paula A. White, *School-Based Management: Institutional Variation, Implementation, and Issues for Further Research* (New Brunswick, N.J.: Center for Policy Research in Education, 1988).

36. Carol Steinbach and Neal R. Pierce, "Multiple Choice," *National Journal*, 1 July 1989, pp. 1692–95; John E. Chubb and Terry M. Moe, *Politics, Markets, and America's Schools* (Washington, D.C.: Brookings Institution, 1990); Ray Marshall and Marc Tucker, *Thinking for a Living: Education and the Wealth of Nations* (New York: Basic Books, 1992), pp. 128–42; Peter W. Cookson, Jr., *School Choice: The Struggle for the Soul of American Education* (New Haven: Yale University Press, 1994).

choose their schools is appealing from the perspective of making it easier for schools to tailor their programs to the interests and needs of specific groups of children. Still, there is reason to worry that choice is being sold as an alternative to more important, more costly approaches. For large schools serving geographically mobile disadvantaged youngsters, it is hard to see how choice alone offers much value; many of these students would be unable to exercise meaningful choice because of their transitory status. Those with serious learning problems would probably have difficulty succeeding because their school lacks sufficient resources to meet their needs, regardless of whether there was a choice plan. It also is hard to see how choice would help if curriculum and instruction continued to be regulated at the district or state level. School-based management in some form seems to be a precondition for choice to be worth pursuing.

Nevertheless, in a situation in which disadvantaged minority youngsters are routinely able to attend the same (small) schools for many years, schools in which building-level educators have substantial decision-making authority and in which the resources available to schools are directly related to the needs of their student bodies, public school choice could be useful. Some public schools could specialize in ways designed to be responsive to specific student aspirations, important student attributes, or family preferences.[37] For example, children from an immigrant group that represents a small language minority in a relatively large community might be able to attend a bilingual school designed with their specific language needs in mind. Schools that take a particular approach to multicultural education could be established among like-minded parents and teachers. Schools that specialize in specific learning problems might emerge, especially if more resources are made available for schools serving the poor.

Early childhood education offers one of the most important avenues for improving the academic performance of disadvantaged children.[38] Three decades of research have established that high-quality preschool programs for disadvantaged three- and four-year-olds increase their preparedness for elementary school and are associated with long-term improvements in their academic and social success.[39] But many poor children continue to be unserved by high-quality early childhood programs. For example, Head Start had sufficient

37. The modest movement toward the creation of "theme" high schools is consistent with this approach. For example, see Berger, "Plan Seeks Small Schools with Themes," pp. B1, B5.

38. There is broad agreement on the importance of early childhood education. See *Children in Need: Investment Strategies for the Educationally Disadvantaged* (New York: Committee for Economic Development, 1987), pp. 33–37; *An Imperiled Generation: Saving Urban Schools* (Princeton, N.J.: The Carnegie Foundation for the Advancement of Teaching, 1988), pp. 17–19; *Education That Works: An Action Plan for the Education of Minorities* (Cambridge: Quality for Minorities Project/Massachusetts Institute of Technology, 1990), pp. 56–57; National Commission on Children, *Beyond Rhetoric: A New American Agenda for Children and Families*, p. xxvi; and Boyer, *Ready to Learn*, p. 138.

39. David P. Weikart, *Quality Preschool Programs: A Long-Term Social Investment* (New York: Ford Foundation, 1989), pp. 2–7. Such programs, of course, cannot themselves provide disadvantaged students with the educational and related life chances of advantaged children. Ron Haskins, "Beyond Metaphor: The Efficacy of Early Childhood Education," *American Psychologist* 44 (February 1989): 274–77.

funding in the early 1990s to reach only about 30 percent of all eligible children.[40]

In spite of the obvious need to make high-quality early childhood education available to all disadvantaged youngsters as quickly as possible, providing full coverage could take years, owing in no small measure to a shortage of qualified teachers. This problem is closely linked to the fact that early childhood educators receive very low pay—much lower than public elementary and secondary school teachers—and this contributes to high staff turnover and makes it difficult to attract qualified new people to the field.[41]

Further, many existing programs, including a number operated under Head Start, are not of sufficiently high quality to provide the long-term school-performance benefits that have been demonstrated by the best model programs. In the absence of more money, this situation is unlikely to change. In the late 1980s, Head Start was spending about $2,600 per child annually, even though high-quality preschool programs were estimated to cost about $5,000 per child per year at that point.[42]

The fact that the United States does not have early childhood education or child care systems that offer high-quality, affordable services to all those who need them is sobering, because 20–25 percent of the preschool-age children in America have been living in poverty at any given time, and over half of the mothers of preschool-age children in the country are now in the work force. Meanwhile the French government, for instance, has supported the creation of a preschool education system that is nearly universal for all three-, four-, and five-year-olds. About 85 percent attend free public preschool programs, which also offer low-cost before- and after-school child care services to working parents. Parents of children who are too young for preschool can avail themselves

40. See Committee for Economic Development, *The Unfinished Agenda*, pp. 36–37. Although estimates of the number of children eligible for Head Start vary and good data on eligible children who are enrolled in other early childhood programs are hard to come by, it is clear that a great many disadvantaged children were not in early childhood programs in the early 1990s. According to one estimate, only about two-fifths of the three- to five-year-olds from families with incomes of $10,000 or less were in preschool programs in the early 1990s, compared to three-quarters of those from families with incomes of $75,000 or more. See National Commission on Children, *Beyond Rhetoric: A New American Agenda for Children and Families*, pp. 187–93; National Education Goals Panel, *The National Education Goals Report 1992*, p. 267; and Boyer, *Ready to Learn*, pp. 50–51.

41. See Weikart, *Quality Preschool Programs*, p. 25; Lawrence J. Schweinhart and Jeffrey J. Koshel, *Policy Options for Preschool Programs* (Ypsilanti, Mich.: High/Scope Educational Research Foundation, 1986), pp. 19–20; and Edward Zigler and Pamela Ennis, "Child Care in America," in *Early Childhood and Family Education: Analysis and Recommendations of the Council of Chief State School Officers* (Orlando, Fla.: Harcourt Brace Jovanovich, 1990), pp. 157–59. Head Start teachers have recently been paid about $10,000 a year, one-third of the average elementary and secondary school teachers' salaries. Committee for Economic Development, *The Unfinished Agenda*, p. 37; National Center for Educational Statistics, U.S. Department of Education, *Digest of Education Statistics 1991* (Washington, D.C.: U.S. Government Printing Office, 1990), p. 81. Sharon L. Kagan, *Excellence in Early Childhood Education: Defining Characteristics and Next Decade Strategies* (Washington, D.C.: Department of Education, U.S. Government Printing Office, 1990), p. 10.

42. For a summary of research on Head Start, see Haskins, "Beyond Metaphor," pp. 277–79. On expenditures, see ibid., p. 281; and Weikart, *Quality Preschool Programs: A Long-Term Social Investment*, pp. 11–12.

of either full-day group child care centers or family day care networks. The French also have made a commitment to pay for high-quality professionals to staff both components of the system. As a result, toddlers through five-year-olds spend their days in developmentally appropriate activities, and their health care needs are also met.[43]

Further, although disadvantaged children in America often face substantial family-resource gaps vis-à-vis middle-class children from the time they are born (and even prenatally), traditional early childhood education programs do not begin to address their needs until they are three or four years old. As a result, there has been growing interest in building a family-support/early-education system in the United States that serves children (and their parents) from birth until the youngsters enter elementary school. Programs that are consistent with this approach can be differentiated in at least three important respects: whether they provide parent education services only or also include developmental education for children; whether services are offered to all families with very young children or only to a subpopulation such as the poor; and whether they are designed to serve children from infancy to age three or from infancy to age six (or even older). For example, Minnesota's Early Childhood Family Education program provides a variety of parent education services to families with children from infancy to age six. The Missouri Parents as Teachers program offers parent education services (and health screening for children) for all families with children from infancy to the age of four.[44] In Texas, Avance operates community centers in San Antonio and Houston for low-income families, most of whom are Hispanic. The core program of this innovative organization, which is for families with children under age three, provides extensive parent education and developmental day care services. But Avance also administers parent education and early childhood education programs for three- to five-year-olds and their parents, extracurricular and enrichment activities for elementary and secondary school students, ongoing parent education programs, and a program for parents to obtain their GED.[45]

Two conclusions can be drawn from French and American experiences. First, the United States should move as quickly as possible to create a true system of parent education and developmental day care/preschool education for young children. Universality must be the foundation of this emerging system. (To be universal, the system does not have to be funded or operated exclusively by government.) Second, the system should be designed so that the types and amounts of services can be varied to meet the needs of different population segments. This approach would provide a solid floor of support for all and a more substantial infrastructure of assistance for those with the greatest need.[46]

43. Richardson and Marx, A Welcome for Every Child, pp. 15, 18–19.

44. Heather B. Weiss, "Nurturing Our Young Children: Building New Partnerships among Families, Schools, and Communities," in Early Childhood and Family Education, pp. 177–208.

45. Gloria G. Rodriguez, "Early Family Interactions of Young Children: Critical Stages and Different Contexts," in Early Childhood and Family Education, pp. 103–10.

46. The Minnesota Early Childhood Family Education program is able to provide additional services for some populations, notably those that are disadvantaged. Lawrence J. Schweinhart, "How

A good example of the importance of being able to vary the assistance level based on need comes from the area of preventable health conditions among children. Research has demonstrated that intensive programs directed at developmental and health problems experienced by low-birthweight babies produce cognitive and behavioral gains for the children by three years of age; these benefits have been greatest for low-SES children.[47] If a family-support/early education system were in place, it no doubt would be much easier to make widespread use of these findings.

The strategy suggested here for supporting children and families in the early years would invest financial capital, health capital, human capital, and social capital in both the children and their parents. It would entail in-kind financial capital transfers to parents by providing free or subsidized child care; health capital investments by providing sites for the delivery of health care services and health/nutrition education to populations that are difficult to reach; human capital investments in children through developmentally appropriate preschool and child care; human capital investments in parents through regular advice on and assistance with education-relevant parenting strategies; and social capital investments in parents by enabling them to be in regular contact with educators who have well-developed skills of relevance to the mainstream of society.

Addressing Developmental Education Needs of Older Disadvantaged Students
I want to turn to the difficult problem of meeting the needs of disadvantaged students once they have begun to do poorly in school and have continued to do so over a long period of time. Over the years, educators have attempted to respond to these students' needs in a variety of ways: retention in grade, summer school, tutoring, tracking into less demanding sequences of courses, and assignment to so-called alternative high schools. These efforts suggest, first, that it is very difficult to change the educational trajectory of many at-risk students by the time they reach their teens.[48] Second, the most successful strategies are resource intensive. And third, even among the most successful strategies, it has been easier to produce increases in educational attainment than in academic achievement. For example, one of the most substantial approaches is the alternative high school for extremely at-risk teenagers and young adults, including those who have dropped out of school. These schools are typically much smaller than regular secondary schools, have lower pupil/teacher ratios,

Policymakers Can Help Deliver High-Quality Early Childhood Programs," in *Early Childhood and Family Education*, pp. 194–95. France provides extra resources to preschools that operate in communities with many at-risk children. See Richardson and Marx, *A Welcome for Every Child*, p. 22.

47. Infant Health and Development Program, "Enhancing the Outcomes of Low-Birth-Weight, Premature Infants: A Multisite, Randomized Trial," *Journal of the American Medical Association* 263 (13 June 1990): 3035–42.

48. James M. McPartland and Robert E. Slavin, *Increasing Achievement of At-Risk Students at Each Grade Level* (Washington, D.C.: Department of Education, U.S. Government Printing Office, 1990), p. 15.

smaller classes, and more capacity to tailor curriculum and teaching strategies to the needs of the students.[49]

In the early 1980s, researchers for the Public Education Association in New York City found that the students in a number of alternative high schools accumulated more credits and had better attendance records than had been the case when they were enrolled in traditional high schools. Yet 38 percent dropped out of the alternative schools within four semesters, and even the students who were successful had difficulty earning a high school degree before reaching their twenty-first birthday. Research on some alternative schools in California has produced generally similar findings.[50]

It is not clear how much the results achieved by the better alternative high schools can be improved upon. One probably should not expect that the primary solution to this problem will be found at this stage in the education pipeline.[51] Research indicates that from a long-term perspective, most of the solution lies in reducing the number of high-school-age students who did poorly in elementary school.[52]

Nonetheless, the nation must continue to work to meet the needs of older students, including the many minority high school graduates who enroll in college despite being academically underprepared for postsecondary education.[53] Although the higher education community has made a forceful effort to address the needs of such students, the results have been disappointing in many respects. For instance, degree completion rates have generally been low. Longitudinal data for 1980 high school seniors from the High School and Beyond (HS&B) study who entered a four-year college immediately after receiving their diploma show that 61 percent of those in the top quartile on both achievement tests and family SES earned a bachelor's degree within six years, but only 13 percent of those who were in the bottom quartile on both had done so. The gradu-

49. See Gary Natriello, Edward L. McDill, Aaron M. Pallas, *Schooling Disadvantaged Children: Racing against Catastrophe* (New York: Teachers College Press, 1990), p. 116; McPartland and Slavin, *Increasing Achievement of At-Risk Students at Each Grade Level*, p. 18.

50. Eileen Foley and Peggy Crull, *Educating the At-Risk Adolescent: More Lessons from Alternative High Schools* (New York: Public Education Association, 1984), pp. 48–50; Deirdre M. Kelly, *Last Chance High: How Girls and Boys Drop In and Out of Alternative Schools* (New Haven: Yale University Press, 1993.)

51. Summer programs have also been used to address the needs of at-risk teenagers. In the Summer Training and Education Program of Public/Private Ventures, an ambitious effort, students were provided with summer jobs, basic skills instruction, and life skills instruction. Early results were positive, but long-term evaluation found that within a few years participants were not much better off than the control group. See Michael A. Bailin, "Testimony before the House of Representatives, Committee on Ways and Means, Human Resources Subcommittee," 6 March 1992, excerpted in *Youth Notes—The Monthly Newsletter of the National Youth Employment Coalition* (April 1992): pp. 1–3.

52. James M. McPartland and Robert E. Slavin recommend that every effort be made to ensure that children become successful readers the first time they are taught because research shows that those who do not master reading and other fundamental skills in the primary grades are at great risk of school failure. McPartland and Slavin, *Increasing the Achievement of At-Risk Students at Each Grade Level*, pp. 7–14, 23.

53. See Alexander W. Astin, "Educational Assessment and Educational Equity," *American Journal of Education* 98 (August 1990): pp. 458–78.

ation rates of African Americans and Latinos, who were overrepresented in the latter segment, were 24 percent and 20 percent, respectively. (They were 44 percent and 42 percent for whites and Asians.)[54] These data are in line with a body of research indicating that, as a result of having access to developmental courses and programs, many academically underprepared students are able to improve their GPAs somewhat and to increase their short-term persistence rates but do not reach the overall academic performance levels typical of regularly admitted students.[55]

On the positive side, there is evidence that under favorable circumstances the higher education community can help a number of academically underprepared students succeed in college. Mount St. Mary's College in Los Angeles (an independent Catholic college for women) is an instructive success story for seriously underprepared students, many of whom are minority. Mount St. Mary's has two campuses, one offering a bachelor's degree program and the other an associate's degree/two-year transfer program. Freshmen in the baccalaureate program are generally in the top quartile of the college-bound population (as measured by SAT and ACT scores), while some of those at the two-year campus are admitted under an alternative-access program for individuals who have not done well in high school. (The combined SAT score average for the underprepared students has been about 660 in recent years.) Yet 68 percent of the alternative-access students earn an associate's degree or transfer to a four-year program.[56]

Xavier University of Louisiana (a private, historically black institution also of Catholic affiliation) has been successful in preparing moderately to substantially underprepared blacks for careers in pharmacy. About 40 percent of Xavier's prepharmacy students who score 12–17 on the ACT (648–811 on the SAT) do well enough academically at Xavier to gain acceptance to a school of pharmacy. However, this is only half of the 80 percent acceptance rate of Xavier students who score 24 or more on the ACT (1033 or more on the SAT).[57] What accounts for the success of these two schools with underprepared students? One important factor is that each is a liberal-arts-based institution in the one thousand to three thousand student range. Both have a history of high-quality teaching and excel-

54. Oscar F. Porter, *Undergraduate Completion and Persistence at Four-Year Colleges and Universities: Completers, Persisters, Stopouts, and Dropouts* (Washington, D.C.: National Institute of Independent Colleges and Universities, 1989), pp. 10–12, 26–27. HS&B data show similar completion rate patterns at community colleges for associate degrees. W. Norton Grubb, "The Decline of Community College Transfer Rates: Evidence from National Longitudinal Surveys," *Journal of Higher Education* 62 (March/April 1991): 218–19.

55. See Hunter R. Boylan and Barbara S. Bonham, "The Impact of Developmental Education Programs," *Review of Research in Developmental Education* 9 (5, 1992): 1–3; James A. Kulik and Chen-Lin C. Kulik, *Developmental Instruction: An Analysis of the Research*, Research Report No. 1 (Boone, N.C.: National Center for Developmental Education, Appalachian State University, 1991).

56. Mariette T. Sawchuk, *Access and Persistence: An Educational Program Model* (Los Angeles: Mount St. Mary's College/Prism Publishing, n.d.): pp. 4–5.

57. Very few of those with an ACT score of 11 or less do well enough academically to be admitted to a school of pharmacy. Marcellus Grace et al., "Assessment of the Ability of a Prepharmacy Program to Serve Black Americans," *Journal of the NPhA* (January 1989): 23–29.

lent campus atmospheres. Interestingly, over a period of many years, a group of faculty in the sciences at Xavier has developed innovative curricula and teaching strategies explicitly designed to meet the developmental needs of their students.[58] Both institutions have been able to invest a substantial amount of resources in each student. For instance, at Mount St. Mary's the average class size is nineteen students. And, importantly, the underprepared students who attend these institutions are not representative of the academically underprepared student population in the United States at large. At Mount St. Mary's, admission to the alternative-access program "is based on an interview during which the student's goals, maturity, and potential for college work are assessed." Unlike many urban campuses, Mount St. Mary's does not serve a mostly underprepared, low-income population on an open-enrollment basis.[59]

These experiences suggest that some underprepared students can make considerably more academic progress than would currently be predicted, if well-resourced learning environments are available and the students enroll in institutions that are a good match for their needs. Because these conditions may be increasingly difficult to meet at many colleges and universities, especially in the resource-constrained 1990s, they deserve a great deal more attention from researchers and policymakers. (I shall return to the needs of these students in Recommendation 3.)

Increasing Social Capital and Polity Capital for Chronically Unemployed Parents
A question that was briefly mentioned earlier is whether government should develop a major jobs program for chronically unemployed people, especially those with few skills. In a Panglossian world, the supply of (adequately paying) jobs would always equal demand, regardless of the number of people needing work or their skills profile. This is not a balance, however, that many industrialized nations have been able to achieve, at least for long periods of time. In fact, an insufficient supply of adequately paying low-skill jobs is a growing problem in many countries. In Germany, France, Denmark, and Great Britain in 1989, the unemployment rate for 25–64-year-old adults with less than a high school degree was 10 percent or more; it was about 9 percent for this age group in the United States (7 percent for whites and 16 percent for blacks). In all these nations, the unemployment rate for those with less than a high school diploma was two to four times the rate for individuals with a college degree.[60] Recessions in the early 1990s have only worsened these unemployment problems.

58. See Mary Ann Ryan, Donald Robinson, and J. W. Carmichael, Jr., "A Piagetian-Based General Chemistry Laboratory Program for Science Majors," *Journal of Chemical Education* 57 (September 1980): 642–45.

59. Sawchuk, *Access and Persistence: An Educational Program Model*, pp. 13, 7. Open admissions policies have been very common at community colleges. See Richard C. Richardson, Jr., Elizabeth C. Fisk, and Morris A. Okun, *Literacy in the Open-Access College* (San Francisco: Jossey-Bass, 1983).

60. "Education Survey: Trying Harder," *The Economist,* 21 November 1992, p. 5; U.S. Bureau of the Census, *Statistical Abstract of the United States 1991,* 111th Edition (Washington, D.C.: Department of Commerce, U.S. Government Printing Office, 1991), p. 403.

In spite of this situation, it is not easy to recommend that government establish a large-scale jobs program because such initiatives have historically been both expensive and politically controversial.[61] Still, there are several reasons why the nation must look more closely at this option. First, because many unemployed individuals with a high school education or less have extremely low literacy levels, it is very hard for them to find employment in the private sector. African Americans and Latinos are significantly overrepresented among this segment of the unemployed population.[62] Second, one of the most important lessons of a quarter-century of experimentation with job-training programs is that it is very difficult to raise the skill levels of many of these individuals to the point that they can qualify for a job or significantly increase their earnings. Third, research also suggests that growing structural unemployment among minority-group members with few skills in the nation's central cities has contributed to their isolation and alienation (not to mention much higher levels of crime and violence). Many minority children growing up in those circumstances must overcome many obstacles in order to succeed academically. Finally, there is an emerging consensus among Americans that all able-bodied individuals, including single female parents with preschool-age children, should work. This view is consistent with the fact that most parents, both men and women, are now employed outside the home.[63]

Over the long term, the emphasis must be on economic policies that generate more good jobs and on educational and social policies that reduce the number of the working-age population with few skills. But in the meantime the nation

61. On the political conflict surrounding the Carter administration's efforts to expand public employment programs, see David Whitman, "Liberal Rhetoric and the Welfare Underclass," *Society* 21 (November/December 1983): 63–69.

62. A 1990 survey by the Educational Testing Service of the literacy skills of a national sample of individuals who were unemployed and looking for work, as well as of persons who were seeking better jobs, found the following:

1. Individuals with high literacy skills were able to avoid long periods of unemployment, hold high-level occupations, and earn high wages; the opposite was true for those with low literacy skills.

2. Some 75–80 percent of those sampled believed that their job opportunities would improve if they had stronger reading, writing, or math skills.

3. About 40–50 percent had literacy skills so poor as to make it very difficult for them to succeed in the job market. Among African Americans and Latinos, the percentages were 50–60 percent; they were 25–30 percent for whites.

4. Literacy skills were directly related to educational attainment levels.

5. However, differences in literacy scores between racial/ethnic groups were not simply due to differences in educational attainment patterns; there were also important differences in scores between members of racial/ethnic groups who had the same educational attainment level. In fact, black and Hispanic college graduates had lower average literacy scores than whites with a high school diploma, which suggests that inadequate literacy-related skills are a serious problem for a number of African Americans and Latinos who have apparently good academic credentials. The employment consequences of this finding are largely unaddressed.

See Irwin S. Kirsch, Ann Jungeblut, and Anne Campbell, *Beyond the School Doors: The Literacy Needs of Job Seekers Served by the U.S. Department of Labor* (Washington, D.C.: U.S. Department of Labor/Educational Testing Service, 1992): pp. 1–11, 70–71.

63. See Judith M. Gueron and Edward Pauly, *From Welfare to Work* (New York: Russell Sage Foundation, 1991); Jencks and Edin, "The Real Welfare Problem," *The American Prospect* 1 (Spring 1990): 42–43; Gueron, *Reforming Welfare with Work*, pp. 1–5, 13–32; and Nathan Glazer "Education and Training Programs and Poverty," in *Fighting Poverty*, pp. 169–72.

must find ways to enable low-skilled, chronically unemployed people to work, with the highest priority given to minimizing the number of custodial and non-custodial parents who are among the long-term unemployed.[64] Having a job that has been created (directly or indirectly) by government increases an individual's ties with the mainstream of society, even if the position is low-skilled. If substantial numbers of previously unemployed parents in communities with high unemployment rates secure such jobs, these new ties to the labor market could represent a large amount of social capital. They also might produce an increase in the amount of polity capital because the larger society would see increasing numbers of disadvantaged parents making contributions to their families and communities; and the disadvantaged populations would see that the larger society had made an important commitment of resources to them.

The Environment for Pursuing Social Policy Change   Although the undertaking of major social program initiatives can be highly problematic for government, recently the environment for making some of the social policy changes suggested here has become somewhat more favorable. The most visible shift has been with regard to health care. The high costs of health care and the large numbers of Americans without health insurance have made health care reform a national priority. In the fall of 1993, President Bill Clinton submitted legislation to Congress that would provide all Americans with a basic set of health care benefits. With several alternative proposals subsequently submitted by members of Congress, the national debate is focused on what the reform package should be, rather than on whether there should be reform.[65]

Less visible but profoundly important was the inclusion of a provision to expand the Earned Income Tax Credit in the tax legislation passed by Congress in August 1993. It will provide a substantial increase in after-tax income for working-poor families as it is phased in over the next few years.[66] Also of note is the early work of a group of Clinton administration officials on welfare reform. A major question for this group seems to be how to ensure that jobs are actually available for the chronically unemployed.[67]

Recommendation 2: Pursue Strategies to Improve the Educational Performance of Middle-Class Minorities and to Meet the Needs of Minority High Achievers

Although middle-class African American, Latino, and American Indian students generally do not do as well academically as middle-class white and Asian

64. For a suggested long-term strategy, see Marshall and Tucker, *Thinking for a Living*. Whether the federal government should essentially guarantee a job for all is addressed (affirmatively) in Mickey Kaus, *The End of Equality* (New York: A New Republic Book/Basic Books, 1992).

65. For example, see Edmund Faltermayer, "Health Reform: Let's Do It Right," *Fortune*, 18 October 1993, pp. 54–56.

66. John H. Cushman, Jr., "Wealthy or Not, Taxpayers Will Find Plenty of Surprises," *New York Times*, 8 August 1993, pp. A1, A24.

67. Jason DeParle, "Clinton to Weigh Payments to Spur Hiring of the Poor," *New York Times*, 28 November 1993, pp. A1, A32; Jason DeParle, "Clinton Welfare Planners Outline Big Goals Financed by Big Saving," *New York Times*, 3 December 1993, pp. A1, A26.

students, their needs, like those of high-achieving minority students, have been given relatively little attention by educators, researchers, and policymakers. Some of the research findings reviewed in previous chapters offer guidance for developing recommendations concerning these segments of the minority population:

1. Parents with little formal education and parents with a great deal of formal education tend to use significantly different education-relevant parenting strategies.

2. Parents who are the first in their families to earn a college degree tend to interact with their children in ways that reflect their college education, how they were parented by their own mothers and fathers (most of whom had much less formal education), and the socioeconomic characteristics of their friendship networks.

3. Among individuals with a college degree, a higher proportion of minorities than of whites are first-generation college graduates, which suggests that a larger proportion of the current generation of middle-class minority parents may rely on a combination of working-class and middle-class parenting strategies. Owing to housing segregation, one can infer that black and Puerto Rican first-generation college graduates are less likely than whites and Asians to have friendship networks composed primarily of members of the middle class.

4. There is reason to believe that some middle-class minority students are vulnerable to the anti-academic-achievement orientation that characterizes some poor minority youngsters facing a bleak opportunity structure.

5. Minority students are much more likely than whites to attend schools in which a high percentage of the student body is poor, and students in these schools tend to do much less well academically than students in low poverty-rate schools.

Some of the steps that need to be taken to promote the educational advancement of middle-class minorities are the same as those already recommended for the minority poor, including the creation of a universal family-support/early-education system and the restructuring of schools in a manner that emphasizes smallness, vertical stability/team-teaching, and so forth. Because the family-support/early-education system would be available to all, more first-generation middle-class minority families could easily obtain information and advice on child-rearing practices associated with the academic success of children. Regular use of family-support services also might help middle-class minority parents to become members of friendship networks supportive of the educational advancement of their children. These benefits would complement their children's regular participation in developmentally appropriate child care and preschool programs. Overall, the family-support/early-education system should help increase the number of middle-class minority children who are very well prepared for elementary school.

Elementary and secondary schools that have been restructured along the lines discussed should benefit all children but especially middle-class minority children who attend schools in which a large number of poor minority children are also enrolled. Such schools would be organized and resourced in a fashion that would make it easier for teachers to meet the needs of their students; to the degree that both poor and middle-class children are able to do better academically as a result, anti-academic peer pressure should be reduced; and the combination of greater resources and improved student results should make it possible for a much stronger academic culture to emerge in these schools. (It should be easier for teachers to maintain high expectations for their students, for students to hold high educational aspirations grounded in reality, and for parents to have confidence in the schools.)

Although some of the proposals for improving the educational success of poor minority children are also likely to benefit middle-class minority youngsters, additional steps are required. Some middle-class minority students attend schools in which the enrollment is both predominantly white and middle class, others attend largely middle-class schools with substantial minority middle-class enrollments. In both cases, such schools are often in suburban communities.[68] Additionally, a number of middle-class (and other) minority children, in both predominantly white and predominantly minority schools, are doing very well academically. The nation must consider what needs to be done for these students.

In suburban schools in which a large majority of the student population is white and middle class, few teachers and administrators are likely to know a great deal about minority education issues, and even fewer are likely to be focusing on the special academic needs of their middle-class minority students, especially since most of these youngsters do acceptable academic work (and some do superior work).[69] Suburban schools that have moved from having a predominantly white student population to one in which minorities are 25 percent or more of the students may have been largely middle class (or working class) originally, but often become quite diverse in social class as they change in racial composition.[70] In these communities, the overall minority-majority achievement gap is almost certain to become a matter of concern. If there are a great many low academic achievers, however, possibly owing to substantial contingents of poor minority children, the high achievement problem, especially among the middle class, may still get relatively little attention.

Because of the limited understanding of minority achievement issues in many suburban communities, the twin issues of the general underrepresentation of

68. See James S. Hirsch, "Mixed Results: Columbia, Md., at 25, Sees Integration Goal Sliding from Its Grasp," *Wall Street Journal*, 27 February 1992, pp. A1 and A7; David J. Dent, "The New Black Suburbs," *New York Times Magazine*, 14 June 1992, pp. 18–25; and Morton D. Winsberg, "Flight from the Ghetto: The Migration of Middle Class and Highly Educated Blacks into White Urban Neighborhoods," *American Journal of Economics and Sociology* 44 (October 1985): 411–21.

69. On the need for suburban school districts to pay more attention to their minority students, see Daniel U. Levine and Eugene E. Eubanks, "Achievement Disparities between Minority and Nonminority Students in Suburban Schools," *Journal of Negro Education* 59 (1990): 186–94.

70. In Montclair, New Jersey, a suburban community in which the minority student population has grown rapidly, there are now significant numbers of middle-class and poor minority youngsters. See Beatriz C. Clewell and Myra F. Joy, *Choice in Montclair, New Jersey* (Princeton, N.J.: Educational Testing Service, 1990).

African Americans, Latinos, and Native Americans among high academic achievers and the low academic performance of middle-class segments of these groups relative to their white and Asian peers must be brought to the attention of suburban educators in a constructive fashion.[71] One way to do so would be to establish what I have tentatively called the Suburban Minority Education Consortium (SMEC), to provide research, clearinghouse, and consulting services, with particular attention to helping educators in different schools and school districts learn from each other's experiences. Initially, SMEC might focus on the primary grades when substantial gaps in minority-majority school achievement patterns develop. Eventually, it should work at the secondary level. And expanding into the preschool arena would be appropriate, even though school districts continue to have limited educational responsibilities at this level.

It might be appropriate to establish a companion organization of Advocates for Minority High Academic Achievement (AMHAA) to play an advocacy rather than a technical assistance role. It would do so by regularly calling attention (through reports, conferences, and so forth) to the need to increase the number of high-achieving minority students. AMHAA would collect data on the number and proportion of minority and majority students from each social class who score in the top 1 percent and top 10 percent of all students nationally on such standardized tests as the SAT and GRE or the number and proportion of minority and majority bachelor's degree recipients who graduate with honors, high honors, or highest honors, by fields and selectivity of institutions.

Some non-Asian minority students who are already performing at high levels academically also may need support for their continued success. These students should be monitored during their elementary and secondary school careers so that those who get off track academically can quickly be assisted by their teachers. They should be counseled to undertake academic programs as demanding as those taken by the most academically successful white and Asian students. They should be encouraged to develop close relationships with other high-achieving students, minority and majority.[72] And they should be offered

71. Although some suburban public school systems are well informed about minority academic achievement problems, available data suggest that few have a handle on the problem. See ibid.; Susan Gross, *Participation and Performance of Women and Minorities in Mathematics, Executive Summary* (Rockville, Md.: Montgomery County Public Schools, 1988); and Levine and Eubanks, "Achievement Disparities between Minority and Nonminority Students in Suburban Schools," pp. 106–94. Moreover, there are only occasional (usually indirect) references to middle-class minority achievement issues in the news media. For one of the few, see Hirsch, "Mixed Results: Columbia, Md., at 25, Sees Integration Goal Sliding from Its Grasp," p. A7.

72. Promoting study groups for high-achieving students within a school and networks of high-achieving minority students from several schools are two approaches in this area. Signithia Fordham and John U. Ogbu found that black high school students who wanted to do well academically hide their interests from others, which makes it difficult to become part of an academically oriented group (see chapter 9). And Philip Uri Treisman found that the fact that black students at Berkeley tended to study alone while Asians tended to study in groups explained much of the divergence in grade patterns between these groups. He subsequently developed a study-group strategy for non-Asian minority students that has contributed to significant improvement in their grades. The black students in Treisman's original study were primarily from middle-class homes. See Allyn Jackson, "Minorities in Mathematics: A Focus on Excellence, Not Remediation," *American Educator* (Spring

extensive counseling designed to help them make postsecondary education decisions that are well suited to their interests and circumstances.

Addressing Higher Education Needs   Good counseling is especially important with regard to maximizing the academic success in college of both high achievers and many middle-class black, Hispanic, and Native American high school graduates. As we have seen, middle-class non-Asian minority high school graduates are generally not as well prepared academically as their white and Asian counterparts, as measured by SAT scores.[73] Although there is a tendency for the SAT and some other admissions tests to predict higher grades for black students at historically white colleges and universities (HWCUs) than they actually receive, for those attending some historically black colleges and universities (HBCUs), standardized test scores may be about as predictive of performance as they are for whites who attend HWCUs. At Xavier of Louisiana, for example, ACT scores are the best single predictor of persistence and grades for students who major in biology, chemistry, or prepharmacy.[74]

A definitive explanation for these findings is not available. According to Walter R. Allen, one possible reason is that, in addition to academic preparation, the social context and attendant interpersonal relationships experienced in college tend to shape the academic performance of African American students in higher education—and blacks are much more likely to experience a favorable social context at an HBCU. Although this interpretation is plausible, other researchers have not been able to use it to explain statistically the tendency of the SAT scores of black students to overpredict their grades at HWCUs.[75]

A largely unexamined factor that may be affecting the absolute and relative success of non-Asian minorities in college is that African American, Hispanic, and Native American high school graduates are more likely than whites and Asians to enroll in a college or university and to pursue an academic major for

1989): 22–27; and Beverly T. Watkins, "Many Campuses Now Challenging Minority Students to Excel in Math and Science," *Chronicle of Higher Education*, 14 June 1989, pp. A13, A16–A17.

73. This view is reinforced by a substantial body of research which has found that the SAT and ACT, along with other "traditional" preparation measures such as high school GPA, are reasonably good predictors of academic performance in college. Richard P. Duran, "Prediction of Hispanics' College Achievement," Michael Olivas, ed., *Latino College Students* (New York: Teachers College Press, 1986), pp. 221–45; Michael T. Nettles, A. Robert Thoeny, and Erica J. Gosman, "Comparative and Predictive Analyses of Black and White Students' College Achievement and Experiences," *Journal of Higher Education* 57 (May/June 1986): 289–318.

74. J. W. Carmichael, Jr., et al., "Predictors of Success of Black Americans in a College-Level Pre-Health Professions Program," *The Advisor* 6 (Summer 1986): 5–6, 9–10; and J. W. Carmichael, Jr., "Predictors of First-Year Chemistry Grades for Black Americans," *Journal of Chemical Education* 63 (April 1986): 333–36. The SAT has not been found to overpredict or underpredict Latinos' academic performance in any consistent fashion. Duran, "Prediction of Hispanics' College Achievement," pp. 235–38.

75. Walter R. Allen, "The Color of Success: African-American College Student Outcomes at Predominantly White and Historically Black Public Colleges and Universities," *Harvard Educational Review* 62 (Spring 1992): 39–41. Jacqueline Fleming found that blacks experience greater cognitive growth at HBCUs, *Blacks in College* (San Francisco: Jossey-Bass, 1988). Also see Nettles et al., "Comparative and Predictive Analyses of Black and White Students' College Achievement and Experiences," pp. 302–04.

which they are academically underprepared. Ironically, this phenomenon is partly a result of efforts by colleges and universities to maximize minority students' access to higher education in a context in which there is a large shortage of non-Asian minorities who are well prepared for college. Because some of the most selective institutions have been unable to achieve the desired level of minority representation on their campuses by drawing only from the small pool of extremely well prepared non-Asian minority students, they have tended to admit a number of African Americans, Hispanics, and American Indians who, by traditional standards (high school GPAs and SAT or ACT scores), would not ordinarily be enrolled if they were white or Asian. It is not uncommon for selective institutions to "dip" into the minority pool until a large proportion of their African American, Latino, and Native American freshmen have academic preparation profiles significantly below those of most of their white and Asian freshmen. For example, very selective institutions might have white and Asian freshmen who collectively average 1300–1400 on the SAT but non-Asian minority freshmen who collectively average 1200–1300 or even lower.[76] The minority admissions decisions of the most selective institutions reverberate throughout the system, as each stratum of institutions repeats the dipping process. Although many institutions evidently have been admitting two very different student populations in terms of academic preparation, one nevertheless expects colleges and universities to produce academic success rates with their minority students that are close to those of their white and Asian students. This is the case even though few of these institutions have demonstrated an ability to succeed at high levels with white and Asian students who have preparation profiles similar to those of many of the non-Asian minorities they are admitting.

This situation has contributed over the past two decades to a substantial effort by colleges and universities to expand and improve their developmental education and support services for academically underprepared students. A recent federal survey found that 74 percent of all colleges and universities offered at least one remedial course in reading, writing, or math in the 1989–90 academic year.[77] Nonetheless, owing in part to the limited effectiveness of developmental education programs, there are reasons to believe that the dipping phenomenon is undermining the intergenerational educational advancement of blacks, His-

76. The economist Thomas Sowell found that the average black student at Cornell in the late 1960s and early 1970s scored at the 75th percentile nationally on standardized college admission tests, while the average white student scored at the 99th percentile. In the late 1980s, an MIT study indicated that the average black student at that institution had a math test score that placed the student in the top 10 percent nationally—but a score in the bottom 10 percent of his or her class at MIT. Thomas Sowell, "The New Racism on Campus," *Fortune*, 13 February 1989, pp. 115–16. According to John H. Bunzel, a similar pattern existed for African American, Latino, and American Indian students at Berkeley in the mid- to late 1980s. John H. Bunzel, "Affirmative-Action Admissions: How It 'Works' at UC Berkeley," *The Public Interest* (Fall 1988): 111–29. My discussions with admissions officers, deans, and other administrators have produced similar findings. Moreover, these individuals virtually all said that minority students' grades and graduation rates were much lower, on average, than those of the white students.

77. Wendy Mansfield, Elizabeth Farris, and MacKnight Black, *College-Level Remedial Education in the Fall of 1989* (Washington, D.C.: National Center for Education Statistics, U.S. Department of Education, 1991), p. 24.

panics, and Native Americans relative to whites and Asians. First, because a disproportionate number of non-Asian minority college students are in settings for which they are underprepared, unusually high percentages are at risk of academic failure. Second, the potential for large numbers of minority students to fail academically has led too often to the application of fairly undemanding standards to measure their academic progress: enrollment and graduation rates are usually emphasized, not average GPAs or, importantly, the distribution of GPAs.[78] And third, owing to their inevitable preoccupation with the relatively large number of students at risk of academic failure, many institutions are less able to pay close attention to the academic experiences of their well-prepared minority students, many of whom are likely to be middle class.[79] To the degree that these well-prepared students need additional attention to ensure appropriate academic and social integration but do not receive it, we are undermining the late-twentieth-century version of the W. E. B. Du Bois agenda: To create a large cadre of minorities prepared for leadership positions requiring academic achievement at the highest levels. As the data reviewed in chapter 3 demonstrate, meeting this agenda is especially difficult in areas that emphasize math and science.[80]

It is not easy to identify feasible, acceptable strategies for rectifying this situation in the short term. The demographic shift, the concern for social justice, and the need to improve the educational level of the work force have produced great pressure to maximize minority student enrollment at each stratum of colleges and universities. The distribution of minority enrollment produced by following a "traditional standards" admissions strategy is untenable given these factors; individual institutions will therefore keep dipping into the minority student pool more deeply than the students' academic preparation patterns suggest is appropriate for maximizing their success in college.

Under these circumstances, I recommend, first, an academic accounting system to provide information about the graduation rates and distributions of

78. See, for example, Richardson C. Richardson, Jr., and Elizabeth Fisk Skinner, *Achieving Quality and Diversity: Universities in a Multicultural Society* (New York: American Council on Education and Macmillan, 1991), pp. 11–14.

79. At a corporate foundation for which I worked several years, many proposals were received from colleges and universities to address the needs of academically underprepared minority students, but only a handful to address those of minority high achievers. Several representatives of colleges and universities have explained this by saying that priority must be given to underprepared minority students. Many have also suggested that it is difficult politically to gather data that would show differences in the distributions of GPAs by race/ethnicity and differences in academic outcomes for apparently similarly prepared students. The result is that the high-achievement issue is often invisible and that relatively little attention is given to the question of whether the best-prepared minority students are doing well.

80. For a discussion by Du Bois of higher education for African Americans, see W. E. B. Du Bois, *The Souls of Black Folk* (New York: First Vintage Books/Library of America, 1990), pp. 68–82. In his evaluation of minority engineering programs, Edmund W. Gordon noted the need to develop a "leadership" group of minorities in science and engineering; the lack of explicit attention to that need among most minority engineering programs; and the lack of evidence that this need was being met. Edmund W. Gordon et al., *A Report to the Field: A Descriptive Analysis in Engineering Education for Ethnic Minority Students* (New Haven: Institute for Social and Policy Studies, Yale University, 1986), pp. 1–7.

GPAs for each racial/ethnic group at individual colleges and universities, for different strata of institutions (by selectivity), and for different academic majors. This system would provide information on the relationship between academic preparation (as measured by high school GPAs and SAT/ACTs) and other factors (campus climate, amount of financial aid, and so on) to the graduation rates and GPA distributions for the different racial/ethnic groups.

The key here is the emphasis on group patterns rather than the results achieved by specific individuals. Students and academic administrators must be reminded that, while a few very underprepared individuals may do well in college, as a group they will produce a much weaker distribution of achievement than an academically well prepared group. An appropriate accounting system would provide information about how underprepared, adequately prepared, and very well prepared students perform academically in different institutional circumstances. By doing so, it could lead more minority students to select institutions at which they will find the work challenging but still have a good chance to succeed academically. It also could lead administrators to focus more attention on how to meet the needs of well-prepared minority students as well as to use a more empirical approach for planning and evaluating their minority support efforts, regardless of whether they are for underprepared or well-prepared students.

For some colleges and universities, one near-term effect of the accounting system might be to reduce minority enrollment and/or increase the middle-class proportion of their minority student populations. Indeed, charges of "creaming" and of catering to middle-class populations are potential risks of this approach. However, efforts that focus on academically well prepared minority students at a few colleges and universities are showing good results.[81]

My second recommendation is that steps be taken to make greater use of the most effective strategies for maximizing students' success in college that have emerged from developmental education, minority engineering and science, and similar efforts concerned with improving the academic performance of minority and underprepared students. This requires both more effective information dissemination capacities and greater resources for making use of this information at individual institutions.[82]

81. The Meyerhoff Scholars Program at the University of Maryland Baltimore County is designed for academically very well prepared black college students majoring in science and engineering. Clustered together, these students are given a rigorous undergraduate education and encouraged to study with each other. Early research found that their average college GPA was 3.5 (on a four-point scale), while it was only 2.8 for comparable students at the institution who were not participating in the program. Ann Gibbons, "Minority Programs That Get High Marks," Science 258 (13 November 1992): 1190.

82. At the college level, a valuable approach is the California Minority Engineering Program (MEP) model, which emphasizes the building of learning communities by clustering students in common sections of classes, promoting the use of group study practices, offering workshops in math and science, etc. See Raymond B. Landis, Retention by Design: Achieving Excellence in Minority Engineering Education (New York: National Action Council for Minorities in Engineering, 1991). On some highly regarded precollegiate (middle school level) programs, see Beatriz Chu Clewell, Bernice Taylor Anderson, and Margaret E. Thorpe, Breaking the Barriers: Helping Female and Minority Students Succeed in Mathematics and Science (San Franscisco: Jossey-Bass, 1992).

My third recommendation is that a much larger research and development effort be mounted to create operationally feasible strategies for colleges and universities to improve the educational performance of minorities. The need for more research, of course, is not limited to higher education or to meeting the needs of middle-class minorities and those minorities who seem well prepared to be high academic achievers. For this reason, I would like to turn to my next set of recommendations, which is broadly concerned with the research and development function.

Recommendation 3: Pursue Research and Development Strategies for Expanding Education-Relevant Institutional Systems, Changing the Organizational Attributes of Educational Institutions, Changing the Practices of Professional Educators, Modifying Support Programs for Academically Underprepared Minority College Students, and Increasing Understanding of Racial/Ethnic Prejudice in the United States

The suggestions made for increasing the educational advancement rates of minorities have generally been of three types: those concerned with adding or expanding institutional systems to provide crucial education-relevant services to children and families; those concerned with changing the organizational attributes and resource levels of educational institutions; and those concerned with changing what teachers and other educational professionals actually do. Although acting on these and other recommendations would almost certainly lead to significant educational gains for minority children, I doubt that we know how to undertake them in a form that can produce minority/majority educational achievement parity within the near future. Quickly reaching parity among the highest achieving students, especially in quantitative fields, seems particularly unlikely. We need to expand our knowledge in several areas, which in turn requires a large applied research and development effort directed at minority educational advancement issues.

Several types of research and development should be pursued: those testing different institutional mixes/capacities and different school organizational arrangements; those developing a range of new professional practices geared to minority students; those testing plausible and implementable combinations of institutional and professional practice strategies; those developing strategies for promoting widespread use of the most promising institutional and professional practices; and those increasing understanding of patterns of racial/ethnic prejudice in the United States, from the perspective of their impact on social policy.

One of the most important questions for this research and development effort is, What mix of education-relevant institutions, school arrangements, and edu-

Nonetheless, there is a growing sense that the two-decade-old minority engineering effort has produced few proven, readily replicable strategies for increasing the number of minority engineers; see Calvin Sims, "What Went Wrong: Why Programs Failed," *Science* 258 (13 November 1992): 1185–87; Gordon et al., *A Report to the Field.* Two organizations involved in information dissemination on effective practices and technical assistance are the National Action Council for Minorities in Engineering and the Higher Education Extension Service.

cator practices would consistently produce a distribution of achievement for poor and/or culturally different minority children by age nine that is reasonably close to the distribution normally attained by white children at the same age?[83] As I noted earlier, some of the best-documented educational strategies for disadvantaged minority children tend to reduce the size of the bottom of the distribution significantly but seem to increase the size of the top of the distribution only modestly. Moreover, few of these strategies have been evaluated in a fashion that sheds light on whether changes produced endure throughout the students' academic careers.

Earlier, I described a configuration of institutional systems in general terms that could serve as a starting point for efforts to increase the rate of educational advancement for disadvantaged minority youngsters: more generous supplementary financial assistance programs for poor families with children; a universal health care system; an extensive family support/early education system; small, vertically stable schools; and mechanisms for creating jobs for chronically unemployed parents with few skills. We need to learn more about how these systems can be configured to meet the requirements of different subpopulations of families and children.

Regarding schools, we need "evergreen" model programs designed to test alternative institutional arrangements over a long period of time (in some cases decades). After these experiments have gotten under way, they should address professional-practice questions along with institutional questions.[84]

From a long-term perspective, some of the most important research and development work must be concerned with expanding our understanding of educationally important cultural differences and developing professional practices and strategies responsive to them.[85] Much of this work should look at cultural differences defined simultaneously in terms of race/ethnicity and social class in order to gain a better understanding of how ethnic and social class factors interact. A number of studies should be launched that examine home, school, and community experiences of groups defined in these terms. With

83. On research generally relevant to this question, see Robert L. Egbert, ed., *Improving Life Chances for Young Children* (Lincoln: Bureau of Education Research, Services and Policy Studies and Center for Curriculum and Instruction, Teachers College, University of Nebraska-Lincoln, 1989).

84. On the value of model programs for improving schools, see Robert E. Slavin, *On Making a Difference* (Baltimore, Md.: Center for Research on Elementary and Middle Schools, Center for Research on Effective Schooling for Disadvantaged Students, Johns Hopkins University, 1989). Many educational researchers and school reformers are already operating such model programs. Slavin's own work in cooperative education and improving elementary schooling for the disadvantaged qualifies as an evergreen effort, as does the school reform work of Deborah Meier and her colleagues in the Central Park East schools, James Comer in the School Development Program, and Theodore Sizer through the Coalition of Essential Schools.

85. Professional practice/development schools designed to improve entry level and experienced teachers' skills could provide settings for some cultural-difference-oriented research and development work. For a discussion of these schools, see the Holmes Group, *Tomorrow's Schools: Principles for the Design of Professional Development Schools* (East Lansing, Mich.: The Holmes Group, 1990); and Marsha Levine, ed., *Professional Practice Schools: Linking Teacher Education and School Reform* (New York: Teachers College Press, 1992).

regard to the school-oriented studies, special interest should be taken in assessing the impact of different types of school organization, classroom organization, and instructional strategies on different subpopulations. With regard to home-oriented studies, attention should be given to how parent-child interactions evolve over time for different subpopulations as well as how peer networks for parents and children evolve. Home-school studies emphasizing parent-teacher relationships should be mounted. Ideally, some of these studies should be longitudinal and involve fairly large samples. Some also should look simultaneously at the home, school, and community and the interactions among them. Where possible, gender should be added to the factors that define the groups in these studies.

I touched briefly in the discussion of Recommendation 2 on the importance of a substantial research and development effort directed at higher education, in part because of how difficult it is for colleges and universities to meet the needs of academically very underprepared, economically disadvantaged minorities who wish to pursue postsecondary education. Many of these individuals have time-consuming family responsibilities, including children of their own. If society succeeds in providing larger income supplements and high-quality, low-cost child care, it should become somewhat easier for adults in poor families to pursue higher education. Yet we really do not know how much financial aid and child-care assistance, along with developmental education services, many of these individuals need to succeed in some form of postsecondary education. A research and development effort that provided different combinations of academic, financial, and child care assistance to groups of students with different combinations of needs in these areas would be extremely valuable for policy purposes.[86]

One of the nation's most pressing needs is for ways to gain widespread acceptance of promising approaches to improving minority educational achievement. For practitioners, this means devising and testing new or better-resourced approaches for disseminating new knowledge and for providing technical assistance to those who want it. In terms of public acceptance, it means developing a richer understanding of how different racial/ethnic groups and social classes view each other. The continued existence of racial/ethnic prejudice in this country, which leads many whites and others to doubt the educability of blacks and some other minorities, represents a fundamental polity-capital problem. Moreover, this prejudice structure is probably becoming even more complex owing to increasing racial/ethnic diversity. Most of the research is still con-

---

86. This could build on a diverse body of work from the past two decades concerned with increasing the success of underprepared students at all levels. Michael S. Knapp and Brenda J. Turnbull, *Better Schooling for the Children of Poverty: Alternatives to Conventional Wisdom,* vol. 1: *Summary* (Washington, D.C.: U.S. Department of Education, 1990); Michael S. Knapp and Patrick M. Shields, eds., *Better Schooling for the Children of Poverty: Alternatives to Conventional Wisdom,* vol. 2: *Commissioned Papers and Literature Review* (Washington, D.C.: U.S. Department of Education, 1990); Kulik and Kulik, *Developmental Instruction: An Analysis of the Research*; Means, Chelemer, and Knapp, *Teaching Advanced Skills to At-Risk Students*; and Clewell, Anderson, and Thomas, *Breaking the Barriers.*

cerned with the relationship between whites and blacks; there is a paucity of survey data on the relationship between whites and other minority groups and on relationships between minority groups. In the years ahead, our society should mount a substantial survey research program including both minority-majority and interminority components. This program should link groups' attitudes and beliefs toward each other to their views toward possible societal actions in such vital areas as health care, child care, financial support programs for poor families, and financial aid to inner city schools. This research should also go much deeper than most survey research. It is necessary not only to understand what people currently believe and why, but what kind of information might lead them to alter their views.

Recommendation 4: Develop Information Systems to Monitor the Academic Achievement Patterns of Groups from the Perspective of Intergenerational Advancement and Family/School Resource Variations

Currently, we are able to monitor academic achievement trends of groups primarily via data from standardized tests. However, most such data have several important limitations. The results are typically not reported in a manner that permits within-social-class score comparisons among racial/ethnic groups. The data are almost never reported in ways that take gender into account simultaneously with social class and race/ethnicity.[87] Within-social-class differences in the standardized test scores of racial/ethnic groups are typically difficult to interpret when the social class measure is parent education level, which is usually measured in terms of educational attainment rather than academic achievement. Reports on changes in the test scores of students over time usually do not explain the role, if any, of shifts in the racial/ethnic or social class composition of the test takers or the impact of simultaneous shifts in the race/ethnicity and social class of test takers. Variations in test scores among groups over time are difficult to link to variations in school resources, particularly variations in resource quality rather than quantity—for example, the quality of the human capital possessed by teachers. And finally, changes in standardized test scores over time cannot be linked systematically to changes in the physical health and social stability of children and their families.

One way of improving the quality of information may be to test much less frequently and gather much more (and in some respects different) resource data than is typically done now when tests are administered.Another may be to build a new multiple-use information system that can be used by policymakers, researchers, and professionals in education, health care, child care, and other areas of importance to the well-being of the members of our society.

---

87. This is a serious limitation because NAEP and other achievement test data usually show significant differences in test scores between racial/ethnic groups, between social classes, and between males and females and among groups defined simultaneously by all three factors. See, for example, College Board, *1992 College-Bound Seniors: Ethnic and Gender Profile of SAT and Achievement Test Takers* (New York: College Entrance Examination Board, 1992).

Making More Effective Use of the National Assessment of Educational Progress
Over the years, the NAEP testing program has expanded the number of academic areas in which testing is conducted and the frequency of testing.[88] But it is not clear how valuable these changes are. Because test score patterns in some subject areas (math and science, for instance) can be quite similar, testing in a few key areas can be about as informative as testing in several. And since NAEP score patterns usually change slowly, the incremental value of testing every two years instead of every four (or more) is generally small. I believe that it would be more useful to expand NAEP in other ways:

1. The sample sizes should be expanded to permit tracking and comparison of subgroups defined simultaneously by race/ethnicity, social class, and gender. A larger sample would also enable one to look at racial/ethnic groups on a more differentiated basis (Puerto Ricans and Mexican Americans, reservation- and non-reservation-based American Indians, and so forth).

2. The information collected on education-relevant family resources should provide more nuanced insights. More information should be gathered about parents' education levels (if parents are college graduates, what were their majors? what are their parents' education levels?). Family-income data should be gathered. Students should be asked about their friendship networks (what are the education levels of their best friends' parents? do they study with their friends? if so, how much time per week?). Information should be gathered on the geographic mobility of test takers' families (how frequently have they moved? are they immigrants? children of immigrants?).

3. NAEP information gathering should be extended to younger age groups. One approach would be to gather "school readiness" information on a large sample of kindergartners, focused not on administering academic readiness tests but rather on gathering information about the children's health histories (including exposure to preventable health risks) and their early childhood education/child care experiences, along with race/ethnic and social class characteristics.[89]

4. NAEP should be extended to adult populations. By testing thirty-year-olds, we would have a picture of the developed skills of young adults after most have finished their formal education and at a time when many have young children. If information were gathered about both their employment and educational his-

---

88. NAEP now tests regularly in six subjects—reading, mathematics, science, writing, geography, and history—and tests in reading and mathematics are now being given every two years instead of every four. Ad Hoc Committee on the Future of NAEP, *Discussion Paper on the Future of the National Assessment of Educational Progress* (Washington, D.C.: National Assessment Governing Board, National Assessment of Educational Progress, August 1992), p. 23. On the current NAEP testing cycle, see National Education Goals Panel, *The National Education Goals Report 1992*, p. 283.

89. One approach to school-readiness information gathering is proposed in Study Panel on Education Indicators, *Education Counts: An Indicator System to Monitor the Nation's Educational Health* (Washington, D.C.: Department of Education, U.S. Government Printing Office, 1991), pp. 33–34. The National Education Goals Panel has recommended the creation of an Early Childhood Assessment System that would collect school readiness information on kindergartners. See National Education Goals Panel, *The National Education Goals Report 1992*, p. 259.

tories up to that point, we would gain insights into how academic skills and credentials shape early work force opportunities. By testing forty-year-olds, we would have information on the academic skills adults possess when many have older children and on how academic achievement and attainment levels relate to work force participation and career advancement into middle age. By gathering information on both age groups' race/ethnicity, their social class as adults and as children, the social-class/race-ethnic attributes of their friendship networks as adults and as children, and the number of children they have, we could learn much about the intergenerational dynamics of educational, occupational, and social advancement as well as racial/ethnic integration.

5. School resource information should be expanded, especially regarding the characteristics of the test takers' teachers and those of their student peers. Teachers would be given achievement tests that addressed their areas of academic specialization and verbal/quantitative skills in general.[90] Teachers also would be asked about their own social class and racial/ethnic characteristics as well as those of their friendship and professional networks. The racial/ethnic and social class compositions of the student bodies of the schools would be obtained.

A NAEP system modified along these lines would provide much better data on the academic achievement patterns and trends of the nation's population as a whole and those of several subpopulations.[91] It would allow these data to be accompanied by a rich body of information about the family and school resources associated with the distribution of achievement of children and adults. It also would illuminate linkages between the educational performance of individuals/groups and some important concerns and objectives of American society, including racial/ethnic integration and the economic well-being of individuals and groups. Finally, the NAEP system would provide information that allowed the data to be interpreted from an intergenerational perspective.

90. James Coleman and his colleagues found a modest relationship between variations in teachers' scores on a standardized verbal achievement test and variations in students' test scores. James S. Coleman et al., *Equality of Educational Opportunity* (Washington, D.C.: Office of Education, U.S. Government Printing Office, 1966), pp. 130–49 and 316–19. Based on his extensive review of relevant research, Eric Hanushek concluded that "perhaps the closest thing to a consistent conclusion across the studies is the finding that teachers who perform well on verbal ability tests do better in the classroom, but even there the evidence is not very strong." Eric A. Hanushek, "The Impact of Differential Expenditures on School Performance," *Educational Researcher* 18 (May 1989): 48.

91. Owing to the nature of the sampling techniques used in NAEP tests, acting on some of these recommendations may be difficult. NAEP uses a version of matrix sampling called balanced incomplete block spiraling (BIB). On matrix sampling, see George F. Madaus, Walt Haney, and Amelia Kreitzer, *Testing and Evaluation: Learning from the Projects We Fund*, (New York: Council for Aid to Education, 1992), p. 41. On the BIB approach used by NAEP for its 1990 mathematics assessment, see Ina V. S. Mullis, John A. Dossey, Eugene H. Owen, and Gary W. Phillips, *The State of Mathematics Achievement: NAEP's 1990 Assessment of the Nation and the Trial Assessment of the States* (Washington, D.C.: Educational Testing Service/U.S. Department of Education, U.S. Government Printing Office, 1991), pp. 450–51.

Constructing the Human Well-Being Information System   There are, of course, shortcomings associated with cross-sectional studies in which a group (sample) of people is looked at on a one-time-only basis. Notably, they cannot provide detailed, cumulative information about the educational, social, and economic life courses of specific individuals and group members. As an alternative, longitudinal studies such as the High School and Beyond Study have been undertaken; these follow individuals for an extended period of time. Although most major longitudinal studies of education undertaken by the federal government have produced extremely valuable information, they too have had several shortcomings: typically they have not followed younger children; some have tended to follow groups for limited periods of time (sometimes only a few years); and they have usually not gathered significant amounts of information on health and other areas that can influence the educational fortunes of individuals.

I therefore propose the creation of the Human Well-Being Information System (HWBIS). The basic idea is that every ten years, a large national sample of infants would be selected to participate in a lifetime-long longitudinal study. Detailed data on each infant, including health and family information, would be collected at the outset, with follow-up surveys made at ages five, ten, fourteen, eighteen, twenty-four, thirty, forty, and every ten years thereafter. (The follow-ups through age forty would be designed to be generally consistent with the proposed NAEP age-level testing points.) Each HWBIS sample would be supplemented along the way to ensure that immigrants in the age cohort were included in the study.

Achievement test, health, parent, sibling, and friendship network data would be gathered at all points. A great deal of school-readiness information would be gathered at age five, school progress information (in the form of transcripts, attainment levels, and so on) at ages ten, fourteen, eighteen, and twenty-four. Avocational/hobby/community service information would be gathered beginning at age ten, expanding over time to reflect the importance of such activities in adults' lives. Employment information would be gathered beginning at age fourteen until late in participants' lives. Employment information would gradually become more extensive, reflecting a need to understand the career patterns of individuals and groups. Continuing education information would be gathered beginning at age thirty. Information regarding the sample members' own children would be gathered beginning at age eighteen. Information relevant to retirement years would be gathered starting at age fifty. Information on social maladjustment, including criminal activity, would begin at age fourteen (or younger).

HWBIS would provide extensive information about the investment of family, school, and other societal resources in children and adults over time; the impact of these investment patterns on participants' lives; and the relationship between participants' lives and the institutional and social arrangements and conditions of the nation. Because a new cohort would be added each decade, HWBIS would provide information about changes in resource investment patterns in children and adults as well as the impact of these changes on different types of individuals and groups. Because the information would be relatively detailed, HWBIS would provide important insights into the specific strengths and weaknesses of important institutions, for example, the school. Because the structure of society changes over time, HWBIS would provide information to help assess how these changes affect individuals and groups. For example, if the structure of the economy is changing in important respects, HWBIS would show how these changes affect several age groups, either directly via the workplace for adults or indirectly in terms of family (and, possibly, school and community) resources available to children. HWBIS also would provide detailed information on the intergenerational advancement of individuals and groups from the perspective of education, employment, health, and some forms of social integration (including friendship networks and community involvement).

SUMMARY AND CONCLUSIONS

Four sets of recommendations have been made in this chapter. The first set emphasized using social policy in a much more expansive, aggressive fashion to meet educational and other needs of the most disadvantaged segments of minority groups. The second set focused on raising the academic achievement of middle-class minority youngsters and responding more effectively to the needs of high-achieving minority students. The third set focused on expanding the minority-education-related research and development effort. And the fourth set emphasized developing more effective systems for monitoring the educational performance of minorities over time.

As I have noted, the recommendations are intended to be consistent with the key findings, organizing concepts, and principles for action presented at the beginning of this chapter. Thus, particular care was taken to ensure that the recommendations would incorporate a strong intergenerational perspective; hence the focus on both the minority poor and the minority middle class. Considerable effort was made to ensure that no single institution would be expected to accomplish the task single-handedly, reflecting the reality that there are limits to institutional effectiveness ranges. Thus, I have emphasized expanding the number of universal institutional systems, such as those for health care and for family support/early-education (parent education, child care, and preschool), as a means of spreading the responsibility for responding to the education-relevant needs of minorities. In a related vein, the principles of complementarity and redundancy informed the recommendations.

More than anything else, the recommendations reflect the principles that the overall effort should be designed to produce a full distribution of academic achievement among minorities as soon as possible and that this effort should be very large in size and long term in orientation. In the final chapter of this book, I offer some thoughts on the larger meaning of the changing demographics of the United States, which may help to explain further why these two principles have played such an influential role in the recommendations for how the educational advancement of minorities might be accelerated.

CHAPTER THIRTEEN

A Nation-Building, Region-Building Rationale for Accelerating the Educational Advancement of Minorities

In a previous chapter, estimates of variations in family and school resources were presented which suggest that the education-relevant investment American society makes in some children is several times larger than the investments it makes in some others. Predictably, strongly resourced children tend to do well, while weakly resourced youngsters tend to do poorly. The former are disproportionately white and Asian, the latter disproportionately black, Hispanic, and Native American.

It is possible to explain how the United States has come to be in this position from a number of vantage points. One can emphasize the nation's legacy of institutionalized racial/ethnic discrimination, which until recently through law and custom denied economic, educational, political, and social opportunity to several minority groups. One can focus on the changing structure of the nation's economy over the past several decades and the associated inability to meet the demand for adequately paying low-skill jobs. One can emphasize the growing number of culturally different adults (with children) who have little formal schooling relevant to a technology-based society. And one can focus on the absence of universal systems of health care, child care, early childhood education, and parent education as well as the lack of adequate employment and income support programs for poor families with children.

My recommendations have stressed creation of the "missing" universal systems as well as making a number of school-oriented changes, including lowering pupil/teacher ratios and extending the educational year for disadvantaged children. Although this is an extensive, expensive agenda, it must be remembered that behind the statistics on poverty and low academic achievement are a great many real people. The negative consequences of their educational and economic circumstances are quite real—for them and, increasingly, for all Americans.

The situation is made more complex by the difficulty of determining with precision what must be done, at what cost, over what period of time to meet the needs of America's rapidly growing minority population. There are some parallels here with the Cold War. In the aftermath of World War II, it was virtually impossible to know the extent of the effort that would be required to ensure the political, economic, and social recovery of Western Europe and parts of East Asia from the ravages of the war and to meet America's defense needs under conditions of great uncertainty about the expansionist intentions and military capabilities of a Stalinist Soviet Union. The United States essentially decided to overinvest in foreign policy and military defense, in terms of money, material, people, and national attention. Long-term-oriented policies such as containment were adopted.[1] Several specific initiatives such as the Marshall Plan, which helped finance the postwar economic recovery of Europe, consumed billions of dollars.[2] And U.S. military expenditures over the ensuing decades totaled trillions of dollars. As in the case of the nation's current domestic policy challenges, there was considerable disagreement about the risks confronting the nation and what should be done in response.[3]

Although the Cold War offers evidence that it is possible for government to win public support for an expensive, long-term national effort, it is not clear that Americans are ready to support a costly set of domestic initiatives heavily concerned with minority advancement. This is no doubt due in part to a lack of a shared sense of urgency among most Americans about minority needs and issues. But I believe that it is also due in part to a lack of appropriate conceptual handles for public discussion and debate. For this reason, I suggest that we turn to a familiar term to help convey the enormousness of the endeavor that Americans must undertake together—nation-building. With regard to the contemporary circumstances of the United States, I have defined *nation-building* as "the efforts . . . [Americans] make individually and collectively to include 'all the people' within the central realms of . . . society, and in the process establish a national community in the civic sense of the term."[4] Inherent in this definition is the belief that most people within America's borders must have an opportunity to participate meaningfully in society—to vote, to find a decent job, to have a reasonable prospect of improving their circumstances through effort, to be regarded as the equal of others, and to be largely free from worry about basic survival.

Having a broad consensus about the nature of key societal institutions and the access of individuals and groups to them does not mean that major differ-

---

1. As originally proposed by George F. Kennan, "containment" was concerned with using an appropriate combination of political, economic, and military power over the long term to limit the Soviet Union's influence beyond its borders. See X [George F. Kennan], "The Sources of Soviet Conduct," *Foreign Affairs* 25 (July 1947): 566–82.

2. In 1947, Secretary of State George C. Marshall proposed the European Recovery Program to help rebuild Europe. The program, which became known as the Marshall Plan, began in 1948 and ran until 1952. About $13 billion in aid—a large sum in those days—was provided to European nations via the Marshall Plan. See Dean Acheson, *Present at the Creation: My Years at the State Department* (New York: Norton, 1969), pp. 226–35; and George F. Kennan, *Memoirs: 1925–1950* (Boston: Little, Brown, 1967), pp. 325–53.

3. For a discussion of several ways in which the objectives of containment might have been, or were, defined and pursued during the Cold War, see John Lewis Gaddis, *The United States and the End of the Cold War: Implications, Reconsiderations, Provocations* (New York: Oxford University Press, 1992), pp. 18–46.

4. L. Scott Miller, "Nation-Building and Education," *Education Week*, 14 May 1986, p. 40.

ences will not exist within a nation's population, whether in terms of racial/ethnic identity, language, religion, or style of family life. Indeed, one of the hallmarks of a free society is that individuals and voluntary associations of people have the right to think and behave differently from other individuals and groups, as long as they observe the law of the land.[5] Nevertheless, finding a workable balance between differences and similarities in a nation with a large, pluralistic population undergoing rapid change is no easy task.[6] The growing debate over whether America should aspire to be a cultural melting pot or a cultural mosaic inevitably involves the question of whether minorities that are culturally very different from the majority can be successful participants in mainstream institutions without some substantial changes in their cultural attributes—or in American institutions and in the majority culture itself.[7] Although the general answer to this question is that adaptations must be made by all groups and mainstream institutions, identifying essential adaptations in advance and gaining a consensus to pursue them are problematic.[8]

In spite of some real uncertainties about what Americans must share, this book has been concerned with an area in which it is absolutely crucial for individuals and groups to have a great deal in common: the knowledge and skills acquired through formal education. Achieving success in this area helps ensure that America's democratic institutions are in the hands of an informed citizenry, that its economy has a work force that can "think for a living," and that its society is just, inclusive, humane, and reasonably harmonious.[9] The need for most Americans to have fairly well developed verbal and quantitative reasoning and communications skills of the kinds that schools are charged with nurturing, coupled with the continued undereducation of several minority groups that collectively represent a large and growing proportion of the U.S. population, argues strongly for a nation-building effort focused on minority educational advancement.

The suggestion that improving educational outcomes for minorities can be an

5. According to Lawrence H. Fuchs, "Since the Second World War the national unity of Americans has been tied increasingly to a strong civic culture that permits and protects expressions of ethnic and religious diversity based on individual rights and that also inhibits and ameliorates conflict among religious, ethnic, and racial groups. It is the civic culture that unites Americans and protects their freedom—including their right to be ethnic." Lawrence H. Fuchs, The American Kaleidoscope: Race, Ethnicity, and the Civic Culture (Hanover, N.H.: Wesleyan University Press/University Press of New England, 1990), p. xv.

6. For a discussion of racial/ethnic pluralism in the United States, see Milton M. Gordon, "Models of Pluralism: The New American Dilemma," Annals of the American Academy of Political and Social Science 454 (March 1981): 178–88.

7. For an examination of this question as it has emerged in some European societies, see Hans-Joachim Hoffmann-Nowotny, "Social Integration and Cultural Pluralism: Structural and Cultural Problems of Immigration in European Industrial Countries," in Population in an Interacting World, edited by William Alonso (Cambridge: Harvard University Press, 1987), pp. 149–72.

8. On the reality that groups in America have developed similarities and retained differences over time, see Nathan Glazer and Daniel Patrick Moynihan, Beyond the Melting Pot (Cambridge: MIT Press, 1963).

9. Regarding the work force dimension, see Ray Marshall and Marc Tucker, Thinking for a Living: Education and the Wealth of Nations (New York: Basic Books, 1992).

important means of promoting social harmony (or reducing conflict) in a diverse nation is informed by the near-pervasive tendency among humans to identify (often strongly) with a particular racial/ethnic group, to regard those who are not members of their group as "others," and to treat nonmembers with indifference and outright hostility. In this light, it is the mundaneness of racial/ethnic prejudice that is important. In pluralistic settings, the possibility of costly prejudice-based discriminatory behavior is almost always present; and the threat of truly destructive behavior can become very great at times of societal stress (deep recession, war, and so forth). With the growing diversity of the U.S. population, the ordinariness and ubiquity of prejudice constitute a compelling reason to pursue a minority educational advancement agenda. Such an agenda has the potential to reduce the capacity of social class divisions to exacerbate racial/ethnic tensions. To the extent that increasing access to formal schooling is a means of promoting shared ways of thinking, it also can help to build strong cultural bridges between groups.

What worries me at this juncture is not that the United States will be unable to give some additional attention to educational and related needs of minorities in the years ahead, but that Americans will not grasp the very large-scale and long-term dimensions of these challenges. Sustained intergenerational educational advancement requires an enormous investment over time, especially for groups that have had little previous experience with such education or that have been systematically denied educational opportunity.

There is more to the story: America has entered a period in which region-building should be a priority as well. As Orlando Patterson has written, the United States is the economic center of the "emerging West Atlantic system."[10] Just as the well-being of whites is increasingly dependent on the well-being of Americans who are members of minority groups, so the well-being of all Americans is increasingly dependent on that of the people who live in Mexico and the nations of the Caribbean, Central America, and parts of South America. These nations have provided many recent immigrants to the United States and can be expected to do so for years to come. Education levels in many of these countries are low, and few have the resources to raise them appreciably in the near future. Because many of those who come to the United States are not well educated and American schools often find it difficult to meet the educational needs of their children, the human capital development challenges of their countries of origin are, to a considerable extent, U.S. challenges as well.

The North American Free Trade Agreement (NAFTA) is one of the most visible manifestations of how closely intertwined the fortunes of America have come to be with those of other nations in the region. Understandably, NAFTA has stimulated considerable debate in the United States about its impact on the American job market. Yet the now-several-decades-old migration of peoples from Mexico and other nations in the region to the United States has not produced a similar

10. Orlando Patterson, "The Emerging West Atlantic System: Migration, Culture, and Underdevelopment in the United States and the Circum-Caribbean Region," in *Population in an Interacting World*, pp. 227–60.

discussion among Americans about the profound human capital development questions posed by conditions in many of these countries, much less how the United States could be constructively responsive to those conditions over time.

The fostering of human capital development among disadvantaged and low-status groups will be a central obligation for the United States domestically and regionally (and in some other areas of the world) for decades to come. America is in pressing need of leaders and citizens from all institutions and segments of society who understand this responsibility and who are prepared to meet it vigorously. The late Dean Acheson, who was under secretary of state during George Marshall's tenure and subsequently secretary of state himself, could justifiably call his memoirs *Present at the Creation*. Will a senior official in the U.S. government in the next decade be able to give a similar title to his or her memoirs in the year 2020? Will most of the current generation of leaders and their fellow citizens who are still around at that time be able to affirm that they were present at, and fully supportive of, the creation of a nation-building and region-building effort directed at educational advancement?

Index

Accelerated Schools Project, 238
Accreditation Board for Engineering and
    Technology (ABET), 74–80, 82
Acheson, Dean, 381
ACT (American College Testing) scores, 74, 358,
    365
Action for Excellence, 1, 2n3
Adler, Mortimer J., 237n101
adopted children, 193–98, 277–79
affirmative action programs, 218–21, 365–69
AFQT, 162, 170–71
African Americans. *See* blacks
Alabama, 297
Alaska, 288–91
Alexander, Karl L., 240
Allen, Walter R., 79–80, 365
American Indians. *See* Native Americans
Anderson, Bernice Taylor, 146, 152–54
Anderson, Elijah, 112–13
Anglos. *See* whites
Armed Forces Qualification Test (AFQT), 162,
    170–71
Asian Americans: attitudes about, 90n14, 173,
    183, 185, 211–12; author's use of term,
    xiv–xv; classroom culture of, 42–43, 230,
    257, 291; demographics of, 18, 20, 103, 337;
    educational achievement of, xv, 11, 57–63,
    65–73, 79–80, 85, 118, 202, 210, 211, 231,
    236, 258, 298, 332–33; educational achieve-
    ment and class among, 124–25, 141; and
    educational achievement gaps (within-
    class), 144–46, 151, 155–59; educational
    achievement and occupational aspirations of,
    210; educational attainment by, 6, 33–41,
    266, 358; and housing segregation, 111,
    112n67; as immigrants, 6, 15–19, 21, 65,
    89n14, 201, 212–13, 283n114; languages of,
    65, 264; parenting styles of, 211, 274–77;

282; poverty rate among, 108; tracking of,
    234, 235–36. *See also* Chinese Americans;
    Japanese Americans; Korean Americans
assimilationism, 96n23
Avance program (Texas), 355
Azuma, Hiroshi, 277

Baker, David P., 280–81
Bane, Mary Jo, 110–11
Baumol, William, 5, 8
Baumrind, Diana, 270, 271
Bean, Frank, 30
Beginning School Study (BSS), 240
Berne, Robert, 291
Better Schooling for the Children of Poverty,
    239n109
bilingualism, 262–64. *See also* language
Blackman, Sue Anne, 5, 8
blacks: alleged inferiority of, 172–204, 218,
    221–28, 237, 241–43, 338; author's use of
    term, xiv; class differences among, 104,
    109–12; classroom culture of, 250, 252–53,
    255–57; cultural diversity among, 20n64, 21;
    demographics of, 16–18, 22, 23, 103,
    299–303, 337; educational achievement
    gaps of, 1, 3, 47, 62–83, 85, 118, 198, 202,
    210, 223, 231, 236, 258, 298, 302–3,
    332–33, 337; educational achievement gaps
    and class among, 124–25, 133, 141, 163–65,
    194–98; and educational achievement gaps
    (within-class), 144–50, 152, 153–59, 166,
    170–71, 209–10; educational attainment by,
    27–41, 44, 62–63, 198, 266, 293–95, 358;
    and housing segregation, 111n67, 197,
    343n3; as involuntary immigrants, 205–6;
    Korean American tensions with, 117n82;
    middle-class, departure from ghettos of,
    109–12; middle-class, educational achieve-

blacks (*continued*)

ment gaps of, 10–11, 118, 158–59, 201, 208–10, 361–64; middle-class, first-generation, 194–98, 274, 277–79, 362; middle-class, increase in, 3; migration of, 101–3, 180, 206, 280; parenting styles of, 196–98, 274, 275, 277–80, 362; poverty rate for, 109, 110, 132, 141, 183, 198, 282; prejudice against, 103, 105, 167–68, 172–73, 205–7, 218–19, 258; preventable health problems among, 139; role models for, 110, 113, 210; and school resources, 290–91; and school segregation, 112, 167–68, 170; single-parent families among, 105, 108, 132, 279–80; teachers among, 42–43, 66–67, 239–41; teachers' relations with, 228–31, 240–41; tracking of, 231, 233–34; unemployment rates of, 9–10, 104–6, 109, 170, 198, 360; white violence against, 15, 220; working-class, 109–11, 118, 194–95, 209–10, 241, 274, 277–79. *See also* cultural differences; intelligence; prejudice; underclass

Blau, Zena Smith, 194–95, 197, 198, 199n98, 201, 274

Bobo, Lawrence, 181n35

Bourdieu, Pierre, 89

Boyer, Ernest L., 237n101

Boykin, A. Wade, 250, 253

Bradley, Robert H., 271

"brainiacs," 207–9

Britsch, Susan, 253

Bronfenbrenner, Urie, 99, 100n30

Brophy, Jere E., 227

Brown, B. Bradford, 274n123, 275, 276

Buka, Stephen L., 138–40

Bunzel, John, 366n76

busing (school), 138, 293

Caldwell, Bettye M., 271

California, 112, 260, 263, 302, 357

Canada, 16, 345–47

Caplan, Nathan, 276

Carter, Stephen L., 223

caste system (in United States), 172–73, 221, 222, 241, 282

Central Americans, 34–35, 102, 103, 283n144. *See also* Hispanics

Chapter One programs, 330–32

Chicago (Illinois), 101, 102, 111, 116–17, 207, 280n136, 302

child abuse and neglect, 139, 140

child care, 346, 377. *See also* early childhood education; parenting styles

Children in Need, 238n101

Chinese Americans, 17n51, 19, 33, 211–13

Choy, Marcella H., 276

cities: deterioration of, 2–3, 100–101; effects of minority concentrations in, 84, 101–2, 104, 109–10, 131, 141, 170, 241, 291, 300; housing segregation in, 9, 111–12; lack of low-skilled jobs in, 84, 100–101, 116, 170, 207; peer influences in, 208; poverty in, 206–7; schools in, 1, 288–93, 302–3, 312; social isolation of ghetto residents in, 99, 110, 112–14, 116–18, 120, 131, 201, 215, 221, 279, 285, 286, 360. *See also* suburbs; underclass; white flight

Civil Rights Act of 1964, 9, 29, 32, 85

civil rights movement, 8–12, 82, 92, 96, 119–20, 170, 173–74, 180, 181, 201, 206–7, 242, 339. *See also* Civil Rights Act of 1964; prejudice; Voting Rights Act of 1965

Clark, Kenneth B., 222, 224

Clark, Reginald M., 268

class(es): definition of, 12; and educational achievement, 85–87, 119–42, 298, 301–2, 310, 336–39, 361–64; educational gaps between, 266, 337–38; housing segregation by, 111n67, 221, 312; measurement of, 121–22, 160, 170, 298, 338, 339; and parenting styles, 267, 277–79, 285–86; in racial/ethnic conflict, 15–16, 104, 380; racial/ethnic educational achievement gaps within, 143–59, 266, 278–79, 298, 338, 372–73; and social changes, 12–13; teacher's, 241, 246, 374; *vs.* caste, 172n1. *See also* incomes; educational achievement gaps; parental educational attainment; middle-class; underclass; working-class

Clinton, William Jefferson, 361

Coalition of Essential Schools, 238, 239

Cold War, 377–78, 381

Coleman, James S.: on class status and achievement, 121, 143–44, 197; on intelligence tests, 190n68; on relative importance of family *vs.* school resources, 84, 87–88, 119, 137, 167, 190, 224, 240, 282, 286, 293, 312, 335–36, 338; on school size, 348–49; on social capital, 89, 98, 99, 116–18, 190, 224; on teachers' test scores, 374n90. *See also* Coleman Report

Coleman Report (*Equality of Educational Opportunity*), 109, 158–59, 189–90; on educational aspirations, 208; and equal educational opportunity, 93, 146, 237. *See also* Coleman, James S.

College Board, 238, 239–40

college graduation: in education, 42–43; intergenerational, 95, 366; rates of, 26, 27–28, 30–33, 35–37, 44, 357–58; in technical fields, 39–42, 76, 78–79, 161. *See also* parental educational attainment; postsecondary education

Comer, James P., 204, 208, 238, 283–84, 286, 330, 331, 370n84

computer/information sciences. *See* technical fields

Connecticut, 207, 283–84, 298–99, 303n22

The Content of Our Character (S. Steele), 204

corporate training, 247–48

crime rates, 104, 113, 220–21, 360

Crummell, Alexander, 177

Cuban Americans, 15, 20, 34. *See also* Hispanics

cultural differences, 338, 377; about educational achievement, 206–11; development of oppositional, 206–10, 215, 243, 360, 362, 363; effects of, on educational achievement, 244–86, 298; need for research on, 351, 370–71; in pluralistic society, 24; and racial/class isolation, 104, 110, 114, 215; and test scores, 46, 195, 197, 198n93; whites' perceptions of, 117, 241–43. *See also* class(es); language; parenting styles

cultural inferiority, 174–75, 177–78, 184–86, 213. *See also* prejudice

Dahrendorf, Ralf, 91–92, 115n78

Denton, Nancy A., 111n67

Detroit (Michigan), 101, 102, 302, 303

Deyhle, Donna, 217

discrimination. *See* minorities: prejudice against; prejudice

Dornbush, Sanford M., 274–76

Du Bois, W. E. B., 175n11, 367

Duran, Richard, 261

Dusek, Jerome B., 228

early childhood education, 135–37, 261–62, 267, 280–81, 333, 353–56, 370, 376, 377

Early Childhood Family Education program (Minnesota), 355

Earned Income Tax Credit, 346, 361

economic opportunity structure. *See* jobs; unemployment

Edmonds, Ronald, 224–25

Educating Americans for the 21st Century, 1n2

educational achievement: cognitive characteristics associated with, 254; definition of, 93; hard work *vs.* native ability in, 199n96, 275–77; importance of, xiii, 4–8, 377–81; intergenerational effects on, 95, 160–71,

264, 278–81, 284–86, 334, 339, 374; Jensen's views about, 189; and perceptions about job opportunities, 202, 206–17, 241, 257–59, 275–76, 339–40; and poverty, 131–37; recommendations for improving minorities', 340–76; resources relevant to, 84, 87–88, 93–95, 100, 116–18, 122, 160–71, 287–337, 339, 377; role of encouragement in, 89, 97–99, 120, 275; trends in, 26–44, 105; *vs.* educational attainment, 93, 160, 170, 314, 356; and work performance, 11n32, 80n39, 374. *See also* educational achievement gaps; educational attainment; family; schools

educational achievement gaps: causes of, 84–120, 131–37, 337–39; elementary school development of, 26, 70–72, 135–37, 141–42, 240, 320, 351; between majority and minority populations, xiv, 1, 3, 26, 45–83, 121–42, 198, 337–38, 363–64; and parental educational attainment level, 122–33, 141–59, 266; racial/ethnic, among parents of equal educational attainment, 161–71, 338, 360n62; reasons for narrowing, 4–8, 13, 82, 232–33, 238–40, 242–43, 367–69, 377–81

educational aspirations, 208–10

educational attainment: definition of, 93; and employment rates, 106; of minorities compared to majority, 22–42, 102, 198, 266, 357–58; and racial prejudice, 181, 202–43; *vs.* educational achievement, 93, 160, 170, 314, 356. *See also* college graduation; educational achievement; high school(s); parental educational attainment; postsecondary education

educational opportunity (equal), 84, 85, 92–95, 119, 237

educational opportunity structure: and intergenerational educational progress, 96–98, 168–71, 205, 339–40. *See also* jobs

educational reforms, 1, 85n2, 224, 237–39, 241, 358–59, 365

educational resources. *See* educational achievement: resources relevant to

Educational Testing Service, 146, 360n62

Education for All American Youth, 232n97

Education that Works, 238n101

"effective schools movement," 85n2, 224, 237

Egbert, Robert L., 321

elementary school: completion rates of, 27–28; development of educational achievement gap in, 26, 70–72, 135–37, 141–42, 240, 320, 351; math in, 53, 55, 136; readiness for, 373; reading in, 47, 135–36, 357n52

Elmen, Julie D., 271, 275
employment. *See* incomes; jobs; unemployment
engineering. *See* technical fields
Entwisle, Doris R., 240
Equality of Educational Opportunity. See Coleman Report
Equity 2000 (College Board), 238, 240
Erickson, Frederick, 283
Escalante, Jaime, 257, 258–59
ethnicity, xiv. *See also* racial/ethnic differences
expenditures per pupil. *See* school districts; schools; states

family: and educational achievement, 84, 86–88, 90, 208; estimating resource variations among, 310–25; single-parent, 99, 107–8, 115, 132, 279–80, 308–10, 345–46, 360; social isolation of ghetto, 99, 110, 112–14, 116–18, 120, 131, 201, 215, 221, 279, 285, 286, 360; support for, 341, 355–56, 362, 370, 376, 377; variations in resources available in, 87–88, 93–95, 97, 116–17, 119, 136–37, 160–71, 190, 224, 240, 282, 287, 297, 303–37, 339–40. *See also* class(es); intergenerational resources; parenting styles
fertility rates, 21–22, 97n24, 267
Fillmore, Lily Wong, 253
financial capital, 88, 90, 94, 95, 116, 119, 343–48, 356
Florida, 302, 303
Fordham, Signithia, 207, 309n28, 364n72
France, 346, 354–55, 359
Franklin, John Hope, 204
Fredrickson, George M., 176–77, 221
Freeman, Richard B., 114
friendship networks, 194, 197, 275, 279, 362. *See also* peers
Fuchs, Lawrence H., 379n5

Gallimore, Ronald, 265n91
Gallup poll, 181
Gamoran, Adam, 239n107
Gans, Herbert, 113n72
Gardner, William P., 269
gender, xiv, 371, 372–73
General Social Survey (GSS), 182–87, 218–19
Germany, 345, 350n26, 359
ghettos, 104, 109–16; social isolation of, 99, 110, 112–14, 116–18, 120, 131, 201, 215, 221, 279, 285, 286, 360. *See also* housing segregation; underclass
Good, Thomas L., 227
Goodlad, John I., 233, 266n91, 348–49

Gordon, Edmund W., 256, 257, 270n103, 367n80
Gordon, Milton, 96n23
Gosman, Erica J., 80
grades: impact of peers on, 206–8, 217; of minority students in suburban schools, 115; overprediction of minorities', 80, 365; of parents, 161; racial/ethnic/class gaps in, 28, 45, 70–83, 210, 230–31, 274
Graduate Record Examinations (GRE), 68–70
graduate school. *See* postsecondary education
Greenbaum, Paul E. and Susan D., 251
grouping. *See* tracking (educational)
GSS (General Social Survey), 182–87, 218–19
Guam, 297

Hammond, Ray, 202–4
Hanushek, Eric, 374n90
Harris, Irving B., 350n28
Harris, Louis, 180–83, 185–86
Hawaii, 297
Hawaiians (native), 34, 249–51, 255, 258, 285, 330
Head Start program, 353–54
health capital, 88, 90, 94, 95, 116, 118, 312–13, 343–48, 356. *See also* health problems
health problems: need for national program to prevent, 139–40, 341, 343–48, 361, 376, 377; among poor people, 104, 308; preventable, among poor children, 121, 137–42, 195, 343–49, 356
Heath, Shirley Brice, 251, 252, 256, 265, 279–80
Hess, Robert D., 277
Heynes, Barbara, 136–37
Higher Education for American Democracy, 232n97
High School (Boyer), 237n101
high school(s): alternative, 356–57; class rank in, 73; compulsory attendance of, until age 18, 232n97; dropout rate, 46, 218, 230, 293–95, 302–3; dropouts, earnings of, 106; dropouts, educational achievement of children of, 146–47, 149–50, 155, 266; educational gaps in, 26, 70–72; extracurricular activities in, 268; grades in, 70–72, 74–77, 80; graduates, earnings of, 106, 217; graduates, educational achievement of children of, 146, 147, 149–50, 155; graduation rates for, 26–30, 33, 44, 293–95; improvements in reading and math in, 47, 53, 332–33. *See also* postsecondary education: readiness for
High School and Beyond (HS&B) survey, 34–35, 132, 233–34, 357, 375

Hill, C. Russell, 267
Hispanics: alleged inferiority of, 183–85, 200, 219–20, 237, 242; classroom culture of, 256–59; demographics of, 18–20, 23, 103, 299n19, 300, 337; educational achievement gaps of, 1, 47, 48–49, 51–55, 57–59, 62–63, 65–66, 68–72, 74–76, 78–83, 85, 198, 211, 231, 236, 298, 337; educational achievement gaps and class among, 125, 133, 141, 163–66; and educational achievement gaps (within-class), 144–50, 152–54, 159, 170–71; educational attainment by, 28–35, 37, 38, 40, 44, 46, 198, 266, 358; and housing segregation, 112n67; immigrants, education of, 15–16, 21n69, 214, 215, 260–61; immigration of, 15–16, 18, 21, 102, 103, 201, 260n61, 283n144; involuntary immigration of, 205; literacy among, 10n30, 165–66; marriage and family issues of, 105, 108, 253, 272n116, 273–75; occupational aspirations of, 210; parenting styles of, 253, 272n116, 273–75; poverty rate among, 108–10, 133, 198; prejudice against, 173, 184–86, 213; racial composition of, 21; role models for, 259; and school resources, 169, 291; and school segregation, 112, 213; teachers' relations with, 230; tracking of, 231, 233–34; unemployment rates of, 105–6, 170, 198, 360. See also Central Americans; Mexican Americans; "Other Hispanics"; Puerto Ricans
Hmong, 33
Hodgkinson, Harold L., 1n3, 7
Hoffer, Thomas, 89n14, 239n107, 348–49
Horace's Compromise (Sizer), 237n101
housing segregation, 9, 111–12, 197, 215, 220, 312, 343n3
Howard, Jeff, 202–4
HS&B (High School and Beyond) survey, 34–35, 132, 233–34, 357, 375
human capital, 88–89, 95, 116, 119, 160–71, 247n11, 248, 278, 356
Human Well-Being Information System (HWBIS), 375–76

Idaho, 297
Ide, Judith K., 208
Illinois, 112, 302. See also Chicago
immigrants: Asian, 6, 15–19, 21, 65, 89n14, 201, 212–13, 283n114; Canadian, 16; education of recent, 15–16; European, xvi, 6, 16, 18–19, 24, 100, 101, 205, 221; fertility rates of, 21–22; language diversity among, 259–64; legislation regarding, 17, 19, 23n73,

101; from Mexico and Latin America, 15–16, 102, 103, 201, 214–15, 260n61, 283n144; from Puerto Rico, 20, 102; as source of conflict, 14–15; voluntary vs. involuntary, 205–6
Immigration Act of 1965, 17n51, 18
An Imperiled Generation, 238n101
incomes: changes in, 2, 106; and children's educational achievement level, 121–43, 145, 155, 157–58, 307–10, 337; divergences in American, 13, 104, 108; and educational attainment, 106; estimating variations among, 310–14; as measure of class, 121, 159. See also class(es); financial capital; jobs; poverty rates
India, 14, 15, 33
industrialization, 4–8, 98–100
innate inferiority, 174–78, 182–204, 218, 221–28, 237, 241–43, 338. See also cultural inferiority; prejudice
intelligence: culturally defined kinds of, 245; genetic vs. environmental factors in, 188–98, 201; research on racial differences in, 186–98, 277–79; white perceptions of Asian, 212; white views about blacks', 179–86
intergenerational educational progress, 84, 168–71, 264, 374; American myth of, 92; among minority groups, 30, 195, 214–15, 274, 339, 341, 366–67, 380; time needed for reaching parity between racial/ethnic groups in, 94, 119, 340–41, 380. See also intergenerational resources
intergenerational resources, 95, 119, 160, 268–70, 278–81, 286, 287, 334, 339, 341
Iowa, 295, 297
IQ tests. See intelligence; test scores
Irvine, Jacqueline Jordan, 228

Jackman, Mary R., 185, 186, 219
Jacobson, Lenore, 225
Japan, 4, 6, 8, 19, 276, 277
Japanese Americans, 33, 211–14, 277
Jargowsky, Paul A., 110–11
Jensen, Arthur R., 188–91
Jews, 19, 24n75, 181, 183–95
jobs: guaranteed, 348, 359–61; as measure of class, 121, 159; need for adequately paying low-skilled, 9–10, 30, 84, 97, 98, 100, 101, 103–5, 109, 113–15, 120, 170, 243, 283, 359–61, 370, 377; need for high-paying high-skill, 97, 100, 101, 120; parents', and children's educational achievement, 85, 124–25, 130–31, 144, 145; prejudice and availability of, 218–21; prospects for, and

jobs (*continued*)
  educational achievement, 202, 206–17, 241,
    257–59, 275–76, 339–40; suburban, 101,
    109, 114–15; in technical fields, 38–44, 212.
    See also incomes; unemployment
Joint Center for Political Studies (JCPS),
    203–4
Joseph, Gail, 228
Jung, Richard K., 131–32, 135, 208

Kamehameha Early Education Program. *See*
    KEEP
Kasarda, John D., 100, 101, 114, 207
Kaus, Mickey, 116n79
Keeping Track (Oakes), 233, 237n101
KEEP (Kamehameha Early Education
    Program), 249–50, 254, 258, 265, 284–86,
    330–31
Kennedy, Mary M., 131–32, 135, 208
Kerner Commission, 9, 10
Kilgore, Sally B., 239n107
King, Martin Luther, Jr., 9n25
Klineberg, Otto, 181n34
Klitgaard, Robert, 80n39
Kluegel, James R., 182–83, 185–87, 218–19
Korean Americans, 15, 117n82
Kozol, Jonathan, 334

labor market. *See* jobs
Lambert, Richard D., 13
language: differences in, 24, 65, 133, 207, 249,
    259–64, 285, 329, 338, 350–52; importance
    of, in school learning, 63–66, 245–48,
    250–54, 269–70, 272–73, 338
Laosa, Luis, 273
Laotians, 33
Latinos. *See* Hispanics
Lau v. Nichols, 259
lead poisoning, 138–41, 347
Ledlow, Susan, 216–17
Levin, Henry M., 238
Lightfoot, Sarah Lawrence, 204
literacy, 10n30, 162–66, 360. *See also* reading
    skills
Littman, Mark S., 110
Los Angeles (California), 16, 117n82, 302, 303,
    358, 359
Louisiana, 297–99, 358–59

McCarty, T. L., 264
Maccoby, Eleanor E., 270
McPartland, James M., 357n52
Macy Foundation, 332–33
majority population: definition of, xv, 21;

demographics of, 16–24. *See also*
    educational achievement gaps; whites
malnutrition, 139
marriage rates, 106–7, 214–15
Marshall, George, 381
Martin, John A., 270
Maryland, 72, 81, 240, 291, 368n81
Masrui, Ali, 176n16
Massachusetts, 101, 114n74, 303n22
Massey, Douglas S., 111n67
Massey, Walter, 240
math skills: of American students, 7, 53–63,
    305n24; beliefs about innate ability *vs.* hard
    work in, 199n96; cultural adaptations to
    teaching, 257; improving workers', 247n11
Matute-Bianchi, Maria Eugenia, 211, 213, 215,
    277
Mead, Lawrence, 116n79
Mead, Margaret, 99
Medicare. *See* welfare
Meier, Deborah, 238–39, 348, 370n84
Melanesians, 34
Merton, Robert, 224
Mexican Americans: alleged inferiority of, 187,
    213; demographics of, 20, 22; educational
    achievement gaps of, 60, 62, 63, 65–66, 68,
    72–73, 85, 118, 213, 236; and educational
    achievement gaps (within class), 144, 155,
    157–59; educational attainment by, 29–30,
    34, 102, 103; first language of, 65, 260–61;
    and housing segregation, 111; as immigrants,
    213–15; intergenerational educational
    progress among, 30, 214–15; parenting
    styles among, 253, 272n116, 273; prejudice
    against, 173, 213–15; and school resources,
    169; teacher expectations of, 228; unemploy-
    ment rates of, 213, 216; white conflict with,
    15. *See also* Hispanics
Michigan, 79–80, 112, 302
Mickelson, Roslyn Arlin, 209–10
middle-class: educational performance of
    minorities from, 10–11, 158, 159, 201, 208,
    341, 361–64; friendship networks of, 194,
    197, 275, 279, 362; lack of, in urban ghettos,
    104, 109–12; multigenerational components
    of, 10, 284; parenting styles of, 272–80, 309;
    rise of Hispanic, 3; teachers predominantly,
    246; whites, 209–10, 277–79. *See also*
    blacks: middle-class
Minnesota, 297–99, 355
minorities: and academic motivation, 118,
    202–10, 213–15, 241, 243, 257–59,
    275–76, 283, 285, 309, 360; alleged innate
    inferiority of, 172–78, 182–204, 218,

221–28, 237, 241–43, 338; changes needed
to improve educational performance of, 258,
281–86, 329–36, 340–42, 348–53, 356–59,
362–63; definition of, xv; demographics of,
5, 16–24, 84, 101–9, 337; educational
achievement gaps between majority population and, 3, 45–83, 121–42, 198, 202,
305n24, 332–33, 337–38, 363–64;
educational attainment among, 26–44, 102,
198, 266, 357–58; education of, compared to
majority, xiii, 5, 7, 8; family opportunity
problems of, 98–109; grades of, 28, 80, 365;
leadership among, 3, 39; poverty rates
among, 2–3, 110–11, 114n74, 142, 198, 201,
207, 216, 279–80, 307–8, 342–43; prejudice
against, xvi, 90n14, 100, 105, 171, 211–12;
prejudice against, educational impact of,
202–43, 298, 309, 329, 338; preventable
health problems among, 138–41; professional prospects of, 11, 68–70, 73–79,
189, 207; racial/ethnic tensions between,
117n82; research needed on educating, 341,
369–72; and student mobility, 138, 348–49;
teachers among, 42–43, 66–67, 239–41,
246n6; test scores of, 28, 45–70; unemployment rates of, 104–6, 108, 113–14, 170, 198,
201, 213, 216, 359–61. See also blacks;
educational achievement gaps; Hispanics;
jobs; language; Native Americans; prejudice;
teachers; unemployment
The Mis-Education of the Negro (Woodson),
222
Mississippi, 167, 290
Missouri, 355
mobility, 98–99, 121, 133, 137–38, 142,
348–49
Montana, 295, 297, 300
Moore, Elsie G. J., 195–98, 199n98, 201,
277–79
Moore Adoption Study, 195–98, 201, 277–79
Moreno, Robert P., 274n122
Morgan, Harry, 250
Moskowitz, Jay, 291–92
Motorola Corporation, 5n15, 7
Mounts, Nina S., 271, 275
Mount St. Mary's College (Los Angeles), 358,
359
Moynihan, Daniel Patrick, 104n42
Myrdal, Gunnar, 103, 109

NAEP (National Assessment of Educational
Progress): class and performance on, 122,
125–29, 141; data from, 46–59, 70, 72, 82,
135n13, 314–20; limitations of, 46–47,

150–51, 159, 373–74; literacy study of,
162–66, 170–71; math scores on, 53–59, 82,
128–29, 149–50, 154; reading scores on,
47–52, 125–28, 135n13, 146–49, 154;
results of, compared to per-pupil
expenditures, 295–303; Trial State
Assessments, 297–310, 335; and within-
class racial/ethnic educational achievement
gaps, 146–54
National Advisory Commission on Civil
Disorders (Kerner Commission), 9, 10
National Assessment of Educational Progress.
See NAEP
National Education Longitudinal Study of
1988. *See* NELS:88
National Longitudinal Study of Youth (1980)
(NLSY), 162, 166–69
National Opinion Research Center (NORC),
179–83
National Science Foundation, 240
A Nation at Risk, 1, 2, 4–5, 232–34, 237n101
A Nation Prepared, 2n3
Native Americans: alleged inferiority of, 187;
author's use of term, xiv; classroom culture
of, 230, 250–52, 255, 258, 264–65;
demographics of, 17, 18, 337; educational
achievement gaps of, 1, 33, 57–60, 62–63,
65–66, 68, 70–73, 79–80, 82, 85, 118, 211,
216–18, 231, 337; educational achievement
gaps and class among, 125, 141; and educational achievement gaps (within-class), 144,
151, 155, 157–59; educational attainment
by, 35, 37–38, 40, 44, 218, 230, 266; and
housing segregation, 112n67; as involuntary
immigrants, 205; official counting of, 16n47;
prejudice against, 173, 174, 177, 216–18;
and school resources, 169, 291; teaching
goals of, 67; tracking of, 231, 234; white
violence against, 15. *See also* Navajos; Utes
nature *vs.* nurture, 188–92
Navajos, 217–18, 250, 251–52, 255, 258
Nebraska, 295, 297
NELS:88 (National Education Longitudinal
Study of 1988), 70–72, 122–25, 131,
133–34, 145–46, 158–59, 228–31, 266, 310,
314–15
Nelson, F. Howard, 288n2
Nettles, Michael T., 80, 81–82
"new basics," 233, 234
New Hampshire, 295
New Jersey, 112, 288–89, 291, 303n22
Newman, Lucile, 138–40
New York City (New York), 101, 102–3, 111,
238–39

New York state, 112, 288–91, 312, 313
NLSY (National Longitudinal Study of Youth—
    1980), 162, 166–69
non-Hispanic whites, 21. *See also* whites
nonresident aliens, 35, 37, 40–41
NORC (National Opinion Research Center),
    179–83
North American Free Trade Agreement
    (NAFTA), 380
North Carolina, 167, 297
North Dakota, 295, 297, 299–303, 305, 307–9

Oakes, Jeannie, 233
Ogbu, John U., 118, 255, 257, 309n28; research
    by, 204–11, 213, 215–17, 243, 282, 364n72
Ohio, 81, 101, 102, 111, 291, 302
O'Neill, June, 166
One-Third of a Nation, 2, 5, 12, 238n101
on-the-job training, 247–48
Orland, Martin E., 131–32, 135, 208
Osterman, Paul, 114n74
"Other Hispanics," 18, 20, 21, 62, 63, 65, 66,
    68, 72–73, 155, 159, 236

Pacific Islanders, xiv, 108, 112n67; educational
    achievement by, 57–58, 71; educational
    attainment by, xv, 33–34, 37, 38, 40
The Paideia Proposal (Adler), 237n101
parental educational attainment: and children's
    educational achievement, 85, 87, 122–31,
    141–59, 266, 280–81, 299, 301–2, 308–10,
    337; estimating value of, 314–20; as measure
    of class, 121, 159, 160, 170, 299;
    racial/ethnic gaps in spite of equal, 161,
    278–79. *See also* human capital
parenting styles, 99, 194; and educational
    achievement, 251, 267–72, 285–86, 309,
    320–25; among Mexican Americans, 253,
    272n116, 273; racial/ethnic/class differences
    in, 196–98, 211, 265n88, 266–86, 309, 338,
    362
Parents as Teachers program, 355
Park, Robert, 96n23
Patterson, Orlando, 380
peers, 98, 197; educational achievement
    impact of, 208, 247, 256, 259, 275–77,
    312–13, 364n72, 365, 368n82; oppositional
    black, 206, 207–9, 362, 363
Pennsylvania, 101, 102, 111, 292, 303
Philippines, 19
Phillips, Thomas R., 74–77, 80, 82
A Place Called School (Goodlad), 233, 237n101
Plomin, Robert, 190, 193, 196
pluralism, xiii, xv–xvi, 24–25

polity capital, 88, 90–92, 94, 95, 116, 117, 119,
    242–43, 359–61
Popkin, Susan, 115
Portes, Pedro R., 270, 274
postsecondary education: admission policies in,
    359, 366–69; curricular content of parents',
    39–43, 76, 78–79, 161; educational attain-
    ment gaps in, 34–38, 73–76, 80; estimates
    of Americans intellectually able to attend,
    232n97; grades in, 73–82, 365; graduate
    work in, 32–33, 37–38, 40–42, 68–70,
    75–76, 81–82, 155, 266; minorities in,
    365–69; Native Americans' view of, 217;
    nonresident aliens in, 35, 37, 40–41; readi-
    ness for, 59, 72–73, 75–76, 129, 155–58,
    234–36, 242, 332–33, 357–59, 364; reme-
    dial course work in, 31, 59, 66–67, 366–67;
    SAT scores as guide to success in, 77–78,
    358. *See also* college graduation; parental
    educational attainment
poverty rates: among children, 100n30, 108–9,
    121–42, 248, 307–8, 344, 345, 354; for
    elderly, 344; intensity of, and educational
    achievement, 131–37, 141, 211, 212, 308;
    among minorities, 2–3, 110–11, 114n74,
    142, 198, 201, 207, 216, 279–80, 307–8,
    342–43; among people with few job skills,
    104, 282; by race, 108; and student mobility,
    133, 137–38; white beliefs about reasons for
    blacks', 183. *See also* class(es); jobs; under-
    class; unemployment
prejudice, 104, 171, 371–72, 377; among chil-
    dren, 200n100; educational impact of,
    202–43, 298, 309, 329, 338; and jobs for
    minorities, 218–21; origins and evolution of,
    172–201. *See also* caste system
Present at the Creation (Acheson), 381
Productivity and American Leadership
    (Baumol), 5, 8
Public Education Association, 357
Puerto Ricans: demographics of, 20, 22;
    discrimination against, 169, 216; educational
    achievement gaps of, 11, 60, 62, 63, 65–67,
    69, 72–73, 85, 118, 216, 236, 332–33; and
    educational achievement gaps (within-class),
    144, 155–59; educational attainment by, 34;
    and housing segregation, 111n67, 216; immi-
    gration of, 20, 102; poverty rates of, 216;
    white conflict with, 15. *See also* Hispanics

race: definition of, xiv; among Hispanics, 20.
    See also racial/ethnic differences
Racial Differences (Klineberg), 181n34
racial/ethnic differences: in educational

achievement, 45–83, 202–43, 266, 372; in family and school resources, 326–36; and per-pupil expenditures, 290–91; research on, 181, 186–98; as source of conflicts, 9–10, 13–16, 117n82, 380. *See also* cultural differences; educational achievement gaps; *names of specific racial or ethnic groups*

racism. *See* prejudice

Rand Corporation, 29–30, 214

Randolph, A. Philip, 8n23

reading skills: of adopted blacks and whites, 197; of American students, 47–52, 146–49, 309; and educational achievement, 357n52; improving minorities', 249; improving workers', 247n11. *See also* literacy

refugees, 14–15, 102. *See also* immigrants

religion, 18–19, 24, 177

remedial course work. *See* postsecondary education: remedial course work in

resources (education-relevant), 84, 87–88, 93–95, 100, 116–18, 122, 160–71, 287–337, 339, 377

Rock, Stephen L., 271

Rogoff, Barbara, 268–70

Roper poll, 179, 181, 187

Rosenbaum, James, 115

Rosenfield, David, 178, 200

Rosenthal, Robert, 225

Rothman, Stanley, 186–87, 190

Said, Abdul A., 13–14

Samoans, 34

SAT (Scholastic Aptitude Test): limitations of, 59; test takers of, 30, 72, 234–36. *See also* SAT scores

SAT scores: and class, 122, 130–31, 141; gaps between minorities and majority in, 3, 59–68, 74–75, 78, 79–80, 82–83, 202, 305n24, 332–33; as indication of college success, 77–78, 131, 141, 365; and need for remedial education, 66–67, 131; within-class racial/ethnic educational achievement gaps among, 155–59, 302. *See also* SAT

Savage Inequalities (Kozol), 334

Scarr, Sandra, 192, 193–94, 196, 198, 199n98, 200

Scarr-Weinberg Adoption Study, 193–94, 196, 198, 199n98, 201

Scholastic Aptitude Test. *See* SAT

school-based management, 351–53

school choice, 351, 352–53

School Development Program, 238, 330, 331

school district expenditure variations, 288, 291–93, 335. *See also* schools: resource differences between; states

schools: "appropriately" *vs.* "equally" funded, 97, 120; changes needed to improve minorities' chances in, 258, 281–86, 329–36, 340–42, 348–53, 356–59, 362–63; culture of, 245–64, 268–74, 277, 281, 282, 285, 286, 298; curricula of, 85, 169, 231–36, 246, 283, 351, 359; and educational achievement, 84, 86–88, 119, 208, 254, 336, 337; minority students' increased access to, 116, 166–67; prejudice in, 115, 222–43, 338; private, 358, 359; proportion of poor children in, and educational achievement, 131–37, 141, 312–13, 362; purposes of, 160, 237, 245, 283–85, 377–81; racial/ethnic differences in number of years in, 167–68; relative resources of, compared to families, 94–95, 97, 98, 137, 160, 190, 224, 240, 282, 326–37, 339; resource differences between, 86, 87, 93, 167–71, 175, 190n68, 222, 287–310; resource needs of poor, 97, 120, 170, 286, 334, 340, 341; segregation in, 86, 112, 167, 169–70, 222; size of, 348–49; suburban, 115–16, 292, 312, 363–64; "theme," 353n37; urban, 1, 291–93, 302–3, 312; winning minorities' trust in, 208, 217, 238, 282–84, 286, 330. *See also* school year; students; teachers; tracking; summer; *kinds of schools*

school year (length of), 169, 350, 351, 377. *See also* summer

Schultz, Theodore W., 88

Schwartz, Myron, 291–92

science. *See* technical fields

segregation. *See* housing segregation; schools: segregation in

self-fulfilling prophecies, 224–27

Senter, Mary Scheuer, 182, 185, 219

SES (socioeconomic status). *See* class

SE (Sustaining Effects) Study, 132–37, 141–42, 240

Shade, Barbara J., 252–56

Simmons, Luis R., 13–14

Simpson, James, 175n11

Sizer, Theodore R., 237n101, 238, 249n18, 370n84

slavery, 173, 175–77, 205–6, 222

Slavin, Robert E., 331, 357n52, 370n84

Smith, Mary Lee, 228

Smith, Tom W., 183–84, 219–20

Smith Cultural-Socioeconomic Study, 194–95, 198, 201

Snyderman, Mark, 186–87, 190, 199n98

social capital, 88, 89, 94, 98–100, 116–20, 190, 356, 359–61
social harmony, 4, 12–16, 82
Social Security. *See* welfare
socioeconomic status. *See* class
South Dakota, 295
Soviet Union (former), 14, 99
Sowell, Thomas, 221, 366n76
Spanish language, 260, 263n79
special education, 115, 139, 350
Stafford, Frank P., 267
states (per-pupil expenditures), 287, 288–303, 335
Steele, Claude M., 204
Steele, Shelby, 204
Steinberg, Laurence, 209, 210, 271, 274, 276
Stephan, Walter, 178, 200
stereotypes, 117, 118, 178–79, 197–200, 203, 212, 218–21. *See also* cultural differences; innate differences; prejudice
Stevenson, David L., 280–81
Stevenson, Harold W., 276
Stewart, Donald, 239–40
Stigler, James W., 276
students: demographics of, 21–24, 82, 298–300; inadequacy of American, 1, 5, 7; mobility of, 121, 133, 137–38, 142, 348–49; oppositional attitudes among minority, 206, 207–10, 215, 243; quality of American college, 8n20; ratio of, to teachers, 168, 169, 303, 348–51, 358–59, 362, 370, 377; segregation among, 86, 167–68; socioeconomic status of, and test scores, 86, 121–42, 298–99; study patterns of, 276–77, 364n72, 368n82; as workers, 249n18. *See also* grades; math skills; peers; reading skills; schools; teachers; test scores; tracking
A Study of Schooling (Goodlad), 233
substance abuse, 113, 138, 140–41, 347–48
Suburban Minority Education Consortium (SMEC), 364
suburbs: jobs in, 101, 109, 114–15; schools in, 115–16, 292, 312, 363–64; whites' preference for, 220, 312
Success for All program, 331
summer (educational achievement in), 136–37, 142, 240, 351, 357n51
Sustaining Effects (SE) Study, 132–37, 141–42, 240

Taylor, Robert R., 280n136
teachers: characteristics of American, 245–47, 249–52, 374; and cultural differences, 284–85, 351, 352; educational achievement

of, 66–67, 169; expectations of minority students by, 202, 222–31, 236–37, 239–41, 338; minority, 2n3, 67, 239–40, 246n6, 303, 305, 352n34; parents as, 266–70, 285–86, 320–25, 342; prejudice among, 222–28, 236–37; ratio of, to students, 168, 169, 303, 348–51, 358–59, 362, 370, 377; salary variations of, 303, 354; segregation among, 86; teams of, 349–50, 362; and test scores variations, 85, 374n90; training for, 42–44, 303, 305. *See also* schools; students
technical fields: college degrees in, 39–42, 76, 78–79, 161; college grades in, 73–79, 82; growth in, 38–44, 212; minorities in, 366n76, 368n81; preparation for, 59, 75–76, 246; test scores for those planning to enter, 67–68, 77–78
television, 99, 309
Terman, Lewis, 187
test scores: impact of peers on, 208; limitations of, 45–46, 93, 372; of parents, 161, 314–20; racial/ethnic/class gaps in, 28, 45–70, 72, 85, 122–31, 141–59, 170, 202–3, 210, 236, 297–99, 302–3, 372–73; and students' socioeconomic status, 86–87, 119, 143–59, 202–3; and teachers' expectations of students, 225–26, 228; and variations in schools, 85–86, 295–303. *See also* ACT scores; NAEP; NELS:88; SAT scores
Texas, 112, 303, 355
Tharp, Roland G., 249–52, 255, 257, 265n91
Thoeny, A. Robert, 80
tobacco. *See* substance abuse
Tomas Rivera Center, 352n34
tracking (educational), 231–37, 239, 241, 305, 330, 332–33, 338. *See also* special education
Treisman, Philip Uri, 276, 364n72
Truman, Harry S., 8, 181
Tulkin, Steven R., 272–73
twins, 193, 198n93
Two Worlds of Childhood (Bronfenbrenner), 99

underclass, 109–17, 131, 141, 207, 221, 279–80, 282, 334, 339, 341
unemployment. *See also* jobs; poverty rates; effects on children of parents', 116; among minorities, 104–6, 108, 113–14, 170, 198, 201, 213, 216, 359–61; rates of, by country, 115, 359
United States: changing demographics of, xiii, 7, 16–24, 38, 41, 232, 243; education in, 6–8, 232, 276, 277; effort needed by, to improve minorities' education, xiii, 42, 82, 118, 242–43, 340–81; history of racial/ethnic

prejudice in, 8–12, 172–201, 206, 211–12, 220n64, 221, 222, 241, 282; lack of childcare system in, 346, 354–55; lack of national health care system in, 346, 354; racial/ethnic conflicts in, 9–10, 15, 16, 117n82

U.S. armed forces, 8, 162, 170–71

U.S. Bureau of Indian Affairs, 174

U.S. censuses, 16, 18–20, 26–34, 104–6, 110, 173

U.S. Congress, 330, 361

U.S. Constitution, 173

U.S. Department of Education, 144, 295

U.S. Office of War Information, 179

U.S. Supreme Court, 9, 223

urbanization, 99–100. *See also* cities

Utah, 288–90, 295, 312, 313

Utes, 217–18

Vermont, 290, 295, 303n22

Vietnamese immigrants, 15, 33

Virgin Islands, 297

Visions of a Better Way: A Black Appraisal of Public Schooling, 203–4

vocational education, 175, 231. *See also* tracking

Vogt, Lynn, 255

Voting Rights Act of 1965, 3, 9

Wacquant, Loïc J. D., 116–17

wages. *See* incomes

Washington, D.C., 288–90, 293–95, 297, 299–303, 305, 307–9

Weber, George, 224

Weinberg, Richard, 193–94, 196, 198, 199n98, 201

welfare, 115, 117n79, 344–46, 361, 370

West Virginia, 295, 299–303, 305, 307–9

white flight, 103, 111, 221

whites: author's use of term, xiv; classroom culture of, 230, 257; demographics of,

16–18, 21, 102–3, 299–302; educational achievement of, 11, 47, 48–51, 53, 54–55, 57, 59, 60–63, 65–76, 78–83, 85, 118, 202, 231, 236, 298, 332–33; educational achievement and class among, 124–25, 133, 141, 163–65, 198n93, 302; and educational achievement gaps (within–class), 144–47, 149–50, 153–59, 166, 170–71, 209–10; educational attainment by, 27–42, 266, 293–95, 358; educational privileges of, 168, 169; and housing segregation, 220; marriage rates among, 107, 110; parenting styles of, 273–75, 277–79, 282; poverty rate among, 108–9, 132, 141, 198; prejudice among, 172–243; and school resources, 290–91; single-parent families among, 108, 132; southern, 183, 185; tracking of, 231, 234, 235–36; violence against minorities by, 15, 220n64. *See also* majority population

Whitmore, John K., 276

WIC program, 347

Williams, Luther, 240n111

Wilson, William Julius, 107n51, 204; on black underclass, 109–18, 131, 141, 207, 221, 279, 282, 339

Wisconsin, 111, 137–38, 292

Wolff, Edward, 5, 8

Woodson, Carter G., 222

workfare, 117n79

working-class: blacks, 109–11, 118, 194–95, 209–10, 241, 274, 277–79; lack of welfare programs for, 345; parenting styles of, 272, 277–79; whites, 209–10, 241

work performance: and educational achievement, 11n32, 80n39, 374

Wyoming, 295

Xavier University (Louisiana), 358–59, 365

Zigler, Edward, 190–91, 193, 196